PHILIP LARKIN

Letters Home

1936–1977

by Philip Larkin

poetry

THE NORTH SHIP

XX POEMS

THE FANTASY POETS NO. 21

THE LESS DECEIVED (The Marvell Press)

THE WHITSUN WEDDINGS

HIGH WINDOWS

COLLECTED POEMS (edited by Anthony Thwaite)

EARLY POEMS AND JUVENILIA (edited by A. T. Tolley)

COMPLETE POEMS (edited by Archie Burnett)

THE OXFORD BOOK OF
TWENTIETH-CENTURY ENGLISH VERSE (ed.)

fiction

JILL

A GIRL IN WINTER

TROUBLE AT WILLOW GABLES (edited by James Booth)

non-fiction

ALL WHAT JAZZ: A RECORD DIARY 1961–71

REQUIRED WRITING: MISCELLANEOUS PIECES 1955–82

FURTHER REQUIREMENTS: INTERVIEWS, BROADCASTS,
STATEMENTS AND REVIEWS 1952–85
(edited by Anthony Thwaite)

letters

SELECTED LETTERS OF PHILIP LARKIN 1940–1985
(edited by Anthony Thwaite)

LETTERS TO MONICA
(edited by Anthony Thwaite)

PHILIP LARKIN

Letters Home

1936–1977

EDITED BY

JAMES BOOTH

FABER & FABER

First published in 2018
by Faber and Faber Limited
Bloomsbury House,
74–77 Great Russell Street,
London WC1B 3DA

Typeset by Donald Sommerville
Printed and bound by CPI Group (UK) Ltd, Croydon, CR0 4YY

A CIP record for this book
is available from the British Library

ISBN 978-0-571-33559-6

2 4 6 8 10 9 7 5 3 1

CONTENTS

PLATES

Except where noted, all photographs are reproduced by permission of the Society of Authors as the Literary Representative of the Estate of Philip Larkin and are copyright © the Estate of Philip Larkin.

ACKNOWLEDGEMENTS

I am most grateful to Philip Larkin's literary executors, Anthony Thwaite and Sir Andrew Motion, for their support and patience, and to Lisa Dowdeswell at the Society of Authors, administrator of Larkin's estate, for her assistance and advice.

I owe particular debts, among those who knew Larkin, to his niece Rosemary Parry (Hewett); Molly Terry (Sellar), who knew Larkin in Belfast; Mary Judd (Wrench), former library assistant in Hull, and her daughter Helen, Larkin's god-daughter; Larkin's secretary in Hull, Betty Mackereth; and his Hull friends and colleagues Professor Edwin A. Dawes and John White.

The advice and assistance of the University of Hull archivist, Simon Wilson, and the staff of the Hull History Centre have been invaluable.

Particular points in the text were clarified by: Professor John Kelly, Emeritus Research Fellow in English, St John's College, Oxford; Anthony Head, Peter Foss and Chris Thomas of the Powys Society; and John White and Don Lee of the Philip Larkin Society.

I am grateful to those who have helped me to improve the introduction, particularly Rosemary Parry, Anthony Thwaite, Ann Thwaite, Andrew Motion, Geoff Weston, Philip Pullen, Janet Brennan, Don Lee and Peter Lodge; also Graham Chesters, the late Ivor Maw, Sheila Jones, Philip Weaver and Suzette Hill. I owe special debts of gratitude to Anthony Thwaite for his constant support, quite beyond the call of duty, and to Rosemary Parry for the insight she provided into Larkin's family relationships. Finally I must thank my typesetter, Donald Sommerville, for his invaluable suggestions and unwavering attention to detail.

Unpublished material by Larkin is used with the permission of the Larkin Estate. Unpublished material by Sydney and Eva Larkin and by Catherine Hewett (Larkin) is used with the permission of Rosemary Parry (Hewett). Every attempt has been made to trace all copyright holders, but if any have been overlooked the editor and publishers will be pleased to make the necessary arrangements at the earliest possible opportunity.

THE ARCHIVE

The letters published here are extracted from various deposits in the University of Hull collection currently held at the Hull History Centre, as follows:

Deposited by Rosemary Parry (Hewett) in 1994

U DLN/1/31 Picture postcard (24 August 1936) from Philip Larkin to his sister Catherine (Kitty) Larkin (later Hewett): in a group of seven cards sent from Germany between 1933 and 1939, from Sydney to Eva Larkin, Sydney to Kitty (3), Sydney to Philip, Kitty to Philip and Philip to Kitty.

U DLN/3/2–3 Eleven letters from Philip to his sister Catherine: February 1941–September 1943, together with a telegram of 7 July 1943 ('IT SEEMS I HAVE GOT A FIRST').

U DLN/3/5–7 Fifteen letters and eight picture postcards from Philip to his niece, Rosemary Hewett (later Parry) (1960–83), including correspondence of 1966 concerning a visit to Warwick University where she was then an undergraduate studying English and European Literature.

U DLN/3/8 A letter from Philip to his sister Catherine dated 2 May 1947 welcoming the birth of her daughter Rosemary, together with two picture postcards and ten letters from Larkin to Catherine dated 1972–82. The file is devoted mainly to correspondence with Berrystead Nursing Home, and legal papers concerned with the sale of 21 York Road after Eva's death.

U DLN/4/5 Picture postcard sent to Catherine Larkin on 20 August 1946, showing a portrait of Philip.

Deposited by Rosemary Parry (Hewett) in 2008

U DLN/6 Approximately 4,000 letters, lettercards, postcards and picture postcards written by Philip to his parents (1938–48), and later to his widowed mother Eva (1948–77); with fourteen letters to his sister Catherine (dated 1940–4).

U DLN/7 Approximately4,000 letters, lettercards, postcards and picture postcards written to Philip by Sydney and Eva, separately or together (December 1943–February 1948), and later by the widowed Eva (1948–77); with two letters from Catherine to Philip from 1944.

INTRODUCTION

On the morning of Sunday 13 September 1964, Philip Larkin sat in his flat at 32 Pearson Park, Hull, writing a polite, ceremonious letter to his mother, 'My very dear old creature':

> Once again I am sitting in my bedroom in a patch of sunlight embarking on my weekly task of 'writing home'. I suppose I have been doing this now for 24 years! on and off, you know: well, I am happy to be able to do so, and I only hope my effusions are of some interest to you on all the different Monday mornings when they have arrived.

His 'writing home', as he notes with his customary precision, began exactly twenty-four years earlier in October 1940, when he started his first term at St John's College, Oxford. He sees the correspondence as continuous since then, but his phrase 'on and off, you know' conceals a major discontinuity. For the first seven and a half years 'home' had been a household of two or three: his father, Sydney Larkin, City Treasurer of Coventry ('Pop'); his mother, Eva ('Mop'); and also on occasion his sister, Catherine ('Kitty'), ten years older than him, who became a teacher of art and design in Leicester, and married in 1944. This phase ended abruptly with the death of Sydney early in 1948. There followed two years during which the poet and his mother lived together and the correspondence was at a halt. The second phase of the correspondence began when Philip departed for a new post in Belfast in September 1950, and lasted for twenty-seven years until Eva's death in November 1977 at the age of ninety-one. From this phase the letters which survive are almost exclusively those between mother and son. Kitty seems to have destroyed her letters from Philip after 1947 and only a small handful survive from 1969–82.

Larkin's letters home make a consistent thread through his life. From the beginning, he would usually write, when not living at home, at a rate of more than one letter a week. From the 1940s the archive contains between 59 and 73 letters, lettercards or postcards per year, some very long. For most of the second phase, between 1950 and 1972, he wrote a regular Sunday letter to his mother, and/or a letter or card during the week. From this phase the archive preserves between 77 and 111 letters per year. Then, between February 1972 and her final months, Philip wrote to Eva most days, sometimes twice on the same day. There are, for instance, 277 letters from 1972. Of Larkin's nine major correspondences[1] this is by far the largest in volume and most extensive in duration. It dwarfs the others, being twice as extensive as that with Monica Jones. From 1938 to 1977 there are about 4,000 letters or cards home from Philip, and 4,000 replies from Eva. Philip writes almost always with a fountain pen and never types his letters. Eva similarly writes with a pen, occasionally a ballpoint.[2] The handwriting of both is clearly legible and, with few exceptions, both begin each letter with the full date: day, month and year.

Only a fraction of the archive could be included in this selection. In all, 607 letters or cards written by Philip are represented, either complete or in extracts: 82 addressed jointly to 'Dear fambly' or 'My dear Mop and Pop', 485 to Eva, 20 to Sydney and 20 to Kitty. The selection is to an extent arbitrary. References to literary matters, and to emotional relationships, are included, while repetitive accounts of the weather and familiar routines or responses to Eva's news about relatives are cut back. But inevitably many letters of interest, and many amusing drawings, have been excluded. To allow the poet's correspondents to be heard in their own voices, and to give context to his letters, an appendix, 'Letters from Home', is included, comprising one joint letter from Eva and Sydney, ten letters from Eva, seven letters from Sydney and two from Kitty.

The main strand in the correspondence is the humdrum and domestic ('Many thanks for the load of beautiful lilies', 'How long in minutes do you pummel & squeeze a woolly?' 'how exciting about the lavatory!') However the story they tell is psychologically fascinating. When Anthony Thwaite quailed at the sight of all the shoe-boxes full of envelopes, and decided to exclude the family correspondence from the *Selected Letters* (1992), he still had no difficulty in producing a bulky

1 The others were with James Sutton, Kingsley Amis, Monica Jones, Judy Egerton, Robert Conquest, Anthony Thwaite, Maeve Brennan and Barbara Pym.

2 Hull History Centre, U DLN/6 and 7, deposited by Rosemary Parry (Hewett) in 2008.

volume covering every aspect of Larkin's literary and personal life. But the letters he omitted constitute Larkin's most intimate and committed correspondence, and take us to the tragic core of the poet's life. His love for his mother is matched by his sense of obligation to ensure her well-being. He wrote on 13 February 1965: 'Nothing I can give you will equal all you have done for me. I only wish I had achieved a more satisfactory position in life. And of course I ought to find some solution for you.' Here we find a clue, perhaps, as to why, as he put it in 'Love Again', 'it never worked for me'.

The continuous series of family letters begins with Philip's arrival in Oxford on 9 October 1940. The letters are addressed firstly to the initial family home, 'Penvorn', 1 Manor Road, Coventry,[3] then, after the blitz and consequent dispersal, and 'near-fall of the House of Penvorn',[4] to the new home which Sydney bought in June 1941: 73 Coten End, Warwick. For six and a half years it was to Coten End that the young poet wrote; and it was to an attic room in this house that he returned during vacations. Our view of Larkin's early home life is perhaps unduly coloured by his autobiographical fragment in the first pages of his fifth poetry workbook, written probably in Belfast in 1953, a time when he was particularly concerned to distance himself psychologically from his family: 'I never left the house without a sense of walking into a cooler, cleaner, saner and pleasanter atmosphere.'[5] The affectionate tone of his letters of the 1940s contradicts this sour recollection. A card of 10 November 1941 ends 'Love, love, love, Philip'. On 27 May 1947 he wrote to his parents: 'Once again I have to thank you for a very happy weekend. What struck me this time was really how young you both are – not young in the sense of silly, but young in keen response to things.'

Oxford was a high point.[6] He was exempted from military service because of his poor eyesight, and completed the full three-year course,

3 The name was derived from the names of the house's builder, Percy Vernon Venables.

4 Philip's letter of 26 October 1940. Over Christmas 1940 Sydney moved Eva away from the bombing to his brother Alfred's house at 33 Cherry Orchard, Lichfield, and after Christmas she lived at Wear Giffard, Cliff Hill, Warwick.

5 Hull History Centre, U DPL/1/5/1.

6 He lived first in St John's College. Then, from January 1942 until his graduation in July 1943, he shared lodgings in 125 Walton Street with his friend Philip Brown, a medical student.

achieving the first-class degree which gave him a secure self-confidence for the rest of his life. But despite this success he had no idea what to do next, except to become a writer, and it was not until after four months 'sitting at home quietly writing *Jill*' that he was prompted by a letter from the Ministry of Labour to apply for the post of Librarian in Wellington, Shropshire.[7] His letters from his time at Wellington, beginning at the end of November 1943, breathe disappointment at talent wasted, but also show him rising with determination to the challenges of the job, improving the library's holdings and facilities, and coping with a growing number of borrowers.[8] But he was eager to improve his position, and after three years he gained appointment, in 1946, to the post of Deputy Librarian at University College Leicester.[9] Throughout his time in Oxford and Wellington, and during his first year at Leicester, he wrote regularly to 'Pop' and 'Mop'. Then, late in 1947, a little more than a year into his appointment at Leicester, his father became ill, and died on Good Friday, 26 March, 1948, at the age of sixty-three. The first phase of the family correspondence was at an end.

Despite the starkly contrasted personalities of Larkin's parents, the shared 'family' identity of the letters of the 1940s is striking.[10] Though Philip addressed letters concerned with money or career advice to Sydney alone, and wrote separately to Kitty in Leicester, most letters are, as he writes, 'common property', intended to be read by the family as a whole. Numerous envelopes are addressed to 'Mr and Mrs Sydney Larkin'. An envelope directed to 'Sydney Larkin Esq.' will contain a letter beginning 'Dear Mop and Pop'. While addressing his mother Philip will direct questions at Sydney, or engage in asides ('Tell Pop

7 Philip Larkin, 'An Interview with the *Observer*', *Required Writing* (London: Faber, 1983), 51.

8 In Wellington he stayed in three successive lodgings: first Alexander House, New Church Road, then for two years (January 1944–January 1946) at 'Glentworth', King Street, and finally at 7 Ladycroft (January–September 1946).

9 Over his first two years at Leicester he occupied three temporary lodgings. During the first month he stayed with his sister Kitty and her husband Walter Hewett at their home at 53 York Road, Loughborough, travelling the ten miles to work by bus. In October 1946 he moved into rented rooms at 172 London Road, moving again in 1948 when his landlady required his room, to 6 College Street, Leicester.

10 It seems that virtually all his letters to Sydney and Eva have been preserved, and a large proportion of the letters from Eva and Sydney to their son, though their letters from the first three years, when Philip was at Oxford, are lost.

that . . .', 'Pop would be interested to know . . .') There are hints that Eva may have read their son's letters out loud to her husband. Similarly, it was normal for his father and mother to place their replies in a single envelope, even on occasion to write on the same sheet. Their marriage was not as dysfunctional as it has seemed to some observers. When it came to parenting their son they made an effective team. Philip diagnosed a common weakness of temperament which kept them united: 'My father was intensely shy, inhibited, not robust, devoid of careless sensual accuracy (though not of humour), and I don't think he did well to choose a wife of the same pattern.'[11]

Family unity extended to cultural and social attitudes. Though, in writing to his parents, Philip is understandably reticent about the women in his life, the letters show no sign of the conflict between generations which is so familiar an element in the early lives of other writers, John Betjeman and Kingsley Amis for instance. There is never a hint of serious censure or disapproval from either Eva or Sydney. This must be partly a result of the intense affection of parents for a son born late, when his father was thirty-eight and his mother thirty-six. His sister Kitty remarked: 'Really, Philip could do no wrong in his father's eyes. Or his mother's. They worshipped him.'[12] But they were also unusually open-minded. Moreover Sydney's restless enthusiasm for books made their home a stimulating environment for a would-be writer. As Larkin later noted, his school friends 'were brought up to read Galsworthy and Chesterton as the apex of modern literature, and to think of Somerset Maugham "a bit hot"'.[13] In contrast his father filled their house with works by Hardy, Shaw, Samuel Butler, Wilde, D. H. Lawrence, Aldous Huxley and Katherine Mansfield. In a letter of 28 February 1944, Sydney mentions that he is reaching the end of volume five of Gibbon's *Decline and Fall of the Roman Empire*. He then goes on to mention Carlyle and the Koran which he compares with Law's eighteenth-century *Serious Call to a Devout and Holy Life*. Elsewhere he gives his verdict on a novel by Agatha Christie ('silly as all crime stories are'), the *Letters* of Katherine Mansfield and Radclyffe Hall's lesbian novel, *The Unlit Lamp*.

11 Autobiographical fragment, Workbook 5, Hull History Centre, U DPL/1/5/1.

12 Andrew Motion, *Philip Larkin: A Writer's Life* (London: Faber, 1993), 8.

13 Philip Larkin, 'Not the Place's Fault', *Further Requirements* (London: Faber, paperback edn 2002), 10.

D. H. Lawrence is a constant reference point. On his arrival in Oxford Philip tells his father that he has seen a manuscript letter by Lawrence for sale in Blackwell's. He buys Lawrence's *Apropos of Lady Chatterley's Lover*, commenting: 'I don't think we have this, have we?' He gives his sister and his father amusing accounts of his attempt to order the unexpurgated *Lady Chatterley's Lover* and the volume of Lawrence's paintings in the Bodleian: 'I couldn't get them, however, without being engaged upon a "study" of Lawrence. Anyway, I preserved a chilly air of hauteur and remarked that the restrictions appeared singularly childish. They aren't, actually, but I was rather disgusted' (to Sydney, 8 March 1941). A year later, on 15 May 1942, he joked to Eva:

> You might tell Pop that a friend of mine found an Obelisk Press Edition (i.e. unexpurgated) of 'Lady Chatterley's Lover' behind the bookcase in his digs, and I am impatiently waiting for him (and his wife) to finish it. 'Mine eyes have seen the Glory of the Coming of the Lord.'

It is very difficult to imagine any other son of his generation writing to his mother in such a tone.

Most crucially, mother and father followed their son's literary ventures with keen interest. Sydney would ask for Philip's literary opinion in a tone of respect, and pasted a cutting of his first published poem 'Ultimatum'[14] into his diary. Later, in 1947, Eva describes how she and Sydney pounced on a review of Larkin's novel *A Girl in Winter* in the *Sunday Times* which had dropped through their letterbox: 'Daddy peered over my shoulder and spotted it first and said "read it out to me." Well, I began to read it, but it was so marvellous that I had great difficulty in reading to the end – in fact both of us became very deeply moved. I consider it the most wonderful achievement, and am very, very proud' (3 March 1947). She added a halo to a self-ironic drawing of the young writer puffed up with pride which Philip had drawn in his previous letter home. Sydney had sent his own, brief 'hearty congratulations' a day earlier.

For many readers a key point of interest will be the light these letters throw on the character of Sydney Larkin and his impact on his son. Though Sydney was notorious among his colleagues for his right-wing eccentricity, he was a public figure of some distinction, nationally

14 *The Listener*, November 1940.

respected for his achievement in balancing Coventry's books by his far-sighted reforms. In 1936 he had been elected to the presidency of the Institute of Municipal Treasurers and Accountants, and later his work as chair of the wartime National Savings Committee helped to earn him the OBE. He maintained his reputation by the difficult route of rigorous integrity. In February 1944 he wrote to his son:

> I am at present about to engage in a battle with the Labour party and the Council on a question of 'dishonesty' in expenses on the part of a Councillor. The trouble in this matter is that Councillors stick together on matters of this sort but I have 'right' on my side. Local Government is made up (or should be) of this sort of thing.
> Love S. L.

He termed himself, as his son recalled, 'a Conservative Anarchist', meaning, Philip explained, that although 'he consented to do his part in maintaining the fabric of society he despised it in his heart and wished it at the devil'.[15]

Now that his twenty-volume diary, 'The Fools' War', written between 3 September 1939 and 1 October 1946, is available,[16] Sydney's character can be better estimated. His enjoyment of his visits to international accountancy conferences in 1930s Berlin, together with holidays in Germany, had given him an uncritical admiration for the early Nazi achievement in re-establishing the German economy and national confidence. On the first page of his diary he gives a crude version of history in accordance with Nazi propaganda:

> The trouble arose through the rise to power of Adolf Hitler, who was determined to put Germany on her feet, and to his constant success in this direction from 1933 to the present date. This roused the jealousy of the British people who were also annoyed at the doctrines of the National-Socialist Party in Germany which were directed against all subversive and foreign elements, notably the communists and the Jews [. . .] Those who had visited Germany were much impressed by the good government and order of the

15 Autobiographical fragment, Workbook 5, Hull History Centre, U DPL/1/5/1. Motion, *Philip Larkin*, 11, mistranscribes this, substituting for Larkin's explanation: 'but what that means I don't know'.

16 Hull History Centre, U DLN/1/10–29. It was embargoed until 2015, thirty years after Larkin's death.

country as by the cleanliness and good behaviour of the people – both in marked contrast to our own country.[17]

His opinions, however, were not predictable. The anarchist element in his conservatism made him a champion of individual conscience against authority. He was outraged by the tribunals set up to decide on cases of conscientious objection, which he felt were biased towards religion and designed to catch out sincere objectors with 'trick' questions. On the other hand he was crudely anti-Semitic. His diary is scattered with newspaper cuttings about British Jews hoarding gold instead of handing it in to the authorities as required. Even after the revelations concerning the Holocaust at the end of the war, Sydney never acknowledged Nazi barbarism. Instead he chose a moral high ground consistent with his prejudices, sniping at the verdicts of the 'dummy court set up at Nuremburg':

> The prosecutors – chiefly ourselves, Russia and United States – are also the judges [. . .] the prosecution-and-judges are themselves guilty of [. . .] burning alive hundreds of thousands of innocent men, women and children in Germany and Japan [and] murdering in Russia millions of opponents of the communist regime of their country.[18]

These political views are, however, quite absent from the family letters. In his relationship with his son, Sydney was the opposite of a fascist bully. Despite his racism, he had taken out a subscription on his schoolboy son's behalf to the Chicago jazz magazine *Down Beat*, and even bought him a drum kit, a sacrifice of domestic calm which even liberal-minded parents would have baulked at. The letters show that he respected his son's intellectual independence. And Philip showed no sign of adopting his father's politics, commenting in a letter to his school friend Jim Sutton that 'the German system is, from all accounts, much more evil than last time'.[19] The young Philip's attitude towards his father is seen in his brilliant drawing of his family in a letter to Jim Sutton of

17 Hull History Centre, U DLN/1/11.

18 1 October 1946; Hull History Centre, U DLN/1/19.

19 1 April 1942; in James Booth, *Philip Larkin: Life, Art and Love* (London: Bloomsbury, 2014), 25.

6 September 1939.[20] 'Pop' appears as an endearingly pathetic figure, leaning back in his chair, thinning hair on view, holding a newspaper with the headline 'WAR'. Flinging out his arm, he defends Hitler and spouts a farrago of Lawrentian rhetoric about 'the end of civilisation'. Eva sits knitting opposite him, worrying about what the family ought to have for lunch and hoping that 'Hitler falls on a banana skin . . . by the way I only washed four shirts today.' Later, when Philip mentions to his parents, in his letter of 7 March 1943, that he has inadvertently chosen the 'Official Star of David' for his bookplate, he ostentatiously declines the opportunity to echo his father's anti-Semitism. Instead, with a moral complexity, not dissimilar to his father's, he turns himself into a hypothetical victim of race prejudice: 'On the wave of Anti Semitism that is almost bound to come after the war I may be hung up on the nearest lamppost.'

In some ways the example Sydney set his son was unambiguously positive. In his account of the blitz on Coventry in 'The Fools' War' it is clear, reading between the lines, that Sydney played a leading role in the firefighting. But, almost perversely, he avoids any hint of self-dramatisation:

> On the night of the 14th November Coventry was heavily bombed and the centre of the city destroyed. I was in the Council House all night and although the whole town was in flames the Council House was only hit at extreme ends by high explosive bombs, while the 8 or 10 incendiary bombs which fell on the roof were dealt with by the staff volunteers. The town remained in a state of chaos for a fortnight at the end of which period fires were still smouldering. Gas, electricity, water, sewerage were all disconnected and transport thrown out of gear by reason of impassable streets.[21]

This is the language of a City Treasurer, dispassionate, conveying the facts with an eye to future action. The first-hand objectivity of Philip's account of his experiences in wartime Oxford owes something to his father's example. His undergraduate letters show little of the self-involved narcissism one might expect of a youthful poet; and when they do show it, it is subjected to brisk irony.

20 Reproduced as the endpaper of Anthony Thwaite's edition of Philip Larkin, *Selected Letters* (London: Faber, 1993).
21 'The Fools' War'. Hull History Centre, U DLN/1/16.

Larkin also learned from his father his meticulous grammar, spelling and syntax. Sydney took an obsessive interest in the history of words, and pursued ultra-correct usage. He was very clear on the distinction between 'should' and 'would', looked askance at the use of 'implement' as a verb, and queried whether his son's 'orientate' should not, more correctly, be 'orient' ('In your letter this morning, you mention that death is lonely and that to death we should all orientate'; 8 September 1944). In one of his earliest letters an embarrassed Philip accepts his father's rebuke that he has addressed a letter to him with an incorrect epistolary formula: 'Sorry I called you "S. Larkin" – I could have sworn I put "Esqu." in'. But he cannot resist the impulse to challenge his father's pedantry: 'Anyway, I've half a mind to address this to the "Lord High City Keeper of ye Moneybags" just to nark you' (15 October 1940).

But Philip was impressed by his father's terse, elliptical style. It prompted him to an elaborate mythification which must owe something to W. B. Yeats's 'The Fisherman'. With a faint note of impertinence he takes the liberty of appraising his father's personality:

> You know, reading your letters through, I am coming to the conclusion that you have a powerful style! You sound utterly detached, cold, impersonal: as if you were writing in an old farmhouse on a windy and stone littered moor, far from any human noise or movement. Only the wind answers your sentences: 'I find that the days go rapidly by and I have not answered your last letter'; 'I am sorry you have a cold and can offer no remedy'; 'You are none the worse for knowing nothing about the war. We don't either'; 'It is usual to put Mr. or even "Esq." in case of public officials'. Then you fold the parchment, seal it with the old heirloom of a seal, and put it for the carrier to take when he calls in two days' time. Then you sink into your austere, wooden chair by the fire and listen to the wind around the high chimney pots or watch the racing clouds through the tall windows.
>
> (*12 November 1940*)

Amusement and respect are blended with intimate affection.

Philip's parents worshipped him, but in different ways. Sydney required his son to earn his respect and was concerned to win his respect in return. It is no wonder that Philip stammered badly from the age of four. Eva's love, in contrast, was unconditional. Dominant though Sydney's personality was, if the correspondence had been left in his hands all that would survive would be a string of short, pithy interchanges. It is Eva, with her detailed accounts of daily events and unfailing interest in her son's activities, who sustains the momentum. It is as if a gender theorist had created the letters to illustrate the performative extremes of masculine self-command on the one hand, feminine domesticity on the other. As Philip commented: 'My mother constantly toiled at "running the house", a task that was always beyond her, even with the aid of a resident maid and a daily help.'[22] In a joint letter from mother and father of 7 February 1944 Eva gives an account of washing clothes and reflects on how her son might make certain of getting enough bread at meal times in his lodgings. She continues with a sad reference to a neighbour's son who has been reported missing in the conflict. Sydney then intervenes to advise his son to reclaim a rebate on his first year's subscription to the National Association of Local Government Officers, since he signed on late in the year and so is owed 2/6d. Eva then concludes the letter: 'I think I have no more to add except that I am now going to darn some socks. Much love from both. Mop.' A hint of defiant resistance is audible in her tone ('Well, I hope Hitler falls on a banana skin'; 'I think I have no more to add except that I am now going to darn some socks.')

The degree to which Philip adopted Eva's attitudes is startling. She is as significant an influence on his style of letter writing as his father. On 7 March 1943 he boasts about the care he has taken over his socks: 'I darned 2 pairs last Tuesday with great satisfaction. Only not having any khaki wool I had to darn in grey.' On 23 February 1947 he writes from Leicester: 'I bought two pairs of socks yesterday [. . .] they are *pure wool* and therefore, Miss Sutcliffe tells me, will wear through in no time. She advises me to strengthen the heels & toes by preliminary darning: do you advise this?' Nor is this influence confined to the 1940s. The darning or washing of socks recur as leitmotivs from the beginning of the correspondence to the end. On 18 July 1972, shortly after entering Berrystead Nursing Home, Eva wrote to her son: 'I got all your socks out this morning and mended one before breakfast.' On 14 December 1975 Philip told his mother: 'last night I mended eleven pairs of socks'.[23]

22 Hull History Centre, U DPL/1/5/1.

23 A significant proportion of the socks recovered from 105 Newland Park by the Philip Larkin Society in 2004 following the death of Monica Jones have been carefully darned, some with non-matching wool or in two colours. See Plate 5A.

In a letter of 18 November 1940 addressed to 'Dear fambly' describing his visit to Coventry with his friend Noel Hughes after the blitz, Larkin adopted an indicative concision which his father would have appreciated. 'We heard the blasting all afternoon. Hughes' house was standing but empty: however, we got some bread & cheese at a neighbouring house, & then visited the Riders'. From these sources we gained some impression of the chaotic state of things.' But later in the letter his tone becomes more complex and literary as he depicts himself holding forth over dinner 'to an astonished commoners' table' – 'By God . . . Just back from Coventry . . . What a sight . . . pass the peas . . . any factories hit? . . . Ha, ha! . . . all be out of production for a month . . . blowing up the city . . . streets full of broken glass . . . pass the potatoes . . .' He then wrenches gear again and imitates his mother's domestic, fussy tone: '*Remarks to Mop*: No marmite yet. We subsist on weird & peculiar pots of fishpaste (2 for 5½^{d}) in all flavours. Anchovy is the favourite [. . .] I broke the handle from a tea-cup the other day, unfortunately. This was the first breakage of any sort we have had. We *lost* the strainer the other day, but on questioning the Scout found it had only been mislaid. It is still the best thing we have.' In addressing Eva he gives the breaking of a tea-cup handle the same dramatic impact as the dynamiting of ruins in Coventry.

Larkin's father did not bother to comment on the drawings with which Philip adorned his letters home. His mother, however, responded readily to their ingenuous frivolity. The image of himself as a 'creature' formed itself as a distraction from the stress of revision for his final examination in 1943, and in the first instance it was his undergraduate friend Diana Gollancz who inspired him.[24] Eva was enchanted by the drawings: 'How I do love your "creatures". It is amazing how each one conveys so much meaning in such few lines – and they are all the same and yet have such different expressions, and all are so full of action' (14 February 1944). She tried to emulate him, painstakingly drafting images of herself with long hair in pencil before inking them in. But she was intimidated by her son's mastery and her own drawings remain few. Larkin will have included similar drawings in the lost letters of the late 1940s to his fiancée, Ruth Bowman, who saw herself as a cat, and he was later to develop images

24 'I was shocked on Wednesday on returning from York to find a cutting saying Diana Gollancz had died. [. . .] It was for her that I drew my first "creatures" – she used to call everyone "dear creature"' (to Eva, 6 April 1967).

of Monica Jones and himself as rabbits and Maeve Brennan as a mouse. But it is in the 'creature' drawings in the letters to his mother that his sketches are at their most varied and adventurous.

Kitty, the third correspondent included in this volume, has attracted little comment until now. In a letter to Sutton in April 1943, the twenty-year-old Larkin traced the impact of his parents on both himself and his sister: 'I realized that I contain both of them [. . .] It intrigues me to know that a thirty-years struggle is being continued in me, and in my sister too. In her it has reached a sort of conclusion – my father winning. Pray the Lord my mother is superior in me.'[25] His wording is misleading, seeming to imply that Kitty has become like their father, when Kitty was in fact very much her mother's daughter.[26] He actually means that their father has bullied Kitty into internalising his low estimation of her ('winning'). Eva, their mother, in contrast, had succeeded in stubborn domestic resistance, maintaining her emotional space in the face of her husband's disregard; hence Philip's wish that his mother should be 'superior' in him.

In his autobiographical sketch of 1953 Philip accused his father of contempt for Kitty: 'His first child, my sister, he thought little better than a mental defective, who was showing regrettably few signs of marrying and clearing out.' This is highly coloured and perhaps not fair to Sydney, though it must be significant that, after the crisis of the Coventry blitz on 14/15 November 1940, Sydney sent a telegram of reassurance to his son in Oxford but not to his daughter in Leicester.[27] It is evident that the mutual respect and affection between father and

25 To Sutton, 12–14 April 1943. In Booth, *Philip Larkin*, 15–16.
26 A letter survives from Kitty to Eva from 25 March 1943, addressed to 'My dear Mother Cat'. Kitty, describes a visit to Leicester with Walter Hewett, whom she was to marry in 1944. After a visit to the bookshop, and tea, they had seen a comedy at the Repertory Theatre, which ended early, at 7.00; 'so we had time to wander round and then go dancing at a lovely hotel "the Bell Hotel" it really was a lovely floor and quite select, not like the usual palais-de-danse. Of course I hadn't gone intending to dance but didn't feel out of place in my black dress and snow-white collar. We came back on a late train – 10.27 and were such tired cats having to walk from the L.M.S. station which is miles away.' She ends the letter with anxieties about some 'mauve-flecked green material' she has bought 'which rather worries me as it is so loosely woven. I keep on peeping at it to see if it is as bad as I think it is.'
27 Kitty was hurt by this and always remembered it. Rosemary Parry, email, 7 December 2017.

son never existed between father and daughter. Philip wrote that 'the ten years' difference in our ages made me for practical purposes an only child'.[28] This was no doubt increasingly the case, particularly after Kitty moved out of the family home. But in the earliest years Philip and his sister were inevitably close. When he was five, Kitty was fifteen. Kitty told her daughter, Rosemary, that she had 'really brought him up when my grandmother wasn't able to cope'.[29]

Though Philip shows something of his father's impatience with Kitty, he also has sympathy with her plight.

> My sister, whose qualities of literal-mindedness and fantasy-spinning had infuriated my father until he made her life a misery, did not have many friends and endured, I should say, a pallid existence until she took up art, and even then day classes at Midland Art School did not lead to the excitements they should have.[30]

While we seem to have virtually all the letters from Philip to his parents, only twenty-nine of his early letters and cards to Kitty survive, dated between 1936 and 1947. Twenty-two of them are from 1940–1.[31] They show Philip at his most empathetic, praising his sister's ideas and asking her advice on artistic and theatrical matters. Just as he imitated his father and mother's styles, it seems he copied Kitty's florid handwriting on his envelopes and in his signature. He thanks her for 'your letter and elaborate envelope', and tells her that he enjoyed one of her letters 'very much, notepaper included'. He asks for her view on his own experiments: 'My idea with the orange & red paper was to use orange paper & red envelopes & vice versa. What is your opinion on this?' (6 March 1941). On 24 October 1941 he tells their mother that Kitty had written to him 'on her swagger crested paper

28 Hull History Centre, U DPL/1/5/1.

29 Rosemary remembers that to the end of his life he and Kitty would share private jokes from his early years. 'My grandmother always had a maid and one evening when Sydney and Eva were out she asked Philip "Do you want a *knife* with your supper?" in a sinister tone. This phrase became a regular joke between them.' Rosemary Parry, email, 17 December 2016.

30 Autobiographical fragment, Hull History Centre, U DPL/1/5/1.

31 There is a holiday postcard from 1936 (Hull History Centre, U DLN/1/31). Fourteen letters are preserved among the main family correspondence in U DLN/6. Eleven more letters and a telegram are preserved in U DLN/3/2–3. There is a picture postcard, showing Philip himself, sent on 20 August 1946 (U DLN/4/5). The 1947 letter survives along with later letters and cards from 1972–82 in U DLN/3/8.

in answer to one of my orange telegrams'. His letters project a high-spirited aestheticism and artiness. He eagerly looks forward to the shantung silk tie she has bought him for Christmas: 'You will have my tie by now, I suppose. I like 'em subtle, sister. Wheel 'em in and lay 'em out' (12 December 1940). He boasts: 'I have bought a pair of crimson trousers – dark crimson. They are the only pair in the University' (15 May 1941). The experiments with his sister's name in the earliest letters show a teasing intimacy. She is addressed in various letters as 'K', 'Kit', 'Kath', 'Kathryn', 'Katherine' and 'Katharine' ('the best spelling don't you think?').[32] (Later he settles back on 'Kitty'.) The various forms of the name recur in his later writing. It is surely highly significant that the hypersensitive, vulnerable refugee heroine of *A Girl in Winter* is called Katherine. Moreover, in 'Dublinesque' (1970) the name 'Kitty, or Katy' echoes down the streets of a dreamlike Dublin, 'As if the name meant once / All love, all beauty.'

Philip explores ideas in his letters to Kitty, echoing her enthusiasm for the liberal educationalist Homer Lane. In a long letter of 15 May 1941 he takes her into his confidence about the Jungian philosophy he is imbibing at the lectures of John Layard, adding elaborate diagrams: 'Could tell you lots more but I haven't time. But it was like an evening spent with truth.' In a particularly affectionate letter he breaks off from his Anglo-Saxon revision to respond to her account of her latest educational challenge, 'teaching a whole secondary school in Art'. He draws a brilliant sketch of his sister as a cat holding her own among the clamouring pupils. It is to his sister that he writes his most lyrical descriptions of Oxford:

> [. . .] south-east down St. Aldates, gusts of snow blow past Big Tom and away onto the Meadows, where are no footprints; and south-west by the river flakes fall in the quadrangles of Magdalen. And in hundreds of brightly lit rooms, or solitary by reading-lamps, hundreds of undergraduates smoke, read, talk and laugh, oblivious of the outer dark but part of it, forgetful of all but a tiny section of living but influenced by life and its implications, as am I, sprawled on a sofa in St. John's College, a pad on my knees and my feet on the fireplace, writing to you.

32 Rosemary remembers that 'She got annoyed with other people who called her "Katherine" or "Kathleen"' (email, 3 January 2017).

It is unfortunate that so few of these early letters survive, and that only one formal letter concerning holiday arrangements exists from the twenty-five years between 1947 and 1972 (20 April 1969). Following her marriage in 1944, when she was living in close proximity to Eva, it seems that Philip saw no reason to communicate with her separately. As he wrote on 1 October 1944 'I expect all my general news is passed on to you by bush-telegraph.' But Rosemary also explains that Kitty was 'a very private person' who did not wish her correspondence to be read by others. In particular she 'didn't want any attention paid to her as Philip's sister'.[33] It is irresistible to conclude that the malign early family dynamic played a part in this self-effacement. In his letter of 31 October 1940 Philip indirectly points out two spelling mistakes she has made: 'By the way, what is "contempory"? ("Tradition v. Contempory") Perhaps, too, you might enlighten me on "psycology"?' One can imagine the exasperation such solecisms would have caused their father. Such considerations may explain why Kitty wanted to erase herself from her famous literary brother's story.

Equally regrettable is the fact that only two letters survive from Kitty to Philip.[34] (They were preserved in the family envelopes along with letters from his parents.) In one (23 October 1944) she shows herself taking great pains to satisfy his request for her to decorate a cigarette case with his initials, locating an appropriate letter font and gold paint. Why are all the other letters from Kitty lost, when Philip so religiously preserved the letters from his father and mother? For Philip to have routinely destroyed them would have contradicted his usual principle: 'To destroy letters is repugnant to me – it's like destroying a bit of life' (24 June 1963). Nonetheless a casual reference in a letter to Eva of 9 September 1956 suggests that he might have done this in the case of Kitty. He had asked her for a particular book for his birthday (9 August), and this had arrived rather late with a comment that she 'had read it but didn't think it much good'. Her comment induced a sudden irritation on his part, and he continued spitefully: 'Tearing up one of her letters recently I found I'd torn up some pictures of Rosemary that were inside – ssh!'

33 Email, 17 December 2016. Rosemary records, however, that Kitty did not seek out and destroy letters addressed to her when the family correspondence came to her following Philip's death. She is certain that her mother never even looked into the envelopes.

34 See Appendix, 17 April and 23 October 1944. It is conceivable that Kitty asked her brother to destroy her letters to him.

But it would be a mistake to read much into this self-dramatising comment. The sibling relationship is always a particularly sensitive one. He quite often wrote slightingly of Kitty, implying that she was over-talkative or slow-witted, and when she failed to write to thank him for a present in August 1958 he called her 'mean bitch of hell, if you'll excuse the expression'. A recurrent source of tension was the necessity for one of them to be on hand to care for Eva at all times, which made for regular disputes about holiday timings (particularly in 1964 and 1969). But such quarrels were transient and were always amicably resolved with apologies on his part. On 26 November 1954 he wrote: 'I wonder if you w^d tell Kitty that I'm sorry to have been awkward about Xmas – I felt v. bad on Monday morning: but I did appreciate seeing her new suit.' When he first took up his job at Leicester in 1946 he stayed with Kitty and her husband for three weeks, writing on 11 September: 'Kitty says (and Walter seems to agree) she doesn't mind how long I stop here.' Their relationship was essentially warm and affectionate.

He took charming photographs of Kitty with her daughter, and in the Larkin family tradition he always sent her carefully chosen presents on her birthday and at Christmas. One file in the archive consists of twenty-two Christmas and birthday cards to 'dear Kitty' and/or to Rosemary.[35] Philip frequently asks Eva to pass on points of interest in matters of design and artistic taste to his sister. On 9 January 1955 he writes: 'Please show Kitty the stamp on this envelope & ask her if she doesn't think the lettering vile!' A repeated refrain is: 'Remember me to Kitty', 'Give my regards to Kitty', or to Kitty and Walter, or to the Hewett family. When the direct correspondence resumes briefly in 1972, it shows a familiar co-operative relationship in caring for their mother (if with Larkin's customary brusqueness in

35 Hull History Centre, U DLN/3/1. He also wrote occasionally to his god-daughter, Rosemary. He attended her confirmation in December 1960, and followed up with a sententious letter on the importance of Christianity in British culture. In a charming letter of 25 April 1962 he writes: 'one of the nice things about being a girl is that you can wear all the nicest colours & smell of the most beautiful flowers – you are much luckier than men who go about in perpetual camouflage smelling of Tweed & Gorse & Oldspice, not very inspiring smells' (*About Larkin* 1, April 1996, 8). He included 'creature' drawings in letters to Rosemary written in 1966 when he visited her at Warwick University. Rosemary preserved fifteen letters and eight picture postcards from her uncle dating from 1960 to 1983. Hull History Centre, U DLN/3/5–7.

discussing money matters, inherited from his father). And his letter to his sister of 4 April 1977 following Rosemary's wedding shows the same warm empathy as the earliest letters of the 1940s. Kitty's feelings for her brother are shown in her response to the typescript of Andrew Motion's 1993 biography, which she read in 1992, weeks before she died: 'There's no love in it.'[36] Philip's feelings for her are clear from his letter to Eva of 5 June 1966, in which he echoes the colour imagery of the earliest correspondence: 'I dreamed about Kitty the other night, but have forgotten what. Fancy her saying we were utterly unlike each other! Only as one red is utterly unlike another red, I sh[d] have thought.'

The death of Sydney Larkin in 1948 hit Philip hard. The grief of 'An April Sunday brings the snow', the only mourning elegy he addressed to a human being, is made intimately personal by the image of the 'sweet and meaningless' jam which his father had made in such unnecessary quantities. He completed no poems after this for nearly a year. As he explained to Sutton, he felt he was required to 'become an adult'.[37] Six weeks after Sydney's death he proposed marriage to Ruth Bowman, his girlfriend from Wellington. But rather than setting up his own establishment he was to end up living with his mother. Eva was incapable of coping on her own and expected her children to sort out her life for her. Kitty, married in 1944, had recently given birth to Rosemary (28 April 1947) and could scarcely be imposed upon. So Philip took on the burden and bought Eva a house close to his work in Leicester where they could live together.

Mother and son moved into 12 Dixon Drive in August 1948. Here they lived for two years until September 1950. The arrangement suited Eva and they got on well enough together. But it was a frustrating situation for a man of his age. By 1950, the year in which he turned twenty-eight, he was desperate to escape, not only from his mother but also from Ruth. Haunted by the example of his parents' union, he could not bring himself to marry. He wrote to Sutton on 4 May 1950 'My chief handicap at present is this bloody set up here, Christ knows how it will all end. But it can only be broken up by a good excuse like a new job, you see [. . .] I do realize that my mother must live with someone –

36 Rosemary Parry, email, 3 January 2017.
37 Larkin, 24 February 1948. *Selected Letters*, 144–5.

only I'd rather prefer it not to be me.'[38] Eva's dependency can be judged from the fact that the few cards Philip sent to her in 1948–50 from trips away are addressed not to Dixon Drive but to the home of his sister and her husband, Walter Hewett, at 53 York Road, Loughborough.

Philip made his escape at the end of September 1950 by taking up a sub-librarianship at Queen's University Belfast, across the Irish Sea, thereby throwing the immediate responsibility for their mother back on his sister. He had proposed afresh to Ruth in June, only to take back the offer after three days amid acrimony and bitter self-reproaches. This was the signal to cement the relationship with Monica Jones, a lecturer at Leicester, who shared his Oxford background and who was to become his wife in all but name, albeit at a distance. They became lovers weeks after the break with Ruth, and weeks before he moved to Belfast. It suited him that this new relationship would be conducted largely by letter, physical relations being confined to his visits to the mainland. The proximity of Monica in Leicester to his mother in Loughborough meant that he could visit both in the same trip, and such visits became a fixed feature of his life for many years.

As time passed Eva abandoned the hope that Philip would bring her across to join him in Belfast. Just over a year after his departure Kitty and she found a suitable house at 21 York Road, a hundred yards or so from her daughter. Eva moved in in December 1951, and was to live here for the next two decades. For many years, terrified of loneliness, and more immediately of thunderstorms, she could not sleep in the house on her own. A bedroom at the back of the Hewetts' home became 'her' room. Kitty, it was understood, was grateful for her mother's company since Walter was often away from home for long periods.[39] It was a minor triumph when Eva wrote to Philip from her own house on 24 November 1956: 'I have slept here last night and shall do so to-night, for I think it is more comfortable not having to turn out in the cold, and there is really no need when Walter is at 53.' Philip was delighted to hear that 'you had been sleeping in your own basket for once' (28 November 1956). Eva remained apprehensive that her son-in law, a management consultant with Urwick, Orr & Partners, would take a job elsewhere and she would be abandoned. Eventually, after fourteen years, in 1965, Walter did buy a new, larger house, 'Oddstones', in

38 Larkin, *Selected Letters*, 161.
39 Rosemary Parry, email, 3 January 2017.

Forest Road, Loughborough, and Eva was compelled to live more on her own. However, the Hewetts' new home was only one and a half miles from York Road.

Even before she had found a house Eva was exploring the possibility of a paid live-in companion to occupy it with her. She placed an advertisement in the newspaper, and over the months discussed the various applicants in letters to Philip. But, unsurprisingly, none satisfied her requirements. The one person with whom she might have been able to share her life comfortably was her great friend Auntie Nellie, widow of her brother Arthur Day (d. 1943). But Nellie lived in Hyde, Cheshire (now Greater Manchester) and had a son and daughter of her own, and eventually also several grandchildren. She never considered uprooting herself and joining her sister-in law. Eva would go to stay with Nellie, Nellie frequently visited Loughborough, and the sisters-in-law shared summer holidays together by the sea.

Eva lived at 21 York Road, Loughborough for two decades, from December 1951, when she was 65 and Philip was 29, until January 1972, when she was 86 and he was 49. Their exchange of letters was unaffected by Philip's moves between lodgings in Belfast,[40] and continued without significant change when in 1955 he returned to the mainland. He made sure at this point not to be drawn back into the domestic trammels of 1948–50 by taking up the post of Librarian in the University of Hull, far enough away from his mother and Monica to keep both versions of the domestic trap at a distance. Finally, after eighteen months in temporary lodgings around Hull and in the village-suburb of Cottingham,[41] he found the place he could stay, moving into his high-windowed flat at 32 Pearson Park in October 1956. Here he was to live until 1974, three years before Eva's death.

40 He lived first in Queen's Chambers (October 1950–August 1951), then briefly at 7 College Park East (August–September 1951) and at 49 Malone Road (September–October 1951), before finding comfortable lodgings in an attic at 30 Elmwood Avenue, where he stayed for his remaining three and a half years in Belfast (October 1951– March 1955).

41 After staying briefly in a university property, Holtby House, he moved into 11 Outlands Road, which gave him the model for Mr Bleaney's room (April–July 1955). Then he moved to 200 Hallgate, Cottingham (July 1955– April 1956); then to 192A Hallgate, Cottingham (April–October 1956).

The second phase of Larkin's writing home began exactly ten years later than his first letters from Oxford. The early letters from Belfast were frequent and could be very long. His relief at escaping the domestic proximity of the previous two years led to an outpouring of affection. On 29 September 1950 and on 3, 5 and 11 October he sent Eva six pages, on 18 October he sent eight densely packed pages, on 20 October four pages, on 28 October eight pages, on 31 October ten pages. This is the more remarkable since he was, at the same time, writing even longer letters to Monica Jones. The drawings of himself as a 'creature' with which he had enlivened his letters from 1943 onwards became more refined. Eva commented: 'I think it is really wonderful how you can make your creatures say so many different things just by placing the eye in different positions' (23 January 1951). During 1950 he experimented with various depictions of his mother with different hairstyles or wearing a hat. Sometimes he drew her as a straggly 'mop'. In response, on 21 November 1950, she made one of her own rare ventures into drawing. He responded enthusiastically: 'How I did laugh at your "wild Mop" a really skilful & comic drawing' (26 November 1950). Then, on the last day of 1950, he hit upon the image of Eva that was to become fixed for the remainder of the correspondence: an 'old creature' distinguished from the 'young creature' by a neat mob cap. Her new epistolary identity was confirmed in 1951–2 when Philip abandoned the former 'Dear Mop', 'My dear Mop' or 'Dearest Old Mop' in favour of 'Dear old creature' or 'My very dear old creature'.

From the beginning the routine was fixed. His time at weekends had to be organised to ensure his letter reached Eva on Monday: 'I'm writing to you on Saturday evening this week-end, because tomorrow I shall be occupied all day, and of course old creature must have its letter! Anything can be missed rather than that' (2 May 1953). He also wrote a second letter or two, or a card, during the week. Betty Mackereth, Larkin's secretary at Hull from 1957 until 1984, recollects that on arriving back in his office after a meeting he would at once sit down to dash off a letter, taking it himself to the postbox on Cottingham Road outside the university in time for the afternoon collection. Her replies were equally regular. A missed letter would cause a minor crisis and generate elaborate displays of affection. On Friday 24 October 1952 Philip sent his mother a postcard with a drawing of the 'creature' peering disconsolately under the doormat: 'No letter! Are you all right?' Two days later in his regular Sunday letter he thanked her for the 'pretty telegram' which she had immediately sent to reassure him. It had arrived on Saturday along with the delayed letter: 'how kind of you to send a greetings one!'

Their letters always methodically address the other's concerns as well as conveying their own 'news'. The formal considerateness of tone is unbroken except on the few occasions when Philip berates himself for exploding with irritation at her: 'I have behaved wretchedly – I don't know what gets into me. I humbly apologise' (10 January 1968). She would immediately accept his apologies with a dismissive comment or an admission of a fault on her own side. Both correspondents make a point of filling up all the space on their pages. Philip regrets that he might not have time to fill the sheet he has begun before he has to catch the post. On another occasion he sends 'an extra page for you, because I think my 2 pages this morning were a bit thin – I was hurrying slightly' (24 October 1954). He thanks his mother for an 'extra' letter which he could not have 'legitimately' expected. On 29 April 1952 he exclaims: 'Yesterday I received *three* letters from you! Never been such a day.' As time went on Eva tended towards the ends of longer letters to write smaller and with lines closer together, in order to squeeze everything in. Her spelling, grammar and punctuation are perfect except that she uses tentative dots for commas, and sometimes misplaces the apostrophe in 'it's' and 'haven't'. When he gently corrected this fault she became over-anxious, and he had to reassure her that the matter was of no importance. True to Sydney's memory, she not infrequently had recourse to a dictionary. On 12 February 1967 Philip concluded: 'You are a better writer than I.' There is no sign of constraint or duty in his letters. On a card of 11 November 1956 he suddenly bursts out in a gush of ingenuous emotion 'I wonder what you have cooking in the oven? Dear old creature, I do love you. I am now going to make a list of draughts!'

It is inevitable to speculate on the impact of Philip's lifelong love for Eva on his attitudes towards other women. Both Maeve, with whom he contemplated marriage in the early 1960s, and Monica, his lifetime lover, believed Eva to be a rival for his affections. On 16 October 1957 Philip wrote a letter of contorted self analysis to Monica:

> I am simply terrified at the prospect of us going on year after year & not getting married – so terrified that it may almost be something else I'm terrified of but don't recognise [. . .] if I don't want to marry you then I don't see why I should mind not doing so, & if I do then

> I don't see why I don't. You'll say Mum is at the bottom of all this. Well, if she is, I don't know what to do about it, though I wish I did.[42]

It is tempting to speculate on what might have happened had Eva's lifespan been shorter: if she had died, say, at the age of seventy-seven in 1963, when Philip was just forty and in the final throes of his marriage debate. Would he then have been able to resist marriage to Monica? Had he married at this point he would not have written 'Dockery and Son' and his whole story would be different. But instead Eva lived on until 1977, when she was ninety-one and her son's debate with himself about marriage was long over.

It is tempting, also, to search in this correspondence for an Oedipal rivalry with his father. But even in the 1950s Sydney is not so large a presence in the letters as one might have expected. On 9 October 1955, only seven years after his father's death, Philip wrote to Eva on notepaper 'from the old days'. 'It's the kind Pop would use isn't it: it's strange that I can never remember anything of the kind of letters he used to write. They were very short and dry, weren't they? And slightly ironic.' At some key points in his life Philip was pleased to compare his own career with Sydney's. On 29 May 1959, he told his mother: 'Great surprise – yesterday *Who's Who* sent for my details! This pleased me mightily. Pop never got in *Who's Who*.' A decade later on 9 May 1968 he related, with a certain melodrama: 'I delivered in person to No. 10 Downing Street a refusal of the O.B.E.!' Does his exaggerated response suggest that he was holding out for a CBE, determined to go one better than Sydney, whose highest achievement had been an OBE? Perhaps; though he does compare his case with those of other possible literary candidates for the award, R. S. Thomas and Cecil Day Lewis. So other factors were at play.

Without Sydney, Eva fell gradually into the habits and views to be expected of a widow of her class at the time. For a while she attempted to stay true to Sydney's, and her son's, exacting standards. She wrote on 15 May 1951: 'I have been reading Daddy's Diary (1947) this evening and have made a list of the books he was reading. I have asked the library here to get me Franz Kafka's Diary, which you recommended.' But

42 Philip Larkin, *Letters to Monica*, ed. Anthony Thwaite (London: Faber, 2010), 229.

Philip has to tell her to stop struggling with Dostoevsky's *The Possessed* which she is finding unreadable, and over time her reading became more middlebrow. She began to attend lectures on psychology run by Dr Edith Folwell and, though Sydney had taught her a severe religious scepticism, she made several friends among the widows and unmarried older women of the 'Circle of Silent Ministry', and began to attend her local church: 'Oh dear! Oh dear! I seem to be getting more and more involved with "the Church" and the Psychologists!' (12 June 1951).[43] Philip encouraged her to find a cure for her loneliness wherever she could: 'I hope you found the visit to Dr Folwell lastingly beneficial: I am sure it is best to tell her anything that preys upon you [. . .]' (29 October 1950). Eva came to rely with abject hero-worship on the support of Dr Folwell: 'She says she is my friend forever' (15 May 1951).

The only solution to her problems Eva could envisage was to find someone to live with her. But her attempts at employing a paid companion were doomed to failure, and the emotional pressure was clearly on Kitty or Philip to take her in. She dropped hints: 'My new doctor, after reading my case sheet was very emphatic that I should not live with strangers, but with my own family. Some day I'll tell you what he said' (15 May 1951). As the 1950s progressed she became more and more dispirited. It is cruel that it was in 1955, at a time when Philip should have been enjoying his first national success as a poet with *The Less Deceived*, that Eva succumbed to clinical depression. Philip and Kitty coped as a team with her spell in Carlton Hayes Hospital over Christmas, including electric shock treatment. No upheaval or significant change followed and her life soon returned to its regular routines. She complained at one moment of being harassed and at the next of being lonely. Philip responded reasonably: 'I can see that having other Circle members ring you up could be awfully interrupting, but surely it is comforting too' (11 July 1965).

What sustained Eva was her 'work'. Their letters maintain the fiction that Eva is valiantly coping with a life of enforced domestic labour. On 6 January 1959, at the age of seventy-three, she cited pressure of housework as the excuse to give up writing her life story, having reached only as far as her childhood: 'Perhaps when I am too old to work,

43 Dr Folwell and the Circle of Silent Ministry are explored by Philip Pullen, 'No Villainous Mother: The Life of Eva Larkin', in Dale Salwak (ed.), *Writers and Their Mothers* (London: Palgrave Macmillan, 2018), 81–95.

I might have more time to spend on it.' On 7 July 1959, she wrote 'I have been very busy to-day until about 3 p.m. thoroughly overhauling the front bedroom in readiness for A. Nellie. I have rubbed down the walls and ceiling and had all the bundles off the top of the wardrobe and overhauled the bed.' He would respond in kind, describing the chores of turning over his mattress or doing his washing and darning. When Philip described having to arbitrate in a complicated dispute between the cleaners at Hull Library, she responded with her own recollections: 'I am not surprised that your cleaners worry you. I well remember the worries and misery I suffered over the women and maids. And the number of things they stole!'

Most of the time Philip assents to this equivalence between his and her 'work'. On a couple of occasions, however, he cannot help allowing the reality to show through. Overwhelmed by problems in the library he wrote on 10 March 1963: 'It must be nice to be like you, nothing to do but shop, cook & eat!'; and again a week later: 'Wish I had nothing to do all day, like some people!' Aware that such comments struck at the heart of Eva's sense of identity, he immediately ticked himself off for his impertinence, drawing one of his wittiest sketches in which the incensed old creature delivers a peremptory blow with a rolling pin to the top of the young creature's head. On 26 March 1963 Eva wrote in an injured tone: 'Yes, it is a hard job to get any spare time, although I know you will hoot at the idea of me not having any.'

In fact all her time was 'spare'. She was a wealthy widow without responsibilities, who, as her bank manager told her, could have made her whole life a holiday if her spirit had been so inclined. But her spirit was not so inclined. Philip's diagnosis appears accurate. On 11 July 1965 he compared his own depression with hers: 'I've felt fairly depressed recently for no very good reason. I think one is stamped with a particular kind of character, like a butter-pat having a cow or leaves stamped on it, and just has to struggle away with it.' His mother's condition was not a set of circumstances susceptible to change. It was a fixed state of mind.

A more developed sense of humour would no doubt have helped Eva to take greater pleasure in life. She laughs 'outright' at one of his sketches (12 January 1964). But the moments of comedy in her letters are usually unintentional. He told her he had 'howled with laughter' at her account of discovering that she had a twelve-month-old tin of salmon. After looking up food poisoning in a medical dictionary she 'took it out and buried it in the garden!' (5 and 3 October 1967). Eva cooperated with her son's *Goon Show* humour in collecting cuttings concerned with the village of Bunny, but it seems doubtful that she derived much pleasure from the ambiguities and puns he found in them. Nor would she have much appreciated the rare flashes of sharp literary wit in letters to her: the description of E. M. Forster as 'A toothy little aged Billy Bunter' (12 October 1952), or Cecil Day Lewis's report on his reception as Compton Lecturer in Poetry at Hull: 'the students had begun by treating him as a sacred cow, but ended by treating him as a cow' (5 December 1968).

More radically, Eva lacked the simple pleasure in existence which is the lifeblood of her son's poetry. On 24 February 1952 he told her to stop worrying about the past: 'it is, after all, past, and fades daily in our memory & in the memories of everyone else [. . .] Every day', he tells her, 'comes to us like a newly cellophaned present, a chance for an entirely fresh start', and in consequence 'we are silly if we do not amble easily in the sun while we can, before time elbows us into everlasting night & frost.' He added with a hint of hopelessness: 'This is perhaps not very helpful, but I am so sorry for you, and feel you have *no* reason to worry yourself!' She is at a loss as to how to respond, turning back to her obsessive anxieties: 'It was kind of you to write a page full of advice to lessen my depression. Of course I know it all, but the strange thing is it is so difficult to act upon, and one can never forgive oneself. [. . .] I do wish I was a better and braver creature' (26 February 1952). Eva was charmed by the birds nesting in her garden and by the toad she found in her cellar, but she was never overwhelmed by aesthetic *jouissance* as her son was. On 23 August 1953 he told her: 'We must go again up that road to the wood where we found the scarlet toadstool and listen to the wind in the trees. I'm sure it's beautiful at this time of year.' On 14 April 1957 he wrote: 'The view out of my bedroom window over a number of back gardens and allotments is lovely – all the trees and bushes opening their fans of fresh green in the sun. It makes one despair of ever saying how glad one is to be alive!' But for Eva, he knew, such words were 'not very helpful'.

Generally the tone of his letters to Eva is as prosaic as hers to him. But there is a fundamental difference. Prosiness was her only option; Philip's prosaic writing is self-aware: in invisible inverted commas as it were. Larkin is the master of unironic sincerity. When he buys some crockery his plain indicative tone is itself emotionally touching: 'I love to hear the little details of your life. I bought a tea-set yesterday – 21 pieces, Wedgewood, fairly ordinary but quite nice.' His mother is his muse of the everyday. 'I love the commonplace, I lead a very commonplace life. Everyday things are lovely to me.'[44] She is a muse in the time-honoured sense of being beyond the poet's reach. Poetry is made of her, but she herself is unconscious of it.

Directly or indirectly Eva gave occasion to a number of poems. She provided the inspiration for 'Mother, Summer, I' and 'Reference Back', with its dialogue between 'unsatisfactory youth' and 'unsatisfactory age'. The mundane subjects of some of the letters are transformed into poems like 'Coming', 'Ambulances' and 'Long Last'. But, though Eva appreciated her son's most moving works, her own taste in poetry was undiscriminating. Philip expresses no impatience with her on this point. Among the poets of his generation Larkin is unusually tolerant of the middlebrow, the sincerely sentimental. Some of his greatest poems rely on the carefully contextualised cliché. Unless read within Larkin's thunderously negative rhetorical context ('Time has transfigured them into / Untruth'), 'What will survive of us is love' is a mere tag from a newspaper 'In Memoriam' column.[45]

Though Eva never attended such a meeting, 'Faith Healing' gains emotional depth from the poet's experience of her incurable loneliness. On 3 October 1967 she sent him a cutting:

> WHO LOVED IS – armoured is against all foes.
> All darts of Fate and spectres of the night:
> An one who in eternal sunshine goes
> Illumined by a shining inner light.

He thanked her, deadpan, 'for the nice poem about being loved'. But he must have been acutely aware of the contrast between this verbal slop and the poem he had created seven years earlier:

> In everyone there sleeps
> A sense of life lived according to love.
> To some it means the difference they could make
> By loving others, but across most it sweeps
> As all they might have done had they been loved.
> That nothing cures.

44 Larkin, 'An Interview with John Haffenden', *Further Requirements*, 57.
45 Maeve Brennan insisted until she died that Philip 'really did mean' this last line.

In his relations with his mother Philip was prepared to disregard the rigour which makes his own poetry great and accept unmediated sentimentality. On 16 August 1966 he wrote to her: 'I enclose a piece from Patience Strong – I thought it rather good advice for me & perhaps you too!' Eva replied on 21 August thanking him for 'the beautifully expressed advice on the Patience Strong cutting which I shall read every morning'.[46]

One element in this correspondence which will inevitably give readers pause is race. On 7 April 1968, when riots were occurring in the USA, Philip wrote to Eva: 'Aren't you glad you don't live there? I shouldn't like a crowd of Negroes roaming around Pearson Park, or Loughborough,' and sketched a couple of banner-wielding protestors. On 2 August 1971 he mentioned that he had 'a pair of Africans to show round the Library – real fuzzy-wuzzies'. Disconcerted by this explicit racism, Larkin's defenders stress that he never expresses such attitudes in any of his poems and note that such comments in his letters tend to reflect the prejudice of his particular correspondent (Amis, Conquest, Gunner, or his mother). There is, indeed, plenty in Larkin's life and writing to contradict the charge of simple racial prejudice. Among his friends at Oxford, Diana Gollancz and Denis Frankel were Jewish, and he based the situation of Katherine in *A Girl in Winter* on the Jewish refugee Miriam Plaut. His jazz reviews show moral indignation at the humiliations of the colour bar in the USA, and he enthusiastically admired the music of Count Basie, Sidney Bechet, Bessie Smith and Billie Holiday. His comment that Louis Armstrong 'was an artist of world stature, an American Negro slum child who spoke to the heart of Greenlander and Japanese alike' is impeccably liberal in its universalism. In this context the flashes of crude racist language in his letters are all the more shocking. On 30 July 1967 he wrote to Eva that London is 'full of foreigners – chinks, wops, wogs, frogs, huns, the lot – and yanks, of course. Awful, awful.' Sometimes the contradictions in Larkin's attitudes are simply irreconcilable.[47]

In the correspondence surveyed in this volume the moment that causes, perhaps, most serious concern comes on 10 February 1963, when Philip told his mother that he was about to interview applicants

46 The cutting is lost.

47 Rosemary Parry comments that her mother Kitty 'never expressed racism of any kind, so that was one thing Sydney had not influenced'. Email, 5 January 2017.

for a post in the library, two of whom were from India, adding 'I shan't have the Indians.' He was not at ease in the racially diverse society forming itself around him in the post-war period. 'Integration! I just can't get English people,' he complained to her. On the other hand there is evidence in the letters that he assessed applicants for posts without prejudice, and indeed could show a sympathetic interest in the problems of immigrants:

> This week I had to interview an Indian – a Ceylonese, actually – for a job as porter, and have offered it him, though I don't know if he'll turn up. He seemed a nice chap but I couldn't understand a word he said! He'd been in the Royal Navy as a steward and had good references. I hope he turns out a success. I'm also expecting to appoint a Ceylonese lady higher up the scale. (22 *September 1968*)

Later Larkin sympathised with the awkward financial and cultural situation of this second appointee, Lila Wijayatileka, who became Senior Library Assistant: Inter-Library Loans. 'Yes, I appointed a Ceylon girl, to match the Ceylon porter. I don't know how she'll be. She's quite well qualified. If she takes my job she will have to pay back a grant she came to England on – in instalments, I hope! She says life is awkward for a single woman in Ceylon – can't go anywhere.'

On 22 June 1969, when Eva was eighty-three, Philip wrote: 'But certainly you are wonderful for your age! It's all this work that does it, though I wish you could do less. A little bungalow, or someone to look after you . . . I don't know.' She was becoming too frail to cope and he had been suggesting that she simplify her routines by keeping fewer rooms in occupation. Her mental capacity was also in decline. On 7 August 1969 Philip wrote to Monica from a holiday with his mother in Norwich: 'If we are in a room, she doesn't know which door she came in by . . . she is perpetually lost in the hotel.'[48] That Christmas his anxiety about her growing senility caused one of his outbursts of irritation:

> I'm afraid I was not a very nice creature when at home. I wish I could explain the very real rage & irritation I feel: probably only a psychiatrist could do so. It may be something to do with never having got away from home. Or it may be my concern for you

48 Motion, *Philip Larkin*, 392.

& blame for not doing more for you cloaking itself in anger. I do appreciate your courageous struggle to keep going in the old way, and am aware of your kindnesses – I did enjoy the duck, and all the other things – but I am worried about how long you can carry on without help. *(5 April 1970)*

Anticipating the inevitable, Kitty and Philip persuaded their mother to spend a fortnight in a care home in Loughborough in July 1970, while the Hewetts were away on holiday.[49] The following year, 1971, they booked her in once again, in August. But she longed to be back at home: 'I am finding time *is* hanging heavy on my hands and I don't think I should like to live in a "home" for some things' (24 August 1971). On the Hewetts' return from holiday she went back to York Road.[50] Once again she was to be in her own home for Christmas.

He wrote on 5 December: 'As regards "pegging on", well, as you know, I have set out the alternatives often enough, but nobody pays any attention [. . .] I think there's a lot to be said for staying in one's own house as long as possible, but equally I think we should face the fact that it will eventually not be possible, and make some plans.' Yet again, despite his protests, she insisted on cooking a duck. But she had overreached herself. On 24 January 1972 she fell in her kitchen and broke her hip. She spent only a week in hospital before, on 1 February, Kitty delivered her to the care home which she and her brother had chosen, Berrystead, at Syston near Leicester. This was Eva's final home, and from this point until her death nearly six years later Philip's 'letters home' were directed there, either from 32 Pearson Park, or from 105 Newland Park, where he moved on 27 June 1974.

On the day Eva arrived at Berrystead Philip sent her a greetings telegram of welcome. Thereafter he wrote a two-sided single sheet to her virtually every day, often including a drawing. This was still the same formal, ceremonious correspondence as before, and only very occasionally did he substitute a picture postcard for a letter, usually a photograph of a dog or kitten. On the day before his fiftieth birthday,

49 Abbeyfield House, 17 Victoria Street, Loughborough. Eva spent 12–24 July 1970 there.

50 4–24 August 1971. Motion (*Philip Larkin*, 417) mistakenly states that she stayed for four months. The letters she wrote from there are dated 9, 16 and 24 August, and Philip's postcard of 25 August addressed to Abbeyfield House has been redirected to 21 York Road.

8 August, he thanked his mother for her letter: 'I certainly feel the impudence of being 50 rather! I suppose it's all right when you get used to it, but I feel the grave is uncomfortably near!' He drew the creature looking over its shoulder, startled, at a black hole in the ground. It is a thoughtless letter to send to an 86-year-old woman in a nursing home. But their long-established intimacy was such that he failed to notice the irony. Her permanence was too well established, and, more subtly, he was aware that their biological clocks were set differently. She might be presumed indestructible; he was certain he would die at the same age as his father, sixty-three, as he did.

In 1971 he had congratulated her on her immaculate writing: 'Your letter came second post today [. . .] How beautifully written it is for an old creature of 85! Your writing is smaller than mine. Truly you are a marvel.' Her fall at first dispelled this neatness. For a month and more, though she continued to write regularly, her handwriting was spidery, the lines heavily slanted and far apart, and paragraphs often only a sentence long. But by May she had staged a recovery, and for a year or so the letters regained something of their previous orderliness and control, though they were now shorter: like his, a single page of two sides.

Eva's final prolonged struggle with death is intimately tracked in Larkin's last great reflective elegies, and increasingly dominates his mood. In January 1972, just before Eva's fall, Philip had gone to hospital on his own account with a crick in his neck (Eva had one too). The visit inspired 'The Building'. Beginning as an impersonal contemplation of the pathetic attempt of the new Hull Royal Infirmary to 'outbuild' death, it develops at the end an intense elegiac tone which must owe something to the 'many dreary visits to the hospital' which his mother's fall had necessitated:[51]

> nothing contravenes
> The coming dark, though crowds each evening try
>
> With wasteful, weak, propitiatory flowers.

It was published in the *New Statesman* on 17 March 1972.

Larkin's exposure to the geriatric patients in the ward to which Eva was taken in late February unsettled him and led to one of the most original developments in his poetic *oeuvre*. A new tone is heard in the

51 Larkin to C. B. Cox, 3 August 1972, *Selected Letters*, 461.

brief poem 'Heads in the Women's Ward', drafted on a single workbook page on 6 March 1972. In contrast to 'The Building', this is a poem of direct reportage, describing in the nursery-rhyme couplets of second childhood the staring eyes, taut tendons and bearded mouths of the inhabitants of the women's ward:

> Smiles are for youth. For old age come
> Death's terror and delirium.

He gave this poem to the crusading atheist journal *New Humanist* (May 1972).

Later in the year he built on this new brutalism in his most moving and original poetic response to his mother's plight. 'The Old Fools' was written in a long drafting process between October 1972 and 12 January 1973, at the time when Eva was writing her last coherent letters to him. It expresses in poetry a sentiment frequently heard in his letters. As he explained to Brian Cox: 'It's rather an angry poem, but the anger is ambivalent – we are angry at the humiliation of age, but we are also angry at old people for reminding us of death, and I suppose for making us feel bad about doing nothing for them.'[52]

> What do they think has happened, the old fools,
> To make them like this? Do they somehow suppose
> It's more grown-up when your mouth hangs open and drools,
> And you keep on pissing yourself, and can't remember
> Who called this morning?

Senility is a rare topic in poetry. It is customary to confront it with heroic defiance, as in Tennyson's 'Ulysses', Yeats's 'Sailing to Byzantium' or Dylan Thomas's 'Do not go gentle into that good night'. Larkin's approach is disconcertingly incorrect, making this a unique masterpiece. Few poets could have achieved such a wide poetic range in one poem, from crude jeering at the old fools' 'hideous inverted childhood' to the aching beauty of the evocation of dementia: 'thin continuous dreaming / Watching light move':

> Perhaps being old is having lighted rooms
> Inside your head, and people in them, acting.
> People you know, yet can't quite name; each looms
> Like a deep loss restored, from known doors turning,

52 Larkin, 10 February 1973, *Selected Letters*, 473.

Setting down a lamp, smiling from a stair, extracting
A known book from the shelves [. . .]

It was published in the *Listener* on 1 February 1973.

Eva's letters continued to arrive every few days until 25 April 1973. At this point, unless some letters are lost, her condition deteriorated. There is a coherent letter dated 26 June ('If you like I could mend a sock or two for you if you wanted [. . .] I think of you lovingly every day'); then another dated four months later in October. After this there are numerous undateable fragments and partially finished letters which Philip must have collected from Berrystead on his visits. The last letter from Eva to have been stamped and sent comes after a long gap and is dated 17 May 1974. It barely maintains coherence. Touchingly, however, Eva attempts to satisfy her son's exacting standards by using hypercorrect spelling. She writes: 'The birds are flying to and fro'' with an apostrophe to indicate the omission of the m in 'from'. She was to live for a further forty months, but at this point her voice falls silent.

At first Philip continued to write his letters in the same tone as before, gradually making the content and style simpler. On 23 May 1974 he tells her that he is to have lunch at Fabers but does not bother to mention that his new volume, *High Windows* is about to be published. He kept up the formal appearance of the correspondence. Only from mid-1975 are there as many picture postcards as letters. But then in the final months, in 1976–7, colour postcards take over entirely, featuring kittens, horses, the royal family or the TV puppet Basil Brush. Forty-seven of the cards from these last months were collected by Eva or those caring for her into an album. It seems most likely that Philip continued to send cards regularly to the end. The latest to survive are creased or stained, and it is probable that some were destroyed. As Larkin wrote later to Winifred Dawson, 'the last few months of her life were scarcely livable'.[53] No card in the archive is dateable to June or July 1977. There are two dated August and then four dated September, two months before Eva's death.

By the early 1970s Larkin was aware that his *oeuvre* was all but complete and his poetic inspiration was failing. He began writing 'Aubade' in April 1974, at about the time of his mother's last dated

53 Larkin, 13 December 1977. *Selected Letters*, 573.

letter. The poem underwent a more prolonged drafting process than even 'The Old Fools'. Having written the first two of the eventual five stanzas, and drafted the beginning of the third, he abandoned the poem on 7 June 1974.[54] Was he perhaps reluctant to signal his poetic demise by completing this, in a real sense, his 'last' poem? It was not until Eva's final months that he resumed work on the last three stanzas. Between May and August 1977 he filled nine pages with drafts and redrafts. On 24 October, less than a month before Eva died, he wrote to Kingsley Amis:

> My mother, not content with being motionless, deaf and speechless, is now going blind. That's what you get for not dying, you see. 'Well, all I can say is, I hope when my time comes I don't linger on, a pest to myself and everyone else' – oh no my dear fellow, that's just who I do hope lingers on. Well in a way. Well, anyway. Even now I can't believe it's going to happen, not too far off now too.[55]

By the end of the paragraph he is talking about his own death as much as his mother's: 'not too far off'. Larkin's emotional logic is sometimes breathtakingly ingenuous. During the drafting of 'The Building' he wrote at the bottom of a page: 'We must never die. No one must ever die.'[56] Now, it seems, the fact of extinction needed to be demonstrated to him by his mother's death before he could fully 'believe' it, and complete his own self-elegy. 'Aubade' is both a great philosophical poem with an impressive atheist gravity and his 'in-a-funk-about-death poem',[57] an abject elegy on himself. Also, on some level, it is an elegy on his mother, his muse of prose. Eva died on 17 November 1977, and days later, on 28–29 November, he returned to the draft and completed the final stanzas.

In the poem the thought of death drains life of meaning; but nevertheless life is all we have and, however reduced, we cannot willingly relinquish it. The poem's most original feature is the way it conjures poetry from the most prosaic material. The force of the most moving passages is generated not by inventive imagery but by plain indicative eloquence:

54 Hull History Centre, U DPL/1/8/18, pp. 55–64.
55 Larkin, *Selected Letters*, 571.
56 Hull History Centre, U DPL/1/8/2.
57 Larkin to Barbara Pym, 14 December 1977, *Selected Letters*, 574.

the total emptiness for ever,
The sure extinction that we travel to
And shall be lost in always. Not to be here,
Not to be anywhere,
And soon; nothing more terrible, nothing more true.

The poem's only fully developed metaphor is its comparison of religion to a 'vast, moth-eaten musical brocade / Created to pretend we never die'. But this elaborate, decorative phrase is not the most telling image in the poem. The epiphany to which it builds is the wardrobe in the poet's bedroom, emerging in the growing light of dawn. 'It stands plain as a wardrobe, what we know'. Like the jam Larkin's father made thirty years earlier, the wardrobe is a metonym of 'sweet and meaningless' life, now not so unambiguously sweet. Like another similar wooden box, it defines our limits. It tells us 'what we know': that we live in an 'intricate rented world' and that the lease will run out. Until then 'Work has to be done.' Librarians have to answer telephones in offices, and old creatures have to rub down the walls and ceiling of the front bedroom and have 'all the bundles off the top of the wardrobe'. Meanwhile postmen go from house to house, like doctors, keeping it all going. But now his mother has died and he will soon follow. There would be no more letters to or from home.

Home for Larkin was ambiguous. In his lugubrious poem 'Friday Night at the Royal Station Hotel' he plays symbolist games with the concept. A disembodied speaker takes us through the public rooms and 'shoeless' lit corridors of a surreal hotel to confront us with 'The headed paper, made for writing home / (If home existed) letters of exile'. His experience taught him the fragility of home. A month after he left it for the first time, the city in which he had been brought up was blitzed. The death of his father seven years later reduced his 'home', for the remaining three decades of his life, to a single needy parent. From the age of twenty-six to twenty-eight he shared a house with her and was determined thereafter to keep his distance. He lived almost his entire life in rented attics, never setting up a permanent establishment of his own where his mother, or another, might claim a place. The Pearson Park flat in Hull was designated by the university for the temporary accommodation of new lecturers. He lived there for eighteen years, a vagrant of no fixed abode. 'I don't really notice where I live.'[58] The protagonist of his poems is forever in transit: in 'The Whitsun Weddings', in 'Here', in 'Dockery and Son'. On the other hand in 1964 he still feels that every Sunday he is 'writing home'. Poems such as 'Home is So Sad', 'Love Songs in Age' and 'Talking in Bed' speak poignantly of home. Larkin is a great poet of domestic joys and sorrows. Eva haunts his poetry, as theme and muse. He continued to return from exile every few weeks throughout his life, and wrote to her every few days. In 1970 he guessed that the 'very real rage & irritation' he felt with his situation 'may be something to do with never having got away from home'. He had left home but he never 'got away' from it. This paradox is one key to the greatness of his poetry.

58 Larkin, 'An Interview with the *Observer*', *Required Writing*, 54.

TIMELINE

25 April 1884	Sydney Larkin born in Lichfield, Staffordshire.
10 January 1886	Eva Emily Day born in Littleborough, Lancashire.
Early August 1906	Sydney Larkin meets Eva Day in Rhyl, north Wales. She is on a holiday with her parents and brother, he on a brief stopover during a cycling tour.
5 October 1911	Sydney Larkin marries Eva Day in Leigh, Lancashire. In the same year he becomes Chief Audit Accountant in Birmingham City Hall.
21 August 1912	Catherine Emilie Larkin ('Kitty') born in Birmingham.
1913	Sydney Larkin appointed Assistant Borough Accountant in Doncaster, West Yorkshire.
1919	Sydney appointed Deputy Treasurer of Coventry.
1921	Sydney appointed Treasurer of Coventry.
9 August 1922	Philip Larkin born at 2 Poultney Road, Coventry.
1927	The Larkin family move into 'Penvorn', 1 Manor Road, Coventry.
September 1930	Philip enters King Henry VIII Preparatory School, Coventry, moving into the senior school in 1932. His closest friends are the aspiring artist Jim Sutton, and the reckless Colin Gunner.

1936	Sydney Larkin elected to the Presidency of the Institute of Municipal Treasurers and Accountants.
c. 1936–40	Kitty attends Art College in Birmingham and subsequently enters Leicester College of Arts and Crafts where she completes a teacher's diploma. (Precise details lost.)
1936 and 1937	Philip accompanies his parents on holidays in Germany.
1938 or earlier	Sydney Larkin takes out a subscription on his son's behalf to the Chicago jazz magazine *Down Beat*. He also buys his son a drum kit.
December 1938	First published poems, 'Winter Nocturne' and 'Fragment from May', appear in the King Henry VIII School magazine, *The Coventrian*. Philip becomes deputy editor of the magazine and further poems follow in 1939–40.
Summer 1939	Philip goes on a school trip to Belgium.
3 September 1939	War declared. Sydney begins a new diary, at first in large hard-cover manuscript books. It would run to twenty volumes, and continue into 1946.
9 October 1940	Philip enters St John's College, Oxford, as a commoner, and the sequence of letters to his parents begins, at a rate of more than one a week. His schoolfriend, Jim Sutton, is studying at the Slade School of Art, which has been relocated to the Ashmolean Museum.
Late October 1940	Sydney moves Eva away from the bombing to the house of his brother Alfred at 33 Cherry Orchard, Lichfield. After Christmas Eva lives for several months at Wear Giffard, Cliff Hill, Warwick.

November 1940	'Ultimatum' published in *The Listener*. Sydney Larkin pastes a cutting of the poem into his war diary.
14/15 Nov. 1940	Coventry experiences its first major 'blitz' of the war. Sydney stays all night at his post in the Council House, which is hit by two bombs and several incendiaries.
Sun. 17 Nov. 1940	Hearing no news from home, Philip and his schoolfriend Noel Hughes, also at St John's, hitch-hike to Coventry. Their homes are undamaged but empty. On their return Larkin finds a telegram from his father: 'Am quite safe. Daddy.'
January 1941	Sydney Larkin awarded an OBE in the New Year's Honours list, partly in recognition of his work as chair of the National Savings Committee.
April 1941	Jim Sutton is called up and serves in the 14th Field Ambulance, Royal Army Medical Corps.
1941	Kitty joins the Commerce Department in Loughborough College and teaches in the College Junior School of Art until the birth of her daughter in 1947.
5 May 1941	At the beginning of the summer term Philip meets Kingsley Amis, who has just arrived as an undergraduate in St John's.
May 1941	Attends seminars led by the Jungian psychologist John Layard.
June 1941	Sydney buys 73 Coten End, Warwick, which becomes the new family home. Philip occupies an attic room overlooking the garden.
November 1941 & February 1942	Amis, as editor of the *Oxford Labour Club Bulletin*, publishes Larkin's 'Observation' and 'Disintegration'.

1 January 1942	Receives notification that he has been exempted from military service on the grounds of poor eyesight.
Jan. 1942–July 1943	Moves out of college and shares lodgings in 125 Walton Street with Philip Brown, a medical student.
Summer 1942	Kingsley Amis commissioned into the Royal Signals and leaves Oxford.
1942–3	As Treasurer of the Oxford English Club Larkin entertains R. H. Wilenski (May 1942), Margaret Kennedy (May 1942), Dylan Thomas (November 1942), Vernon Watkins (February 1943) and George Orwell (March 1943).
27 May 1943	First appearance of a 'creature' drawing, on a postcard to his parents.
29 June 1943	Eva visits Oxford with Nellie Day ('Auntie Nellie'), who lives in Hyde, Cheshire. Nellie is the widow of Eva Larkin's only brother, Arthur Day (1888–1941).
4 July 1943	Graduates with a first-class degree in English.
Aug.–Oct. 1943	Encouraged by his Oxford friends Bruce Montgomery and Diana Gollancz, he writes girls'-school stories and poems under the pseudonym Brunette Coleman.
1 December 1943	Arrives in Wellington to take up the post of librarian, lodging at first in Alexander House, New Church Road. Shortly after his arrival he meets Ruth Bowman, then a schoolgirl of sixteen.
Early January 1944	Moves to 'Glentworth', King Street, Wellington.
April 1944	Sydney Larkin takes early retirement at the age of sixty. He is succeeded by his deputy, Arthur

	Hedley Marshall, who remains City Treasurer until 1964.
14 May 1944	Philip completes the manuscript of *Jill*. His Oxford friend Bruce Montgomery, who has just published a successful crime novel under the name Edmund Crispin, sends the typescript to his publisher, Gollancz, who turn it down.
12 August 1944	Kitty Larkin marries Walter Hewett, a mechanical engineer.
1945	The Hewetts move into 53 York Road, Loughborough.
1945	*Poetry from Oxford in Wartime*, ed. William Bell, published by the Fortune Press, including ten poems by Larkin, all included also in *The North Ship*.
31 July 1945	*The North Ship* published, after much delay, by the Fortune Press.
October 1945	Sends his second novel, then titled *The Kingdom of Winter*, to Bruce Montgomery's agent, Peter Watt.
Jan.–Sept. 1946	Lodges in 7 Ladycroft, Wellington, where he is woken early in the mornings by the sun through an east-facing window.
September 1946	Takes up the post of assistant librarian at Leicester University College, staying during the first month with his sister Kitty and her husband in Loughborough. Shortly after his arrival he meets Monica Jones and lends her a copy of *Jill* and the proofs of *A Girl in Winter*, which has been accepted by Faber.
30 September 1946	Moves into lodgings at 172 London Road, Leicester.
26 October 1946	*Jill* published by the Fortune Press.

Late September–early October 1946	Philip and Ruth Bowman become lovers and briefly fear a pregnancy.
21 February 1947	*A Girl in Winter* published by Faber.
28 April 1947	Kitty and Walter Hewett's daughter, Rosemary, is born.
2 May 1947	Philip's letter congratulating the Hewetts on the birth of Rosemary. After this no letter to his sister survives until 1969. However, Kitty will have read most of the letters from Philip to their mother, and Eva will have related the contents of others to her.
7 September 1947	Philip moves into 6 College Street, Leicester.
October 1947	Philip buys a 'Puma Special' camera for £6.7.9d.
Early January–26 March 1948	Sydney Larkin terminally ill in Warwick Hospital.
21 January 1948	After abandoning plans for a back-street abortion, Kingsley Amis and Hilary Bardwell (Hilly) are married.
February 1948	Faber reject Larkin's collection *In the Grip of Light*, as do five other publishers.
26 March 1948 (Good Friday)	Sydney Larkin dies of cancer of the liver at the age of sixty-three. On 4 April Philip writes the elegy 'An April Sunday brings the snow', and then completes no other poem for almost a year.
April 1948	Eva receives hot wax treatment for an injured wrist.
17 May 1948	Philip proposes marriage to Ruth Bowman.
August 1948	'Penvorn' is leased, and Eva and Philip move into the newly bought 12 Dixon Drive, where they live for the next twenty-five months.

1948	Walter Hewett joins Urwick Orr & Partners as a management consultant. On 27 July 1949 Philip congratulates him on earning £1,000 a year.
28 December 1948–early January 1949	Philip and Ruth travel to Thomas Hardy country for a short holiday and visit Dorchester and Weymouth.
March 1950	Visits Kingsley and Hilly Amis in Swansea, where Kingsley is working as a university lecturer.
17 June 1950	Proposes for a second time to Ruth Bowman, but retracts the offer after three days.
July 1950	Philip and Monica Jones become lovers.
4 September 1950	The furniture from 12 Dixon Drive is put into store in anticipation of its sale and Eva moves in with her daughter at 53 York Road, Loughborough.
1 October 1950	Arrives in Queen's University Belfast (QUB) to take up the post of sub-librarian. Shorty afterwards he meets Ansell and Judy Egerton. Ansell is a lecturer in economics, and Judy is later to become one of the poet's regular correspondents.
October 1950	Eva advertises in the press for a live-in companion to share the house she intends to buy, and over the following months interviews several applicants.
October 1950	Eva begins to attend lectures on psychology organised by Dr Edith Folwell. In 1951 she writes 'She really is the most marvellous woman I have ever met.'
Oct. 1950–Aug. 1951	Philip lodges in Queen's Chambers, Belfast.
31 December 1950	First appearance in a letter of a drawing of the 'old creature' distinguished from the 'young

	creature' by a neat mob cap. At first she is still 'dear old Mop', but from 3 August 1951 becomes 'Dear old Creature'.
February 1951	'Latest Face', inspired by Winifred Arnott, library assistant at QUB. Several of Larkin's best early poems are addressed to her.
27 April 1951	Larkin takes delivery of 100 copies of *XX Poems*, privately printed by Carswells, Belfast. He dedicates the collection to Amis.
April 1951	Eva visits Belfast, breaking her return journey in Hyde to stay with her sister-in-law, Nellie.
11–14 May 1951	Monica visits Belfast. On 12 May they take a trip to Dublin together.
July–August 1951	Philip and Monica holiday in Dorset and Devon and also visit the Amises in Swansea.
August 1951	Eva stays in Newark with the Cann family. John Cann had been a friend of Sydney Larkin.
Aug.–Oct. 1951	Philip lodges briefly at 7 College Park East, and then at 49 Malone Road, Belfast.
13 October 1951	Colin Strang of the Philosophy Department in QUB, and his wife Patsy, help Philip to move into an attic flat at 30 Elmwood Avenue, Belfast.
10 December 1951	Eva moves into 21 York Road, Loughborough, bought with Kitty's and Philip's advice. However she frequently sleeps in 'her' room in her daughter's home a hundred yards away, or takes refuge there from thunder.
March 1952	Monica visits Belfast. On 15–17 March she and Philip take a trip to Dublin together.
23–27 May 1952	Philip visits Paris with Bruce Montgomery.

July 1952	After a clandestine affair of some months Patsy Strang tells Philip that she is pregnant by him, but immediately suffers a miscarriage.
August 1952	Eva visits Belfast, breaking her return journey in Hyde and staying with Nellie for three weeks.
January 1953	Winifred Arnott announces her engagement to be married. Philip tells his mother he feels 'a bit balked concerning her'.
July–August 1953	Philip holidays in Mallaig, Inverness-shire, with Monica, and then with Eva in Weymouth.
August 1953	Completes 'Mother, Summer, I'.
26 October 1953	Completes 'Whatever Happened', which alludes obliquely to his affair with Patsy Strang.
January 1954	Kingsley Amis's *Lucky Jim* published.
19 February 1954	At Donald Davie's request, Larkin gives a talk at Trinity College, Dublin, where Davie is a lecturer.
1954	*Listen Magazine* (Hessle), published by George and Jean Hartley, prints 'Toads' (Summer 1954) and 'Poetry of Departures' (Winter 1954).
November 1954–September 1961	Monica lives at 8 Woodhall Avenue, Leicester. On his return to the mainland in 1955 Philip combines visits to his mother in Loughborough with visits to Monica in Leicester, though the two women seldom meet. It becomes a fixed routine for Philip to be at his mother's for Christmas and with Monica at the New Year.
30 December 1954–5 January 1955	Philip and Monica take a holiday in Winchester and Salisbury, and visit Bruce Montgomery.

21 March 1955	Larkin takes up the post of Librarian at the University of Hull. He stays at first in a university property, Holtby House, in Cottingham.
Late April–early June 1955	Lodges at 11 Outlands Road, in the room which inspires 'Mr Bleaney'.
May 1955	*Lucky Jim* wins the Somerset Maugham Award for fiction.
4 July 1955	Eva's GP refers her to a psychiatrist, who prescribes tablets.
July 1955–Apr. 1956	Larkin lodges at 200 Hallgate, Cottingham, a 'village-suburb' of Hull.
21 August 1955	Completes 'Reference Back', which he later calls in a letter to Eva 'The one about you saying "that was a pretty one".'
September 1955	Philip and Monica holiday in Dixcart Hotel, Sark, Channel Islands.
1 November 1955	*The Less Deceived* published by subscription by George and Jean Hartley's Marvell Press.
Late 1955	Eva is diagnosed with clinical depression and in early December is admitted to Carlton Hayes Hospital, Narborough, where she receives electric shock treatment. Philip stays with Eva over Christmas at the Angel Hotel in Grantham (where he writes 'Pigeons'), with an excursion on Christmas Day to a hotel in Melton Mowbray where Kitty has booked a family Christmas dinner. At the end of December Eva is moved to convalesce in 'The Woodlands', Forest Road, Narborough.
January 1956	In the New Year Philip and Monica visit Chichester Cathedral, and on 20 February he completes 'An Arundel Tomb'.

28 January 1956	Philip takes Eva home to 21 York Road before returning to Hull by train on 29 or 30 January.
1956	*New Lines*, edited by Robert Conquest, published. It includes eight poems by Larkin.
April–October 1956	Moves to 192A Hallgate, Cottingham.
July–August 1956	Philip and Monica holiday together on Skye. Then Philip spends a week (11–18 August) with Eva in Stratford, after which she goes to stay with Nellie in Hyde.
24 September 1956	Mary Wrench appointed as a library assistant at the University of Hull.
1 October 1956	Eva is initiated by Dr Folwell into the 'Circle of Silent Ministry' with whose members she remains in touch until her final years.
27 October 1956	Larkin moves into a high-windowed flat at the top of 32 Pearson Park, Hull.
1 January 1957	Completes 'Love Songs in Age'.
20 May 1957	Betty Mackereth appointed as Larkin's secretary.
30 August 1957	On a trip to London with Monica Philip buys the second-hand Rolleiflex camera with which he takes his later photographs.
4 November 1957	Larkin, Betty Mackereth, and library assistants Mary Wrench and Wendy Mann drive to Busby Hall, North Riding to collect books for the library. Betty drives the hired car.
February 1958	Anthony Thwaite invites Larkin on behalf of the BBC to contribute to a programme for the European Service entitled *Younger British Poets of Today*.
January 1959	The Listen Records recording of Larkin reading *The Less Deceived* is issued.

28 May 1959	*Who's Who* send for Larkin's details. He comments to his mother: 'This pleased me mightily. Pop never got in *Who's Who*.'
September 1959	After meticulous preparation the transfer of books to the newly built University of Hull library begins. 'We are doing about 10,000 books a day, & it will last about 2–3 weeks.'
18 October 1958	After many months of drafting, 'The Whitsun Weddings' is completed.
Oct.–Dec. 1959	Monica's parents die, her mother on 11 October, her father in the second week in December. She falls into depression. Having nowhere to go, she spends Christmas in Loughborough with Eva and Philip, the only time she does so.
29 December 1959	Mary Wrench marries Stephen Judd.
March 1960	Larkin travels to Reading University, having applied for the post of librarian. But, after being given a tour round the library and seeing the town (9 March), he catches the train back to Hull and misses the interview. He tells his mother: 'It's strange how panicky I got towards the day: I can see now that I didn't at all want to move from Hull.'
10 May 1960	Completes 'Faith Healing'.
20 June 1960	The Queen Mother officially opens Stage 1 of the Hull library. Both Eva and Monica travel to Hull for the occasion.
July 1960	Philip and Monica take a holiday in Stocks Hotel, Sark, Channel Islands.
13–18 August 1960	Eva and Nellie holiday in Llandudno, staying in Hyde before and afterwards.
11 December 1960	Philip attends the confirmation of his niece Rosemary in St Peter's Church, Loughborough.

2 February 1961	On hearing that she has passed the Library Association examination, for which he coached her, Maeve Brennan takes Philip out for a celebratory meal in the Beverley Arms. She writes later that at this point 'our friendship entered a new and headier phase'.
11 February 1961	The first of Larkin's monthly jazz reviews appears in the *Daily Telegraph*.
6 March 1961	Larkin collapses in a library committee meeting and is rushed to Kingston General Hospital.
24 March 1961	Walter drives Kitty and Eva to Hull to visit.
10–24 April 1961	Larkin admitted to Fielden House, the London Hospital, for tests under the neurologist Sir Russell Brain. Monica stays in a hotel and visits every day. Robert Conquest, Judy Egerton, Stephen Spender, the Amises and John Betjeman also visit. He complains that his hearing has been damaged by infections contracted in the hospital.
21–26 June 1961	Philip and Monica stay in Durrants Hotel, London, and attend the England *vs* Australia Test Match at Lord's. This cricket outing becomes an annual ritual.
September 1961	Monica moves to 1A Cross Road, Leicester. She also uses money inherited from her parents to buy a second home in Haydon Bridge, near Hexham, Northumberland, on the banks of the Tyne. In subsequent years it becomes routine for Philip to spend New Year with Monica in Haydon Bridge after Christmas with his mother.
6 November 1961	Completes 'Broadcast', addressed to Maeve Brennan, which he later describes as 'about as near as I get in [*The Whitsun Weddings*] to a love poem'.

1961–4	Philip and Eva exchange cuttings concerned with news from the Leicestershire village of Bunny, with jokes about Bunny's presumed rabbit inhabitants.
25 February 1961	Mary Judd (Wrench) gives birth to a daughter, Helen. Betty Mackereth and Philip are the godparents.
2–9 Sept. 1962	Eva and Nellie holiday in Bournemouth.
3 February 1963	Completes 'Long Last', based on Eva's account of acquaintances of hers.
10 May 1963	Maeve Brennan persuades Philip to attend a staff dance, which occasions his unfinished poem 'The Dance', concerned with his inability to marry.
August 1963	Eva holidays with Nellie at Cliftonville Hotel, Cromer.
28 February 1964	*The Whitsun Weddings* published by Faber.
3 March 1964	Buys his first car, 'a Singer with an automatic gearbox'.
3–10 June 1964	Filming of the BBC *Monitor* feature 'Down Cemetery Road', directed by Patrick Garland.
August 1964	Eva holidays with Nellie at Sunnyville Hotel, Alexandra Road, Southport, Lancashire.
Aug.–Sept. 1964	Philip and Monica holiday in Dentdale and Swaledale, Cumbria, and visit the home of Beatrix Potter in Sawrey.
15 December 1964	'Down Cemetery Road' broadcast.
3 June 1965	The Queen's Gold Medal for Poetry arrives by post, encased in corrugated cardboard.
26 August 1965	The Hewetts move from 53 York Road to 'Oddstones', 283 Forest Road, one-and-a-half miles from Eva in York Road.

September 1965	Philip and Monica holiday in Dixcart Hotel, Sark, Channel Islands.
7 November 1966	Visits his niece Rosemary in Warwick University where she is studying English.
March 1967	Hull's library is renamed after the Vice Chancellor, Brynmor Jones, Larkin himself having suggested the idea some time earlier.
21–25 June 1967	Philip and Monica stay at Durrants Hotel, London, and attend the 2nd Test Match of the India tour of England at Lord's. They also have dinner with John Betjeman and Lady Elizabeth Cavendish.
23 September 1967	Monica and Philip visit Bellingham Show for the first time. This and subsequent visits inspire 'Show Saturday' (completed 3 December 1973).
October 1967–March 1968	Eva has problems with her new 'Parkray' fire. Larkin engages in correspondence with the contractor and the National Coal Board Heat Advisory Service asking that the fire be removed and requesting a reduction of the bill.
9 May 1968	Philip tells his mother he has 'delivered in person to No. 10 Downing Street a refusal of the O.B.E.!'
July–August 1968	Eva and Nellie holiday in the Windsor Hotel, Great Yarmouth.
Late 1968	After hearing that she has achieved her two 'A' levels in August, Jean Hartley leaves George, and moves into an unfurnished flat with her two daughters. She goes on to register for a degree in English at the University of Hull.
31 December 1968	Philip and Monica attend the New Year tar-barrel festivities in Allendale, Northumberland, for the first time.

9 July 1969	Receives an honorary D.Litt. at Queen's University, Belfast.
21 July 1969	Undergoes an operation to remove a polyp from his nose, staying overnight in hospital.
7 August 1969	While on holiday with Eva at the Duke's Head Hotel, Norwich, Philip notices that his mother is frequently disorientated. They take trips from Norwich to Southwold.
25 August–14 September 1969	Philip and Monica tour Ireland, viewing Yeats's grave and visiting Richard Murphy at his home in Cleggan near Westport.
26 October 1969	Larkin tells Eva that he has written a poem 'based on our visits to Southwold [. . .] It mentions your first meeting with Pop.' This is 'To the Sea'.
9 February 1970	*All What Jazz* published by Faber.
12–24 July 1970	Eva stays in the Abbeyfield residential home for the elderly at 17 Victoria Street, Loughborough, allowing Kitty and Walter to take a holiday.
17 July–5 Aug. 1970	Philip and Monica holiday on Uist and Skye, returning via Haydon Bridge.
16 September 1970–22 March 1971	Larkin takes sabbatical leave at All Souls College, Oxford, to work on the *Oxford Book of Twentieth-Century English Verse*. He stays at Beechwood House, Iffley Turn, Oxford.
12 December 1970	Lord Cohen of Birkenhead opens Stage 2 of the University of Hull library.
16–20 June 1971	Philip and Monica stay at Durrants Hotel, London, and attend the 2nd Test Match of the Pakistan tour of England at Lord's.
15–22 July 1971	Philip and Eva holiday together at the Duke's Head Hotel, King's Lynn.

4–24 August 1971	Eva is booked again into the Abbeyfield home while Kitty and Walter take a holiday in Hungary.
January 1972	On one of a sequence of diets. On 16 January Larkin weighs 'halfway between 14 st & 14½ st'.
January 1972	Goes to the Hull Royal Infirmary for treatment for a crick in his neck. Here he has the first idea for 'The Building'.
18 January 1972	Eva is told by the doctor to stay in bed with flu. But it seems that she has also suffered a fall.
24 January 1972	Eva falls in her kitchen and breaks her hip. After a week in hospital she enters (1 February) Berrystead Nursing Home, Syston, Leicestershire, the care home chosen by Kitty and Philip. From this point on Philip writes to her almost every day, except when he is visiting.
6 March 1972	Drafts 'Heads in the Women's Ward' on a single workbook page.
September 1972	Monica moves to 18 Knighton Park Road, Leicester.
10 October 1972	John Betjeman appointed Poet Laureate.
October 1972–12 January 1973	'The Old Fools' written in a long drafting process.
29 March 1973	*The Oxford Book of Twentieth-Century English Verse* published by Oxford University Press.
23 August–16 September 1973	Philip drives up to Haydon Bridge and then (29 August) he and Monica drive on to Scotland, staying in hotels in Peebles and

	Fortingall. They then return to Haydon Bridge on 14 September. Philip returns to Hull on 16 September.
17 May 1974	Eva writes the last letter to Philip to be stamped and posted, though she leaves a number of uncompleted draft letters.
3 June 1974	*High Windows* published by Faber.
27 June 1974	Moves out of 32 Pearson Park and into 105 Newland Park.
July 1974	Philip and Monica travel to St Andrews, where he receives an honorary D.Litt. on 6 July.
2–15 Sept. 1974	Philip and Monica holiday for a week in Gatehouse of Fleet, Dumfries and Galloway, followed by a week in the Yorkshire Dales.
1–6 August 1975	Philip and Monica stay at Durrants Hotel, London, and attend the 2nd Test Match of the Australia tour of England at Lord's.
4 November 1975	Travels to London with Monica and receives his CBE at Buckingham Palace.
1–7 August 1976	Philip and Monica holiday in Dorset, visiting Dorchester and Bere Regis in the footsteps of Thomas Hardy.
2 April 1977	Rosemary Hewett, Kitty's daughter, marries David Parry.
16 September 1977	The last dated postcard from Philip to Eva in the archive. It is probable that other cards were sent after this which have not survived.
17 November 1977	Eva Larkin dies at the age of ninety-one.
29 November 1977	Completes the drafting of 'Aubade', abandoned on 7 June 1974.
1983	Appoints Anthony Thwaite and Andrew Motion as his literary executors.

2 December 1985	Philip Larkin dies of cancer of the oesophagus in Hull Royal Infirmary at the age of sixty-three.
25 December 1992	Catherine Hewett dies.
1994	Rosemary Parry (Hewett) deposits Larkin family papers U DLN/1–5 in the Brynmor Jones Library. The university collection is now held in the Hull History Centre.
2008	Rosemary deposits more Larkin family papers (U DLN/6–7) in the Brynmor Jones Library.

Letters Home
1936–1977

1936

24 August 1936

Picture postcard[1]

Hotel Eichburg Werningerode

Dear Kit,

Thank you very, very, much for the dance band report. It makes me wish I was with you; & puts me in touch with civilization once more. They sound lovely. Bands here are lousy, except one I saw on Saturday evening in Cologne. personnel: BASS & TROMBONE: SAX & VIOLIN: SAX, VIOLIN & CLAR: TRUMPET & CELLO. PIANO DRUMS. They are all doubled, as I have shown. leader: violin & sax. lovely tone.

1 Werningerode Rathaus.

1938

21 September 1938

[Penvorn,[1] 1 Manor Road, Coventry]

Dear Pop & Mop: –

Kit said that she was posting a letter to you, so I thought I'd stuff in a note for you.[2] I am now a Sixth-Form "man" plus honours plus glory plus a locker plus a blasted place in the Rugger second team which I don't want. We aren't set homework – whoopee! (excuse lousy writing), and have several private study periods in the library. Can survey the world with scorn now.

A new kid called Slater who came into the modern VI has been shoved onto me. Comes from Mansfield & is bespectacled & white. Grogh!!

Heard that Sankey(!) and I were the only ones who got distinctions in English. Favours in the usual way, please ....

We read Molières [*sic*] "Un Médècin(?) Malgré Lui"[3] in class today with Horne. To my mind, humerous a few [*sic*]. Hughes[4] says I can be a sub Editor on the Mag as Davies wants to chuck it. (Excuse "healthy schoolboy" tone of letter – you asked for it!) The attaché case meets with much approval. Montgomery has been doing German for a year & doesn't know what "eingang" means, so you can see I shan't be taught much.

Saw M. Dietrich in "Shanghai Express" yesterday.[5] Not bad. We received your card & are pleased that you are all o.k. (revolting phrase!) also one from the Ashton people who are at Blackpoo'.[6]

Have almost finish[ed] "Jane Eyre" and "Erewhon".[7] I like the first more: but I like the bit in the second (for Pop only) about the college of Unreason & the teachers: "The expression of the faces of these people were repellent (i.e. the graduates & dons); they did not, however, seem particularly unhappy, for none of them had the faintest idea that they were in reality more dead than alive." Reminiscent of certain gentlemen whom I have an acquaintance .....

All Love & wishes from
Philip.

1 'Penvorn' is a portmanteau of the names of the house's builder, Percy Vernon Venables.
2 Sydney and Eva were on holiday in Germany.
3 *Le Médecin Malgré Lui* ('The Doctor in Spite of Himself'): farce by the classic French writer Molière (1622–73), first presented in 1666.
4 Noel ('Josh') Hughes, Larkin's friend and rival at King Henry VIII School, Coventry. At this point he was editor of the school magazine, *The Coventrian*.
5 A 1932 film, directed by Josef von Sternberg and starring Marlene Dietrich, Clive Brook, Anna May Wong and Warner Oland.
6 Eva Larkin's only brother, Arthur Day (1888–1941), lived with his wife Nellie ('Auntie Nellie') and their family in Ashton-under-Lyne at this time.
7 *Jane Eyre*: novel by Charlotte Brontë (1816–55), published in 1847. *Erewhon*: satirical novel by Samuel Butler (1835–1902), published in 1872.

1939

18 June 1939

<*Letterhead*> Penvorn, Manor Road, Coventry

Dear Mop (& Pop, if he happens to be there),

Hope you are painting Southport the correct shade of red. Pop seems to be, to judge from this evening's Telegraph: –

"'FALSE GLAMOUR' ATTACHED TO ELECTRICITY!"
"THIS CODDLING OF THE INDUSTRY!"
"VAGUE & WOOLLY" LANGUAGE!!!
"MR LARKIN TELLS THE WORLD"!

– just a few of the headlines.

For mai seniah Coventrian praize (haw haw! Eh, what?) I have chosen, in a fit of frenzy, an anthology of the Prose of D.H. Lawrence. The old man[1] made a few caustic remarks, i.e. "He led rather a dissipated life, didn't he?" and I said "Mmm." (meditative sound) and added, like a FOOL!!! "He was a schoolmaster." The old man burst into a cackle of laughter (old chump!)

Oh, well. I don't think I've much to say, but I 'ave been suffrin' aggernies, dearie, somethin' chronic!!

'Ay fever!! Cor, more like a non-stop sneezing display!!

Your 'orrid offspring,
Philip

1 A. A. C. Burton, Headmaster of King Henry VIII School, Coventry, 1931–50.

[Summer 1939] Tuesday Night & Wednesday Morn.

Hotel du Cinquantenaire, 21 Rue Juste Lipse, Brussels

Dear Fambly,

Excuse pencil but pen is empty & I don't feel like haggling with Belgian hotel manager about "de l'encre". Thanks for both of your letters:

1 Pop: glad you enjoyed Bishes[1] tergy[2] – he was Judas, as you probably know. He produced and wrote it all himself – bar my swingeing verse, and where is Albania anyway? *I* don't know.[3] Thanks for the Hersill instructions.[4]

2 Kit. (Good God, I am tired – time: 11.15) sorry about 'rollicking schoolboy' tone of letter. I have rather been overdoing it at times, but an early night is promised tonight.

Still, a holiday is by definition, a complete change, so it is all logical. Thanks for news of what you have been doing. – I suppose Ashworth is saying "Don't draw laike a mep – a mep of Albaniah!" every time he sees Wilson's work. Did you get my postcard? Might show it to him!

Thanks for both cuttings. I presume an arrest is expected quite soon as far as Hodge goes – ("Ooh – it wasn't my fault – the teacher rubbed it out!")

You needn't worry about *me* getting locked up at all, or dancing with any hostesses. The nearest I got to the latter was sitting for about an hour in a beastly stuffy room, right under the band, drinking an orangeade – yes, an orangeade – and watching Sheppard gnawing his fingernails and wanting to dance, but as the floor resembled Smithford St[5] on Saturday night and the band kept playing tangos & rumbas, he couldn't do anything. Afterwards a section of us left him to it & went on to a café to play cards.

Yesterday we went a full time trip to Spa[6] and a few other joints near the German frontier ("them Nazis"). [. . .]

We went over another mineral water factory at Spa & got ourselves blown out. Lousy muck, this mineral water. Tonight we hope to get seats for the "Folies Bergère" who happen to be in Bruxelles.

I'll see what I can do about the notepaper.

("er – pourriez-vous me donner –"

"le prochaine, s'il vous plaît" (next please))

Philip

P.S. Hope K.[7] is cutting out my countryman's diary.

1 Nickname of Frank Smith, one of Larkin's school friends.

2 Conjectural reading; perhaps a deliberately illiterate abbreviation of 'dramaturgy'. Possibly 'elegy'.

3 Larkin had written blank verse choruses for a Holy Week passion play by his High Anglican school friend Frank Smith. See Noel Hughes, 'The Young Mr Larkin', *Larkin at Sixty*, ed. Anthony Thwaite (London: Faber, 1982), 17–22.

4 Obscure.

5 Street in central Coventry.

6 Spa had been the headquarters of the Imperial German forces in the later stages of the First World War.

7 Kitty: Philip's sister Catherine.

[Summer 1939] Picture postcard[1]

[Brussels]

Dear Mop,

This is another of the Wiertz collection[2] – Sent it to you because it's rather like how we look in the mornings. Weather continues fine, and Brussels is a marvellous city. You wouldn't like me to bring you back a Belgian maid, would you?

Philip

1 *Une Tête Coupée – A Severed Head*: Musée Wiertz, Bruxelles

2 Antoine Wiertz (1806–65), Belgian Romantic painter and sculptor.

1940

11–12 October 1940

St John's College, Oxford

Dear Mugs in General,

I might as well start writing to you now though I probably shan't finish it at one sitting. Not that it's going to be very long or very detailed. Up to the present I haven't done very much at all except join the O.T.C.[1] and see Gavin Bone about lectures, tutorials &c.[2] The former was rather a swindle altogether. We gang of shivering freshmen were herded into the enormous hall: august figures in stately robes gazed down at us from the picture frames. August gentlemen (gowned) gazed at us from the high table. Forms were served out to us by obsequious college servants. We were augustly & curtly commanded to fill up & hand in both forms (one matriculation: one O.T.C.). This most of us did. Only now, when we're gaining a bit more confidence do we realise that the whole thing is a purely voluntary affair & that not even the Chancellor himself can make us join if we don't want to. We feel rather strongly about this. But we hope to be slung out when any medical exam comes off.

The second event, seeing my tutor, was more congenial. I am to drop Pass Mods altogether because the College now decides that two groups (i.e. of special subjects for War Degrees) is equal to Pass Mods & when they are passed (in 2 terms I hope) I can go on with the Honours Course as usual. You may not like this but the advantage is that I do get started on English at once: and especially Anglo Saxon, which will take (for me) God's own time to learn.

Tutorials take place once a week on Friday at 12 noon. Lectures I shall attend aren't particularly brilliant (not by their famous names, anyway) but the subjects look interesting. The one that most interests me actually is Lord David Cecil on "English Poets since Tennyson". (This however is only about a thousand years out of my period.) So as regards work I shall do Shakespeare & Anglo Saxon this term, taking a Shakespeare Group at the term's end.

As regards friends & society, everybody of my year – bar one or two – seems very pleasant. (The Seniors don't even look at you – yet.) Up to the date of writing, I have not been asked:

a) Who I am
b) What I'm reading.
c) Who my father is.
d) Who I think I am.
e) What I'm doing in *this* part of the College?

Money is being spent pretty freely. Still, I suppose it's all necessary initial outlay. I've bought a new cap & gown (the other one was really just *too* short, even for a commoner) which were 12/6: (Hughes' were 22/6 – who'd be a scholar)[3] then I bought three pictures – Cézanne's "The Smoker": Van Gogh's "The Artist's Bedroom" and one by Gauguin. They were 8/- each. Hughes gingerly inquired the price of a glass virgin & child and was equally gingerly told "3 gns". Then we bought a clock (10/-) and then of course there are odd expenses that one hardly notices. The other large thing remains, perhaps, a College scarf. But I'm leaving that for the present. Neither do I feel like playing any games. I feel I've got no team spirit so what the hell's the good of joining teams. And anyway the O.T.C. will probably take up all surplus joie de vivre.

Last night (Friday night) we had a sort of clan-gathering of Old Coventrians in Dupénois' rooms at Jesus, proceeding for coffee at Smith's rooms in Hertford.[4] While we were there, the secretary of the O.U. Labour Club called: previous to going out, we at St John's had received a visit from the secretary of the corresponding Conservative league. A very smooth young man, like a guinea pig. When we got back, we found that the respective secs of the O. Union & the St John's league for Nukel[5] affairs (or something) had called in our absence.

Yesterday, too, Roe[6] turned up for tea, bringing some cakes &c so we scoured Oxford for milk & managed to make some tea. We have since placed a standing order for ½ pint of milk per day at the buttery.

I am enclosing the receipt for the £40 cheque. I suppose that's the right thing to do. \PS. Note the spelling!/

The food here defies comment. Hughes & I agree that we are the only people here who can really plumb its depths, all the others having been ruined as regards taste at their public schools. Breakfast begins with porridge. We had some the first day. I had one mouthful & Hughes had 3. Since then we have had no more. The coffee is black. When milk is added it turns grey. It neither looks nor tastes like coffee. Yesterday we had "grilled herrings". They tasted simply awful: as if all the fishwives and fishmongers in Billingsgate had contributed a gob of spittle to their glutinous horror. Other meals are less horrible: the bread & cheese at dinner is perhaps the only food that is positively pleasant to eat.

Hughes was yesterday informed at dinner that "all freshman scholars must meet at staircase 1 tomorrow morning at a quarter to 7". Needless to say, he didn't go: this is only the first of the long series of practical jokes freshmen are subjected to. When mine comes perhaps I'll let you know. Things probably won't start in earnest till Sunday; however, we have hidden our caps & gowns away in the most inaccessible place we could think of.

I don't know if it's an official secret to tell you that Oxford is continually bothered by airplanes (pardon the slang)[7] all day & night. English of course. Very queer to hear the noise of a 'plane at night, & look out to see a moving light in the sky. English, you see. Rumour had it that a German plane circled over here yesterday afternoon quite unnoticed by anybody, but it did nothing. Rumour also has it that Baginton aerodrome was dive-bombed on Thursday afternoon: if so I hope you're all right.[8]

We have been here three mornings: I have had 3 baths, Hughes 2. (He overslept today.) We find that a charge is made of 7/- for using the college baths, so we are wasting our money.

The clock is going very nicely & fits in well with the mantelpiece. But I wish I'd brought that calendar, because 3 pictures, however good, don't exactly fill up 4 huge blank walls. I suppose you couldn't send it, could you?

So far (Saturday morning) I have had no post at all, bar a circular from St. Aldate's Church. Cheerful. Hughes periodically slinks off to drink sherry with Alphonso de Zuluetta (commonly known as "Zulu") who is Catholic chaplain of the University, and talk of "Ronnie" (Father Ronald Knox).[9] Also he consorts with the Black Friars over the road.[10] Comic Black Friars, they all wear white!

As yet I am doing no work. Before I can, the College library has to open, & I've got to be admitted to the Bodleian as a reader. The latter I can't do till I've matriculated: this happens on Tuesday afternoon at 3 pm or so. If you like you may think of me then serenely parading down Broad Street in cap, gown, & white tie, to meet the Vice-Chanc. & be addressed in Latin.

Later. We have just been "activating our social side". We asked someone called Ross to tea and gorged him on sausage rolls & cream buns – with a cigarette thrown in for good measure. I don't think we're really a success at this social game – it's too hard to keep up. But we form our friendships now on the: "Are – you – in – the – O.T.C. – awful – rot – isn't – it" plan that seems to work all right. I've spoken to no one yet that really is keen on it & a good many that are decidedly antipathetic. Anyway, we're having the Old Coventrians in our rooms tonight, so we can relax.

Another bogey at the place is {sconsions / sconcians} (?) – anyway, the idea is that, after today any fresher at dinner may be demanded to "sink a sconce" – i.e. 2 pints or more of beer – at one go. Or you pay for the sconce for the whole table. The Senior Scholars do the dirty work: anyone whom they pick on (beforehand) is "sconced" for the most trivial offence – wearing gaudy clothes, staring at the oil paintings, being a minute late for dinner – anything they can trump up. God knows how long it goes on .... [11]

———

Has anyone sent off any of those poems of mine? If so, where? And shoot along any two guineas that turn up – we need more pictures.

———

Today I went into the College library. Pretty good. Can see myself doing very little real work – but reading a good deal.

Well, I don't think I'll prolong this letter further, even though I'd like to include Norwood's Sermon tomorrow.[12] But tonight is my last night as a sort of half-member: term & work starts tomorrow. This time on Tuesday, too, I shall be full-blown.

Worry not about me: everything seems relatively harmless.

All love,
Philip

1 Officer Training Corps.

2 Gavin Bone, an Anglo-Saxon scholar, was Larkin's tutor in St John's.

3 Larkin was sharing his rooms with his school friend Noel Hughes ('Josh'). Hughes had gained a scholarship in modern languages. Larkin was merely a 'commoner' with a shorter gown.

4 Georges Dupénois and Frank Smith ('The Bish'): Old Coventrians who had also come up to Oxford.

5 A guess at Larkin's word, which is illegible, perhaps deliberately so.

6 Ernest Roe, another Old Coventrian, was at Exeter College.

7 'Aeroplane' was regarded as the correct usage, 'airplane' being an Americanism.
8 The Baginton aerodrome was close to Coventry.
9 Fr Alphonso de Zulueta (*d.* 1980) succeeded Ronald Knox, broadcaster and writer of detective stories, as Catholic chaplain of Oxford in 1938.
10 The Dominican priory is on the corner of Pusey Street opposite St John's across St Giles (built 1921–9).
11 This Oxford tradition is usually termed 'sconcing'.
12 Sir Cyril Norwood (1875–1956), President of St John's between 1934 and 1946, was an Anglican layman and President of the Modern Churchmen's Union. His *The English Tradition of Education* (1929) praised the character-building effect of public school discipline. Larkin and Hughes ridiculed his elegy 'To a Fallen Airman' (*The Times*, 16 January 1941) in the College Junior Common Room Suggestions Book: 'Surely, sir, the ability to scan throughout eight whole lines is not to be despised, and to produce three good rhymes out of four is no mean achievement.' See John Kelly, 'Philip Larkin vs Sir Cyril Norwood: St John's College, Oxford, 1941', *About Larkin* 44 (October 2017), 5–6.

15 October 1940

St John's College, Oxford

Dear fambly,

Thanks for the bulky parcel of correspondence that arrived yesterday. Very sorry to here [*sic*] about Saturday's raid: it must have been hell. Jim came up on Sunday & told us what he knew, which wasn't much. So I was relieved to here [*sic*] that nobody was injured at all apud Penvorn.[1]

To answer Mop first: at present we are using Hughes' "toilet cover" which is as bad as mine in a different way – silky and très chic. As for the rest of the paraphernalia, the coffee strainer is *invaluable*. Ours are the only rooms in Oxford where coffee free from choking grounds can be drunk. Work – as yet – is rather tentative. One might as well try to work in a hotel. So far – I am warm. I have the eiderdown on the bed which is also invaluable.

Now for Pop: Thanks for the poems, & the addresses. The latter look fishy to me, bar "new verse" – rather too traditional. You see, a traditional paper would never print a modernist poem. Still, I'll try.

As for the line in question, I am surprised that Mr S.[2] should find it difficult – if he really does. The last sestet is far more obscure – involving a whole rigmarole of private philosophy and so on. \However,/ when Rupert B. returned from Tahiti to join up in 1914, he wrote five sonnets, of which the most famous is "If I should die, think only this of me . . .".

These sonnets have been "taken" by "the old" politicians, editors, archbishops &c to delude the young of the last generation & of this too into fighting the "old"'s battles for them. This may not be true but anyway that's what the lines mean. Confirmation can (I hope) be found in the intro. to Kitty's edition on her bedroom shelves, whence all the data for the poem was found.[3]

Before continuing this letter, I am going to do some work. (!!!!!) By the way, Hughes was introduced to Arnold Lunn[4] last night. As far as social activities go, Hughes is outstripping me by *yards* .....

Wednesday. On Sunday I attended my first and (I trust) last chapel. Norwood drivelled in a cultured manner. On Monday I attended my first lecture – Edmund Blunden talking about biography.[5] Very strange. B. was a nervous man with a shock of hair, a nose like a wedge, and a twitching mouth. He delivered his lecture in staccato phrases, semi-ironically, only half concealing his genuine enthusiasm for his subject. After that I heard Nichol-Smith talking about Dryden, and yesterday Prof. Wyld on the History of English. The latter was very interesting but hard to follow.

Yesterday, too, we were Matriculated. This entailed dressing up in all the full apparel – I didn't look half bad at all – and shambling down to Divinity Schools to receive the Statutes of the University and being blessed in Latin by the Vice Chancellor. This was only a very hasty affair – cut down to a mere nothing – and conducted to the accompaniment of bombers overhead. God, there are *hundreds*! My Latin name, by the way, is Philippus Arturus Larkin.

I withdrew three pounds from the P.O. yesterday & the fellow complained that the Coventry people had not stamped their stamp in the first place, which he then left blank, advising me to send it back to be done. This I am doing. If this is necessary, could you please get it done? He suspected me of further hanky-panky when I signed "Philip Larkin" instead of "Philip A. Larkin". Not that he was at all nasty about it.

Last night went to resee "Charley's Aunt".[6] Great humour at the Oxford scenes.

Jim complains that he is the only wholly male person at present at the Slade.[7] "70% women: 30% half-women." They look a peculiar crew.

Later on Wednesday. We are just awaiting our first game of hockey. This is a result of being pestered by other numerous gentlemen who are anxious not for our souls but our bodies. One particularly unpleasant fellow was from the Boat Club. He sat down at our table & talked, beady eyes glittering. We protested that we'd never touched an oar in our lives. He said that a year ago nor'd he. We whimpered that it would interfere with our work. He said that *he'd* passed all his exams. We whispered that we were weedy, unhealthy, weak & generally debilitated. He replied that one of the best oars suffered from infantile paralysis. Following his advantage, he said that we couldn't frowst all the time. We inaudibly replied that we sometimes opened the windows. Anyway, when the hockey fellow turned up we rushed into his arms in eagerness to "do" something & so provide ourselves with an excuse. Now it's so near, we rather feel nervous. Pray for us sinners now and at the time of our death . . . .

After tea Wednesday. Hockey over. Not so bad anyway. May play for the College tomorrow against Wycliffe (?),[8] they aren't short of men. But very unlikely, this. Roe & Georges are very worried about the absence of news. I've told them they can ring up you if they want for information about their districts.

The calendar arrived at lunch time today: thank you! Am glad you found my letter "most interesting": I'm afraid they must be very disconnected & hard to follow. Sorry I called you "S. Larkin" – I could have sworn I put "Esqu." in. Anyway, I've half a mind to address this to the "Lord High City Keeper of ye Moneybags" just to nark you.

The airraids sound ghastly: am divided between relief at not being there and remorse at having gone at all.

Have bought two more expensive things. 1) A St John's tie. (6/6) This is the red, yellow & black one, not the one with lambs & flags on. 2) An umbrella. This may seem quite absurd to you – perhaps it is. But in Oxford it rains so much – it's raining now – that it is unpleasant to dress in a continually damp mac. And it's no good staying in because there are always lectures. A second reason is that everybody has one. In Oxford, mackintosh = umbrella: overcoat = huge college scarf. Have not [got] the second yet: but may get it before the purchase tax goes on.

Thursday. Have just endured half-an-hour from a) the Democratic Socialists & b) the John's Society for World Affairs. Gods, give me strength! Beyond comment. If only people would think more about *why* they believe, instead of *what* . . . .

Will close now. Have bought a box of St John's College notepaper so you will see the dear old college crest next time.

Philip

Do hope you are still undamaged. P.T.O.

Thursday night attended the first meeting (which was public) of the Oxford Union.

Edward Hulton[9] was the guest speaker. After a great deal of cultured pleasantries about the new officers (all neatly attired in evening dress) the motion ("that after the war no single political party will be capable of dealing with the problems that will arise") got under way. It was proposed by an Indian, opposed by a young Carlton Club conservative, sec. prop:[10] a huge Pickwickian secretary with an affable smile & great wit "Adam said to Eve .... When they were leaving the Garden of Eden .... My dear .... We are living in an age of transition ...") Sec. opp: an oily, olive skinned Socialist from Balliol who was very convincing. Then Hulton got up & talked utter rot for an hour: and – which was worse – talked it badly. Incoherent and frequently punctuated with "er"'s. His attempts at humour failed lamentably: his attempts to discredit the Labour Party were greeted with hisses & fiery questions. ("Can the speaker explain how the Labour party refused armaments to the country when the conservative party was in power?") It was terribly boring. We remained until the end at 11.30 p.m., sneaking back to John's at about 10 to 12 – avoiding the 2/6 fine & "an interview with the President" by 10 minutes. Probably the only time *I* shall ever go to the Union.

1 *Apud*: Latin for 'at the house of'. James (Jim) Sutton (1921–97) was Philip's closest friend at King Henry VIII School, Coventry.

2 Possibly Sidwell. See letter of 23 January 1944.

3 This paragraph refers to Larkin's Audenesque sonnet 'Ultimatum', which had been accepted by the *Listener*, and appeared in the issue of 28 November 1940.

4 Possibly Sir Arnold Henry Moore Lunn (1888–1974) skier, mountaineer, supporter of Franco and Catholic apologist.

5 Edmund Blunden (1896–1974), poet of the First World War and friend of Siegfried Sassoon, was a fellow at Merton College at this time.

6 The farce by Brandon Thomas first performed in 1892.

7 Jim Sutton was studying at the Slade School of Art, relocated during the war to Oxford.

8 Wycliffe Hall: a Church of England theological college and a 'Permanent Private Hall' in the university.

9 Edward Hulton founded the Hulton Press in 1937. It published *Lilliput, Picture Post,* and *Eagle* and *Girl* for children. He was a member of the '1941 Committee' which pressed for more efficient production to enhance the war effort.

10 'second proposer'.

26 October 1940

<*Letterhead*> St John's College coat of arms

Dear Mop,

Received letter from Pop this morning telling me of the dispersal and near-fall of the House of Penvorn. I am very sorry to hear it, indeed. I was becoming rather worried because Roe, who receives daily letters, told me of virulent attacks on the station &c. and on our district in general. How we are dispersed – Leicester, Lichfield, Coventry & Oxford![1] Gloomy thought.

We are free from air raids here – only 3 since I came up. Only a few bombs, miles away. I don't see why they shouldn't attack here, though, (whisper it quietly) its [*sic*] lousy with aerodromes. [. . .] Oxford seems singularly cool about airraids – they've had none.

Am settling down now, except for work, which is very hard to get down to. Spend most of my time at lectures, eating, sleeping, & vainly trying to write poetry. Sometimes play poker with the others. [. . .]

I haven't found many friends up here yet. The person (Iles) I know the best I simply loathe.[2] Everybody else seems pleasant & unintelligent or distant & unintelligent. Oxford seems very little more intelligent than Coventry, in fact.

I take a bath now on (generally) alternate mornings, and it is quite comforting. My battels[3] last week came to about 4/6: this seemed a lot, but I heard somebody languidly complaining that his battels were 35/- & that he would have to cut down his laundry! All else was on beer, wine &c. There are some mugs here.

I should [think] Lichfield is pretty peaceful after the inferno of Coventry, & I hope you're getting on well there. Who is it you're staying with? I can't remember just for the minute.

With much love,
Philip

PS What a lovely-sounding address you have.

1 Sydney remained at his post in Coventry, Kitty was at the Leicester College of Arts and Crafts, and Eva was staying with Sydney's brother Alfred (1873–1955) at 33 Cherry Orchard, Lichfield, where this letter is addressed.
2 Norman Iles, Larkin's tutorial partner.
3 College bill.

28 October 1940

<*Letterhead*> St John's College coat of arms

Dear Pop,

Your letter of Thursday reached me this morning with its calamities. Actually, I was beginning to get worried about you, for Roe, who receives letters every day, reported concentrated attacks on Coventry and particularly the station. If nothing had come this morning I should have sent a telegram: "Is no news good news?" in desperation. But now the news has come it is sufficiently horrible.

What is happening in the world at present? I never read the papers and am quite ignorant of any developments at home or abroad. And I hope your temporary displacement won't mean the abandonment of your war diary. That will probably be the only good thing resultant from the war at all.[1]

We are \not/[2] free from airraids here. On Thursday night some bombs were dropped but no "alert" (!): on Thursday morning there was a short alarm. I am told that old Brett-Smith, lecturing on mediaeval romance, paused in his discourse, peered over his spectacles, and said "Do I hear an *unacademic* sound? . . ." Everybody roared with laughter & the lecture continued. I was listening to Lord David Cecil who just didn't bother at all.

You should have read that letter you readdressed to Mop, because the actual address doesn't mean a thing.[3] I tried to address to you each alternately, but the contents are common property – this actual one, I think, contained several things for you – receipt of bank book &c.

I have joined the English Club, the largest mixed club in Oxford, for 3/6 per term. Wilson Knight spoke on "Hassan" (James Elroy Flecker) on the first night to an enormous audience – nearly 300, I should think – at St. Hilda's. I have also subscribed for one term to "The Cherwell" (University magazine) which invites articles, short stories & poems. Four poems, too, have been sent to "New Verse", "The Cherwell" doesn't seem much to (literally) write home about, being mistakenly funny and veiledly 'left'. Reports of the Union, for instance – all the Left speakers praised, all the 'right' ones depreciated.

Work here is very hard. The trouble is, they expect you to do ten times as much as at school & make it ten times as difficult to work at all. But no doubt I shall settle down. [. . .]

Please write often if only to say you're still safe.

Philip

By the way, my stammer, which vanished for a few days when I came up, has returned in full force.

1 On the day war was declared, 3 September 1939, Sydney began a formal diary in a large hard-bound volume, headed on the first page 'The Fools' War'. It was to run to twenty volumes, and continued into 1946. Hull History Centre, U DLN/1/10–29.
2 'not' inserted in pencil superscript, with a question-mark in the margin.
3 This letter is addressed to Mrs E. E. Larkin, but begins 'Dear Pop'.

30 October 1940

St John's Coll. Ox.

Dear Pop,

[. . .] The "Listener" poem is still unprinted. "New Verse" have not yet replied. There is a letter of D.H.L.'s being offered for 15/- in Blackwell's: "Del Monte Ranch, Questa, New Mexico, 21st April 1925." A perfectly-written piece of work.

Must now try to do enough work to write an essay.

Philip

<*At top of first page*> PS as regards money, I still have £18.2.6. Can you give me some estimate of how much I ought to spend this term?

31 October 1940[1]

<*Letterhead*> St John's College coat of arms

Dear Kath,

Thank you for your letter, which I found very interesting and ought to have answered earlier.

If we are going to swop "day-in-the-life-of"'s, perhaps you might like to hear my general day, which starts with the scout making one big hell of a row at the grate in our sitting room at about 7.0 a.m. At about 7.30 he[2] pretends to wake, although I at least have generally been awake for threequarters of an hour already. We get up between then &

8.10 (breakfast at 8.15) and take it in turns to have baths on alternate mornings.

Breakfast over (usually quite insufficient) during the morning I work, unless I write a letter to start with. Perhaps I visit the college library (as many books as you can carry) first. Anyway I work in my room, or down at the Bodleian English reading room (of which I am a member) until it is time for any lectures I am going to. Lectures are not much help, as a rule. On Fridays at 12 I have a tutorial, which means that I spend an hour with Bone & he reads my weekly essay. Then comes dinner – 1 course & as much bread & cheese as you can lay your hands on.

Afternoons are rather dull. Most people play games. I either fall asleep, read & fall asleep, work & fall asleep, or potter round the numerous bookshops with my umbrella, peering shortsightedly at the dusty titles. Perhaps I buy something for tea (from Marks & Spencers).

Anyway, at four (about) I generally meet Jim from the Slade & we go back to tea at my rooms – or at least he has a cup of tea & Hughes & I eat largely.

Between tea & dinner (7.0 or 7.15, it varies) is quite a fruitful time for work. The night has fallen & the fire chuckles in the grate; there is a pleasant aroma of tea & cigarette smoke in the room (& coal-smoke, if the wind is in the wrong direction). At length we put on our gowns and grope across two quads in *pitch dark* for dinner. Also generally insufficient. It is over by 7.45 always.

The nights are spent in various ways. Generally I work, but sometimes I go to the pictures, or round to somebody else's rooms. If I am out after 9.0, I have to kick on the gate & have my name taken, although fines don't start till 10.15. After writing our diaries & having a final cup of coffee & a cigarette (to use up the milk – the coffee I mean) we go to bed at about eleven, tired but happy – or something like that.

"Freedom v. Discipline" sounds ghastly.[3] Hope you supported freedom, anyway. By the way, what is "contempory"? ("Tradition v. Contempory") Perhaps, too, you might enlighten me on "psycology"? The discussions sound interesting, up to a point. I have had no "intellect at advanced standard" yet, thank God, except when Jim & I had a long & fruitless argument with Hughes concerning the motive power (if any) of Reason.

Yesterday I had a horrible *cold*!!![4] It lingers today, but after some hot whiskey (smuggled into the college by Jim) it seems to have subsided somewhat.

Tell old Christopherson he's wasting his time if he doesn't know Homer Lane.[5]

Philip

I've bought three postcards – two Paul Nash, 1 John Nash – & stuck them over the mantelpiece.

1 Addressed to Miss C. E. Larkin, c/o Y.W.C.A, Granville Hall, Granville Road, Leicester. The precise details of Kitty's early career are lost. She attended art college in Birmingham, leaving probably in 1936, and going on to obtain an art teacher's diploma at Leicester College of Arts and Crafts.
2 Philip's room-mate, Noel Hughes.
3 Presumably a debate at Kitty's college.
4 Doubly underlined.
5 Homer Lane (1875–1925), American educationalist who believed in giving children more control over their own education. He influenced A. S. Neill, the founder of Summerhill School.

8 November 1940

<*Letterhead*> St John's College coat of arms

Dear Mop,

I am hoping to write to you during this half-hour before dinner, in answer to your letter of the 4th. My cold has folded its tents and stolen silently away, you will be pleased to hear, so I shan't be joining my ancestors just yet!

Friday afternoon and evening are pleasant times because, having had my tutorial in the morning, I can do nothing with a clear conscience. I've been reading a very funny book called "Cold Comfort Farm" by Stella Gibbons: a sort of debunking of the sort of novel written by Mary Webb. If you'd like to read it, it's in the Penguin series.[1] The authoress came down to the English Club on Tuesday and talked about "First Things". She said that she'd always put her housework before her novel-writing because if she hadn't people would have said "Ah but look how she neglects her husband and home!" Whereas now they say "Isn't Stella marvellous, she does all the work *and* finds time to write those wonderful novels!"

I don't think we shall get a toasting fork, on the whole. I don't really *like* toast, on thinking it over. The kettleholder has been hung up by the fireplace on a little hook & is still very useful. We have starting [*sic*] using my kettle too now. [. . .]

After dinner. Ah! replete with lentil soup, mutton & cauliflower & fruit salad, I will end this little note. I feel strangely content, although Oxford, as a place, is not up to much.

Rot it, anyway.

Love to all at Cherry Orchard,
Philip

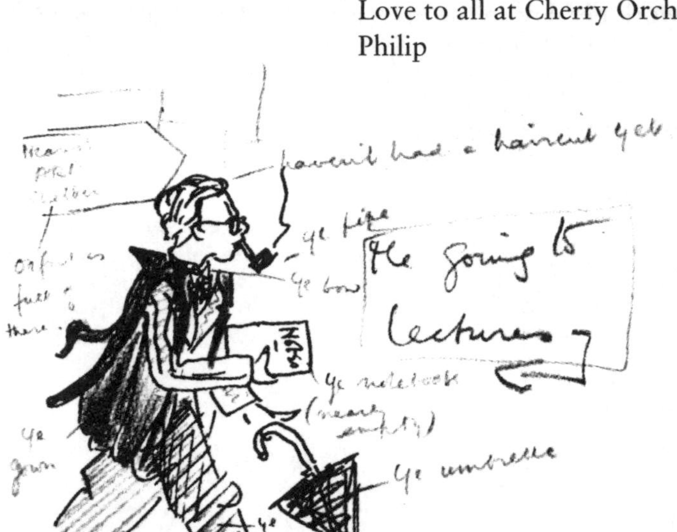

1 Stella Gibbons (1902–89). Her first novel, *Cold Comfort Farm* (1932) won the Prix Femina Étranger and eclipsed her later writing.

10 November 1940[1]

<*Letterhead*> St John's College coat of arms

Dear Kath,

About time I answered your letter, for which ay thang yow.[2]

Firstly – I inquired, in humorous vein, what "psycology" was, because "psycology" is usually spelt "psychology". All I receive in reply is remarks about "psycology" again, and (!!) "phycology" (!!!)! Arabic news[3] is a poor excuse for ramblings such as this!

I haven't been doing much. (Pause.) There isn't much to do! (Comic Oxford!!!) I work & write letters, eat & sleep, play cards & smoke my pipe all the time. Oxford as a place is pretty gruesome. If you like "social life" – that's all right. I don't. If you like intellectual discussion – that's all right. *I* don't. If you like games, beer, & hooliganism, that's all right. *I* don't. If you like working like Hell & reading all day in the Bodleian – that's all right. *I* don't. If you like spending money, that's all right. I don't (on principle). What I want to do is to *be given* a little manual work per day, in the open air preferably, plus plenty of fruit & vegetables to eat, and with congenial & varied companions who talk very little & think less. That's all right, but you can't get it *here*!

In other words, Oxford & me don't quite hit it. I thought it unlikely.

...x...

To continue talking about myself, "New Verse" are still struck dumb with admiration over four poems I sent them on October 21st. The swine probably won't answer, not for nearly six months.

Jim seems to be getting on alright up here. He says they're all no good at the Slade except an Irishman in his 3rd year. This Irishman's chief justification is that he once said a drawing had "shape", when 9,999,999,999,999 art students out of 10,000,000,000,000 would have said "form". This seems a good quality to me, too.

—

[. . .] Well, well, I think I must curtail this sprawling note. I suppose the next thing I shall hear is that you're writing a book on "The Teaching of Art in Nursery Schools", uh?

Ah well, Yours
Sincerely,
Philip

1 Addressed to Miss C. E. Larkin, c/o Y.W.C.A., Granville Hall, Granville Road, Leicester.

2 Imitating Arthur Askey, popular wartime radio comedian. Larkin mentions him several times in his letters.

3 Presumably Kitty had written about the campaign in Africa.

12 November 1940

St John's College

Dear Pop,

I have just bought this notepaper to conserve my college supply a little. It cost (with envelopes) 2/5½d. None to be had in Woolworth's. My money is being spent with alarming rapidity. At present I have fifteen pounds fifteen shillings & sixpence halfpenny: and it is just gone half term. My battels, too, will rise a little.

I have been squandering money on books, that's the trouble. My bookcase now reads Auden's "Poems" (6/- but pre-College days); Auden's "Look Stranger" (3/6); Auden "Spain" (1/-); "Excerpta e Statutis"[1] (free); "The Malcontent" – Marston (2/-); Beaumont & Fletcher's "Philaster" (2/-); "Othello" (2/3); "Selected Plays of Middleton" (2/6); "Lyrics & Poems of Shakespeare" (1/-); "Selected Poems of Andrew Marvell" (6d); "Songs of Innocence & Songs of Experience" – Blake (1/-); Blake's "Poetical Sketches" (2/-); "Basic English", Petronius' "Satyricon", Donne's "Devotions", Lawrence's "Apropos of Lady Chatterley's Lover" (I don't think we have this, have we?) – about 2/-, and the Cambridge Book of Lesser Poets which includes some rubbish and some valuables (3/6). I am still coveting "Rare Poems of the Sixteenth & Seventeenth Centuries" going in an obscure bookshop for 2/-.

You know, reading your letters through, I am coming to the conclusion that you have a powerful style! You sound utterly detached, cold, impersonal: as if you were writing in an old farmhouse on a windy and stone littered moor, far from any human noise or movement. Only the wind answers your sentences: "I find that the days go rapidly by and I have not answered your last letter"; "I am sorry you have a cold and can offer no remedy"; "You are none the worse for knowing nothing about the war. We don't either"; "It is usual to put Mr. or even 'Esq.' in case of public officials". Then you fold the parchment, seal it with the old heirloom of a seal, and put it for the carrier to take when he calls in two days' time. Then you sink into your austere, wooden chair by the fire and listen to the wind around the high chimney pots or watch the racing clouds through the tall windows.

I hope you see what I mean by all this!

Well, I want to do some work before I attend Prof. Wyld's lecture at 11.0. He is the dictionary man, actually.[2] His dictionary is going in Blackwell's for 11/-. So I will close this epistle which I fear isn't very cheerful. I am more or less College Secretary of the English Club, by the way. [. . .]

With all love
Philip

<*Vertically up the left margin*> PS "New Verse" still struck dumb with admiration.
<*Bottom left*> P²S Am hearing Clifford Bax[3] at English Club tonight.
<*Vertically down bottom right margin, in pencil*> P³S Hughes asks me to thank you for the £6 for fees he received. I suppose you [know] nothing about this.[4]

1 The Oxford guide to statutes and regulations.
2 Henry Cecil Wyld, author of *The Universal Dictionary of the English Language* (1932).
3 Clifford Bax (1886–1962): playwright, journalist, poet and hymn writer; brother of the composer Arnold Bax.
4 An arch joke, implying that Sydney had been paying his room-mate for reporting back on Philip's behaviour.

18 November 1940

S John's College, Oxford

Dear fambly,

This letter is addressed primarily to Pop, but I don't know where he will be when this is due to be delivered. I am addressing it to Lichfield.

First, I was tremendously relieved to know that you were safe. While you had the bombings, fires, rescue parties & all the rest of the grim trappings of air raids,[1] we up here merely had the unpleasant rumours, the horrific newspaper, & the lack of news. We heard of the raid at lunchtime on Friday: we immediately sent telegrams off to Coventry but this was patently futile. Roe & Dupénois went down on Saturday.

By Saturday dinner time I hadn't any news so I sent another telegram to Lichfield. Smith was going down on Sunday by train, so Hughes & I decided to go down as well, if no news awaited us on Sunday morning. It didn't: so, with our warmest clothes on (& me with my beret), we started stopping cars on the Banbury Road outside College at 9.0 am Sunday morning. By noon we were dropped at Stoneleigh Avenue. We tried Penvorn first, but no one was at home, although we deduced from the fact that the windows were sealed up that someone (probably Pop) had been there & that Pop was probably alive. No one seemed in at Barnes',[2] Williams', or Snape's, & the maid at Bass's[3] didn't know where you were. Nor did a policeman of whom we inquired.

Next we tried Hughes' house in Churchill Avenue. We had to get to Foleshill via Gulson Road & Stoney Stanton Rd., over Stoke Common & back into Foleshill. We couldn't go within a mile of the City Centre because they were dynamiting it. We heard the blasting all afternoon. Hughes' house was standing but empty: however, we got some bread & cheese at a neighbouring house, & then visited the Riders'. From these sources we gained some impression of the chaotic state of things.

This brought us to about 3.15 pm & although we had leave to stay a night away from College we decided that as there was no point in staying we had better get out of the way. We had arranged with a lorry-driver who brought us from outside Banbury to Kenilworth that we should be in Kenilworth at 5.0 p.m. It was quite impossible: we couldn't get back across the town in time. So we got a lift to somewhere in Radford, & then picked up a crazy lorry trying to find the Birmingham Road. We piled in (I was clinging onto the running board) & got as far as Stonebridge, where we stopped & waited for the lorry which was due to return from Castle Bromwich. Luckily it came & we got back to College by 7.15 – just in time for dinner, with an individual outlay of about 3/- each. Your telegram[4] made the day a success, & I was able to hold forth to an astonished commoners' table – "By God . . . Just back from Coventry . . . What a sight . . . pass the peas . . . any factories hit? . . . Ha, ha! . . . all be out of production for a month . . . blowing up the city . . . streets full of broken glass . . . pass the potatoes . . . no gas . . . all candles . . . no electricity – can't hear the news on the wireless – absolutely no communications . . . bread, please . . . getting water from shellholes . . . danger of typhoid . . . all clocks either stopped or wrong . . ." and so on. We afterwards repeated the performance in Exeter J.C.R. where we met Burgess – the only O.C. who hasn't been to see for himself. It is possible that he too, will go down soon.[5]

In this letter I will acknowledge Pop's letter of the 13th & Mop's (undated) posted on the 12th. The tension of awaiting news increased my Bibliomania & I bought the Muse's library Blake (2/-), Max

Plowman's "An Introduction to Blake" (3/-), the Mermaid "Dekker" (2/-) & Sweet's "Anglo Saxon Primer" (-/6). All these were, of course, secondhand. Blake, by the way, I regard as a coming poet. You probably know that Donne is the fashion today: – nearly everybody has the Nonesuch Donne (as well as corduroy trousers) – but I think that Blake really ought to receive more notice than he does. Do you know anything about him? He seems a man after your own heart. Lit his own fires & cleaned his own boots.

There have been no bombs on Oxford yet, though some do fall around the outskirts. We had a harmless *five*-hour warning on Friday.

Remarks to Mop: No marmite yet. We subsist on weird & peculiar pots of fishpaste (2 for 5½^{d}) in all flavours. Anchovy is the favourite.

I should like to see you but *why* must you go to such an unpronounceable place like Lichfield? About the most difficult town in the British Isles to ask for! Quite impossible for me, anyway.[6]

As you say, we do not know there is a war on. Not at all. I broke the handle from a tea-cup the other day, unfortunately. This is the first breakage of any sort we have had. We *lost* the strainer the other day, but on questioning the Scout found it had only been mislaid. It is still the best thing we have. Breakfast is in Hall. Sometimes we go without – just don't get up.

The calendar would be a very good idea. No, I don't want another Shakespeare one. Any other author will do *bar* the Bible & Milton. Blake of course if possible but I don't suppose such things exist.

Well, I must close now for I have to get to a lecture in 15 minutes time.

Very much love to both –
Philip

1 During the night of 14/15 November 554 were killed in Coventry, and a thousand injured. Sydney was in the Council House which was hit by two bombs and several incendiaries.

2 Reading conjectural.

3 Conjectural; possibly the same name as that earlier in the sentence.

4 'Am quite safe. Daddy.' 17 November 1940. Hull History Centre, U DLN/1/32.

5 Hughes gave his own account of this visit to Coventry: 'Going Home with Larkin', *London Magazine* (April/May 1989), 115–19.

6 Because of his stammer.

23 November 1940[1]

St John's College

Dear Katherine,

From the lawned quads of Oxford the sky is blue, slim clouds tinged salmon by the low sun in the east. Smoke rises from the chimneys and birds argue in the college garden. General morning peace presides over all.

Therefore I was unpleasantly surprised to hear of your acquaintance with a landmine. I supposed one of the "four Midland towns" raided last Tuesday was Leicester, but I still hoped they might be B'ham, Cov., Northampton & Rugby or something like that. Anyway, I'm very sorry to hear you are disturbed from your home of rest. I'm getting the positive jitters about air raids – all you beasts will be as cool as cucumbers ("Can that have been more than 50 yards away, do you think?") while I shall be a gibbering maniac. [. . .]

Roe appealed yesterday at London: his appeal was upheld & he is registered if he does A.R.P. work.[2] This he is already doing.

We were all very worried by Thursday's raid, & having received no news by Sunday, on that day Hughes & I hitchhiked down to ye old place via about four private cars & a lorry. Found nobody there, of course: the streets miry with brickdust & water from hoses & so on. You probably know all about it. At length we picked up a lorry going [to] Oxford at Stonebridge and got home just in time for dinner. Cheap excursion.

Yesterday I bought some rather nice Christmas cards (12). There are some good shops here for that sort of thing. You know, I should like to see you here before term ends if only for a few hours. I think you'd find the place very interesting.

The poem – ha! Swine, God knows when the lice will print it. I've half a mind to write them a stiff letter about it. Ages ago too I sent four poems to "New Verse" which have still not come back. Also I met Michael Meyer (editor of Univ. magazine "The Cherwell") who genially invited me to "send something along". This I have done but nothing has come of it. Poetry don't seem to catch here and now. Apes asses & dogs. Goats & monkeys.[3]

The promised weather has gone away from here: against a grey sky the sombre back of Trinity College rises. Smoke drifts away on the ruffling wind. Farther out, across the university park and over the swift river, the playing fields wait for the games of this afternoon; through the unecstatic street the gowned bicycles are whirling.

I pick up some books and climb to the College library.

Philip

1 Addressed to Miss C. E. Larkin, c/o Mrs H. C. Page, 719 Loughborough Road, Birstall, Leicester.
2 As a conscientious objector.
3 *Othello*, Act IV, scene 1.

12 December 1940[1]

33 Cherry Orchard, Lichfield[2]

Dear Katharine, (honestly don't you think this is the best spelling?)[3]

I picked up your last letter from Leicester at Coventry on Tuesday. It arrived as I did. I came down earlier than expected – on Saturday – & had one big hell of a journey, arriving after dark and mumbling to passers-by "Am I right for Cherry Orchard?" Anyway, I'm here now, sleeping & reading (& writing this) at Mrs Cope's, 9 Sturgeon's Hill, and eating & generally seeing human faces at 33, C.O. A fairly satisfactory arrangement. At first I didn't like being here at all. I missed the talk & the books and the general air of carelessness that is so congenial at Oxford. I missed Jim's conversation & huge belches. Roe's face round the door & playing poker, even Smith's absurd conceit. I missed the little things that make you feel such a man, like the College scouts, & the loud meals in Hall. Now I still miss them but not so much. War does not suit me. I was made for peace. It will be interesting to see how I turn out.

You will have my tie by now, I suppose. I like 'em subtle, sister.[4] Wheel 'em in and lay 'em out. Lichfield is a hole for shopping, as you from Leicester and I from Oxford realise or will realise. But for Peace and Quiet, Incorporated, it's fine. I shall sink into a primeval slime.

Since I left Coventry – on October 9th – I have had my hair cut once.

I went to Coventry on Tuesday, returning Wednesday p.m. Nearly sick at Nuneaton! I was carrying two enormous greasy sausage rolls (you never [–] sausage rolls – woe hoe hoe) in a bag, & I hurriedly tipped them out loose into my pocket and held the bag at the ready. As the 'bus started off again I gave two enormous hiccups & felt comparatively all right for the rest of the journey. Near thing, though.

Coventry looked queer. Not terrible – at least not to me. It looked like some big government clearance scheme to me – except that it seemed done rather carelessly. I do hope they never have another raid like it. Went one or two of my old walks. I can't help wondering if I – or any of us – shall ever live again in Coventry. Pop was cheery. We dossed at Marshall's.[5]

Well, I expect you'll be shambling along to see me soon. I've quite forgotten what your voice sounds like. You won't find things much changed here – unless I am a little more insufferably big-headed.

Thoombs oop & we'll beat Jerry yet –

Philip

1 Addressed to Miss C. E. Larkin, c/o Mrs H. C. Page, 719 Loughborough Road, Birstall, Leicester.

2 Home of Sydney's brother Alfred, where the family had taken refuge.

3 Philip addresses his sister Catherine variously as 'Katherine', 'Katharine', 'Kathryn', 'Kath', 'K', 'Kit' and 'Kitty'. Often the writing on the envelopes addressed to her is mannered and florid, as was hers.

4 He had asked Kitty to buy him a shantung silk tie for Christmas.

5 Dr Arthur Hedley Marshall (1904–94), Sydney Larkin's deputy and successor as City Treasurer of Coventry (1944–64). Obituary: http://www.independent.co.uk/news/people/obituary-hedley-marshall-1410193.html.

1941

19 January 1941

St John's College, Oxford

Dear Pop,

Enclosed find Battels, to be paid by cheque before Friday, January 31st 1941. Hughes' were £58.7.9 & I haven't spent so much as I thought.

Oxford remains much as usual. At present I have a slight cold which I am doing my best to disbelieve in: snow is deep on the ground, just turning to slush. My pipe () broke – Heaven only knows how – someone must have trodden on it – & I have replaced it by  which I am told fits my face very well.

Today is the first day of term and the president is to address us on A.R.P. duties at 11 am. I hope this only refers to firewatching which I understand is to be compulsory this term. When there's a warning at night some poor fool has to shamble up to the tower and watch for firebombs till he freezes. Then they send somebody else up. Doesn't sound very nice to me. [. . .]

Jim is here and flourishing in a purplish sports coat and an orange polo-sweater. Looks all right. My parcel arrived safely on Friday afternoon & I am well set up now.

The O.T.C. sent me a form demanding size of boots! I have disregarded this because I don't belong to the O.T.C. though they may think I do. Blast 'em, anyway.

I don't know Kitty's address or Mop's, if she has gone. Send me latest details from the front. I must attempt to work now.

Your Affec. S.
Philip

22 January 1941

S John's College, Oxford

Dear Mop,

Thank you for your letter. I hadn't the least idea where you were – even whether you'd left Coventry or not: but I hope that wherever you are you are well & cheerful.[1] (By the way, why read "Way of all Flesh"?[2] Awfully gloomy.)

Well, ye olde university is looking much the same, except for the nasty shock it received yesterday about calling up the 19s. Everybody is very annoyed and worried by this, and it seems likely that when the calling up takes its full effect Oxford may close down. Everybody is cursing the war like hell. [. . .]

No, I don't get much exercise, but I get the hell of a lot of fresh air. I spend most of my time going from place to place & room to room and it all entails breathing that strange & alien body known as "fresh air." Actually I never have much time to crouch over fires.

I hope you can read all this. I bought some brown ink as you see & a pen to use it with. The pen doesn't suit my hand at all (as you can see).

I am definitely S. John's College Secretary of the English Club! This gives one a pleasing sense of importance. I have just put up a notice on the college board signed "P. A. Larkin (Coll. Sec.)" in two inks. I have roped in several members & can find more, I think. Pity all this has to stop.

Well, I must shut up now and attempt some Anglo Saxon. Horrible! Bone has a chill – haven't had a tutorial yet – but I shall have 2 per week.

Give me Kitty's address – I don't know it.

Your affectionate but uneasy son,
Philip

1 The letter is addressed to Mrs Sydney Larkin, 'Wear Giffard', Cliff Hill, Warwick.
2 Semi-autobiographical novel by Samuel Butler, published in 1903.

24 January 1941[1]

S John's College, Oxford

Dear Katharine,

[Excuse (a) this ink.
(b) this penknib, I'll change it if it gets too awful.][2]

Thanks for your letter. As Jim once said "Your letter was marvellous, with just enough compliments to make it appear great." Anyway, very much appreciated in these literally dark mornings.

Oxford is all right at present. I have gained 2 offices – Coll. Sec. of English Club and Coll. Agent of "Cherwell": both jobs vaguely disquieting. John's remains much as before: several new freshmen who all look far brainier than I do. I am beginning Anglo Saxon – it's impossible. I can never pass an exam in it in 7 weeks. Mad! The only bit I know at present is "Heofane rice ist ge-lic" which means "the kingdom of heaven is like . . ." Even there the accents are probably all wrong. Mad! German is very slight help.

Last Saturday Jim & I shambled into Acotts[3] & demanded a long list of practically unobtainable hot records – they had at least ½! Yeah man! In a fit of madness we bought four & damn good they are too. Then the Turl bookshop was selling off first hand but shopsoiled Lawrences for 2/6 instead of 4/6. I bought 2 we haven't got – "Reflections on the death of a Porcupine" & "Studies in Classic American Literature". Jim bought "Fantasia of the Unconscious" & "Kangaroo". We sit whole evenings reading on each side of the fire reading bits aloud. Josh[4] gets frightfully annoyed.

Glad you like my pipe. I do, much more than the last. It holds more. Going down to the Cherwell Offices yesterday I was struck by my reflection in shop windows. Suits my face fine! Still, enough of this egoistical babble in which you can't take part.

Pleased to hear the {pchysology pschchology / pycshology pyschology}!! is going forward once more. I've forgotten what my ideas about education were but anyway glad your lecturer liked them. But nothing will be done for years yet – probably not in our time at all. Blast 'em all.

I've heard of that Sherard Vines[5] book all right. You're very cute, actually: from what I remember it *is* a first novel (not quite sure, though) and certainly all the critics blamed it for being "clever". I rather wanted to get hold of it.

Jim's sports coat isn't *quite* purple – a kind of red, more. Not *very* fine, but it looks excellent with an orange sweater. Unfortunately, Jim's likely to sell the latter.

God, this pen!

Bevin,[6] the old b— he'll have us both in the services before we can say "Ather-ather-ather". But I reckon Herr Hitler will press all the buttons on his desk before then. So does everybody else. At an A.R.P. lecture (compulsory) yesterday, the lecturer said that the authorities expected the use of gas in the spring. Er . . . ha, ha. Very funny . . . Er – UH? Ather-ather-ather . . . . Blast 'em. Everybody I meet curses the war like blazes.

I like the sound of your owl. Good drawing, too. I suppose if I send you a pea green boat you'll start snooping round for the honey & the £5 note as well, eh? You can't fool me! Still, love to the owl & both pussy cats.

This letter is becoming long – & frightfully dull, too, I expect. T.S. Eliot is coming to speak at the Ark – a religious group – & I may join the Ark (2/6) just to hear & see him. I want to confirm my opinion that he really is an unpleasant guy.

Stopped a buck the other day in Hall:

Member of Democratic Socialists (trying to get me to join): "And we're having the Lord Privy Seal to come down too!"

Me (ladling soup, cheerfully) "Oh ar, & you're having Attlee too, arncha?"[7] (collapse of Dem. Soc. & an awed hush.) Ah well these little things will happen won't they.

Ernie Roe is becoming unbearable. Sits at tea making mad remarks like "What is Truth?" and "Is Truth the same as reality?" I don't know whether he does it because he can't help it or because he thinks it's smart. Georges burned "F. G. SMITH IS A" on Bish's mahogany fender yesterday with a red hot poker while B. was out of the room. The idea is that the visitors can supply the missing word to taste.

Well I must knock off & do something in the way of work. Blast it. Blast everything. This life is getting me down. I'm going mad! Ather ather ather.

Yours affec.
Philip

<*Up right margin*> Write again. [. . .]

1 Addressed to Miss Katharine Larkin, c/o 85 Stanfell Road, Leicester.
2 The ink is brown and the pen has a very thin nib.
3 Music and record shop on the High Street, Oxford.
4 Philip's room-mate, Noel Hughes.
5 Walter Sherard Vines (1890–1974): academic, poet, novelist and critic. His first novel was *Humours Unreconciled* (1928).
6 Ernest Bevin (1881–1951), Labour politician: Minister of Labour in the wartime coalition government.
7 Clement Attlee (1883–1967), Labour Party politician. He was Deputy Prime Minister under Churchill for much of the war, and later became Prime Minister (1945–51). In January 1941, however, he held the office of Lord Privy Seal.

26 January 1941

S John's College, Oxford

Dear Pop,

I am taking advantage of Sunday morning to apprise you of the fact that I am still alive & moderately well. I suppose by now you've paid my battels. I hope you don't consider them excessive – I don't think they are, actually.

We are working a scheme of fire-watching now with Balliol & Trinity. 8 undergraduates (in John's at any rate) are "on duty" if an alert takes place. Two are always awake. (4 shifts of 7–10, 10–1, 1–4, 4–7) and if an alert takes place, one goes up onto the tower & the other stands ready to run messages. After a half-hour they change places. If nothing happens during an hour they chuck it.

We are told that sand is now considered the most effective way of dealing with incendiary bombs – especially sandbags. Put a sandbag on a bomb, & the bag burns through at the crucial point & a steady & well directed stream of sand pours onto the bomb. Sound in theory at any rate. I mention this because I imagine you'll be interested, but you probably know it anyway. [. . .]

I note the Government have done several drastic things, although I never read the papers. The suppression of the "Daily Worker"[1] has caused a good deal of annoyance here: and Attlee who was here the other night apparently made a very poor show. Indians kept popping up with awkward questions about India and so forth.

I am College Secretary of the English Club & College Agent of the Cherwell. I may have told you this before.

Well, I must divert my attentions to Anglo Saxon at present so this letter must cease. I do hope you're all right.

Yours very affectionately,
Philip

1 Organ of the Communist Party of Great Britain, founded in 1930.

5 February 1941[1]

S John's College, Oxford

Dear Katharine,

I'm sorry I was so long in answering your letter which I enjoyed very much, notepaper included.

I'm afraid this letter won't be "more like a book". It'll be more like a telegram. Going through your letter & the points I feel I want to answer – there is a general view here that undergraduates will be allowed the usual 9 months extension – i.e. to 19.9 months if they call up the 18s though I think they will have to close down [the University]. Pity – I'm just beginning to enjoy it. Has Joyce found a chance to become the life & soul of the party yet?

At present it is 8.28 p.m., and snowin' 'ard. On every cornice, crag, gargoyle, ledge, and bit of dog-tooth moulding in Oxford snow settles. In the High 'buses run silently: down the Broad rectangles of light fall across the wide pavements from the lodges of Balliol & Trinity. Further away, south-east down St. Aldates, gusts of snow blow past Big Tom and away onto the Meadows, where are no footprints; and south-west[2] by the river flakes fall in the quadrangles of Magdalen. And in hundreds of brightly lit rooms, or solitary by reading-lamps, hundreds of undergraduates smoke, read, talk and laugh, oblivious of the outer dark but part of it, forgetful of all but a tiny section of living but influenced by life and its implications, as am I, sprawled on a sofa in St. John's College, a pad on my knees and my feet on the fireplace, writing to you.

There is a nice little literary description of the scene for you. Tell me if you like it. It's quite easy.

I don't think I've got much to tell you, apart from the fact that "The Cherwell" (university rag) accepted 2 of my poems and I'm getting to know the editors. Soon be in the literary swim my boys!

I'm sorry to hear you are overburdened with work. I have quite a lot but I rarely do any of it. It's too hard. All I do is mess about, read, eat, and talk to Old Coventrians, with possible intervals of listening to hot records. Yas sir! Oxford on the whole is pleasant. But it's *impossible* to do any form of serious writing (prose) when you're here. Quite impossible.

Talking about writing, I sent 3 poems off to the Listener the other day. I hope they accept them – *all* of them. Sidney Keyes[3] – literary ed. of Cherwell – says he knows Ackerley well.[4]

Well, it's about time I knocked off and did something to the enormous pile of work that eyes me from a corner of this large, panelled room. I will sign off now with my signature tune "Forward Lads": (tune – "Rock of Ages")

"O won't it be just posh
When we beat the ruddy Boche?
When the battle we have won
When we've licked the bloomin' 'Un,
Then earth's treasure will be mine,
And the sun forever shine,"

Sung in tones of beautiful youthful hope.

Philip

1 Addressed to Miss Katharine Larkin, c/o Stanfell Road, Leicester.
2 Larkin confuses south-east and south-west in this sentence.
3 Sidney Keyes (1922–43), poet; killed in action in North Africa.
4 J. R. Ackerley (1896–1967), Literary Editor of the *Listener* (1935–59).

6 March 1941[1] Thursday

[St John's College, Oxford]

Dear Katherine,

It is raining. It is Thursday. I am confronted by loads of Anglo Saxon to do by Monday – it squats in corners and looks at me: the story of the Queen of Sheba (seo cwēn, genaten Sabā), Ælfric's life of King Oswald (sum æþele cyning, Ōswold gehaten), and little rivulets and standing pools of grammar. What's more, I feel tired and vaguely dispirited. Likewise, I don't like this pen much. My writing, so far from looking like D.H.L.'s, as I hoped it might, resembles that of a slightly imbecile child.

Anyway! You seem to be doing a phenomenal amount of work – quite frightens me. Er – teaching a whole secondary school in Art[2] – Gawd! I had visions of you.

But surely Miss Larkin, that theory was exploded in '38 by Heinzholz in Vienna . . .
form + content = shape
please miss come an' draw a cow!
please miss can I be excused?
please miss it's raining
please miss yer 'airs cummin down

But perhaps it isn't so bad!

My idea with the orange & red paper was to use orange paper & red envelopes & vice versa. What is your opinion on this? Actually I suppose orange and green, or orange and yellow would be better, but I want to be bright and sunlike.

Talking of D.H.L. I applied for the original "Lady C." and "Paintings" at the Bodleian yesterday. After about ¾ of an hour I was disturbed at my seat/desk by a girl – an unpleasant girl with spectacles – with a face as red as a peony who demanded "*What* is your reason for applying for *these* books?" I said "I want to read them." This rather puzzled her – nobody in the Bodleian "just reads." She didn't consider this a serious answer & pressed me for a *reason*. I repeated that I wanted to read them: with motions of the hands suggesting one who explains to a child, I pointed out that these works were not available to the general public and, as I had a considerable admiration for Lawrence, I wanted to read them. She said I couldn't have them without being a student of Lawrence or writing a thesis on him or something. I frowned and said: "Isn't that rather *childish*?" She became even redder and whimpered that it wasn't anything to do with her and would I come and see Mr Wright? I said: "Certainly". So I came and saw Mr Wright, an objectionable little man like a constipated bank clerk. I repeated the foregoing in essentials and so did he. Then I remarked with pontifical scorn: "You see, *I* don't consider these works obscene." This touched him in his sensitive spot – his "tolerance" – and he snivellingly began explaining that neither did he nor the Library. I said that their action implied as much, and brushing aside his mumbling about copyright, responsibility, defacement etc. I shambled back to my seat, snarling. Actually, I suppose I could have got them by pretending I was writing a thesis on Lawrence – anything as long as I wasn't going to "read" him, and admire him. If I were "studying" him – i.e. engaged on a longdrawnout effort to reduce Lawrence to my own size and the size of my readers, motivated at bottom by an envious and snivelling *hate* – well, that would have been all right. Tolerant Mr Wright wouldn't mind at all. As it was, he could only squirm up to me with a yellow eye and mutter obscenely "I expect there are *plenty* of copies in the university if you only *looked* for them??!" I gave him one look and he lost his nerve. Canaille! Lice! Slimy professional haters! I regard the Bodleian Library as a home of a considerable amount of evil.

I went to see the O.U.D.S. production of "Othello" last night – stagemanaged by "Ernest Roe". Pretty bad, apart from Iago. Desdemona was far too adult and poised – her "Willow Song" was quite inaudible and rather ludicrous. Othello, afraid of being too violent and so undignified, was rather stiff and weak. The grouping &c was wearily conventional. Parts were occasionally forgotten. I wonder why people do this sort of thing? Exhibitionism? Mere animal spirits? Anyway, I don't care.

Jim had his medical yesterday. There is every possibility that he will be in the army within a month. He was put in Grade I: he said that the medical on the whole was not too bad at all – nothing like Lawrence's descriptions. I still don't think the army can be anything but revolting and intentional Hell.

Norman Iles and I climbed into college last night over the wall. Easy as falling off a wall – which it necessitates. The brilliant moonlight was unpleasant – and one had irrelevant memories of similar situations in the "Magnet" and so on. You'd probably like Iles. It's only this term we've got to know each other really: I thought him rather an oaf last term and he says he thought me "fearfully dull". He never gets up before 10 which I constantly tell him is all wrong – but luckily to a certain extent he can see his faults. And mine!

Jazz shops here are damn' fine. We've bought quite a lot of records, & I know several people who are interested in jazz, though nobody with quite my tastes, unless it's Frank Dixon. We generally meet Fridays and Sundays in Magdalen and Christ Church respectively.

Well, I must abandon this letter and regard my work. I stay here till about March 23rd, to take my Shakespeare exam – er, of course, I shall pass. Have a vague feeling I'm certain to fail.

Well, much love and so forth,
Philip

[. . .]

1 Addressed in an elaborately florid hand to Kathryn Larkin, c/o 85 Stanfell Road, Leicester.

2 The *History of Loughborough College* (1952) records Kitty as having joined the Commerce Department in 1941. Photographs from 1942–3 labelled 'College Junior School of Art' show that she was teaching there at that time.

2 April 1941

S John's College, Oxford

Dear Pop,

Thank you for your letter of March 31st. You sound in a very hard condition back at Coventry – I heard from Smith who mentioned the number of food queues about. In Oxford they aren't so numerous – except outside Lyons and in Woolworths. I never join a queue myself, it's too much trouble. I haven't bought cakes for weeks. Nor cigarettes or tobacco, chocolate, sweets &c. It's certainly very easy not to have them when you can't get them easily.

Re my abortive distinction. Bone said that Prof. Brett-Smith (big bug in the English School) was of the opinion that my General paper on Shakespeare was well up to distinction standard, but my second one (Text of "Othello") fell from grace considerably. He was, apparently impressed by my "capacity for developing a theory". The point about distinctions is that (as I've told you) they count *two* sections[1] and thus you are ready to go in the army all the sooner. Thus I have known at least one person who deliberately avoided a distinction on these grounds. However, I *could* have got a distinction if I'd tried, so that satisfies me.

The S. African prof. is Leishmann not Leichmann[2] if that makes any difference. He has edited a volume of poetry by Rainer Maria Rilke (modern Austrian poet, influenced Stephen Spender) but apart from that I don't know much about him, except that his mental capacity is obviously below standards. He reads the "News Chronicle" and remarked apropos of nothing that he'd like to invent a ray that exploded powders – then he'd just fly over enemy ammunition dumps and blow them up. He really is a blockhead. [. . .]

With very much love,
Philip

P.S. Mop says you have a new sports coat. Congratulations!

1 Examinations.
2 J. B. Leishman (one n) (1902–63): translator of Rilke.

9 April 1941[1]

<*Letterhead*> Penvorn, Manor Road, Coventry

Dear Katherine,

Subsequent to my first air-raid with real live bomb (last night) I am sound in mind and body. So is Pop, and Mop who is here as well, but the general opinion prevailing at present is that you shouldn't return as you had intended.

As regards the raid, an attack appeared to be directed at the station, and the Goods yard was burnt. So was the Grammar School. Bombs fell ("Cor! I was just a-thinkin' of 'aving a look outside when I 'eard . . Wheeeeeeeeee . . and o' course me an' ole Charlie ducked back into the Anderson, and there was a whackin' great bang . . . . An' ole

Charlie, 'e says . . .") in Manor Road (2) Park Road (2) and presumably frequently in S. Patrick's Road. Anyway it wasn't very pleasant.

Philip

P.S. It's not *meant* to be!! . . .
<*Top of first page*> P.P.S. This is very vague, but the most definite thing, it seems, is: Don't return until further orders – or (I suppose) move at all.
<*In pencil up left margin of last page*> P.³S. house undamaged apart from windows, tiles, etc.

1 Addressed to 85 Stanfell Road, Leicester.

30 April 1941

S John's College, Oxford

Dear Mop,

[. . .] This afternoon has been very fine & Roe, Hughes and I went on the river in a punt. Not my idea of pleasure. The pole retreats along to the edge of the punt where it is most insecure and water swirls directly beneath him. He holds the pole upright & slides it vertically into the water. The punt glides over it and bends it away from him:

He has to withdraw the pole hurriedly in order to avoid breaking the pole. However he jerks the 20-foot pole up again, sliding it through his hands & getting his sleeves soaking in water (the pole is wet). Once more he slides it in, and shoves. Ah! this is fine! the punt glides rapidly away and the poler is forced to relinquish the pole and the others get out the paddles & paddle back:

If the poler has any sense he will then give up learning to punt and will take out a canoe.

Well, I must be off to dinner. Do keep happy & don't pay any attention to Churchill. I don't & don't forget to feed the typewriter.

Philip

12 May 1941

S John's College, Oxford

Dear Pop

[. . .] With regard to my trousers, they are too good to firewatch in, you impudent scoundrel! Chah! Brr!! Where's my horsewhip?!! They are a speciality of this particular shop who made one pr. of each colour and can make more to order. I don't say they aren't monstrous but I like them. The blazer is well fitting – possibly if I did grow a paunch it would be too small, but I doubt if I shall. The Army and subsequent hard labour and privations will keep away any surplus fat, I should think. And touching the war, there are numbers of nasty rumours flying about: Such as no one but scientists allowed to come up; compulsory O.T.C., no more war degree sections, and so on. I had noticed that my registration provisionally falls on Jan 1st 1942, but this may easily be altered if the demand arises. [. . .]

I hope you continue to keep well and that a house soon presents itself to your notice.[1]

Love, Love, Love,
Philip

P.S. I apologise for a certain childish tone I discover in this letter on re reading it.

1 Sydney's search led to the purchase of 73 Coten End, Warwick, in the following month, June 1941.

15 May 1941[1]

S John's College, Oxford

Dear K.,

Thanks for your letter and elaborate envelope. I rather like this combination of ink and paper at present – paper is "blue shade" according to the cover. Woodja believe it?

I have one or two odd things to tell you – I have bought a pair of crimson trousers – dark crimson. They are the only pair in the University. Also, I have joined an elementary psychology group under John Layard ("Barnard" in "Lions and Shadows")[2] which is really extremely interesting and the answer to my question "Why did I come to Oxford?" He favours Jung and has worked with him. Briefly:

As the foetus before birth goes through all stages of evolution (amoeba, fish, reptile, animal, ape, man) so does the psyche.

Post-natal disorders & dreams cannot therefore be explained in terms of post natal experiences (differs from Freud.)

The further and deeper one penetrates into the psyche, the greater is the help one gains from it. ∴ Psychology is necessary.

There is much more. The point of this "impersonal unconscious" is that fundamentally all men are alike. Yugoslavian peasants dream of symbols that were incorporated in ancient Egyptian religions and so on. Never believe that you are unique, said Layard. That is a fundamental neurosis. You aren't.

In the beginning, man *may* have been perfect. But he had to combine with his fellows to conquer nature. This entailed "Sinning against his instincts." Thus every rise in moral, social, and spiritual-God values is accompanied by an equal fall in animal, individual, and natural instincts.

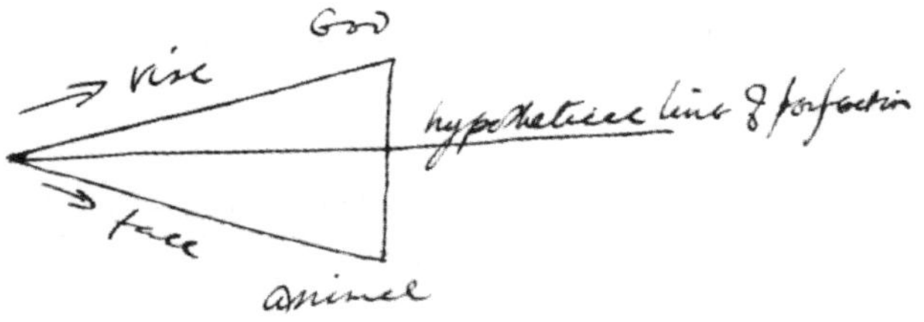

The natural thing to do is to placate nature for having sinned against her. Therefore religion arises – crudest religions entail sacrifice of *animals*. Symbolising the sacrificing of the instincts. Likewise Christ (sacrifice of).

The way of salvation lies not away from the instincts but into them. (Layard vague here, or else I can't remember.) Any man who disbelieves his animal side e.g.

will pretty soon

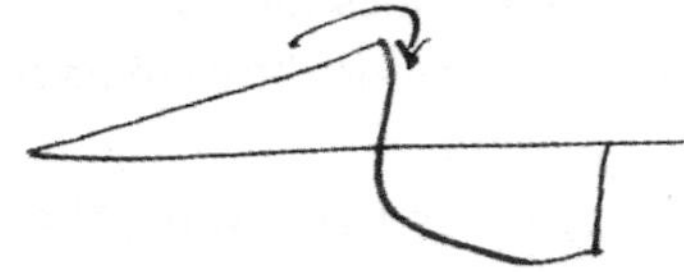

and become a criminal or neurotic.

Knowledge of the instincts, e.g.

(Symbols: Christ descending 3 days into Hell: savages religious initiation in models of animals)

is wise.

(Could tell you lots more but I haven't time. But it was like an evening spent with truth.[)]

[. . .]

Write again soon,

Love,
Philip

1 Written in bright blue ink and with elaborate handwriting; addressed to Katherine Larkin, c/o 85 Stanfell Road, Leicester.

2 A lightly fictionalised autobiography by Christopher Isherwood (1904–86), subtitled 'An Education in the Twenties', published in 1938.

25 June 1941[1]

S John's

Dear Mop,

Thanks for your letter. After your callous suggestion that I should "wash one or two out if you are short", I have spent a soapy hour battling with 7 of the little beasts. I have changed their colour from dark grey-green to medium grey-green. God! You should see me.[2]

I have bought a bottle of Endrine[3] but even that seems to have lost its customary potency. Hell! Luckily today seems likely to be less luridly hot and tortuous than yesterday & the 10 days previous.

In Bagley Wood we carry trees about[4] –

And generally tire ourselves out in unpleasant ways. However, I suppose it's frightfully healthy and so on.

How queer to see the new address on the paper! I shall address this there – I suppose it'll find you. I can hardly believe it doing so. I shall be quite interested to see what sort of a place it is. Have I got one of the attics?

The most unpleasant feature of life at present is that all the milk is sour. I couldn't eat my porridge this morning because of this, and my coffee was vile.

By the way, if you'd like another little trip to Leamington, you might order HMV X6252 and Parlophone R2807.[5] The former is on their special list, the latter is not yet issued but is available on order.

Yours sneezingly,
Philip

1 Addressed to Beauchamp Lodge, 73 Coten End, Warwick. In June 1941 Sydney Larkin moved the family home from 'Penvorn', 1 Manor Road, Coventry, to this newly-bought house.

2 The nose in the drawing is inked in red.

3 A nosespray remedy for hay fever.

4 Bagley Wood: ancient wood between Oxford and Abingdon (in Berkshire until 1974, now in Oxfordshire). Since 1557 most of the wood has been owned by St John's College.

5 HMV X6252: Fats Waller and his Buddies, 'Harlem Fuss, The Minor Drag' (recorded in New York 1929, featuring Eddie Condon). Parlophone R2807: Eddie Condon and His Orchestra, 'Home Cooking / The Eel' (UK reissue, 1941), Parlophone Jazz Classics Series (2), No. 17 / No. 18.

14 October 1941

S John's

Dear Mop (& Pop),

Thank you for your letter, received this morning. As regards rooms, I am in the *President's lodgings*, in one of the converted servants' rooms, and a sitting room that I share with another man. (That is where I am now.) I arrived, however, roomless, and it was only after seeing Poole that I obtained accommodation.[1] I think Poole is losing his grip. Anyway, Bone is ill, and I may have another tutor. The rooms are quite comfortable, but directly over the President's study, so I can't play my records there. Consequently I live mainly in other peoples' rooms.

I saw Dorothy Rowley yesterday, and fled!

The Cherwell, you will be interested to hear, has closed down owing to a mighty deficit of £40 or thereabouts. I don't wonder; and I am pleased that I shall spend no more weary Thursdays chasing round College trying to sell it. I shouldn't have contributed either, in all probability, as poetry seems to have given me up, and I never write any prose short enough for it.

Next week end will be a furious rush. I said independently to Gunner, Hughes, and Jim "Come up for a week-end sometime." Needless to say, they have all chosen next wk-end, so I shall have an unholy task trying to make them feel they each have my undivided attention. This week promises well as regards entertainment, for I have treated myself to a stall at the New Theatre, where the Old Vic Company in entirety are doing "The Cherry Orchard." (Tchekov) You probably remember having to dust it on the desk. Then on Friday the Film Club are giving a show of "The Cabinet of Doctor Caligari" – an early German film (1919) with Conrad Veidt in. Altogether I am enjoying myself hugely.

For Pop's benefit; the Communist agitation for a Western front is much greater here, and the University is plastered with posters and deluged in pamphlets. Their argument is: "If we can't invade when ¾ of Hitler's troops are occupied in Russia, when in Heaven can we?" I have been badgered to join the Labour Club, whose membership has gone up immeasurably.

The jam is being ate swiftly, but with appreciation. Fine![2] The butter & biscuits are no more. The barley sugar isn't opened yet. I think I'll try it now, as I have only had a college breakfast. The food is most unimaginative here.

Best wishes,
Philip

1 Austin Lane Poole (1889–1963), a historian, was Senior Tutor at St John's (1931–45) and later President (1947–57). He edited the poems of Gray and Collins for the Oxford Standard Authors series. Larkin wrote in his memoir 'Biographical Details: Oxford', 'My room, due to a misunderstanding with the Senior Tutor, was an attic in the president's lodgings.' *About Larkin* 23 (April 2007), 7.
2 Sydney Larkin was a keen jam-maker.

24 October 1941 Friday

S John's

Dear Mop,

Thanks very much for your news from the front. Weather as I have mentioned before, is nippy, but beautifully clear; everything here (except work) is highly satisfying. Last night I went to bed at 10 p.m., quite early for me. My friends saw the evening to bed at 2 a.m.

I heard from Kitty today quailing under the invasion of inspectors and so forth. She wrote on her swagger crested paper in answer to one of my orange telegrams. Mrs Yeomans termed it "a startler." I don't wonder, myself.

As I may have told you I have been (unknown to myself) elected to the College Essay Society. This is AN HONOUR, the Essay Society being *the* College Society and composed of serious-minded young intellectuals under the Presidency of a don. Considering the circles I move in, I'm surprised.

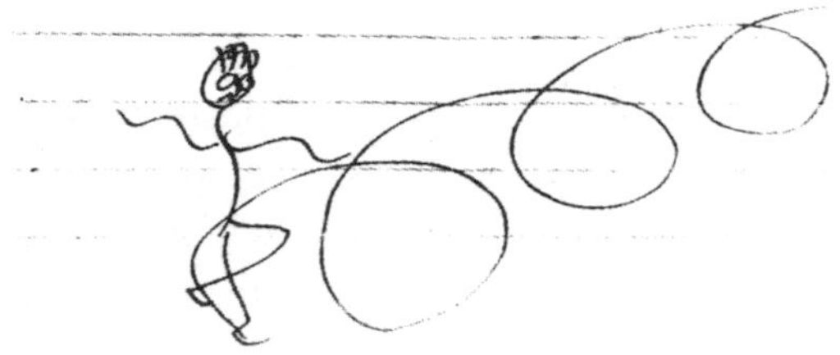

(me moving in circles)

Jim will arrive (I hope) today. I'm very much looking forward to seeing him, and hope this weekend will be more successful than last, which was generally a mess. My Oxford friends didn't like Colin, and don't like Josh anyway, and so relations were strained.[1] Added to which, the Proctors[2] complicated matters. But this week end will be peaceful, friendly, and broken only by the wildly pulsating strains of the negroidist jazz.

This term is easily the best yet, and I shall be really ~~happy~~ sorry \(Is this Freud?)/ to leave.

People are generally friendly and pleasant, work easy, jokes funny, food nice (this is my imagination, I expect) and everything Edenian (not Anthony.)[3]

With this happy thought I close hurriedly – Someone has just called.

Yours very warmly (the radiator's full on)

Philip

1 Colin Gunner and Noel ('Josh') Hughes: schoolfriends from King Henry VIII School, Coventry.

2 Internal university police.

3 Anthony Eden (1897–1977), Conservative politician; Foreign Secretary 1935–8, 1940–5 and 1951–5; Prime Minister 1955–7.

6 November 1941 Postcard[1]

Oxford Union

Life proceeding very merrily after the week's tute. Just played 2 games of billiards & am going to "La Traviata" tonight. Last night (Nov 5th) an unpopular member of the College was debagged by instruments of divine justice (Norman, myself &c) and there followed a full scale fire practice with real bombs and hoses. We squirted the Bursar.

Sorry I forgot you yesterday!

Much love,
Philip

1 Addressed to Mrs Sydney Larkin.

14 November 1941

St John's College, Oxford

Dear Katharine,

Thank you so much for your bulletin of light College chit-chat, touching upon latest developments in the modern theatre. "The Monkey's Paw," eh? Plenty of scope for a'tistic staging, I presume: for those penetrating flashes of psychological direction we have come to expect from Eisenstein, Korda and Louis Milestone. I trust you will put "A Katharine Larkin production" on the programme. S. Hugh's as far as I know haven't got a play yet – nor have they opened fire on me yet.

Life proceeds merrily with a maximum of expenditure. I was polyfotoed again this morning – no mean task.[1] Just the kind of thing you would hate. From what my face felt like, I faced each shot with a shy smirk that will look peculiarly revolting. I also did my hair (as far as possible) in the Rupert Brooke Coiffure you approved of once. The results will be posted home I suppose – so you may see them before I do. I don't anticipate them with any pleasure.

I saw the play "Spring Meeting" last week. As a play it is much less 'disturbing', being nearly a pure comedy. Bijou was as grim, but had less to say. The film gave too many close ups of her.[2] I also saw "The Ghost Train", for the ?th time. I shrieked at A.A.'s gags – "one night ..... as they were pushing the bodies in ....." – and all the rest.[3]

Margaret Iles is no relation of Norman, who is flourishing like the green bay tree. I had a[n] evening of the riotous amusement last week which laid me on my back for one Sunday morning and afternoon, and caused me to miss the meeting of the O.U. Rhythm Club. Also Old Coventrian teas which I haven't yet attended. I hope you are holding up under the strain of the authorities & Vidjin-Jenks (spelling???) and Mrs Jones; from your timetable it would appear that you have plenty to occupy your mind: it must be difficult to be ceaselessly adapting your personality to the different subjects and classes. You are very clever to be able to do it.

With very much love,
Philip

PS College people seemed to think your stamps were a V sign!

1 Polyfoto ran a chain of high street photographic studios which specialised in taking forty-eight head and shoulders shots printed on a single sheet. Customers could choose the best poses for enlargement and individual pictures, when cut out, were of a size to fit into a wallet or purse.
2 A 1941 British comedy film directed by Walter C. Mycroft and Norman Lee, starring Enid Stamp-Taylor, Michael Wilding, Basil Sydney and Sarah Churchill. It was based on the play by M. J. Farrell and John Perry. Aunt Bijou in the film was played by Margaret Rutherford.
3 A 1931 British comedy-thriller film directed by Walter Forde and starring Jack Hulbert, Cicely Courtneidge and Ann Todd, based on the play by Arnold Ridley. Arthur Askey played a vaudeville comedian, Tommy Gander.

17 November 1941

<*Letterhead*> St John's College coat of arms

Dear Mop & Pop,

I have a sinking feeling of not having written you a line for about 3 days – so here is a brief bulletin.

I enjoyed my trip to London very much. I caught the 8.15 a.m. bus from Oxford and with 2 other men – one of whom *knows* London – arrived at Victoria at about 10.30. Following a late breakfast at a Lyons, they left me to my own devices; so after vaguely wandering I attempted to get to Tottenham Ct Road by tube, which I accomplished after losing my way – or rather the way to the correct line – several times. Having reached T. C. R[d] I entered the Horse Shoe where the

O.U. Rhythm Club was congregating, and we all went off to St. John's Wood. The Jam Session was really very fine – not that the Jam was of a very high standard, but one occasionally got visions of what a real American one would be like.[1] We had to leave before it finished to catch our 6.0 bus, which we did in the hell of a rush by taking a tube to Piccadilly Circus & a taxi thence to Victoria. We *just* got the 'bus. Back in Oxford at 8.30.

Thanks to Pop for his letter (12/XI/41) and cuttings; I don't know anything about Vernon Watkins, but we are having his "mester", Dylan Thomas, at the English Club tomorrow. Incidentally the sec^y of the Club, David Yeomans (whom Pop knows, at least by repute) is dead – died of heart failure last week. This quite shook me, as I had been talking to him only the day before etc, &c.

Talking of etc, the Experimental Theatre Club did a play called "Enrico Quatro" by an Italian – translated, of course; about the madness of modern life: it was very good.[2] Other undergraduate performances will be forthcoming, I expect: all I'm doing is helping to shift scenery from one house to another for the girls of Westfield College. All my relations with women coll's have produced unhappy results – I quail at what time may bring from this.

Yrs with love,
Philip

1 This jam session, at the Abbey Road Studio of HMV, was the first to be recorded in Britain. It is available on Tolley and White (eds), *Larkin's Jazz*, disc 2 'Oxford', track 24.

2 *Enrico IV*, by Luigi Pirandello, premiered in 1922.

24 November 1941

<*Letterhead*> St John's College coat of arms

Dear Mop & Pop,

I must apologise for having left you so long unadvised, and regret that I may seem to have neglected you. Things have been rather busy. [. . .]

Talking about writing, the Labour Club Bulletin will probably print a new poem by me this week. I know the editor, Kingsley Amis: but the Bulletin is only a stencilled rag of no great circulation or influence.[1] The poem itself is nothing to do with Communism but might be interpreted that way. I'll send you a copy if it ever materialises.

The squash racquet is being used quite a lot and I enjoy using it. Only now is my right hand beginning to develop anti-blister flesh to guard against friction – I wish I weren't such a tender slice off the joint.

Thank you for your letters – write again soon. Many loads of love –

Philip

1 'Observation' was published in the issue of November 1941.

5 December 1941 Postcard[1]

[St John's College, Oxford] Friday

Still no time to write to you – my days are full as eggs, like eggs too, I feel they are rationed. Have you got my polyfoto? It has been sent to you. Please send it to me as soon as possible with comments, as it is awaited with interest here. I have had my last tute – by the way, there are now no grounds for appealing for an extra term. Excuse writing.

Love in abundance,
Philip

1 Addressed to Mrs Sydney Larkin, 73 Coten End, Warwick.

16 December 1941 Postcard[1]

St John's College, Oxford Tuesday

Temporary loss of pen makes pencil unavoidable. Medical are giving me a special "Eyesight Exam", this afternoon – they thought I was fooling them. I wasn't.

I don't know if this is hopeful or not.

Philip

1 Addressed to Mrs Sydney Larkin, 73 Coten End, Warwick.

17 December 1941 Postcard[1]

St John's College, Oxford Wednesday

You will be astounded to hear that so far from failing my section,[2] I have got a distinction. So has Norman. This is probably due to mistakes on the part of the examiners but they still stand.

Philip

P.S. This seems a good time to warn you I am down to my last £3.

1 Addressed to Mr & Mrs Sydney Larkin, 73 Coten End, Warwick.

2 On 14 December Philip had written to his parents: 'I have failed the exam, unless there is a wartime policy of letting through mental defectives as well as everybody else.'

1942

17 January 1942

125, Walton St, Oxford[1]

Dear Mop & Pop,

I am installed, but without my trunk. I don't know when this will turn up or how long to give it before becoming worried, but I left the receipt with you. So if you have it, hold it.

These lodgings seem all right. We haven't been asked to pay yet, and we haven't really settled all our problems, as regards having tea and things, but most things seem to be very nice. Details are – we are called at 8.0 a.m. with hot water and breakfast at 8.30. Baths – except on Sundays – are awkward and never before breakfast, which consists of shredded wheat, a second course, and toast and marmalade. The second course was bacon and eggs on the first morning and what she[2] called "a bag o' mystery" this morning. It was. Eatable up to a point, it spread over the plate like an enormous rissole. The only grouse I have is that she serves tea for breakfast instead of coffee. I don't know whether to ask her to change it or not.

Other meals – lunch & dinner – we have in College. She provides – apparently – sheets, towels and so on. In herself she is a kindly and rather sloppy woman, not bad looking but with gleaming false teeth.

With regard to work, I had a nasty shock when Poole told me last night that I was *not* exempted from Pass Mods.[3] and that if I wanted to read for Schools I'd better start brushing up my French & Latin. I have seen my tutor, however, – the Reverend Houghton, S. Peter's Hall – and he thinks I can plead a special case.[4] I should —— well think so too: if not I have wasted four terms and about £200. I will keep you posted in this direction, and I shall see Poole tonight. I shall be firm.

Until my trunk arrives I've nothing to read or wear but this does not bother me as I have my records. My new tutor is well known as a pedantic, uninspired, literary, Christian fool, so we shall get along fine. Norman had him last term and after a terrific quarrel about D. H. Lawrence they were never really on good terms. [. . .]

Love,
Philip

<*On back of envelope*> Received Card & letter – thank you!
P.P.S. Trunk arrived, slightly damaged. No underclothes. Where are they? Send some, please!

1 On 1 January 1942, Larkin received the notification that his poor eyesight placed him in medical category IV, so he was exempt from military service. At the beginning of term he moved into a flat at 125 Walton Street, Oxford, shared with Philip Brown, who, as a medical student, was also exempt.
2 The landlady, Mrs Burchell.
3 Austin Lane Poole. See note 1 on letter of 14 October 1941.
4 Rev. Ralph Edward Cunliffe Houghton (1896-1990), at this time a Fellow of St Peter's Hall. In 'Biographical Details: Oxford' Larkin recalls him as 'a tutor I disliked from the start'. *About Larkin* 23 (April 2007), 9.

26 January 1942 — Postcard

125 Walton St, Oxford — Monday

Just had my first tute with my new tutor.!!! He's too like Kingsland[1] to be bearable. But I agreed with everything he said, so we didn't quarrel. Pants[2] still unposted but will follow soon. Breakfasts still very nice, but nearly always cold by the time we get to them. Jim now says he's going to be a conscientious objector. How he will get on I don't know.

Love,
Philip

1 English Master at King Henry VIII School, Coventry. He had recommended that Larkin apply for Oxford.
2 Underpants (British usage).

9 February 1942

125 Walton St, Oxford

Dear Mop & Pop,

[. . .] The Bulletin printed the poem, which was a hack string of images scrawled for the occasion.[1] The L.C. Executive Committee didn't like it, however & my days as a Left Poet seem numbered. The Cherwell is just terrible these days, and if I had anything to send them I would.

A meeting of the Rhythm Club yesterday succeeded in getting three players from London – two negroes & one semi Arabian pianist by the name of Katz. It developed into a one-man show by the negro trumpeter, who was quite unabashed by the depressing university surroundings, and danced, sang, clowned, roared with laughter, addressed women in the audience, insisted on shaking hands with latecomers, and played his trumpet all without the least trace of self consciousness. I, needless to say, heartily enjoyed it.

Bacon & eggs this morning, for Mop's benefit. Are you a stronger animal now? My rude health, apart from an early morning cold, continues. I had a letter from Colin this morning which runs: "Now I want to speak a very serious word to you. I have known you since infancy. I like you immensely: I like your people, so for God's sake KEEP OUT of THE —— —— —— ARMY." He goes on to enumerate the drawbacks – shovelling snow for four days, sleeping on floors of condemned barracks, drilling in the snow at 8 a.m. &c. &c. Altogether I feel well out of things.

Jim has seen various high officers, all unsympathetic. He intends to persist, however: but I warn him to act quickly before being sent abroad as a dangerous element. He agrees.

Well, I must go & work in the Bodleian now. Love to all: be a stronger animal.

Love,
Philip

1 'Disintegration', published in the *Labour Club Bulletin*, edited by Kingsley Amis. 'Observation' had appeared in the issue of November 1941.

21 February 1942

125 Walton St, Oxford

Dear Mop and Pop,

It is about time I sent you a letter, I think: the spectacles have just arrived, for which many thanks: but I have found my fountain pen, praise be. [. . .]

I haven't forgotten the oculist, but am waiting for the spectacle business to be cleared up. I have had no news as yet from the Army, and am living in hopes. Pop will be infuriated to hear that I have joined the Labour Club, due to the amusing exertions of a Czech woman, Chitra Ruderingova, who is the crankiest communist I have ever met.[1] Also they now have club rooms where one can get coffee at 10 p.m. every night – most convenient.

I hope you (Mop) are improving daily; I am still battening and fattening on bacon and eggs. Mrs B. is very shy about *money*: it pains her deeply when we ask for a bill, and she hides it like a squirrel in a drawer for us, and insists that we do the same with the money. It vanishes. By the way, I think our vac. starts about March 15th. I don't know what I shall be doing with regard to firewatching, &c. but you asked for the date so there it is. Work continues fairly nicely. Hope you liked the poem (did I send it?) I do. The Czech woman thought it "morbid and unhealthy". She's crazy.

Yours v. affectionately,
Philip

1 Larkin invited Rudingerova to tea (he misspells her name): 'We ate toast and marmalade and she told me I was decadent. Nothing else happened.' 'Biographical Details: Oxford', *About Larkin* 23 (April 2007), 9. See also Zachary Leader (ed.), *The Letters of Kingsley Amis* (London: HarperCollins, 2000), 13 and fn.

26 April 1942

125 Walton St, Oxford

My dear Mrs Larkin,

Thank you for your very prompt despatch of my few Goods and Chattels! I was truly surprised they arrived so soon. Everything was quite all right, nothing was broken "in transit", as they say, and I am settled once more in my "digs" as of yore.

That fool Mrs Burchell has put a screen in front of the 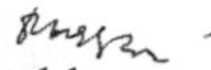 –[1] in front of the fireplace, so I am not expected to warm my aged bones at this time of the year, apparently! My breakfast was stone cold yesterday & the teapot was half full of leaves this morning. That dam' fool Joyce[2] put blacking on my brown shoes last night & I have had to get busy this morning with my gown rubbing it off. She thinks I don't notice it. But I do. She may think this is an easy job. But I tell her she'll get called up into munitions as soon as look at her. That shows her which way the wind's blowing.

I have another new tutor – a b. fool called Hughes from Birmingham, ninety years old and blind, quite incapable of doing anything.[3] He can't even see me, let alone read my essays. A case of the blind leading the blind, oh, dear lady?! I am also going to another tutor sometime to pick up my Anglo Saxon again – it can do with a little "brushing up"!

Negotiations are under way for us to hire a punt for the whole term, in order to laze on the river without having to rush about trying to find one like a crowd of b. fools. As far as I can see, the college won't even have *one*. They're too lazy. I know the type. They're too slack to do a hand's turn even if they didn't know where their next meal was coming from. But if we get one and they leave it so late that they can't, they'll laugh on the other side of their faces, I'll be bound. That will be a slap in the eye for them, with a 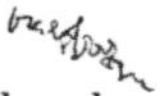 – with a vengeance.

Well, dear lady. I must thank you yet once again for your kindness during my stay at your delightful residence. I hope to be with you again before very long and "tempus fugit", you know!

Yours very truly
C. D. Penn[4]

1 The letters are misformed and the word lurches downward into the next line, as if the author had lost control of the pen.
2 Mrs Burchell's daughter.
3 Arthur M. D. Hughes (1873–1974) had edited *Cobbett: Prose and Poetry* for the Clarendon Press (1925). He retired from his chair in Birmingham in 1939 and was at this time an emeritus professor. Larkin exaggerates his age. See letter of 15 May 1942.
4 Larkin gives no explanation of the letters, in slightly disguised handwriting, sent in the name of C. D. (or G. D.) Penn M.A. See Philip Pullen, 'The Mysterious Mr Penn', *About Larkin* 35 (April 2013), 12–14.

29 April 1942 Wednesday

125 Walton St, Oxford

Thank Pop for his letter, cutting, & check. I must ask you for one more thing – Sweet's Anglo Saxon Reader (blue book) & Sweet's A. S. Primer (small dis-covered brown book) from the shelves of my desk. I am restarting Old English with a vengeance under the kindly hand of Miss Bisson, a kindly middle-aged lady whom I hope to get on all right with. I think I prefer women tutors to men – they're gentler.[1]

Mrs B. has removed the wall-flowers & brought some exotic pink lilies, Gelder lilies & blue things that might be scabious. They look lovely.

Love,
Philip

1 Mrs (not Miss) Isabella Jane Bisson, née Smith (1895–1986) was described in the Somerville College Register as 'coaching in English at Oxford, 1935' (no end date given).

10 May 1942

125 Walton St, Oxford

Dear Mop & Pop,

Thanks for letter and forget me nots, which arrived squashed and flat, but still recognisable as f-m-n's. I will answer any burning questions first.

Wilenski[1] was a genial, toad-like man. I "had conversation" with him, mainly desultory, but quite intellectual. He wanted to know why young artists were so ready to fly into political camps; saying that in his day no one expected the artist to justify his work or make it intelligible to the common man any more than the research scientist. I told him why I thought it was – the double successful attack on the artist, internally by the psychologists and externally by the Fascists (I know Pop won't agree) that had destroyed their self confidence and made them ready to back up the party that promised to deliver them in the new extra-university real-life battle between aesthete and athlete. Needless to say, he was not impressed by all this.

News on the literary front is fairly encouraging. The position is that "Z" (Lehmann) hopes to appear before the term's end.[2] What I have in it I don't know – probably one poem. I had a couple back with some pencillings – presumably Lehmann's – reading "Auden again! I am thoroughly sick of the flat middle-class phraseology of the Auden jargon. But this has some fine lines." Both poems were marked "A" which is a Class number, I suppose, opposed to B & C, and not meaning "Accepted" or "Auden"!

Charles Hamblett returned the story but kept the five poems, sending a very fulsome letter. He says they will be published in the Fortune Press. I don't really trust him, but I suppose all is grist etc. at this stage of the proceedings. Many people were included in his search for "non Hogarth press" protégés.

Jim is at present at Moreton-in-the-Marsh. Nothing has happened yet about his case. I like my new spectacles immensely. They are slick and shiny.

I think that is all you wanted to know.

One of the things I have learnt about Dylan Thomas, you might tell Pop, is that he rarely reads any poetry but when he does it is Thomas Hardy and A. E. Housman (very simple people) who are his favourites. I suppose this is because he is so under educated . . . He is also writing for the Govt. in MofI[3] film capacity. Beowulf is now hissing at me from a corner, so I must end.

Ever with love,
Philip

My dear Mrs Larkin,[4]

Don't you worry about Warwick being raided, dear lady. Jerry has a lot more fish to fry yet, I'll be bound. I'd like to see him lay a finger on Oxford, either. He'd soon have a pretty mess about his ears, you mark my words.

Yours very sincerely,
C. D. Penn M.A.

1 R. H. Wilenski (1887–1975): art critic and historian, author of *The Modern Movement in Art* (1928). Larkin was Treasurer of the English Club, and responsible for managing the visits of guest speakers.

2 An anthology of Oxford and Cambridge writing, edited by John Lehmann (1907–87), who founded *New Writing* in 1936 and the *London Magazine* in 1954. See Geoff Weston, '"Z": Another Larkin exclusion', *About Larkin* 44 (October 2017), 25.

3 Ministry of Information.
4 In disguised handwriting.

15 May 1942

125 Walton St, Oxford

Dear Mop & Pop,

This weekly letter is a trifle schoolboyish in plan, but I hope you appreciate the fact that I really can't fit it in for certain any other way. The postcards are also too infrequent, I know.

Thank you for the fat little pipe. For some reason, it arouses terrific disgust in all my friends, but I like it. The mouthpiece *is* wrong, I know, but it actually doesn't make much difference. Thank you for the chocolate.

I am getting to like my tutor, inasmuch as it is in my nature to like any tutor. He was born in 1873 and before the last war held a position at Kiel University. His appreciative powers make up for what he lacks intellectually – which is a pleasant change from the rest, who just don't make up for what they lack intellectually.

No poetic news. You might tell pop that a friend of mine found an Obelisk Press Edition (i.e. unexpurgated) of "Lady Chatterley's Lover" behind the bookcase in his digs, and I am impatiently waiting for him (and his wife) to finish it. "Mine eyes have seen the Glory of the Coming of the Lord". I have also stupidly consented to write a paper for the Essay Society for May 31st, and am going to expand the Isherwood paper the English Club underwent.

Margaret Kennedy is next week's guest.[1] I expect Pop is one of her regular readers, but I really can't remember anything she has written. The Finances are tough going, but with Philip Brown's assistance (like Pop's assistance at my homework – remember? even to the "Yes, but do you see *why* we do it?") it hasn't come unstuck yet.[2]

I haven't had much in the way of tea-parties this term, but I went to supper with a friend called Hilary last night who casually produced a crab he had bought and *boiled himself*. Needless to say he darns his own socks. Truly an amazing kind of person.

By the way, vac. plans loom. I shall be conscripted into the coll. firewatching scheme for 3 weeks. I don't know when, yet. Also my South Wales holiday may really happen.

Condole Pop on his indisposition & new sports coat. Philip had one arrive yesterday – very nice, but v. expensive (£5.0.0)

Very much love
Philip
PTO

My dear Mrs Larkin,

Please pardon my writing in pencil, but my pen has just run out and someone – that b. fool Joyce, I expect – has run away with the ink. I shall be overjoyed to accept once more the kindly hospitality of you and Mr Larkin this coming vacation.

Don't be nervous about this fellow Hitler – I'll wager he's sorry he ever crossed swords with us, eh?! The bells will ring, dear lady, very soon, but it won't be for an invasion, you mark my words. It'll be peace.

Now I must try and get off some of the blacking that b. fool Joyce has put on my brown shoes.

Yrs v. sincerely
C. D. Penn, M.A.

1 Novelist and playwright (1896–1967), best-known for her novel, *The Constant Nymph* (1924).
2 Larkin was Treasurer of the English Club.

21 May 1942

125 Walton St, Oxford Thursday

Dear Pop,

Thanks for your words in season. I haven't got hold of the book yet, but I can't imagine Lawrence doing anyone any harm, who knew what he was talking about. And I do know what he's talking about – I hope. However, I will walk warily, as you suggest.

A drifting, rainy day here – not particularly objectionable. I have to prepare a question on 'Bacon as a moralist', and having carefully constructed the epigram "Bacon was a moralist without being an idealist" am finding it refuted in all introductions, prefaces, essays &c. By the way, Hughes (my tutor) edited that Cobbett I used at school – remember? – in the Clarendon Series.[1] Also three others – Shelley, Burke and someone else.

You know, I regard "Lady C." as the last piece to be put in my Lawrence jigsaw. All his work I have read and reread. This last book is the final flower, crown, jewel – whatever you like. Anyway, I have just read the most disgusting and revolting book ever written, which should be immediately banned instead of selling thousands to the RAF – "No Orchids for Miss Blandish".[2]

All Love,
Philip

1 A. M. D. Hughes (ed.), *Cobbett: Prose and Poetry* (Clarendon Press, 1925).
2 A lurid crime novel published in 1939 by James Hadley Chase (1906–85).

26 May 1942 — Postcard[1]

<*Letterhead*> St John's College, Oxford — Tuesday

Things miserable here, for a variety of reasons. Raining solidly for several days. Feel like death. Essay a bore. Work too heavy. Life in decay. Hope you're both happier.

Love,
Philip

<*Down right margin*> P.S. I'm not *quite* so gloomy as this may suggest.

1 With printed letterhead, but text written in pencil by Larkin.

7 June 1942[1]

[125 Walton St, Oxford]

My dear Mrs Larkin,

How is the sun finding you these days, eh? Don't forget to get out a bit, even if it's only for half an hour in the afternoon – in the afternoons. My laundry troubles have been cleared up satisfactorily, but I am a little short of handkerchiefs, you know, due to the pestilential hay-fever. hugh!!

My regards to you & Mr Larkin.

Yours very sincerely,
G. D. Penn[2]

1 The final side of a four-side letter.
2 *Sic*. In other letters he signs himself 'C. D. Penn'.

9 June 1942

Postcard[1]

125 Walton St

Tragedy. 'Z' appeared, without me.[2] Please send 2 botts. arsenic, 2 botts. strychnine, 1 revolver plus 7 rounds of ammunition, a rope with a noose in it, and a deep pond with a bridge over it.

Philip

1 Addressed to Mrs Sydney Larkin, 73 Coten End, Warwick.
2 An anthology of Oxford and Cambridge writing, edited by John Lehmann. See letter of 10 May.

5 November 1942

Postcard[1]

125 Walton St, Oxford *Thursday night*

Thank you for your nice letters. Sorry I don't tell you more of what I do etc. but there's no use in it. Still raining, Dylan been & gone – I'll tell you more when I write. Thank Pop for cutting – Alex. Comfort[2] is no one but anyone can lecture "Truth" in matters requiring the least sensitivity of feeling or perception. My cold comes & goes in direct ratio to smoking. I am really quite all right but work makes me worse. Thanks for the underwear which I am wearing under. As regards dreams, I had an excellent one last night when two girls (one dark, one fair) kissed each other due to my benevolent presence. This symbolises integration of conscious & unconscious and I may expect to blossom into Tarzan of the Apes in the near future.

Very much love to you both,
Philip

1 Addressed to Mrs Sydney Larkin, 73 Coten End, Warwick.
2 Alex Comfort (1920–2000), physician, anarchist and conscientious objector, was known, at this stage in his career, as the author of the novel *No Such Liberty* (1941) and the collection of poems *A Wreath for the Living* (1942). Later he achieved fame with the popular manual *The Joy of Sex* (1972).

8 November 1942

[125 Walton St, Oxford]

Dear Mop & Pop,

I am in a better mood this morning: the sun is shining and I am sitting in front of the hell of a fire. Let me tell you about my meeting with the greatest poet at present writing. Dylan Thomas is an incredibly small and tousled, grubby Welshman. He has a mass of tangled curly hair ranging from blue to fairest lemon. He wore *two* sailor's jerseys, a shabby purple-yellow checked sports coat, and speckled grey trousers. His face is round, with a comical snubby nose, fat cheeks, incipient double chin and two flabby lips. He smoked literally all the time, except when eating or drinking. His voice sounded 'cultured' to me but Philip said it was pure Welsh.

The meeting was a great success; he read extracts from a novel he was writing and they were brilliant. He has perfected a dream-technique which enables him to be fantastically funny and poetical at the same time. I have always thought that any great book at present must be funny too, but it's harder than you'd think. Afterwards we went to the Eastgate Hotel for coffee. Next morning the Committee including myself and Philip who came too met in the Mitre Tavern for a drink. Philip & I were honoured by Dylan's talking to us the whole time. I should imagine he'd had enough of the Committee the night before. I didn't dare talk shop, and the conversation veered uneasily from one thing to another, like his saying he'd agreed never to firewatch when there was a raid, not caring a —— —— about the premises of Samuel P. [illegible],[1] Tailor, etc. and there were always a couple of ——s in every squad who really enjoyed it etc. etc. Then we dispersed for lunch, feeling slightly drunk from our contact with a great & original talent. There is an enormous contrast between him and his work.

I expect you find this boring. Last night we went to "The Seagull" a Tchekov play & felt gloomy. I began writing a poem which I hope to finish some time today. Let me think of something to interest Mop – I am determined to get needles and wool from somewhere to darn my socks, but so far I haven't had the courage. The trouble is, my socks are too small, really, and my toes always come through. I haven't got a cold any more & feel fine. I am wearing my old Edwardian sweater till it's grey with filth, but really it's my favourite jersey. The brown windcheater is too short and the blue poloneck can't be worn in Hall. So I go around looking like a dirty Old Etonian.

For Pop – academically, I am sunk. I suppose I shall get a third – might even scrape a second, but I doubt it. You and I, who have been brought up to regard reading as one of the major *pleasures* of life, are bunkered by the insistence of the necessity of *attitude*. I can read a whole author without having an *attitude* towards him. I do not want to know where he got his vocabulary from or whether he didn't make the best of his subject. My tutor has openly stopped trying to make an intelligent man of me & I have openly stopped pretending to be interested. He can think I have finished an essay when I have stopped at the end of my first line of argument. I am so disgusted that I let him think it, the bloody old fool. I hope this winter takes him off.

However – Colin Gunner is still training for that Commission – I wonder how Jim has got on during the recent Libya doings.[2] Please ask Pop to tell me what's really happened. I suppose the losses have been enormous – Jim will be pretty sick even if he's safe himself.

No more now – have to write elsewhere.

Love to both,
Philip

1 Illegible.

2 Jim Sutton had joined the Royal Army Medical Corps in April 1941.

1943

18 January 1943

125 Walton St, Oxford Sunday

Dear Mop & Pop,

I am writing this before breakfast (9.10) because I happen to be up "early". The day is overcast & windy.[1] [. . .]

Pop might like to know that the Everyman Yellow Book isn't at all interesting – it's the *old* Yellow Book: some drivelling Italianate documents whence Browning derived the Ring & the Book. I was expecting a 'feuillet' [*sic*] of decadent verse & prose poems, if *feuillet* is the right word.[2]

No news of my own immortal nonsense.

Mop's book token has bought rather a luxury which may not be fully worth it – Frank Harris' 'Oscar Wilde'.[3] You remember I was reading Wilde just before I left, and fell under his fascination as a talker and writer. I think it's delightful that the best biography of Wilde should be "all lies", in view of Oscar's Essay on the decay of lying . . .

I have changed my eating arrangements. Nowadays I lunch at a British Restaurant[4] (like a pig among pigs), sometimes have tea & toast at tea time, and dine at the Anglo Chinese. This costs about 4/- per day: in college – last term – I was paying anything from 4/6 – 5/-, excluding drinks of course. So I am economising, in theory. I wonder what my battels were. Stupidly I forebore to open them, I can't think why. I feel they are enormous –

My breakfast has arrived now – looks like liver & "bag of mystery".[5] I will rise up, and eat, and eructate.

Love from all the apes,
Philip

1 The letter was written mostly on Sunday 17 January. '8' has been superimposed over '7' in the date.

2 Larkin has 'corrected' 'feuillot' both times to 'feuillet', or vice versa. '*Feuillet*' means a leaf or page in French.
3 Frank Harris (1855–1931), *Oscar Wilde: His life and confessions* (1916).
4 Communal kitchens that offered cheap, nourishing meals without requiring any ration coupons to be presented.
5 The landlady of 125 Walton Street, Mrs Burchell, called any unidentifiable ingredient in her breakfasts a 'bag o' mystery'. See also letter of 17 January 1942, above.

31 January 1943

125 Walton St

Dear Mop & Pop,

We are in the middle of a 2-day invasion exercise. Yesterday we had the preliminary air-raid & divebombing of the city, with huge Whitleys and Wellingtons roaming over the roofs and bombs being let off in the streets. Today the Americans are due to capture the town from the North & West: gas, tanks, etc. will be used in profusion. Luckily we're safely indoors and have no official part to play.

I think I shall have to be a warden or a trailer-pump trainer or something, but on the other hand I feel I am being swindled as other wrecks from other colleges are getting off scotfree.

I shall take an obstructionist attitude to it all. But the whole survey is for statistics to answer that old dolt in the "Times" who proved with a lot of phony figures that the Universities were slacking. [. . .]

I haven't any 'homely' things to tell you, as far as I remember: Karl Lehmann recently stayed a night with us, and assures us from the height of his B.B.C. experience that we've already won the war.[1] Can't say I've noticed it. At present I am tousled and unshaved in an armchair, dressed in my green trousers, green dressing gown, and red shirt.[2] I appear languidly at the window occasionally to scandalise the enthusiastic bands of dripping-wet wardens who are hanging about outside. It's a wet day with a strong gale that rattles the windows and tears the smoke away from the chimneys. I have so much to do today. I just dare not start doing any of it.

Loud explosions punctuated this letter – I don't know where they come from, but it adds a distinct Stalingrad atmosphere.[3] A friend has just called, having run the gauntlet of police etc.

Forgive this slightly newspapery letter. My best love to Ginger P.[4] I wrote to Kitty recently a miserable little note.

With much love,
Philip

Me, Jan 31 1943

1 Karl Lehmann was a friend of Larkin's flatmate, Philip Brown, and a keen disciple of Carl Gustav Jung.
2 This letter is written on red notepaper.
3 The Battle of Stalingrad, one of the bloodiest of the war, ended with the surrender of the German Sixth Army on 2 February 1943.
4 'Ginger P': probably Eva herself.

7 February 1943

125 Walton St, Oxford — Sunday

Dear Mop & Pop,

Excuse this ink,[1] it's a relic from my colourful days of 1941. I filled a pen full of it to brighten up my daily round. [. . .]

Today I have discarded my cardigan and clawed on my white sweater. You will be pleased to hear it has shrunk a little but looks beautiful & swan-white. Oh, incidentally, du Cann didn't go down after all.[2] His father pulled a few Admiralty strings and got him another term. He celebrated his return by swallowing a pin and having X-rays at the local hospital. He is now quite well – luckily the pin fell head-first.

I read a review of a new novel based on K. M.'s life.[3] I think it's called "daughter of the earth" or some such nonsense.[4] The reviewer said it was a bad & embarrassing book, but all the same it might be interesting. Have you heard of Vernon Watkins? He is a poet who has published 1 book, and came to the English Club last week. I rather liked him, and he left a lot of books of Yeats' poems with me which I shall eventually return. He is a timid little man.[5]

According to Karl Lehmann we have already won the war.

I was charmed by your remarks on squirrel and bird-life. Some rooks *are* building near here, though. Philip has been teaching me to recognise elms and poplars and other trees. I'm not very good at it.

Give my love to Pop – and I do hope he's well again.

Love to you too,
Philip

1 Bright blue.
2 After the war Edward du Cann, Larkin's contemporary at St John's, became an MP and Chairman of the Conservative Party.
3 Katherine Mansfield.
4 Nelia Gardner White, *Daughter of Time: The Life of Katherine Mansfield in Novel Form*, 1942. Larkin has confused the title with that of the autobiography of Agnes Smedley, *Daughter of the Earth* (1929).
5 Vernon Watkins (1906–67): Welsh poet, translator and painter; close friend of Dylan Thomas. His visit to the Poetry Club stirred Larkin's enthusiasm for W. B. Yeats.

10 February 1943 — Postcard

<*Letterhead*> St John's College, Oxford — Wednesday

Thank you for your lively letter. Today is another of *those* days – I went to a friend's 21st b'day party last night with disastrous results. At 1 p.m. I am still in pyjamas etc. having eaten a breakfast of 3 peppermints. I think I shall see "Bambi" this afternoon.[1] Kitty wrote me a sad little letter.

Large Love,
Philip

1 The classic of animation, *Bambi*, produced by Walt Disney, was released by RKO Radio Pictures in August 1942.

28 February 1943

125 Walton St, Oxford

Dear Mop & Pop,

It is 5 to 10, but nevertheless I am writing this before breakfast. Philip has a 9.15 lecture every day of the week except Sunday so he takes Sunday to luxuriate on. I am a trifle hungry but feel bound to wait for him out of politeness. There is some kind of cold tongue for breakfast.

Thanks for letter & cutting. I agree with what you say about Mrs B.[1] but really what can one buy? It's all very difficult. Scent – well, I can't think she'd use it really. She might like it, I can't tell. She's *worth* something really expensive, but we can't afford that. It's a great problem. As a matter of fact, we might even *not* leave her. Philip's finding difficulty in getting unlicensed digs in the area & price he wants.

"Arabesque" came out.[2] I bought 1 for myself & 1 family copy which I sent to Kitty – thought she needed cheering up.

Mrs Bisson has been ill recently – *Good*!! – but suddenly sent me a mountain of work to be done by Monday. Blessed are they which do not expect. I am sick of this Cook's tour of literature – one gets as much or as little benefit from it as from any other Cook's tour.

Well, Philip has just tottered down so I will hold my horses till I have eaten my breakfast.

The tongue was a little desiccated. Yesterday I was seized with a crazy desire to have a bookplate printed – you know, one of those ex libris things – so I sketched a very simple design and intend putting things in motion tomorrow. Kitty will moan that I haven't made all I might of it. It is merely a symbol – ✡ – my name, and a couplet from Blake.[3] The O.U.P. will do it fairly cheaply. – 10/- – 15/-.

I may stay up here some time – I'm not sure when I shall come home. I daren't leave the libraries because I have so much work.

But I will return –

Love,
Philip

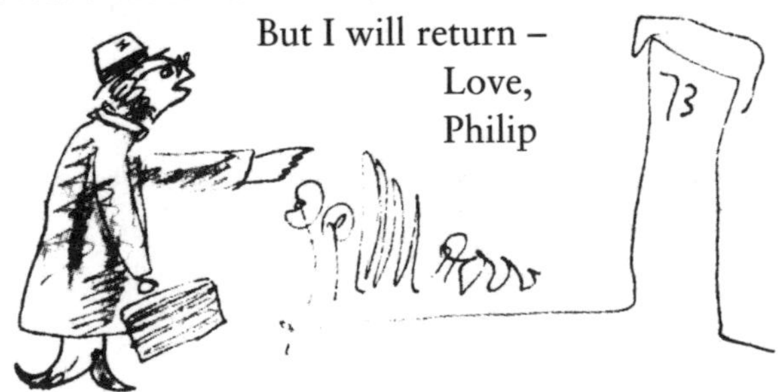

1 Mrs Burchell: landlady of 125 Walton Street.
2 'I dreamed of an out-thrust arm of land', and 'Mythological Introduction' appeared in *Arabesque* in Hilary Term (January–March) 1943. On 21 February he referred to the journal as 'that ballet club thing'.
2 'How do you know but ev'ry Bird that cuts the airy way / Is an immense world of delight clos'd by your senses five?' ('The Marriage of Heaven and Hell')

3 March 1943

Postcard

125 Walton St, Oxford

Wednesday

Sorry I missed a p.c. yesterday but I was very busy rushing about. I met George Orwell who is very nice, though not quite Pop's political line.[1] Your letters arrived as a pleasant surprise this morning. I thought Pop had sunk into a senile apathy that only permitted him to make a mark on the bottom of municipal documents.

Kitty sent me another mournful letter which depressed me a little. But otherwise I am fairly happy, having a great deal to do in all ways – work, poems, essays, etc. I have ordered my bookplate at last. – Don't know when it'll be done.

Of course I'll be home for Pop's birthday – I know what I'm going to buy him too. So does he, if he thinks a little.

Love,
Philip

1 Orwell had spoken at the English Club.

7 March 1943

125 Walton St, Oxford

Dear Mop & Pop

I feel very special this morning, as I am dressed in a white shirt – my exam shirt, you recollect. The sun is shinely [*sic*] and bright, and I am aware of clouds of work on the horizon. I am very sorry I only sent you 1 postcard last week: I spend my time doing many things which seem important and have no time to write to anybody, except Sunday morning which I set aside especially for the purpose.

This paper is a little battered, but it has been lying under a pile of books and papers. I found it while setting my books in order this morning. I can assure you I am not going about in holes – I darned 2 pairs last Tuesday with great satisfaction. Only not having any khaki wool I had to darn in grey.

I'm sorry I didn't send the poems to you, if you'd been expecting them – Kitty grumpily acknowledged them: "I feel miserable enough without having poems like that come." [. . .]

My bookplate arouses dislike – apparently it is the official Star of David. On the wave of Anti Semitism that is almost bound to come after the war I may be hung up on the nearest lamppost. To me it's no more Jewish than a verse of the Bible. But people don't seem to like it.

I think I should like to go out & walk now – get some of God's air into my lungs, ah hah! (violent fit of coughing). All good wishes & much love – are my bulbs coming up yet?

Philip

16 May 1943

125 Walton St, Oxford

Dear Mop & Pop,

Time runs on, and the weather seems settled in a groove of summer. I am wearing my red trousers defiantly and daringly, but not killing myself with work. Everything is very peaceful. I must say, the dark glasses are a great help against hay fever. My nose has snuffles, my throat itches slightly, but *as yet* I haven't experienced the real blitzkrieg of sneezing that I usually associate with May & June. The Lord be praised. Aldous Huxley can go to the devil.

There is very little to tell you as far as events go. I have tickets for Emlyn Williams' production of "Night Must Fall" at the New Theatre next week, and am rather interested to see how it wears after all these years.[1] I don't expect you enjoyed "Holiday Inn"[2] very much, if I'm thinking of the right film.

The cake situation is worse than I had imagined, for after standing in the Cadena queue yesterday for half an hour I staggered out with bloodshot eyes clutching two "trifles" and a couple of currant buns. I then bought a very sad-looking lettuce. "It's got a good heart," said the shopkeeper, pinching it cruelly, like a warder speaking of a prisoner's conduct. I bought it out of pity, and gave it Mrs Burchell to revive, with instructions to make 6 sandwiches with it. I now hear she is very alarmed because she thinks I want sandwiches for six from it. This illusion will be cruelly shattered when she comes to clear the breakfast things. The tea is for my intelligent friend, Bruce Montgomery, but I am expecting him to forget.

The proofs of "Oxford Poetry" are done; I have only got 3 in: the two Arabesque ones and a third, inferior one. The book should be out in a couple of months.[3]

Is Pop finding anything to read these days? I should imagine the papers provide a good deal of amusement. Everyone here is very pleased with the news, and I must say I'm glad Africa is disposed of.[4] I don't fancy England being left to the protection of the Home Guard, though.

Well, I must work. It's a beautiful Sunday: hope you manage to get out in these days for a little. I expect at this very minute Pop is bowling along like a sea god, somewhere in the vicinity of Barford.[5]

Love to both,
Philip

1 It was first produced in 1935.

2 A 1942 film directed by Mark Sandrich, starring Bing Crosby and Fred Astaire, with music by Irving Berlin, including 'White Christmas'.

3 'I dreamed of an out-thrust arm of land', 'Mythological Introduction' and 'A Stone Church Damaged by a Bomb' appeared in June 1943 in *Oxford Poetry 1942–3*, edited by Ian Davie.

4 In early May Tunis and Bizerte fell to the Allies, and the Axis forces in North Africa surrendered; 230,000 prisoners of war were taken.

5 Village about three miles south of Warwick. Sydney was a keen cyclist.

27 May 1943 — Postcard

125 Walton St, Oxford

A terrible breakfast, that Philip identified as *eels*, at present reposes in a cardboard box waiting to be disposed of. Ain't we naughty? The weather continues showery & I feel slightly ill owing to the proximity of Finals. 3 weeks today! Unk! On second thoughts I think it must be the eels. Kitty wrote.

– my new animal. Can't draw him on a small scale.[1]

Love: Philip

1 Larkin abandons the fish image of the previous letters, and this is the first appearance of the 'creature' which will feature in his letters to Eva for the remainder of her life, and also in letters to Patsy Strang and Monica Jones. See James Booth, 'The Origins of Larkin's "Creature"', *About Larkin* 40 (October 2015), 9–11, and Philip Pullen, 'No Villainous Mother: The Life of Eva Larkin', in Dale Salwak (ed.), *Writers and Their Mothers* (London: Palgrave Macmillan, 2018), 81–95.

30 May 1943

125 Walton St, Oxford

Dear Mop and Pop,

[. . .] I came the nearest to literary success this week I have ever been, when Bruce Montgomery had a novel accepted by Victor Gollancz.[1] I read the terms of acceptance with bated breath. £50 advance on royalties. It's a detective novel, written in 10 days. £5 a day, I realise, by a swift brilliant, and untoward mathematical calculation. Nice, eh?

Mop will be interested to hear I still wear nearly as many clothes as in winter. And hayfever has started again, like Hell. I wear the darkened spectacles and carry a battery of handkerchiefs, keeping indoors as far as possible, but twice a day I have to endure a blitz of sneezing and eye-smarting.

Still, you have heard all this before.

News is absolutely lacking. I fiddle at my work. At present I am in a sleepy sea of optimism. I think I am certain to get some degree of a second class, and no matter how hard I work I shall never get a first, so there's no point in working hard. Or so I think.

I ought to dash off a line or so to Kitty (yes, I really mean it this time) so I'll draw this brevity shorter. [. . .]

Much love,
Philip

1 *The Case of the Gilded Fly* (1944).

6 June 1943

125 Walton St, Oxford

Dear Mop & Pop,

[. . .] Bruce has been having a good deal of fun with Gollancz, swearing the book contains no libellous matter, and trying to think up a new title. He is writing it under a pen-name – Edmund Crispin, did I tell you? I may remark that the new "Arabesque" is out, and is so much better than the old one that I deeply regret not having printed anything in it. But poetry has departed and gone away . . .

I suppose I shall be in the Civil Service before the year is out. I can't say the thought gives me overmuch pleasure: the best thing about it is that it's temporary . . . *No* prospects. I s'll starve after the war, urrrgh.

I think I must write to Kitty now: she wants to spend a holiday in Oxford, apparently, with Walter,[1] and she wants the names of hotels. I, unfortunately, can't remember their names – only "that-one-opposite-the-New-Bodleian" etc.

Much love & kisses to both –
Philip

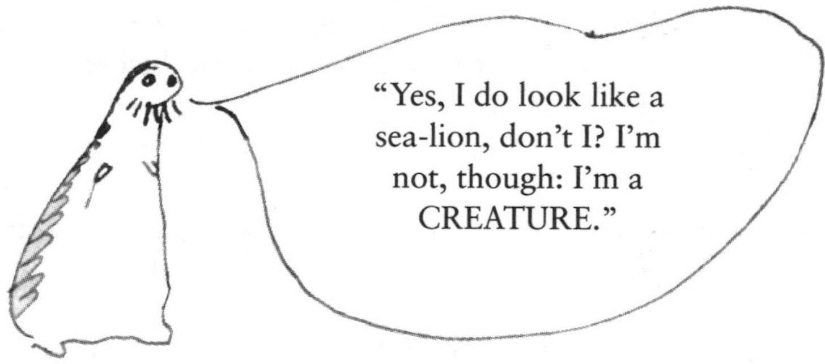

"Yes, I do look like a sea-lion, don't I? I'm not, though: I'm a CREATURE."

1 Walter Hewett, whom Kitty was to marry on 12 August 1944.

11 June 1943

125 Walton St, Oxford

Dear Mop,

Here is a noisome (noisesome?) parcel of Light Washing. For many years I have foreborne to send you anything, but now the laundry flatly admits it hasn't called for a fortnight & won't call for another week, and I am frankly OUT of handkerchiefs. It is an awful position. If you could do the handkerchiefs and return them as soon as possible, I should be most grateful.

It is less than a week till the exam now. I am awfully frightened. [. . .]

Love,
Philip

20 June 1943

125 Walton Street, Oxford

Dear Mop & Pop,

Well, I hope you are feeling set up after your jaunt to Sheffield, and I expect at this minute (11.6 a.m.) you are prowling around the scullery while Pop is whirling among the lanes on his bike. I am enjoying a brief – very brief – respite from the blitz of examinations. Thank you for your letter of encouragement on Thursday morning – they put the time-table up on *Wednesday*, of all the [*illegible*]. I was very afraid on Thursday morning.

How I have done:

Thursday.

Old English – not very well: I should imagine γ or β–
Middle English – slightly better: β– or β.

Friday.

Chaucer – very bad in parts, better in others. β– or β.

Eng. Lit. 1400–1700 – better: β or β+.

Saturday.

General paper. – Fair: β+, I hope.

So you see, as far as I can judge, my marks are in general a second class. I have moments of panic when I think I shall be "thirded" and moments of foolish optimism when I think the examiners might give me a first out of sheer diablerie, but on the whole I think a steady β indicates my level. The exam is held in the Sheldonian Theatre, if you care to look that up in the Oxford book: a big, round building. There is a sea of women, and a little thin file of men down one side of the room – 6 of us in all out of 70 or 80.

Other news there is none, except that I had an airgraph from Colin Gunner – of course, you sent it me – saying he has arrived safely in Tunis and was bathing in the Mediterranean. Philip Brown has found digs for next term, and we still don't know what to give Mrs Burchell when we go.

Yes, bring Auntie N.[1] by all means. Can you come for the day on Tuesday? (that is the 29th, I think – is it?) But I might pass on a warning which is circulating here – don't come if the R.A.F. bomb *Rome*. If they do, I am more likely to come and see you, as soon as possible. Otherwise, come and be welcomed.

Best of wishes and love to both of you. I must now return to my bewks.

Philip

1 Nellie Day ('Auntie Nellie'), the widow of Eva Larkin's only brother Arthur Day (1888–1941), lived in Ashton-under-Lyne at this time, later moving to Hyde. She and Eva were firm friends.

24 June 1943

125 Walton St, Oxford

Dear Mop & Pop,

Oh dear! Oh dear! Oh dear! Having gently prepared you for my getting a second, I feel I shall have to prepare you for a third or lower. I didn't do at all well on Monday or Tuesday. Monday in particular – two literary papers that I ought to have done well – I felt sluggish and mentally incapable so that I handed in two gamma or near gamma papers at the end. Tuesday was better, but I knew the morning's paper (Modern English – language) would be hell and it was. The Spenser-and-Milton paper in the afternoon was much nicer, and I wrote like a mad thing from start to finish.

But altogether I feel anything but optimistic, when I think of the garbled, inaccurate, thin, drivelling, facetious, misinformed rubbish I showed up. Beware! Thirds *are* given, and I *may* get one.

No more now. I'll book a table for lunch at the Randolph for 4 unless I hear otherwise. Thank you for your long and delightful letter. Glad you had a nice time at Sheffield. No news about Civil Service. Yes, 2 handkerchiefs received.

Love,
P.

7 July 1943

Telegram[1]

Warwick

APPARENTLY I HAVE GOT A FIRST PHILIP

1 Addressed to Miss C. Larkin, 13 Cedar Rd, Loughborough.

8 September 1943 | Typescript[1]

[73 Coten End, Warwick]

Women's Mineworkers
Appointment Dept.

Ref. No.: Y7844.

Warwick.
8.9.43.

Dear Madam,

We have to inform you that you have been drafted to the Colliery at Pwllycracrach, Mon., for light duties at the shafthead and also in the pit itself. You will present yourself to the Manager of the Dowlais Pit, Pwyllycracrach, on September 13th, for further instructions. Enclosed please find a travelling warrant. (We can't).

Yours faithfully,
K.W. Ellis [*holograph*]
Staff Appointments
Officer.

P.S. Well, I hope you are having a pleasant time at the old place and that this didn't give you too much of a turn. I have got to go for an interview at Bletchley next Wednesday so I am shaping fair to be a Civil Servant of the genre Sadie.[2] You know 8–4, 4–12, 12–8 shifts. Oh God. There is nothing very much to say except that we went to see "Casablanca" last night and I enjoyed it no end, even at the third seeing. I adore Humphrey Bogart. Oh, and I also had a tooth out ur-hur-hur. It ached quite a deal and so I went along and complained. He tapped it gravely and said: "Mm, it ought to have cleared up by now. Just step into the other room and I'll take it out."

P.

1 In an officially labelled manilla envelope: 'On His Majesty's Service', but with stamp, addressed in type to 'Miss C. E. Larkin, 73, Coten End, WARWICK', the direction crossed out and 'c/o Eastgate Hotel, High Street, Oxford' written in ink.
2 It seems that, with his recent Oxford first, Larkin was being considered for code-breaking work. 'Sadie' remains obscure.

1 December 1943

Alexander House, New Church Road, Wellington, Salop.[1]

Wednesday

Dear Mop & Pop,

Just a short note to indicate my best address, as no one seems sure if the correct number is 40 or 110 . . .

We are on the telephone – Wellington, 594.

Worked this morning 9–10.15 then went off to the doctor who was too busy to see me, and asked me to call again tonight. So I wrote for an hour or so at home.

Mr Bennett[2] is a charming old man, and has assured me that Cecil Roberts[3] is a very fine writer. I agreed. He seems in no hurry to relinquish the reins of office or to let me do much. I agreed to this also.

Mr Buttrey[4] called & said a few words. From his hints the whole of the W.E.A.[5] seem to have been trying to find me rooms, and he mentions several other shadowy figures who are aiming to meet me – the W.E.A. Secretary, the Grammar School Headmaster, and the County Librarian at Shrewsbury, one Mr Adams. Mrs Buttery thinks 2 gns excessive for the room I have, and I think so too after being awoken at 7.0 a.m. by the news, the screaming of a child, the thumping of heavy-footed men about the house, and Harry James' Orchestra later on. Nevertheless I get the impression that a powerful organisation is planning to find rooms for me.

I visited Bruce in Shrewsbury yesterday, and wept at the contrast: the enormous beautiful school, set among avenues of rich houses, the regal view of the town from the hill, the classrooms & the bellowing voices from them – and the house he lives in! Sumptuous ain't the word. Like two Wear Giffards rolled into one.[6] I had to sit and watch him eat his dinner – 3 courses – served from silver dishes by a uniformed maid on a table polished so highly I daren't put the bottle of beer he gave me down on it. He pays 2 gns too, which made me writhe with envy. He is one of the rich in spirit who will always have a happy lot.

As far as I can see, the evening 6–8 hours are the snag of this job. I really don't see why the reading room can't close at 8 too instead of dragging on till 8.30. I suppose changes to fit the librarian's convenience won't be sanctioned by the Committee . . .

Mrs Jones, tell Pop, made some remark about joining a Friendly Society re Health Insurance – I suppose the N.A.L.G.O. ranks as one of these?[7]

Tell Mop my heart was with her when the sirens went this morning.[8]

With all love,
Philip

1 Larkin had been appointed librarian in Wellington, Shropshire from 1 December.
2 The elderly 'librarian-caretaker' who Larkin replaced had been in post since the library first opened forty years earlier in 1903. See Larkin's essay 'Single-handed and Untrained', *Required Writing*, 32.
3 Cecil Roberts (1892–1976): prolific journalist, poet, dramatist, novelist and autobiographer.
4 Chairman of the Wellington Library Committee.
5 Workers' Educational Association.
6 Eva had stayed in 'Wear Giffard', Cliff Hill, Warwick, during the bombing in 1940.
7 National Association of Local Government Officers. See Sydney's letter of 2 December 1943, Appendix.
8 See Eva's letter of 5 December 1943, Appendix, pp. 561–2.

5 December 1943

Alexander House, 40 New Church Road, Wellington, Salop. Sunday

Dear Mop & Pop,

I suppose I should give you a coherent account of this place, now I have been here some time. On the whole, it is not too bad, at least at present.

I get to the library by 9, to find Mr Bennett already in full possession – at what unearthly hour he gets there I don't know. But that is a hangover from the days when he was caretaker as well as librarian. We potter about together till about 11 o'clock, him doing most of the work, and I sorting the previous day's tickets. I have become quite fond of him; he is a kind, gentlemanly, humorous old chap, given to anecdotes and humming a few notes (always the same tune) in a blowing fashion, like a distant trombone. Then we leave the library, and I return here for lunch and meditation. From 3–5 and 6–8 we are open to the public, and that is the principal work of the day. At 5 o'clock he eats his tea there, and I go off to a slatternly café full of soldiers for coffee and spam sandwiches. At 8 I knock off, leaving him to lock up and close the reading room. After eating my supper I lounge till 10.30 or 11, when I go to bed.

The library is a curious place. It is a dreadful mess: the majority of the books (novels) are roughly arranged in alphabetical order of authors – all the A's, all the B's etc. – but by no means exactly. There is no attempt to classify the Juvenile Section at all. The two faces of non fiction (i.e. sides of cases) are also chaotic but less so as they are rarely disturbed. Some years ago (1935) some enterprising person classified them according to Dewey's decimal system, and I actually found – as I had never expected to do – a big 3-guinea copy of Dewey lying covered with dust on a low shelf of "the office". Mr Bennett regards it as a kind of *Kabbala*, and my ability to understand it as something rare and abstract, like the ability to do Higher mathematics. He says, quite rightly, that it is far too complicated for such a small library, but nevertheless I shall get busy.

The public consists of women and children, and a few old men and youths who are not working during the hours of opening. I have made one or two friends already, but there is always the old harridan who stalks in, slams down a couple of Warwick Deepings,[1] and glares: "You the new librarian?" "I am indeed." "Mr Bennett" – glare – "was *very* popular . . ." and stalks away. The children are fairly tractable, considering the complete chaos of their section.

The books are in a bad state – grubby, torn, and often antiquated. But here and there I am surprised by what I find – a copy of "Aaron's Rod", for instance, a copy of "Crome Yellow" and "Bliss".[2] "The Garden Party"[3] is on the stock book but I can't find it. I found an early out-of-print Maugham novel called "The Magician" which I read with interest. There is also a copy of "To the Lighthouse" by Virginia Woolf.

On the whole, the library is shockingly administered in a *laisser-faire* manner that presents some difficulties. Fines are never charged – I can imagine the outraged stares when I start charging them. Overdue-cards are never sent. If a book fails to return it is forgotten about. There is *no* workable catalogue. All this *can* be remedied – at great time and labour on my part, though.

My lodgings are better than I expected, though rather cold. My tiny bed-sitter is now in use, but it is one of those corner rooms with corner-windows and tends to be cold, and my radiator is very small indeed. But Mrs Jones is remarkably efficient and keeps me well fed with ordinary meals and extra-ordinary cups of Oxo, cocoa & biscuits, cheesecakes etc. She read about me in the "Wellington Journal & Shrewsbury News" and was impressed. I will send you a copy of the paper. Considering that there are three other men in the house, and one child, I do very well, but perhaps she favours me. I have early morning tea and a hot-water bottle. In my spare time I am continuing my novel quite easily.

Tonight I am going to see Mrs Barker, who bears a faint but disturbing resemblance to Mrs Allen. A spectacled schoolteacher also came in yesterday afternoon and hushingly welcomed me on behalf of the W.E.A., and handed me an enormous poster to put up. I swallowed my bile and thanked her – part of this job, I imagine is enduring your friends because, ultimately if not immediately, they *are* on your side. Buttrey has also been in, and encouraged me (a) to attend the meeting the poster was about (b) to join the Y.M.C.A. I shan't, but I didn't tell him so, yet.

Well, that's quite enough about this place. How are you all? I regret not being able to see you, but I may get as much as three days at Christmas. Don't get anything special done for me – just keep a bed ready and the piano tuned and the gramophone intact. [. . .]

Rest assured that I am well-fed, fairly well cared for, and relatively content. I shall see Bruce on Tuesday again. By the way, towels *aren't* supplied here, so another of the same might be useful.

I shall now mend a *whole* [*sic*] in one of my gloves.

Much love,
Philip

1 Warwick Deeping (1877–1950): prolific middlebrow novelist, specialising in historical romances. His best known book is *Sorrell and Son* (1925).
2 By D. H. Lawrence, Aldous Huxley and Katherine Mansfield respectively.
3 By Katherine Mansfield.

18 December 1943

Alexander House, 40 New Church Road, Wellington, Shropshire

Dear Mop and Pop,

I am writing this on Saturday night, as tomorrow promises to be a full day. Bruce is coming over in the afternoon, and so a nature ramble with a friendly schoolmistress has had to be shifted to the morning. Last Sunday she guided me to the top of the Wrekin, a celebrated hill hereabouts, which was very nice but left me feeling like a piece of chewed string. Her surname is Musselwhite, which is all I know, but she is another of the kind people.

This has been a less eventful week; I have arranged to move into different digs after Christmas – one Miss Tomlinson, of King Street, who is charging me 35/- per week for a larger bedroom than my present one and a share in a sitting room with Spaull, the Art Master. The 7/- reduction will pay for lunch at the British Restaurant, which I shall have to have out – at least at the start, as Spaull has his at the school, and she prefers to cook two evening meals. As far as I can see, this will be quite a suitable arrangement, and as good as my present one. Mrs. Jones is really awfully kind and keeps me fed to overflowing – indeed, I'm sure she can't make lodging-house keeping pay. But this is her first shot.

As regards the library, the week has passed fairly uneventfully. I have ordered a lot of library stationery, including some writing paper with my name on it: a mild vanity but justified, I think. (Incidentally, tell Pop that the A.I.C.C. (was it?) after Astley-Jones'[1] name stands for an Ass. of the Inst. of Company Clerks – he has it hanging up on his wall, and is probably very proud of it.) Also I have started keeping cash accounts, statistics, a book of reservations, and doing many other normal things which appear like lunacy or super-genius to other people, according to whether they approve or disapprove. I find the work quite interesting, and spend all day at the library, except for mealtimes. I usually spend an hour or so a day writing, so I don't do too badly.

I heard today I had been elected to N.A.L.G.O., and paid a year's subscription, which Pop will probably say was ill-advised, of 15/-, *and* resisted an appeal to give to the Widows & Orphans Benevolent Fund until I'd had expert advice from you.

(There is a graät wind a-roärin' up from Ercall 'Ills,[2] like the breäkin' o' great waäves.)

I had an embarrassing experience this afternoon when I noticed a man smoking in the library.

Me. "I'm afraid I must ask you not to smoke."

Man. "*'E* never said anything to me about it."

Me. "Well. There's a perfectly-plain notice telling you."

Man. "Ho, yus, where is it?"

Me. (after discovering that there *wasn't* a notice to this effect in the *Lending* Library, only in the Reading Room) "Ah . . . er . . . well . . . There doesn't seem to be one at the moment."

Man. "I could 'a' told *you* that." (continuing to smoke with undiminished satisfaction.)

Me. "Well, anyway, it's against the regulations, and I'd be glad if you wouldn't do it in the future . . . er . . . ah . . . regulations . . ." (retreating vaguely. Man smokes on placidly.)

It wasn't as funny as it sounds.

Your letter was very nice, and not at all a dry one! I'm so glad Pop has got the "E. T." Lawrence book[3] – it was a gap in our library – Pop's I mean. I have bought a book for him, which he may not enjoy, for Xmas. By this time Kitty will doubtless have arrived; tell her I stupidly sent a letter to Cedar Road, but doubtless it will follow her home. Is Auntie Nellie coming? I should like to buy her a present, but really I doubt if I could afford it. ("'Appen tha could pay for it out o' thy next pint!")

Yes, the Red Lion is still functioning, and I shall probably have tea with Bruce there tomorrow. There is a great attraction coming to the local cinema shortly – "Pittsburgh".[4] You can imagine that we aren't exactly riding on the crest of the wave of fashion, even tho' they have got a new stuck-up chap at the library 'oo can't talk proper.

Much love – longing to see you.
Philip

1 Chief Clerk to Wellington Urban District Council.

2 Ercall Hill is a small hill situated between the Wrekin and Wellington.

3 *D. H. Lawrence: A Personal Record* (1935), by 'E. T.' (Jessie Chambers: 'Miriam' in *Sons and Lovers*.)

4 A 1942 film directed by Lewis Seiler and starring Marlene Dietrich, Randolph Scott and John Wayne.

29 December 1943

Alexander House, New Church Road, Wellington

Dear Mop,

Yes, I arrived quite safely, rather late, last night. I had to stand till Birmingham, but the general exodus there gave me a comfortable seat for the rest of the journey. [. . .]

Tell Kitty I regretted not saying goodbye to her formally, and that I hope she enjoyed the "panto". ("An' ole 'Itler said: 'Ere, wassat under the bed?' An' li'le ole Goebbels says 'Oh, it's Gestapo." "WAW-HAW-HAW-HAW-HAW!!!! ENCORE!!!") I expect Walter will have returned to his *moutons* (collecting a few more on the way) so I shall not hear his opinion of the matter.

I will write more fully on Sunday, contenting myself with saying now how much I liked Christmas in the old 'omestead, and how appreciative I am of all you did to make it happy.

Love
P.

<*On back of envelope*> Could you *please* send K. M.'s *Letters*?[1] I want to compare them with the Eng. edition which we have on loan here – I suspect ours is abridged. Don't bother *if* there is an open statement of abridgement on our copy, but write and tell me. If there isn't, please send them. I think it's rather an important point.

1 Katherine Mansfield.

1944

2 January 1944

Alexander House, New Church Road, Wellington Sunday

Dear Mop & Pop,

This morning is windy, and I have not been up long. Certainly I have not yet been out, and if I do I shall only go as far as the paper shop, to see if they can supply me with a "Sunday Times" every week. The chances are slight.

I am on my own at the library now.[1] Yesterday was my first day. Lord, it keeps you busy! My additional duties I performed fairly efficiently, though I forgot to lay out the evening papers till six o'clock, and also failed to make the heating apparatus work properly. That is to say, I kept it insufficiently stoked with coke so that I shivered all the evening – I spent the evening at the library, writing, because (a) I had to close the reading room at 8.30 and (b) I couldn't stand the idea of an evening chez Jones. New Year's Eve was terrible – wireless all the night from Attlee onwards, loud as if in a canteen. But I really must get this stove under control. [. . .]

With all love to you one & all,
Philip

1 Mr Bennett left at the end of the year.

13 January 1944

Glentworth, King Street, Wellington

My dear Mop,

It was so kind of you to write as soon as you got back; I must also write to you and say how I liked seeing you. I don't think it was very nice of me not to have a present or even a card for you, so I can only reiterate that I wish you all you deserve in 1944. Which is quite a lot. For sheer, unselfish, unremitting, uncomplaining labour of love, I've never known anyone like you, and I do hope some day soon you will be rewarded. I think of you a lot, and love your letters and emaciated creatures.[1]

I have finished my report and it has been duplicated and sent out. Today I had a fearful row with a woman who wouldn't pay a penny fine. She won, of course. But now I've had it and needn't worry about it any more – I mean I knew I should have to have it with somebody. I shall win next time.

All the library business sends me panting back to my novel, feeling "God! if this is all my life is . . ." I am devouring all George Moore I can find – I think he's really good – just my type –

Mr Spaull comes a week today.[2] I have arranged the lunch business, sent & received my laundry, and had a bath.

All love to you,
Philip

1 Eva's reply of 17 January begins with her own self-portrait drawing:

'My Dear Philip, I very much appreciated the little extra letter, adorned with well-fed creatures, wearing various expressions as the script progresses.'

She continued 'Since writing to you a heavy cold has almost broken my morale', illustrating her text with another tiny self-portrait.

2 Local art teacher; see letter of 18 December 1943, above.

23 January 1944

Glentworth, King Street, Wellington

Dear Mop & Pop,

Another eventful week has flown by, and once again I am sitting by the fire after an unconscionably late breakfast. Thanks to both of you for your letters last week, and to Sidwell and Pop for answering my questions.[1]

As you remember, the committee was on Tuesday, & I enclose a paragraph I sent to the Journal.[2] It was really not so bad, although one Percy Potts, a councillor and past chairman of the committee went for me baldheaded over some imaginary insults in the report. The other members of the committee sat on him, however, so I felt that he was by no means swaying the mob. What a dull process committees are, though: still, we did get all we asked for, and I can look forward to a busy two months until the next one, trying to spend £100 between now and March 31st. I'm not sure it will be easy, without throwing the money away a bit. I expect all the best books are out of print. The "four periodicals" added are the Times Lit. & Ed. Sups., the New Statesman & the Spectator. So you can see we are soaring into vastly higher intellectual spheres. [. . .]

I joined the Y.M.C.A. (!!) on Thursday for the purpose of playing Astley-Jones at billiards. My opinion of his intellectual capacity sinks every time I meet him. I was incent[ivis]ed to join after a particularly harrowing evening at the Library when I was deluged with children, all badly-behaved except one, who wore a Y.M.C.A. badge. I feel that if only in that field the Christian mystery is most valuable.

I also met Miss Forster, the Headmistress of the Girls' School, who taught for a short time at Warwick. So this is rapidly developing into a home from home.

Your letter was most interesting: I am distressed to hear you have both had colds, coughs, snuffles, wuffles, wheezes and hacking coughs. Bruce came over last night and we caroused over a pot or two. He had a fearful row with Diana[3] during the holidays, because he said Diana was uneducated (which she is), and has now got the wind up over his next Gollancz book and is bombarding her with conciliatory letters. Otherwise his life runs on oiled wheels.

May I come home next week-end? I really want another pair of brown shoes – th[is][4] one is still unrepaired as I can't see a F.H.W.[5] shop anywhere on the horizon, and the only shoemender in Wellington is Percy Potts. It looks as if Leamington is indicated. I also want to collect some records, needles, etc. and if possible the typewriter and reams of paper. The novel will be finished by then & I want to type it out. Agreed, or no?

I must rush out & post this.[6]

The weather is very unsettled, and I have mislaid my walking stick. But anyway it was *too short*.

Mrs Barker has lent me Yeats's Last Poems & Plays, & I am slaking my thirsty soul. Bone's book[7] is already out of print, and neither of us can get copies.

See you on Saturday – just give me a rug & a basket in a corner, and a bone to gnaw————————

Philip

<*On back of envelope*> Pardon reckless stamping – they are all I have.[8]

1 In his letter of 2 January Larkin had asked his father to consult his colleague Sidwell on detailed issues concerning different kinds of Library Association membership.

2 Larkin enclosed a cutting: '£100 For New Library Books. – A meeting of the Library Committee [. . .] discussed the report of the present librarian, which advised greater concentration in the future upon non-fictional reading and stressed the usefulness of the Regional Library Bureau in lending such books as the Library did not possess.'

3 Diana Gollancz, daughter of the publisher Victor Gollancz, a friend who had been at the Slade School of Art, relocated in Oxford during the war.

4 Larkin has written 'the' in error.

5 Freeman, Hardy and Willis, shoe retailers and repairers.
6 In her letter of 7 February Eva responded with her own feminine 'creature' drawing. See Appendix, p. 562.
7 Gavin Bone, *Anglo-Saxon Poetry: An Essay, with Specimen Translations in Verse* (Clarendon Press, 1944). Bone had died in 1943.
8 Two 2d stamps. The standard letter rate was 2½d.

27 February 1944

Glentworth, King Street, Wellington, Shropshire

Dear Mop & Pop,

The porridge was burnt this morning. Never before have I realised how horrible burnt porridge is: it seems to embrace every foul gradation of taste under the sun. I suppose you have quite forgotten what it is like.

Then I had an egg. One egg is no meal for a man, with two pieces of toast.

In fact, Spaull and I honestly condemn this place & all connected with it. Our outbursts are of course exaggerated, and we should be stupid to leave it, but nevertheless there is plenty to grumble about. It is undeniably dirty: the food is undeniably scarce & occasionally badly prepared (we had an incredible kind of rayfish last week that smelt & tasted strongly of ammonia) and Mrs T. is uncouth and moody. I would as soon ask her for bread at meal times as suggest she brought me up breakfast in bed at three in the morning.[1] I think wistfully of Mrs Jones' intelligent and considerate manner, and feel I shall keep in touch with her. [. . .]

Still, enough of my own woes. The chief excitement of the week has been Bruce's reviews. I mentioned Edward Shanks' unenthusiastic comments in the Daily Dispatch, I think; well, all was quiet till Thursday, when John Betjeman reviewed it in the Daily Herald: "neatly constructed . . . full of wit and observation . . . I assume he [the author] is a don, for the writing is lucid and distinguished . . ." The Daily Sketch said: "Told with unusual distinction and literary finesse. Effective first attempt." [. . .] To round off the week, Jeremy Scott in "John o' London's Weekly" gives 5 inches of praise: "Here is no unsophisticated initiate: Mr Crispin's touch is self-assured and agreeable, his background one of learning and wit, his portraiture adult, mundane and humorous" etc. etc. "Would it be too indiscreet to enquire whether Edmund Crispin can be read elsewhere under another name – or am I wronging a very brilliant new-comer?"

You can well imagine that Bruce is cavorting about in the seventh heaven of delight, indulging in computations of royalties (£300 if it sells 6,000 etc.) and racing ahead with his next book "Holy Disorders". I hover enviously on the fringe of all this, wondering if I have made a mistake, because I still don't think it, on the whole, a success. Bruce, in his more lucid moments, agrees with me.

But isn't it all nice?[2]

My life continues sedately enough here, contentedly I might say apart from minor irritations. The new books have come and I am slowly getting them on the shelves; I have started an entirely new stock-list, starting from 1, and involving red ink. It becomes clear to me that I must stay here for some time if what I am doing is to be completed or even continued. This prospect does not appeal to me very much, but does not appal me.

Thanks to both of you for your delightful letters: I like very much to hear from each of you. In reply to Mop, I think mending etc. is done as regards socks, but there are buttons being cracked weekly on pants and vests which are not being replaced. I shall speak about this. In reply to Pop, yes, keep the order standing for Bone's book: I don't think I have given anything resembling an order to anybody; merely enquiries, and not all booksellers are as obliging as the Ch. Bk. Shop.

Kingsley is paying me a visit next weekend, and I have booked a room for him at the Crescent Hotel, where you stayed. I like the people there, and they remembered you quite well, though they were under the delusion that I stayed there too.

No more now: I must repair my glove again. Snow is lying about – der Schnee liegt auf dem Erde, as I dimly remember from my German – wrongly, I suspect.

Much love to all,
Philip

1 On 28 February Eva replied: 'I am sorry about the burnt p. Certainly one wants bread and butter with an egg. I think *I* should surreptitiously buy a small loaf or a few rolls, and smuggle them into the library – or would they encourage mice! It is very difficult to know what to do.'

2 Eva responded in her letter of 28 February: 'I was so thrilled over the reviews of Bruce's novel. As you say, it is all very nice, and I should think that Bruce is walking on air just now. / I am panting to read it, although I must confess that I do not really

like mystery or detective novels. / What about *your* novel? I expect you are still typing it out. Do you think it will be good enough to send to a publisher? (I know how critical you are!) or do you think you can find one to publish it?'

5 March 1944

Glentworth, King Street, Wellington

Dear Mop & Pop,

The sun is shining and Kingsley is awaiting me at the Crescent Hotel, but I must perform my Chinese obsequies to my ancestors before I set out.

Thank you for your delightful letter, the chocolate, and the cigarettes – a most kind thought. I am rather ashamed to admit that as things are going I shall eat all the chocolate myself. The smaller block vanished almost without my noticing it: the large is nearly gone. [. . .] I just can't let the stuff alone.

Do you remember forwarding a book in the middle of last week to me? It is the most curious thing: a copy of "The Yellow Night" by Drummond Allison (poems). Accompanying it was a cyclostyled letter from Drummond saying he hoped I'd buy a copy, with a postscript by his mother saying that Drummond had been killed and that perhaps I would like a copy (signed) in memory. Any money received, she added, would go to the Red Cross. So of course I was blackmailed into sending off the cost price. If he hadn't been killed, I should have written sternly to him on the morals of self-advertisement, but in the present case one must put off one's feelings & be conventional. The poems are awfully bad.[1]

It was nice to hear from Pop too, and to know that the old warrior had once again dropped his visor and was jousting in the Municipal lists with Graft, Nepotism, and Fat Pickings. In my own timid way, I am backing him up – trying to make the chairman of the Council pay a quid for the "Country Lifes" he has been getting free of charge. I am being very reasonable – 20/- is the normal annual rate for used library copies – but of course I can't expect him to see it in that light. Luckily he's a decent old stick – I think. Ask Pop to let me know how he gets on. Incidentally, doesn't Newcastle seem a Pandora's box of Local Government ills? "The point has been reached when we are no longer disgusted by their wrong-doing, nor incredulous at its revelation." (Guess who.)

Life has been a bit more cheerful this week: it has been so nice getting the new & interesting books out onto the shelves. While the majority of people pass them over ("Two westerns for granddad and a lover for my mother")[2] others are loud in appreciation and a wholly unwarranted feeling of personal satisfaction possesses me. But I have to work so beastly hard I don't have time to write, not even letters. I only wrote a poem last week, on and off. [. . .]

For once I have had a satisfactory breakfast & feel more or less fine. Doesn't that gladden your heart – that for once I can unreservedly say I can look through the day into next week with robust confidence & cheerfulness?

"What matter! Out of cavern comes a voice,
And all it knows is the one word: Rejoice!"[3]

W. B. Yeats wrote that, though I think he ought to have put "tavern" instead of cavern. I've got to prepare a report next week – next committee on March 14th. I hope it won't be too terrible.

Dying to see you – soon. I shall be coming.

Much love
Philip

1 Eva replied on 6 March: 'I was very surprised to hear about the book of poems by Drummond Allison, and very sorry to know he has been killed. I have just read the two poems of his in the book of Oxford Poetry and, as usual, cannot understand them.'

2 In her letter of 6 March Eva wrote: 'I love to hear all about your doings at the library. I can almost see those nice, new books. Whatever are "Westerns"? I presume Grandpa indulges in Wild West thrillers.'

3 'The Gyres'. Yeats wrote 'that one word'.

26 March 1944

Glentworth, King Street, Wellington, Shropshire

Dear Mop & Pop,

[. . .] I feel like a racehorse pulling a Corporation refuse cart, if I can say so without being conceited, and as everybody agrees that I was stupid to take it, I think I'm not.

I wonder if I can explain more clearly: I feel that I shall never take any job seriously enough to warrant any responsibility; I feel that this present job demands my whole energies and attention, *which I am not prepared to give*; I feel I could get another job which would leave my evenings free and give me (perhaps) more pay, and allow me to get on with the all-important job of writing. You must be sick of hearing that word. But writing is the only thing I shall ever take seriously enough to give my whole energies and attention to, and so will be the only thing I am likely to do well. Certainly (as you will agree) it's the only thing I have ever been singled out for by others. And at present I have not enough time for it. It's maddening. And I haven't been wasting my time – by using almost every hour, I have written, I calculate, nearly 90,000 words since arriving here – which is the length of a normal novel. But because they are only done in bits and pieces they are not as good as they might have been, and of course I could have done more. I could finish this novel in no time if I had free evenings.[1] You don't realise the urgency I feel.

Bruce as you know lodges at the house of a man who has been sheriff of the County etc. I've a good mind to try and get a job through him.

But what d'you think of all this? I expect you will counsel me to stick it out for a year; I am wondering if I couldn't leave after the end of August. August is the month when the library is closed, you know: I think I could get everything relatively shipshape by then. If I gave the Council plenty of warning they couldn't feel offended: they must be wondering (a trifle cynically) how long I shall stick it, and be expecting me to leave. They are fortunate in having had me at all, I sometimes think.

Well, I have no space or time or inclination now for homelier matters. Bruce was glad of your continued appreciation of "The Fly": no, of course I have had no oranges. Children leave peel in the Reading Room sometimes. [. . .]

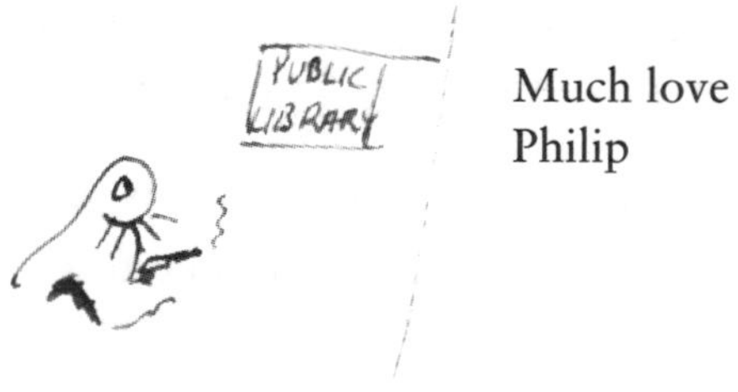

Much love
Philip

1 He completed *Jill* on 14 May 1944.

23 April 1944

Glentworth, King Street, Wellington, Shropshire

Dear Mop & Pop,

I was decidedly heartened to receive your three letters last Wednesday; I picked them up from King Street on my way to the Arleston Estate after a recalcitrant borrower. She was not in, so I turned into The Buck's Head and read your letters again and began a poem in the notebook you thoughtfully, though needlessly, I'm afraid, enclosed. I thought 'a dry crumb of bread (rather large this)' exquisitely funny.[1]

The sun is shining and I do not feel so growlingly morose as usual. Think I do not get so hungry as the weather gets warmer, and this adds to my good temper. The chief plague of the week has been dogs at the Library. During the lunch hour when the place is unattended they come in and make hay. This has been infuriating me so much that I purchased a can of disinfectant, ordered the cleaner to soak the place from top to bottom in it, and yesterday lunch time sat for 3 hours at the top of the stairs reading a novel with a walking stick across my knees, prepared to give any dog hell on sight. Not one came near. The sole result was that I got dizzy from lack of food and smoking, and bitterly cold, and the afternoon was 100 years long. [. . .]

Thank you for forwarding Gunner's letter: he is all right, though alone among my friends he mentioned scenes of battle. "The trouble is that in time he knows where we are and his shelling is bloody accurate and very heavy. The other evening he got within 30 yards of us and the guns jammed. What with us shouting 'Where are the ———s' and him bawling Prussian slogans, grenades being slung and rifles going off it was some pantomime. Cold sweat wasn't in it. I am off for some leave in a few weeks' time . . ."

Perhaps Wellington Library is not the worst place to spend these stirring times. Jim continues to write and seems safe enough; at least his letters are mainly about Lawrence and Giotto. Ernie Roe wrote last week, also Norman Iles, both well.

I don't suppose I'll get any oranges but thanks for the tip –

Much love to one & all
Philip

1 See Eva's letter of 17 April in the Appendix.

18 May 1944 Postcard

[Glentworth, King Street, Wellington] Thursday

Many thanks for the load of beautiful lilies which arrived yesterday. I have found only a tobacco tin to put them in, but they stand beside me as I write and are a real touch of delicacy in this sordid world.

I finished my novel on Sunday[1] and sent copies to Bruce & Philip. On Monday I began the Wellington one, and so far have done 1 chapter.[2] I'm afraid I don't know where Jane Eyre is – I suppose you have searched the stables? I don't remember having seen it at Warwick at all.

Love to both, P

1 *Jill.*

2 This was to become *A Girl in Winter*.

7 September 1944[1]

[Glentworth, King Street, Wellington]

Dearest Mopcreature:

Many thanks for letter & flannel. I enclose a poem which Bruce thinks the only good one of the four. He likes line 7. You won't quite understand it, but it is meant to describe loneliness. I think the impulse of loneliness in everyone is stronger than the impulse of love or 'cosiness'. If it isn't, it should be, because death is lonely and to death we should all orientate.[2]

Aren't you glad about the black-out?[3]

Love,
Philip

P.T.O.

<Letterhead>
Wellington (Salop) Public Library, Walker Street, Wellington.
P. A. Larkin B.A., Public Librarian

Did Pop see Cashmore's column in the B.P.?[4] Did he notice the popularity of J. C. Powys?[5] Queer. And did he notice the typical H.M.C. "signed by me and five other of the biggest librarians"?

Philip

<Enclosed>

One man walking a deserted platform;
Dawn coming, and rain
Driving across a darkening autumn;
One man restlessly waiting a train
While round the streets the wind runs wild,
Beating each shuttered house, that seems
Folded full of the dark silk of dreams,
A shell of sleep cradling a wife or child.

Who can this ambition trace,
To be each dawn perpetually journeying?
To trick this hour when lovers re-embrace
With the unguessed-at heart riding
The winds as gulls do? What lips said
Starset and cockcrow call the dispossessed
On to the next desert, lest
Love sink a grave round the still-sleeping head?

1 The first page, 'Dearest Mopcreature . . .', is in typescript; the second page, 'Did Pop see . . .' is in holograph; the enclosed poem is in typescript.
2 See Sydney's comment on 'orientate': letter of 8 September 1944, Appendix.
3 In September 1944 the 'black-out' regulations were replaced by a 'dim-out', which allowed lighting to the equivalent of moonlight.
4 On 6 September the *Birmingham Post* featured an interview with the City Librarian, H. M. Cashmore. Cashmore listed thirty-seven well-known authors and 'assessed their popularity with the public by comparing the total stock of their works in the Central Library with the number of volumes left on the shelves and available to be taken away on a given day'. The library held twenty-one books by Jane Austen, all but two of which were out on loan, and eleven by J. C. Powys, all of which were on loan. Cashmore lamented the difficulty of replenishing the Library

stock and commented: 'you will probably see in "The Times" shortly a letter signed by me and five other of the biggest librarians supporting Mr Stanley Unwin and others in their claim that the situation ought to be remedied.' See Sydney's letter, Appendix, pp. 567–8.
5 John Cowper Powys (1872–1963), writer and philosopher; brother of Llewelyn and T. F. Powys.

1 October 1944[1]

Glentworth, King Street, Wellington, Salop.

Dear Kitty,

Seems an unholy while since I wrote to you last: here goes my Dear to write you a letter tho the wireless is playing very loud in the Naffy and I do'nt kno if I can think strait. Ah! Ah!

I was sorry I missed you at home last Sunday but of course you had to go at 2.0. whereas at that time I was in Balliol with Pop, Mr. Long ("Don't, Ern!"), and Dr. Marshall ("I shall be very interested in the reporrrrrrt . . .").[2] I heard sundry details from Mop – the tripe – general busyness – which amused me. Also I wanted to see the wedding photographs but they were naat there. I apologise, by the way, for making a mess of the ones I took – I understand they were a failure. It's the malaria. Comes on me out o' nowhere and makes me 'and shake weak as a babby . . . But I did try to avoid brick walls.

Incidentally, don't forget I still have a wedding present to give you both.[3]

I expect all my general news is passed on to you by bush-telegraph so I won't be informative. *Jill* has come back from Faber's. *Katherine* (temporary title of Novel 2) is going very slowly (". . . of an infinite snail-like locomotion, my lord, an't please you" – any clown of the Bard) but – I *think* – steadily. It is very short at the moment and will need fattening. It'll take about a year.

God damn! The wireless really has come on now – some foul play, played with that noxious melodrama that only English radio broadcasting can achieve. "Dr Jekyll & Mr Hyde" – I wonder if in desolate Loughborough you too are having this gormless rubbish forced down your gizzard. How is Sandra?

I have heard several times from Jim, and he seems all right still – swigging Marsala and Vermouth and collecting bodies.[4] The Library goes steadily: I continue to thrust "deep books" into the unwilling hands of the public. Some fool of a woman came in and whacking down Henry Green's "Caught" said "Well, that's a bad book!" "No, it isn't," I snapped, and gave her a short lecture on it. I'm sick of these cocksure dumbbells.

Do you think it is possible to put my initials on that cigarette case I passed on to you? It may sound silly, but I'd like "P.A.L. 1944" on it. But please don't trouble if it means asking favours of people you don't like, or anything of that sort.[5]

Does Mr Devine still do Mr Facing-both-ways to everyone? And is Potter thrusting sundry spanners into sundry wheels? And how is Walter's job? Give him my regards.

With much love,
Philip

1 Addressed to Mrs Catherine Hewett, c/o 13 Cedar Road, Loughborough.
2 Dr Arthur Hedley Marshall (1904–94), Sydney Larkin's deputy in Warwick.
3 Kitty had married Walter Hewett on 12 August 1944, and remained in her teaching post until the birth of her daughter Rosemary in 1947. Walter had trained as a mechanical engineer and in 1948 joined Urwick Orr & Partners as a management consultant.
4 Jim Sutton served in the 14th Field Ambulance, Royal Army Medical Corps.
5 See Kitty's letter of 23 October 1944 in the Appendix.

8 October 1944

Glentworth, King Street, Wellington, Salop.

Dear Mop and Pop,

[. . .] I wrote to the Chambers' Encyclopaedia people, and have had a letter back asking me to go up to London some time during the next month. The managing editor is Mrs M. D. Law, and "there have been several applications". I suppose I must go on one Tuesday – though I'm bound to get lost in London and probably pursued by V1, V2 and V3 in rapid and cataclysmic succession.[1]

This has been a mixed week as regards the Library. On Monday I was depressed by hearing some third hand gossip that I was "filling the Library with filthy books" (I admit there may be some slight grounds for this, modern literature being what it is) but yesterday I had a number of bouquets about the Library being the only place in Wellington where ratepayers see value for their money and that several people were giving up their Boots' subscriptions and coming here all the time. To quote Pop's words, what couldn't I do if I was really interested! But I think I must go soon: no one expects me to stay long – indeed, a London Univ. girl remarked quite out of the blue "Well, I shan't be in again until Christmas, but I suppose you'll have gone by then."

Had a cheerful, bibulous evening with Bruce last night, also another young master, which ended with our being jammed in a noisome fish shop near the river and later wandering back and forward over a bridge, eating. There is a new master at Shrewsbury called Moles from Dublin, who knew Yeats and Gogarty & "AE".[2] Bruce has promised to introduce me on Tuesday. Bruce is also going to be put up for election to the Saville Club in London. I think I shall tell them about the fish shop . . .

I heard from Kitty, who enclosed a wedding-photograph. I thought I was supposed to have made a mess of it? This one looked all right.

Am reading "The Ballad & the Source"[3] – very heavy going and I doubt if I shall finish it.

Very much love –
Philip

Enclosed is a typical A-J raving.[4]

1 A reference to the German V1 and V2 missiles which were striking the London area at this time.
2 Oliver St John Gogarty (1878–1957), Irish poet, doctor and politician; AE (pseudonym of George William Russell, 1867–1935), writer and Irish nationalist.
3 Novel by Rosamond Lehmann published in 1944.
4 Larkin includes a press-cutting in which Astley-Jones, Chief Clerk to Wellington Urban District Council, vigorously rejects criticisms of the council policy on street lighting in view of the government relaxation of black-out regulations.

15 October 1944

Glentworth, King Street, Wellington, Salop.

Dear Mop and Pop,

[. . .] I have arranged to visit the Encyclopaedia on 31 October, at Tower House, Southampton Street, Strand W.C.2 (or 1). I am not sure if the job attracts me or not, rather because I know so little about it – not even the salary. I should like to try the experiment of living in London for a bit, although I am mortal scared of bombs, and also I feel slightly impatient of Wellington. Yesterday was another record-breaking day: I haven't had an exact count, but it is certainly 240 books issued in 210 minutes and probably a few more. So you see I have passed my book-a-minute mark!

Incidentally I should be very pleased if Pop would give me directions of the lie of the land between Paddington & Tower House.

Another letter from the Fortune Press came on Friday saying that *Poems From Oxford* will be out next month.[1] They also add that they still want my "own collection" (which I had refused on grounds of paucity) and they "expect I have enough for their purposes". I think I shall send them all I can muster, little as I like the idea of rushing into print alongside my gormless contemporaries. But such objections are rather quibbling, I feel: what does it all matter? I don't think it matters two hoots whether the poems are published or not, so if I can get a little fun out of having a book done, why should I refuse? What do you think?

There's little news here; I spend nearly all my time reading or writing poems.[2] The novel has temporarily dropped from sight: I have reached a long boring section I cannot interest myself in. I have not read "What Say They" but should like to.[3]

I am developing a gift for epigram. Yesterday during a conversation someone said that two Bebb daughters (not the ones you know) had joined the Womens' Land Army and were doing forestry. "Bebbs in the wood," I said, with a triumphant leer.

Le temps fait beau so I will go and post this. Don't work too hard. I like to think of you as two drowsy dormice, laying up a store of nuts against the winter.

Much love,
Philip

1 It was not published until 1945, with the title *Poetry from Oxford in Wartime*, edited by William Bell. It included ten poems by Larkin, all of them included also in *The North Ship*.
2 In October 1944 Larkin began drafting his poems in the first of the eight workbooks in which almost all his subsequent poetry was to be composed, ending in 1980. The first dated draft was written on 5 October 1944.
3 Reference not traced.

22 November 1944 Postcard

[Glentworth, King Street, Wellington]

13 December 1944 Postcard

Glentworth, King Street, Wellington

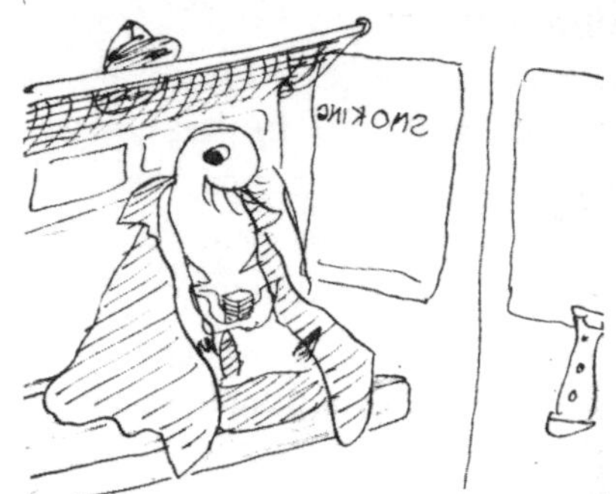

Thank you so much for the delicious tea, especially the orange. It all vanished before Birmingham. I have saved your bags & paper. Thanks also for the heroic lunch. I loved it, especially the shallots.

31 December 1944

Glentworth, King Street, Wellington, Salop.

My dear Mop & Pop,

"The last day of the old year dawned bright and frosty, and at 11.0 a.m. a long muffled figure might have been seen starting its porridge with an expression of distaste." The idea of a New Year takes me aback rather, and induces a febrile session of mental stocktaking, with unavoidable depressions. One novel finished: another started: one book of poems to be printed. That is all there is on the credit side. I daren't look at the debit.

The day of my return – Thursday – was as I predicted terrible. 256: an easy record.[1] However by working like a galley-slave it passed away. Don't let Pop forget this assistant question: I've got to produce something coherent within a week.[2]

The keynote of my return has been a disinclination to eat. Like a camel before a long journey, or a polar bear when the short Arctic summer vanishes, I have stuffed myself up against the hardship to come, and I've hardly finished a meal here yet. I'm just not hungry. Isn't it queer? And talking of animals this household has been enlarged

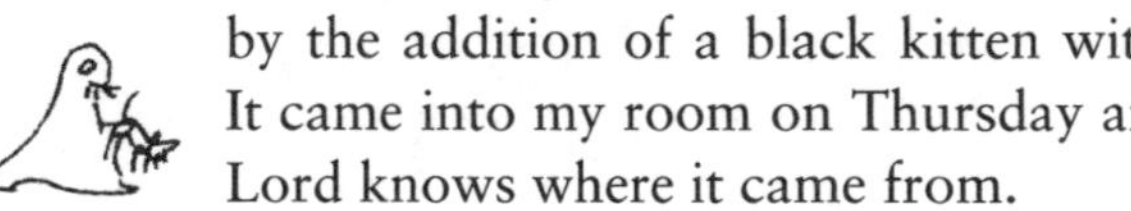

by the addition of a black kitten with a white waistcoat. It came into my room on Thursday and I lifted it out. The Lord knows where it came from.

I view the borrowers with distaste, as before: and the stock with positive loathing. I am tired of trying to rejuvenate a lot of ancient novels. Away! Away! for I would fly to thee, *charioted* by Bacchus and his pards![3] And from the Hertfordshire C. C., get plenty of spare time and rich rewards! (Rather a 17th-Century rhyme that.)

Speaking of poetry, the Fortune Press write: "No agreement is necessary." But in that case who holds the copyright? In due course I correct the proofs – that's one good thing. They gave me two misprints in Oxford P. Then they curiously add: "You might send us your criticisms of *Poetry from Oxford*. Would you send us a few details of your career not for publication?" But if not for publication, why do they want them? To pass on to the police? I sent a few ferocious remarks about my contemporaries, and said that my career was indicated by the heading of my notepaper – I wrote from the P. Lib.

Another letter I wrote was to the sales dept. of the Daily Express, who sent a letter asking if we took their rag, and when I didn't immediately answer, sent a second inquiry. I answered: "The Daily Express is taken by this Library for the convenience of the public." I wanted to put public convenience, but daren't. I don't like the Daily Express.

Much love,
Philip

P.S. Happy New Year!

1 Number of books loaned.
2 Philip had asked Sydney to help document his case for the appointment of a library assistant at Wellington. Eva writes on 1 January 1945: 'Regarding the Assistant question, Daddy made the plan of the working hours all the evening of the day you left, but did not realize the urgency of the question. I am enclosing it. He says that it can be amended to suit circumstances of which he is ignorant.' The plan is now lost.
3 Keats, 'Ode to a Nightingale'.

1945

9 January 1945

Wellington

My dear Mop,

Many happy returns! I hope you are less "mithered" than the creature being honoured in the picture! but Birthday cards are a refinement of civilisation unknown to Wellington, except "To my dear grand-daughter, on her birthday" and "To my dear Nephew".

Have a scrumptious time, my dear Mop, remember all your creatures are with you in spirit and would gather under your wings if they could. I shall be in Shrewsbury today & may find you a gee-gaw.

Many happy returns!
Philip

<*Enclosed*>[1]

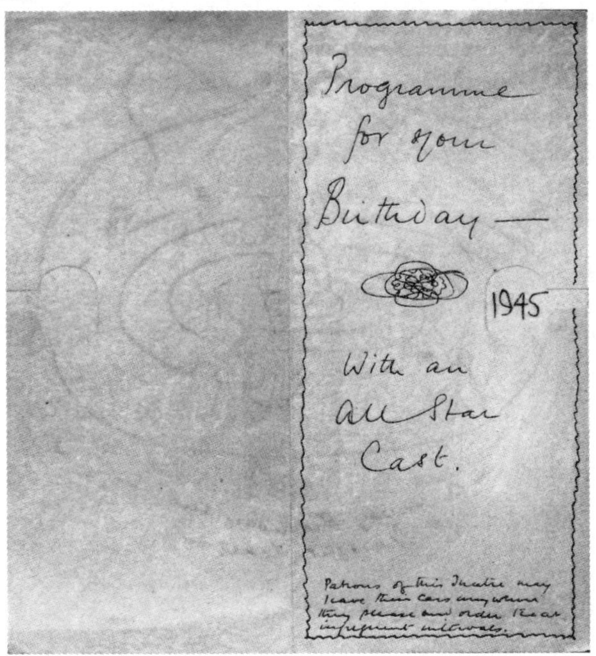

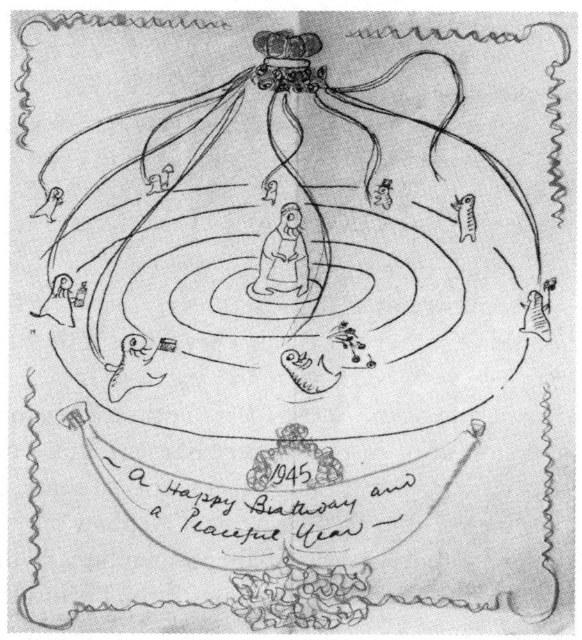

1 In a letter of 11 January, Eva recorded her delight at receiving 'your own made birthday card': 'Really I felt quite excited over the breaking of the seal wondering what I should see inside. Oh, what a lovely whirl of happiness you have drawn! *All* the creatures are charming, even to the dear little one who has fallen over, and scattered it's [*sic*] offering of flowers. Then the one which is vainly stretching upwards to catch an elusive ribbon! then the one with a mop! and the one with the victory flag, how sweet they are! But is that *really* me in the centre? Surely I have waxed very fat on the rations.'

14 January 1945

Glentworth, King Street, Wellington, Salop.

Dear Mop and Pop,

[. . .] The Fortune Press replied and said that "all they ask" is that I don't reproduce the poems in *The North Ship* in any collection of *my* poems for three years. This seems reasonable, and Bruce approves. I forgot to include a 'Contents' to the book, and there is some bother over that which I hope will not impede the production of the book unduly. Did you get a copy of the Oxford Book?[1] I had a letter from Ian Davie, one of the contributors, from Ireland, who said kindly that he thought my poems and Wm. Bell's *Elegies* were the best things in the book and that he felt quite ashamed of his own. This is the kind of thing I never really believe.

The assistant question comes up on Tuesday at a Committee. I rather dread it. I have not Pop's facility for arguing with the clot-pated: surely it is obvious that an assistant is necessary – if they don't see it surely nothing but Divine Revelation will be of any help. The Oxford Appts. Board sent me notice that the Miners' Welfare Commission have a vacancy for an Administrative Assistant (salary £300 inclusive of War Bonus) which doesn't sound too good. They are at Ashtead, Surrey.

Do you like this paper? It cost 2/- for 35 sheets so it ought to be good: it pretends to be handwoven. Notepaper is very scarce round here.

Mop's little dream of us in the country is a very nice one – I should like to pay you visits there but I'm afraid to stay there permanently would sap my morale. But this business of making one's way in the world is a desolate and depressing affair, and any hint of illness – such as on Thursday – sends one to the bottom of the Pit instantly without any hope of recovery.

Oh, well, this is the evil season of winter, and my hands are cold. Let's hope for the Spring.

With very much love,
Philip

1 *Poetry from Oxford in Wartime*, ed. William Bell (London: Fortune Press, 1945). On 15 January Eva wrote: 'Yes, dear Creature, we have the Oxford Book, and Kitty said that Miss Hart had seen it in a shop in Wimbledon. What a lot of poems you have in! I think they are very, very good. Particularly the sonnet, "Love, we must part now", which makes me think of Thomas Hardy's poems. Another one I like very much is "All catches alight." I shall read them many times, and endeavour to find your meaning in them.'

7 February 1945 — Postcard

Wellington — Wednesday

Many thanks for your two inspiriting letters. I will "draft out" an application and you can "check up on" it.[1] I'm glad you think I stand some chance. Don't *they* V.2 Liverpool?

Thoroughly agree with all you say about the advance of spring. There are snowdrops outside my window. And I am so glad you penetrated to the G.B.S. I went to see the Marx Bros. in "A Night At The Opera"[2] last night with Bruce & the Lawrensons, who have invited me to dinner next Tuesday. A social creature. Things here get busier and busier – was surprised to find that Non-Fiction Issues Jan 1945 were 173% higher than in Jan 1944.

Much love
Philip

1 The letters from Sydney and Eva show that Sydney actively helped in the drafting of this Liverpool application. On 7 March Sydney drew his son's attention to the post of Senior Library Assistant advertised by Durham University.
2 A 1935 film starring the Marx Brothers, directed by Sam Wood.

15 April 1945

Glentworth, King Street, Wellington, Salop.

My dear Mop and Pop,

[. . .] The Fortune Press say they "expect to undertake" *Jill* this year". That I suppose means next. They said they would do the *North Ship* in February. Charlatans: they won't pay for it either. Still, it will delight me to see my morbid little tale in book form.

On Wednesday we finally appointed my assistant – a pleasant girl called Greta Roden. She won't start till September. To tell the truth, the responsibility of having to train an assistant weighs on me: I know practically nothing about the technical side of Librarianship, and either I have got to learn it first or she will learn it herself and shame my ignorance. [. . .]

Bruce is alarmed by my sudden teetotalism & abstention from smoking. He says with asperity that if I expect him to go pretty country walks when we meet I am wrong.

Much love to both –
Philip

29 April 1945

Glentworth, King Street, Wellington, Salop.

My dear Mop and Pop,

[. . .] Things meander along here harmlessly enough. I have heard nothing from Liverpool. Last night I finished the first version of my novel, after a fashion, and today start the doubtful pleasure of rereading and making notes for the second version.[1] Bruce chortles away in Devonshire, "being hardly able to write for laughing", and there is no sight nor sound of The North Ship. Le Bateau Nord – or would it be Le Bateau du Nord? Like Rimbaud's Le Bateau Rose.

Noël Hughes wrote to me again suggesting a meeting the weekend before Whitsun, but I refused as I can't afford, or decently manage it. I may see him at Whitsun. I hope the weather returns to some semblance of an English spring by then. Miss T. said yesterday apropos of the frost: "An' all the things in the garden have come up!" I said jovially, "Well, they'll all have to go down again!" which amused me highly and sent me cackling to work.

With much love,
Philip

1 *Katherine*, later to become *A Girl in Winter.*

27 May 1945

Glentworth, King Street, Wellington, Salop.

My dear Mop and Pop,

[. . .] I had a letter from Jim saying he had been to Venice & floated about in a gondola. He says that he "hopes to see me in a very short time" but also that he will be going to Austria as part of the occupation army. These things seem to cancel out, don't they? The sandwiches by the way vanished before Birmingham and the orange is no more, and all the ginger-biscuits except one has gone the way of all flesh. Great and merciful is the Lord. I have started reading the Bible while dressing in the morning. There is only time to read perhaps a chapter a day, but so far it is quite fascinating. I have just arrived at Noah and the Flood. It's curious how even I, in whose upbringing the Bible played a negligible part, feel a sense of the past upon me when I read it – not my own past necessarily, but I think of all the churches where these stories have been read over and over again in times when people could not read them. I think also of the old morality plays, translating them into inarticulate buffoonery and mime. It's like encountering something fundamental in English life – like ploughs or barns or villages. Sorry if I make myself diffuse. I hardly know what I mean myself.

Bruce has no more news, except that he has had a letter from the Chaplain of Ohio State Penitentiary asking for a *free copy* of the Fly as the prisoners are agitating to read it. Further, Professor someoneorother of Ohio University took it as a text for a wireless talk on the detective novel, and finally a girl named Betty E. Smith of Wichita, Kansas, has written saying how much she liked it and how clever he is. I wondered if it was Betty Smith who wrote a popular novel called "A Tree Grows in Brooklyn",[1] and if it was Wichita Faces?

Talking about "mehr licht", as Goethe said,[2] my skylights were scraped yesterday. The counter where I work is now flooded with light, which is a good thing in some ways if not in others. A borrower gave me some eggs yesterday.

I say, as a graduate have I two votes?[3] How do I use them? I particularly want to vote for A. P. Herbert.[4]

[. . .]

With much love to both
Philip

1 Novel by Betty Smith, published in 1943.
2 'More light': the last words of Johann Wolfgang von Goethe (1749–1832).
3 Philip was entitled to vote both in the University of Oxford constituency and in Wellington.
4 Alan Patrick Herbert (1890–1971): humourist, novelist and playwright, standing as an independent, had been elected as one of the two MPs for Oxford University in 1935, and was returned again in 1945. University constituencies were abolished in 1950.

17 June 1945

Glentworth, King Street, Wellington, Shropshire

My dear Mop & Pop,

From what I can see, this is to be a blazing hot day, so I shall keep my head indoors like a tortoise. Come to think of it, I looked out at 5 this morning when the light was just beginning to grow, and across the playing-field opposite my window the birds were very noisy in the poplars, as if expecting such weather. I wonder what you are both doing. [. . .]

Hay fever has started good and proper. Last week I thought I had discovered the best relief yet – smelling salts. The theory is that you take a good whiff, and are immediately plunged into a fantasy of ammonia-water, unable to see, breathe, think, or smell – or *sneeze*. When you come round, you find the hay fever has passed for the moment. But it has been less effective recently and I don't think it's much good.

Creature in June.
I wear dark spectacles too – they were here, after all.

Thanks to Pop for his last note: I'm sorry he'd read the Corelli.[1] I also have gathered some information about Univ. Coll. Library, to wit (to woo!), all that you mention was destroyed during the air raids, and they are existing on books lent by Westfield, King's, etc. Opening for a bright young man with bright ideas for reconstruction! I have as many bright ideas as a woodlouse. However, I should be most grateful if you *would* put [in] an application for me. If I had a good job, I might take more interest in it.

I am still reading John Inglesant, very slowly.[2] An unusual book, not exactly my meat. Did you know him, or was it just Levett you knew? "Lark Rise to Candleford"[3] continues to enchant.

With much love,
Philip

1 No letters survive from Sydney and/or Eva between 26 March and 27 August 1945, so it is impossible to identify this novel. Marie Corelli (1855–1924) was a prolific, hugely popular novelist with transcendental leanings.
2 *John Inglesant*: a historical novel by Joseph Henry Shorthouse (1834–1903). Published in 1881, it is set in the time of Charles I and focuses on Catholic/Anglican tensions.
3 The trilogy of semi-autobiographical novels by Flora Thompson (1876–1947), first published together in 1945.

24 June 1945

Glentworth, King Street, Wellington, Salop.

My dear Mop and Pop,

I blink at the page through watering eyes as if perpetually grieving, but it is only my old friend h.f. gingering up my Sunday morning. The handkerchief you so kindly sent me has been swept into the maelstrom, the *danse macabre* of six handkerchiefs from pocket to pocket under the blazing sun. But it was soft and grateful. The only good think [*sic*] at present is that laundry is going and coming with unusual rapidity – I don't understand it. My basket, instead of lying unattended for weeks, is emptied every few days, and small bundles of clothes appear in their place on my dressing table. This means I have a good supply of clean handkerchiefs.

I duly signed the application and despatched it on Friday. Please excuse me if I sometimes sound ungrateful or lazy in these matters. I know you think – at least I expect you think – that things reach a pretty pass when I don't even write out my own applications, but I really am grateful to you when you do it for me. I shrink from it – I hate laying myself open – I hate being prodded and turned over and pinched like fish on a slab. And then again I hate the insincerity of it – I find it extraordinarily difficult to conceal my attitude of "I will do this job as well as I can, which is probably quite well, because if I am responsible for it I shall take care it does not reflect badly on me, but I can promise now and for ever that it will never interest me." However, something too much of this: but I am grateful.

My novel, since you enquire, is quite well. The second draft is finished except for the final scene, which I shall do during next week. Then I shall reread it most critically, trying as far as possible to avoid writing another complete draft. I am not altogether displeased with it, but I have yet to make sure that I have done effectively what I set out to do. I don't think there has been anything quite like it before, which may of course be a good thing. I'm afraid I can't hold out much hope for Auntie Nellie. She wouldn't find it unreadable, but there is nothing in it that makes a book "nice". Still no news of course from the Fortune Press. Grrr.

I hope you enjoyed your jaunt to Loughborough: Kitty is on my conscience. In these days I have no time to write to anyone outside yourselves: Jim seems to have closed down, though he may of course be on his way home. I look forward to coming home myself, but it's hard to say when that will be. [. . .]

Much love to both. I think of you a great deal, and look forward to our next encounter.

Affectionately –
Philip

1 July 1945

Glentworth, King Street, Wellington, Shropshire

My dear Mop and Pop,

There's a snort of wind blowing this morning, and insofar as it pierces my window into the room it feels pretty chilly. However, better that than beastly sun. My hayfever has cleared up this last week – touch wood! Touch forests, in fact! [. . .]

I fell upon my novel in a frenzy last night and got it nearly finished. The last pages will be written today. As I started it on May 1st – this second draft – I am pleased to think I have written about 75,000 words in two months, in my spare time. After very careful revision I think I shall have it typed. The job of typing it myself seems too much to face – and in lodgings I always feel guilty of rattling away every time I get a spare moment. It will be costly and I'm not sure how I feel about it. Probably somewhere in the region of £5![1] No doubt the eventual sales will about recoup me. [. . .]

Well, I should like to go to Loughborough too: August would perhaps be the best time. Bruce has been pressing me very strongly to visit him at Brixham again, and I certainly should like to: we had better plan these things when I know exactly what is happening here. So far I don't.

A fortnight in August – but which I don't know. Perhaps Kitty will be a world-famous button-designer by then. Now I must go and post this.

Till Tuesday!

Love,
Philip

1 Sydney and Eva paid the £5 typist's fee.

9 September 1945

Glentworth, King Street, Wellington, Salop.

My dear Mop and Pop,

I write this after lunch, for a change, and though the morning has been dull and dry it really looks as if rain will come this afternoon. [. . .]

I am watching the T.L.S. for them to acknowledge receipt of *The North Ship*, but I am doubtful if they will, though Bruce claims to have "fixed" them. I don't trust the Fortune Press an inch. They may not even send them out. I had always thought that when a book of mine was published I should not be able to put it down – that I should be perpetually glancing at my name on the dustcover & stealing glances at the title-page. However, I find that barring a careful perusal for misprints I have hardly looked at it since it came. Strange . . .

I had a letter from Colin Gunner & said I should be at home on the 16th. I will try to steer him away if he comes: we will all go out somewhere. Nevertheless I look forward to seeing both Jim and Colin considerably. They will have tales to tell & experiences to compare. I shall feel a very sick dog, an enfeebled civilian.

Creaturing into Boots' one day last week I saw small 1-oz. jars of Marmite – just creature size – and so I bought one, hiding it assiduously from my landlady and eating it with delight. It reminds me of "le temps jadis" when tea was never without it, and Kitty & I were always snatching it backwards and forwards while you watched it like a staid cat watching a rally at Wimbledon Centre Court – left . . . right . . . left . . . right . . .

Shall descend on you next week. 6.26 Leamington – Jim says he will meet me.

All love,
Philip

20 October 1945

Glentworth, King Street, Wellington, Salop.

My dear Mop and Pop,

I reached home eventually in good order. I did not touch the sandwiches till after Birmingham, then sat and stuffed next to a student who seemed to be reading economic psychology but who eventually fell asleep. There seemed a lot to eat and it was all very nice, as was the brief time I spent with you. Many thanks!

There is not a great deal of news from this whirling metropolis: issues are increasing and we are settling down to real hard work insofar as Wellington Public Library understands the phrase. My assistant is really very sensible and I like her.[1] Admittedly she can't spell and is illiterate generally but she is far politer than I am and has a habit of doing things unexpectedly for me which I like. She is gradually assuming complete control of the Library while I moon around thinking how unhappy I am.

Bruce read my book (*The Kingdom of Winter*) and while dubious said I should easily find a publisher. So now it has gone to his agent. I think perhaps it will not rock the world, but all the same I have affection for it. There is no other literary news.

As for details – I found my other set of underwear: after all, they were at the laundry. I have got a receipt from Bruce's sister and await the Inland Revenue man clothed in righteousness. So far I have not written to Kitty but am full of good intentions.

I had a letter this morning from Kingsley, who is back at St John's, and who gives long lists of people who are back there. It makes me feel rather nostalgic. Noël Hughes has returned, and several other people I know. Still, I have eaten my cake while they were in the army, so any complaints on my part would be ungracious as well as ridiculous. Because I don't really want to go back there. It's only the thought of easy, delightful living that attracts me.

I caught and slew another flea on Thursday – really, to have a job where fleas did not jump on one would be rather a relief. Really, there have been moments in the past few days when I have felt quite seriously that either I resign, taking no thought for the morrow, or I stay here for all eternity. I expect I'm wrong on both counts. [. . .]

Did you tell Pop that we nearly had another accident in the bus going to Leamington? The Fates are against me. Very narrow-minded of them.

With much love,
Philip

1 Greta Roden. See letter of 15 April 1945.

28 October 1945

Glentworth, King Street, Wellington, Salop.

My dear Mop & Pop,

[. . .] Life here is very boring at the moment. I feel I am living as ordinary people do, without inspiration, and it is a depressing process. When the angel will next revisit me I have no idea. In the meanwhile, there is nothing to do.

It is such a dark morning that I can hardly see to write, and except for the necessary journey down to the post office to send this on its way I shall most likely stay in, reading. I am making another attack on "Moby Dick" – my first was defeated about a year ago – and I also have G.B.S.'s dramatic criticism, Quenell's "Four Portraits" and a Boots' novel.[1] These should keep me going. The odd thing is, I have a novel fairly well planned in my head, but am no nearer writing it than of becoming Head Librarian of Bodley.

I spent last weekend in London, on a visit to Ruth who is now at King's College.[2] She is billeted, so to speak, in upper Norwood in a comfortable flat, the owners of which put me up also. As you remember, it rained all the time, and the only tangible thing we found to do was inspect St Paul's. Ruth, if you don't remember, is the girl I used to help with essays. She got 2 distinctions – history & English – in her High Cert. exam, as I did.

My fire is at last giving off a little heat. There is a malignant draught. The rain is pelting. Love to both ——— Philip

1 Sir Peter Courtney Quennell (1905–92): English biographer and essayist. *Four Portraits* (1945) is a study of Boswell, Gibbon, Sterne and Wilkes.

2 Ruth Bowman, whom Larkin had met as a sixteen-year-old schoolgirl on his arrival in Wellington, and to whom he was to become engaged in 1948–50. He is notably reticent in his references to her in letters home.

30 December 1945

Glentworth, King Street, Wellington, Salop.

My dear Mop & Pop,

I expect you are surprised to see this awful paper,[1] but the truth is that by a series of mischances the notepaper that Kitty gave me for Christmas is at the library, and I have not a solitary scrap in my room. So I am forced to use this, and hope you do not mind

I arrived back here safely if rather wet and dejected, and have been very busy since, but it wasn't till yesterday that Miss Tomlinson sprang the rather nasty bombshell that she wanted my room for a paralysed relative and would I please go by Jan. 16th. This has not quite sunk in yet but I am sure it will be very difficult to move anywhere in a fortnight except into a hotel or professional boarding-house. However, it all makes a change and I don't really care, though I doubt if I should be as comfortable anywhere else. I will keep you informed.

I sent off my application for Evesham and yesterday received an answer from the Lib. Assoc. Courses start in March 1946 for exams in June 1947. There's a quid to pay at the outset. I feel I am setting off down a long dark road lined with broken rocks and ending in perpetual night. Further, I asked for a Year Book, and shall be able to see what kind of place Evesham is – No, that's not true, it is a different publication that lists libraries, sizes, staffs, etc. Most people here seem to think Evesham would be deadly dull.[2]

There was a copy of *The North Ship* in the *Smiths'* here when I got back – an order that hadn't been taken up. I promptly bought it and despatched it to a friend. Don't want that tack lying around this place.

I am rather late about things this morning so it will be better if I break this off and depart to clean my shoes. The morning is bright & frosty, and in my grate lies the ruins of a good fire.

Thank you once again for the Christmas (I ate the last mince pie yesterday) and I hope both of you have a very happy and comfortable new year.

With lots of love,
Philip

1 The letter is written on both sides of a single large sheet of lined paper.

2 Sydney wrote on 7 January 1946 that he had 'run over to Evesham to refresh my memory of the town'. He described the centre with its medieval buildings and two parish churches, and praised the local branches of Smiths and Boots ('the Boots' Library being particularly spacious'). He continued: 'The Library is in the same building (not a bad building) as the British Restaurant. Libr. Hours 10–1, 3–6, Wednesday afternoon closed. There are 2 reading rooms. / From the borough treasurer I learn that in 1943–4 the issues were 58,161, 46 vols. were purchased, 47 borrowed from Region. Estimated expenditure \(this year)/ £800, penny rate £320. The woman librarian is leaving to go to Exeter. There is one middleaged woman assistant.'

1946

6 January 1946

Glentworth, King's Road, Wellington, Salop.

My dear Mop & Pop,

[. . .] Now I am leaving here shortly I feel tempted to behave outrageously, slamming doors, demanding more coal, and mumbling "God! I'm not *that* hungry!" when a meal is put before me, but oddly enough the place is quite tolerable, the fires are enormous, and the food quite edible. I have a small hot water bottle that she makes no bones about filling. Nevertheless, it will be nice to leave.

I've heard no more about Evesham so far: Buttrey wasn't very keen on the idea, as you can imagine; but Warwick C.C. sent back my application yesterday saying the post had been filled. The words "I am 23 years old" had been scored under.[1] [. . .]

Tell me all your news. A very happy and creatureful New Year to you both.

Philip

1 In his letter of 7 January Sydney reflected: 'Regarding the Warwickshire application, It is only to be expected that they would not have the courage to appoint one so young as you, although it was the one thing I emphasised with Davey (County Treasurer) that you were much more advanced than many older people and that if I were in the position of "nabbing" a young man of your qualifications, I should do so, even if I had only a more subordinate position to offer than the one advertised. But W.C.C. is 50 years behind the times.'

9 January 1946

<*Envelope front (no address, presumably enclosed with presents)*>

Wellington

My dear Mop,

Many happy returns of the day! May you have lots of kippers and cream.

My presents to everyone reach a new seedy level every time, but honestly these nasty things I am sending you were all I could get in Shrewsbury in the "beer mat" line. I hope you will find *some* use for them. And then I couldn't find a birthday card, so am reduced to writing to you to say how much I hope you have a peaceful, happy, *quiet* year, with all you wish for and comfort & kindness. In short all you deserve!

And thank you for your letters. I will try to answer them soon, because this weekend I go to Berkhamstead. Also I go to London to confer with the FP. I am furious with them.

I move into my new lodgings – 7, Ladycroft, Wellington on Friday night. We started off with 20/- difference between our starting prices: each relinquished 10/- & I agreed to pay 45/- a week, which seems rather a lot to me. But I *think* it'll be worth it. I wonder if there'll be a "garden jakes" as Ll. Powys calls it.[1]

My dearest love to you and may you have a happy day, week, month, year.

Philip

<*Envelope back*>

1 The toilet at 7 Ladycroft was indeed outside, and there was no bath. Llewelyn Powys (1884–1939), novelist; brother of the writers J. C. and T. F. Powys.

20 January 1946

7, Ladycroft, Wellington

My dear Mop & Pop,

The frost was just intense last night and the windows are icy and everything outside crumbly with frost.

However I am up at 10.35 a.m. in a clean room feeling reasonably warm (three things that wouldn't happen at Glentworth) so I don't feel inclined to complain.

My Berkhamsted trip went off very well, except that connections at Stafford were abominable & the train was late. The Amis' (plural) were awfully kind. On Sunday morning a tray of tea & toast was put into our room and we lay in our beds till 12 playing the gramophone & talking. I mention this not because I admire it but because that is how some people dispose of their guests. The one horrible thing was that the beds were *cold*.

On Sunday afternoon Kingsley & I went from Watford to Euston and picked up Ruth, then I called on the Fortune Press. When I rejoined them I found that they had been to the Picasso exhibition which infuriated me, because I w^d much sooner have gone there than kept an entirely needless appointment with the Fortune Press. All we decided was that I sh^d use my discretion in the alterations, which was what I had suggested by post anyway. I learnt with enjoyment that my typescript had sent a girl into hysterics and gravely offended a chapel-trained compositor and generally played merry hell.[1] They say the book will be out by March (grossly untrue) and that it will cost 9/6. This is to *ensure* that nobody buys it, I suppose. Not that I care. I get no profit from it and the book itself is childish and ordinary.

Talking of books, "Holy Disorders" comes out on Jan 21st, and I already have a copy. Don't forget to buy it![2]

They also said *The North Ship* was an edn. of 600, but whether to believe that or not I don't know. In my next letter I shall be able to include an account of what John Heath-Stubbs read at the Arts Society on Friday.[3] I am having a trained observer there.

Thanks for your letter: I do hope the mess about the boiler has cleared up, and that you have managed to get someone to do the work regularly. With regard to my lodgings, they are really very nice: an index to Miss Davies may be found in the fact that she *washed my brushes* without asking or being asked. I live chiefly on eggs & bread & butter.

The delay over *Welsh Ambassadors*[4] is due to my assistant's having sent it back without my knowing, but I have reordered it and it shd be along shortly. My dentist has started work on me again and has not hurt so far, but I can't help feeling that this tooth he is so painstakingly "saving" will never settle down and will have to come out in the end.

I have entered for Part 1 of the Registration exam as it seems impossible to do all 3 parts at once by spare-time study. At this rate it will take ages. How boring.

Much love to both,
Philip

1 On 21 January Eva commented on this reaction to *Jill*: 'What a strange book it must be to cause such an uproar amongst the girls who were fortunate enough to read it.'

2 Bruce Montgomery's second novel, published under the pseudonym Edmund Crispin.

3 The poet John Heath-Stubbs (1918–2006) had co-edited *Eight Oxford Poets* in 1941, with Sidney Keyes and Michael Meyer.

4 Louis Umfreville Wilkinson, *Welsh Ambassadors: Powys Lives and Letters* (1936).

19 May 1946

7, Ladycroft, Wellington, Salop.

My dear Mop & Pop,

This is a very great change from last Sunday. Outside, it isn't actually raining but it's very dark and there's a cold wind. Last night produced a tremendous cloudburst which all the farmers and gardeners say they've been needing.

And thank you again for the lilies – they are still in good condition and are in my sitting-room. I was amused by your phrase "the electricians are tapping about" – I see them as a set of woodpeckers hopping over the furniture. [. . .]

There is not much news here: on Tuesday I face another committee, probably slightly differently constituted from the old one. That does not greatly cheer me. More pleasing is news from Peter Watt that Fabers have enquired about my "previous work" after reading *The Kingdom.*[1] This no doubt means very little. But I do wish they would take it: heaven knows their fiction list is as uncommercial as it could be, and not very good either. You'll be amused to hear that Cape, Secker, Chatto & Windus & the Cresset Press have declined it. I should be more hopeful if I remembered the book as being any good . . . but sincerely the only parts I recall are amateurish in the extreme.

Thursday sees the advent of a new Isherwood book, since we speak of literature.[2]

I should think my overcoat could be turned, at considerable expense – however I don't seem to have finished with it yet "this winter"! I'm still dressed as for January. It really would be nice to expose the other side – but would the "hang" be affected? That overcoat always 'hung' well, in my opinion.

I think, if it would not flutter the dovecotes too much, I should enjoy visiting you next weekend as I promised at Easter to visit you 'soon'. Will you let me know if all the electricians have "tapped away" by that time?

Am reading the Pelican book on local government by W. Eric Jackson.

Very much love to both,
Philip

1 *The Kingdom of Winter*, Larkin's preferred title for *A Girl in Winter.*

2 *Prater Violet* (1945): Isherwood's satire on the vacuousness of American film-making.

30 June 1946

47 Wellington Sq. Oxford

My dear Mop & Pop,

Yes. I'm afraid I have run down here again, mainly to see Bruce who has been negligently adding a degree of B. Mus. to his honours during the past week.

Well, thank you for your card! I am neither elated nor depressed by the success.[1] I shall no doubt be happier when I have settled there. Including myself, there were four candidates – two men & two women. I think I was the worst one as regards library training & the best as regards general knowledge and education. The people seemed friendly and I sh^{d} imagine that the academic calm will suit me far better than my present sordid hullaballoo. You can imagine the incredulous amazement that fell on me when they summoned me a second time – a signal I have learned to recognise as the committee's choice.

So far as anybody in Wellington *knows*, the reaction there is embarrassingly regretful. I am beginning to long for someone to come up & say "You're goin', eh? Good riddance to rotten bad rubbish!" [. . .]

~~*Yes*~~*No*. I shall not apply for Scotland now, but thanks all the same for the information.

Very much love,
Philip

P.S. There is a John Bunyan collection at Leicester!

1 Philip had been appointed Assistant Librarian at Leicester University College.

7 July 1946

7, Ladycroft, Wellington

My dear Mop & Pop,

[. . .] Soon after I had posted my letter I discovered that Bruce had *not* become a B. Mus. after all – he had merely passed the first of two hurdles!

Leicester have offered and I have accepted the post, and I have resigned my "headship" here as from Aug. 31st. My colleagues & Committee men seem oddly non-committal – "glad to see that swine's back" or "letting us down properly, that swine is" – but the borrowers are much kinder and seem quite sorry. My key phrase is "I'd have missed it for anything" – my 30 months here, that is! There was an indistinguishable photo of me in the local paper and a garbled account of my stay here.

Faber's have also offered a formal contract for my book which, though it is rather miserly, I have of course accepted. They are paying £30 in advance, and royalties of 10% on first 2,000, 12½% on next 3,000, and 15% on any copies above that total number. Recourse to the "Author's handbook" tells me that this is a poor rate – one ought to end up on 20%. – but Watt says that Faber's are always like that. If it only sells 2,000, about £80 will flow into my coffers – then Watt & the Inland Revenue dept. will sharpen their claws. In contrast to this, I have been reading Arnold Bennett's *Journals* (3 vols).[1] They are all about money, & how many words he writes, and awful people like Beaverbrook.[2] Also I read Kingsmill's *Frank Harris*[3] – for sheer incredible behaviour, one would have to go far to equal F. H. Horatio Bottomley sounds like a trusty bank cashier in comparison.[4]

I was interested in your news & glad that you have "a new woman". I telegraphed to Kitty from Leicester but she hasn't said anything. The College people were vague on the subject of lodgings but said they would try. I think bread rationing is a nuisance but I am in favour of anything that hurts the common people – we too exceed our ration. Holidays at Leicester are a minimum of 7 weeks p.a. – all August! There was a big "fête" here yesterday at which Anthony Eden burbled through his famous hat.

With love,
Philip

1 Arnold Bennett (1867–1931), English novelist, best known for his works set in the Potteries.
2 Max Aitken, Lord Beaverbrook (1879–1964), Canadian-born British newspaper owner, and government minister during World War II.
3 Hugh Kingsmill [Lunn], biographer (1933) of the controversial journalist Frank Harris, whose memoirs had been banned because of their sexually explicit content.
4 Horatio Bottomley (1860–1933), English newspaper editor, rabble-rouser and fraudster.

21 July 1946

7, Ladycroft, Wellington, Salop.

My dear Mop & Pop,

A search through my pockets reveals that I have put your last letter somewhere very carefully, so carefully that it escapes me now, but I recall that it was a nice long one.

This week has been fairly uneventful except that I had a last committee on Tuesday, when people were very polite and generous, and I had to rise to my hind paws and make some sort of reply. It is extraordinary how words and particularly ideas fly before the hour of need. However, I managed to preach some rigmarole and sat down, reflecting that it was in any case the first time I have officially spoken to anybody about anything. And the last, if I'm lucky. Consequent upon this, I have received another official letter thanking me for my services etc. which will serve as a testimonial if I ever need one. It occurs to me – rather belatedly – that I shall probably never do any job so spectacularly well again, and shall certainly not enjoy such responsibility for probably 20 years![1] Looking back, I can't think which is the most surprising – that I sh^{d} have gone there, or that they sh^{d} have appointed an unknown quantity of 21!

Also, consequent upon the unguarded reference to *The North Ship*, there have been many friendly enquiries that make me sweat as if ridden by a nightmare. I have lent the book out to one woman who reports that there are some "very striking similes" in it. They must have crawled in when I wasn't looking, like Colorado beetles.

As far as I know, I shall be at home all my holiday, but I might stay a weekend with Kingsley or a day or two with Bruce. This however is pure guesswork as I haven't been asked yet! [. . .]

There's no news of a successor to your creature: Our advert appeared in the TLS yesterday: if that doesn't bring 'em in, nothing ever will. Paradoxically, I feel disinclined to hand over the place to someone else. In some respects it is a remarkable collection of books, not to be paralleled in the U.K.! My never to be realised ambition was that I could somehow be borrower as well as librarian – in some fantastic way walk in and find the very library moulded to my own taste . . .

Very much love to both –
Philip

1 Pencil superscript: '9, actually!' in Larkin's handwriting. He must have re-read this letter decades later.

20 August 1946

Picture postcard[1]

Wellington.

A very happy birthday to you, dear – pardon this unusual greeting card but everything connected with birthdays here is inexpressibly horrible. I will search Full Diligentlie for a Preſent for you & Dispatch Itt.

Love – Philip

1 Photograph of Larkin. See Plate 5B. Addressed to Mrs C. E. Hewett, 53 York Rd, Loughborough.

25 August 1946

7, Ladycroft, Wellington, Salop.

My dear Mop & Pop,

Though somewhat uncertainly, the sun is shining; I can hear church bells & the sound of the B.B.C. It is warm. I reflect that this is the last Sunday I shall write to you as Chief Librarian, Wellington, Salop.

Many thanks for your letter & news. Yes, the rations were much appreciated. I am very glad you washed the tie, because it is a subtle shade and dear to my heart.

I have not a great deal of news. Faber's have passed the revised portions of my book, and it is now in the hands of "the production department". They now say they want a new title! This will cause me a great deal of trouble if they're adamant. What they don't realise is that every detail of the book was studied for months by a finer mind than they can command, and that for them to suggest alterations is impudent & silly. So there![1]

I laid hold of my sports coat last Tuesday. In the end it cost 68/6 (I c[d] have got it for 25/6 if I'd had the courage to be dishonest) and is I think a success. It is not so long as it might be, but it is a good inch longer than my last two. The cloth is very nice (within limits) & it has 6 pockets. Wearing it, I have that odd sensation of being well dressed, that has deserted me since leaving Oxford.

I have so far exposed 3 photographs. One of the Wrekin taken across a cornfield and Ruth; one of "The Raven", my favourite hostelry; & one of myself, which I'm afraid won't come off, being an interior time exposure. But there's been hardly any sun for such activities.

I am very busy these days: I'm afraid Mr. Haynes will not take over the library at its best, but with part time help order & efficiency go largely by the board.

Much love to both,
Philip

Needless to say, no *Jills* yet.

1 On 26 August Eva replied: 'We are surprised to hear that Faber's are not satisfied with the title of your novel. / Daddy says that he sees nothing amiss with it, particularly when one thinks that the novel entitled "If Winter Comes", sold like hot cakes, and I expect it is from the selling point of view that *they* select a title.'

7 September 1946

53, York Road, Loughborough, Leics

My dear Mop & Pop,

It's early on Saturday evening, and as I haven't anything to do I thought I would write my letter to you in order to make sure you get it on Monday morning.

I have not so far found any lodgings. When I arrived on Thursday I went to the College office and worked on some addresses they gave me, but without success. On Friday I did the same, but the kind of place I found myself visiting made me think that I was not on a good trail. They were certainly not "private" places – mainly living with the family or with other lodgers, for 35/- a week. So on Friday afternoon I threw up the sponge (for the time being) and entered a "small ad." in the Leicester Mercury, saying exactly what I wanted. There seem plenty of lodgings in Leicester – of a sort – so I am not quite hopeless. The Mercury is a recognised organ for such transactions.

I am enjoying my visit here, and feel very lucky to have such a refuge, but am terrified lest I fail to find anywhere to go & so overstay my welcome.[1] Today I didn't leave the town, but looked round at the Library, bookshops, etc., feeling rather bored. I think the main discomfort of new surroundings is the boredom consequent on new surroundings – one doesn't know where to go to be amused. [. . .]

I have been receiving a lot of letters, though: one from Bruce was waiting for me at the library. He has been racketing round London with literary folk. [. . .]

Much love to both.
Philip

1 Philip stayed with Kitty and Walter during the first month of his appointment at Leicester, travelling the ten miles to work by bus.

29 September 1946

53, York Road, Loughborough, Leics

My dear Mop and Pop,

Many thanks for the fat envelope duly received on Wednesday. I don't quite know who to answer first. Thank you, at any rate, for the photographs. I'm sorry they are not all I hoped for. The portrait of Ruth would have been passable if only I'd had a tripod or at least a steady base for my camera. I am furious. Why aren't there any films to be had? It is only by ceaseless practice that one discovers what one can and cannot do.

Thanks to Pop for his advice on the policy. I don't like the idea of funding my income in my old age:[1] – but if you say so it is probably the best way. I haven't seen the Registrar yet. He is a vociferous man, likely to bully me into taking an annuity. His name is the unusual one of Drewery – there is one obvious rhyme but one w[d] need a third for a limerick.

I am glad Mop has been enjoying *Kangaroo*. I am inclined to think that a study of Lawrence should start from that book sooner than almost any other. I have never known anyone give such a complete picture of himself. And doesn't he get the feel of the beaches and desolate Australian countryside skilfully?

Talking of books, the Fortune Press make renewed promises of JILL for the "middle of October", and say they expect to send copies "within the next ten days." I'm afraid that Pop will find it very different from *To the Dark Tower*.[2] There are two ways of learning to write novels. One is to spread your talent as far as possible over as many different characters, aspects, attitudes etc. as you can in your first book, and however thin the result concentrate on filling in during your later ones. That is I think Francis King's method. The other is to concentrate your talent on one subject within easy range, to do nothing you are not sure of, however limited or elementary. That is mine. Charles Madge[3] acknowledged *The North Ship* and pleased me by saying that they have "an altogether different quality". But I shall not believe in their value until someone is willing to pay me hard cash for them.

I shall be moving into my new lodgings tomorrow. I dread this for fear they may be irretrievably bad. I don't mind "roughing it" but to pay 45/- and rough it seems double-roughing it to me. The address is 172, London Road. In case you have not a record. But it will be a relief to be shut of the 'bus-journies.

Yesterday was a beautiful day, wasn't it? I sat in Leicester's Victoria Park for a while, read a book on Yeats and watched the people playing hockey. The town gets very busy on a Saturday. [. . .]

Perhaps next weekend I shall be glad of a visit home. This oscillation of mine is keeping Kitty away! Why she wants to come I don't know: why have a home if you don't stay in it? It seems to point to a radical breakdown somewhere. Now I really *do* want things like clothes, etc., and come to fetch them . . .

Much love to both,
Philip

1 Eva comments in a letter of 30 September: 'Oh! the *dear dear* Creature in it's old age! It is a clever little sketch but not at all cheering. How fat and bent the poor thing looks. The drain adds the final touch of degradation. But I don't believe it. I feel sure my Creature will never be like that.'

2 The first novel by Francis King (1923–2011), published in 1946.
3 Charles Madge (1912–96), poet and sociologist.

27 October 1946

As from 172, London Road, Leicester

My dear Mop & Pop,

You will probably notice from the postmark that I am paying a visit to Ruth in Norwood. As usual words cannot describe the weather: cold, wet, & a thick blanket of mist. I thought it seemed very cold in the night, & I found on drawing the curtains this morning that my window was open. Brrr . . .

I am happy to say at last that *Jill* arrived yesterday & when walking up Charing Cross Rd I saw it in Schwemmer's window. I will post a copy to you tomorrow and you should get it on Tuesday. It is really quite nicely produced, if your standards are not very high: several misprints & the pages crowded with print. It costs 9/6. This seems sufficient guarantee that nobody will buy it.[1]

I have said a lot about it in the past and I will not weary you with further excuses except to say that do remember it is a very "first" attempt, "young" in conception & treatment, with numerous faults, and concerning matters in which you will probably find it difficult if not impossible to interest yourself – and you will be right!

Yes. I have bought a mushroom from Woolworth's – a multi-coloured speckled one of which the top screws off. So far I haven't used it.

Ruth & I went to see *Henry V* again yesterday.[2] I often wonder what Pop thought of the verse speaking in that film, assuming he saw it. To me it seemed very remarkable. I enquired at one or two shops for books by Ll. Powys, but none were forthcoming. After glancing at some prices of 2nd hand books I thought it was probably just as well. (By the way I have ordered Elwin's book too.[3])

Bruce wrote to me "commanding" board & lodging from the Grand Hotel, so I rang them up & secured a room (no mean feat this). He arrives on Friday, Nov. 1st till Tuesday. I am dreading it financially. When Bruce visits me it seems to cost as much as my visiting any one else. He has just finished another novel called *Swan Song*. This is I think a good title, as it concerns a murder during *Lohengrin*. Another for Marshall!

The King & Queen are coming to Leicester on Wednesday, but I shall have no chance of seeing them. All the streets are decorated with flags and there is scaffolding rigged up all over the L.M.S station. I hear that the King broke the golden key in New Bodley door when opening it last week – someone had to shin up & get in a window & let them in from inside. What a paltry business this ceremony racket is!

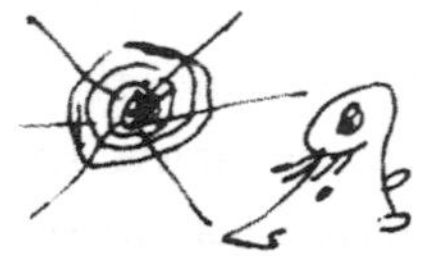

With much love to both creatures. How is your spider?

Philip

1 On 28 October Sydney asked Philip to acquire 'half a dozen copies, or less ... if possible on author's terms', and corrected his son's recollection: 'The window you saw *Jill* in would be Zwemmer's, I think, not Schwemmer's, as you say. I must see Collier [local bookshop] has it and, if you agree I would get it reviewed in [a] Coventry paper.' In a letter in the same envelope Eva wrote: 'How very happy we were this morning to read that Jill has at last arrived. When I read that you had actually *seen* it reposing in a bookseller's window, I tried to imagine what your feelings would be. *I* should, in such a happy situation, have felt that I was walking on air and thought that the whole company of birds in the world were making sweet music in my ears.' She followed up on 4 November: 'Well, I have read "Jill". I like it very much indeed. I think it is beautifully written and some parts are deliciously fresh and pleasing, "All at once it seemed very cold. *The stars marched frostily across the sky.*" The bow-tie episode is *very good*, also the part where Jill takes shape in his mind. I felt very sad over the many times she eluded John, and wished so much for a happy end to all his worries.'

2 The 1944 film adaptation of Shakespeare's play, starring and directed by Laurence Olivier, with music by William Walton.

3 Sydney must have recommended a book by Verrier Elwin (1902–64), English-born Indian anthropologist and tribal activist.

11 November 1946

172, London Road, Leicester

My dear Mop & Pop,

I do apologise for not writing more than a note yesterday. I carried paper & envelope around with me but what with going from place to place to see different people I never had a chance to settle down. I was only there 26 hrs, of which about 3½ were spent in sleep.

I am enclosing this with *A Girl in Winter*, proof copy. It sh[d] form a contrast to *Jill*, being a very different sort of book. In *Jill* everything is clearly stated and comprehended: this deals with less explicit feelings & so I have tried to represent them by indirect reference & allegoric incident. I wonder if you will find it dull. All my friends do except Ruth.

I have 6 *Jills* which I will bring when I come on Saturday. They are bound in two shades of green, some light, some dark, and rather more ruthlessly guillotined, less nice on the whole than the blue variety.

You will be interested to hear that the College are attempting to speed inflation by giving everyone a £100 cost of living bonus. This has yet to pass the Grants Committee, and I imagine that it will be cut to £50 or £25 in the process.

Don't buy *Back*.[1] It is a rotten book. If I'd read the T.L.S on Sat. I shouldn't have.

I shall really have to settle the question of NALGO when I come: they wrote me a letter asking for money, though what for I don't gather. Also, can you hunt out my Savings Cert. number? I have to have it if I buy any more, I find.

Much love – see you Saturday,
Philip

1 By Henry Green. Shortly after this Philip gave his father his copy, for which Sydney thanked him on 28 November.

1947

12 January 1947

172, London Road, Leicester

My dear Mop and Pop,

– But principally, this time, to Mop, in answer to her very kind letter & to make up for the letter I didn't send on the 10th. The creature knew it ought to have written! but it was mithered and worried and so sent a poem instead (yes, the verse was by me).[1]

I am *so* sorry you have not been well – is all better now? I don't like to think of you being ill. [. . .]

Last night when I was going to sleep I remembered something I do periodically remember from my earliest childhood – a picture book about some Robber Rats who surprise an old-woman rat on the way to market and make her spill her basketful of round red Dutch cheeses. Do you recall this book at all? I always felt there was something sinister about those rats.

On Friday I saw *Great Expectations*,[2] but as I had no great exptns. was not disappointed when it proved to be a mediocre film. It does start well, but gets rather ordinary later on.

Do you remember my application at Southampton? Well, Peter Roe, one of the young men here, asked his sister (who was the person vacating the job) why they had not appointed me. The reason apparently was that they thought I should not keep the juniors in order! Perspicacious but annoying. She reported, however, that Miss Henderson, the Librarian, passed round my application, saying she had never seen one so well-written before. And since we are on the subject of trumpet-blowing, Bruce reports as he sends me a copy of the American *Toyshop* that the *East Hampton Star* says "But in the entire 250 pages . . . it is those few he devotes to the writing of poetry that are really an achievement . . . Fine, inspiring, understanding stuff. I suspect Mr. Crispin is a poet at heart." Now as you know I was largely responsible for that bit, so that makes me laugh.

You will be pleased to know that as from Aug. 1946 my salary has been £450 p.a. – back pay will be forthcoming and the new scale starts this month. Aren't I a rich creature!

Finally, are you responsible for the sudden reception by *The Times Literary Supplement* of *The North Ship*? As it is approx. 16 months since it was published it seems rather late in the day.[3] At any rate I had nothing to do with it! It gave me an awful turn, next to Landor and all. Well, since they *have* it, Bruce's girl on The Times sh[d] wangle a review for it, but I expect she has quite forgotten.

Is it any use my sending to Pop the Leicester Public Library copy of J. C. Powys' *Autobiography*? It is over 600 pages long but very easy to read. He is a sort of Honey-Campion type, only even more extraordinary. Let me know.

My dearest love to both,
Philip

1 The verse that Philip sent to Eva for her birthday cannot be identified.

2 The 1946 film, based on Dickens's novel, directed by David Lean and starring John Mills, Bernard Miles, Finlay Currie, Jean Simmons, Martita Hunt, Alec Guinness and Valerie Hobson.

3 Eva's reply of 13 January is prefaced with two lines by Mary Webb: 'Into the scented woods we'll go / And see the blackthorn swim in snow.' She writes: 'Last night, after a large dose of Mary Webb's poetry, I took up your North Ship being curious to see what I should think of it after reading hers. I was, as a matter of fact, quite startled to find how good and fine some of your poems are. Yes, I really do think you are a poet – first and foremost.'

16 February 1947

172, London Road, Leicester

My dear Mop & Pop,

My letters will have rather a piebald appearance until I use up all my varying kinds of paper. I hope you don't mind.

[. . .] I expect you noticed the advance notices of *Winter* in the T.L.S. and again this morning in the S.T. I have at last regained the proofs from the English dept. here and dislike the look of it. Miss Jones said it reminded her of Eliz. Bowen's *Death of the heart*[1] which I am in consequence reading. Dr Collins[2] said it was "gloomy" – plague take the fool!

I'm enclosing the birth cert. which was accepted without comment.

There is really not much to say, having said all this: I find it easy enough to keep existing but I fail to do anything original off my own bat: my correspondence course has suffered. I am sure we are only half alive in this weather: it'll be interesting to see if anybody comments on the apt conditions when *Winter* appears. As a matter of fact I think it shows up my descriptions as rather badly done. The reality, for a change, is more effective than the imagination.

Best love to both –
Philip

We have more oranges!

1 Elizabeth Bowen (1899–1973), *The Death of the Heart* was published in 1938.
2 Arthur Collins was appointed the first lecturer in English at Leicester University College (founded 1921) in 1929. Monica Jones, who was to become Larkin's lifelong lover, arrived as the second lecturer in 1943.

23 February 1947

172, London Road, Leicester

My dear Mop and Pop,

Well, here is another Sunday and the snow still here, looking brilliant in the half-sun. Do you know, it was quite warm yesterday? The streets were full of slush. But I think last night brought the old familiar frost again.

I am pleased to enclose this letter in a copy of the book. It arrived on Friday after going to Wellington first (my fault, that): I have since found it in the shops. So far as I can see there are no misprints in it – but there is one thing that mightily annoys me: an intentional mistake in grammar, that I saw safely through the proofs, has been *corrected*. It occurred in one of Anstey's speeches and was no little addition to the general humour thereof.[1] I am trying to get another 2 dozen copies of which you w^d doubtless like a dozen. You will tell me, won't you, if you see any reviews.

I was amused by the account of Pop's speech: Colin Gunner came over on Friday and said you had been "blowing off your mouth" in a manner which showed your mental faculties to be no way impaired by retirement.[2] So I looked forward to seeing the high spots.[3]

Thanks too to Mop for her letter. I bought two pairs of socks yesterday – a typical "silly" purchase, for although they are delightful colours, 12" foot, long legs, they are *pure wool* and therefore, Miss Sutcliffe tells me, will wear through in no time. She advises me to strengthen the heels & toes by preliminary darning: do you advise this?[4]

I do not know that I have much news: I went to the pictures in order to see *The private life of Henry VIII*, and Charles Laughton was as good as a tonic.[5] The scene where he eats and dismembers the capon made me roll about in my seat with laughter.

(Now the beastly power has suddenly gone off, at 11.15 a.m. What a country we do live in.)

I may go to London next weekend: the Slade are holding an exhibition somewhere in Bond St. and Jim wants to show me round.

The College is just barely warm enough. We shiver around in many cardigans, jumpers, &c, and in the library at any rate the students cling to the radiators like limpets. But on the whole I stay just warm enough.

Well, all is over now bar the shouting, & I shall have to bend my attention towards the future when I have time. One thing: it will be very easy to write a better book than *A girl in winter*. Don't they say some nice things about me, though?

Your affectionate offspring –
Philip

1 This hypercorrection still irritated Larkin when the paperback reprint of the novel appeared in 1974. In a letter to Charles Monteith of Faber & Faber (16 April 1974) he asked for the word 'with' to be reinstated in a sentence ending 'you would have to deal with', spoken by Anstey. The word was, he writes, 'cut out by your super-efficient editors in 1946'. He had intended it as 'a deliberate grammatical mistake [. . .] to show the muddle-headedness of the speaker'; 'it has irked me for over a quarter of a century'. *Selected Letters*, 503–4.

2 Sydney Larkin realised his ambition to retire early, in April 1944, at the age of sixty.

3 Sydney had been invited to propose the toast to 'The City of Coventry' at a dinner to celebrate the twenty-fifth anniversary of the Coventry Rotary Club. On 17 February Eva wrote: 'He has now the chance to tell the City the *truth*!' On 24 February she reported: 'Of course, Daddy created much laughter and interest by his speech which went down very well.'

4 In her letter of 24 February Eva wrote: 'I am interested to hear about your new socks. I have not known woollen socks to wear out rapidly, but then the wool which is used now-adays is not nearly as good as the pre-war variety. I should certainly darn the heels and toes before wearing, to strengthen them. What a capable creature you are becoming!'

5 A 1933 film directed and co-produced by Alexander Korda, starring Charles Laughton, Robert Donat, Merle Oberon and Elsa Lanchester.

2 March 1947

Royal Hotel, Woburn Place, Russell Square, London

My dear Mop & Pop,

Well! You can imagine how I am licking my fur this morning after reading what Michael Sadleir has to say about *Winter*![1] You will have to be very respectful to me in future, –

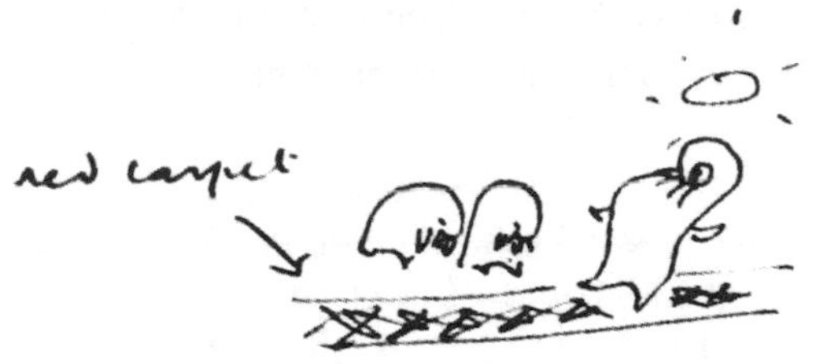

Seriously, I didn't think anyone w^{d} like it as much as that. I shall never disparage *Fanny by Gaslight* again.[2]

I was very pleased to get such a nice long letter from you last Wednesday. How good & kind of you to spend so much time writing to me. Concerning *Winter*, which occupies my thoughts mainly at present, I had *not* noticed the misprints (I never do) but they annoy me. The jacket is inoffensive to me at any rate. I have BEEN PAID for it – £27 – so can at last count myself at least a semi-professional author. The 2 doz. copies have not arrived yet, but I'll dispatch a dozen when they do. \<*Up left margin*> plus one signed for Auntie Nellie./

This hotel is "not quite our class". Though not annoyingly so. It seems mainly populated by football teams & (seemingly) a circus – at least when I came in last night there was a gentle giant in the foyer, at least 8 ft high. I blenched horribly & scuttled to my room, which is one cell in an endless corridor of cells.

I spent some time with Jim at the Slade exhibition. He is as taciturn as ever, and is living what *really* constitutes a bohemian life – cooking his own meals, spending his offdays at the National Gallery, & drawing in the evenings. The rest of the time has been spent with Ruth[3] & one of her friends, to whom I have promised (overgenerously, perhaps) free *Winters*. The weather has been really beautiful, sunny & springlike in the day, and we watched people feeding the pigeons in Trafalgar Square. The people hold their arms out with seed in the palms of their hands, & the pigeons perch on their arms & wrists to peck it up.

Tell Pop I have bought both of the Charles Williams reprints, so if he had felt inclined to do so he need not.

I continue taking the adexolin but it does not seem to dissipate my mild everpresent catarrh, nor prevent my rare, abstract sneezes – I call them abstract sneezes because they don't seem to be accompanied by a cold.

This fuel cut certainly seems to have come to stay, at least for the domestic consumer, such as we be, unluckily for us. I must say I don't suffer greatly – they do keep the college relatively warm – but it is such a nuisance to have no light in the shops. Don't you find it so?

Now I must fold this & post it. My very best love to both creatures from a long,[4] cold, but none the less cheerful creature. –

Philip

1 For their reactions to the *Sunday Times* review of *A Girl in Winter*, see Sydney's note of 2 March and Eva's letter of 3 March 1947, Appendix.

2 Michael Sadleir's 1940 novel about Victorian prostitution, made into a film in 1944.

3 Ruth Bowman was at this time in the second year of her degree course at King's College, London.

4 Perhaps 'loving' was meant?

13 April 1947

172, London Road, Leicester

My dear Mop & Pop,

Well, back again: Leicester and the college do not seem to have changed at all. Since Thursday I have worked solitarily in the Library, doing very little but clear up after the holiday. Almost nobody has been about: one felt like a lost soul. Jack Simmons, biographer of Southey, looked in and looked out again. He is a friend of A. L. Rowse[1] & indeed resembles him in a distant way.

Thanks for forwarding the letters: one contained the news that Messrs Lars Hokerberg have cabled an offer for Swedish bookrights of

Winter, which I have accepted on Watt's advice – 10% per copy, £30 advance. I *suppose* it will be a translation. So we shall all have to learn Swedish! Truly, it's a language I know nothing of at all.[2]

I also had another batch of press cuttings including Evening Standard (19/3/47), Liverpool Daily Post (26/3/47), Manchester Evening News (26/3/47), Daily Dispatch (27/3/47), and Oxford Mail (3/4/47). They are all fairly favourable – Edward Shanks suggests I am a woman using a pen-name.[3] Benighted old idiot. I have put them all in a little notebook – there are now sixteen in all. [. . .]

Did you notice that Somerset Maugham[4] had founded a prize of £500 p.a.? I wouldn't mind getting that. I think I shall ask someone to send my book in for it. A condition of winning is that you must travel at least 3 months – perhaps to Sweden!

I do hope everything is going well at Loughborough – give Kitty & Walter my love. What does Pop want for his birthday present – not a book, by any chance? Let me know.

The Budget "news" in the *S.T.* is a bit heartening, isn't it?

Best love to both,
Philip

I have finished the biscuits!

1 A. L. Rowse (1903–97), Cornish author and historian.

2 *Sommar blir vinter*, trans. Britta Gröndahl (Stockholm: Lars Hökerbergs bokförlag, 1947).

2 Edward Shanks (1892–1953), English journalist and critic.

3 W. Somerset Maugham (1874–1965), successful British author and playwright.

2 May 1947[1]

172, London Road, Leicester

My dear Kitty,

This is a gentle wave of the paw to hope you are both very comfortable & well.[2] Pop came over today and we shrank about the dusty, bitter streets for a few hours. Unless your nursing home is a sort of punishment-house you are very much better off there. We seem to be settled in another cold belt for good and all.

There is not much news here: I went with a party of students to Stratford on Wednesday to the theatre. I have also accepted an invitation to the students' dinner. So before long I shall be organising campfire rallies, tennis tournaments, community singing, and reunion rugger matches. The descent is very easy.

Otherwise my exam is looming very large in my view, though I expect you feel a million miles away from the world where exams take place – almost on a different planet. I wish I was. And nearly everybody wants me to visit them, or wants to visit me, which I think is a bore, but better, of course, than the other way round.

Many salutations. I look forward to seeing this new sprig of our ancient family.

Very much love,
Philip

1 Addressed to Mrs C. Hewett, 53 York Rd., Loughborough.
2 Kitty had just given birth to Rosemary (28 April 1947). Apart from the formal letter to Kitty and her husband Walter concerned with holidays, which Philip copied to Eva on 20 April 1969, this is the last letter which survives from Philip to his sister until 1972, twenty-five years later. Kitty seems to have destroyed all the others. It is preserved in a file containing letters from the 1970s related to Berrystead Nursing Home and the sale of Eva's house following her death. Kitty perhaps kept it because of its celebration of Rosemary's birth.

27 May 1947

<*Letterhead*> University College Leicester

My dear Mop & Pop,

Got back here after some 4 hrs! at about 9.30. I suppose it w^{d} be. Not exactly a joyride, but I munched my biscuits and was relatively at peace.

Enclosed are some B.U.'s.[1] I do hope they are enough, and of the right kind.

Once again I have to thank you for a very happy weekend. What struck me this time was really how young you both are – not young in the sense of silly, but young in keen response to things. Let Mop see a pretty patch of garden, or Pop get his nose into a new book, and the interest aroused is as quick and vivid as my own, and sometimes more so!

It makes home a very nice place to come to.

By the way, by a strange piece of fortune I have obtained some films for my camera from Belgium. So please don't worry Mr. C. on my account this year!

Love,
P.

1 Bread units: ration slips.

20 July 1947

Charlton Hotel, Wellington, Salop.

My dear Mop & Pop,

[. . .] Yes, as you will probably have heard, I paid a visit to Kitty on Friday and spent a happy 4 hours or so. I invented a game of "shake-a-paw" with Rosemary, who gave an occasional toothless grin. This Kitty found surprising and said it meant she had taken to me. I took her a few mangy cherries & she gave me two lettuces and some spring onions. [. . .]

But we'll talk a lot more when I arrive for next week end – if Kitty will let us.

All love,
Philip

13 September 1947

6 College Street, Leicester[1]

My dear Mop and Pop,

It is only Saturday night, but I thought I would start my letter to you – if not finish it – while I have a little time and feel in a talkative mood.

There is really quite a lot to tell you, though I don't expect I shall get it all down or even remember it.

Thank you, in the first place for your letter. [. . .]

My room here now is quite comfortable – or perhaps I should say it looks more like a room. I have two good lights, a little table to work at, a bookcase, 4 pictures & your calendar, a bowl of fruit (of my own buying), my gas fire (newly repaired), and plenty of books to read. This lodging will suit me, I think – it's not quite so good (I'm taking good in the widest sense) as 172 London Rd., it's less physically comfortable in some ways than Miss Davis, and while seemingly clean has a foul kitchen-stench that I abhor. The food is fairly adequate & there's always bread to fill up on. Tonight I intend to have a bath in the enormous dark brown "baths our grandfather used" type of bath. [. . .]

Sunday

I arose uncalled this morning and am writing this before breakfast. On Thursday I bought one of those 22/- large white sweaters (coupon free) that I mentioned. It is a good heavy garment and designed, I imagine, for those in peril on the sea.

And on Friday I went to tea at Kitty's. I enjoyed this quite a lot. Rosemary looked very well to me, what I call the 'wan look' quite gone, and after tea she had a fit of giggles when we went to look at her. She lay and chuckled and squeaked for quite five minutes and w^{d} have gone on if we had not departed. Earlier I took a photograph of her, but whether or not it will prove even in focus I can't guess.

I hope the photograph of me I sent a postcard asking for will not frighten the Swedes out of their skins.[2] I can't think of a better one, although I am not particularly fond of it. Before I send it off I will order three more prints from its number so that you may have another one. [. . .]

I don't think I need any of the things I left behind for the moment. I wonder when you will be at home & prepared to receive boarders – or one boarder, anyway. Perhaps there is nothing really to fetch, but I should very much like a taste of home sometime after this rather strange week in strange surroundings.

Very best love to both creatures,
Philip

1 Philip's landlady at 172 London Road required his room, so he moved into 6 College Street on 7 September 1947.

2 Publishers of the Swedish translation of *A Girl in Winter*.

26 October 1947

6, College St. Leicester

My dear Mop & Pop,

This is being started before breakfast, although ten o'clock has just passed. No – breakfast has just come and gone. I do not feel very cheerful this morning, though nothing lasting has happened to disturb my composure – I mention it only to account for any steely brevity that may make itself felt in my phrasing. The principal cross to bear is that my oafish lodgings-mate, Rose, has announced his intention of coming cycling with me this afternoon. Now, as it happens, Sunday afternoon is one time when I like to be alone. To have him with me – to have anyone with me, of course, but him in special – will largely destroy my delight. But what can one do? I feel that to refuse would be not only rude but self-important. I only hope he won't enjoy himself. I don't fancy he will.

I *am* sorry you expected me on the 19th. Instead, I went in the Melton Mowbray direction, to Hungerton and Beeby. One feature of the Leics. Countryside is the enormous sheds of ammunition & explosive, quite unguarded, along the roadside.

This week has been crazy week, for I have bought a camera. (I can see Pop's eyebrows becoming stiffer & more aggressive.) It is a "Puma Special", & I fear it is rather a *faux pas*.[1] (Wasn't one of grand-dad's endearing habits that of buying phony cameras?) Not that it's bad in itself, I imagine, though I can't say till I've seen what it does, but it is not really the kind of camera I need. It is a fixed focus with 3 exposure speeds – 1/25, 1/150, 1/450. So you can see it's only good for open air movement. It *won't* take time exposures, which is a great drawback. It takes 16 exposures on a roll, but I suppose the developing is more expensive as they have to be enlarged. Until I see what kind of results it produces, I can't make up my mind about it, but something tells me that I shall part with it when I have learned all I can learn off it. In case you think I am afraid to tell you the price, may I add that it was £6.7.9?[2]

This letter does not seem to contain much news so far, but in truth there is not a great deal to report. I get some amusement out of writing my book, but it is almost completely shapeless and without tone, The Library Association Record have asked permission to reprint a passage from *Winter* – the bit about teamaking fairly early on, ending "Why does he have to talk in that silly way?" I met Mr Kent in the street recently, and he had recovered from his influenza. He regretted not having seen Pop, whom he seems to regard as a stimulating agent. I look forward to any comments that Pop hears about his masterly article in his journal.

I am glad Rosemary liked her bowl (by proxy) – the drawing was not really meant for her, but for any infant. The sun is shining here today, but it's very windy – probably a cycle ride will be more of a curse than a blessing. Then tonight I shall stay in and write. How beautiful life becomes when one's left alone!

My very best love to both creatures. Let me know how life fares at "Creature Lodge, Coten End" –

Philip

1 Mark Haworth-Booth describes Larkin's cameras, and analyses his skill as an amateur photographer, in 'Philip Larkin as Photographer', *About Larkin* 42 (October 2016), 5–15. See also Haworth-Booth's foreword to Richard Bradford, *The Importance of Elsewhere: Philip Larkin's Photographs* (London: Frances Lincoln: 2015).

2 Sydney replied (27 October 1947): 'Comments on your camera are (1) I don't recognise the make. Whose make is it? (2) What "focal lengths" are given i.e. apertures, mine, e.g., are F23. 16. 11. 8. 5.6 and 4.5. Yours should be fairly wide for an exposure of 1/450. A useful time is about 1/10 except in midsummer. (3) It doesn't matter about time exposures, you can use your other for those. (4) As you say, proof of pudding is in the eating. Don't sell it until Dalton has put on another dose of purchase tax or otherwise made them less obtainable.' Hugh Dalton was Chancellor of the Exchequer at this time.

26 November 1947

6, College St., Leicester

My dear Mop and Pop,

Many thanks for your letter, received this morning rather latish (late-ish?). The post has been getting later recently. Yes, my weekend was spent almost entirely with Kingsley, who on Thursday (tomorrow) starts his Finals. I shall be very interested to see if he gets a First Class or not.

It's pretty chilly here, but I keep *fairly* warm. Lunches have started at the College today, in the new "Refectory" as they call it – good food but not very plentiful. I suppose we shall have to start wearing gowns now, to get splashed with gravy, etc. I shall feel rather queer.

When I was in Oxford I saw some St John's Xmas cards, very small & plain, but found they were 1/- each, so put them down hurriedly and walked away. Isn't everything a price!

My novel[1] is not going very well at present, & is causing me much worry. In fact I worry all day about it. I can't "focus" it: it blurs & shifts: I don't know the "key", so to speak, to which it shd be tuned. O by the way! Kingsley said: ". . . or psychology, as we would say nowadays." Me: "As we *should* say nowadays." Kingsley: "No, that means we *ought* to say it. We *would* say psychology, if we *were* to say it." Who's right, please? We always quarrel over this.

Mrs Sutcliffe has been displaying extraordinary virtuosity this week with a pig's trotter – it has appeared 3 times this week, finally in soup.

Yes, all being well, I'll see you on Saturday afternoon.

Love to both
Philip

1 This is almost certainly the fragment provisionally entitled *No for an Answer*, which fictionalises Larkin's relations with Ruth Bowman and his father around Christmas 1947. See James Booth (ed.), *Trouble at Willow Gables and Other Fictions* (London: Faber, 2002), xxxiii–xxxv.

9 December 1947 Postcard[1]

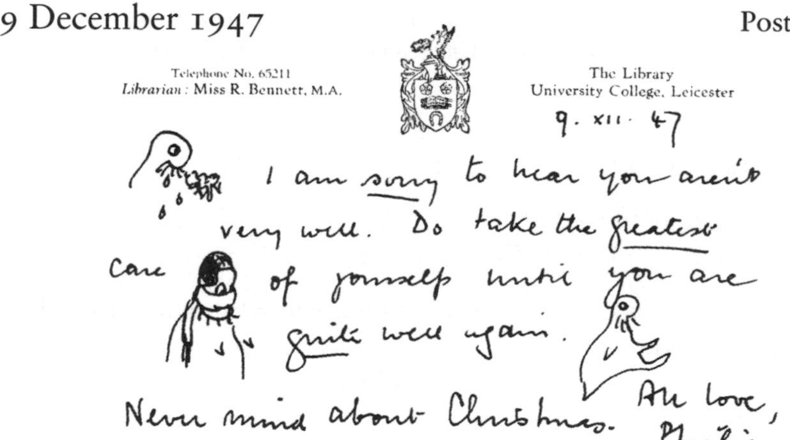
Telephone No. 65211
Librarian: Miss R. Bennett, M.A.

The Library
University College, Leicester

9. xii. 47

I am sorry to hear you aren't very well. Do take the greatest care of yourself until you are quite well again.

Never mind about Christmas.

All love,
Philip

1 On 3 December Eva wrote: 'Well, I have not felt at all well since my cold came on and have spent every morning in bed – but the bedroom is so cold, it is impossible to get the temperature above 42° and meals are a misery; that I get up about lunch time and spend the rest of the day in the dining room – crouched over the gas fire.'

1948

7 January 1948 Postcard[1]

[6 College St, Leicester]

Got a lift from Coventry Rd. bridge to Coventry in a saloon car, that did 60 m.p.h. some of the way, à la Jack Cann.[2] Good thing I did, too, for there were nearly 20 people at the stop. Passed Marshall walking to work, & picked up a copy of Connolly's *Condemned playground* for 2/- at W.H.S. Hope you are feeling peaceful & stronger, & are chivvying the nurses. All love – Philip

1 Between 7 January and 18 March 1948 thirty-seven postcards survive addressed to 'Sydney Larkin Esq., Ward 2 [later Ward 1], Warwick Hospital, Lakin Rd., Warwick', ten of which are printed here. Sydney was admitted to the hospital in January, initially for a gallstone operation. But his condition deteriorated and he died of cancer of the liver on 26 March.

2 John Cann, a friend of Sydney Larkin, had retired from a senior post in a brewery and had property interests in Mold, Newark and Scarborough. Cann visited Eva regularly in the 1950s and 1960s, and invited her to stay in Newark with his family.

12 January 1948 Postcard[1]

<*Letterhead with coat of arms*>
The Library, University College Leicester

Am thinking of you continually & hoping you are feeling better. Wet & miserable here.

All love,
Philip

1 Addressed to Sydney Larkin Esq., Ward 2, Warwick Hospital.

15 January 1948

<Letterhead with coat of arms> University College Leicester

My dear Mop,

Many thanks for your letter this morning: I was very glad to hear that Daddy was at least not conspicuously worse when you wrote.

The news about Uncle Ernie is sad & astonishing – how very ironic life can be. I can see that it is another trouble for you, not telling Daddy.[1] Poor pussy, you must be very worried: I am myself, when I have time to think. But we are still short-handed and are likely to remain so for many days yet, I fancy.

I expect, if it is convenient, that I shall be home about the same time on Saturday.

Was surprised to hear that Kingsley & Hilly are engaged today.

With very much love to you, also to Kitty,

Philip

1 On 13 January Eva wrote: 'Kitty & I have been very upset over bad news from Auntie Alice – London. Uncle Ernest was taken ill on Sunday – a slight stroke, and passed away about 4 o'clock in the afternoon. / Upon the advice of the Doctors I have decided not to tell Daddy of this sad happening. He is not well enough to be told yet. I have written to Auntie Alice & also Uncle Alf.' Ernest was one of Sydney's five elder brothers.

20 January 1948 Postcard[1]

[6 College St, Leicester]

Have got another batch of developments back from the photographer's today – 2 complete flops, 8 more or less flops, & six quite reasonable.

Hope things are going peacefully with you. One picture I took outside the hospital remains a blank.

My very best wishes & love,
Philip

1 Addressed to Sydney Larkin Esq., Ward 2, Warwick Hospital.

23 January 1948 Postcard[1]

[6 College St, Leicester]

Many thanks for letter: I'm glad things are no worse – or were no worse.

I shall be arriving about five tomorrow as usual. I do hope you are feeling well.

With much love,
Philip

1 Addressed to Mrs Sydney Larkin, 73 Coten End, Warwick.

26 January 1948 Postcard[1]

[6 College St, Leicester]

A quiet journey – though very quick – Walter set me down at the clock tower at 8.30 a.m. precisely. Things busy here. I hope you are managing better now the heavier & more useless creatures have departed. Poor pussy, I wish I c[d] stay & cheer you, but I don't suppose I c[d] cheer you if I did stay & I certainly shd make *work*. But receive my best love and closest thoughts.

P

1 Addressed to Mrs Sydney Larkin, 73 Coten End, Warwick.

26 January 1948 Postcard[1]

[6 College St, Leicester]

Had a swift ride here in the shooting brake – Coventry very busy at 8.0 in the morning, but after steering Walter through it I fell asleep. I do hope your improvement is holding ground and advancing. I find I have an extra pencil in my pocket & am conscience stricken lest I have taken yours by mistake. Do forgive me if I have.

All greetings & love,
Philip

1 Addressed to Sydney Larkin Esq., Ward 2, Warwick Hospital.

4 February 1948 Postcard[1]

[6 College St, Leicester] Wednesday

It has gone much colder here: I hope you are not feeling the draught through your windows. This afternoon I encountered a garrulous & learned schoolmaster who said he was a brother of Gillie Potter: this chap was comical enough.[2] There is little news here: I go out to Leon's tonight, Leon of *Plato*, for "intellectual enjoyment", as Cobbett calls it. Precious little, I'll bet. Faber's have turned down my poems, as I thought they would. Hope you are enjoying your eggs.

All love,
Philip

1 Addressed to Sydney Larkin Esq., Ward 2, Warwick Hospital.
2 'Gillie Potter' (Hugh Peel) (1887–1975): comedian and broadcaster.

12 February 1948 Postcard[1]

[6 College St, Leicester] Thursday

A quite unremarkable day: a letter from Kingsley bitterly complaining about the amount of married life spent with either his wife's parents or his own! I sympathise with the poor chap. I wonder if you have started on *Penguin island* yet. I hope you are well & 'finding your feet', as the saying goes.

With all best love,
Philip

1 Addressed to Sydney Larkin Esq., Ward 1, Warwick Hospital.

24 February 1948 Postcard[1]

[6 College St, Leicester]

Warmer weather here is melting the snow, so I hope Mop has been able to pay you a visit. I hope also you are not feeling lonely in your new room – did you have to leave *Esquire* behind you? I think a lot about you & hope you are feeling better. There is not much news here:

Nottingham have taken up my references, I hear from Buttrey.[2] They seem to want a shopwalker – someone to 'please all people with whom he comes in contact', or something like that.

All love,
Philip

1 Addressed to Sydney Larkin Esq., Ward 1, Warwick Hospital.
2 Chairman of the Library Committee at Wellington.

1 March 1948 — Postcard[1]

[6 College St, Leicester]

Have been hoping all day that you are more comfortable than on Sunday. I think it is cooler out, and I hope you feel the benefit of it. I had an uneventful journey back here, dozing much of the time, thinking about you & hoping you are recovering equilibrium. Not much to be seen in Coventry except the usual pinchbeck shops & the sour cathedral.[2] I wrote to Auntie Nelly saying you appreciated her card.

With all love & good wishes,
Philip

1 Addressed to Sydney Larkin Esq., Ward 1, Warwick Hospital.
2 Coventry's medieval cathedral had been reduced to a shell by the German bombing of 1940.

11 March 1948 — Postcard[1]

Leicester

Today I tried to photograph the cat I told you of yesterday: I lay down to get a portrait & it promptly walked over me. So I passed the camera to an onlooker & asked them to take the cat, washing itself, on me. Whether it will come out I don't know. I hope you are feeling well today. Nothing of note has happened – I have booked a seat to watch the Australians ("What Australians?")[2] A chap came for interview today I used to see about Oxford in 1940. This weekend, warn Mop, I shall be obliged to return on *Sunday* evening, for work on Monday.

My very best wishes to you & all love,
Philip

1 Addressed to Sydney Larkin Esq., Ward 1, Warwick Hospital.
2 The Australian cricket team which visited England in 1948 was captained by Don Bradman, who was making his fourth and final tour of England.

18 March 1948 Postcard[1]

[6 College St, Leicester]

Chilly & sunny here – have taken a photograph or two. Hope you are getting on satisfactorily, and think of you hourly. Tonight I am dining out with Leon, the Christian philosopher: I hope he won't trumpet his tenets too loudly through the room, but he is a very clever man.

Much love to you,
Philip

1 Addressed to Sydney Larkin Esq., Ward 1, Warwick Hospital. Sydney Larkin died of cancer of the liver on Good Friday, 26 March 1948.

11 April 1948[1]

6 College St., Leicester

My dear Mop,

I wonder if you will be expecting a letter on Monday as usual! Although there is nothing to say, I can send you my good wishes on this bright Sunday morning. I have just written to Poynton to thank him for his letter: then I really have no other letters to engage me, and I may go out into the country for a while on my bike.

The journey home last night was quite uneventful, except for a girl in the seat next to me who would read my book, and by mischance it seemed to bristle with love affairs & marriage problems with every page I turned. Therefore in desperation I let it lie open on my knee and stared out into the gathering darkness, as if such stuff could not even hold my attention. She read & reread the two exposed pages.[2]

I have just wrapped up 4 prs. winter wools & stowed them in 4 inches of dust on the top of my compactum, or cupboard (brown gents').

Love to you, to K & W & to baybay.
Philip

1 Addressed to Mrs Sydney Larkin, 53 York Road, Loughborough, Kitty's home. Written in ballpoint.
2 Eva replied on 12 April: 'How very nice it was of you to send me the usual "Monday" letter! [. . .] Kitty & I had to smile over the fact that you were not able to read your book (by Sidney Campion?) on the journey back. Your bus companion would have quite a lot to tell her girl friend when she reached home. [. . .] I took Rosemary out into the park yesterday morning. I have been busy this morning "doing" my room.'

14 April 1948 — Postcard[1]

[6 College St, Leicester]

Many thanks for your two letters & all the enclosures. It looks as if Maton[2] intends to be there, doesn't it? Yes, book my seat to Leicester if that is all right by you. Gunner is in Rhodesia, building, as I expect you noticed.

There is not a great deal of news here – I hope at long last to get my photographs on Friday (2 of Rosemary included) & if so will bring them over on Sunday: I'll definitely come on Sunday afternoon, if that suits you. The "whisperings" concerning the job here grow more unfavourable, I'm afraid – it'll be settled by the end of the month.[3] Still, it can't be helped. Goodbye dear puss, & DON'T WORRY – there's NOTHING TO WORRY ABOUT.

All love,
Philip

1 This and subsequent letters are addressed to Mrs E. E. Larkin or Mrs Sydney Larkin, 53 York Road, Loughborough, Kitty's home. Eva also wrote to her son from this address.
2 Maton has not been identified.
3 It seeems that, as well as applying to Nottingham (see card of 24 February 1948), Philip had also applied for internal promotion at Leicester. See letter of 13 May 1948.

Formal portraits of Sydney and Eva Larkin from the late 1920s.

Philip photographing his sister Kitty in the early 1930s; presumably taken by Sydney Larkin.

Plate 8

Larkin's photograph of the entrance to Warwick Hospital, where his father died on 26 March 1948.

'First day at 12 Dixon Drive' (August 1948). Though Larkin chose to record this moment, he did not take his usual care to focus the camera correctly.

29 April 1948

6 College St., Leicester

My dear Mop,

Thank you for your two letters – I am returning the circular to Warwick, though I don't think it really merited so much trouble.

The 15/- is $10/7^{d} + 4/6^{d} = 15/1^{d}$ – fare to Lichfield, you see, puss.

Regarding the rent of Penvorn, I am as much in the dark as you about it. £20 a qr. sounds logical: if it came on Oct 1st it should also come on Jan 1st & April 1st & July 1st. I don't remember any such money coming in and I imagine that the Manager of the bank would be the only person who w^{d} know, as I don't think it comes through Odell's,[1] does it? If they are paid into Lloyds at W., I should have thought Blenkinsop could have found out by ringing the manager up. Anyway, I should reply by saying that the last entry you can discover was £20 for Oct. 1st, and that you don't know that any other sum was received. Suggest that he checks it if he is dubious. Odell's are the auctioneers, and they are at present supposed to be enquiring whether the rent can be increased. That $w^{dn't}$ affect the payment, though. (The "paying in book" might be called a deposit book.)

Yes, include Lees' bill.

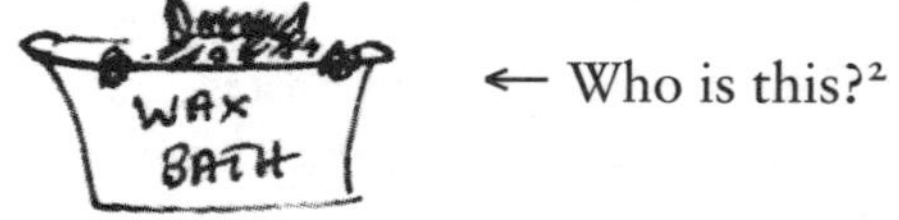

← Who is this?[2]

I still don't know if my friends are coming or not: will send you a postcard. Had a letter from poor Doctor Goetz, wondering what has happened, also one from Alf,[3] sounding inarticulate but friendly.

My best love to you: be a restful puss: lie in the window in the sun.

Philip

1 Solicitor.

2 Eva had injured her wrist. On 27 April she wrote: 'The hospital are giving me treatment twice a week for my wrist. This morning I had it immersed for ½ hour in a hot wax bath and at the end of that time it came out looking as if it had a wax glove on it. This I had to peel off and then do certain exercises.'

3 Alfred Larkin: Sydney Larkin's brother in Lichfield, with whom the family had stayed during the blitz in 1940.

30 April 1948 Postcard

Leicester

I have received word that Kingsley is going to pay me a visit this weekend and so I feel I shan't be able to visit you on Sunday. I do hope you don't mind. Write to me about anything you are uncertain of – two wooden heads are better than one. Get fat! Get fat!

 All love Philip[1]

1 The following Thursday, 6 May 1948, Eva replied that she felt 'very depressed and miserable – although I suppose I ought not to tell you this – but I find it impossible to keep it to myself. Is there, do you think, any hope for a broken & remorseful heart?'

13 May 1948

<*Letterhead*> University College Leicester; coat of arms

My dear ,

I expect my telegram came along at the leisurely pace this morning to tell you the sad news – I don't think I ever had a chance, once the applicants had applied. I think it is unusual to be shortlisted but not interviewed: What Pop w^{d} call "a rotten way of doing things".[1] A man named Barker was appointed, from Edinburgh Univ. – not Scots. He stutters. So we shall be yammering at one another like 2 curious birds in the zoo.

Dr Marshall sent me a copy of *Local Govt. Finance* today & a short letter.

Isn't the weather fine today? I have done nothing at all – a plague on life at present, as for many years past &, I expect, to come.

Tomorrow to the Red Lion, Wellington, for the weekend: I wonder what you will do. Seven enormous pairs of socks smile sweetly at me as I go in my room, all together. Dear puss, I hope you lay your head on your paws and snooze long snoozes: has your cold gone? I do hope so.[2] Have you introduced Rosemary to Bruin properly yet?

I am writing in the library – 8 p.m., very summery evening. We shall meet next week at Warwick, shan't we: if you feel the urge to visit me at

Leics (always welcome) my best possible day is I think Thursday – free 1–5.30 p.m.

<*Up right margin*> My best love to the puss, Philip[3]

1 It seems that Larkin had applied for an internal promotion at Leicester, and been shortlisted but not interviewed.
2 On 16 May Eva wrote: 'I *do* so hate to worry you but if you could come over on Monday or Tuesday, \(it would be evening)/ there is much I should like to talk to you about. I felt extremely miserable yesterday – I do hope I shall get more at peace soon – else I do not see how I can keep going.'
3 'Puss' must be Eva herself.

10 June 1948[1]

<*Letterhead*> University College Leicester; coat of arms

Dearest Mop,

I'm really not a great comfort in time of trouble, am I. *Please* do not mind my miseries. They are far of less account than yours.[2]

I'll try to see another house tomorrow.

I was only 10 minutes late here – I do hope you found your 'bus safely.

All my love,
Philip

1 Addressed to Mrs E. E. Larkin, 53 York Road, Loughborough, Kitty's home.
2 On 11 June Eva wrote: 'Dearest Creature, [. . .] Don't think for one moment that I blame you for being somewhat out of humour on Thursday, I only feel too sorry that circumstances are making me one more problem for you to deal with. I wish I could manage to be on my own. I felt very, very miserable when I returned to Loughborough – but it was not your fault.'

15 June 1948

6 College St., Leicester

My dear Mop,

I sent you a telegram late this afternoon asking you to ring me up at a college no. at 7.0 tonight, but as nothing happened between 7–7.10 I expect it didn't reach you. It was not urgent, as it turned out. Harrison's told me when I went there about two o'clock that 35 Byway Rd (the second of the two we saw last week) was going for nearest to £3,000, without auction, and I wondered if you'd like it. But after trying to ring up Ivor & failing, and sending you a telegram, I rang Harrison's again & found it had been sold. It w^{d} have been a bargain, but the garden *was* large, wasn't it?

Then Turnor's[1] rang up & said that Warren's bottom price for 12, Dixon Drive was £2,950. This is not a bargaining offer, just a statement. It seems a lot to me, & the overall price will probably be £3000 (with stamp duty & paying them for the coal & what not). On the other hand it *is* well placed, and for that I shd be sorry to lose it.

If we bought it, do you think you would like it? If you don't think you would, if you think you'd feel "Oh, Philip's landed me in this horrid little hole", then we'd better leave it. If you think you would like it, perhaps you'd ring me up.

I am very anxious not to worry you: we'll leave it till July if you like till you get fatter. It's a heavy job, thinking about moving.

All my love,
Philip

<*Up left margin*> I don't know even if we have sufficient cash for the deposit!

1 Auctioneers and estate agents, Loughborough.

21 June 1948

<*Letterhead*> University College Leicester; coat of arms

My dear Mop,

Well, we now *have* the house, the offer was duly gobbled up, and I have paid £295 to Turnor & signed a deed of some description "for and on behalf of Mrs Eva Emily Larkin".

I noted from the deed that we have bought the gas cooker & the cooker & the curtain rails & rings (& something else, I can't recall what, but I don't think – oh, I remember: the garden shed) but not the electric light shades & bowls nor the shelves in the garage.

Will you write to Blenkinsop, saying you have named him as solicitor in connection with the purchase of 12 Dixon Drive?

Here's luck to us![1]

All love,
Philip

1 Eva and Philip moved together into 12 Dixon Drive on 17 August 1948.

23 September 1948

Picture postcard[1]

[Eynsham]

Spending a good time here, and I hope you are "putting your fur on" & trotting round the neighbourhood. Ruth has picked up an awful cold but is otherwise alright. We eat lots of apples & I'm quite well again. The cat here is lovely.

Love especially to you,
P

1 High Street, Eynsham. Addressed to Mrs E. Larkin, 53 York Road, Loughborough. Eva was too anxious to spend her nights alone in 12 Dixon Drive, so when Philip was not there she moved back in with her daughter.

29 December 1948

Picture postcard[1]

[Dorchester]

Not a good picture of a very pretty town! We got here about 5.30 yesterday after a crowded journey, & today have seen the museum, Hardy's birthplace, "Mellstock" churchyard & walked altogether nearly 10 miles![2] Tomorrow to Weymouth & the sea.

Love,
Philip

1 High Street, East, Dorchester. Written in ballpoint.
2 Philip was taking a winter holiday with Ruth Bowman.

1949

27 July 1949[1]

<*Letterhead*>
Lupton Hotel, Churston Ferrers near Brixham, S. Devon

My dear Mop,

Yesterday I bought a little bottle of suntan oil, & of course today thick clouds obscure the sky. However, it does not look really serious, and anyway I don't think I shall bathe today. I expect you will have received my postcard by now, though it is a mystery to me that anything or anyone ever leaves this place. *You* never would. From the front door to the front gate is a brisk walk of seven minutes – from our house, say, to Victoria Park gates: it is a pleasant enough stroll by day, but *by night* quite eerie enough to set my nerves on edge. It lies through fields & plantations of conifers, etc.

I expect you will want to know "everything" – I have a double room, furthest away from the bathroom, am kept awake by the noise of the electric plant going in a separate building all night, the meals are *inadequate*, & take so long to appear that they might be coming up from the lodge by hand, & the company liberally sprinkled with uninhibited children. On the credit side, the house is certainly very large – I hesitate to say very beautiful – & peace & silence can easily be obtained. (As I write the library-cum-billiard room is suddenly infested with women: still, they have gone now.)

Since arriving I have not done much that *sounds* much: Yesterday I walked to Elbury Cove after lunch, found it (with great difficulty) and bathed in warm calm sea. Then I went over to Brixham, where Bruce was just finishing his novel, and we spent the time at the Yacht Club and back at his home, where his mother, deafer & more genial than ever, provided a supper of cold fowl, salad, fruit salad, gorgonzola & coffee. I borrowed five books (plus his own in typescript) & made my nervous way back home.

I very much wonder how you are faring at Loughborough – expect you will have a tale or two when I return. (A dog is now whining under the window & a small assembly of guests engaged in some hostile demonstration.)

I am enclosing, if the maids leave it on my mantelpiece where it is at present, a small sprig of lavender, which you can picture if you like growing in clumps on the high wall of Churston Churchyard. This is in one of the lanes, turning & tangling you deeper into the countryside, that I walked along when going to Elbury: it all reminded me of earlier holidays with squashed snakes on the road, grasshoppers, crickets & a dozen sorts of small butterflies & moths such as we don't see in Leicester, or I don't anyway. All the lanes are extremely nice & a treat to stroll in.

Mind you see a bit of life in Loughborough, always supposing there is any which seems highly improbable to me, as Bruce w^{d} say.

With all love,
Philip

P.S. – Your letter has just arrived by second post – pretty momentous things afoot, eh? Anyway, about the Insurance, I am not a very legal creature, you know, and feel that I really don't know enough to advise you against old Blenky's monitions. I think I sh^{d} write back saying that if in his opinion you wouldn't be the loser in any circumstances (if any other calamity than fire occurred, for instance) you think you had better do as he suggests & suspend the Alliance policy in favour of the M of Works one. Only I sh^{d} send him the *Penvorn* policy (if you can!) & ask him to do the letter to the Alliance people. Say you are uncertain how to phrase it & feel he'd do it better!

Congratulations to Walter – whatever happens, it's nice to think *someone* values you at £1,000 p.a.

Love to all, incl. Rosemary,
Philip

1 Addressed to Mrs E. Larkin, 53 York Rd, Loughborough, Kitty's home. The archive preserves just this letter and six picture postcards from 1949, sent from Cambridge, Dedham, Churston Ferrers, Lyndhurst and Oxford (2).

1950

28 March 1950 Lettercard[1]

11 Haslemere Rd, Sketty, Swansea, Glamorgan[2]

My dear Mop,

I do hope you are finding a rest at Loughborough, & managing to get about for walks, if the weather is warmer than it is here. Rather wish I'd not changed those pants, atween you and me.[3] Swansea is definitely colder than the midlands were when I left them.

About the weekend: I think I shall return on Friday night, but shall devote Saturday to visiting Lincoln at last. To avoid giving you a lonely day in the house, would you like not to return till Saturday night, Saturday afternoon, even Sunday morning? I can probably manage the few bites I shall need – meals here aren't so enormous. With best love to you & all.

Philip

1 Addressed to Mrs Larkin, 53 York Road, Loughborough.

2 Larkin was staying with Kingsley and Hilary Amis.

3 Eva replied on 29 March: 'Of course you ought not to have changed those pants – remember that I thought it very unwise at the time. I am glad that I brought sufficient warm clothing here for it has been bitterly cold ever since I came.'

4 June 1950 Postcard[1]

Belfast[2] Sunday

Arrived safely after comfortable & good journey – but am feeling like a mouse set down in a bus station. Wish you were here to be frightened too! The boat was extremely comfortable: had to share cabin with an RAF officer. Mrs Patterson has received me, shown me the outside of the University, & tried to enhearten me: this latter is no easy job, however. Would I were back at Dixon Drive, & all well! Belfast is an unattractive city & I am sitting at present in front of what I suppose is the City Hall, watching the pigeons & wondering where the devil my lunch is coming from. Everywhere looks shut! The clock has said 11.40 for about 35 mins so it cannot I suppose be relied on. Now I hope you are treating yourself to a good restful weekend: be careful Mr Cann doesn't get you on a horse. My regards to Mr & Mrs, & the family. Much love to you. Oh dear Oh dear,

Philip

1 This card and the next are addressed to Mrs Larkin, 95 London Road, Newark on Trent, Notts., ENGLAND. Eva was staying with Sydney's friend John Cann and his family.
2 Philip had travelled to Belfast for his interview for the post of Sub-Librarian at Queen's University. He was appointed with a start date of the beginning of October.

5 June 1950

Dublin

Here for some sightseeing in brilliant sun: hope you are getting some of it! Sorry to say my hayfever has started up *in full force*. There's not much news except that I am advised that if there *is* a favourite for this beastly job, *I'm it*. This really disconcerts me more than certain failure. Make sure you are getting plenty of sun & rest.

Much love,
P

24 September 1950[1]

Digby House, Stoughton Drive South, Leicester

My dear Mop,

What rain! What gloom! It has been pouring all morning & I've had a to & fro walk in the rain to breakfast & back. I also tried a bath but there was hardly any hot water.

I hope your cold has gone & that you are feeling well again. [. . .] A rather souring depression has begun to invade me at the thought that this is the last Sunday, &c.

Regarding your person, I sh^{d} say myself that it w^{d} be advisable to set up house with someone considerably poorer than yourself only if you liked them very much and found them extremely heartening & sympathetic – the sympathy would be necessary to overcome the financial adjustments that would continually be cropping up. I don't think money should be put before sympathy or liking, but I think it would be wise, other things being equal, to team up with someone of relatively equal means. Not having seen your present candidate. I can't say how she might do, but I expect you can decide that yourself.

There's no news here – I go on living quite comfortably & extravagantly, like one under sentence of death. This next week will be devoted to final packing & despatching. When I was crossing Victoria Park in my Duffle coat a little girl pointed at me & cried "A man going on a ship!" I thought: You've said it. Rosemary's query about the beetle has gone down very well.

I am extremely angry about this rain, as I had planned to go & say goodbye to King's Norton Church this afternoon. Then there is tea at Mollie's (!) for I hope the last time. Barker is going too. We had a furious party on Friday till early morning: no one shall say that I did not go out in a blaze of glory. On Wednesday I'm standing all my colleagues dinner somewhere or other. On Thursday I'll come to see you, isn't that right?

I'm writing to Clemersons[2] about the bookcase now. [. . .]

Very much to you & to all with you,

Philip

1 This and subsequent letters are addressed to Eva at Kitty's home, 53 York Road, Loughborough.

2 A removal and furniture storage company in Loughborough.

1 October 1950

Queen's Chambers, Queen's University, Belfast

My dear Mop,

I'm sure I can't imagine when this letter will reach you: probably Wednesday morning! Anyway, here & now it is Sunday afternoon & I am alive & well.

Let me say again that I was disappointed not to see you on Saturday though the weather was so beastly that it was hardly a day to come out, was it? I got off in good order at 4.17: the train *did* go through Loughborough but didn't stop. Manchester looked the depths of dreariness: grey, drizzling, empty, ruined, with just a few lights here & there. Liverpool was much better. We sailed – that's the "royal plural"; I hadn't anyone with me – on the "Ulster Duke" in good time. I ate some hyoscin[e] tablets & some fish & chips, & sat on deck in my duffle coat writing up my diary as we edged out of the complicated docks. It takes a full hour to leave Liverpool, I timed it: I felt rather mournful as I saw we had cast off, but a spell at my diary cheered me up,[1] & I went to bed about 10.45 in a nice single cabin. There was a little velvet convexity in the wall, circular, with a hook above it. I couldn't think what it was for a moment, then I realised it was for a watch to hang on! So I hung mine up!

We had a quiet crossing & after breakfast. I taxi'd up here & spent the morning installing myself. At first I didn't like my room, but now I don't mind it. Imagine a main road, like Leicester London Road at, say, Dr James' with trams still going down it. Build on Victoria Park a big building like K.H.S. Coventry, with a big divided lawn & a statue in front of it – that's Queen's. Plant trees on the other side of the road, turn Dr James' house into a tall red-brick Dutch-style house, with an identical one on each side of it, knock them into one, & that's Queen's Chambers. Inside it is like a very cheerless very bare hotel: it reminds me very much of some cheap hotels I have stayed at. But I shan't mind much. My room is at the front. I overlook Queen's & the trams, second floor (fairly high). It is about the size of the Dixon Drive drawing room, but not so well furnished! It contains:

1 single bed
1 wardrobe (quite good)
1 armchair (not so good, wooden arms)
1 desk (not bad, but no lock)
1 cupboard-cum-bookcase
1 tiny rug beside the bed
1 bedside table
1 bedside lamp
1 radiator (6d meter)
1 wastepaper basket
1 steel-tubing chair at the desk (horrid!)

This may sound a lot, but in fact it leaves a great expanse of green rubber-lino which appears to "floor" the whole house, & there are no pictures on the wall. Obviously I shall have to do some furnishing. But I can't grumble. I have been put in the *wrong* room! The Warden says since I am in I had better stay: but if I had arrived *after* a certain Mr Grahame \instead of before!/ I should have had another, less *nice* room. I've seen it.

The Warden seems pleasant enough: a small, old-maidish historian with a passion for Jane Austen & chess.[2] I think we shall get on. The only meal I've so far had was lunch: if I were marking it like an essay I should give it β or β–. However! . . . Another thing I can see myself needing is an electric kettle: no evening grub here, after about 6.30. Hungry to bed, hungry to rise. The weather looks beautiful outside & methinks I will go a stroll. It's extraordinary to think I'm in Ireland. It looks just like Leicester, except for a yellow A.A. sign saying "Bangor. Newtonards. Donaghadee. ←."

My luggage arrived safely, though I *believe* I've lost a strap – & if so I may lose more, as 2 more suitcases had straps on, sent on Friday. Bloody thieving Irish!

I hope you have not been anxious about me (or anything else). The heather saw me through all right. Tonight I have an invitation to dinner at the Graneeks',[3] so I shall be spared that awful dreary first evening. I must say it would not displease me to see you peering up at this house as I sit looking down at the people! Write & tell me all you are doing.

My love to Kitty, also to Rosemary, a manly clap on the back for Walter, & my very best-quality love for yourself.

Philip

1 He also began drafting the unfinished poem 'Single to Belfast' (Motion, *Philip Larkin*, 197).
2 J. C. Beckett.
3 Jacob ('Jack') Graneek was Librarian at Queen's University.

15 October 1950

Queen's Chambers, Belfast

My dear old Moth,

Your letter turned up quite late – Friday evening – & I was beginning uneasily to wonder if you had gone down the bath plug, & to meditate enquiring. Still, I needn't have worried: you will always get my letter, I suppose, on Tuesday – right? & I shall always get yours on Friday. This is another sunny Sunday, really lovely weather: perhaps as I have no social engagements today I may go out this afternoon. Yesterday (Saturday) I cycled along Belfast Lough to Carrickfergus, a little historic port where William of Orange landed in 1690. The weather was cloudy & windy, & I sat on a seat on the esplanade trying not to shiver & watching the little waves slapping the pebbled beaches. The town is drab & mainly stone-coloured: it has a castle & a squarish dull-looking harbour. I found a dirty-looking café & had some fish & chips for tea, then pedalled home. The way back was nicer, though the wind was against me: the sun had come out, & the sky over the Lough was very shifting & full of pretty clouds, while on the landward side the hills were a dark green. I met a peacock too, just as if I were walking about the back lanes of Warwick under the Castle wall!

I am enclosing three rather poor photographs for your interest: (1) is a general view of the front. You can see it's not unlike K.H.S. Coventry, can't you. (2) Is the Library: this is at the extreme left-hand end of the front, not shown on (1). The Library is the sunlit, religious-looking, hideous building. (3) is Queen's.[1] [. . .]

My best love to all of you, & especially to the old moth,

Philip

1 See Plate 9A for Larkin's later carefully composed photograph of QUB.

22 October 1950

Queen's Chambers, Belfast

My dear Mop,

[. . .] So there are more "persons" on the horizon, are there?[1] That is encouraging news, and I shall be eager to hear how they strike you. I do think that in one way you would stand a better chance of a happy "new life" with a congenial new person as long as Kitty & I were enough in evidence to talk now and again of the old days – I find, myself, incidentally, that I quite often think of Dixon Drive now, the roses & the long summery evenings when Peter[2] might call or I should be clipping the hedge: it seems still very real – and that such a congenial person would give you a great many new interests & would help to run the day to day routine in a way that would leave you more relaxing time, which is very important. I quite understand that after a lifetime spent in the family a venture like this must seem a fearsome risk, and a fearful *bother*: Well, I agree it is a bother – though I & the rest will certainly help all we can, I'm sure – but if you do meet a similarly-situated lady, whom you like and who is good tempered, quiet & sympathetic, then I don't think it should be too much of a risk. £2,500 should get a nice house. [. . .]

Love to all, & a special consignment for old Moth.

Philip

1 Eva had advertised for a live-in companion. She sent the cutting to Philip on 20 October:

WIDOW would like to meet lady, with view to sharing Furnished House in Loughborough, and for Companionship. Free accommodation; other expenses shared by arrangement.—Write 84, Echo

2 In a letter of 12 January 1947, shortly after his arrival at Leicester University College, Larkin mentions Peter Roe as 'one of the young men here'.

29 October 1950

Queen's Chambers, Belfast

My dear old Mop,

Sunny & dry here – for the moment. But in Belfast the most reliable-looking day has a habit of sudden cracking right across and ending in rain and dismalness. I don't think I ever saw a gloomier day than *last* Sunday: it rained all day, and the sky was like one enormous bruise. Today looks considerably better.

This week has been an expensive one for I have bought clothes. Total spent £11.10.2 – and really very little to show for it. On Wednesday I went to Austin Reed's & bought three pairs of Wolsey short pants – 82/6!!!! – a shirt & 2 pairs of 12" socks. Really I don't know why I bought such expensive ones: there are plenty of utility ones about for about 6/9. The socks were the height of dullness, a plain grey & a plain brown. Then yesterday I went tweed-hunting: having been told of a place near here I went there on the bus, & found in a little country town a real tweed-centre, where it is woven. I was shown a kind of Aladdin's cave of tweeds, fascinating, two rooms full, in all textures and colours, at 12/6 & 15/- the yard. At least I say all textures & colours, but in fact none of them really caught my fancy: some I liked were too loose for a suit, & one I did like was "suitable" (fearsome pun) but there wasn't enough of it. In the end I bought 7 yards of a very sober one – the colour of stagnant bogwater, a kind of very very dull silvery brown with a faint aura of heather. This I shall get made up in Belfast for 8 or 9 guineas – so the total cost will be considerably lower than Austin Reed's offer of £23/15/-. O extravagant creature! Incidentally, yes, I do think it would be wise to buy clothes now. Anything containing wool is going to increase in price next year, I'm afraid.

Q.U.B. not O.U.B.![1] Queen's University Belfast. Now let me look at your long and interesting letter. [. . .]

I hope you found the visit to Dr Folwell lastingly beneficial: I am sure it is best to tell her anything that preys upon you, for she can only help if she knows your chief enemies. I don't think the subscription will bust you – all in all \with the 1/-'s/ it works out to about 8d a week, doesn't it? If you had *one* glass of beer on a Saturday night it would cost more than that.[2]

[3]

[. . .] This week has provided more noise-news: Tuesday night I was kept awake from 12–1.30, SIMPLY FURIOUS, so on Wednesday night I tramped up & bearded the lions, or one West Indian lion at any rate. He was very charming & pleasant, but returning from a game of billiards on Thursday night I found my bed playfully standing on its end! However there has been a considerable improvement since then after midnight.

Hoping you don't get any more mouse trouble.[4] Regarding your advertisees, if one can call them that, I'm very sorry M[rs] Pell was a flop: I shouldn't answer the rogue Gamble.[5] I wonder what you thought of the other two. Don't despair. I'm sure we shall succeed in the end. [. . .]

My best regards & affections to Kitty, Rosemary & Walter, & particular remembrances to yourself ——— Philip

1 On 22 October Philip had mentioned that the copy of Dostoevsky's *The Possessed* that Eva was trying to read was 'a Q.U.B. Library book'. She asked on 28 October: 'By the way, what does O.U.B. mean. Oxford Union ———?'

2 Eva was attending a series of lectures on psychology organised by Dr Edith Folwell of Victoria Park Road, Leicester. On 28 October she described a visit to her mentor: 'She received me in her usual gracious way and brought me a cup of coffee and biscuits and was oh *so* altogether kind and comforting. I stayed there till 12.15. I told her all my worries, and broke down & wept. However she cheered me up once again and made me promise to go to the lecture here on Monday evening (Derek Neville) and said I was to sit with her. I told her that she must send in her bill – but she wouldn't hear of it. I can go and see her again, when I like, she said.' At the lecture the secretary announced that subscriptions were due: 'I really feel that I ought to pay as I have been so regularly since I came here [. . .] It is 6/= per year and a silver collection each fortnightly lecture. I think one is supposed to give a shilling. I wonder if it is too extravagant?'

3 On 31 October Eva wrote: 'My very dear Creature, Your letter once again gave me so much joy, and when I came to the sketch of *me* I laughed outright!' She recounted her interviews with prospective live-in companions, Mrs Pell, Mrs Gamble and Norah Barlow ('about forty-something and exceedingly bright and cheerful'). She continued: 'I hope you insist upon the tailor making the jacket long enough, and do have it loose-fitting so that it is comfortable. / *I* am puzzled when I think of buying a costume. I don't know whether to get a good one (£15.15.0) or a utility, composed of unknown material £8.8.0.'

4 Eva had been kept awake by gnawing sounds outside her bedroom (letter of 28 October). Walter put down three mouse traps, but no mouse was caught.
5 Eva had been 'rather disappointed' by Mrs Pell, who 'looked so much older than me, and very countrified' (28 October). Two people named Gamble had responded, one of whom was a man. He had requested that Eva engage in 'respectable' but 'private' correspondence.

5 November 1950

Queen's Chambers, Belfast

My very dear Mop,

It's another very fine Sunday morning here, quite warm, and people are strolling up and down the road outside. Have two open windows and have just opened a third but I fancy I shall close that one. Moderation in all things! I'm wearing my fat white sweater so feel well muffled. The central heating is on as usual.

There was quite a lot to digest in your last letter and I have just been reading it through again – in fact, if this letter is disconnected or not very long it will be because I sit & think in between each sentence! I realise that the question of choosing a companion is extremely difficult and delicate, & I must say I shouldn't like to do it except after two or three fairly long meetings, when I had begun to grasp the person more clearly, and to form an opinion whether I liked them or not once their strangeness had worn off. Of the people you mention, the French one sounds as if she would not give any companionship & was anyway not what you asked for. No two to one! You say you liked Norah Barlow – that is the great thing: she sounds a bit "fierce", though, and I do think you want someone who'll grow *more* friendly rather than becoming self-sufficient once she has found somewhere to live. As for E. Jepps (is it?) perhaps you will have seen her by now and can report on her: she does not sound too bad from what you say.[1] It is an extrememly hard choice to make & I do wish sincerely there was some old acquaintance of yours who wouldn't be too strange, for I realise very well that a new person is much more of a risk and also more of a strain to live with until you know them better. It all worries me a good deal, not so much from the financial angle which I think would be all right, but I do not like the thought of you forced to live with someone who does not allow for your private ways of doing things & with whom you can't share jokes from time to time. A *good* person wd be very good and would I think help you to get much more fun out of life, but a misfire would create more problems than she would solve.

Your balance-sheet certainly looks encouraging[ly] low – of course clothes & fares – & a holiday, cats *should* have holidays – will swallow up the balance very quickly.[2] I don't think the figures you quote are wrong, & I can't think of any omissions: the new Chancellor has remarked, however, that prices will rise still further, which of course is no news to anyone. I should buy a *good* suit *now*. I might add that I do not think a serious "candidate for the post" *ought* to be put off by the absence of [a] house if you convince her of your goodwill & if she herself is as I say serious. Though I can imagine it might dash the spirits of some one eager for a house.

The house you described sounded a nice one – what condition is it in? Good? <[*in left margin*] The price sounds all right if the state of it is good.> I'm afraid there will always be *some* drawbacks in any house, you know: the garden sounds rather large though a lovely asset if you could benefit by it. Regarding Clemerson's list, have you to "accept" it? If so I suppose you might say that you queried the absence of certain items. Have they really been over everything? Ten shillings does not sound too bad – it's a sort of compromise increase, I fancy.[3]

About Christmas, what I mean is to come & spend seven consecutive nights in Loughborough: I might look in on Monica on the way home & on Kingsley on the way away again. That is, I might arrive in Loughborough on the 22nd & depart on the 29th. I shall have to confirm all this as soon as I can as booking will be brisk at Christmas: I shall look forward to seeing you once more though not to seeing our dear Lichfield relatives once more! However, I promise to take you.

This is not a very interesting or even very helpful letter, I'm afraid. I spend much time wondering how you are.

I have not much news this week. I was measured for the suit & it *may* be ready for Xmas, I don't know. On Thursday night I had to go out on a ghastly drinking evening with the people I *lied* to previously. God! why can't one be *really rude*? Yesterday Graham, Bradley & a man called Terry[4] & I walked to Lisburn – some 7 or 8 miles I suppose – & Bradley & I stayed there for the evening. This was *all right*, but O! I do get *bored* so *easily*. A few hours of anyone is always enough for me. Then I long for a book & my own uninterrupted thoughts. Regarding my "new life", it is superficially quite bearable, but at bottom all lives are impossible. I don't mean I'm not quite happy, but it doesn't do to analyse it all.

I've read all the papers about Shaw & shall make a selection of cuttings for my diary.[5] By all accounts he was very thankful to see the end of life: what a splendid show he put up of recovering. GBS to the last. The *Manchester Guardian* gave him the best write up.

Must "dress for lunch" now. Sunday lunch is v. respectable – gowns!

My very best & dearest love:
Philip

<*On the back flap of the envelope*>

1 Elizabeth Jepps, who appears in Eva's address book as living a minute's walk away from her at 123 Ashby Road, later became her friend, and initiated her into a charitable sewing group.
2 Eva's letter of 31 October included a list of her expenses at 12 Dixon Drive for the previous year.
3 In her letter of 31 October Eva wrote: 'This morning I also received a list of all the articles stored at Clemersons. Their revised price is 10/- per. week or part of a week. Do you think I ought to let Walter raise objections about it or not? *I* think not.' Clemersons was a removal and furniture storage company in Loughborough.
4 Arthur Hubert Terry (1927–2004): assistant lecturer in Spanish; later professor at QUB (1962) and Essex (1973–94).
5 George Bernard Shaw died on 2 November 1950.

12 November 1950

Queen's Chambers, Queen's University, Belfast

My dear old Mop,

The sun is looking in with a watery eye, & I am looking out with a watery eye at the Q.U.B. cadet corps drilling. Perhaps it will be a nice day after all. If it is fine after lunch I shall take out my bicycle. – Quite exciting opposite: a wreath-laying ceremony has suddenly started, with some bright robes and a military band. I remember giving half a crown towards a Chambers wreath, and this must be when it is due to be laid. I didn't buy a poppy this year: no particular reason, except that the hags are so confident when they approach you. – Now the last post is sounding: echoing all along the front of the building in velvet rather \than/ bright notes. [. . .]

My best love to you & kindest thoughts

P

26 November 1950

Queen's Chambers, Belfast

My dear old Mop,

How I did laugh at your 'wild Mop': a really skilful & comic drawing.[1] Well, today is fine but frosty, the grass opposite in front of Queen's is quite white & the wreaths I described being here a fortnight ago are all frosty. It would be nice to go out a walk or ride but I don't expect I shall, having quite a lot to do today. And I expect the best of this day will be gone before lunch. [. . .]

A very furry week to you, best loving wishes & a lilt of slightly cracked Irish laughter to Kitty, Walter & Rosemary. And extra love to y^r goodself – Philip

1 On 21 November Eva told Philip that she did 'feel wild' that the linen she needed to make Philip the bag he needed for his clothes was in storage. She added a pen-sketch:

On 9 January 1951 she drew a similar mop version of herself drinking sherry with her friend Effie McNicol.

31 December 1950

Mumbles Road, Swansea[1]

My dear old Mop,

This is just to report that I did arrive – 90 mins late – after a boring journey which didn't get any warmer as time went on! I hoped you returned to your burrow and found comfort in a fire.

I haven't much to report from here – conditions are the same or worse – & a very very small cold has perched on my shoulder. Curiously enough I don't at all want to go back to Belfast!

However, I must thank you all for such a pleasant Christmas. I hope your upsets have subsided, & that Walter has thrown off his embryo influenza. I shall think of you & your Real Turtle Soup![2]

Will write more lengthily later on.

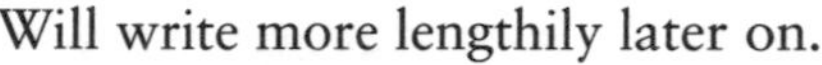

All love,
Philip

1 Philip was staying with the Amises.
2 This is the first appearance of the 'Old Creature' wearing a mob cap.

1951

2 January 1951

Picture postcard[1]

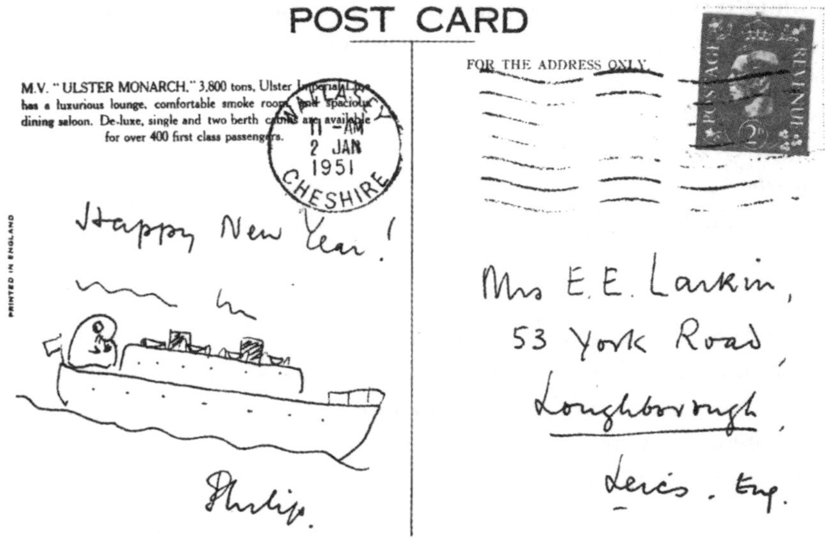
POST CARD

M.V. "ULSTER MONARCH." 3,800 tons, Ulster Imperial Line has a luxurious lounge, comfortable smoke rooms, and spacious dining saloon. De-luxe, single and two berth cabins are available for over 400 first class passengers.

PRINTED IN ENGLAND

Happy New Year!

Philip.

FOR THE ADDRESS ONLY.

POSTAGE REVENUE 2½d

11 -AM 2 JAN 1951 CHESHIRE

Mrs E. E. Larkin,
53 York Road,
Loughborough,
Leics. Eng.

1 MV *Ulster Monarch*. Larkin was returning to Belfast via Liverpool.

7 January 1951[1]

Queen's Chambers, Belfast

My dear old Moth,

I am sitting in the Senior Common Room for a change, still in this place however, listening to a good coal fire flapping behind me. Outside, the sun is shining wanly, & the snow just beginning to shrink at the edges. I don't think I've ever seen a more depressing sight than Belfast when I returned – worse than England by a long chalk. They'd had 9 inches of snow in the main streets the day before: everything was grey, hopeless & slushy – then it froze again. Then there was fog. Then about half the population is ill with influenza, all hospitals are closed to visitors. After a day or two I cultivated the little cold I told you about & have spent about 3 days indoors. This is just as well as where I should have got my food from I don't know. As it is I have lived pretty comfortably, but have not much *news* for you as I've done nothing since arrival. Except that the Graneeks had me to lunch on Tuesday, when the fog was so bad. He is not going to Canada, I'm happy to say. I mentioned the likelihood – or should I say suggestion – of your coming here & he nodded vaguely but said he didn't suppose I should stay here, as if he had just put in a confidential report on my complete incapacity to the Senate. If you're interested in the lunch it was soup, shepherd's pie, apple tart, & cheese, with the offer of beer, which I refused – ay! You've got to con-sider what yer boss it thinkin' of yer! Ruth was much in evidence. She is a most utterly spoilt little girl.[2]

The Amises are living even more sluttishly than usual, & *their* children are wondering, wandering tow haired little boys, really rather pretty, but quite squashed & timorous.[3] Even their crying seems subdued. Kingsley & Hilly had just visited both sets of parents and felt done in: Hilly's lot only burn *peat* & Kingsley was frozen all the time: & Kingsley's mother had made a lot of tactless remarks about Hilly's general incompetence to run a home or bring up children or do anything at all: all of which is probably quite well founded, only not at all the right thing to say & especially not likely to win Kingsley's sympathy as she seemed to suppose, somehow, that it might. However, as I may have said, Hilly has come into some money & they will be buying a house shortly, so that cheered them up a good deal.

So far I've not had a chance to settle down: my belongings are littered over *four* rooms at present, and I shall have to do an enormous amount of work to settle into this new one. I haven't unpacked my suitcase yet, except to discover that a record I brought back has not survived the journey.

I wonder very much how you are faring? Have you undertaken the fraud of the British Railways yet? And have you had the turtle soup yet? I expect if I mention it much more you will pour it down the sink. By now I hope the weather is better on your side of the Irish Sea than here: once it all clears up we shall see the first signs of spring sooner than we expect.

There's a suggestion now that I should go to Dublin on Feb 4th.

Please excuse a shortish letter this week – for I've really nothing to report, & they got me up very late this morning. Let me have a good bulletin of news, & give my love to R. & K.[4]

Especially love to dear 

Philip

1 In an envelope postmarked 14 January; the delay presumably caused by the snow.
2 The Graneeks' daughter.
3 On 9 January Eva wrote: 'I was interested to hear all about the Amises. Somehow they make me think of the "Constant Nymph" or am I making a big mistake and mixing this up with some other book. I often think though that little boys *are* quieter than little girls – they seem when very small, much more shy and inclined to hide behind Mother.' Margaret Kennedy's 1943 novel *The Constant Nymph* depicts a bohemian domestic ménage.
4 Rosemary and Kitty.

28 January 1951

Queen's Chambers, Belfast

My dear Mop,

A sunny day here, with frost on the ground. I am wondering if I might go out somewhere for lunch after writing to you, it seems a shame to waste the fine air. Since writing last I have progressed satisfactorily & am now quite all right again, enjoying life as far as it's my character to do so. Really I work quite hard here: there are days when I am rushing about from about 9–5.30 (with a break for lunch, of course!) doing all my various jobs. Then at night I sit up here undisturbed by anyone. Curious! While writing that last sentence I suddenly became overcome by an enormous sadness, from hearing a phrase of opera wafted up the stairs, making me think of London & operas I have seen. Strange. The sense of happiness is easily overthrown.

People here do seem (I mean Queen's people) less interesting than at Leicester: I don't know why. I suppose I really am among the barbarians, or else I'm becoming *blasé*. There is not much to report on this week: you know I planned to go to Dublin next weekend and meet Bruce at Stephen's[1] – as before Christmas – well, now Bruce writes to say that when all the world has 'flu he had got *mumps*, so won't be able to come.

Nuisance! Still, I shall go (D.V.) and see what the real Ireland is like. Talking about the real Ireland I was looking in a Catholic trinket shop in Chapel Lane here yesterday, & spied a little card about the size of a visiting card headed "When I say 'Jesus'" – it went on to explain how the holy name was in itself a prayer & meant firstly &c and secondly &c. Keep this card in your pocket & under y^r^ pillow at night, it said, for the holy name will ward off evil spirits: and try to say 'Jesus' as often as possible through the day. It seems to me that I'm in a fair way to achieving sanctity myself! (Better not tell Miss J. this).[2] I remember Pop making great game of the hymn 'How sweet the name of Jesus sounds'. It is curious how the *atmosphere* of Catholicism is so oppressive & irritating: one begins to chafe as soon as one looks into one of these shops, with their awful saccharine saints & little leather purses stamped "my rosary". I shall be joining the Orange Lodges soon!

I'm returning y^r^ coding notice: if your bank is going to do y^r^ Income Tax this year – & I don't see why they shouldn't – you should pass it to them. What £27 means is a mystery to me. The main thing you will have to watch is that now Dixon Drive is off y^r^ hands anything depending on that will be altered. I think there's a space in the declaration form (which you won't have had yet) to say if you have lost or gained any property through the year.

Thanks for the *Egoist* – or *Eogist* as you called it! – extract: it was remarkable.[3] Meredith is supposed to be a master of words; they come pouring out of him like bees out of a hive, though oddly enough I've never read any of his books.

If you come to Ireland – & I do hope you will, just for a few days – you will have to get a passport photo & a travel permit : No more now –

Fondest love to you & all the others,

Philip[4]

1 St Stephen's Green Hotel.

2 Elizabeth Jepps, Eva's religiously inclined friend.

3 In a letter of 23 January Eva had quoted from George Meredith's novel of 1879: 'He placed himself at a corner of the doorway for her to pass him into the house, and doated on her cheek, her ear and the softly dusky nape of her neck, where this way and that the little lighter-coloured irreclaimable curls running truant from the comb and the knot – curls, half-curls, root-curls, vine-ringlets, wedding rings, fledgeling feathers, tufts of clover, blown wisps – waved or fell, waved over or up or involutedly, or strayed, loose and downwards in the form of small silken paws,

hardly any of them much thicker than a crayon shading, cunninger than long round locks of gold to trick the heart.'

4 On the flap of the envelope Eva has written 'passport. photo'.

11 February 1951

Queen's Chamber's, Queen's University, Belfast

My dear Mop,

[. . .] Today I've half decided to go to Bangor again, but by bus this time; lunch, then walk either along the coast to Donaghadee, or inland to Newtownards. Each way w^d^ be about 8 miles. I don't really know if I can manage 8m!

I found your quotes from G.B.S. very interesting, & very sympathetic too. I shouldn't join any Brains Trusts – say you have no brains, & stick to it. Of course I understand how you feel about these Churchgoers. I sh^d^ always keep an eye open for anyone you like *personally*, & if there should be anyone, take all steps to transfer the relation to a personal footing & drop the social side out.[1] Anyway you can easily say you are very busy & can ill spare any time. Say Kitty is on nights at the Brush,[2] & you have to look after Rosemary. But I certainly shouldn't indulge in any heartsearching; not beyond: Am I more unhappy with these people than I sh^d^ be alone?

Speaking of Kitty[:] her stockings are *nines* – well, better too large than too small, eh?[3]

Jim writes to say that he has bought 4 cottages for £1000 & is living in one of them on the rent of the other three! They are at a village called Harbury, not far from Leamington. I think you'd reach it from Warwick by going along the Banbury Road about 5 miles then turning off. Doesn't it sound idyllic? But I bet they are cold, & how about repairs? If I had any sense I'd join him & live by writing: but nay.[4] I'm a useless creature.

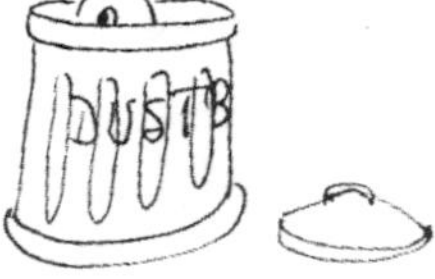

£2000 seems quite *enough* for a house of that class, in Heathcoat St.,[5] but it w^d be near Kitty & it is quite unusual for *another* house to be free so near, isn't it? Have you looked inside it?

Now to Bangor. Have you seen snowdrops & daffodils yet? I have.

All very best to you & Kitty & R,

P.

[. . .]

1 In a letter of 6 February (misdated January) Eva had written '*I* am doing what everyone has advised me to do, that is to get out and find new interests and mix with folk but, I am now wondering whether *I* too, shan't end up by feeling more confused, puzzled and consequently miserable. This afternoon I have been to the sewing party. I have nearly finished my cushion cover for some unknown baby's pram. I quite enjoyed it and had chats to various people but – now I have been asked to join in with them in dusting the church and generally getting it all spic and span against the coming of the new curate in a fortnight's time. Miss Jepps is helping and says they all take overalls, so it looks like a real job. Then there is a whist drive and I have also been asked to be on the Brains Trust next Monday – What shall I do? Shall *I* turn into an ardent church worker or disgust them all by wriggling out of it[?]'

2 Larkin invents an imaginary job for his sister in the Loughborough factory of the Brush company, which manufactures electrical equipment.

3 Eva replied on 13 February: 'How I adored your sketches and Kitty was highly amused at herself at the "Brush". By the way, how *cross* she looks.'

4 Jim Sutton and Philip had shared an ardent admiration for D. H. Lawrence, hence the touch of Laurentian dialect here.

5 The Larkins had sold 12 Dixon Drive, and Eva, living with her daughter and Walter, was searching for a suitable house of her own. In her letter of 6 February she wrote: 'The house which is for sale here in Heathcote street [the name can be spelled either "Heathcote" or "Heathcoat"] is very near York Road. I enquired about it at the agents. It is next door to the Catholic Church hall. There are three bedrooms, lounge, dining room, kitchen with triplex grate and scullery, cycle shed (wooden) W.C. coalhouse and small private garden. The drawback is that there is no indoors lavatory, although there is a bathroom with modern panelled bath and washbasin. Rateable value £17. Rates £7.7.4. per half year. Price £2000.'

11 March 1951

Queen's Chamber's, Queen's University, Belfast

My dear old Mop,

[. . .] I have just looked at your photograph by holding it up against the sun & think that in reverse you look a quizzical, merry old bird!

This Sunday I am not really any fuller of the joy of life than I was last Sunday: I am entering – or entered – on a very anti-Queen's phase at present, along with sour depression & all the rest of it. The scarcity of any good companions, my own inability to do anything myself, all contribute to clay-cold depression. When I am in I want to be out & when I am out I want to be in – last week I was out three times: once to hear Beckett read a paper about Jane Austen[1] – that was at a meeting of the Belfast Literary Society, where a man was knitting a sock on the back row all the time; once at a send-off party for Miss Webster of the Library, who is going to the States for 5 months – do you know, that party wouldn't have happened if I hadn't suggested it – presumably they would just have nodded goodbye to her at the end of her last working day. I contributed a bottle of champagne, which was gawped and giggled at as if they had never seen one before: I tell you, Belfast is a dull unsociable place, much worse than Leicester: they have nothing that appeals to me at all. The third outing was a somewhat comic outing to a dance with Ellen Wilson who preserved her meek inaudibility as we shuffled backwards & forwards in front of the band which was my only reason for going. I think I should be able to dance if I only learned.

It was a pleasure to get Kitty's letter, and I am glad the stockings are acceptable: certainly I don't want paying for them: they are what Lewis Carroll calls an unbirthday present. Rosemary's room sounds very nice: I am glad the furniture is solid – it will need to be, I expect. She will look delightful as a bridesmaid, & her own comments will be worth hearing.

You sounded a little more bold this week about the house situation! The one you describe sounded nice but I fancy you'd need a shed for the garden tools at least, and an immersion heater is always useful, though that can always be added later at little (I imagine) cost. I should not buy a big house nor a house you don't like. [. . .]

With all my love to dear old 

Philip

1 J. C. Beckett, Warden of Queen's Chambers.

17 April 1951

Queen's Chambers, Belfast

My dear mother monst-haugh,

I was most relieved to get your card & know that you had crossed safely to the other side. That took a great load off my mind! [. . .][2]

I know you would like a letter at Hyde, but, to say truly, I've forgotten (or never knew) Auntie N's address, so I am sending this to your little room in Loughborough to greet you on your return. I wonder if you have been to Leigh and Manchester and all your old haunts? But the Sunday papers say that your weather has been just as bad, & really it's been just the same here. A snivelling North wind drivelling over the town.

With all love to old

Philip

1 On 27 May 1951 Philip responded to a puzzled query (21 May) from his mother: 'a Monst-Haugh is a Monst-Haugh, e.g. the Loch Ness Monst-Haugh.'

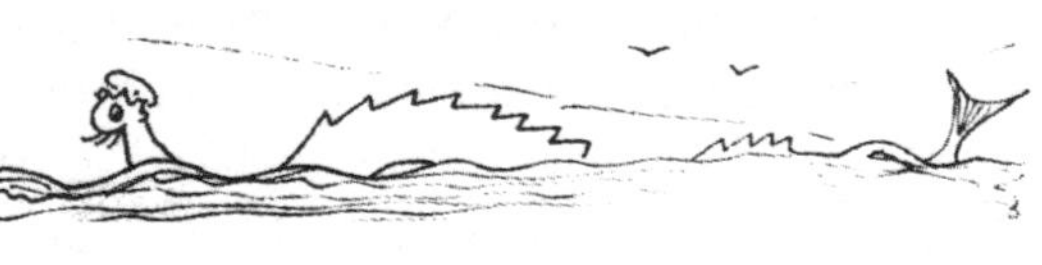

2 Eva had visited Philip in Belfast, and was now staying with Nellie Day in Hyde. In her letter of 17 April she wrote 'I *did* like being in Belfast and shall often think of you in surroundings which I now *know*.'

29 April 1951

Queen's Chambers, Belfast

My dear Mop-Monst-Haugh,

[. . .] Jim wrote saying he enjoyed seeing me: the idea crossed my mind that he would gladly (I imagine) take a room in any house we have over here. I haven't yet mentioned the vague idea we had to Monica. She will be over here in May. Jim is a nice old bird, but his letters grow fuller & fuller of windy philosophical tosh about mankind . . . However it shows a nicer, more unselfish nature than mine.

I hope Rosemary had a good birthday & that my little remembrance turned up.

Much love old Creech-Haugh,
From Young Creech-Haugh

15 May 1951

Queen's Chambers, Belfast

Dear creaturely one,

Alone at last! For after I saw Monica off last night, the Warden lugged me in for a bottle of stout: then, all today there was *work* . . . As you can imagine, the weekend was very full & exhausting, & I think Monica enjoyed it all very much. The weather was superb: quite un-Belfastlike. On Friday I had to leave her very much to her own devices, but showed her one or two "picturesque" pubs in the evening; then on Saturday we went to Dublin & walked all about it in the finest of weather. (For lunch I had a tomato cocktail, a mushroom omelette, & fresh pineapple & cream.) I'd never *stayed* there before & was interested to get the "feel" of it. In a way I rather disliked it: beautiful Georgian streets are all decaying into flyblown slums; men squatted about playing cards for money (betting is legal); everything was very expensive & I found the waiters faintly ironic, as if to them I was just another mug. Many of the main streets were up: others ought to have been: dust blew everywhere. Flags drooped at half mast for the funeral of the Papal Nuncio, & we sat in College Park and watched Trinity College playing cricket like old English Gentlemen. Monica was much distressed at the price of shantung & gabardine – about 12/- the yard. On Saturday night we had a steak each, & fruit salad, & Bordeaux – 42/3d – at Jammet's, but I really don't think it was good cooking, it was just lots of food. After that we took a long long walk along the nine-bridged Liffey, circling Guinness's & Steevens Hospital, seeing a lot of drunks. On Sunday we walked about more, & I took photographs. These I fear will all be failures.[1] The journey back was long & rather tiresome, but the weather remained fine. On Monday we walked from Crawfordsburn to Helen's Bay & looked at the sea, & had tea at the Ship Hotel where you and I had tea on that wet Sunday. Really, it *is* a good place. After that we had to return & put Monica aboard, & I watched the boat out. In Belfast she'd found a sort of dressing gown that's apparently scarce, & was pleased in proportion. I asked her vaguely about the self-raising flour (not having your letter with me) and she said that if she wanted anything to rise, she put "raising" in it, & didn't trust any flour.[2]

Now for your letter! Tell Kitty that athlete's foot is, according to Piggot,[3] "very intractable": I didn't really listen to Maybin when he explained it, but it is some sort of skin disease. If she is really interested I will enquire about it, but it's my sincerest hope that she hasn't anything of that at all (Irish expression). Incidentally I met Miss MacDonnell who said she was very pleased to have heard from you, and asked me to advise you to rub your foot with something I have *also* forgotten. Addled creature![4]

(can you follow this?)
No! it was
pumice-stone.
Not so addled
after all!

By far the most surprising thing in your letter was the meeting with Mrs Knight at the doctor's surgery. That is really odd. I have chumbled y[r] affairs over a good deal in my mind: Monica had no particular suggestions to offer except to buy a house & make some money by it. Generally speaking that is what most people say. I think she'd gladly live in it – or live in it, anyway – but was much too polite to say so without being asked. Probably Jim would, too: if it was in the country & he was not "badgered". Perhaps they'd both live there! But I'm not sure I feel inclined to add Monica onto the family in that way: anyway, it would be your business. I think I had better not arrange anything this Summer in case you want me to do anything for you. For my part I quite agree with y[r] Dr about not living alone. I don't really think you want the responsibility of a house, either, from the work aspect or the business aspect either. There remains the possibility of your coming to Ulster: this I still feel to be a *faute de mieux* by reason of the expense, the isolation, the trouble & I shouldn't be here much in vacations . . . I don't know! It seems such a way of throwing good, irrecoverable money away. Tell me what you think of the lady at tea. She is the one that I said you'd be one-to-three or four with, isn't it? [. . .]

I'm so pleased you are better: what tablets are you taking? I can ask Piggot what they're supposed to do. And I hope you keep on with your diary: I have at last *stopped* mine, out of weariness with it.

1 One of these photographs is reproduced in Mark Haworth-Booth, 'Larkin as Photographer', *About Larkin* 42 (October 2016), 11.
2 On 8 May Eva had written: 'Could you ask Monica whether it is Self-Raising Flour which is used in the fruit crumble recipe? We often make it.'
3 Jimmy Piggott (double t), Deputy Warden of Queen's Chambers.
4 On 21 May Eva wrote 'If you ever do see Miss MacDowell again thank her for her hint about pumice stone. G. Dad used to use sandpaper!'

10 June 1951

Queen's Chambers, Queen's University, Belfast

My dear old Monst-Haugh,

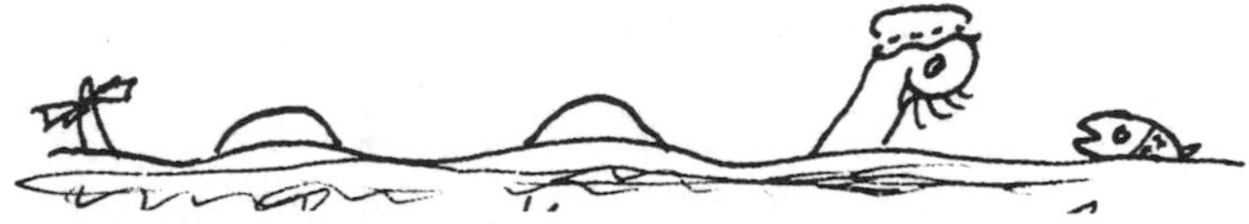

Your yellow notepaper was much appreciated: it added a summery air to a nice letter. Aren't bird calls beautiful in the evening? Sometimes I hear repeated "over and over again, a pure thrush word" (Edward Thomas),[1] but I think the blackbirds are the best, or what I imagine are blackbirds. Their calls seem like smooth odd polished sound-shapes, don't they? cast up on the beach of the evening. I liked your ending "Now I must end and get *wine*" –

I thought of you creeping down a cellar stair.

Thank you also for describing the wedding in such detail, & for sending the "programme".[2] Please tell me if the "Army" have *power* to marry people – I thought they had not – that they could solemnize it, so to speak, but not perform it. Have they clapped a bonnet on Rosemary yet? (Don't show that bit to Walter!) Is she playing at weddings? If so I expect Grandma will be called in to fulfil a variety of functions.

No: the Royal Visitors did not visit Queen's because they have been before. They came during an interim period before Graneek was appointed & Miss Megaw had to receive them at the Library.[3] Do you know she was at Roedean? The Megaws are a definite "family"

here. Another Megaw – though perhaps not related – is Arthur Stanley Megaw – the 'Arthur Stanley' who compiles the Bedside Book etc. He lives in Belfast too. [. . .]

No more tooth news yet – I go to the dentist tomorrow & shall be snaggle-toothed or not as he decides. I do hope he can save it. It all depends whether the *bone* is healing.

I was interested to hear of the freight price to Belfast. It certainly seems a lot, but I expected it would be. Dear! It is a worry. Other people have suggested a companion & a third party to pay for the Companion, & it does sound sensible, but it is a lot of people to contend with, and would there be room for *me*?

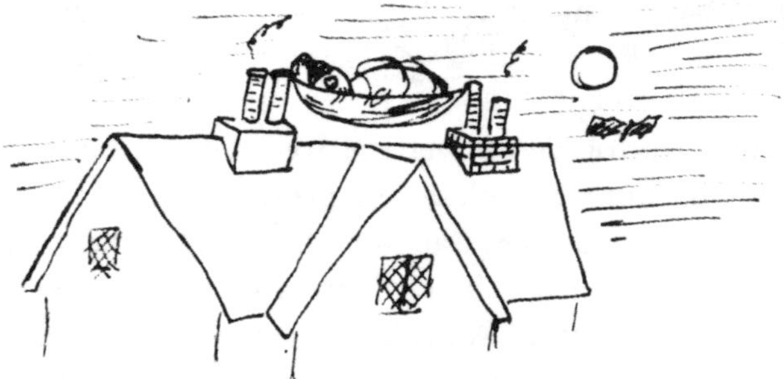

I think before I write any more I had better shave & lunch (debauched creature!)

Ten to three. – In many ways I should like to keep an eye on you, but it would not be very sensible to lay out all that money bringing you to Ireland & back within a few years, & you would not want to be left here – it is really more sensible to leave you in England where you have a chance of keeping up with old creatures of like interests.

But have you any companion in view from Mrs S's bag?[4] It would be easier to get the "paying guest" first & the Companion after: in fact, once you had the p.g. you might find you did not need the Companion, & could keep the money for yourself.

Nevertheless, how unpleasant all this importation of strangers is! Setting up with somebody known & liked is one thing, but apart from that it is all a weariness.

If A. Nellie (as we are all calling her) does *not* come, it would be awfully nice if you came here. I could put a bit towards your fare, though at present I've forgotten the dates. I have a notion to fly back towards the end of July, landing at Birmingham.

A bill arrived from Leicester yesterday – £2–7–6 from a bookshop. Beasts! I thought they'd forgotten all about me.

Now I must post this, & pull myself together a bit (3.30 p.m.!)

With much love,
Philip

1 The final phrase in Thomas's poem 'The Word'.
2 Eva's letter of 8 June gives a detailed account of 'how the wedding [. . .] went off'. Ivor Hewett, Walter's brother, had married Connie (Constance) Barnett in Salvation Army uniforms. Eva commented: 'Rosemary looked very sweet and played her little part very well.'
3 Chief Cataloguer at Queens. Motion (*Philip Larkin*, 200) has 'McGraw' in error.
4 On 21 May Eva had written: 'Mrs Swainson [. . .] has advertised in "The Lady" and the Church Times for a permanent Housekeeper Companion. She is "inundated with replies" and wants to know whether she shall pass any on to me if she thinks they are suitable.'

15 July 1951

The Library, Queen's Univ. Belfast

My dear old Monst-Haugh,

[. . .] After the party broke up I took a stroll down Sandy Row, the Protestant Quarter: bonfires were burning in the road at nearly every street corner, all the shops were open, and people with paper hats on were dancing in the streets to drums & fifes and loudspeakers. All very thrilling and primitive! Thursday was of course the great day, the Twelfth. I cycled out to Finaghy where the procession would end & fell in with some Queen's people who live there & we watched the Orange procession together. It was a very grey day & drizzle fell from time to time, but the procession was astonishing: nearly 300 "Lodges" with banners & bands all marching along to express their detestation of Communism (i.e. anything mildly savouring of the organisation of the labour movement), & their insistence on 'Civil & religious liberty' (i.e. denying civil & religious liberty to Catholics & Nationalists, & damn the Pope, etc.) I watched for an hour & a quarter & then gave up: but in the end I believe there were 100,000 people on the field hearing the speeches. [. . .]

Much love to old Creature,
Young Creature

28 July 1951

Postcard

<*Postmark*> Swanage, Dorset[1]

Am sitting *frying* in the sun on the coast of the Isle of Purbeck, by Durlston Lighthouse. A lovely day, & I wish you were here to see the waves exploding, but you'd need a sunshade. Those lobster salads were so *small* (6/- each) we had to have a big feed of fish & chips afterwards. It is so beautiful to sit in a strong unhindered sun. I love it: life ought to include lots of this.

Much love,

1 Philip was on holiday with Monica in Dorset and Devon, ending with a brief visit to the Amises in Swansea.

16 August 1951 Postcard

[Queen's Chambers, Queen's University, Belfast]

Many thanks for the letter! A more gruntled creature now.

Are you trying 1500m. for Mrs D – *Long*[1] wave?

Will write at weekend as usual. I am surprised about Dr F.[2]

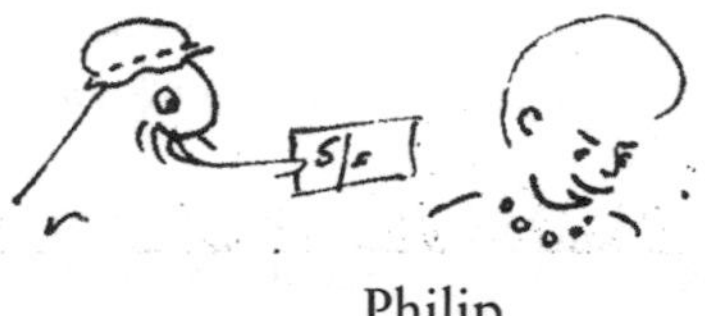

Philip

1 Triply underlined. On 14 August Eva wrote: 'I wish you were here, so that we could listen to the little wireless in the evenings. I have one complaint about it. I cannot get Mrs Dale's Diary at 4-15 p.m. on the Light Programme [. . .] 'tis much too faint.' After following Philip's advice she wrote 'I have got Mrs Dale better now' (21 August). *Mrs Dale's Diary* was a popular BBC radio serial drama, broadcast daily between 1948 and 1967.

2 On 14 August Eva had written that the secretary of 'our Psychology Group' had visited and told her that next month it was the golden wedding of Eva's mentor, Dr Folwell; 'in a burst of gratitude I gave him 5/- although the subscription asked was 2/6. [. . .] I have been thinking Dr Folwell must be about 70, which surprised me very much. I always thought she was my age. She really is the most marvellous woman I have ever met.' Eva was 65 at this time.

26 August 1951

7 College Park East, Belfast[1]

My dear old Mop,

[. . .] Your money seems *very* comfortable – MORE THAN I GET – and I can hardly believe it,[2] perhaps Gaitskell's[3] dividend cuts will affect you – mind you. I hope they *won't*, for creatures need all the money they can get. About the house – I find it impossible to decide *for* you: it depends on how you feel. On the balance I think it would be as well to *try* – as I am trying this flatlet – if it turns out badly then it will have to be abandoned. The annuity idea sounds good.[4] But for this reason I don't think a house that needs much spending on it is a good idea – although you might sell it at a profit – & also I don't want you to be *alone at nights*. It would be too trying for you – you w[d] never sleep!

Oh dear, this doesn't sound much help. I'll thank Miss Bennett when I see her.[5] Do give yourself up to having a happy week at Newark![6]

With very best
love & constant
thoughts,
Philip

1 The university required Larkin's Queen's Chamber's flat and he stayed a short time at College Park.

2 In her letter of 21 August Eva wrote that she had taken her income tax statement to Mr Otley at Lloyds Bank. She gave complicated details of her calculations and concluded that her income after tax was £433.11.7 per. annum. 'This is about £8.5.4 per week, isn't it?'

3 Hugh Gaitskell (1906–63), Chancellor of the Exchequer, 1950–1.

4 In the letter of 21 August Eva told Philip that Mr Otley had suggested that she might sell the remaining 45 year lease on 'Penvorn' and 'buy an annuity with either part, or the whole of the money from the sale. [. . .] He thought £4,000 for the lease, but then he has not seen it!'

5 Eva's friend Miss Bennett had told her of 'an elderly lady, a doctor's widow' who wanted someone to share her flat 'as she does not want to be alone during the winter'. But Eva turned down this flat-share: 'it would not solve the question of my furniture, and then there would be nowhere for my dear Creature to come – when it was hard up!!' (21 August 1951).

6 In her letter of 21 August Eva told Philip that she had been invited to stay in Newark with the Cann family. In a letter from Newark of 27 August she explains that Mr Cann 'has retired from the Brewery'. She has visited his farm at Newark, where the piglets 'all set up a shrill squealing, expecting to be fed'. On 30 August Eva sent a postcard from Newark: 'I am having a delightful time here.'

23 September 1951

Cockburn Hotel (pro. "Co-burn"), Edinburgh[1]

My dear Monst Haugh,

So Creature Castle is ours![2] Well, good luck to it, & to all the creatures and persons who inhabit it. I think the world can be divided into "Creatures" and "Persons", don't you? [. . .]

Yes, I am enjoying the tour, but yesterday I felt I had a chill – pains in the bones & shivering. However I did my duty by the University Library, then had a plate of soup, a hot bath, aspirins, & went to bed till about 6.30. Rising, I had dinner (melon, sole, pineapple) and walked up to the castle in the dark, but returning went to bed again about 8 p.m. Today I feel vastly improved. The weather is certainly beautiful – if it were cold & wet I sh[d] be much worse off, for I've had a lot of walking to do.

Well, there's only Glasgow now, and then back to old Megaw, 49 Malone Road (my 94/6 a week home until the flats open) & Belfast. The trip has been extremely interesting. For one thing it's shown me what all these places are like & what conditions in them are like. I almost think that Durham is as nice a place as any. The town is small, quite like Warwick, except for the huge Cathedral looming over all, & there is a lovely river-walk: the library is v. old & almost entirely non-scientific, & the University small – about 1,000 students (Queen's is above 2,500). Altogether very decent. I can see myself sorting out the Cosin's Library, which the Bishop has a right to use for meetings, among the old chairs & crumbling leather backs. [. . .]

Best love – pray for a smooth crossing!

Philip

1 Larkin had been sent by Graneek on a tour of northern universities to study issuing policies, facilities etc.

2 On 8 September Eva, asking for a '*reply by return*', described a four-bedroomed house, 'in York Road on the same side as no. 53' which she had looked over with Kitty and Rosemary. This was no. 21 and the price was £2,500. After considering two other possibilities she paid the deposit on 20 September and moved in on 10 December. She lived there for two decades, until 1972.

12 October 1951 Lettercard

[30 Elmwood Avenue, Belfast]

My dear Mop-creature,

I am sitting in "my flat" at present, which is furnished (just about) but not lived in! I move in tomorrow: Colin Strang is going to help me with the moving & Patsy with the first provisioning.[1] I have a bed a wardrobe a carpet a gas fire 2 armchairs 2 straight chairs & a table in this room & a sink an oven a kitchen cabinet & kitchen table in the other – & another gas fire.

Until I'm sure post arrives here *safely*, please write to the Library. This address is 30 Elmwood Avenue. No telephone. My flat is at the top & is No. 13! If there is a fire I shall regret my choice.

Many thanks for your letter wch I'll reply to on Sunday. How queer it is having one's "own burrow"!

Much love! P.

1 Colin Strang was a member of the Philosophy Department at QUB. His wife, Patsy, wealthy daughter of a South African diamond magnate, had trained as a doctor in France. She read Larkin's diaries without his permission, seduced him into an affair in 1952–3, and became pregnant by him, but suffered a miscarriage.

2 December 1951

30 Elmwood Avenue, Belfast

My dear Mop,

I feel somewhat drowsy this morning, perhaps because of the gas fire: I had quite enough sleep last night. Or perhaps the progress of term is slowing me down generally. Certainly I'm not as sprightly nowadays as

I was at the start of October. Last Monday I bought another clock – an electric one – and this goes silently in its corner, giving tongue only at 7.45 a.m. each morning when it starts buzzing in a steady insistent way and keeps going till I crawl out of bed & shut it up. The first clock I keep in the kitchen, to warn me during breakfast how time is going.

So Dec 10 is the day when we go "over the top", or rather when you go:[1] I was expecting the move to take place a week later – say Dec 17 – so that I could help *in* it, but it seems I shall come in on the "mopping up operations" only – I only hope Mop won't have to be mopped up as well as other things!

I was surprised to hear that we got both War Damage *and* dilapidations – quite a pleasant surprise! The garage business sounds a *great* advantage when it comes to selling. [. . .]

Now I must "try conclusions" with a cauliflower. Nice weather here! Take care of your dear self, & pass my kind wishes to the h's.

Much love,
Philip

1 On 10 December Eva replied: 'Well, here I am, safely on the other side of the moving. Clemerson's men were very efficient and had delivered everything by 4.30 p.m.' In the same letter she wrote that she had received a telegram from the solicitor Odell's telling her that they had received an offer of £3,000 for the Penvorn lease. 'Walter rang them up straight away accepting for me.' But this fell through and Penvorn was not sold until September 1971, when it was demolished.

1952

25 January 1952 Postcard

[30 Elmwood Avenue, Belfast]

Yes, it has arrived![1] And it is really lovely, nicer than the last, even. I asked a Yorkshireman in last night, with some mustard & Guinness, but he made so much noise eating it that I wished I hadn't. Still, there's plenty left for me to eat alone. I have just had your nice letter & think that is a bit 'cool' of the Corporation.[2] Will write at more length on Sunday.

"These are the weeks when even the poorest of us should be allowed a little something on the hob – a drop, perhaps, of hot West Indian rum, well sweetened with sugar . . ." (Llewellyn Powys).[3]

Tonight I have "eaten out" & mean to busy myself with my spare time literary activity. Dear creature, what are you doing, I wonder?

1 On 22 January Eva wrote: 'Your pork pie is on the way to you, so watch out for it [. . .] By the way, while I remember it, Kitty wonders if you got her letter thanking you for the cheese.'
2 In her letter of 22 January Eva referred to the situation regarding her continuing lease on Penvorn: 'Daddy used to say that the Corporation would grant compensation when the house was taken over for the re-building scheme. I wonder if it would be better to let it, and wait for the compensation money?'
3 *The Twelve Months* (London: The Bodley Head, 1936), 'November', 78.

1 February 1952 — Postcard

[30 Elmwood Ave, Belfast] — Friday

I dare say your letter is awaiting me below, but I'll write this before I go out. This hasn't been a busy week, just rather a slack & sluggish one.

There is a fresh robe of snow on the earth for February – sign of good weather to come, they say. I hope you have not been 'in the grip of ice and snow' as the papers say.

Life goes on very quietly, with the usual quota of *work*.[1]

Later. Found your letter! & many thanks for the cutting.[2] I am indeed sorry to hear that you've had a cold – but what a brave creature to stay alone! Cheers! Am very sorry you didn't get my note in the 1st place.

Love P.

1 Doubly underlined.

2 With her letter of 29 January Eva enclosed a press cutting concerning the Loughborough Poole Academy pantomime at the Theatre Royal, Loughborough, in which Rosemary had played a part among 'over 160 juveniles'. 'The audience enjoyed a well-dressed tuneful show that went with a swing from the start.'

24 February 1952

30 Elmwood Avenue, Belfast

My dear Mop-Creature,

I sit down to write to you before doing anything else, except have breakfast: my bed is a tangled heap; cigarette ash covers the boards; 14 empty bottles stand in a corner; and the kitchen I dare not think about – it is a sea of crumbs & coffee stains. The bells have been ringing for church & it is about 11.30 on what looks like a perfect spring day. I vow I shall get out today! My bicycle puncture is mended, & I have hardly been out all winter.

The reason for the generally debauched appearance of my room is that last night a gathering was held in my room until about 2 a.m. It was the evening of the "housewarming" of the new Common Room: Colin & Patsy brought – at long last – the steak & kidney pudding, & I had prepared potatoes, sprouts, & carrots: also purchased a doz. stout. We did not really want to go to the Common Room, but we did, & really it was very enjoyable, with plenty of drink & company,

& really I quite enjoyed it. Then the Strangs & the Morrisons – Clare & Archie – came back to here: it was a "mixture", for the Strangs are v. English & the Morrisons v. Irish, but to my delight it was quite successful & as I say lasted till 2 without boring anyone as far as I could see. I feel a very social & adept creature!

Needless to say I feel a bit flat today, & a bit doleful about my future, & life, & all the rest of it.

[. . .]

What an original way your letter card was written! Like a little book. I was indeed sorry to hear that you have been depressed of late & that your old friends have found out your new address. Do not worry about the past: it is, after all, past, and fades daily in our memory & in the memories of everyone else. Further, it can't touch the future unless we let it. Every day comes to us like a newly cellophaned present, a chance for an entirely fresh start. Finally, do remember that we are *not very important*. Hundreds of living people have never heard of us: those who died in previous years & those who will be born in the next century have no chance to, and in consequence we are silly if we do not amble easily in the sun while we can, before time elbows us into everlasting night & frost. This is perhaps not very helpful, but I am so sorry for you, and feel you have *no* reason to worry yourself![1]

My holiday will *probably* be: arrive about 2 p.m. on Sunday April 6, depart about 2 p.m. Saturday April 12. If you want to plan a visit to Lichfield during the time I am quite agreeable, My very sweetest love, old creature.

P.

<*On first page alongside address*>
My *groceries* have not come. O death & torments!

1 Eva replied on 26 February: 'It was kind of you to write a page full of advice to lessen my depression. Of course I know it all, but the strange thing is it is so difficult to act upon, and one can never forgive oneself. I don't quite agree with you though that we are not very important. I know that whatever I say or do, and whatever happens to me will affect Kitty and you – either make you happy or unhappy, and because of this I do wish I was a better and braver creature.'

16 March 1952

30 Elmwood Ave, Belfast (Wicklow Hotel, Dublin)

Well, old Creature,

We are here, in Dublin – but not quite as we imagined it: the hotel is *shut*, because there's a strike on of hotel staff & so on. Everywhere is very *cold* (no heating) & there's no regular cuisine, only breakfast. [. . .]

We stay here tomorrow (St Patrick's Day) & I return to Belfast in the evening. On Tuesday another visiting creature arrives – John Wain, whom I knew in Oxford,[1] & who is convalescing after an operation. By that time the Strangs will have gone home, leaving their dogs in store.

What! A whole letter & no creatures. Well, let me see.[2]

I shall be interested to hear what the advertising lady is like – What a gamble it all is, with the odds heavily stacked against ourselves! Anyway, let me know.

Colin has now appeared & we shall shortly be moving off – the weather is damp but fine. Outside the hotel pickets move up & down carrying notices – "Lock-out in progress". Lockout & freeze up as far as I'm concerned – & an awful crowd singing in the room above me at 3.30 a.m. Dublin!

My best love to a dear old creature,
Philip

1 John Wain (1925–94), prolific novelist and poet, had been a freshman in St John's when Larkin was in his third year. In 1973 Larkin supported his successful candidacy for the Professorship of Poetry at Oxford.

2 Eva commented (18 March): 'The Irishman reminds me of a photo of U. Alf. in the garden at Lichfield when he was growing a beard.'

18 May 1952

30 Elmwood Ave, Belfast

My dear Mop-Creature,

Once again I have crawled into Queen's & spent the best part of an hour snoozing in the sun. For once again the day is fine, expansively fine, deliciously fine, splendidly fine. It is queer how a fine day always makes me think of the past – of wide brimmed garden party hats in the '90s & clusters of afternoons falling like drops of river water from an oar way back in the '70s & '60s – boating parties of curates and daughters and young men down for the Long Vacation, with straw hats and picnic baskets and fringed parasols. And in the early morning my thoughts go back much further – to mornings in the middle ages, when monks might be shuffling past a ray of sunshine on the stone floor in the mist of the early hours, with the "dawn chorus" of birds starting outside. I am wasting much space to no very good purpose, but fine weather does always send me beyond the confines of this particular day & place.

Well, I thought your poem very good – very skilful by the way; do you notice how he does it all on two rhymes? – and feel that it is surely what one would wish anyone one loved in the lean years of age.[1] It sounds indeed very like the poem you are always looking for! Are you sure it isn't? That Henley was a good deal in Pop's hands at Warwick. [. . .]

I hope your visit to Dr Folwell was successful – you never told me what happened about her son.

Well, I won't dredge up further remarks for I shall be seeing you soon. Monica might look in on the Thursday evening but that will liven up your mind pleasantly enough, won't it? Drop me a card to say you're expecting me.

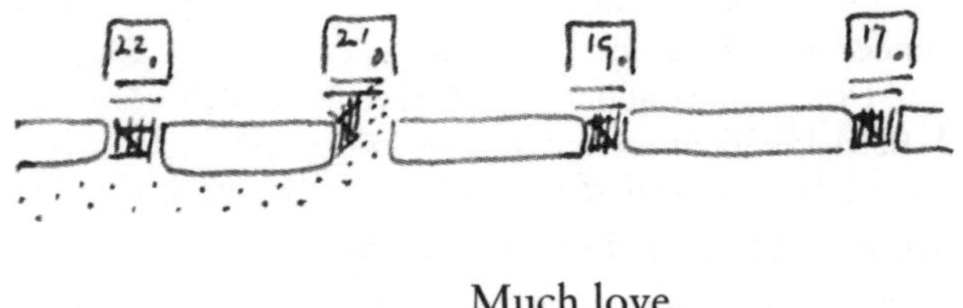

Much love,
Philip

1 On 13 May Eva had written to thank Philip for the 'lovely letter and sweet violet', which she had 'put in Henley's poems to mark a most lovely poem which I came across last Sunday evening whilst looking for the poem which Daddy showed me one evening at Warwick. / I will copy it, because I somehow can imagine that Daddy might want it to be like this now for me. (Maybe you know the poem already.)

When you are old and I am passed away –
Passed, and your face, your golden face, is gray –
I think, whate'er the end, this dream of mine,
Comforting you, a friendly star will shine
Down the dim slope where still you stumble and stray.
So may it be: that so dead yesterday,
No[t] sad-eyed ghost but generous and gay
May serve you memories like almighty wine,
When you are old!'

'When you are old' by William Ernest Henley (1849—1903), English poet and critic.

23 May 1952 — Postcard

Leicester LMS[1]

I must thank you for once more for my stay – everything was so nice, except for the *incident* pictured in Fig one! However, I hope the second figure is also true. I hope you will have y^r bath & a good relaxing rest, & that clouds will all flee away like spiders before y^r broom. Enjoy your weekend – hope I do mine! All love to old C. from young C. Philip.[2]

1 LMS = London, Midland and Scottish Railway. Presumably sent from the station.
2 On 27 May Eva replied: 'How kind of you to send me a card on Saturday and how I both *loved* it and was amused by it. The irate creature looks really terrible – just as it sounded – to me at least. The two dear creatures in the second sketch look much nicer. Don't bother about the "incident". I have nearly forgotten it, and I expect it was partly my fault for speaking as I did. / I got your card from Paris ce matin.'

24 May 1952

Picture postcard[1]

<*Postmark*> Gare Montparnasse

Saturday

Arrived safely dear creature, & apart from everything being about 2ce as *dear* as I expected things have not gone too badly so far. Thank you again for the lovely tea & supper. Love xx P.

1 Paris – La Tour Eiffel. Philip visited Paris with Bruce Montgomery on 23–7 May.

27 May 1952

Hotel Madison, Paris

Tuesday morning.

My dear Creature,

I can't get any answer to my knocks at Bruce's door, so I suppose he is still asleep! It's after 10 on our last day, & I'm a bit ashamed I haven't sent you more than a postcard in this brief crowded visit. The flight was quite all right – a salmon supper served on the way – & we got here about 11 – to the hotel, I mean. We then sat about in cafés till nearly 3. People seem never to go to bed! On Saturday we walked about in the morning – fine sun – warm but not hot – in the afternoon slept & ascended the Eiffel Tower, & in the evening ate a very slow dinner & went to a night club where there was reputed to be "le jazz" – & there was indeed. I enjoyed it all tremendously, though the best people advertised as appearing "chaque soir" did not do so. Drinks cost about 15/- apiece, though the place was only a cellar full of wooden tables & stools. To bed late – & *quite* unable to sleep, far too excited!

On Sunday we sat about in the sun & ate at a new café one of my Belfast acquaintances had recommended – quite cheap & good. I had hors d'oeuvres, pork, & bananas & cream. In the afternoon we walked about again, & in the evening went to a theatre, after which there was further café-sitting till about 1 a.m. Monday was a very nice day: I went into Notre Dame in the morning, then we went off to lunch. Unfortunately *hayfever* greeted me in the afternoon – by now the weather was very hot – so I went back & lay down till evening.

Going out again, we paid our second visit to the Ritz bar (the first was on Saturday, midday) & then went to the Opera – *Salomé*, by Richard Strauss. You've no conception of the enormous size of both the total interior of it & the actual auditorium – all marble & red plush & a chandelier as big as a cottage depending from the middle of the roof. The music was very fine.[1] Having left that, & had another drink or two, I inveigled Bruce back to the jazz club & we stayed till it closed at about 2 a.m. this morning. Today we leave! by the evening 'plane.

Of course there is so much more to say that this is a mere skeleton of our stay: many times I have thought of your "un peu" though I have really done no more than order breakfast by room telephone in the mornings. Paris is much less crowded & busy than London, & parts are very sweeping & impressive. But the traffic! Apart from being quick & ruthless, it comes at you from the wrong side all the time, so that, bothered already, you fall into a worse confusion & fall on your knees in prayer. I shall need a certain time to recuperate after these late nights, but it has all been great fun. If I went again it might be with a more frugal person, but this time I've seen one kind of Paris & on the whole it's the kind I expected. Art galleries & Museums will wait till next time!

Now I think Bruce is stirring & I must close. Happy weekend! Hope this reaches you.

Love,
P

1 Eva responded on 29 May: 'How lovely to visit Notre Dame and to hear the opera Salomé. I hope you'll tell me all about everything when you have time. / When I last wrote to A. Nellie I mentioned that you *had* suggested I might set up house in Belfast, but added that she mustn't take it seriously, as it *was* only a suggestion.' She also mentioned that Nellie's son-in-law George had suggested she might buy 'a house in Hyde as near to them as possible'. She asked Philip: 'What do you think of their suggestion?'

26 June 1952

30 Elmwood Avenue, Belfast[1]

My dear old creature,

I have now got 2 single-berth cabins from Heysham for the 17th, so we shall be travelling in peace. You owe my mother 12/-! as Kitty's nightdress case used to say,[2] but of course it doesn't matter till I see you. I'm not sure of the way from L'boro to Heysham – I expect we change at Manchester.[3] If you return alone, I wondered if you could break your journey at Manchester at least to the extent of perhaps lunching with Auntie N. & being put on the night train by her. I'm so glad Miss McN[4] is staying with you. You'll have to "entertain" her.

No, I'm only joking. You needn't really. I am sorry you can't "relax" because of the weather – truly very sorry. Silly old creature – not *really* silly – no harm can come to you from clouds!

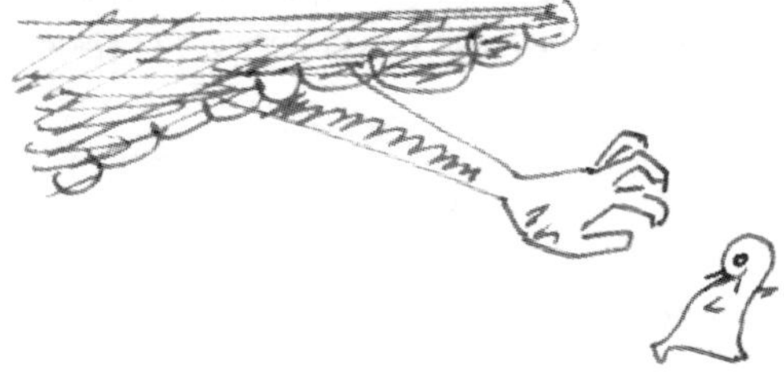

Not like this. Well, you will have a good rest here. Nothing to do at all but CLEAN MY KITCHEN: I expect you'll find lots of little corners of dust that I generally ignore.

The weather's been really hot today & my hayfever has reappeared, somewhat to my annoyance. Nearly all my friends have gone now & I can settle to a lonely *cheap* existence, I hope. The laundry has not returned my bedcover, which I sent them in a fit of *diablerie* last week to clean.

"Now my dear Eva", you *will* have a good rest this weekend, won't you? Imagine there are legions of sturdy creatures sleeping in all the other rooms.

<*Up left margin*> Love, Philip. [. . .]

1 Queen's Chambers letterhead crossed out.
2 Kitty's daughter Rosemary recollects that this nightdress case, called (in its own spelling) 'Blak Pussy', was used to house notes with messages about money owed by Eva or Kitty. Kitty continued the tradition into the next generation, putting notes about Rosemary's pocket money in it. It still survives. See Plate 11B.
3 After much strategising and many changed plans, Philip had arranged to come across and accompany Eva to Belfast. Her doubts and anxieties multiplied. On 21 June she wrote: 'You ask me whether I could fly back alone. To tell you the truth I don't like flying at all. [. . .] Why I should be more afraid to fly back I don't know. There would be other people in the 'plane of course. Would you be able to see me off? Where does the plane start from? Can I get from Birmingham to Loughborough without changing? I don't much fancy coming back alone at all. I ought to stay until you come over in September!! I might find the house burgled!' In the event she returned by ferry and spent three weeks in Hyde with Nellie before returning to Loughborough. She wrote from Hyde on 16 August: 'I have thought about you and your dear little flat so much. [. . .] I did so like my stay with you and enjoyed our little trips abroad.'
4 Effie McNicol, a friend of both Kitty and Eva, lived at 3 Radmoor Road, Loughborough, opposite the end of York Road. She had been the secretary of Dr Herbert Schofield, founder of Loughborough College (now the University) and had served with the British forces in France in the First World War. Eva affected superior amusement at Effie's forthright, brusque personality ('Isn't she a caution!').

29 June 1952

30 Elmwood Avenue, Belfast

My dear old creature,

[. . .] One odd thing that is happening next week is that Kingsley is coming for an interview for a job in the English department. Of course for years we've been saying that it would be marvellous to have a job in the same university; & I suppose it would in many ways: however, I shall not be utterly desolated if he is unsuccessful, not because of personal feeling so much as of certain knowledge of the inroads he would make on my time & possibly money. (They are penniless again, by the way.) The interview's on Tuesday. Somehow I don't think he will get it.

With my best love & kindest wishes,
P. [. . .]

22 September 1952

Picture postcard[1]

<*Postmark*> Ambleside

Have received the Guide today[2] – thanks – & used it to come here. Near here is Beatrix Potter's house, & we had a lovely time there.

Weather dry so far. We are now going to look at Wordsworth's old school.

Love,

1 Esthwaite Water.
2 On 20 September Eva wrote: 'Thanks for your p.c. this morning. I have to-day sent off the guide book to Grasmere, although I wasn't quite clear whether that was *where* you wanted me to send it.' Philip and Monica were on holiday in the Lake District.

12 October 1952

30 Elmwood Avenue, Belfast

My dear old Creature,

[. . .] I had an interesting evening on Friday, when I had the honour of being invited to meet E. M. Forster, the novelist who was over to unveil a tablet to a local writer. He was very pleasant, but I found it hard going to talk to him. I expect you have read his books – he is by elimination the "greatest English novelist" today. A toothy little aged Billy Bunter.

Today is not the kind of day you'd like! a dark sky, rain, very dreary. You would be having recourse first to the sherry, then to the damson gin, trying to decide which was the nicer, then back to sherry, trying to deshide . . . to . . . deshide . . .[1]

But I have enough to do to fill three Sundays! O my! I had better go & start doing some of it.

Yes. I *did* enjoy my stay, & how lovely that walk was. We'll go again. And I even enjoyed doing the garden.

Love of a special good sort,
Philip

1 Philip had left a bottle of sherry after his last visit. Eva wrote on 21 October: 'I have not had my glass of sherry yet to-day. Of course it won't last long if I have it daily.'

19 October 1952

30 Elmwood Avenue, Belfast

My dear old creature,

[. . .] The Strangs are back & have been hunting for a flat, complicated by Patsy's having picked up some germ – possibly by drinking tapwater on the boat, she says, so remember never to do that!

I am not doing very well with my pools! Yesterday the line I had calculated carefully scored 13 out of 24, & the line I had just dashed in made 14. In Vernons, I only do the Treble Chance pool. This consists of putting an "o" against 8 matches in the first column for 6^{d} or 1/- or whatever you like to stake. What you are trying to do is forecast 8 draws. If you succeed you score 24 pts. Needless to say the odds against are astronomical. You then copy your forecast onto the check list, which you keep. However, somebody has to win! Perhaps it would be wiser to do a few other combinations – or even to save my money.

I am glad you have your circle of cronies in Loughborough. It makes all the difference if you can knock on a door & know you will be welcomed.

Today I have a piece of best steak to try conclusions with, so I think I had better go and put the potatoes on.

Later. – Yes, all over now: a creature filled with steak & potatoes, positively *gorged*. I'll certainly try your way of roasting things: I think perhaps I overcook my pieces of meat. – Not this one though.

A sombre brown afternoon has succeeded a sombre brown morning, & the wind & rain are as powerful as ever. Really I should like to go out but I doubt if my shoes are sufficiently waterproof. Wouldn't it be nice to be walking along that road you showed me between the plantations of trees moaning & whispering like the sea? Do you remember the acorns? & the one crimson toadstool? How very beautiful autumn is.[1]

Ellen Wilson has had a daughter. There is really very little news this week otherwise: 3.15 on Sunday & all still to be done – laundry & bed changing & dusting & so on. I do hope you are keeping on with the sherry. Don't forget that 1 glass w[d] probably bring you to normal, as you are no doubt screwed up a few points above normal as a rule.

My very best love, old creature,
Philip

1 Eva replied on 21 October: 'As I always do, I again enjoyed your meditations upon Autumn. I am so glad you really liked that walk along to the forest. I should have enjoyed it more had I not been haunted by the fear of those cows! I expect you will laugh, but I have already been wondering where I could go next spring and summer so that I need not be so worried over the storms. I'm certain it's no good my being here alone.'

24 October 1952 Postcard

[30 Elmwood Avenue, Belfast]

Friday
WELCOME
No letter! Are you all right? Not –
Please reassure me!
Very unsettled weather here.
Much love
Philip

26 October 1952

30 Elmwood Ave, Belfast

My dear old creature,

[. . .] Well! Your letter arrived on Saturday morning – obviously it had gone astray, for it bore a Belfast postmark (4.45 p.m. Friday) as well as the L'boro one: the address was quite in order. I wonder where it had been? Then by lunchtime your pretty telegram arrived – how kind of you to send a greetings one![1] It was the autumn one of harvesters and fruits of the earth. I expect you felt sorry for the poor creature peering under the mat: it wasn't all *tha*t worried, since I know you'd let me have *some* word even if you were in bed. As it happened Thursday was my party day – the Graneeks & the Grahams came in the evening, & Patsy, Colin having gone to Dublin to a meeting. I rather recklessly gave them hot frankfurter sausages to start with, with half bridge rolls & mustard, so that they could make their own hot dogs. I thought this would be a very good idea for a cold-night party, with beer, for less delicate company, but was afraid it might be too crude for an evening with ladies (not to mention the fact that the Graneeks are, of course, Jews), but damn me, when I got back from putting [on] a second lot of coffee the dish was empty! Of course, they are expensive – over 5d apiece. I also bought some Gentleman's Relish – *Patum Peperium*[2] – very old world, reeking of bachelor quarters, Oxford, Inns of Courts, tea in the gun-room, and all the lovely life of the 19th century.

"Creature's relish"

I can see I shan't have to waste time drawing if I'm to answer your letter properly. Thanks for the pools cutting – I'd like to see them always – yes, I do send up my efforts, but I see that it is extremely unlikely that I sh^{d} ever win anything. You enclose a P.O. for *last* week always, & listen to the results on Saturday on the Light Prog. at 5.30 p.m. I can't score more than 14 points in the Treble Chance out of 24![3] [. . .]

It doesn't matter if you finish up the sherry: you buy another bottle then. Are you keeping count of the glasses you take from it?[4]

You are *not* such a very old creature! I wish you were here today to take advantage of the lovely sunshine – I'm angry that I can't get out myself. If only Sunday were 48 hrs long! There's far too much to do in one day. The weather is mild & gentle here – no frost yet at all, hardly.

With my most affectionate thoughts, & best-quality love,

Philip

1 On 25 October Eva had sent Philip a colourful greetings telegram: 'HOPE YOU HAVE LETTER NOW AM QUITE WELL MUCH LOVE = MOTHER + +'
2 Anchovy relish.
3 On 28 October Eva wrote: 'Hurry up, Creature, and win that £75,000! I hope you aren't spending much on them. I don't think I shall ever be able to fill one up myself. Perhaps when you come again you will help me to have a flutter.'
4 Eva wrote (28 October): 'Regarding the sherry. I have had 9 glasses, including the two we had when you were here last. The bottle is now rather more than half empty.'

28 November 1952 — Postcard

[30 Elmwood Avenue, Belfast]

So we shall be alone for Xmas after all? How jolly. We'll mull some wine & eat nuts. I'm sorry my cards don't reach you on time: they're surely postmarked Friday? Perhaps the post-creatures read them & decide they aren't important. But they *are*, post-creatures.

I'm sorry too that you aren't going to see M. – She asked me if you'd come if asked & I'm afraid I said you would. I'd forgotten you didn't like dark nights.[1]

Looking forward to the pie,
Philip

1 On 25 November Eva told Philip that Monica had asked her to tea, 'giving me the times of various buses and different ways of getting to Westgate Road but somehow the journey rather bothered me, particularly the journey back in the dark. I wrote, as nicely as I could, and said I wasn't at all happy about the return journey, and I would rather postpone any visit until the lighter evenings.'

1953

4 January 1953

30 Elmwood Ave[1]

My dear old creature,

And a happy new year to you too!

Well, I'm back again in my flat: the crossing was quite uneventful, though cool: I had an outside cabin, & I think these are colder than the rest. Belfast is covered in white frost and my two rooms need a good bit of warming up. Your letter & the gloves awaited me: I will change them for the next size larger as soon as I can.

London was not very eventful, but it was certainly warmer than Warwick. So that was a good point in its favour! Of course we spent a ridiculous amount of time & money eating and drinking: we also saw the negro opera *Porgy & Bess*, wch was good, and a film *Quo vadis* which wasn't![2] I noticed one night after midnight that the air is full of twittering in London – flocks of sparrows & starlings that never sleep but sit chattering till all hours. I also devoted some time to trying to fit London together in my mind – walking about, trying to connect it up, but I find it extraordinarily difficult. There's so much of it, & it all looks the same. [. . .]

Monica was delighted with Warwick, & indeed it did look a very picturesque & pleasing spot. To my great delight peacocks were picking about in Castle Lane, but when I turned to Monica to see what she thought of such oriental quaintness I found she'd backed about 10 feet in half a second, nor could she be induced to approach them. However, she admitted such a sight was *unusual*, if she personally could not call it *delightful* . . . They fly over the wall and the cottagers feed them. Don't you think it strange for any old lady? A queen in her palace couldn't have more than peacocks at her door.

I noticed Mr Harrod's name amongst the CBE's, but nobody else's. He's Chairman of some Committee to do with *Poles*. How Pop would grin.

Of course I was too lazy to buy any rations in London, so lunch today has been a poached egg, macaroni & tinned spinach, quite nice, but not unduly filling. However, I daresay I could do with a day's fasting after some of the meals I've had. My New Year resolutions are: Eat fruit and sugar! but I do hate sugar so! Perhaps it will be enough if I eat my chocolate ration regularly – that may help anyway.[3]

Well, my dear creature, I am a bit flat today, but I enjoyed my Christmas & look forward to seeing you again. Daddy's watch is going well & has already been much admired. I didn't see anyone in London except Bruce & Peter Watt, & a man called Jiggs who is Bandmaster of the Irish Guards. Quite a change for me.

Much special love,
Philip

1 Address inserted in pen; Queen's Chambers letterhead crossed out.
2 George Gershwin's 1935 opera and MGM's 1951 Technicolor epic film starring Robert Taylor and Deborah Kerr.
3 In her letter of 6 January Eva remarked: 'I think a better New Year resolution would be to get up in time to prepare and eat a good breakfast. After all, to have to be at Queen's by 10 o'clock is no great hardship, is it? If you got breakfast by 9.15 a.m. you would be in good time.'

18 January 1953

30 Elmwood Ave, Belfast

My dear old creature,

[. . .] Things have been going on much the same as usual here: no, you didn't meet Winifred last year.[1] As you may divine I am feeling a bit balked concerning her – my paw was raised to be brought down on her – and now she scuttles away into the shadow of a rock! Bah![2] [. . .]

My very best love, dear old creature:

Philip

1 Larkin addressed 'Lines on a Young Lady's Photograph Album' and 'Maiden Name' to Winifred Arnott, an English Library Assistant at Queens. They discussed the pros and cons of marriage and went on long cycle rides together. Their relationship never became physical and on her return to Queeen's after Christmas 1952 she announced that she was engaged to be married.
2 Eva wrote on 25 January: 'You mystify me somewhat about Winifred. Why should you feel balked? I can only think of one reason. However I hope you are not too miserable about her engagement.'

1 February 1953

30 Elmwood Ave, Belfast

My dear old creature,

I have just turned your calendar over to February, & sat down to do as much of your letter before lunch as I can. You'll be interested to know that I am trying a tiny *pot au feu* today – beef for boiling, turnip, carrots, a leek, onion, & a cabbage I shall have to do separately. It smells lovely. I've also ½ a bottle of claret (4/-) & some new potatoes. I wonder what you have got? Anything like this?

[. . .] I must thank you for your last long letter. I'm sorry the telegram was not an unmixed blessing.[1] My "other ailments" are the music hall jest of *non-acting bowels* – this has been going on for five weeks now & I'm heartily sick of it.

So are all my friends, I can assure you, as I keep them well informed of my day to day progress or otherwise.[2]

My social evening went fairly well, but it was hellish dear. As well as ham sandwiches (which go with anything) I did cheese sandwiches – cheese & pickles, cheese & celery, cheese & tomato. Also chocolate biscuits. I had another one last night – the Strangs, Winifred, Leo[3] & Archie – more free and easy, & much cheaper. How did you get on with Effie?[4] I'm sure, though she must be difficult to talk to, that you get a good deal of private fun out of her. Next Sunday I have to go out and listen to some records of *Bartok*, a very nobbly modern composer that I doubt I shall enjoy. Today I dedicate to myself & to my cooking.

I'm sorry Kitty is in such a poor way. I can quite imagine that the strain must tell on her. If I had the time to write letters I'd take her onto my rota, but perhaps I might send one. I wore her tie on Friday, having assembled suitable clothes to match it, & it didn't look too bad.

At present I'm starting *The adventures of Philip* by Thackeray. The title caught my eye, So far he is just a young man who doesn't like his father, but I don't know why.

Well, now I will go and see to my lunch: & leave a little space to tell you what it was like.

Later – I wish you could have seen my lunch table: blue & white check cloth, claret, brown bread, celery, cheese – it looked like an advertisement! The lunch *was* nice – much too much of it, of course! – but not quite so nice as those made by a certain old creature of my acquaintance, not long ago. I didn't have any peppercorns, but I had cloves & bay leaves.

I enclose a para. about Spring. I have a bunch of snowdrops in my room & another in the kitchen. My special spring time love,

Philip

<*Cutting enclosed*>

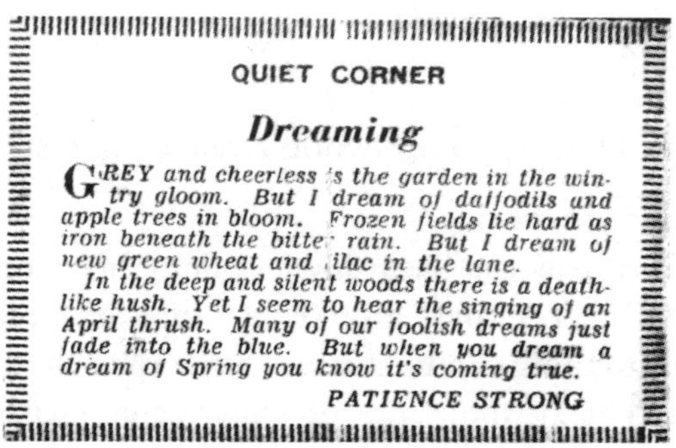

QUIET CORNER

Dreaming

GREY and cheerless is the garden in the wintry gloom. But I dream of daffodils and apple trees in bloom. Frozen fields lie hard as iron beneath the bitter rain. But I dream of new green wheat and lilac in the lane.

In the deep and silent woods there is a deathlike hush. Yet I seem to hear the singing of an April thrush. Many of our foolish dreams just fade into the blue. But when you dream a dream of Spring you know it's coming true.

PATIENCE STRONG

1 Eva wrote on 27 January: 'The telegram, you might like to know gave me, and my next door neighbour a slight shock. I was standing at the front door speaking to Mrs Coleman, who is rather under the weather just now, and also has a sister very ill indeed, and a brother just recovering from a very serious operation (the Doctor gave him up) as well as a mother, over 80 who had just had a fall and hurt herself, when the telegram boy cycled up. Of course *she* thought it was for her, and turned pale.'

2 On 3 February Eva sent detailed dietary and physical advice from 'the Encyclopaedia' on how to avoid constipation, concluding: 'I hope you won't be tempted to try a cold bath for it might make you ill, as you are not in the habit of taking it cold. Wait till summer!'

3 Leo Japolsky, Lecturer in French at QUB. On 5 March 1954 Larkin wrote: 'I went to Leo's piano recital last night, which was taken at top speed in a very cold hall, but was quite good.' See Plate 9c for Larkin's expressionistic photograph of this unstable colleague, who was eventually committed to a secure hospital after killing his father.

4 Effie McNichol.

14 March 1953 — Greetings telegram[1]

10.0 AM BELFAST N 13 =
GREETINGS = LARKIN 21 YORK ROAD LOUGHBOROUGH =
CHARMING LETTER ENJOS [*sic*] YOUR WEEKEND **
LOVE = PHILIP +

1 15 March was mothering Sunday. On 17 March Eva wrote: 'In what a delightful manner you remembered "Old Creatures' Day"! As a matter of fact on the Saturday morning I hurried away from Kitty's early (they were only just getting up!) in order to be in, if the postman *should* knock, perhaps a card too large to be pushed through the letter box, because knowing what a kind-hearted Creature you are I somehow thought there might be something un-usual. At 11-a.m. the postman knocked and handed to me your lovely "greetings telegram" which made me very happy.'

2 May 1953

<*Letterhead*> Flat 13, 30 Elmwood Avenue, Belfast

My very dear old creature,

I'm writing to you on Saturday evening this week-end, because tomorrow I shall be occupied all day, and of course old creature must have its letter! Anything can be missed rather than that. My inside feels a trifle congested at the moment, for I have eaten nearly a whole tin of salmon for supper, & nearly a whole tin of asparagus.

But I'm not so bloated that I cannot send you my most special love & sympathy this week, hoping that you have had a more enjoyable time this weekend than you had to chronicle in your letter. There is nothing more grisly than the rattle of house agents' keys – I mean that nothing is more unsettling than the slightest hint that one *isn't* settled in one's domicile. And of course I know that you are ridden by this particular dislike of thunderstorms, which seems quite reasonable to me as long as there's one actually in progress, but *not* when there isn't.[1] You really must remember that in a temperate climate like ours there are always plenty of clouds about, & that they don't necessarily mean any harm: they are always forming and dissipating, and I think if you kept a little diary and marked every day when you were worried about storms, and every day that there *was* a storm, I think you'd be astonished at the amount of worrying about nothing that you'd done. As for the larger questions, I am coming to think that you would be happier in a flat (less work, less worrying responsibility) & that if all our special belongings are an obstacle to your happiness then it's time they went. Your object in life should be happiness, now you have come into the quieter waters of old creaturehood, & I hope to see you achieve it.

This week held one or two small worries for me – my cleaner & my caretaker are squabbling, also some people in the library who are nominally under my aegis. And then my driving lesson gives me the jitters – I get frightfully nervous & do things all wrong. And also of course I am wondering what Walter will do.

The volume called *Springtime* that includes six of my *XX Poems* turned up on May 1st – in the introduction they call me an Irish poet, "rooted" – I don't quite know in what, but rooted anyway! They seem to imagine I am some kind of rural Irish creature!

Tonight I have to go to a play by St John Irvine,[2] which you will hear us talking about on Thursday at 9.15 p.m. (N.I. Home Service). I hope *that* goes well. Probably I shall gibber gibber gibber. I understand a man is going to differ from me violently.

I think I'll break off now, & go to the theatre: perhaps I can finish this when I return. Goodbye for about 4 hours!

20 to 12. Phew! Home again, and after a fairly boring time. It was a first night, crowded, in the little theatre we went to with the Wilsons (funny night that!). I was so hot & bored, I ran away at the end, probably offending the B.B.C. creatures I was with, but really I couldn't stand any more of anything. Tomorrow I have a day out: six of us have hired a car down to Dublin, where we shall see *Tristan & Isolde* done by the Munich State Opera Company. Can't say this will be exactly my cup of tea, but I'm always interested in new experiences & I've never seen any Wagner before. Of course I'm not going to drive, in case you think I am! I couldn't drive a dodgem car at present. [. . .]

When I go onto a third sheet I really have to ferret things out to tell you![3] I bought my nylon pants in Oxford, and they've been wearing quite well – I wash them at night, & am thinking of putting in a special hook in the rafter to hang them on to dry. My housekeeping is an endless round of bacon & eggs, cheese, spaghetti & soups – but now the season is coming in again there'll be more variety. Isn't it nice to have spring again? You remember Housman's lines "And since to look at things in bloom Fifty springs is little room . . ."[4] and I do agree. As the dawn song of birds is supposed to represent their joy at finding that the light did come back, so I feel we ought to make some similar rejoicing – well, I suppose Easter is our festival, the Resurrection thanksgiving. How I do drivel on. But, dear old creature, do remember that there are more things in life than thunderstorms – trees, stars, rivers, all costing nothing to look at. It takes quite a bit to crush any human spirit, so take courage! Now I must go to bed.

My best love,
Philip[5]

1 In a six-page letter of 28 April Eva considered her future should Walter take a job in Wolverhampton, where he had been living in digs during a long assignment away from home: 'I could stay here if only I weren't so afraid at times. Ever since Saturday I have lived in fear and trembling, all because of the weather, and the thought that I may be alone if a storm comes along. If I don't get better soon, I really shall have to do something about it. Can you, or Patsy tell me how I can overcome these fears. I *do* wish I wasn't like it. / About letting the house furnished, I think it would be very difficult to clear *all* the rooms of our especial belongings. [. . .] Then again, I think what I really want is company in the house. You see, I should be just as worried if I came to Belfast and just as much alone. I wonder if I tried to get a companion help, even though it might be costly, it would be worth it if my mind was more at ease. I might cease to think of the weather in time.'

2 St John Ervine (*sic.*; 1883–1971), Irish author and playwright.

3 He is now at the bottom of the recto of his third page (the 5th side).

4 A. E. Housman, *A Shropshire Lad* 2: 'Loveliest of trees, the cherry now'.

5 He finishes, as almost always, at the very bottom of the verso of the final page.

7 July 1953

Postcard

[30 Elmwood Ave, Belfast]

Tuesday.

A little more stable by now! but not much. Glad you received and liked the book. It makes one want to go on the moors, doesn't it?[1] Our weather has cleared up somewhat but is very windy. Yesterday I bought a new pair of bathing trunks – fashions have changed rather since my young days! These are very scanty & sporty & I trust will not get me arrested. The moths have been wearing my old ones.

Very best wishes to our special old creature P.

1 Perhaps this book was Emily Brontë's *Wuthering Heights* or Richard Blackmore's *Lorna Doone*.

17 July 1953

Postcard

[30 Elmwood Ave, Belfast]

Many thanks for your letter. Don't be flurried, old creech-haugh! I shall be in B'ham long before you, on the 25th July, & will meet you.[1] Before I send this card I'll look up the train-times for you. – *Friday*. In Glasgow, after safe though slow journey. As far as I can see, your train to B'ham must be the 8.30 a.m. from Leicester, arriving at 9.39 a.m. – but I really cannot find how you manage to be at Leicester (London Rd) by 8.30! Wd you please ask at the Nut Shop? As I said before the train on the day is the 9.49 but it arrives *too late* – our train goes at 11.35. No, I ain't forgotten Kitty: mea culpa. Quite fine here.

All love,
Philip

1 On 13 July Eva, worrying about travel arrangements for her forthcoming holiday with Philip in Weymouth, had written: 'I feel more than a bit perturbed about meeting you in Birmingham. I'm so afraid I shall miss you. I suppose though, if your train gets in first, you will enquire which platform mine comes in [at] and wait there until it *does* come in. I do hope I don't have to change. If *my* train gets in first I must find out where yours is expected to come in. *Where* will your train be coming *from*? If, however, I can't find you within a reasonable time, and the worst comes to the worst I shall get the station authorities to call you on the loud speaker.'

6 August 1953

<*Letterhead*> Flat 13, 30 Elmwood Avenue, Belfast

Welcome home, dear old creature![1] I hope you had an easy journey and that your little home looks snug & neat. Last night I asked for the lawn mower, but was told it had gone to be mended. I breathed again!

Now don't go worrying about any old weather: summer's pretty well done, so old creatures can sit round the fire & roast chestnuts.

All love, P

1 An unusual one page letter with blank verso. It awaited Eva on her return from the holiday she had spent with Philip in Weymouth, following his holiday with Monica in Mallaig, Inverness-shire.

23 August 1953

<*Letterhead*> Flat 13, 30 Elmwood Avenue, Belfast

My very dear old creature,

This is a dull day of the kind I expect you like: no one could find a thundercloud if they rooted about all day, & I think a fine steady rain is falling. I've not dressed yet: I've made my bed, but apart from breakfasting & shaving that's all. There is a curry made in the kitchen, ready to be restarted: how it will taste I don't know. I think there's too much lemon in it. I've no "duties" today except innumerable letters [. . .]

Can you feel the autumn where you are? It seems to hang in the air here, and sharpen my senses, and again I feel a sense of a great waste in my life. We must go again up that road to the wood where we found the scarlet toadstool and listen to the wind in the trees. I'm sure it's beautiful at this time of year. Here the moon is large and lemon-yellow and drifts up into the sky at night like a hollow phosphorescent fungoid growth. Do you watch it?

[. . .]

Well, old creature; now I must up and dress, & see about my lunch. I'll send you a card about when I'm likely to arrive on Saturday. Keep yourself in good trim & good fettle.

My very best love,
Philip

13 September 1953

<*Letterhead*> Flat 13, 30 Elmwood Avenue, Belfast

My very dear old creature,

[. . .] Kingsley is very well: rapidly becoming a successful writer! On Wednesday he is going to London to see his *English* publishers, his

American publishers, & be photographed & interviewed for *Vogue*. You can imagine the mixture of feelings I contemplate all this with![1] His two children seem well enough; The elder reminds me of Hilly, the younger of Kingsley – the younger likes blue cheese, beer, pickles, vinegar & little girl friends, all of which things Kingsley likes himself. The house is a bit cleaner, but full of things needing repair: for instance, I had been raising & lowering my bedroom window every night & morning some days before I found out a whole pane was missing! [. . .]

All special love,
Philip

1 Eva wrote on 15 September: 'Kingsley *is* forging ahead. Somehow I fancy I can hear Daddy saying, "You ought to be glad *you're* not being photographed and interviewed by Vogue!"'

15 November 1953

<*Letterhead*> Flat 13, 30 Elmwood Avenue, Belfast

My especial old creature,

[. . .] Yes. I am sad Dylan Thomas has died. Eliot, Auden and he were the three living poets who had altered the way other people write poetry – other poets have written as well or better, but these three are the influences. Lawrence, for instance, never had a tenth of the influence of Dylan Thomas. I stood him a drink once! As for poetry, I have been rhyming away myself recently, and have sent a group of 8 poems to some undergraduate concern at Oxford. Should have grown beyond this by now, but still: it may lead to something.[1] [. . .]

Farewell, my dear old creature: my thoughts are often with you,

Philip

1 Eventually five of these poems were published in *Fantasy Poets*, no. 21, 1954.

30 November 1953

Flat 13, 30 Elmwood Avenue, Belfast

My dear old creature,

This is just a little note with no reason behind it, except that I envisaged you pottering about your little home & wished I could let you know how much I'd like to be there! Dear old creature, remember you are very often in my thoughts: I hope you'll come here again next year, even if I have to escort you myself. In the meantime I look forward to seeing you at Christmas. There'll be no thunder at Christmas, & we can sit tippling damson gin.

With my best love – shall consider some "writing" now – Philip

6 December 1953

30 Elmwood Avenue, Belfast

My dear old creature,

[. . .] For me the great news this week has been the death of T. F. Powys;[1] although he did in fact die on 27 November, I didn't hear of it till a week later. You know he was a great favourite of mine, though he was an old man and would obviously not write any more. I felt very sorry for him because he did in his work describe the *fear of death* better than anyone else I know, and it was a matter he couldn't regard without distress. Bishop Barnes died too,[1] as I expect the *Church Times* will have told you. [. . .]

I expect I shall have Leo Japolsky up here some time today – he always comes at an inconvenient moment – because he is only recently back from Oxford where he was interviewed in connection with his Doctorate. I wonder if they are going to give it him. I could hear him playing the piano this morning and it didn't sound very cheerful playing.

From what I saw of his thesis I thought he would be a borderline case. He will be extremely dejected if he doesn't get it. [. . .]

With my best love to the dear old creature,

Philip

1 T. F. Powys (1875–1953), novelist; brother of J. C. and Llewelyn Powys.

2 Ernest Barnes (1874–1953), Bishop of Birmingham from 1924, known for his controversial views on theological and other subjects.

1954

24 January 1954

30 Elmwood Ave, Belfast

My dear old creature,

Today has got going suspiciously early: I mean I've only got up, breakfasted, shaved & dressed, and here it is, 20 to 1, with hardly any progress made. Outside, the day is grey and dry, with a bleak with blowing, or at any rate a wind: perhaps quite a mild one. I did go out to secure the papers, but hardly noticed what was happening as I had only just got up. In the papers I found the first 2 reviews of Kingsley's book.[1] I expect you'll see the S.T., which is adverse. The *Observer*, though not much more perceptive, praises it very highly indeed. My copy turned up last Monday, & I do find it extremely funny. I think Kitty would enjoy it, though I don't know if you would.

My life proceeds on its usual winter course, quiet and not especially demanding. I feel much more cheerful now my pain has gone. My young assistant continues to gobble up all the work I can find for him.[2] Which is very nice for us: shortly I hope to maintain connection with the library by telephone only. Of course when he goes I shall fall down flop.

Monica continues to be a good deal exercised about where to live. Various flats present themselves but are either given to others or are not suitable. It worries her a good deal, since now Charmian has gone the rent of her house is of course still the same but with only 2 people to pay it – & I don't suppose the other girl is going to pay any more as she is "only temporary". I do feel sorry for her: she dislikes her job, it wears her out, and she is not very good at fending for herself in the matter of flat-finding and the rest of it. And the future seems to hold nothing better.

I find your Courtaulds letter hard to understand – honestly, y[r] bank people would understand it better than I – it seems incredible that they should be giving away £24m., and yet that's what they seem to be doing.[3] O enviable creature! You could take a cruise all round the world for that, & forget that such goblin-eared miseries as crouch about York Road ever existed!

Not a very successful drawing. Believe me, I do sympathise with your difficulties in your lonely life: I feel very beastly at being so far away and able to do so little to help. Certainly, as I said at Christmas, I think a rest would do you good, and am interested to hear that Dr Folwell does too. After all, if circumstances can affect you adversely (as you say they can), a change in them might affect you favourably. You do not take sufficiently into account the fact that your depression results from the kind of life you lead: surely if you alter, even for a bit, the kind of life then you may alter, even for a bit, the depression it produces – and that is better than nothing. 3 months pleasure and 9 months misery is better than 12 months' misery. Isn't that so? Of course I agree about the unpleasantness of having a stranger to live with you, unless the stranger were a person you found sufficiently nice to make a friend of, which *might* happen, of course. Did you see Dr Folwell again? I'm sure you are less trouble than some of her more desperate patients who chew the carpets. In short, I think a brief holiday first of all would be the thing – especially as you HAVE THE MONEY. Talking about money, I haven't yet spent the £1 you gave me for Christmas, but I keep it separate, in your original envelope, & shall 'plunge' in due course.

Let me know how you get on. Remember that every day is something chalked up to your account; a victory, instead of a defeat; a medal, not a black mark. I think of you a great deal. Would you like me to ring up for a chat next Sunday?[4]

Very best creaturely love,
Philip

1 *Lucky Jim.*
2 On 19 January Eva had written: 'I was interested to know that you now have a young man under you. I hope he doesn't make you as distracted as some of the maids made me. I wonder if you and I *are* alike. I always think you resemble G. Dad more than anyone else.' Grand-dad is Eva's father, William Day.
3 Philip returned the letter, which Eva had enclosed with hers of 19 February. It informed her that 'they are going to give me a fresh share for each one I already possess. As I think I have 300 this seems a nice little gift.'
4 Eva responded on 26 January: 'How I wish I could chase all my fears away [. . .]! then life might be worth living. Even now, I am shrinking from inviting Effie in on Thursday evening, fearing that the weather will do something dreadful which will un-nerve me, and prevent me making the necessary preparations.' Later, on 4 May, she related how Effie had called on her, 'all in a thrill', to insist she 'go over and celebrate her television set which had just been fixed up. [. . .] The T.V. programme was rather boring but the climax arrived for me when the weather report came on. I hardly know how I listened to it – I was all in perspiration.'

21 February 1954

UNIVERSITY OF DUBLIN

TRINITY COLLEGE
DUBLIN

My dear old creature,

Well, here I am, set down in the middle of the Anglo-Irish tradition, and considerably relieved that my ordeal of Friday is over.[1] It went quite well, I think: I was nervous to start with, and the beginning of my paper was not very good (2 young men got up & went out & I thought O dear it can't sound up to much), but the second half of the paper was much better written & got some laughs, & they were really very kind & agreeable afterwards. So the ordeal went off not too badly after all my moanings, as I expect any one who wasn't a craven creature would have realised to start with.[2]

On the other hand I don't feel particularly happy as I have nothing to do today and to be alone in a strange town is always a little upsetting. I am booked here over tonight, but I've more than half a mind to go home. [. . .]

If you are passing a bookshop you might look out for a Penguin copy of *Love lies bleeding* by Edmund Crispin & read what he says about himself on the back (don't buy it as we have it): I think it will amuse you.[3] He's a rare old card is Bruce, like all my friends, successful swine all of them.

Talking about colds, the fellow who arranged for me to come down here, a lecturer called Donald Davie, has along with his wife & 2 children most frightful colds – I fancy even the cat sneezed once, so I hope I haven't caught it myself. But Dublin always seems a chilly wet place to me, though no worse than Belfast, I'm sure.

I still feel no more decided about what to do today – it seems absurd to go home, yet I've no resources save the church & the cinema . . . creature alone in Dublin! Creature feels a bit lost. There is a mild sun coming out, but I can hear the wind, & I don't feel that rain is far away. I wonder what kind of a day you are having, & whether anything is sprouting in your back garden.[4]

Very much love, dear old creature:
P.

1 Donald Davie had invited Larkin to give a talk at Trinity College, Dublin, where he was teaching at the time. Davie was on the editorial board of Dolmen Press and had been in favour of publishing what was to become *The Less Deceived*. He was overruled by his two co-editors. See *Selected Letters*, 229.
2 On 23 February Eva wrote: 'Words cannot express how magnificently brave you are! Really, I *do* think you are wonderful to give that talk in spite of the awfulness of your feelings. How glad you must be now that it is over, and how uplifted to think that you *didn't fail*.'
3 Montgomery had written: 'He is thirty-one years old, unmarried, constitutionally torpid: for recreation he does crossword puzzles, reads and sleeps. Unlike most authors, he has not been a lumber-jack, bar-tender, advertising agent, ship's cat, lecturer in metallurgy, gigolo, and Member of Parliament. For a time after leaving Oxford he was, however, a schoolmaster.'
4 In her letter of 23 February Eva turned Philip's query into a focus of anxiety: 'What a sweet little sketch of me in the back garden! There are lots of things coming up in my back garden, Creature, but there are *lots* more that ought to come up and be thrown away. I fully intended to 'phone the gardener to-day and ask him why he had not been to set it in order – but the weather frightened me off it!'

30 May 1954

30 Elmwood Ave, Belfast

My very dear old creature,

[. . .] Will you think of Thos. Hardy on Wednesday? It was his birthday, in 1840.

I fancy I hear Leo[1] playing his piano in the distance – he has been away for a week – he is a moody fool – but I want to borrow his room –

Patsy[2] is on the point of going to Italy for a holiday. She has bought *a knife* to defend herself with! I think she is very courageous. She can't even buy a return ticket on the 'bus without losing the return half – so perhaps she will never come back from Italy!

Now I must dress, & pack my lunch. My very best love, dear creature. Keep up your tail!

Philip

1 Leo Japolsky.
2 Patsy Strang.

8 August 1954

30 Elmwood Ave, Belfast

My poor dear old creature,

I say 'poor' because of the storms I hear you've been having in Nottingham and Lincoln, & which I expect did not pass you by either. Certainly I thought we were booked for one yesterday, but the rain came down instead. I was listening to a cricket commentary from Bradford & could hear the thunder there & the 'ooo's of the crowd as it lightened! I thought you would have your head in a bag safely somewhere.[1]

[. . .]

Tomorrow I have a stall reserved to see Tommy Trinder at the local Hippodrome. This is by way of being a "birthday treat", though it will be rather a lonely one, I fancy. However, it's nice to know you will be thinking of me & drinking my health.

Give my love to Kitty & the other two.

With all my love,
Philip

1 On 10 August Eva wrote: 'Yes. I'm writing this at Kitty's, for the weather has kept me on tenterhooks all day so that I have at last given up the fight and come here. / As you guessed I've been a "poor creature" since reading about the awful storms of last Friday and Saturday. On Friday evening I could both see and hear that a storm was coming up, and I was trying to hurry with the usual routine of leaving all safe before closing the door for the night when Walter came up to see where I was, (and wasn't I thankful!).'

10 October 1954

30 Elmwood Avenue, Belfast

My dear old creature,

This day is a little upset – I found the time was a quarter to eleven before I knew what had happened. Now it is a quarter to two: I have my joint (of pork) in the oven, but I'm not sure I shan't turn out the gas and go for a ride round when I finish this, as the weather is warm and balmy. Recently my bicycle has had a flat tyre, but yesterday the repair shop said they could find nothing wrong – they simply blew it up! Fool of a creature.

I feel a little better-tempered today as J. B. Priestley in the *S. Times* remarks that Kingsley has been "luckier than his own *Lucky Jim*" – good stuff.[1] He hasn't written to me since we met in Cheltenham: I'm hanged if I will be the one to write first. I'm so glad you found *Corduroy*[2] – what can it have been doing in the ottoman? Finally, I don't know if I mentioned it, but the Dublin book of poems has fallen through: the selectors didn't like the group I submitted, so that's that.[3] I was disappointed at first, but now do not care. My skin is thick enough to withstand such criticism.

I'm sorry to hear Dennis Folwell is ill again – it coincides with "Jack"'s prolonged absence in the mental hospital, I suppose.[4]

Yesterday I did worse on my pools than ever before – 10 scored on each line: you *can't* score less than 8, however badly you do, so you see that I was pretty near the bottom. I buy a bunch of postal orders and so don't have to worry about buying them separately. If I won £75,000 I expect old creature w^{d} find itself among marble halls somewhere![5]

I really must send you a Llewelyn Powys: I have plenty of them here. Perhaps when I ring you up tonight I'll ask you which you would like.

Yes, I should like another *Country Life* "Beautiful Britain" calendar when the time comes.

Trinity College was very interesting. The dinner was: celery soup, Lobster Newburg, pheasant, & apple pie with real cream. It was accompanied by sherry, white wine, & a Corton (burgundy, I suppose). Then we piled upstairs and sat round tables lit by red candles in silver sconces – or do I mean candlesticks? – and drank claret, madeira, or (and, I'm afraid in my case, *and*) port, & smoked cigars, while the Provost made a speech saying what a fine fellow Donald Davie was, and Davie made a speech saying what a good place Trinity College was. As a fellow, he is now committed to the place, but he seems quite happy about it.

Oh, drat! I've switched out the gas in the oven, now the *rain* has started! [. . .]

In retrospect this looks a dull letter, but I shall be talking to you tonight, & anyway the sun has come out now. My special love.

Philip

1 Eva replied hesitantly, not sure of Philip's tone (12 October): 'I read J. B. Priestley's remarks about Kingsley's novel and in consideration of *your* remark assumed that it was not a very good review of "Lucky Jim". When I got to Kitty's last night she had kept their S. Times to show it to me. Walter spotted it first, and they both took it that it was a very good review and thought Kingsley had got the first prize. Are they right? I did not think so when *I* read it.'

2 A novel by farmer and author Adrian Bell (1901–80), published in 1930. It was followed by *Silver Ley* (1931) and *The Cherry Tree* (1932), the three books forming a *Corduroy* trilogy.

3 Donald Davie was in favour of the Dolmen Press publishing twelve of Larkin's poems, but his co-editors, Thomas Kinsella and Liam Miller, outvoted him.

4 Eva had mentioned (22 January 1951) that Dr Folwell's son Denis, who played Jack Archer in *The Archers* radio serial, was very ill.

5 Eva replied on 12 October: 'Oh, I *did* love your sketch of the old Creature in those marble halls. I expect, like the sketch, I should look a bit uneasy and afraid to put my paws down.'

17 October 1954

30 Elmwood Avenue, Belfast

My dear old creature,

I am not in the best of shape this morning, as I went out last night to a "routine" party, & had for the previous three nights been occupied in some way or other in a social fashion. The weather is wet & warm, & I haven't even the consolation of thinking I can spend the day in relaxation, since this evening I must draft my application for this Hull job. No doubt I shall be letting myself in for much trouble and embarrassment for nothing. Really I can't envisage myself as a university librarian! I said this to Graneek & his reply, in effect, was that *good* university librarians were very rare, but that he had no doubt that I should make a university librarian of *some* sort, more so than *some* people who *were* university librarians . . .[1] So we shall see. I rang up Dr Marshall[2] on Saturday to ask if he would support my application, & he readily agreed. He asked after you, & I said you were "not too bad".

I had your card (postmarked Ambergate) and was relieved to know you were *not* stranded in the wilds of Derbyshire. Are you surrounded, I wonder, by *rather queer* people? I despatched *Impassioned clay*[3] to you on Friday, after glancing into it and thinking how very good and thrilling it seemed: I hope you enjoy it.

Do you remember Alec Dalgarno?[4] The two of us seem to be bracketed together in the public mind, as I hear there is a proposal to put us both on the Common Room Committee. We have also been "taken up" by a pair of well off Australians called Egerton (they drove me to Dublin & back), and they give us food and drink and play bridge with us.[5] (This is what I was up to on Thursday.) I put them down as people who find their ordinary life rather boring, but I'm not sure I want to be bracketed with Alec, agreeable fellow though he is.[6]

How I liked your self-portrait at the end of your letter![7] I'm afraid there are no marble halls this week either. It's not a very hopeful prospect. However, I shall persevere for a time, in the hope of landing a shower of gold.

Monica is not very happy at present, though I haven't heard from her for a few days: she has not had any leads in the matter of flats, and finds living with the Evanses a little oppressive, not because she doesn't like them, but because living with anyone that way can hardly help being oppressive.

It's now a quarter to three: I must dash off a letter to Miss Bennett in time to catch the post and inform her that I am taking her name in vain as a reference.[8] Hope she doesn't turn nasty. Oh dear, it seems queer to be thinking about moving. One goes on and on in life, from place to place and salary to salary, getting no nearer to any sense of having "arrived" or of being contented, though of course I am comfortable enough here . . .

My very dearest love Philip

1 Eva commented on 19 October: 'You have decided to apply, then, for Hull. I'm sorry you cannot feel more enthusiastic about it, Creature. I really cannot think what else you could do, if you went out of the Librarian business. Of course, if you won a shower of gold you wouldn't need to have a job at all!'
2 Arthur Hedley Marshall had succeeded Sydney Larkin as Treasurer of Coventry.
3 *Impassioned Clay: An Essay*, by Llewelyn Powys (1884–1939), published in 1931.
4 Colleague in the maths department at Queens University.
5 Larkin remained friends with Judy Egerton (1928–2012) for the rest of his life. She moved to London with her husband Ansell, who wrote a business column in the *Times*. Judy was an art historian and in 1974 was appointed Assistant Keeper of the British Collection at the Tate Gallery.
6 A photograph of Alec Dalgarno, taken by Larkin, miscaptioned 'Robert Conquest', is included in Bradford *The Importance of Elsewhere: Philip Larkin's Photographs*, 160. See James Booth, 'Belfast Friends: Alec Dalgarno', *About Larkin* 43 (April 2017), 18.
7 Eva had ended her letter of 12 October with a self-portrait, carefully sketched first in pencil. She added diffidently: 'What a funny creature.'
8 Rhoda Bennett, Librarian at Leicester University College.

24 October 1954

30 Elmwood Ave, Belfast

My very dear *thrifty* old creature,

[. . .] I have sent off my Hull application & can only sit back and wait now. It is not very probable that I shall be successful, but I feel I might get an interview – free trip to England. I am rather uneasy because during the summer I published three poems in a Hull magazine of a nature calculated to repel all but the jolliest and most advanced of Library-Committee members – one begins

"Why do I let the toad *work*
Squat on my life?"

– not the best kind of testimonial! It may be that no one will have read them, of course, but they leave the reader in no doubt about what I think of salaried employment ("Six days of the week it soils, With its sickening poison"). It will take an awful lot of explaining away.[1] [. . .]

It is nearly three now, & I must get this to post, & perhaps I might go a ride round. The weather is still fine & clear. My best love to you, dear old creature. What a rich creature!

Philip

1 In her reply of 26 October Eva was reassuring: 'Possibly no one on *the* committee will have read them. *If* they have, I expect they will put you on the short list out of curiosity to see the author.'

23 November 1954 — Postcard

Hull, Tuesday 10 a.m.

Arrived safely after very dull journey – train broke down at one point! We didn't change at Doncaster. Hull has its Christmas decorations up, for what that's worth. I've paid my hotel bill & bought my ticket to L'pool & put my bag in the station – w^{d} that I were safely rolling away! All that remains is this 4½ hrs in between. It's a bit chilly here & smells of fish. I am going to put down the alternatives & then cross off which doesn't apply, so that I can post this quickly later in the day.

Appointed ~~Not appointed~~
~~Don't know~~[1]

Very much love!
Philip

1 'Appointed' ringed in pencil; crossings out in pencil

26 November 1954 Postcard

[30 Elmwood Avenue, Belfast] Friday

Horrid wet here: and has been all the week. Many thanks for your letter & congratulations! I feel commiserations are more what I want! Glad Mrs Lowe is on the mend. & hope you are keeping warm indoors.

I wonder if you w^d^ tell Kitty that I'm sorry to have been awkward about Xmas – I felt v. bad on Monday morning: but I did appreciate seeing her new suit. Hope she doesn't think handkerchiefs dull – I certainly need them. Further news on Sunday. Have been correcting some proofs for Bruce.

Very best love P.

1955

1 January 1955

<*Letterhead*> The Royal Hotel Winchester Ltd.

My dear old creature,

What a surprise to find my scarf for breakfast this morning![1] In truth I knew I had left it, but I was very glad of it today because the weather is so frightfully cold, really arctic, so your most kind thought was appreciated after all.

This hotel is quite comfortable but the food is no great shakes. This morning we traipsed about & looked into the cathedral (where Jane Austen is buried): this afternoon we went to a nearby village & walked in the country – but it was bitterly cold & the way was strewn with dead rabbits, so that we came back feeling unhappy.[2] This evening we have stayed in. Tomorrow we are thinking of taking a look at the New Forest – Lyndhurst & Brockenhurst. I hope it isn't similarly disfigured. [. . .]

I do not remember my general demeanour at home with much pleasure! but I remember all the things you did to make me comfortable & happy.[3] Have you got the cheese disposed of yet? And how about the chicken carcase?

I hope Walter will be more amenable about the door this weekend, and that you have not had any more surprise visits from Effie.[4]

Best new year wishes to you, dear old creature, and very much love:

Philip

1 Eva wrote on 30 December 1954: 'Have posted your scarf and nail file which you left behind.'

2 Larkin's poem 'Myxomatosis' had been published in the *Spectator*, 26 November 1954.

3 On 3 January Eva replied: 'I'm sorry you didn't enjoy the visit to Bruce, for, as you know I should have been happy to have you here longer. / I appreciate all the little things you did whilst here – mending my coal gloves, putting a new plug on the radiator, and tidying and dusting the sideboard cupboard. Also cracking the

great lumps of coal! / I am sorry to hear about the poor rabbits. Hope you don't see any more.'
4 Effie McNichol.

6 January 1955 Postcard

[30 Elmwood Avenue, Belfast]

Arrived safely after good crossing, to find no signs of snow here – good. I gave my last card to a porteress on Crewe station, so I hope she posted it. Have had breakfast & changed clothes, so feel fit for another term's work – brr. No interesting letters waiting for me, except a man pressing me to let him publish a book of my poems. Only he lives in *Hull*! It's entirely a coincidence. If there *is* a rail strike, y^{r} birthday present may be late, Very much love. P.

9 January 1955 Postcard

30 Elmwood Avenue, Belfast

My dear old creature,

First of all, many happy returns of the day! and may I ring you up at *10 p.m.* on Monday to say so personally? [. . .]

How are you finding *Lucky Jim*? Does it make you laugh? Perhaps not so much as the Archers. I think Mrs. P. is terribly good;[1] Dr Folwell said she knew her quite well. Isn't Grace a nasty girl? If I were Philip (sounds odd) you "wouldn't see my arse for dust" getting away from her, if you'll pardon the expression.[2]

Well, I must see about my lunch now: two chops, & a small cabbage. It will probably be put on the table around 3.15 p.m.! Are you having a birthday tea? Anyway, I shall think about you, and ring you up in the evening.

All my very best love, dear old creature:

Philip

<*On the first page opposite address*> Please show Kitty the stamp on this envelope & ask her if she doesn't think the lettering *vile*![3]

1 Mrs Perkins, unsuccessfully wooed by the Ambridge character Walter Gabriel.

2 Denis Folwell, Dr Folwell's son, played Jack Archer in the radio serial. In the story the glamorous, wealthy Grace Fairbrother married Philip Archer in 1955, only to die in a stable fire in September.
3 The pink die-stamped 2½d franking on the pre-paid envelope has elaborately florid lettering.

3 February 1955

30 Elmwood Avenue, Belfast

My dear old creature,

Quite better now, thanks! and I hope you are, too. I felt "very poorly" when I went back to work, but have picked up marvellously, & am back to normal. The news of the week is that "Arthur" – this is a friend of mine who lectures in Spanish, name of Terry – has got engaged to Molly![1] This has been in the air for some time, so it wasn't exactly a surprise, except that such things are always something of a shock. This is the third engagement in about a month! Graneek is rolling his eyes philosophically.

I'm arranging to send my things home by removers, if they are not too costly, & come home myself on Saturday 12 March, flying as far as Manchester & catching the 1.50 train, with as little luggage as possible. The thing I shall try to work is to get my belongings home before me so that I can unpack during my week. You won't want all my stuff standing not unpacked till I don't know when, will you? The bicycle will be the biggest problem.

I don't really know why I applied for Hull – I think Graneek made me! Anyway, he is very pleased with his new acquisition, who will no doubt put me in the shade.[2]

In the paper yesterday I noticed that your Mr Follick is to introduce his bill advocating the decimal coinage.[3]

It was very nice of you to send me an extra letter for Monday – I was feeling a bit low & it cheered me up. I heard from my Hull publisher(!) saying that the poems would make a nice volume – I shall be interested to meet him. Bet he's a horrible little squirt! Wonder if he has money? It's a curious hobby. More on Sunday, dear old mob-capped one.

Love from Philip

<*Top of first page opposite address*> So sorry you were shivery at the pantomime – it must have been bad enough without that.

1 Molly Sellar was an assistant in the library. See Larkin's photograph, Plate 9B.
2 On 27 January he told Eva that a Hungarian had been appointed as his successor: 'He seems quite a decent bloke – better at the books than me.' However, sixteen months later, on 17 June 1956, he heard from a former Belfast colleague passing through Hull that his successor was 'ABSOLUTELY NO GOOD AT ALL, which is comforting.'
3 Montefiore Follick, Labour MP for Loughborough, moved a bill for the introduction of a decimal currency on 2 February 1955.

6 February 1955

30 Elmwood Ave, Belfast

My dear old creature,

I can't help feeling rather regretful and cast down on Sundays just at present, because I think how few of them are left to me in this room. After today I shall write to you only four more times in the peace of my top floor, able to breakfast & lunch when I please and lapped in perfect silence! In five weeks I shall be loafing in your dining-room: in six I shall be where? – well, travelling, I suppose: in seven I shall be I know not where. Oh dear! I don't like the prospect. I have a premonition of dreary dullness, of nasty people, nasty living conditions.[1] [. . .]

I really shouldn't worry about your investments: as long as they are producing *something* that is enough for unworldly creatures like ourselves.

I'm glad you occasionally do a bit at my pullover! Did I tell you Molly finished a very smart grey & white one, copied from *Vanity Fair*, with a giraffe neck, & now has gone and singed it by sitting in front of the fire? This is a coincidence as the old Molly, at Leicester, singed herself in the same way. I hope to take a photograph or two of her in it before I go: it really looks very nice.[2]

The Egertons are proposing a visit to Dublin to attend a première (? odd word) of a new play by Sean O'Casey – Alec & I react identically, neither of us wanting to go much, but not seeing how we can decently refuse. It means getting home about 2 in the morning & having to go to work the next day.

Now, I do hope you are *fully* restored to health and able to appreciate this keen season of snow-drops and lambs. I have strewn a few of the former in your Wedgewood egg cup, but they are rather droopy & I suspect I was "had"! If I ever get round to my meal today it will be tinned steak & kidney pudding & real mushrooms, raspberries & real cream. What are you having? I expect you have withdrawn something from your cellar!

Well, I hope you enjoy it. My most affectionate greetings & much love, Philip

1 With some prescience Eva replied on 8 February: 'I don't suppose you *will* like the living conditions, at first in Hull. Perhaps in time you could get a flat and live in much the same way as you have been doing in Belfast.'
2 See Plate 9B for a photograph by Larkin of the library assistant Molly Sellar, who later married his colleague Arthur Terry. Further photographs of Molly are reproduced in Richard Bradford's *The Importance of Elsewhere*, 103, where she is described as a 'still-unidentified woman'. She is named in the paperback (2017).

13 February 1955

30 Elmwood Ave, Belfast

My very dear old creature,

[. . .] "My plans" came on Friday: that is, the plans of the proposed University library at Hull. It's intended to house a million books & seat 500 readers, and as the expense will be considerable they intend to build it in 2 stages. I expect in the end they will never get beyond the first stage! It's quite a good design, but lots of the details are not to my liking – the main staircase is a spiral one, for instance! and, I should imagine, entirely unsuitable for rush hour traffic. In the final stage I have a lavatory all to myself! It looks so funny. I wonder if I shall ever use it. There is also a room next door for *my secretary.* [. . .]

People now say "I thought you'd gone" in quite an aggrieved way, till I feel quite ashamed of lingering on for four more weeks – less, now . . .

With all love from

17 April 1955

Holtby House, Cottingham

My dear old creature,

This will be the first time I've written to you from Hull on a Sunday, won't it? Imagine a grey cheerless day, & me sitting in my first-floor room looking out of my open sash-window. There are a pair of tits I think are mates on the gutter nearby: on Friday they were flying about with grass and straw, as if nesting, but today they seem content to sit and look at the garden. Perhaps they know it is Sunday. [. . .]

Oh dear, the future now seems very bleak and difficult – I really don't know what I'm doing in this job at all! Still. I shall try to bear in mind the words of Ll. Powys: "Nothing matters but physical pain and death: all else is experience, enviable enough to those lying under the churchyard sod."[1] With all best love, Philip

1 This exact quotation seems not to appear in any work by Llewelyn Powys, nor in his letters. Anthony Head and Peter Foss suggest that Larkin may be misremembering his source, or paraphrasing a sentiment frequently expressed in Powys's work. In *Impassioned Clay* (1931), for instance, he writes (98): 'It should be an open secret that nothing really matters, that once in a graveyard all is at quits.'

25 April 1955

11 Outlands Road, Cottingham, E. Yorks

My dear old Creature,

I'm sorry I left you without a proper letter for today – after I'd posted the one I wrote I found I had yours with me after all. Anyway, I'm settled now in my armchair in the rather chilly bedroom upstairs, with cotton wool from my bottle of aspirins stuffed in my ears, the radio on downstairs, and the noise of witless children audible from the street – or the *road* – outside.[1]

Probably I've not said much about this lodging so far, but it's not bad *for lodging*, which I'm afraid is not saying enough for my peace of mind. Mrs. Dowling is very kind and obliging, the food she provides is quite good, there is an orange cat for company, and her 15 y^r old son is not too bad, but oh dear! this wireless curse is as strong here as anywhere else – in the sense that I can't concentrate in the evenings as I want to – and I feel *not at home*, like someone trying to sleep in a hotel lobby. Last week I answered an advertisement for a flat, & had an appointment to go to see it, but it went before my turn came. [. . .]

God, the radio below is hideous. So loud! I think *they* must be deaf, or else it's turned up so that she can hear it in the kitchen, or something. How horrible it is, to be helpless in the power of people in this way! I must do something to better myself, though I don't expect I'll ever be as comfortable again as at Belfast. I feel as if I were back in Glentworth, King Street. It is awful to have nowhere to go to be quiet: it makes the day's work twice as hard. The radio goes bellowing on: wish there'd be a strike on *that*, a permanent one.

Well, dear old creature, I don't sound very cheerful, do I? and there are you with too much silence & here am I with not enough. Truly, life is a curious thing and doesn't improve much on acquaintance, though I know I could be worse off by far. I hope there are one or two interesting shoots in your garden. I had your letter-card today of course.

With all love, Philip

<*Top of first page opposite address*> Wireless gone off now! Come on again! Hell! [. . .]

1 Number 11 Outlands Road is near its junction with the main Hull Road, Cottingham.

12 May 1955

11 Outlands Road, Cottingham, E. Yorks

My dear old creature,

I've been thinking of you a lot this week, wondering how you are. Wasn't the cold snap that we had yesterday terrible? I was simply frozen. It's been a fairly dull but no doubt important week, for last night we gave a dinner to the Treasury Committee responsible for University Grants, and today they came round the University looking at things, my library included. I'm afraid there's an awful lot of hard work ahead of your creature. New plans for the library arrived today, & I've been looking at them – the fruit of my Easter deliberations! More and more I feel that they have got the *wrong man*.

I hope you are managing to keep up your afternoon rests, and have been able to put into operation the routine for shutting up the scullery: *one*, off with the main gas tap, *two*, lock the scullery door. Then it's all over. No need to worry any more.

> Turn the gas tap half round,
> Then creature can sleep sound;
> Plugs that are lying on the floor
> Needn't trouble creature more;
> Shut the door, put out the light,
> Happy creature sleeps all night.[1]

– and I do hope it will. Don't worry. You are no madder than the rest of us, and much nicer!

Very dull evening here: I can't settle to anything. I'm due to have a bath, for once.

I did like being in my little crowded room at home – better than here, by a long chalk.

Very much love, Philip

1 This poem is published here for the first time.

23 May 1955

<*Letterhead*> Memorandum, The University, Hull

FROM C:

TO OC:

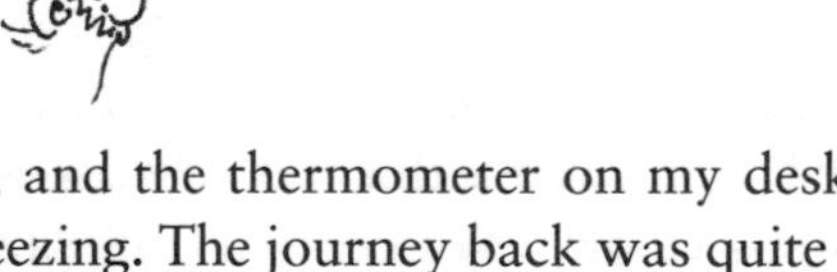

It's just after 5, and the thermometer on my desk says 80°, so you can see I'm not freezing. The journey back was quite successful, though tiring, & the London train I get between Grantham & Selby *very crowded* – I sat on my case in the corridor all the way. Well, it was only an hour really. Really, it's just luck if you get a seat & I wasn't lucky. On Selby platform I met George Hartley (the man who's supposed to be doing my poems)[2] & we talked literature all the way home.

I finally got to Outlands Road about 25 to 11, as I miss a bus very inconveniently, arriving when I do.

Dear old creature, I did love seeing you, & I'm sorry we didn't have our walk up the garden. Home seemed pleasant and restful: you are always very kind to me, for very beggarly returns.

> Creatures who tremble every day
> At gloomy clouds across the sky,
> Remember they are miles away
> With very different fish to fry.[1]

Mrs Dowling asked how Rosemary got on with her dancing exam, so do tell me, won't you?

All love,
Philip

1 This poem is published here for the first time.
2 George Hartley (b. 1933), with his wife Jean, published the poetry magazine *Listen* from their tiny house in Hessle, just outside Hull. Larkin published poems in the 1954 issues and Hartley proposed setting up the Marvell Press to publish a volume of his work. Having been rejected by mainstream publishers, Larkin agreed, and *The Less Deceived* was published in Hull in November 1955, six months after Larkin arrived in Hull. See Jean Hartley, *Philip Larkin, the Marvell Press and Me* (London: Sumach Press, 1993).

5 June 1955

200 Hallgate, Cottingham, E. Yorks

My very dear old creature,

I hardly know exactly how to write this week: as you see, I've moved, and as you can guess I don't feel especially cheerful, but I think it should be laid down that the wretchedness of moving is not really related to where one moves to or from. Of course it is in a *way*, but not so much as you might expect. The wretchedness of moving is like losing a skin – one is in fact losing a whole set of circumstances and things one takes for granted, all very simple, but by their immediate relation to the way you live very influential – bed, food, noises, warmth & so on. Deprived of these at a blow & thrust into another set, one feels as if skinned and clad in a coarse shirt. Of course this new shirt of circumstances becomes one's skin in time. But until it has one feels, as I say, wretched, and I don't intend to minimise this! I think I slept about 3 hours last night – 2 till 5 – and lay awake the rest of the time, simply unable to settle. Nor can I eat: my stomach has screwed itself up into a ball. However, this will pass. Of the *place*, well, I suppose it is an improvement on where I was – it's certainly quieter, or will be when I get used to it. The bedroom is not so bad, though too small, & the tiny kitchen they have tried to fit out usefully. Yes, it is quite clean. I can't write very enthusiastically about it because the first wretchedness hasn't worn off. The only thing is it has rather an odd smell – on the stairs, anyway. Mrs Squire is a nice old thing, & obviously hopes I shall stay a long while. I don't feel so keen on this myself at present! But what is the alternative? [. . .]

Your cowed but courageous (& very loving)

Creature

24 June 1955

In Train.

Very dear old creature,

[. . .] So you are going to see a psychiatrist! It's very bold of you, but I expect if he proposes shock therapy he won't "see your arse for dust", to use a vulgar expression – but I shall be waiting very anxiously to hear what he says. Suppose he says you sh^{d} become a voluntary patient in a mental hospital? Somehow you seem much too sane for such measures. Perhaps you will find it helps you just to see him.[1]

God! I feel pretty grim – & this letter is no pleasure to read, I know, scrawled as it is,[2] but my thoughts are very near to you, dear creature, nearer even than my body, which must in fact be quite near. I'll write on Sunday as usual, to tell you the news. Love – P.

1 On 20 June Eva had written: 'I went to see the Doctor last Friday, really for a fresh supply of capsules. He has, however, arranged for me to see a Psychiatrist on 4th July. I don't know whether it is a man or woman doctor. I may as well hear what treatment is advised – but whether I shall agree to take it is another matter. Dr Jenner says I needn't take it unless I wish. Really I haven't much hope that anyone can give me the courage which, above all things, I need.'

2 The effect of the train's movement is visible in the handwriting.

26 June 1955

Eastgate Hotel, Oxford[1]

My very dear old creature,

It is a very paper-thin creature who addresses you this morning, for I was in a poor way last night & am not by any means recovered this morning – breakfast was a mere token meal, at which I ate 2 pieces of toast & toyed (that's the word, isn't it) with a grapefruit, but the coffee, which should have been a life-saver, was so villainous that I felt sicker, not stronger, in consequence of its ministrations. I hardly feel capable of describing the day, but the weather was gloriously hot, & I sh[d] say it was a complete success. I met a number of people I had forgotten about, & some I hadn't. The Dean, an old enemy, hailed me & said a few kind words – nothing succeeds like success! Noel Hughes, my old room-mate, was there, with an irritatingly-attractive wife. I spent a lot of time with John Wain, who is a literary gent & writer, you may recall, & as time wore on got so intoxicated I can't attribute my safe return home to anything but divine providence. I remember John & I sitting in an unlighted room eating strawberries & cream & drinking champagne at one point: then later on there were fireworks, a splendid sight. I must have written something legible in the hotel book when I got in, for the *S. Times* & *The Observer* were delivered under my door at an early hour. I expect I made a terrible row coming in. I remember staggering about the corridor treading on people's shoes. However, don't think I was incapable – far from it.

Today is another hot sunny day. Yesterday morning I took a walk in Christ Church meadows and it was simply marvellous – the squirrels were about, & I got quite near to one & could watch it clambering down a tree trunk & sitting up in the grass to eat something. To walk along the deserted paths by the river with the dew still on the grass & the cows grouped in the middle of the field (sign of fine weather!) was a wonderful treat for me, & I felt really glad to be alive. How I love summer, hay fever or no hay fever! Gorgeous rich expansion of everything! I felt I wanted to stay there for ever. However, having come with no pyjamas I had to go to the shops & buy some – a lovely pink pair.[2] Then I had some lager in the Randolph & met David Williams, a portly barrister by now, & then the fun started.

Dear old creature, I'm afraid this isn't a very interesting letter but it is a happy one for a change! and considering the way I feel it is rather wonderful to write a letter at all. With all love,

Philip

1 Larkin was attending the 400th anniversary celebration of the foundation of St John's College.

2 Eva commented: 'What a poetical, but absent-minded Creature you are! However, another pair isn't a bad investment, and I only hope the laundry won't spoil the lovely pink colour' (28 June).

3 July 1955

200 Hallgate, Cottingham

My dear old creature,

[. . .] The subscription forms for my book of poems have been printed, and indeed Kitty may have one by now. Of course I don't especially want the family to *pay*, but I thought she might like her name in the back along with a motley crew of mugs and literati who (we hope) will send along their six bobs, so if she *w*^{d} like her name in the back, w^{d} she subscribe in the normal way. If not, then she needn't trouble. W^{d} you like *your* name in the back? Personally I'd as soon keep anyone called Larkin out of the list, it looks so silly, but if you have ambitions in that direction, let me know.[1] There's plenty of time. I expect the publication will produce some worries & bothers as well as pleasure. Some of the poems, as I think I said, are rather subversive for a righteous official like me.

Well, it is 12.15 & the rain is pelting down still. I got thoroughly soaked the other evening, stupid creature, cycling back from the library.

Is it tomorrow you visit the psychiatrist? I wonder if you feel wobbly about it. I expect I sh^{d} – afraid he w^{d} clap me into a padded cell right away. You have all my sympathy, & I hope it does you good to go.[2] I'm glad Rosemary passed her dancing exam so well.

All my best love – I hope the sun will shine on your furry head – Philip

1 Eva was not included; Catherine Hewett (no longer 'Larkin') was.

2 On 5 July Eva wrote: 'I have just returned from Leicester, where I have spent a most happy afternoon with Dr Folwell. I really bless the day that you took me to see her. She is the most marvellous woman I have ever met. I got a very nice letter from her on Saturday suggesting that when I had seen the psychiatrist I should go

over to see her and tell her all about it. So I went today. / There really wasn't much to tell, for the psychiatrist was very non-committal – It was a lady, and she wrote down all I said, but beyond saying that she thought I ought to have someone to live with me, and get out as much as possible, she said very little.'

11 August 1955[1]

200 Hallgate, Cottingham, E. Yorks

My dear old creature,

[. . .] I'm going down to London for the weekend but hope to write from there. If my poems *are* broadcast, it will be on August 17th (Wednesday evening) in a programme presented by Richard Murphy.[2] If you should hear one containing a disrespective reference to "home", I was quite honestly thinking of my room in Belfast – which I'd give a lot to have back now, anyway![3] Nothing to do with Loughborough, or Old Creature.

I did almost nothing on my birthday but pursue my orderly & decent progress towards *The Grave* . . . went to the cinema in the evening & had an expensive and nasty meal, alone. Booo!

Much love, enjoy yourself. How is the weather chart?

Philip

1 Addressed to Nellie Day's home at 33 Grange Road, North, Hyde, Cheshire.
2 Richard Murphy (1927–2018), Anglo-Irish poet. He married Patsy Strang in 1955, and was later the second Compton Poetry Fellow at Hull. See letters of 18 May and 14 September 1969.
3 'Poetry of Departures'.

14 September 1955 Postcard[1]

We arrived after [a] very rough sail – an hour long – fortunately we both stood it. Cold & wet here, thunder & wind! *Not* the best time of year. Fellow guests nothing to write home about so I won't. Real cream on Guernsey – didn't have any: others who did *lost it* on the sail over.

Love, P

1 Dixcart Hotel, Sark.

30 September 1955

200 Hallgate, Cottingham

My very dear old creature,

[. . .] I was also very grateful for the news that you had washed "the basque", as it is a worthwhile garment and should be taken care of.[1] [. . .]

Much love, dear creature – hope to be home soon, P.

1 On 27 September Eva had written: 'I have had a *very* busy day to-day, to compensate for my little holiday yesterday. Have been washing most of the time and really got to the bottom of the linen basket. I have washed the things you left, also the green socks and the "basque", and the trousers, so feel very satisfied that they are all cleared up at last!' The basque must have been Monica's.

9 October 1955

200 Hallgate, Cottingham, E. Yorks.

My dear old Creature,

I seem, temporarily, to be rather short of writing-paper, but I expect you remember this sort from the old days. It's the kind Pop would use isn't it: it's strange that I can never remember anything of the kind of letters he used to write. They were very short and dry, weren't they? and slightly ironic.

Well, to give this village its due, it's certainly lovely at present. Yesterday we had a fiendish "ceremony" in the morning relating to degrees, but once I got back home & rested, I went out to the local branch library to change my books & was overwhelmed by the soft beauty of the afternoon. Mrs Squire's garden is tidied up for the winter now, but is still strewn with squashy plums, apples (a curious tiny shiny high-coloured sort) and pears. The churchyard[1] has clumps of Michaelmas daisies, chill blurs of mauve, and the leaves do not seem to have turned yet. I bought 2 tea-spoons (4/½^{d} the two!) and a root of celery, and experienced a feeling I've felt before – that, outside my own miserable cramped absurd life, the world is still its old beautiful self. This morning the sun shines, & I think I shall go a cycle ride, if it doesn't rain. I wish it were possible to convert the happiness we find in ordinary things into a comfortable way of life for all of us.

You sound a gay creature with your new clothes, what Lawrence would call a "bobby-dazzler".[2] Surely you are always having new hats and handbags! Vanity, saith the preacher![3] Still, as Kingsley w^{d} say, where is the point in not?

I've sent K. her copy of Kingsley's book,[4] & I hope she enjoys it. There's not nearly so much of me in this one, hardly anything in fact, but there are one or two things. [. . .]

Love, Philip

1 St Mary's Church, Hallgate, Cottingham, where Larkin's funeral took place thirty years later.
2 On 9 October Eva wrote: 'You remarked that I sounded full of beans, well I certainly *do* feel better than I have felt for a long time. Whether it is due to the tablets which the psychiatrist prescribed and which I still take, or whether the fact that there is now less risk of storms as we draw nearer to winter, I do not know. Neither do I know how I should feel if I heard a rumble of thunder at this moment!! [. . .] From Ye olde Creature.'
3 Ecclesiastes 1:2.
4 *That Uncertain Feeling* (Victor Gollancz, 1955).

17 October 1955

<*Letterhead*> ~~Librarian~~ \Horrible Beast/ P. A. Larkin, M.A., University Library Hull

My very dearest Old Creature,

What a silly "performance" I made before I left. I do feel ashamed of myself. You w^{d} hardly credit how miserable I feel at the time, though – like a limpet in process of being torn off a rock – that might explain in some measure my behaviour, though not excuse it.[1] *Of course* I shall always visit you for the delight of seeing *you*[2] and hearing of your doings: I was sorry we could not go out together yesterday, but I felt you w^{d} benefit more from a rest after lunch, as I think you did.

I dozed much of the way back, lying full length in an empty nonsmoker for the last stretch. On arrival I bought bacon, cheese & coffee & came up to the University. Nothing had happened.

It's very windy, clear & cold up here.

I feel *bitterly ashamed* of leaving my breakfast – if it were here I w[d] eat it 10 times over. It is just that *at the time* I get into such a state I cannot eat or think clearly or behave properly. Really, it is *not* easy to leave home with equanimity when I know what I am coming back to, not that it's very terrible I suppose. You were goldenly good to me and I am *very* grateful – but I am now retreating under the table where I shall stay till I hear from you.

With very best love:
Philip

1 Eva responded on 18 October: 'I am so sorry you feel as you do over Monday morning's "performance", as you call it and I *do* sympathise with you very much indeed, and I am sure there is no need for you to flay yourself, and I hope you have by this come out from under the table. What a pathetic little sketch. I feel sad when I look at it.'

2 Doubly underlined.

30 October 1955

200 Hallgate, Cottingham, E. Yorks.

My very dear old creature,

Well, the dreaded day of the 29th is over, and I'm grateful for that anyway. It went off fairly well. I had to give my little talk, realising as I did so that *three* people who had been turned down for my job were listening. I think I don't stammer in public so much now: but I find it hard to think clearly & speak sufficiently impressively. The visitors (who were mostly from Leeds) seemed to enjoy looking at the exhibition we had laid out of addresses from other universities on the occasion of our installation of our Chancellor in July. Just as well we had them, because we have nothing else.[1]

My pools yesterday were about the best I have ever done – one line was 12, which of course isn't exceptional, but the other was 20! Another point & I'd have won something! All through chance as well: I never know anything about the teams. Of course if I had won anything it wouldn't have been more than about £2·3·4d, I expect. Not enough to STOP WORK.

Since I wrote last Sunday George Hartley has re-entered my life, and at a meeting on Thursday we settled the business of the contract, not exactly to the satisfaction of both parties, but I am happier about it than I was. The book is binding at present, and should I hope be out before too long – perhaps by the middle of November. I think it will be very successful in a small way, and am looking forward to it greatly. [. . .]

Tonight I am going to a jazz concert at the Town Hall, featuring Humphrey Lyttelton the trumpeter – this was the sort of "carrot" I instituted to get me past yesterday. I do hope it will be good. Recent jazz concerts I've attended have been something of a disappointment. The last time I heard H. L. in the flesh was in a hall in London with Ruth in 1947! I expect he's improved since then.

I had the pleasure of finding the cheque the laundry sent me for that shirt they lost. I thought I'd lost the cheque! It was only 30/- but still.

Now I must dress & so on. I might come home next week end – wd it be suitable? I want to discuss a few things with Barker at Leicester.

Very best love from Philip

<*Printed slip enclosed*> 'WITH THE LIBRARIAN'S COMPLIMENTS'

Greetings! old creature. Here is a magazine containing a poem about an incident you'll recognise. Of course I don't mean my room is unsatisfactory really except in so far as it really isn't my permanent room.[2]

I hope you are feeling better today and more chirpy. Can't say I am! Oh, those awful librarians. [. . .]

Best love, old creature.
Creature

1 Larkin had addressed a visiting group of librarians from other universities.

2 He had enclosed *Listen* 1.4 (Autumn 1955), which included 'Reference Back'. Eva replied on 1 November: 'Just fancy you writing a poem about something I said when you were here. How very nice of you. I like the poem, too, very much.'

25 November 1955

200 Hallgate, Cottingham, E. Yorks.

My very dear old creature,

Yes, they have misspelt Dr. Marshall's name – isn't it annoying?[1] I have written apologising, but had no answer so far. I think it's quite a nice book, but I've found one silly error that is my fault. [. . .]

I expect Kitty thinks I ought to write a poem for Rosemary![2]

Today I had a letter from a publisher[3] saying they liked my poem in the *Spectator* this week & would I like to submit a collection? I grind my teeth.

The weather is very nice here – I am going to a hellish ball tonight, all clobbered up. I fill my life with distractions to prevent myself thinking.

On Sunday I will write at more length, but do be sure that I am thinking of you constantly & hoping that you aren't worrying yourself sick, like a silly old pussy, because there's NO NEED. You are as nice a pussy as ever trod.

Love, P.

1 In the list of subscribers to *The Less Deceived* the name had appeared as 'A. H. Marhall'.

2 On 23 November Eva wrote: 'Thank you very much for the lovely book of poems. I see there are one or two new ones in it and also my old favourite "At Grass". I particularly like the first poem ['Lines on a Young Lady's Photograph Album'] and think it very good, also the one for Sally Amis. / What a long list of subscribers! Haven't they misspelt Dr Marshall's name? Kitty will be very pleased to get hers. / I am very sorry indeed to know the sad news of Mrs Squire.' Philip's landlady had died.

3 Charles Monteith at Faber & Faber.

4 December 1955[1]

53 York Road, Loughborough

Don't answer if
you feel you can't

My very dear old creature,

As I'm in the habit of writing on Sunday morning, I thought I'd keep it up, though of course there's not a great deal to say after seeing you so recently. First of all, don't worry about the Medical Card. Kitty says she had it from you and handed it in to the hospital yesterday. So that's one less thing to worry about.

I went off with the rest of the visitors – a motley crew – and called in on Monica who asked about you & if you'd liked the dormouse, & I said you had, & that you'd probably prefer *being* a dormouse at present, as they seem to have such quiet lives. We conspired to send you some "extras", then you can pay back the people who have been kind to you. I'm glad there are some.

I felt very sorry you are finding the hospital so bewildering and un-private. I can quite sympathise with you. No doubt the idea is that the company of others (however quaint the others are) is meant to draw you out of the prison of misery you find yourself in, but for my part if I didn't want the company of such people when *well* I shouldn't want them when *ill*. However, I do hope you can manage to cotton on to one or two of them, since that is the way salvation lies.

I rang Dr. Folwell up this morning, because I thought she "deserved" to know the latest news about you after all her kindness.[2] She sounded very concerned, and repeatedly said how sorry she was. When I asked if I sh[d] send you her best wishes, she said "Give her my LOVE" very emphatically. She also said she would send details of a small private hospital outside Nottingham for us to look at. In closing she insisted that you had taken the best step towards *getting better*.

Have you had any more to do with the old creature in blue? I thought she looked sympathetic, but of course you can form your own idea about that.

I slept in "your" room at Kitty's (temperature 50°!) & found it quite comfortable. I dreamed I had bought a big cream-coloured car and was whizzing about in it – no doubt caused by a remark of Walter's that now was the time to buy a car. But I don't think I shall.

Kitty says the laundry will be all right, since she can send it on Monday & receive it back on Friday. So DON'T WORRY. I am looking forward to seeing you again – now do *eat plenty* & keep up your strength.[3]

Very best love from Philip

1 Addressed to Carlton Hayes Hospital, Narborough, Leicester, which specialised in treating depression and nervous problems.
2 See footnote to Philip's letter of 29 October 1950.
3 On 7 December, Eva wrote, on roughly torn paper: 'This morning I had my first electrical treatment but beyond feeling a bit shaky and sick afterwards I felt nothing of it. [. . .] I feel very proud to know that you are now recognised as a foremost English poet. How very pleased you will feel about it. / Like you I shall be glad when I am quite well again for the time passes very slowly here.'

16 December 1955[1]

<Letterhead with coat of arms>
Librarian: P. A. Larkin, M.A., University Library, Hull

My dear old Creature,

I've just had word from your medical superintendent that you may have "leave of absence for Christmas" from 10 a.m. Dec. 24th to 6 p.m. Dec 28th. I should like you to think this over & let me know what you think about it tomorrow when I come to see you.[2]

Terribly rushed!
All love,
Philip

1 This letter and the next are addressed to Carlton Hayes Hospital, Narborough, Leicester.
2 On the same day, 16 December, Eva wrote, on small sheet of wide-spaced lined paper: 'I wonder where you will be at Christmas? I fancy most of the people here will go home and I don't quite know what to do. I do hope you will find a Christmas dinner somewhere and enjoy yourself. [. . .] / This scrappy notepaper I got from the canteen. It is the largest they have.'

20 December 1955 Postcard

200 Hallgate, Cottingham, E. Yorks.

My dear old creature,

I expect this will hardly reach you before I call on you on Saturday morning, but I've just had your nice letter thanking me for the carrier. Not at all, old creature: you are very welcome!

I am looking forward to our time together at Grantham.[1] You will enjoy a trip into the outside world, and I shall be all the happier to be with you at this time of year. I've only once been to the Angel at Grantham, but it's a nice place & should be cosy.

The weather is simply frightful here – snowy, frosty, & the most terrible slush underfoot. I find it hard to keep warm in my rooms, but I have three different sorts of heater & am managing to keep alive, though not very cheerfully. Nowhere is really warm in weather like this: what is the hospital like? Pretty dreary, I expect.

Now remember I am calling for you on Saturday morning (if all goes well), bringing with me the blue case, & we'll call at Loughborough first before going on to Grantham so that you can collect a few more clothes.

Dear Creature! Happy Christmas, Creature! Philip

1 Philip had booked Eva and himself into the Angel Hotel in Grantham over Christmas, with an excursion on Christmas Day to a hotel in Melton Mowbray where Kitty had booked a family Christmas dinner.

1956

8 January 1956[1]

21 York Road, Loughborough, Leics.

My dear Old Creature,

Just a note to say I got to Kitty's all right, & had a good night's sleep in a warm bed, so feel refreshed. I'm afraid when I visited you I was very dull and tired: but it was very nice to see you, and I certainly think the Woodlands is a nicer place for you to be than the hospital.[2]

Kitty seems more cheerful this time than the last, & my bedding was actually airing when I arrived! She says the agreement is for you to "come out" on January 21st – a fortnight yesterday, in fact. I suppose I shall fetch you in the afternoon & stay the weekend at 21 York Rd.[3]

I wonder if you've heard the owl yet? "Alone & warming his five wits The white owl in the belfry sits".[4]

When I get back to Hull I expect I shall find your letter waiting my return. Let me take this opportunity of wishing you a happy New Year – happier than last, at least! I expect the snow drops will be out soon at the Woodlands. I hope you'll get rid of your cold promptly & be a fine fit old creature when I next see you. All love, Philip

1 This and the next three letters are addressed to The Woodlands, Forest Road, Narborough.

2 On 31 December 1955 Eva had written: 'You will be surprised to see my new address and I, too, was surprised when I was sent here yesterday very quickly. / I saw the Psychiatrist yesterday and she said that my treatment was finished but that she thought I should benefit by a little while here. "The Woodlands" is a lovely, large house in the country standing in large grounds. / There are about 12 people here and it is more like staying at a private house than a hospital.'

3 On 5 January Eva had written from The Woodlands: 'The fancy dress ball went off well and some of the characters were marvellous. They included "Alice", the white rabbit, the mad hatter and Old Mother Riley who made us all laugh. I am quite happy here, and we are all sitting round a lovely fire. / Yes, I too, enjoyed our stay at Grantham.'

4 'The Owl', Alfred, Lord Tennyson.

11 January 1956

200 Hallgate, Cottingham, E. Yorks.

My dear old creature,

What a disappointment that we couldn't hear properly yesterday! At least, I could hear you fairly well, but I could tell you couldn't hear me. Anyway, I was glad you had had a proper birthday, with a special tea & flowers & a telegram.

I hadn't really much news: I'm frightfully busy at present with all sorts of work – I never remember being so busy before. All library work, I need hardly add. I heard from Hartley today that my book is in demand & that the first 300 have nearly gone. He is having another 400 bound. I don't expect you'll be able to hear a poem of mine read on Sunday night on the 3rd Progr. by John Wain – I don't know what time the programme is until the Radio Times comes out. It is *Church Going*, the long one.

Weather here has been very snowy & cold. My cough has pretty well gone: how is your cold? Cleared up, I hope.

A new Vice Chancellor has been appointed here: just the man I *didn't* want![1] Oh dear. The future looks stormy.

I'll be thinking of you on Saturday, even if I don't see you. Have you been out again yet?

Very much love,
Philip

1 Brynmor Jones, later Sir Brynmor Jones, after whom Larkin's library was named, at the poet's suggestion, in 1967. He had taught in the chemistry department in Hull since the 1930s.

15 January 1956[1]

200 Hallgate, Cottingham, E. Yorks.

My dear old creature,

[. . .] The biggest news this week is something that won't really interest you much, but is of enormous importance to me – namely, that a new

Vice Chancellor has been appointed here. The VC, as you may know, is the "headmaster" of a university and it's an extremely important office. I'm sorry to say that they have appointed one of the existing professors, a man I find it hard to get on with and whom I dislike & think no good. So the future here looks rather black! It's really a serious setback & I still can't imagine how they could have been so foolish. [. . .]

Goodbye for now & much love, Philip

1 Addressed to The Woodlands, Forest Road, Narborough. Eva had caught cold and her discharge was delayed until Saturday 28 January.

25 January 1956

200 Hallgate, Cottingham, E. Yorkshire

My dear old creature,

I am sitting, rather chilly, in my room – snow outside, as you say, but it's been lying since Monday & is easy enough to get about. Thanks for your letter: I expect the weekend was rather lonely. Still, you would have the pussy!

There's not much news here except more & more work for yours truly – God knows how I shall ever get through the next few years, building this new library. A sad life for an unambitious creature!

Had a terrible scare this week: thought I was going to be forced to read some of my poems on the wireless, but managed to get out of it. The one about you saying "that was a pretty one" is being broadcast early in February – you never thought, when you said it, that you'd be repeated over the BBC, did you?

I hope the weather's fine on Saturday. I'll arrive as near two p.m. as I can. Try to be ready to leave without delay! It'll be a dreary journey back, but a happy homecoming.[1]

All creaturely love,
Creature

1 On 28 January Philip took Eva back to York Road before retuning to Hull by train on 29 or 30 January.

5 February 1956

200 Hallgate, Cottingham, E. Yorkshire

My dear old creature,

[. . .] I was interested to hear that you had seen Dr Morton, & that he had been sympathetic. Glad you have some more tablets! I myself went to my Doct^r^ on Thursday about my stomach, wch has not been any better, and he prescribed some medicine. He has also arranged an x-ray for me next Thursday at hospital – I rather dread this, as it means much tiresome feeding or non-feeding, and eating a "barium meal", a revolting (by all accounts) mess which is designed to show up on the x-ray – but things are bad enough to send me there of my own accord. I hope it isn't an ulcer. [. . .]

My book continues to be noticed here and there: it's reviewed in today's *Observer* and reference is made to my "vivacious melancholy". I think that's a very good description of me. They misquote a passage: fools. Tell Kitty *Vogue* has written for a copy: it may mean a mention in *People are talking about*.

Next Friday night it is being reviewed on the Northern Ireland Home Service – the Arts in Ulster, 9.45 to 10.15. Do try to listen. I expect I shall get pulled to pieces. I am also agreeing myself to introduce a programme on the 3rd in the early summer. [. . .]

Do let me know how you are getting on: I long to know.

Very much love, Philip

14 February 1956

200 Hallgate, Cottingham, East Yorks.

My dear old creature,

Just a line, written in the deepest of winter, the coldest I have ever felt as I can remember, to say that my x-rays show nothing seriously wrong with me. Apparently the pain or discomfort is caused, as I felt, by nervous spasms that contract the oesophagus when I eat & prevent my food getting into the stomach at all. The only sure cure is to stop worrying! So I'm to try to relax before meals, & go on taking belladonna medicine, & hope for the best.

In compensation I have got the beginnings of a horrible cold.[1]

Really, I don't know that the weather *could* get any colder. There isn't much more than a fairly light covering of snow everywhere, but the roads are glassy with ice and the air is like the finger of death. Yesterday & today a "friend" of mine, the novelist Wm Cooper,[2] visited the university and I stood dinner at a hotel at night. Can't say I greatly enjoyed it, but it makes a change.

At Needler Hall tonight when I unrolled my napkin I found a valentine in it! Much mirth among the students.[3]

Now dear old creature, do take special care to *keep warm* – leave electric radiators on all over the place, & be glad you *have* them to leave on! Warmth is life these days.

All best love,
Philip

1 On 16 February Eva wrote: 'When your letter came this morning I really felt afraid to open it. *When* I did open it I felt overjoyed, and so relieved to know that the xrays showed nothing seriously wrong. Of course I had to look up oesophagus in the encyclopaedia and it means what I thought it did. Somehow I suspected that worry was the main cause of the trouble, so now dear Creature, you must *not* let things worry you – but it is easier said than done as *I* know. Above all don't worry about me for I'm quite all right. [. . .] I've had another busy day, thoroughly cleaned the bathroom, also did landings and stairs. I took a radiator with me, had it on the stairs even!'

2 Harry S. Hoff (1910–2002), author of *Scenes from Provincial Life* (1950), wrote under the name William Cooper about his experiences as a teacher in Leicester in the 1930s.

3 On 16 February Eva wrote: 'P.S. Fancy having a valentine! Would it be from the girl students – or aren't there any at the University?'

13 May 1956

192A Hallgate, Cottingham, E. Yorkshire[1]

My dear old creature,

Quarter to twelve when I sit down to write to you! This is because I invited the Hartleys round last night and they stayed till about 1.30 a.m. Fearful! They are the first visitors I've had since arriving in Hull, & I didn't do it very well. Still, they wouldn't mind. Hartley, who is as you know my "publisher", talks largely of giving me cheques, wch I agree to receive, but shall believe in when I see. I have really been very foolish in allying myself with him, I now realise, but such foolish behaviour is all of a piece with the general conduct of my life. I wish this next edition w^{d} hurry up & come out.

[. . .] I send you all my dearest love on this bright warm Sunday –

Philip

1 Between April and October 1956 Larkin lived here, a short distance from his previous lodging.

29 July 1956

192A Hallgate, Cottingham, East Yorks.

My dear old creature,

[. . .] This has not been a very remarkable week, by any standards: did I tell you that last Sunday I cleaned my gas-cooker, or tried to? A vile coat of slime slid down the sink at the finish. Every evening I come back to my room & try to write poetry, but am varyingly hindered by the row in the house. It's quite awful at times – well, not awful, but enough to put me off. Talking of poetry, there is a sharp criticism of me (for a change) in this week's *Time & Tide*, apropos of this *New Lines* book.[1] If you pass the public library it might amuse you to read it. I am on cool terms with George Hartley at present, so don't know if the 3rd edition is ready or not. Curse the whole stupid farce! [. . .]

Dear old creature! My thoughts are with you as always. Much love,

Philip

1 *New Lines*, edited by Robert Conquest, was published in 1956. It included eight poems by Larkin, and works by Amis, Davie, D. J. Enright, Thom Gunn, John Holloway, Elizabeth Jennings, John Wain and Conquest himself. For Conquest, see note on the letter of 11 April 1961.

19 August 1956

53 Glanmor Road, Uplands, Swansea, S. Wales

My dear old creature,

Well! I hope you made the journey safely, & that you found someone waiting at the other end. I expect we are both in very different environments now, from our luxurious little apartments in Stratford![1] Kingsley & Hilly are both well, & so are all the children – especially Philip, who seems a charming little boy now.[2] There seem other children about too, also lots of dogs and cats. The new house is a bit larger than the last, but not unduly palatial: certainly the guest room is as rigorous as before. Breakfast was frightful, but I shall be more explicit about food henceforth. The weather seems sunny but with showers now & again: it rained heavily last night.

In retrospect Stratford seems quite fun! The Sunday papers today both praise Alan Badel (*Lucio*) very highly.[3] Do you remember the swans all asleep on their little island?

There's some mention of me in the TLS this week, in the supplement. Give my love to everyone.

Love to you too, of course! Philip

1 After a holiday in Skye with Monica in July Philip had spent a week with Eva in Stratford, 11–18 August. She was now on a visit to Nellie in Hyde.
2 The Amises' first son was named after Larkin, who was also his godfather.
3 While at Stratford Eva and Philip had attended a performance of *Measure for Measure* at the Shakespeare Memorial Theatre.

2 September 1956

192A Hallgate, Cottingham, East Yorkshire

My dear old creature,

[. . .] Miss Wrench writes to say she will start on September 24![1] I feel a little scared. It's not that I'm afraid of *her*, but I'm afraid she will discover that she is out on a limb, socially. You see, all the rest of my staff are either graduates, & members of the common room, or local girls with their own friends. Poor Miss Wrench will be neither, and I'm rather afraid lest she will find herself intolerably lonely. Perhaps she will leave quickly! Perhaps, on the other hand, she won't.

I'm "nursing" my stomach along, trying not to get worried or angry, & so far am not doing too badly. I enjoyed my Sunday with you – it seemed a real holiday, after all my troubles. All the papers say "Lucio stole *Measure for Measure*!" M. has gone to relations in Durham.

All love, P.

1 Bored with her work in the London Institute of Education, Mary Wrench, a poetry-lover, had applied for an assistantship in the University of Hull library out of curiosity, just to see what a poet was like. Larkin, flattered, had charmed her at the interview and she had taken the job.

9 September 1956

192A Hallgate, Cottingham, East Yorkshire

My dear old creature,

Another dull Sunday, but it may very well clear up – there was a faint grin of sun on the wall not long ago. I am glad of a day to myself. Last Monday I went along to Hartley's, to pick up 6 copies of the new edition: it is now available again, so Aunt Alice (her aunthood is a very tenuous one really, isn't it?)[1] will be getting her copy. On Wednesday I had a forced dinner with a fool – a chap who is going to Nottingham as head of the fine arts department – a *good* dinner really, but I couldn't get it down – & on Thursday I had a well-meant but really rather nasty dinner with the Hartleys again – this was pure "sociability", to mark the end of a period of coolness between us, caused by me I suppose, but me irritated by him. So I've had more than enough company for a while.

I'm glad you heard the two programmes. I purred with pleasure at Stephen Potter's appreciation,[2] & have sent him a copy – he read the few lines very well, didn't he. The Hull programme was all right, but I though[t] the poems were read badly. The one about *Pigeons* was written at Grantham, when we were there at Christmas – they were on a roof opposite the hotel, and I watched them through the short afternoons as we sat in the lounge. Do you remember them? I expect not. You were asleep most of the time![3]

Monica is in Co. Durham at present, visiting one of her mother's sisters who is in hospital and worse than they expected. So she is not very cheerful. They are in the very heart of the country – Rookhope – and staying with near-farmers.

My present finally turned up from Kitty, with a note saying she'd read it but didn't think it much good! I wish I'd worn her stockings for a bit. Tearing up one of her letters recently I found I'd torn up some pictures of Rosemary that were inside – ssh!

Auntie Nellie wrote thanking me for the book, and said she had enjoyed your visit & that, though you still worried about things, you were better than last year, she thought.

I am pretty well decided to take the flat:[4] the thought of winter here is too dreary – it's so damp! The pegs that were put in the wall in April are rusting: I've never known anything like it. But when I shall move in I don't know. It'll have to be painted first, & I shall have a gas fire put in (shades of you!). I expect it will have its drawbacks, but so will anything, really. I looked at furniture again yesterday but this time it all looked horrible. I'm very afraid of the whole business, but I think it is just fear and not indecision – I'm sure this is the right thing to do, at the moment.

Is your ear improved, old creature? What a funny thing to get all of a sudden. I hope it goes as quickly as it came.

I had a letter from the Librarian of Coventry yesterday asking for one or two minor items for their "local collection" – it's nice to think I am a "local author", like George Eliot. His name is Simpson. Next time I go to Coventry I must call on him. [. . .]

Yesterday I paid *another* call on Hartley, but in his shop this time, Austin Reed's:[5] there I ordered an overcoat, as Pop's, wch never really fitted me, is too shapeless to be worn another winter really, though what to do with it I don't know. He also let me have a shirt reduced to 25/- for 20/-! I think I like George better as a shop assistant than as a publisher.

There's no more news of Miss Wrench, but she's due to start two weeks tomorrow – fortunately I'll be away at a conference in Liverpool for her first day. I'm sure she won't stay – hope not, anyway! My very best love,

Creature

1 As the second wife, now widow, of Ernest Larkin (1878–1948), fourth of Sydney's five elder brothers, Philip considers Alice's aunthood tenuous.

2 Stephen Potter (1900–69), author and broadcaster, best-known for the satire *Gamesmanship* (1947).

3 Eva replied on 11 September 1956: 'I have a dim recollection of the pigeons at Grantham and I don't think I was asleep most of the time, but only had my eyes closed!'

4 On 27 October 1956 Larkin moved into a high-windowed, top-floor flat at 32 Pearson Park, a Victorian house belonging to the university overlooking a leafy park between the university and the city. Here he stayed for nearly eighteen years, until he moved to 105 Newland Park on 27 June 1974.

5 George Hartley worked as a sales assistant at the gentleman's outfitter, Austin Reed.

23 September 1956

The Charlton Arms, Wellington, Shropshire

My dear old Creature,

You'll be surprised to get a letter from me from here! It hardly lies on the *way* from Hull to Liverpool, but it can be brought into the journey without too much trouble. Anyhow, I'm here till 5.57, when I entrain for Liverpool. Ruth is here too of course, much the same as usual. I haven't seen anyone else I know, thank God. It's a curious little town, ugly & graceful all mixed up together. The Library was shut when I arrived, but I could see they have altered it a good deal. I'd love to have gone in: inspected my erstwhile prison! I remember Pop rather romantically saying that the centre of the town reminded him of Germany. Most of the names over the shops are still the same.

There is not much flat news, except that my cooker is on its way from Falkirk. It's curious that both the cooker & the gas fire should be the same as I had at Belfast: the whole thing will be alike a superior Belfast – I hope! If only I can find a superior cleaner to go with it!

The weather is astonishingly warm here: much warmer than Hull. I expect it will cool off again as I go north. [. . .]

The "Residents Lounge" at the Charlton Arms is so depressing a place that I am eager to be up & out of it, so when I've finished this I shall take a walk up King Street, & look at Glentworth – what grisly remembrances that name calls up!

Goodbye for the present, dear old creature.

With all love, Philip

28 September 1956

192A Hallgate, Cottingham, E. Yorkshire

My dear old Creature,

Yes, Wellington was not much altered, except for the people – I found I recognised nobody, except an idiot who used to misbehave in the Reading Room. [. . .] Ruth was all right, very nice in her way, (nicer than I am in mine), and undeniably living more for others. Her mother & grandfather (I didn't meet them) are still alive: he *was* almost blind, but has slightly improved since I mentioned it to you.[1] [. . .]

Miss Wrench has arrived! and seems all right so far, though not liking her digs(!): what will happen to her I don't know. She has a cheerful way with her. Actually there are times when one dreads *all* one's staff, for fear they ask you to do things, or organise things, or for fear they grumble. Trials of a boss! Still, my secretary returns on Monday, & I shall feel less badgered, I hope. [. . .]

With all love, Philip

1 It was Ruth Bowman's grandfather who insisted that she destroy all Larkin's 400 letters to her.

28 October 1956

32 Pearson Park, Hull

My dear old creature,

Well, this is the first morning in the new home: I suppose I've been in occupation just a day, as I arrived by taxi at just about 10.30 yesterday morning, with the residue of my belongings. The rest of the day I spent shopping, & trying to sort things out: the task today will be cleaning, for a good deal of surface dirt seems to have collected since my last efforts.

I expect you wonder what I think of it: well, it's very nice in itself, & will be nicer when it's cleared & cleaned & curtained & carpeted. The sitting- & bed-room are much larger than I've previously had, though, and I can see they won't be easy to keep warm. The hall & bathroom are cold places, too: the bathroom in particular, for the window is stuck open a little. This also lets smuts in. These are new to me, & I don't like them. I tried to have a bath last night, but through misjudging quantities & behaviours found myself with only a lukewarm one. All sorts of little draughts sneak in & out! One can't really understand where they are coming from, or how. But I had a very good night's sleep in my striped sheets: a double bed seems warmer than a single one, though I don't see how it can be. I have about 5 blankets on, plus a candlewick bed cover. The down pillow was fine!

I nearly had a dreadful accident: when making up the bed, I upset a bottle of marking ink with w[ch] I had been marking sheets, & it missed my sheepskin rug by inches only! In fact it left a spatter of nasty spots on it, but I quickly soaked them up and *cut them off*. It w[d] have been the most awful calamity & suppose I'd *had* my yellow carpet? It's funny how there's a lucky side to everything.

I have just found your letter. I am so glad you listened to the wireless: there are few things more comfortable than doing some simple job (like cleaning the silver) & listening to some witless wireless programme. Do you ever hear Wilfred Pickles? I find his programmes interesting in a sometimes rather awful way.[1]

Actually, I bought a small portable wireless on Friday (12 gns) to have in the kitchen. I thought of you & your old Bush.

You would like to see my view as I sit, a wide vista of tree-tops, most of them nearly bare, & nothing else. All trees. I shall feel like a bird. But then, I hope you will come when I have somewhere to put a second creature. In the meantime, I shall be seeing you next Friday night – as it happens, I'll be arriving about 8.15 for once, as I have a committee in Leeds on that afternoon & shall come straight on. I expect I shall be going to Leicester on Sunday, as before. Looking forward to seeing you – hope you enjoy the play! If you leave the key with Kitty I can go in & make myself at home. All best love, Philip

1 Wilfred Pickles (1904–78), actor and radio presenter, was the first newsreader on the BBC Home Service to speak in a regional accent, and his radio show, *Have A Go*, was the first to give out money prizes. It ran from 1946 to 1967, giving currency to such catchphrases as 'How do, how are yer?', 'Are yer courting?' and 'Give him the money, Mabel.'

18 November 1956

32 Pearson Park, Hull

My dear old creature,

[. . .] Yesterday some of my curtains came, & I was able to put the sitting room ones up myself. They are "oyster velour", lined with wine sateen. So the room now looks more civilised, though several points about them displease me. For one thing, I ordered them too short, & they rest on the sill (no doubt the *bill* will be long enough); and they would look better with a long frill at the top to hide the rail. But if I have that I also hide the top circle of the centre light – as you recall, my window is 3 lights:

and the ceiling is tangential to the top of the circle. So a frill or pelmet such as I have pencilled would spoil the whole effect. They are coming to fit the bedroom ones tomorrow.

I have been having a great time with draught excluders. I bought some of the metal strip variety, only to find that the first direction was "remove the door from its hinges", which I thought rather a tall order! However, even if I could have done it, it would hardly have been back the same night, for it's a very slow and painful job hitting a small tack through a thickness of metal every 1½" for about 80", especially when (if one *doesn't* remove the door from its hinges) the bottom end has to be done lying on one's back on the floor. Subsidiary operations have been carried out with long strips of putty, newspaper, and plastic foam. The job isn't nearly finished yet, but whether it will make any noticeable difference I am already beginning to doubt.

Well, I mustn't go on about the house all the time. [. . .]

All love to dear old creature P

<*On back of envelope*> Have 2 pork chops to deal with.

23 November 1956 Lettercard

Hull

My dear old Creature,

Hasn't the weather turned nasty! It's very grey and shivery here this morning. This has been an irritating week: *Kingsley* announced his intention of paying me a visit this weekend, & I had to borrow a bed; now he says he isn't coming![1] I don't mind – in fact I'm glad – but I wish he hadn't put me to the trouble in the first place. Curse all friends, at least of that variety.

Isn't the petrol business a mess?[2] I'm glad I haven't got "a little car", even though I could then go for drives with a certain old party –

Very much love, d.o.c.
P.

1 Amis never visited Larkin in Hull, travelling for his funeral in 1985 only as far as St Mary's, Cottingham.
2 Supplies of fuel from the Middle East were cut off when Gamal Abdul Nasser, President of Egypt, blocked the Suez Canal when threatened by an Anglo-French-Israeli attack in late October 1956. The government in Britain restricted fuel sales from the end of November, which led to panic buying.

28 November 1956 Lettercard

Hull

My dear old Creature,

Many thanks for the extra letter – it was nice to hear that you had been sleeping in your own basket for once, though not because you had a cold.[1] I love to hear the little details of your life. I bought a tea-set yesterday – 21 pieces, Wedgewood, fairly ordinary but quite nice. Also the 3 Sassoon books! After lunch I shall take things to the cleaners

& buy some bacon. How kind of Kitty to buy violets. Expect me on Friday.

With all love Philip

1 Eva had partly broken her habit of sleeping at Kitty and Walter's house rather than her own. She wrote on 24 November: 'It seems to be a "head" cold and my nose and eyes "streamed" all the time on Thursday and Friday. I stayed here last night, and shall do so tonight, for I think it is more comfortable not having to turn out in the cold, and there is really no need when Walter is at 53.'

1957

3 January 1957

32 PEARSON PARK

HULL

My dear old Creature,

This is my new paper: rather nice, isn't it? I love the smallness of the address: highly smart, I think.[1] It was very nice to have a letter from you on New Year's Day. I smiled at you thinking the end of the world was imminent – and sympathised about the snail in the cellar.[2] Poor creatures, where do they come from? Surely there can't be anything for them to eat down there. Perhaps they can sense the Guinness.

I stayed in all Tuesday afternoon waiting for my studio couch, and occupied my time with cleaning. It came eventually, & *looks* all right, but I don't think it's a very *comfortable* object. However we shall see. Monica's picture was also here, & looks splendid.

I find it hard to get up here just as at home! I set my alarm for 7.30, but this seems too early, so I usually lie till 8.15 as I should have done anyway.

A travel agency has sent me some literature. Have you any idea when old Walter's holiday will be? I expect he won't know. All the literature is of "tours" – W[d] you like a trip down the Rhine? I really don't see how you can possibly book a holiday to match Kitty's if you don't know when it's to be until very late. Could you ask her?

Oh by the way, The Critics are doing *A Girl in Winter* on Sunday next. Oh dear![3] I must end now, but thank you for your letter & all creaturely wishes for the new year. It's good to be alive, no matter what we may say to the contrary now & then.

All love, Philip

1 When writing from his flat Larkin used paper with the above letterhead consistently until the early 1960s. By 1964 he was using it very rarely, but in mid-1965 he seems to have obtained new supplies and resumed its regular use.

2 On 31 December 1956 Eva wrote: 'To-day has been a most miserable affair regarding the weather. At lunch time it became so dark that one would be forgiven for thinking that the end of the world was imminent. It has rained most of the day and is still doing so this evening. / I've put another snail out of the cellar.'
3 The text continues up the right margin, across the top and down the entire left margin.

10 February 1957

<*Letterhead*> 32 Pearson Park, Hull

My dear old Creature,

I feel rather sluggish today – the time is just after 1 p.m., and I haven't done anything but rise, breakfast, and wash up. This despite my eat-more-and-better-food campaign! Yesterday I bought a large pyrex dish, a large saucepan, & piece of silverside, a bag of potatoes, a cabbage, a bag of carrots a bag of onions . . . Very shortly I shall buy a cookery book. I'm tired of hating my Sunday meals.

The week has been rather trying in that my building has been worrying me – it is such a rottenly-planned affair, full of wasted space and old-fashioned ideas that I shall be held responsible for, and wch I accepted only to hurry the thing up. I've no faith in the architect: he is a bungling fool. It's all very worrying, and keeps me constantly on the jump.

I shouldn't pay any attention to Walter & his money-making schemes. It is all right for him: his needs exceed his income, & he is driven to find other ways of making money. Yours don't, so I should just forget about it. Money should be like a skin, something one's not aware of unless it goes wrong.

My photograph was taken by Elliott & Fry, a well known firm, but I've no hopes that the results will be successful. I tried to look grave, kindly yet humorous withal, but shall doubtless emerge as the popeyed small mouthed fat-cheeked balding gold-rimmed version of Heinrich Himmler we all know so well. No proofs have arrived so far. [. . .]

I am beginning to be terrified of the "short paper" I have to give to a local club on Feb 25 – I haven't written it yet, & the prospect of doing so makes me turn cold, let alone the prospect of delivering it. Then the *London Magazine* wants 500–1000 words on should writers be political or not – and I've got several reviews hanging over me. "I'm coming! I'm coming! Beware o' me!"

Monica is going home next weekend, wch is a pity, as it means I shan't see her if I come: but I think I had better come for all that, as I'll need the pre-25th weekend to prepare my talk. Only if you too found something unsuitable in next weekend w^{d} I postpone my trip. Let me know if you do. W^{d} you, please?

It's a quarter to two. What shall I do with this beef, eh? We shall see. I hope you are finding plenty of little things to interest you. All my love,

Philip

14 April 1957

<*Letterhead*> 32 Pearson Park, Hull

My dear old Creature,

I refused to get up this morning until 11.30 – not because I needed more sleep but because I felt I could do with more rest. Anyway, up I got in very brilliant sunshine which seems to have abated rather by this time (5 to 1). The view out of my bedroom window over a number of back gardens and allotments is lovely – all the trees and bushes opening their fans of fresh green in the sun. It makes one despair of ever saying how glad one is to be alive! At the front of the house of course the park is equally impressive, but there are more fish-faced citizens & their brats wandering about. [. . .]

Some time today I ought to face my income-tax return: awful bore it is. I earned £178 by writing etc. last year – I shouldn't get very fat on that; should I? [. . .]

The weather still looks only half-fine.

With very best creaturely love,

P

19 May 1957

<*Letterhead*> 32 Pearson Park, Hull

My dear old creature,

[. . .] Well, the royal visit went off quite all right: the weather was bright but sometimes showery & with a very strong wind. There was a small crowd of about 2,500 at the University, & the plan was that the Queen & the Duke sh^{d} arrive at the central building and meet certain big bugs & middle sized bugs (not me), then walk about 200 yds to the Students' Union where the "coffee party" w^d be held, students presented, & so on. That's where I was. For me the biggest thrill was seeing, after a wait of about an hour, the line of big black cars crawling in at the distant gates, & the royal standard being swiftly run up to leap out in the wind from the university flag staff, all red and gold. Then it was quite exciting to see her close at hand – she is quite slim, & looks very young still, & was wearing a blue coat, white hat, & black bag & shoes. Rather ordinary clothes really. If I had edged nearer to her during the time the party was on I'm pretty sure I should have been presented, for she had apparently expressed a wish to meet more students, but since none were available made do with staff, & anyone within reach was being presented. I'm sorry I wasn't in a way, but I was only meekly obeying orders to keep back & not crowd the centre room. Others not so scrupulous were more successful! Ah, well, one day I shall meet her as Philip Larkin, & not as the paltry librarian of a piffling university. Or so I like to think! I only wish I was doing more about making it possible.

My new secretary starts tomorrow, but I can't say I feel in the mood for her. The old one has less than 14 days now, & I expect is feeling pretty low about it, as she avoids all mention of her departure.[1]

Well, you will be seeing me for Whitsun: actually I shall be going to London next Friday \but one (31st May)/ & probably staying overnight: my plans are vague, but I shall be "on the move" at any rate, Next Saturday I am going on this book-collecting expedition. My very best love – be of good cheer!

Philip

1 Hilary Penwill was leaving to get married, and had encouraged her friend Betty Mackereth to apply for the job.

26 May 1957

<*Letterhead*> 32 Pearson Park, Hull

My dear old creature,

[. . .] I wrote to Bruce not long ago & had a reply from his Secretary saying he was too busy to write himself – I don't know what things are coming to. I may see him next weekend in London when I go. Then again I may not.

I have washed my terylene pyjamas and hung them over the sink to dry. The seam has not come undone any more, but they look a poor job really, & the trousers do need shortening. I'll bring them at Whitsun! I must remember to send laundry today, as I shan't be here to do so for the next two weekends.

My new secretary has begun, & seems all right in a way: no doubt she will learn.[1] She'll probably stay all her life, though, now.[2]

Haven't much in to eat today, but shall no doubt *survive*! Shall now put my shoes on & go out for a pint.

All best love, Philip

1 On 28 March Philip had written: 'She seemed rather concerned about the loss in pension if she gave up her present job, where she has been for 12 years.'
2 Betty Mackereth did indeed stay, retiring only on her sixtieth birthday, 27 June 1984, the year before Larkin's death.

2 June 1957

<*Letterhead*> 32 Pearson Park, Hull

My dear old creature,

We are just moving out of London – 10 a.m. on another beautiful morning. I'm bound for Leicester, to see M. who'll be away next week when I come to see you.

Well, my stay in London was short, but very enjoyable. On arrival I went to lunch with some businessmen & some librarians at the Junior Carlton Club in Pall Mall, wch is of course a v. high-class place. We had lunch in the library at a table where Disraeli used to sit planning his political schemes. It consisted of (the lunch I mean) *foie gras*, *salmon trout*, & strawberries, with hock to drink. Of course all this was done with a purpose! But I don't expect they will bear me any hard feelings if they don't get the job. After that, I attended my committee, wch went on till about 5: checked in at my hotel, & immediately went out again. I spent the first half of the evening drinking beer in a bar near Gower Street with a few acquaintances, and the second working my [way] through an enormous plate of food at a Spanish restaurant with the Egertons. Almost anything seemed likely to turn up in the plate –

mussels, chicken, lobster, for instance. Yesterday (Saturday) was again fine, & I felt very keenly the pleasure of strolling about in London, not dead yet, with money in pocket & nothing to do. I went to Hatchard's, & looked over the books, then to Simpsons in Piccadilly, where I bought a suit (2 piece) at what seems a fantastic price now of £25. They are retaining it for a few alterations. At lunchtime I met Bruce, who had come up from Devon for the day, & we had lunch at one of his clubs (cold salmon). After going to see one of his absurd science-fiction films, we went to the Authors' Club and sat on a kind of covered-in verandah sipping & talking, till Bruce felt an urge for high life & we went off to somewhere I think was the Ambassadors, where we had a quite nice dinner costing £7 (I'm afraid B. paid for all this, but he says he's earning £10,000 a year) with a hock so marvellous that I shan't easily forget it. Unfortunately B. then felt tired & gloomy & went to be *de bonne heure* as the French say, wch suited me quite well. He enquired after you, & seemed in fairly good shape. In all this was a day I shall remember for a long time. The great drawback to this weekend is that I'm wearing a suit that's much too hot. At present I feel as if I may dissolve before we reach Leicester – if we ever do, that is, as the train is crawling. You can tell by my legible writing. Ah, now we're quickening up.

I can't think that Whitsun is a very convenient time for going to Lichfield, as I shall be at home only for the 3 days wch are bound to be very busy ones as far as travelling goes. Still. I wonder if it would be possible to go on *Sunday*? Honestly I don't know which of the 3 days would be least unsuitable. But I agree we ought to go some time. Perhaps you c^d find out what the Sunday 'buses are like.

We seem to be loitering about on the edge of Kettering. I can't think we shall be in Leicester by 12.16. I wonder what you are doing? I hope on such a fine day you have at least been out in the garden to see what the bees are doing.

See you on Friday evening, all being well – probably about 10.15 or so.

All love,
Philip

1 September 1957

<*Letterhead*> 32 Pearson Park, Hull

My dear old Creature,

Well, here I be, back again in my own surroundings. We had quite an interesting time in London, which is still full of foreign visitors, mainly Americans. As you know, we stayed at the Ivanhoe. It's an odd place. I notice that it's run entirely by women, except for the porters – woman manager, woman receptionists & accountants. It's a temperance hotel, in that it hasn't a bar, & a lot of the guests seem to have a feminine appearance. I wonder why Pop chose it? What was it like in your day?[1]

On Thursday evening we roamed about. We had a drink in the Café Royal, where Oscar Wilde used to dine, & then went to a pub in Leicester Square we like for beer (a low drink the C. R. w$^{dn't}$ dream of selling). After that we went to a Lyons for roast beef & baked potatoes. On Friday I went to the big camera shop that supplies the Duke of Edinburgh, & bought a new camera: at least, it isn't new itself, but it is a German camera, a Rolleiflex, & they are regarded as being very good indeed & above £120 each when new. I won't tell you how much I paid! But I insured it on the spot.[2]

Then, as I said on my card, we went to Lord's, & saw a really good day's cricket, in wch the match was won in the last over by Monica's county, Worcestershire. It was also the last match in wch Compton & Edrich play for Middlesex: they have been very famous for the last 10 years. In the evening, we went to see *The Prince & the Showgirl*, the Laurence Olivier – Marilyn Monroe film, & rotten it was.[3]

The journey back was dull & slow, but we endured it, & spent the evening in my flat. M. admires my Welsh tapestry bedspread, wch is now on the floor & looks quite at home.

M. wants to know how you like your navy skirt – I couldn't tell her, though I remember you having it on one day at Portmeirion.[4] She ordered a dress in New Bond Street on Saturday morning, a cream brocade affair by Frederica. When we got in we ate some cold beef brought from London, & a pickled walnut or two. She was sorry to see that her cake had grown whiskers! She said she had never dreamed it would have any competition – I related how you took yours to Portmeirion & then took it home: she said "I think I should have given it best by then."

Have you asked about the immersion heater? How is the cellar?

Very best love to O.C., Philip

1 Eva replied on 3 September: 'What a queer place the Ivanhoe sounds now. I cannot remember much about it, except that it was then a temperance hotel. Perhaps we went there because it was cheaper than other places.'
2 The shop was Wallace Heaton in New Bond Street. The Rolleiflex was a German camera introduced in the late 1920s. It became very popular with reportage photographers such as Brassaï, Bill Brandt and Lee Miller. See Mark Haworth-Booth, 'Philip Larkin as Photographer', *About Larkin* 42 (October 2016), 5–15.
3 A 1957 film directed and produced by Laurence Olivier, with a screenplay by Terence Rattigan based on his 1953 stage play *The Sleeping Prince*.
4 Eva wrote on 3 September: 'Tell Monica I like my new skirt very much. I think it wonderful that it does not crease, and is washable. / I was interested to hear that she had ordered a new dress in London. Is it for evening wear? Cream brocade sounds elegant.'

29 September 1957

<*Letterhead*> 32 Pearson Park, Hull

My dear old Creature,

[. . .] I hope you liked the photographs I sent you. I thought they showed a very agreeable old creature, very well dressed and affable, and I'm glad to have a souvenir of the week we had among the fleshpots of Portmeirion. It's rather ironic that it should be taken with my *old* camera, or rather Pop's old camera, now that I've just spent so much on a new one.[1] It seems to prove that all I need to do was to learn how to use the old one! I can hear Pop judging my new one to be "too good for you", in a gruff fashion. [. . .]

With all my best love
Dear old creature
Philip

1 In fact Philip had bought his old camera on his own initiative (see letter of 26 October 1947), though spurred on by his father's enthusiasm.

20 October 1957

<Letterhead> 32 Pearson Park, Hull *Telephone 41719*

My dear old creature,

You had better make a note of my telephone number! Now it is in, of course I don't use it, and if it rings I know it's the Library, Coveney[1] or the Penwills,[2] since they are the only people/places where my number is known: I'm not putting it in the directory. [. . .]

As regards Monica & America, she has had another offer of a year's exchange in a small college on Long Island. Whether she will go or not I don't know. She may have decided by now. I don't feel over-cheerful about it from any aspect.

Do watch the way you write abbreviated negatives – "haven't" *not* "have'nt"! The latter is just awfully uneducated, not like you at all. Actually I find I have been writing "sophistocated" all my life wch is of course hopelessly wrong. [. . .]

I've decided what I want for Xmas – a book about Rollei cameras. Details later.[3]

With all best love, Philip

1 Larkin had become friends with Peter Coveney, warden of Needler Hall, a student hall of residence.

2 Hilary Penwill had been Larkin's secretary until the appointment of Betty Mackereth.

3 On 26 October Philip wrote: 'After mentioning my "present" I felt I had perhaps been rather presumptuous – it costs about 35/-, wch may be more than an old creature wants to pay. If so, I also want a particular kind of filter, but I might have to order that myself. It sh^{d} be cheaper. What w^{d} old creature like?'

26 October 1957

<Letterhead> 32 Pearson Park, Hull

My dear old Creature,

[. . .] Of course, you mustn't worry about shortened negatives – but it's an increasing solecism these days.[1] I am trying to convert my secretary to saying envelope and not onvelope, wch I also think low. My meeting with the Finance Committee went off quite all right – they are a rather simple-minded bunch. I can't believe that the building will actually start before the year is out. Perhaps it won't! Don't I see that the builders are asking for more money? This will probably cause a general strike, or a rise in prices so that the £300,000 we have won't be enough, or something. [. . .]

Expect this letter reads rather dully, but it has all my love,

Philip

1 Eva had written on 21 October: 'O, Creature, I suddenly became a most abject being when I read your admonition regarding my slip up with the abbreviated negative. I'm quite puzzled at it, because, of course I *do* know how they should be written. When you mentioned your own mistake with "sophisticated" it reminded me of how for a very long time I wrote "tremend*r*ous" in letters to Daddy before we were married. He never alluded to it, and I found it out only by accident.'

3 November 1957

<*Letterhead*> 32 Pearson Park, Hull

My dear old creature,

My life is now temporarily back on an even keel, I'm glad to say: the prospect of uninterrupted leisure in Hull is quite comforting after the trip to Belfast, which really struck me as very long and tiring. It's quite 4 hrs from Hull to L'pool, then of course 10 hours on the sea . . .[1] [. . .]

I've suddenly had a burst of meat-eating! Steak on Friday, steak on Saturday & a pork chop, pork & lamb chops today. Perhaps I am unconsciously restoring the losses of Thursday night!

Tomorrow I have a big day. A lorry & 2 men, & myself & 3 others in a hired car, are going up to Busby Hall in N. Riding to pack about 2000 books & bring them back to Hull. They are mouldy & filthy & will constitute a frightful headache: we've paid only £100 for them, so I suppose it doesn't matter. My secretary, Betty, is driving, & Miss Wrench & Miss Mann are coming with us: we shall have to take our lunches, and I only hope we can get the books onto the lorry & all of us back by about 5 or 6 – then they have to be unloaded & stowed away.[2] I only hope we don't get a puncture or any holdup like that. It will be a fearfully long journey. [. . .]

With all my best love, Philip.

1 Larkin had acted as best man at Alec Dalgarno's wedding.

2 Mary Wrench (later Judd) recalled this jaunt in a letter she wrote to Maeve Brennan and Betty Mackereth in 1986 after Larkin's death. See Booth, *Philip Larkin: Life, Art and Love*, 231.

17 November 1957

<*Letterhead*> 32 Pearson Park, Hull

My dear old creature,

[. . .] This has not been a very eventful week, really: I haven't seen any results of the photographs & don't suppose I shall – U.S. papers seem awfully far away. No doubt the results will show the usual balding chinless creature familiar to all. I had Miss Wrench in on Thursday wch was all right, though she departed with 3 of my books. She didn't say very much, less than she does at work: perhaps she was nervous. Anyway, she didn't display the madness for which she is renowned, as you'll remember![1] She asked after you & wondered if you were better now. She regretted not having seen you when you came. *Her* trouble is not being *able* to get home from Hull: she lives near Northampton, wch strangely enough is awfully hard to reach from here. [. . .]

Coveney was much cheered by having a good review of his book[2] in the *New Statesman* on Friday. It looks as if it may be quite successful.

Every morning when I eat shredded wheat, as I do just now, I remember your first encounter with it and smile. It *is* rather like eating a bird's nest! And one needs to open one's mouth awfully wide to get a piece of it in. I took some photographs of myself at breakfast this morning. Perhaps they will capture the squalid spirit of Sunday breakfast![3]

I look forward to seeing you.

All v. best love, Philip

1 On 30 November 1957 he related how he and Miss Wrench had rescued 'a cat that had been driven up a lamp standard by dogs! . . . about 100 students were idly watching the entertainment.' Larkin was attracted by Mary Wrench's quirky, independent spirit. On one occasion he surprised her by donning a cat mask while her back was turned. Booth, *Philip Larkin*, 231.

2 Coveney's book was *Poor Monkey: The Child in Literature* (Rockliff: London, 1957).

3 Richard Bradford reproduces two of these photograph in *The Importance of Elsewhere*, 194.

1958

5 January 1958

<*Letterhead*>
Cranston's Ivanhoe Hotel, Bloomsbury Street, London W.C.1

My dear old Creature,

Here I am in y^{r} old shredded-wheat place: outside the rain is pouring down. The hotel is fearfully hot! in fact we have gone from lounge to lounge seeking coolness, which may sound strange in January. On Friday we went to see *Blue Murder at St Trinian's*,[1] wch we thought very funny, & last night went to *The Boy Friend* for the 3rd time – it is in its 4th year now, but still seems full of energy & sparkle.[2] At the end they let balloons down from the ceiling & we each got one! we bore these triumphantly back & are now faced with the task of letting them down, no easy job *je vous assure*.[3] I got the impression that the house was mainly filled with provincial 'bus-loads, who were not very quick at the jokes.

Just before I left I had a letter from A. Nellie enclosing copies of the photographs of the Queen & Duke. She wrote saying she'd enjoyed her stay, & asking for prints of "the fat lady on the bridge" – I am having an enlargement made. The goose came out quite well, but much to my disappointment the lunch ones are slightly out of focus as far as the people are concerned – the foreground of plates and glasses is first class!

On Friday we went to Liberty's to see what was being sold, & I'm afraid I laid out £6.10.0 on a dressing gown – camel-hair & wool, marked down from £10/10/- which will release Daddy's old one from Hull & enable me to throw away the green horror wch you see me [in], sulky & silent, facing life at the breakfast table on so many Saturday & Sunday mornings. I also bought a tie & a pair of socks. This goes rather contrary to my principle of never buying at sales! There were some *very* pretty silk ones, but I don't really need a silk one.

London looks rather deflated after Christmas, but we are enjoying ourselves well enough. I hope you are keeping on top of everything &

that Rosemary's pantomime was a success, or is, or whichever tense is appropriate.

It's still raining, & I think we had better go out *for beer*, as Uncle Alf w^{d} say.

All best love,
Philip

1 A 1957 film set in the fictional girls' school, written by Frank Launder and Sidney Gilliat and directed by Frank Launder. It starred Terry-Thomas, George Cole, Joyce Grenfell, Lionel Jeffries and Richard Wattis.
2 The musical by Sandy Wilson, first performed in London in 1954, ran for 2,078 performances. It transferred to Broadway and was made into a film in 1971.
3 Eva (7 January 1958) was puzzled by her son's evasiveness: 'You say we went here and we did this and that without saying who was your companion. I expect it was Monica.' She was right.

21 January 1958

<*Letterhead*> 32 Pearson Park, Hull

My dear old creature,

Isn't it *cold*? There were 29° of frost on Monday night at a place near here – that is, the temperature stood at 3° [F]! I expect you too have snow showers, ground frost, and nasty draughts coming through cracks in the windows. Do take care to keep warm, & don't slip on the pavements. Take *extra* care, & don't stand at street-corners with Mrs Dexter. She has more fat on her ribs than you.[1]

I ate 8 oz. of steak tonight, & a lot of rice, & feel blown out in consequence. Hope it will "do me good". There's no news here, except that the wife of one of my colleagues is having a baby & the other is ill, so both are off. I realise again what a sheltered life I lead. I sent off the photographs to Auntie Nellie, & hope they don't conflict with her idea of herself.[2] One day I must take another of you.

I feel I was a little snappish during my stay – it was perhaps envy of Kingsley, & nothing personal. You know it's no formality that I always end my letters

With all love from,
Philip

1 Eva's long-term friend lived nearby in Frederick Street, Loughborough.
2 Three photographs were included with the letter, one of which is reproduced as Plate 13B.

2 February 1958

<*Letterhead*>
Cranston's Ivanhoe Hotel, Bloomsbury Street, London W.C.1

My dear old creature,

I'm here, as you see: a rather battered creature sitting in the lounge, w[ch] is full, or half-full, of anonymous dreary creatures from the wilds of the provinces. It appears rather a dull day but it may improve.

I got to the BBC all right on Friday – rather late, actually: my own fault as well as the fog's – & we ploughed through the little programme.[1] The readers sit at one table & you sit at another. After the rehearsal we found that the programme was too long – most unfortunately, it can't be allowed to over-run, as it is geared to an outside broadcast – *Peter Grimes*. So we had to cut a poem out – *Coming*. Even now I fear it will be too long: perhaps the producer will fade it out or something! I had very little to do, & wasn't too nervous, but I was all the same too nervous to use the elegant vowel sounds I had been practising all the week! So I shall sound very much as always.

Kingsley is here: really rather dreadful, but it's quite nice to see him again, also Hilly, who is exactly the same, & gloomily contemplating her 30th year.[2] I joined Kingsley yesterday in the Ritz & drank champagne (at Lord Beaverbrook's expense), while K was interviewed by a frightful woman reporter from the *Express*.

I hope you are in good form: I return on Monday night. All my very best love

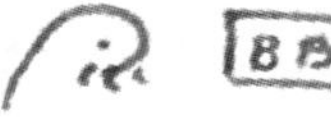

Philip

1 Anthony Thwaite had invited Philip to contribute to the BBC European Service series 'Younger British Poets of Today'.
2 On 4 February Eva reminisced: 'I'm not surprised that Hilly does not welcome the coming of her 30th year. I remember I felt quite depressed when I attained that age, and thought it the end of all youth and gaiety. I've since found out I was quite mistaken.'

9 February 1958

<*Letterhead*> 32 Pearson Park, Hull

My dear old creature,

[. . .] I'm glad you managed to hear the little poetry programme, & that my voice sounded strong & clear. I think one gets easier as one goes on: some people felt I should have said more, & I agree in a way, but there isn't much to say about the poems, & I w^{d} sooner they were read than that I droned platitudes about them. After this, I really shall have to write some new poems: I really can't go on running these same old ones any longer. Unfortunately I don't feel much in the mood![1]

Glad to hear the cushion had grown softer. I am sending my bed cover to be cleaned today. When I was in bed it looked so filthy! Also my bedroom curtains need doing, but I shall postpone them somewhat. The dirt in this town is terrible. [. . .]

Your ever-loving * Creature

1 On 18 February Eva wrote: 'I wonder if your ears burned on Sunday morning about 12.15 p.m.? As I was coming out of church Mrs Stapleton came to me and said that she and Mr Stapleton listened to your poems the other week. She thought they were wonderful, but said they made her feel so sad. Then Mrs Dalton, another lady whom I know and like, said, "I've never seen your son" and Mrs Dexter said "O! he's got a lovely smile and I do like his voice, in fact he has a lovely manner altogether and I've always liked Philip." Can you imagine how I swelled with pride!'

16 February 1958

Newcastle

My dear old creature,

As I probably intimated, this is one weekend I could very well have done without: it is proving all *right*, just dull. Colin's 2nd wife Barbara is about as unlike his 1st (Patsy) as could be, but that doesn't improve her much.[1] The house is an older terraced variety, crammed with 2nd hand furniture of various kinds. Newcastle I've not seen much of, but they say it is quite as dirty as Hull, & it certainly has a drab appearance. I travelled up by York on Friday, a very dull journey. There are still traces of snow about. Yesterday afternoon Colin drove us out in his rattle-trap Daimler to see the countryside (we went along the Roman wall for a long way), but the weather was so frightful I was glad to get back to the fireside, where I fell asleep. Tonight I get the 7.10, arriving Hull 10.57 – bloody late: another weekend wasted. [. . .]

Do take good care of yourself & keep a little flower of cheerfulness among your leaves!

All love, Philip

1 Barbara was a lecturer in English Language at Newcastle University. Richard Bradford reproduces a photograph taken by Larkin on this visit inthe hardback edition of *The Importance of Elsewhere,* 101, but misidentifies her as Strang's first wife, Patsy. In the paperback (100) he describes her as 'an unknown friend'.

22 February 1958

<*Letterhead*> 32 Pearson Park, Hull

My dear old creature,

This is an unbelievably dreary day. I sensed it would be and stayed in bed till a quarter to eleven! [. . .]

Very little has happened this week, as I recall: to some extent I have been irritable in a general non-focussed way, but this hasn't led to anything. *Wood* has been getting on my nerves again:[1] I had occasion to discuss with him whether or not a girl who works under him should have a merit-increase or not, & this has temporarily taken the lid off his cupidity, & he has been pestering me with proposals for getting him more money, all of which I refuse. He's scotch, of course. [. . .]

You're certainly well forward with your birthday cards! I forget if I told you of Miss Wrench's latest piece of lunacy – she had planned to send me a Valentine, & having addressed it put it in another envelope with a covering letter to a friend of hers in London. Unfortunately she put her friend's address on the Valentine & mine on the covering envelope! So it turned up a few days in advance. She had the grace to avoid me for a whole day afterwards. (If I've told you this before, please excuse me. Old brain going!)

I wonder if anyone showed you the article published in the *Daily Mail* supposedly by Hilary Amis about why she married Kingsley? Memories are very short. They seem to be becoming a sort of "popular couple" – They'll probably be on TV soon. Hum!

I do hope your arm is better. I should certainly seek medical advice about it if I were you, & refrain from putting any strain on it. Don't go to any especial trouble for my arrival! (Porridge for breakfast?)

All my very best love,
Philip

1 Arthur Wood, Larkin's deputy, inherited from his predecessor, Agnes Cuming.

30 March 1958

Kensington

My dear old creature,

I am in a better humour now that the weather is warmer. The sun is shining in quite a balmy way, though I shouldn't be surprised if there was some rain later on. I am staying in the Murphys' flat in Kensington,[1] but return to Hull this evening – I have been away for over a week!

Since coming to London I haven't done much but go to Barkers & order an Anglepoise lamp for my flat. I hesitated a long time over other sorts, but decided in the end that I should be always bumping into any kind that stood on the floor, and might not like the feeling of it peering over my shoulder!

It's a mistake to have too many things standing about.

My little talk – only about 15 mins – went uneventfully & seemed to provoke quite a lively discussion, though I had to think it all over carefully several times beforehand & work out how I was going to begin. We had a delicious dinner & altogether I liked Southampton very much. The Librarian once turned me down for a job there, & we talked this over with amusement: the person they *did* appoint – back in 1945 – has just died, poor woman. [. . .]

There are crocuses in Hyde Park, but not much else, except foreigners. And not visitors, either – inhabitants! Scum of Europe, I kept thinking à la Sydney L. I suppose they are the staff of the embassies etc.

With all very best love,
Philip

1 The Irish poet Richard Murphy had married Patsy Strang in 1955. He was later the second Compton Poetry Fellow at Hull. See letters of 18 May and 14 September 1969.

2 April 1958

Librarian:
P. A. LARKIN, M.A.

UNIVERSITY LIBRARY
HULL
Telephone: 18960

Hurray about Matlock!

We shall have a nice Easter after all.
Arriving Thursday 8–11 pm.
Philip.

18 May 1958

<*Letterhead*> 32 Pearson Park, Hull

My dear old creature,

[. . .] Tomorrow I have my last Committee of the year, which may prove a stormy one, as I am trying to get an increased grant for the Library, & money is very short. I expect I shall upset the Vice-Chancellor if I am not careful. Oh well. My building is getting more interesting:

they have one whole section of the steel girders up now. I go and look at it every day, much to the amusement of the men, who offer to take me up on the crane-hook! I don't think I shall accept the suggestion. They are an amusing lot. One said that the Clerk of Works disagreed with the way one v. high bit had been done, so he scrambled out along the girder & invited the C. of W. to come & have a look. The C. of W. declined, saying that he was keeping a wife & children: "ah doan't know what he thought ah'm keeping!" They tell me that they have left all the bolts out in the part supporting my room. [. . .]

I don't expect you would hear Kingsley's short programme of poetry on Thursday: he included a couple of mine, kindly.[1] I haven't heard any more from my publisher – I sent a letter gently expressing disinclination to finance his overdraft. Nor have I yet got my record, though it is promised, so I may be able to bring it home for Whitsun.[2] You'll be almightily bored with it, I expect. [. . .]

Very best (I put vest!) love,
Philip

1 Eva reported on 20 May: 'As it happens I did hear Kingsley's programme last week. I was searching the Radio Times for something worth listening to, and noticed it. Kitty happened to call that day [. . .] we both listened, and when he mentioned "a younger poet", I knew who it was! / I very much liked the poem about the thrush and thought it worthy of Hardy. I am glad he chose "At Grass", another favourite. Was it the first time it had been broadcast?'

2 A baffling reference. The Listen recording *Philip Larkin reads 'The Less Deceived'* was made five months later on 24 October 1958 at the HMV studios in London. (See letter of 7 December 1958.) Was an earlier recording date perhaps envisaged? Bloomfield, B. C.: *Philip Larkin: A Bibliography 1933–1994* (London: British Library, 2002) lists no earlier recordings by Larkin himself.

8 June 1958

<*Letterhead*> 32 Pearson Park, Hull

My dear old creature,

It looks a dull rainy Sunday outside, but this doesn't greatly displease me as I have nothing especial to do, & anyway it looks as if it will clear up later. In fact the sun is coming out even as I write. I am lying on my sofa in the window & the record-player is playing.

About the most exciting thing of last week was photographing a graveyard! Last Sunday I took Monica for a short walk round a certain large deserted graveyard not far from here, wch I love. It is very overgrown & full of splendid trees & ivy & creepers & urns. She thought it marvellous, so on Tuesday I took advantage of a sunny afternoon to go down and photograph it. Yesterday I got the prints & am pleased with them: at least six are absolutely what I wanted.[1] I shall send off for enlargements & let you see them in due course. To my delight I find that I have the headstone of a centenarian in one of them, quite accidentally! Miss Brennan[2] thinks all this v. morbid, but I think I have certain affinities with the poet Gray, who as you know wrote *Elegy in a Country Churchyard*.

Fancy getting 15/- for the jackets![3] Well, of course, they are probably worth more in one sense, but the fellow has got to make a profit, & they have been pretty well used. In *Brave New World* Aldous Huxley forecast the time when we should throw clothes away much oftener, probably instead of washing them, but of course he was expecting they w^d^ be cheaper than they are now.

My building grows slowly – very slowly. I'm sure it will never be ready on time. Did I tell you the workmen said "It walks about at night? They meant that until the stanchions are concreted the structure alters position at night in the wind and has to be adjusted each morning. I wish they would all hurry up & get on with it.

Rather foolishly I agreed to help judge a poetry competition in Suffolk & 38 awful poems, each supposed to be "A Song of Praise", have arrived. They are nearly all indistinguishably bad. The other judges are Mrs Frances Cornford & Sir Charles Tennyson. Another literary feature of the week was a talk by Alan Pryce Jones, editor of the Times Lit. Supp., whom Kitty will have heard on the *Critics*. He asked me to go to lunch with him when next in London, but I don't suppose I shall.

I was wrong about the weather – the sun couldn't maintain itself, & really the sky is so overcast it may rain any moment. I expect it is the same with you – never mind, you must be like the sundial in Hardy's poem that even when it is raining knows the sun is still up there & will shine again to give the sundial something to do.[4]

The Duffins[5] are making a fearful noise downstairs: I should like to go down & lay about me with a cudgel. The squealing of the little girls, the deeper imbecilities of Duffin himself, all mingled with stamping of little feet, crashes and explosions . . . I should like to hurl tear-gas bombs down the chimney.

Well, it is just about noon, & I must bring my ramblings to an end. Take great care of yourself, my dear old creature, for there is much quiet enjoyment to be had from life & in any case you could ill be spared by

Your Creature. Lots of love.

1 Eva replied on 10 June: 'It seems strange to think that the photographing of a graveyard could be even a little bit exciting. It must be a most unusual place if both you and Monica think it is marvellous. I look forward to seeing the pictures of it.' There are numerous graveyard photographs by Larkin in the archive. See Jean Hartley, *Philip Larkin, The Marvell Press and Me*, 98; and James Booth, 'Larkin as Photographer', *About Larkin* 37 (April 2014), 5.

2 Maeve Brennan: the library assistant with whom Larkin was to become romantically involved in 1960.

3 Eva had written (2 June): 'This morning I sold your three sports jackets to a second hand clothes buyer. He gave 15/- for them. I wonder if that is a fair price.'

4 'The Sundial on a Wet Day'.

5 Bill and Janet Duffin, colleagues of Larkin at the university, occupied the flat below his.

14 September 1958

<*Letterhead*> 32 Pearson Park, Hull

My dear old creature,

I am on the floor of my bedroom again, for there is every sign of a fine day outside and I want to make the most of it. I shall be going out on my bike after lunch, I expect. Last Sunday I went out & did about 30 miles, to the coast & back. Pop w^{d} like E. Riding – it's very flat for cycling, like going to see the deer.

I was glad to get away from London – I travelled back 1st-class with a 2nd-class ticket: the railway people are getting very slack – but I suppose I had an interesting time. One of the most interesting things was my first oyster! You know I was meeting Stephen Spender for lunch. Well, he had oysters, & I didn't dare to, but I said I'd never had one, so he gave me one of his. It wasn't too bad! rather like having a swim. I didn't have any more, though. There was an American there who talked all the time, so we didn't actually get much of a chance to say anything. [. . .]

Philip

12 October 1958

<*Letterhead*> 32 Pearson Park, Hull

My dear old creature,

It's just about 2 p.m. Today I went up to the university as soon as I had had breakfast & was properly shaved & dressed, to look at the building while the sun lasted – you will laugh at me, always rushing off to look at this half finished "palace of culture", but it is starting to be more interesting inside now, & I can get inside only when the workmen aren't there, as when they are there they scatter pebbles & cement over me from high scaffolding! [Whether][1] on purpose or not I don't know.

Then I came back & prepared a curious saucepanful of onions, carrots, celery, tinned peas, two lamb chops, tomatoes, slices of black pudding, & broken-up spaghetti. This I set to stew! For lunch I had bacon, egg, tomato & a few more slices of black pudding. This afternoon I shall go out & see George again, about this record business (I enclose a subscription form for you to see). It is a really lovely day, autumn at its best, & I wish I had 10 hours more to cycle about the countryside looking at it.

Last night I went to Hull Fair with a few other of the university people – it is a big riotous fair, of the usual sort with lots of side shows & roundabouts, & very brightly lit, with hordes of young people in hats saying "Kiss Me Quick" surging about. I won a small china poodle & a glass dish through combined luck & cunning. At throwing at tins I was not so successful. I went in several side shows & saw "Lollo the Rat Girl" & other such spectacles. This fair is a big thing in Hull's year and people come in from surrounding villages to spend a few hours there.

Well, I really don't know what to say about your coming to pay me a visit! [<*Up left margin*> The 'bus *might* be *through* to & from Nottingham: anyway, changing at Doncaster is easy. The bus is right alongside you. At Nott. It is about 40 yards off.] Of course, I should *prefer* you to come during the vacation, when I could take an afternoon or two off with a better conscience, & especially in summer when there are fewer people seeking lunch in town. But you won't come in the summer! and the other vacations are so short. On the whole I don't think I ought to be asked if I "mean" my invitation. If you would prefer not to have the upset of leaving home again so soon after your summer holidays, or something like that: that's all right. I shan't be offended. If you would secretly like to come, do say so! Only don't say "if it will be trouble": *every* visit is trouble: issuing an invitation means thinking that the trouble will be *worth while*. I expect this paragraphs [*sic*] sounds just as if I were hectoring you over the dining room table![2]

I have just turned off the "pot au gaz" or whatever I should call it. I expect it will provide enough for two meals. The sun has gone in now, but only in that misty winter afternoon's way that presages no harm for old creatures. I don't suppose you see the *Sunday Dispatch*: there's a lot of guff about Kingsley in U.S. in it. Having a whale of a time, *as usual*. I bought 2 rather handsome ties yesterday, one black with yellow *horizontal* stripes!

All very best & special love, C.

1 Larkin wrote 'When . . .'

2 On 14 October Eva responded: 'You sound as if you \had/ "taken umbrage" (one of Daddy's jokes) at something I said in my letter. I don't remember asking whether you "meant" your invitation. I *do* recollect saying that it wouldn't be very nice for you to turn out of your bed to accommodate me.* *<at top of first page>* *I suppose what I really meant was "would it be quite convenient for me to come just now." Of course I know you "meant" it so do forgive the thoughtless question. / Perhaps it is just as well that I stay at home, because I have so much to do *before* Christmas, and the time goes all too quickly. I shall, however, look forward very much to coming some time in 1959.' On 17 October he sent a Librarian letterheaded postcard: 'Very windy up here & inclined to be cold! So perhaps not the best time for a visit. In any case I hope to arrive in L'boro' on 24th October at 9.5 (Midland), so we can roast chestnuts over the fire.'

7 December 1958

<*Letterhead*> 32 Pearson Park, Hull

My dear old creature,

[. . .] I feel somewhat disagreeable in one or two respects – I have now seen the proof of the record sleeve, & find to my annoyance that my charming publisher has put "Cover photo by George Hartley" on it! This seems pretty cool to me, as he did little more than press the button.[1] One or two minor spectres, such as a committee tomorrow, occasionally tug my elbow. And I do feel drowsy – in fact just before I wrote "spectres" I nodded off for a few minutes. Yesterday Coveney & I went to see *Indiscreet*,[2] a rather silly film, & then ate some curious Chinese food at one of Hull's two Chinese restaurants. The food consists of bamboo shoots and dry little curls of stuff rather like wood shavings.[3] Then we came back here and remained talking, reading, & playing records, till between one and two. [. . .]

Wood thinks he will apply for the post of Librarian at the U.C. Swansea! I don't imagine he will be even interviewed – hope not, anyway, as this would mean my having to write a reference for him. Nothing but a plague or act of God I fear will ever get him out of the position he now holds. Dreary blinking fool. [. . .]

All my best love, P.

1 *Philip Larkin reads 'The Less Deceived'* (Hessle: Listen Records, The Marvell Press, 1958). The published wording is 'Cover photograph and design by George Hartley.' The recording had been made in the HMV Abbey Road Studios on 24 October 1958.

2 A 1958 film directed by Stanley Donen and starring Cary Grant and Ingrid Bergman.

3 Philip was a regular customer of the first Chinese restaurant in Hull, the Hoi Sun, Anlaby Road, close to the station.

1959

4 January 1959

<Letterhead>
Cranston's Ivanhoe Hotel, Bloomsbury Street, London W.C.1

My dear old creature,

This is really to warn you that a small parcel will be arriving for you from Liberty's: it is really not meant to be opened till Saturday. I'm afraid it isn't quite what you have in mind, but I think it's sensible enough. I hope you like it, anyway.[1]

London seems much as ever: I spent some time on Thursday talking to a friend of mine in Faber's, who eventually startled me by saying "Have you ever met Eliot? I'll just see if he's next door" & to my alarm reappeared leading an aged but spry Eliot who said he was sorry he couldn't talk to me but he had a visitor himself, but that he was "pleased to see me in this office" – meaning, I suppose, that they'd like to publish me! My friend assured me that Eliot really had a visitor. I felt quite relieved he stayed only a moment, as I couldn't think of anything to say.

I spent most of Friday arguing with shelvers & architects, but didn't go to the conference in the evening – lazy! Monica had materialized by then & we looked about on Saturday morning: in the afternoon I *did* go to the conference, & in the evening we went to see *The Yeomen of the Guard* at the Prince's.[2] This bored me awfully to start with, but I liked the second half very much. I had a double gin before it started & the barmaid asked if I wanted anything at the interval, so I ordered two more! They were waiting without fuss when we joined the scrimmage at the interval.

Today we shall probably go to a Brigitte Bardot film[3] – my choice rather than Monica's. What we do before then I don't know, but I can predict I shall take on board several pints of beer.

Fancy you beginning the story of your life! I expect you'll find the war part dull, but do persevere, as it becomes interesting again. It is written with a deceptive simplicity, isn't it?[4]

I liked your "Waverley notelet". Monica thanks you for your card too. She was entirely unmoved by the news that her card to you had anticipated Kitty's to Rosemary! "Life is full of such reverses" she said briskly. Tell Kitty.[5]

Tomorrow we return to Hull so you'll know where to find me. The sun is shining here & I think we shall go out shortly. I hope it's shining in York Road too!

"Going for the coke".

All love, P.

1 Saturday 10 January was Eva's seventy-third birthday. The present was 'a lovely basket' (lettercard from Eva, 11 January).
2 A Savoy Opera, with music by Arthur Sullivan and libretto by W. S. Gilbert.
3 Presumably *In Case of Adversity* (*En cas de malheur*) released in France in September 1958, directed by Claude Autant-Lara, starring Jean Gabin, Brigitte Bardot and Edwige Feuillère. The censor had cut out a two-minute sexually explicit scene.
4 On 6 January Eva wrote: 'Much as I should like to, I'm afraid I shall never finish my bit of writing. Perhaps when I am too old to work, I might have more time to spend on it. I have not yet got farther than my childhood in Epping! It is a problem to decide what to write and what to leave out. (family skeletons!)'
5 Monica's Christmas card to Eva had been the same as Kitty's to Rosemary. On 6 January Eva wrote: 'I told Kitty what Monica remarked about the Christmas cards. She said that she didn't mind a great deal but she bought Rosemary's card probably weeks before Monica did, and held it back until nearly Christmas Day. Also Rosemary's card had some French on it, and Monica's hasn't. That is rather strange I think.'

19 January 1959

<*Letterhead*> 32 Pearson Park, Hull

My dear old creature,

This Sunday morning I am listening to the sound of my own voice again, for my record has arrived and will be going out to subscribers in the next few days. It is not too bad, but as the tape editor warned us there are a number of distracting noises in the background which to my mind rather spoil it. The sleeve is quite handsome. I don't think I read *at all well*, but I manage to get it all out somehow. Last night I went to Hartley's & signed them all. You will probably see it reviewed by J. W. Lambert in the *Sunday Times* one of these Sundays.

Today is misty and chilly, but the hard frost has gone & the packed snow and ice everywhere is melting. There are large dreary-looking pools on the Park. I have nothing to do today till this evening, when I'm going to a jazz concert at the huge Town Hall – well, nothing to do, I say: plenty of cleaning-up & letter-writing & bed-changing, plenty of that! Last Sunday I went out a walk after lunch, walking out westwards till I got clear of the suburbs and could trudge along in the half-country along frozen streams and snowy lanes. The sun was low and shone fierily on the snow. As dusk fell & I was approaching Cottingham it began to snow quite thickly & I was glad to get [to] the square & catch the 'bus home!

[. . .]

My very best love, dear old creature,

Philip

1 March 1959

<*Letterhead*> 32 Pearson Park, Hull

My dear old Creature,

[. . .] I hear in a roundabout way that Kingsley finds the United States very expensive & is looking forward to coming home. He doesn't write to me of course! Hilly writes to a wife of a friend who tells a friend who tells me. He could never manage even a little money, so a lot is no doubt worse. [. . .]

Yes, I hope you *will* live to a ripe old age! I hope we all shall! Nothing like being alive!

Now I shall give my sofa a good brush. It is looking rather sad.

Very best love,
Philip

29 May 1959

Lettercard

Hull

My dear old creature,

[. . .] I am scribbling this in the G.P.O., so it won't have the calm of my usual notes.

Great surprise – yesterday *Who's Who* sent for my details! This pleased me mightily. Pop never got in *Who's Who*.[1] I am glad you liked the poem.

Weather dry here but not unduly warm. Monica is coming for the weekend. I go to London on Monday for 2 nights.

All love 

<*On back of lettercard*>

1 In the next letter, 31 May, Larkin mentions that most of his friends 'are in already, but it's nice to be included' and tells Eva that he had given 'as my recreations "resting"!'

28 June 1959

<*Letterhead*> 32 Pearson Park, Hull

My dear old creature,

Things have seemed somewhat out of joint during the last few days, & indeed to be writing to you at 1.30 on Sunday instead of earlier (and I haven't had lunch) indicates a departure from routine. Principally, yesterday was degree day, when we spend the morning in the City Hall watching the students get their degrees; then after lunch there was a mangy garden party. I had lunch with Coveney in the town, & supper at a Chinese restaurant in the evening; after that we went to see *Room at the top*, but it was so bad we came out halfway through.[1] He came home with me & remained till about 12.30 a.m. Now that his marriage is less than a month off, he is somewhat uneasy and doesn't like being left alone, like a man under sentence of execution.

On Thursday I had the Duffins & the Johnsons in for drinks & coffee:[2] I gave them cucumber & lettuce sandwiches, fancy cakes, and strawberries and cream to finish with. I think *they* liked it all right, but it left me with indigestion that kept me awake all night, long after dawn had broken. I managed to be sick about 4, but it didn't seem to put things right. I expect I'd gobbled rather & been nervous. Next day I didn't feel so bad as I'd expected.

The weather is still warm, but more overcast, windy & inclined to showers. I can't recollect any storms apart from a rumble now and again – certainly no lightning. I haven't bought the refrigerator, but on the whole food keeps well enough – the bacon goes musty but nothing else to speak of.[3]

When I was in London I noticed several hats modelled on the mob cap – they are fashionable just now and are certainly not unlike what I draw. I do wish you could get one.[4]

Perhaps you have thrown away last week's *Sunday Times* by now – or perhaps Kitty w[d] point out to you the article under "Atticus" asking whom should we send to America to represent British culture. D. Powell[5]

suggested me. I doubt if should represent it very well. Anyway, there's not much likelihood of my going.

I'm glad you have got the sweep over. I shall be glad to come next weekend, on Friday. How is your mangle, I wonder. I have started boiling handkerchiefs, for the laundry leaves them the colour of old ivory. Unfortunately when I put them to dry on the clothes rack they absorbed a yellowish stain from the wood & I had to do them again! There is a second lot cooking now. I hope I can iron the first lot satisfactorily.

Sun is shining now. I must have lunch – found a big slug in my lettuce recently!

All love Philip

1 A 1959 film based on the novel by John Braine, directed by Jack Clayton and starring Laurence Harvey, Simone Signoret, Heather Sears, Donald Wolfit, Donald Houston and Hermione Baddeley. It was nominated for six Academy Awards.
2 His neighbours in the flats below.
3 On 26 April he had written: 'I feel I am *very near* buying a refrigerator, & wonder if you wouldn't do well to have one.'
4 On 30 June Eva added a postscript to her letter: 'You amused me over the mob cap hats. I could easily get one from John, but if it is only to wear in the house for a joke, it would be a bit extravagant!'
5 Dilys Powell (1901–95) wrote film and literary reviews for the *Sunday Times* for over fifty years.

12 July 1959

<*Letterhead*> 32 Pearson Park, Hull

My dear old creature,

Last night I "entertained" again, on a minor scale – the Hoggarts (he is shortly to go to Leicester, to become a colleague of Monica's),[1] who had to go early to another party, and of course the Hartleys, who didn't go till at least 2 a.m., & then only when ordered out. In consequence I am rather late this morning, and a trifle sandy about the eyes, and there is a sink of washing up waiting to be done, and a lot of ash on the carpet, and all that. George gave me about £19 in notes, to enable me to escape paying income tax.

[. . .]

All love from
Philip

1 Richard Hoggart was a staff tutor at the University of Hull from 1946 to 1959, publishing *The Uses of Literacy* in 1957. He was appointed a senior lecturer in English at the University of Leicester in 1959.

30 August 1959

<*Letterhead*> 32 Pearson Park, Hull

My dear old creature,

I expect you are feeling a somewhat flat old creature this morning with A. Nellie gone. It was nice to have such a long letter from you on Thursday and to have some idea what Hunstanton was like.[1] I'm sure you relished having the weather forecast every morning with your tea – that must have been worse than being at home.

I'm afraid that this week I just FORGOT your card on Friday; I'm very sorry about this, but I am so busy at present from morning till night that I must have had a lapse of memory – I remembered it in the evening when it was too late, of course.[2] The building is *nearly* finished – the men are working all day today & night, so that we can start moving tomorrow morning at 8.30 a.m. This week the cleaners have been trying to work in the building for 3 hours a day, but I'm afraid that much of their work is undone by the men almost immediately.

The part that is causing most trouble is the stack – two decks of 8' steel shelving, with innumerable lights and so on to be fixed. It does really look lovely at present, with "candy pink" end panels on the ground floor & "forgetmenot" blue upstairs, the shelves being light grey in each case. Miss Wrench said she couldn't sleep on Friday night for thinking about it (I had taken them round on Friday for their final instructions). For the next 3 weeks we shall be getting in at 8.30 every morning to start with the workmen, so think of me with my alarm clock going at 7!

Forgive this jabber about work: it just fills my mind at present. I went round this morning & found them all hard at it. [. . .]

Very best love, P.

1 On 1 September Eva replied: 'You were quite right in thinking that I should feel a "flat old Creature" after A. Nellie's departure. Breakfast on Monday seemed very wanting and the house is lonely without her cheerful presence. However, I feel I acquitted myself very well in the way I "locked up" each night and particularly when we left for Hunstanton. (pronounced Hunstan') If A. Nellie had stayed a few more weeks I feel I should have been "cured". Not that she helped me do it, but it just seemed to sink into secondary importance, and I omitted doing all the unnecessary things I do when on my own.'

2 In her letter of 1 September Eva wrote 'Well, Creature, after reading about the hectic time you had in the new library, I am not surprised that you forgot my card. Of course I missed it, and many were the conjectures concerning it.'

3 September 1959

<*Letterhead*> 32 Pearson Park, Hull

My very dear old creature,

It was so nice to get your letter: I didn't in fact find it till this evening, as I am leaving the flat at about 8.15 these mornings! "The Move" has started. The entire library staff is engaged in packing all our books in 3-foot boxes (100 of them) wch are then loaded by removers onto a van and taken to the new library, where they are loaded on trolleys and wheeled to the new shelves. We are doing about 10,000 books a day, & it will last about 2–3 weeks. My new photographer is taking pictures of it (with my camera) so you will get an idea of it when you see them. [. . .]

Happy weekend old creature & all love Philip

5 September 1959

<*Letterhead*> 32 Pearson Park, Hull

My dear old creature,

[. . .] I am rather proud of the way the move has gone. It has been an awful job – of course, it is only half finished at present – and involves moving what I guess to be 250 tons of books! And since each has to be lifted 5 times before it reaches its new home, that means we are employed in shifting 1250 tons! *The Hull Daily Mail* is coming on Monday & I shall tell him this. Next week the furniture comes, wch will be an added stimulus. We are due to open to readers on Sept. 21.

Well, my head is full of all this, as you can imagine, pretty well to the exclusion of everything else, but I'll rake round in my brain to see what else is there. I don't think much has happened since I wrote on Thursday night. I have begun to buy local farm eggs from a shop near at hand – they are 6 for 2/7½d – is that cheap or dear? I eat them with the horn egg spoon Monica bought me in Orkney. [. . .]

Very best love Philip

13 September 1959

<*Letterhead*> 32 Pearson Park, Hull

My dear old creature,

[. . .] By the way, the Library has a cat at the moment! The workmen took in a poor stray cat, & it actually had kittens in the basement, but now the workmen are gone & the cat & two kittens are left. I really don't feel we can keep it, but there is [a] strong cat lobby in the Library (led by Miss Wrench) who claim that there are mice already built in (the cleaners support this) and that a cat is necessary. I don't know what to do. The kittens are too young to be moved yet. Quite a problem![1]

Hope you are mastering the locking up and feeling in the best of creaturely spirits.

All love,
Philip

1 Eva replied on 15 September: 'Of course, I had to read the bit out about the stray cat to Kitty & Rosemary. I *do* hope you will keep it, although it may be a bit of

trouble, especially if it has many lots of kittens. *Do* see that it is fed. It will want extra sustenance whilst it is feeding it's [*sic*] kittens. Are you getting extra milk for it? If there \are/ mice in the library it will soon frighten them away not to mention any it may catch.'

26 September 1959

<*Letterhead*> 32 Pearson Park, Hull

My very dear old creature,

[. . .] I am sure the element of *promising* in your planned Christian giving[1] is because of the recovery of tax. Remember the widow's mite!

It's an awkward situation when one is asked for money in respect of some belief. Samuel Butler said we should not be so ready to pick a fly out of the milkjug if we thought it was likely to ask us for £5! Still, I think you're right to make sure you don't become a charge! It's nice to think of you with a full coal cellar, ready for the dripping days of autumn – but I wish you had a good hot gas fire & no work or mess![2]

I hope I can come home some weekend – 10th, 17th? Love as always,

P

1 Eva had written on 22 September: 'The chief excitement here is this "planned giving scheme" for the churches. I have received a letter saying that £21,000 given over the next three years is the minimum target. A Parish Dinner is to be given next

month free, at which the aims of the programme will be explained in detail. We are asked to attend and to keep an open mind until we have heard all about it. / Did you ever know anything so fantastic! I don't think I shall go to the dinner *and* I'm not going to promise to devote a regular fixed sum to the income of the church. [. . .] I want to give when I feel like it, and what I like to give.'

2 In her letter of 22 September Eva had written: 'I am glad to say I have got my coal shed filled ready for winter and coke ordered also.'

28 September 1959

<*Letterhead*> 32 Pearson Park, Hull

My dear old creature,

I went to work today, and apart from feeling rather gutless in the legs was all right. But I am glad I haven't gone to London and Exeter.

As a matter of fact I had a very good day yesterday! I was taken on the Humber by a chap called Binns[1] in his yacht, and as the day was fine and warm it was really delightful cruising up and down. Binns let the net down but caught nothing but a tiny crab. A friend of his showed us four boxes of fish he had caught, & gave us a few. I took one home for tea & fried it in butter, and it was very good.

It was very nice to have your letter this morning. The cutting about the library sounds like a mad undertaking, but I expect it will look well after Completion. You really must come and see mine before long!

I'm sure I'm quite well now, so don't ponder.

With all love:
Philip

1 Alan Binns was a specialist in Old Norse in the Hull English Department. He lived on the estuary at the village of Paull, where he had mooring rights for his ocean-going boat. He was an adviser on the 1958 film *The Vikings* starring Kirk Douglas and Tony Curtis, and took a small role as a priest intoning medieval Latin.

4 October 1959

<*Letterhead*> 32 Pearson Park, Hull

My dear old creature,

[. . .] I am pretty well restored to health now, and face the week rather grimly – term starts, & there is my party on Monday, & my "short talk" on Wednesday.[1] Think of me between 6 and 8 tomorrow evening, bowing & scraping in the Library & drinking sherry. After 8 we shut the doors & hold our own party! I have ordered a lot of drink & the girls are doing the food. I hope we shall not be too tired to enjoy it. I doubt if these departmental parties are ever wholly enjoyable: I shall have to be careful not to be too well – or too badly-behaved. I shan't enjoy the sight of Wood drinking drink I have paid for! Stupid little gaping ape.

Then there is my "short talk" gibber gibber gibber. Think of me at 2.30 or so on Wednesday. [. . .]

You will be sorry to hear "our" cat was run over on Friday night. It was very much a roaming kind of cat & must have tried to cross the busy road once too often. Of course this solves the problem of whether or not to allow it to stay: it would have been a liability and a nuisance & yet I shrank from the thought of sending it to be killed. I doubt if it was a very loving cat, but Mary is rather upset.[2] [. . .]

My love to all, especially you!!
Philip

1 The Librarian's introductory address to all new students.

2 Eva wrote on 6 October: 'Oh dear! I was *so very sorry* to know that the pussy had met with such a sad fate. I thought about her quite a lot and hoped someone would always remember to feed her, particularly at week ends. What has become of the kittens? However I hope the pussy is happier now, at least it won't be a stray any more. Do cats have souls, do you think?'

1 November 1959

<*Letterhead*> 32 Pearson Park, Hull

My dear old creature,

[. . .] Monica is very unhappy at present, really awfully low. I think I may go and see her the weekend after this one – is that your London weekend? Nov 14–15? I think she is afflicted by the loss of her mother, the "difficultness" of her father, & her work all together.[1] I think she should get time off, but of course then she w^{d} have to go home, wch w^{d} be still as harrowing.[2]

Oh dear, I haven't drawn a single creature. Never mind: here's a small one.

Love Philip

1 In late 1959 both Monica Jones's parents fell ill, and her mother died on 11 October. Her father was seriously ill and died in the second week of December.

2 On 3 November Eva wrote: 'I am very sorry to know that she is so depressed and un-happy. I can quite understand how she feels. She must feel the loss of her mother terribly. It is so sad to know that she will not be at home to welcome her any more. Couldn't she go for a little time to any of her relatives, perhaps an Aunt? Perhaps that would not make her feel any better, though. Really I \think/ that Time is the only healer. Your mention of her Father and his "difficulties" reminds me of the trouble I had with Grandad after Grandma died. You may remember that I found it most difficult to leave him at Leigh, he was really pathetic.'

6 December 1959

<*Letterhead*> 32 Pearson Park, Hull

My very dear old creature,

[. . .] Last night I went out to the Hartley's for dinner: Hartley lives on National Assistance and me, & could therefore offer roast chicken and a bottle of Graves. He also offered me £60 in notes (to cheat the taxman), representing 50% of the profits on the sale of the *Less D.* for 1958/59. I accepted both with alacrity. It was quite a pleasant evening, & I borrowed a letter he had received from John Betjeman expressing his appreciation of a long article I wrote about his poetry in Hartley's magazine *Listen*.

[. . .] The latest news from Monica is that her father has been returned home from hospital, in what circumstances I don't know & I'm not clear if she does.[1] Therefore I suppose she is more likely to be at home at Christmas, but as you say there is a month, or three weeks, to go so one can't be clear. [. . .]

<*Down left margin*> Am just listening to the weather forecast as I conclude with very best love to a dearest creature P.

1 Eva wrote on 8 December: 'I do hope Monica is feeling better, but it is all very sad and worrying for her.'

13 December 1959

<*Letterhead*> 32 Pearson Park, Hull

My dear old creature,

I'm afraid I took you at your word and sent no letter or even card from London, awful creature. It was beastly chilly there – drizzly, too – and I am, as ever, glad to be back. But I was sorry to find a card from M. waiting for me, saying she had been called home by the doctor as her father was worse. I expect his time is short now.[1] I haven't yet mentioned Christmas; it wouldn't be right, but I shall ask in due course what she is planning to do, if anything. So perhaps you had better postpone that turkey if it needs me to eat it up! Of course, M's relations will probably invite her to spend the holiday with them. But I shall feel bound to ask, shan't I?

I had a good journey up from London, for a wonder. There was an Indian opposite me going to Nottingham whom I had to eject from the train at Grantham. Otherwise he w[d] have found himself in Yorkshire! I wanted him out of the way so that I could stretch my legs. From Selby the Diesel was full of tiny sea cadets who chattered & smoked but put newspaper on the seats before resting their shoes on them! Funny sharp little boys, in white peaked caps; I wondered what they will look like in 40 years.

Another sheet soon.[2] Goodnight, my dearest old creature!

Best of love! Philip

1 On 15 December Eva wrote: 'Your news of Monica's Father made me feel so sad, in fact I had a little weep over him. And Monica, too. I do feel so very sorry for her. I hope she does not break down under the strain and worry. If the worst happens to her Father, what ought I to do? Should I write to her, as I did before? I cannot very well send a Christmas card, can I? / Yes, you will have to ask what her plans are about Christmas. I shall go on preparing in case you *do* come.' Monica's father died within days and Monica spent Christmas with Eva and Philip in Loughborough, the only time she ever did so (email to the editor from Rosemary Parry, 7 December 2017). On 31 December Eva wrote 'What a strange Christmas we have had! I must thank you very much for all the things you did for us and do hope you did manage to get some enjoyment out of an unfortunate situation.'
2 This is an unusually short, single-page letter (two sides).

15 December 1959

<*Letterhead*> 32 Pearson Park, Hull

My dear old creature,

Here is the second part of the letter I promised you. [. . .]

Miss Wrench now says she is going to get married on Dec 29th! and has asked me to go, cadging a present I suppose. More trouble. The reception is being held at the Drinkwaters' house. She seems in a good temper now, having been rather temperamental this term: not sometimes without reason.

I've bought a reprint of some beautiful nineteenth century studies of roses by Redouté, but derive more pleasure from thinking of your three sleeping in themselves outside y^{r} back door.[1]

All love Philip

1 Philip sent eight of these postcards to Eva between November 1959 and March 1960.

1960

3 January 1960

<Letterhead> 32 Pearson Park, Hull

My dear old Creature,

Well, this is the first letter I have written in the new decade, and very fitting it should be to you. I've already wished you a happy new year: now let me wish you a happy new decade. But hasn't it started badly, if you are losing M[rs] Mitchell! I know you depend on her for cleaning and company, & it was so nice to think you had someone you could rely on.[1] Perhaps she will reconsider her decision when her domestic situation has quietened down. I thought the son's dramatic act of goodwill seemed too good to last. Anyway, I hope she changes her mind; or, if she doesn't, that you soon find a substitute.

I've not really had much time since returning to think about my own affairs, as Monica turned up on Thursday and has been sitting around recuperating most of the time (she is on the floor reading the papers as I write). Yesterday we went to York after lunch, and enjoyed ourselves very much up to the point of going for dinner to the Station Hotel w[ch] was uneatable and cost the earth. We did some shopping in a second-hand bookshop, & then found a fine old public house with pictures of horses and jockeys on the walls & coal fires in all the rooms. Monica is *rather* thin, & has a cough, but seems content enough at the moment. Of course she was never one for wearing her heart on her sleeve.

Since many of my staff are taking their summer holidays still,[2] the Library is very lonely & not much work is being done. Mary[3] got married (apparently beating all records from church door to altar, so that the organist had to abandon his voluntary or piece intended to accompany her slow advance); Vivienne[4] who was going to New Zealand has met another man & has cancelled her plans: he is a prospective grocer, building up a business in Hull, so she will in all probability never leave this region ever! Maeve's[5] brother has appendicitis. Betty[6] has had her hair done and gone to London. Wood is having a new car! His wife certainly gives him gee-up when it comes to making the money fly. I suppose being married to such a goggling little ass makes her want lots of consolations of this kind. Come to that, I have ordered a two-piece suit myself, in light grey tweed. I suppose that is to console me for having such a goggling little ass for a deputy.

The day looks rather frosty and misty, and we shall now cross the park, post this, buy another paper or two, & enter the Queen's Hotel for a while. After that we shall return and probably not emerge again till M. has to go back to her hotel. Give my regards to Kitty (!) & Walter: I do hope you are settling down again after the trials of Christmas.

All best love,
Philip

1 On 31 December 1959 Eva had written that she had expected her cleaner as usual, 'thinking how glad I was that she would be here on the Thursday after A. Nellie had gone – for company chiefly'. Instead Mrs Mitchell had sent a note saying 'she would not be able to come any more as her Mother-in-law returned on Christmas Eve, which has put them into an awful mess and upset Mrs Mitchell very much.'
2 Because of preparations for the library move in the summer many staff holidays had been postponed.
3 Mary Wrench.
4 Vivienne Wray worked in the library in the late 1950s and early 1960s, and again in the mid-1970s.
5 Maeve Brennan.
5 Betty Mackereth, Larkin's secretary.

10 January 1960

<*Letterhead*> 32 Pearson Park, Hull

My very dear old creature,

I feel sorry that I haven't, or can't, commemorate your birthday properly this year, as I should always like you to feel I am remembering you especially on the 10th January. I ought to have arranged to ring you up this evening, just to exchange a few words with you. Anyway, I am thinking of you, and recalling your dictum that the snow always comes for your birthday. Has it in Loughborough? There is none here – a few flurries in the wind yesterday, but that was all. It's very cold, though! [. . .]

Tomorrow I have to receive an indefinite [number of] – probably about 100 – *landladies* and let them see the Library. This means 'a few words'.

They are people who take in university students, and once a year they are all invited up to the University for tea. I've never seen them before: I expect they're a rum lot.

Last Monday my cleaner-supervisor came & asked me to sack one of the women! I spent a queasy day & night worrying about this, but next morning I saw her again & she said perhaps she had been hasty. So I buttered her up as best I could & we parted until the next time. She is very good – as far as I can tell – rather intense, but much superior to the cleaners she directs. I hope she doesn't leave for any reason.

That reminds me to ask if you have made any further progress towards finding another cleaner.

Monica liked the striped tights, but they don't fit exactly – the feet are too big, and the ankles too large. She wrote in reply to my first Christmas parcel that she thought I might have bought her some striped tights – by then I had & they were already on their way. They arrived on Christmas Day.[1] [. . .]

Once again, dear old creature, I send my love & MANY HAPPY RETURNS!!!!!

Philip

1 In *Philip Larkin: Life, Art and Love*, Plate 13, I mistakenly assumed that the tights had been a gift from Eva.

24 January 1960

32 Pearson Park, Hull — Sunday

My dear old creature,

I'm sorry we didn't have time to say goodbye more ceremoniously. It was a nice though dark (& for me harassed) weekend. Rain last[ed] *all day*, right up to here. No of course!

Here is a cheque to pay for the fire. Don't let him bully you into taking anything you don't want.[1]

Take care of your dear self.

Love
Philip

<*At top opposite address*> M thanks you for your kind thoughts & says she'll write.

1 On 26 January Eva wrote: 'Well, Creature, the man from Keigthleys' [*sic*] turned up this morning with the Belling electric fire. [. . .] I asked the price of it and found it is more than £10.10.0. It doesn't matter though. I can pay the difference. He gave me plenty of opportunity to change my mind, but I think it really is the only suitable one in the shop and I like it, and feel sure it will make the kitchen very cosy and warm. Thank you very much.'

12 February 1960 — Picture postcard[1]

[32 Pearson Park, Hull]

Nasty day here – got up late & have no special desire to go to work, but I suppose I must. Have applied for Reading & now feel rather queasy about it. Glad you have a cleaner – hope I can tell you apart!

Your letter sounded very gay and jolly. I wish it were warmer – filthy snow & sleet & wind & I hate it.

Love from P.

1 Redouté: *Rosa Redutea glauca* painting.

13 March 1960

<*Letterhead*> 32 Pearson Park, Hull

My very dear old creature,

A happier creature this week than last! It's strange how panicky I got towards the day: I can see now that I didn't at all want to move from Hull, & that although there were quite good reasons for not taking the job I was pretty well set against it from the start.[1]

So you must resign yourself to having a Yorkshire creature![2]

Probably one of the biggest factors that turned me against it was the Librarian's room, a hideous little den, dark & bare, not above twice the size of my present desk. I felt it was *impossible* for me to work therein. Actually the staff seemed pleasant & highly competent: I was pleased to see Leila Bishop, the girl whom I replaced at Leicester in 1946. Yesterday I went to a meeting in Leeds & encountered one of the short list. He said no decision had been reached, or at least not communicated to them, but he expected to hear any time now. My guess is that it will go to a character called Richmell & would have done in any case.[3] [. . .]

Actually now the Reading business is over I am beginning to get scared about the opening. I am not sure of my ability to entertain the QM for even a few minutes as I shall have to do![4] [. . .]

My head cleaner at the library is very worried about one "lady" who she says disobeys her. I had this "lady" in to see me yesterday but got nowhere really: she seemed quite mild & astonished that any such notion should have arisen. Possibly my head cleaner is imagining things. Possibly not! Anyway, I hope I haven't made things worse. I'm not especially fond of the allegedly disobedient one, but it's easy to distort things.[5]

There's no other news, Wood is so stupid I want to chop his head off and dribble it round the Library. Why can't some of the road accidents remove him from my sphere? Ugh, Grr.

Lots of love to you – quite springy here. Ph.

1 Larkin had been called to interview on 9 March for the post of Librarian at Reading University, but, after looking round the town and the library, he returned to Hull without attending the scheduled interview.
2 Eva commented (15 March): 'How your sketches amused me, especially the one of the Yorkshire Creature!'
3 Eva wrote on 13 March: 'I think, on the whole, you have done right to withdraw, especially if the thought that you might be successful gave you no pleasure. After all you are not so badly off at Hull – a nice flat situated in pleasant surroundings, and a new, comfortable library to work in. The disadvantage to my mind is that it is so far away from everywhere.'
4 The Queen Mother was due to open the new library.
5 This dispute lasted some time. On 29 March Eva compared her own earlier experience running a household: 'I am not surprised that your cleaners worry you. I well remember the worries and misery I suffered over the women and maids. And the number of things they stole! Coal, tea, tea towels and handkerchiefs, embroidered tray cloths and records.'

12 May 1960

32 Pearson Park, Hull

My dear old creature,

[. . .] Betty suggests I go home next weekend. I think she wants it off herself. So you will probably receive another visit from that sweet tempered, soft-tongued creature you know so well.

I'm sorry about Walter's car. My best love,

Philip

27 May 1960

Picture postcard[1]

[32 Pearson Park, Hull]

Thank you for your nice letter. How exciting about the workmen & the birds.[2] I hope you can watch the young ones grow. There's not much news here – I'm frantically busy, & oppressed by the prospect of the QM. Here is a picture of the gull that goes oghoghogh, actually doing it.[2] Dear old creature I hope you have a peaceful weekend.

Love Philip

1 Great black-backed gulls and herring gulls.

2 On 24 May Eva wrote that she was anticipating the arrival of workmen next day to refurbish and decorate several rooms in her house. She continued: 'To-day when I looked at the blackbird's nest there was a newly-hatched bird in it, and the mother bird was feeding it. They are not at all nice to look at, with no feathers. I looked again just before tea and there were two little birds there – the second egg had hatched. I wonder if they will be spirited away when I look tomorrow morning!' On 30 May she wrote: 'You ask if the birds are still here. Only one little one is here now. I cannot think what has happened to the other one. It was smaller and feebler than the one which has survived, which makes me wonder if the mother has thrown it out of the nest. The remaining one is getting quite nice to look at now. It is covered with down, and has wings tipped with dark blue feathers.'

2 Eva replied on 30 May: 'Oghoghogh! / I liked your Saturday p.c. very much, and was amused to see one of the gulls actually making the famous ejaculation.' This version of a herring-gull's call, 'oghoghogh' (or separated, 'ogh ogh ogh'), appears frequently in Larkin's letters, indicating surprise, amusement or apprehension.

16 June 1960

32 Pearson Park, Hull

Dear old creature,

Just a short word to cheer you on your way (!). I had your letter, thanks, & hope it keeps fine for your journey. Remember a 'bus can always be identified by its number plate, even among 20 similar buses.

We shall wait for you as I said. If you arrive early, wait for us.

We are all rather fed up with the opening now – at least I am – and am longing for it to be over. I still haven't thought up any small talk for the QM. There was a rumour of typhoid among the students today! I w^{d} almost (not quite) welcome it, to escape Monday.

I'm glad you had a good "poussin" at the King's Head. I eat almost every Saturday lunchtime at the White House (where you are staying) & I can tell you I have to pay over 10/- to get anything worth eating. Last Saturday I paid only 6/6 for some "curried chicken" & it was like a dog's dinner, including worm-powder.

My hayfever ebbs & flows, more's the pity. Let's hope it ebbs on Monday – but then I don't want it to rain! Horrible to think it's so near.[1]

Love from
Creature

1 The official opening of stage 1 of the library took place on Monday 20 June in the presence of the Queen Mother. Both Monica and Eva travelled to Hull for the occasion. On 23 June Eva wrote: 'I felt a very proud Creature at the Opening Ceremony, and shall ever remember it. I am so glad that I was there (in spite of all my fears regarding the visit) and am glad that my presence gave you pleasure.'

3 July 1960

<*Letterhead*> 32 Pearson Park, Hull

My dear old creature,

A dull grey morning, with me lying on my sofa, a favourite position with me, but I can indulge it only in summer: in winter it takes me too far from the fire. I expect the weather will cheer up later in the day. Yesterday it was flat and dull and quite cold: the day was our Degree Day, wch means a ceremony in the City Hall, an "official lunch" at the University, and a "garden party" afterwards. I went to all three, & wish I hadn't, they were extremely dull. At lunch I sat next to the Mayor & Mayoress of *Retford*. I thought of you and the many times you must have found yourself in similar circumstances. They were just ordinary people, but quite pleasant. The mayor kept glancing over to his wife and saying "Are you all right, Mother?" which she usually was. The garden party was miserable, I thought: as soon as I got home I plunged into a bath & fell into a daze, feeling all my fatigue and boredom being slowly soaked out of my bones till I almost expected to see it floating on the water like scum.

My telephone has just rung, & proved to be a wrong number. Great relief. I thought it might be someone wanting to go out for the day! Sociable creature! [. . .]

Very much love
Philip

24 July 1960

Stocks Hotel, Sark, C.I. Sunday

My dear old creature,

[. . .] Your letter was full of interest,[1] but I was sorry to hear you hadn't heard from me for so long – I wrote as soon as we got to Guernsey. I should have said that my poem was broadcast last night – 25th – but I forgot. Did you hear it? I didn't.

You sound as if you had a lot of fun at the fair, especially aiming curtain rings:[2]

Here I have my new pair of binoculars & can sit watching gulls, oystercatchers, & cormorants when we are on the headlands. I am also taking some photographs wch I hope will preserve some of the beautiful scenery for me. As usual my stomach thinks that holiday food is a bit too much for it, & looks forward to the simple routine of Pearson Park. I was rather dashed to find that the kitchen staff here seemed to know I write poems! There are 4 lovely kittens here that are a continual joy to us: one scratched a child today wch gave us great pleasure.

Love,
Philip

1 18 July: 'Well, *what* a week I had last week! The plumbers soon installed the new copper cistern and pipes, although they did a bit of damage too – chipped the bath,

scraped some of the lino paint off the linoleum (which I expected) and knocked a bit out of the ceiling in the scullery. / The immersion heater is now fitted in the tank, and this morning a man from the Electricity department came and inspected it, and pronounced it all right.'

2 Eva had written on 18 July: 'Last Saturday I went with Mrs Dexter and Lily to Coleaston to their Church Fête [. . .] tryed [*sic*] to win a bottle of Ribena by aiming a curtain ring at it.' Eva has mistaken the name of the village. Philip Pullen suggests that she meant Coleorton near Ashby-de-la-Zouch, nine miles from Loughborough (personal communication). Mrs Dexter was a friend of Eva's in the 1950s and 1960s.

29 August 1960 — Picture postcard[1]

[32 Pearson Park, Hull]

1 Boating Lake, East Park, Kingston upon Hull. Eva had been on holiday with Nellie in Llandudno from 13 to 28 August, staying in Hyde before and afterwards.

9 October 1960

<*Letterhead*> 32 Pearson Park, Hull

My dear old creature,

[. . .] There doesn't seem to be much news. The proper U.S. edition of my book has come out, wch is interesting I suppose. I am going out to Hessle tonight to collect my free copies. I wish I could write a few more! But just at present I feel that writing about my life is not what is needed, and it's not interesting writing about anything else. Incidentally, the end of this month marks the end of my option with filthy Hartley, so that I can take my next book where I like. Goodbye for now, my dear old Exmoor-roaming creature.

Love,
P.

6 November 1960

<*Letterhead*> 32 Pearson Park, Hull

My dear old creature,

Running rather late this morning! After waking about eight-fifteen I slept till eleven. I don't get up earlier because the papers don't come till after nine. Anyway, here I am just starting your letter at twenty to one. In no very gay mood, really (you'll think "as usual"), but, to echo Kingsley in his new book, who says I have to feel all right, anyway?

I wonder if you have been reading John Betjeman's poem in the *S. Times*?[1] It seems an enjoyable piece of work in its way. I can't understand why in retrospect he doesn't see the family business as romantic and exciting: he certainly makes it sound so. I haven't read it very closely, but I thought the last few lines good. It may be that the *Spectator* will send it to me for review, in wch case I shall have to think about it more deeply. I couldn't write a poem like that myself: I don't seem to have much in the way of childhood memories. There seems to have been a kind of barrier in me between whatever registers such things within one and the events I witnessed or experienced. For that matter there still is!

I wonder how Beauty is: better, I hope. Cat 'flu is very dangerous. A funny thing happened yesterday: as you know, I have a tape recorder, and sometimes amuse myself by reading poems into it. Yesterday I was reading G. M. Hopkins's *The Leaden Echo*, which is a representation of an echoing voice saying that there's no way of keeping beauty from decay, and with a good deal of repetition (like an echo), so that when I came to the words "keep back beauty, beauty, beauty, beauty, from vanishing away" I sounded so like Kitty calling the cat I wasn't able to keep a straight voice. The recording is highly odd at that point in consequence.

I look forward to seeing your purple "high hat".

I don't know what to say about coming. As you may imagine Monica is very keen on my visiting whenever I can, since she is so low and unhappy and lonely, but I don't want to come at an inconvenient time for you. I could I suppose just go & stay at Leicester and not see you, but this means coming again to see you! and then I shouldn't feel happy about returning without seeing Monica, as she really does seem so near giving up, or perhaps paralysis w^{d} be a better word. I w^{d} go to Leicester this Saturday, but I have a meeting on Friday & couldn't arrive till 10.28 p.m. wch is getting late for private hotels. Yet I really feel I ought to go. Would it be too much to ask if you would very kindly \at once/ send me a card saying whether my room w^{d} be habitable on the 11th–12th, and if it w^{d} be convenient for you if I inhabited it? Otherwise I think I shall go to Leicester, & not visit you till the 25th (I must have an intervening Saturday for the sake of my laundry). I apologise for troubling you like this: it is all very difficult.

Thank you for the cuttings. Do continue to look out for them.

Work is worrying me at present because that incompetent fat fool Farrell[2] has let his work get quite out [of] hand again. I wish I could sack him. I suppose it doesn't matter compared with illness & death. On wch gay note I must leave you. <*This last sentence is written up the right margin. He continues up the left margin*> I am going to have some sherry to try to cheer up. My very best love,

Philip

1 'Summoned by Bells' (1960).

2 John G. Farrell, Chief Cataloguer in the library.

13 November 1960

<*Letterhead*> 32 Pearson Park, Hull

My dear old creature,

[. . .] Putting on the wireless at a quarter to eleven (breakfast time) I ran slap into the Cenotaph service again.[1] This moves me more & more as years go by. The thought of all the men who died in the first world war exerts a powerful hold on my feelings. I wonder if it is because you used to tell me about it. Thomas Hardy used to ponder on the Napoleonic war, & collect stories from veterans in Chelsea Hospital: I can quite understand that. I paid a pound for a poppy yesterday. [. . .]

I am surprised you didn't think much of Betjeman's poem.[2] I thought the first instalment quite good. The second instalment today doesn't seem as good. I suppose there must have been some verse autobiographies before this one: the most famous is Wordsworth's *Prelude*, though this mainly describes the growth of his mind & views. Betjeman's is more concerned with little things wch he hits off very well I think. [. . .]

Much love, Philip

1 Remembrance Sunday was 13 November in 1960.

2 On 8 November Eva had written: 'Yes, I *did* read the John Betjeman poem in the S. Times, in fact I was awaiting its arrival. I liked it, up to a point, beyond that it seemed long and rather tiresome. Is he the first to write his life story in the form of a poem? Truly he cannot touch you, Creature, for *real* poetry. Some of yours are very beautiful.'

11 December 1960

32 Pearson Park, Hull

My dear creature,

I got back safely, more or less on time – but the journey is definitely taking ½ hour longer. We stopped at Nottingham, Mansfield & Doncaster. I sat next to a very irascible man between the last two, who thought I took up too much room.

Perhaps I did. But I think he was a bit dotty.

When I got to Hull I went to a Chinese restaurant & had something to eat – and I had eaten two apples on the way – so much for my not-eating-much line.

I do hope you are better by the time you get this. It was very kind of you to have everything so neat & comfortable when you haven't been feeling well. I found the service extremely interesting,[1] & only hope it doesn't diminish our numbers at all!![2]

Very best love,
Philip

1 Larkin had attended the confirmation ceremony of his niece Rosemary on Sunday 11 December. The following day he performed his duty as her godfather, sending a book concerning Christian beliefs. He wrote: 'There is no doubt that anyone who wants to understand England – its history and literature and lots of other things – *must* understand Christianity because England is a Christian country. [. . .] In the course of a year one hears the Bible read aloud in Church, and the fact that this has been going on for centuries has meant that what it says has soaked into our ways of thinking and speaking. I expect you have realised this already. [. . .] But one can go farther & say that Christianity is *our* way of being good: when we say a person or an action is "good" we mean good in a way Christ taught. This is what being a *Christian* country means, as opposed to a Mohammedan or whatever the Chinese believe. [. . .] I liked your dress: it was quite one of the few best.'

2 He fears that Rosemary will diminish the number of sceptics by becoming a believer.

18 December 1960

32 Pearson Park, Hull

My dear old creature,

[. . .] Monica is very undecided about what she should do for Christmas, but she thinks that if you are really sure she wouldn't be causing extra trouble, & also that she wouldn't be intruding on a family Christmas (!), she would be really very thankful to come & eat Christmas dinner. I said you had said she would be welcome if prepared to accept things as they are – and of course she is, & is ready to help with the washing up. I've explained that we prefer A. Nellie to have a rest after meals.[1] [. . .]

Love as ever Philip

1 In the event Monica did not go to 21 York Road for Christmas dinner.

1961

1 January 1961

32 Pearson Park, Hull

My dear old creature,

It is a solemn moment when one writes a new year for the first time, isn't it? I hope we shall see the last of it as well as the first. I "sat up" for it, rather pointlessly, drinking up the remains of two bottles of whiskey on the double excuse that I was celebrating and also curing a cold. I haven't exactly *got* a cold, but *something* is lurking about outside my physique, & I fancy I have a slight temperature. However! do not worry as I am quite confident I shall live.

[. . .] I really think someone should form a Christmas Abatement Society – there'd be plenty of members. You might even join it yourself.

When I went down for the papers this morning I found two little "toy" letters from the Duffin daughters, Amanda & Deborah, thanking me for the chocolates I'd left them. A kind thought on their part! I only spent a few shillings on each. Duffin made most of their presents – he had made a beautiful farmyard, & an equally beautiful shop. He says that toys are so dear & rickety they are really not worth buying.

Well, I must bring this letter to a close, & perhaps write a note to Monica. She is utterly depressed, more so than I have ever known her, & with reason.[1]

I washed those gloves last night, also my black jumper wch exuded blackness like a giant squid. The gloves get longer & longer – soon they will come up to my elbows.

Love & Happy New Year, P.

1 Andrew Motion cites a letter to Eva of this date as including the sentence: 'I have built her in my own image and made her dependent on me, and now I can't abandon her' (Motion, *Philip Larkin*, 310, n. 12). These words do not occur in the full text of the above letter and their tone is more intimate than that which Larkin uses to Eva when writing of Monica.

5 January 1961

32 Pearson Park, Hull

My dear old creature,

Your letter-paper is so like pink-edged woollen underwear it made me laugh, but very welcome all the same. It arrived a day earlier. I'm glad you have enjoyed the remainder of Auntie Nellie's stay: she is a cheerful bird in her way. As for the whiskey, I *think* I finished it last Christmas – pretty strong stuff it was, too, by that time. I'm sorry if I did you & her out of a drink of it.

My cleaner seemed to take to the Hoover, & did the place up very nicely.[1] I used it myself on Monday night, when it was delivered, & got quite a lot of dirt in a short time. It's rather like going hunting, isn't it?

Monica & I are spending two nights at Lincoln on Friday & Saturday, so I may write for your birthday & *not* [come] Monday. Thanks for the Bunny news – I always love it.[2] And thank you for the lovely Christmas!

Dear old creature!
Love Philip

1 In the letter of 1 January Larkin mentioned that he had bought a Hoover vacuum cleaner the previous day, and it was to be delivered on 2 January.

2 On 10 October 1960 Eva included with a letter a brief newspaper cutting. 'BUNNY BUS SHELTER', concerning a protest by residents of the village of Bunny at the proposal to move a bus stop. On 6 December she sent a cutting, 'BUNNY' recording the competition winner at a Brownies' bring and buy sale in the village. Other cuttings followed, and through 1961–4 Philip would also send 'Bunny news' cuttings to Eva, with jokes about Bunny's presumed rabbit inhabitants. The latest surviving cutting (an advertisement by Bunny Garage) was included by Eva in a letter of 12 October 1964.

8 January 1961

<*Letterhead*> 32 Pearson Park, Hull

My very dear old creature,

A very, *very* happy day for you, dear old creature: a happy contented comfortable birthday, surrounded by the good wishes of your nearest & (I hope) dearest: no storms, or worries, or fires going out, & despite the time of year I hope it won't be too cold. You say that the snow usually comes for your birthday, but this looks like one year when it won't be there.[1] [. . .]

Our visit to Lincoln was successful & quite interesting in parts. We stayed at a hotel up by the cathedral (wch as I expect you know is on a steep hill), wch wasn't as luxurious as it thought it was, but was all *right*: we wandered round the cathedral on Saturday morning, & in the town after lunch: then at 4 p.m. we went back to the hotel for a lovely tea in front of a big fire, and at 4.30 went across to the Cathedral for evensong. It was dark by then, but we were beckoned up into the choir & sat in the lovely old carved pews while the Dean and Archdeacon & choir went through the service: there were only about half a dozen people there. They had special prayers for members of the cathedral who had died on that day – one of the 18th century, one ages ago in the 15th century! Today we went to the Art Gallery after lunch, & found a whole room devoted to Tennyson, wch was just up our street. I didn't know you actually had a kind of certificate when you were Poet Laureate. You become a technical member of the Royal Household, & so aren't eligible for jury service. It didn't seem so cold today – Saturday was awful, freezing – and we were able to stroll round in comfort. I sent Betjeman a postcard of a monument to Tennyson that stands outside the Cathedral.

Well, now I must see how best to pack up your present, I do hope you have a good day – why not dip into a bottle of something? Spoil yourself.

Monica says she enjoyed everything to eat you gave her & w^{d} join me if she knew I were writing.

Very best love from Philip

1 Eva's seventy-fifth birthday fell on 10 January 1961.

29 January 1961

32 Pearson Park, Hull

My very dear old creature,

I have just scrubbed *half* my stairs – they are covered by a sort of red lino – I ought to have done them all, but the water got very dirty and a little work goes a long way with yours truly. So now I'm sitting down at 11.30 a.m., the gramophone churning out a succession of records made in 1927 wch I am supposed to be reviewing.[1] The weather outside looks windy but not unfriendly: I expect if I searched about for green spikes in the garden I should find them. "Looking forward to the Spring, One puts up with anything!" (Hardy). I think I sent a card reporting that I had returned safely from London. A piece of good news on my return was that Maeve had passed her library exam. She had to get half marks in 3 papers to pass: out of 120 in each, her marks were 65, 60 & 69! So it wasn't exactly with flying colours, but as she says a pass is as good as a mile. To my alarm she now wants to stand me a dinner for tutoring her, or trying to. This will be on Thursday. I'm glad I'm coming home on Friday, at least I hope I am, coming home I mean. [. . .]

I hope Mrs Slater[2] is better, for your sake, and take care you don't go down yourself. When I come, I will try to do the jobs you speak of.

I shall try to get the sequence of trains that brings me to L'boro by 10.15, if all goes well.

My best love till then. Philip

1 The first of Larkin's monthly jazz reviews for the *Daily Telegraph* appeared on Saturday 11 February 1961.
2 Eva's cleaner at the time.

2 March 1961 Postcard

[32 Pearson Park, Hull]

Thanks for your letter & card – I was sorry to hear Kitty had been ill, though my sorrow lessened somewhat on learning she hadn't been too ill to attend Rosemary's nonsense.[1] Fine day here. I am going to see why my new spectacles hurt my eyes. I don't think Mr Wood will be interviewed even!

Kingsley has been made a Fellow at Cambridge!!

— Grrrrrrrrrrr!!

Love P

1 A rehearsal of *Hansel and Gretel*.

7 March 1961

<Letterhead> ~~32 Pearson Park, Hull~~
Ward 6 Kingston General Hospital

My dear old creature,

This is just a page to show I'm all right.[1] The doctors can't find anything wrong with me but they are going to do a lot of tests to see if they *can* find anything. I feel much better though still a bit dizzy, & my eyes hurt if I read much. I expect I shall be here all the week, and don't look forward to the prospect. My fellow patients sound much worse than me.

Coveney (Cottingham 47181 – Needler Hall) is anxious to help if he can.[2] He rang Monica (Leics 76060 – 8 Woodland Avenue) to tell her the news. I've been told by someone that my family plan to come here this weekend – this is *very* kind of you but it's a *long* way, for a short time. Anyway, goodbye for a short time now. Sorry for all this.

Love as ever Philip

1 On 6 March 1961, Larkin collapsed during a library committee meeting and was rushed to Kingston General Hospital, where he remained until 17 March.
2 Peter Coveney was warden of Needler Hall, one of the university's student residences.

10 March 1961

<*Letterhead*> ~~32 Pearson Park, Hull~~ Ward 6 KGH

My dear creature,

Just thought I would send a line for the weekend, though I haven't much to say. I still have a rather dizzy feeling, though the headache has gone. Nobody has paid any interest in me for a day or two now. I suppose as long as the nurses report I am all right the doctors concentrate on the poor people who are not all right.

I do most profoundly hope I get well & am allowed to depart, though I believe they have plans for a thorough examination of me before this happens.

My best wishes & love for the weekend,

Philip

12 March 1961

Ward 6 KGH, Hull

My dear old creature,

This is the first time my Sunday letter has been \written/ in such surroundings, isn't it. I don't suppose it will be the last, either. Thank you for writing yesterday. It isn't easy to know what to say at present. I am still undiagnosed, & most of my symptoms persist, though my temperature has gone down. I'm quite well looked after, & if I knew what was wrong with me & that it was nothing serious I shouldn't be at all uncomfortable. As it is I can't help worrying a little.

Visiting hours are 7.15–7.45 in the evenings, but (I think) 2.30 to 3.30 on Wednesdays & Sundays. I have had lots of visitors so far, everyone is most kind: my side table is crowded out with fruit & books. So please don't send anything like that.

It looks a chilly day outside, windy too. It's not too warm in here! I am in a small 4-bed ward, one empty, where there is a TV set.

In the event of your wanting news of me, someone at the Library (Hull 18960) will probably have seen me in the last 24 hours. Betty Mackereth is my secretary & w^d^ report for you (between 9.30–5.30).

All love as ever
Philip

17 March 1961

Notecard[1]

Needler Hall, Cottingham, East Yorks.

My dear old creature,

This is just to say I have been discharged from hospital without much ceremony or interest.

I felt terribly shaky & panicky at first, & still have that sense of strain behind the eyes, but I am happier already & hope I have nothing to do now but get my specs altered & recuperate. Of course the hospital will want to see me.

My doctor says I mustn't think of doing any work for three weeks.

I'm afraid this has been a worrying time for you: I'm so sorry. Everyone here has been very kind, & the Coveneys are being quite marvellous about letting me live here in their flat. Much love x x

Philip

1 Bunch of wild flowers (watercolour).

18 March 1961

Needler Hall, Cottingham, E. Yorks.

My dear old creature,

The Coveneys have gone out for the evening & I am left in with the cat, a beautiful and affectionate animal, marmalade colour. I thought I would just – oh dear, the cat has jumped up & is making it (he's gone now) impossible for me to write – write a page to you. Today I've had another eye test, and my spare pair of spectacles have been sent to be altered, though there's not necessarily anything wrong with them.[1] I have, I think, moved a bit more confidently, though I still don't feel completely well: still a bit swimmy in the head and strained in the eye. And a long way from coping with anything, like a 'bus ride or shopping!

My doctor suggested today whether in the interests of getting this period of waiting for a complete check up over I had considered going to London as a private patient, & having it done at a clinic or hospital there. He said he might be able to get me into such an establishment quite quickly, & it w[d] then be over. Please don't interpret this as sending me to London as a serious case! It is just to shorten this trying period of waiting. I don't know what to think. I should feel a bit lonely & scared in London, though Monica might come with me. Of course London w[d] be a good place for such a business, & better than Hull if by any chance any treatment were needed. But it is such a relief to get out of hospital I don't feel like going into another one really, yet I mustn't be silly, I suppose.

I didn't really mean to start a second sheet, for I haven't anything to say.[2] [. . .]

Very best love
Philip

1 It seems that Larkin's collapse may have been precipitated by a misjudged optician's prescription. See Colin Vize, 'Larkin's Refraction', *About Larkin* 36 (April 2013), 23.

2 Despite his comment he went on to fill the recto of the second two-side sheet, and two-thirds of the fourth side.

25 March 1961

Needler Hall

My dear old creature,

I hope you all managed to get home safely yesterday, & that you didn't feel too tired as a result of such a long journey. It was awfully good of you to come so far to see me. I welcomed your familiar faces![1] [. . .]

I hope I didn't leave you with an unduly depressed view of my condition. I tried to let you know all the various things that had been said & done, but the main thing to hang on to is that the doctors are still checking, not following a suspected symptom. [. . .]

Thank you for coming to Hull and love to you & all the family. Philip

1 On 24 March Eva, Kitty and Walter had made the journey from Loughborough to Cottingham to visit him, returning the same day.

5 April 1961 Picture postcard[1]

[32 Pearson Park, Hull]

Just to remind you of your visit.[2] Thank you for your letter: I'm glad you got back safely. It's lovely & *warm* here today! No news from the hospital. Give my regards to Kitty. M. says don't forget the curtains \and the egg & sherry/!

All love,
Philip

1 St Mary's Church, Cottingham.
2 Eva visited Philip over Easter (30 March–3 April), staying at the Fuchsias, a university-owned house in Cottingham.

11 April 1961

Fielden House

My dear old Creature,

Kitty will have told you most of my news, I expect, so I can't add much at present. My tests will be repeated here, & then Sir R. B.[1] will look at the results either at the end of this week or the beginning of next, & then pronounce his opinion. I was x rayed yesterday & shall have the E.E.G.[2] again & an audiogram (for hearing) either today or tomorrow.

I have quite a comfortable room at the end of a corridor looking out onto St Philip's Church and commanding a not very inspiring view of roofs & something called Empire House. My meals come in on a tray & I eat them on a table out of bed. They are nothing very special. Monica comes in every day and we do, or try to do, the *Times* crossword. Yesterday she brought some beautiful yellow roses but they have wilted during the night, isn't it a shame.

I still feel peculiar, but no more peculiar than before. There isn't much to do here but read, & this tends to strain my eyes, still the main symptom of trouble. Bob Conquest came in yesterday & brought me a book called "The Miseries of Human Life", dated 1807. Actually it is very funny![3]

With love as ever & always
Philip

1 Sir Walter Russell Brain, brain surgeon.
2 Electroencephalogram: recording the electrical activity in the brain.
3 Robert Conquest (1917–2015), historian and poet: best known for his works on Soviet history, including *The Great Terror: Stalin's Purges of the 1930s* (1968). He had edited the anthology *New Lines* (1956) which featured Larkin. See note on the letter of 29 July 1956. Eva wrote on 13 April 1961: 'I am trying to think who Bob Conquest is, for I have heard you mention him before.'

16 April 1961

Fielden House, Stepney Way, London E.1

My dear old Creature,

Thank you for your letter-card and for your encouragement – much needed yesterday, for a diversion was provided in the shape of infected and inflamed ears, wch called for codeine every 4 hours & sent my temperature up to 3 figures. I can't but blame the Ear Dept. for this, since my ears were all right when I came in, & I feel very irritated. It's a bit thick to be made ill. I was in a poor mood yesterday. Still, I suppose it stopped me brooding on the advent of Sir R. B. tomorrow & his dreaded verdict.

Monica came in yesterday, as she has done three times every day since I've been here, & brought a Cineraria in a pot. Or was it some flame coloured tulips? She has brought both. And Judy Egerton[1] was also in and brought a mixture of yellow tulips & freesias. Stephen Spender called in on Friday & talked about his father & Lloyd George for the best part of an hour.

A nurse has just come in, & dressed both ears, so I hear but dimly, even dimmer than usual. The nurses are quite nice & kind. I fear there are some bad cases along the passage. Awful noises during the night – now stopped.

Do continue to spend time AND MONEY making yourself comfortable. If you don't like sherry & eggs, just have the sherry. Oghoghogh.[2]

Well, think of me tomorrow morning. If there's anything to say I'll ring up Kitty at 7.30 in the evening. Will you be there?

All love Philip

<*On the back of the envelope*>

c.11 p.m. Monday night 3rd programme – poem by me, new one.

12 noon – RB just been in – says wait for ears to clear up then another x ray. He seemed quite affable.

1 Larkin had first met Judy Egerton (1928–2012) in Belfast. She was now working as an art historian in London; see also n. 5, letter of 17 October 1954, above.
2 See Philip's postcard of 27 May 1960.

1 June 1961

<*Letterhead*> 32 Pearson Park, Hull

Dearest old creature,

Ghastly weather! Rain all day, & cold.

I have got over my tired feeling, but yesterday & today was much distressed by a sort of "anxiety condition" that made me unable to work or even go out with any confidence. I went to the doctor this afternoon, & he said he didn't think it was anything to do with my faint (i.e. it wouldn't lead to another) but was due to the strain of resuming work & being ill & all the rest of it. He gave me a new formidable green & yellow pill w[ch] seems to have calmed me.

He did say, however, that he didn't like my being on my own, as the effort of providing for myself was an additional burden.

Monica sh[d] come tomorrow, & I'll see how I get on over the weekend. In the meantime, don't worry: I'm just having a Guinness. [. . .]

Best best love Philip

<*At top of first page*> Friday. Fine sun, what a change. I feel much better, don't be alarmed, or come rushing here. I'll send further word for Monday.

25 June 1961

<*Letterhead*> Durrants Hotel Ltd, Manchester Square, London W.1

My dear old creature,

I was glad to hear you had returned safely from London, & had enjoyed being there. We tried to think how on earth you could have seen all the places you mentioned, & concluded in the end you must have been on a circular tour.

Our visit is not really proving as successful. The match for wch we have tickets on Monday[1] rather collapsed yesterday, & what play there is on Monday seems certain to lead to a win for Australia. Thursday was quite an interesting day, but not a heartening one from the English point of view, Friday & Saturday were splendidly fine days, but we tended to waste them: today is equally fine, & I expect we shall waste it too. Our rooms are fearfully hot at night, & in general I am not really enjoying myself. Fine weather makes me unhappy.

However, I mustn't sound too gloomy [. . .]

Very best of love, Philip

1 England *vs* Australia Test Match at Lord's.

27 June 1961

<*Letterhead*> 32 Pearson Park, Hull

My dear old creature,

This is just to say that I have returned safely, and am back in my flat again. The visit to London got me down rather, partly by tiring me and partly by upsetting me inside by some germ or other. When Monica had gone on Monday I just went back to the hotel & dived into bed, where I spent the evening, reflecting on the awfulness of London. It's so big & so hot & so expensive, everything is so complicated and confusing. I never leave it without a lifting of the spirits as we get among the fields and trees.

As I write this, I am hearing the tail-end of the installation of Archbp. Ramsey – how Daddy w^{d} have disliked his voice!

I'm glad you approve of the photograph – a huge enlargement was awaiting me when I came in, too big to go in my album. I have one for you as well. Creature surrounded by flowers![1]

Do hope you are well, and not worried by the weather.

My dearest love,
Philip

1 See Plate 15A. On 29 June 1961 Eva wrote: 'I shall be thrilled with the enlargement of "me amongst the flowers". Whilst on the subject of photographs I wonder if you could order me a copy of the photograph I saw on the mantelshelf (was it?) in your room at the library. The one of the Queen Mother signing the visitors book. Hope it isn't too late.'

19 July 1961

Picture postcard[1]

Thanks for your letter. Blazing hot day today. Hope to swim later. Glad to hear you are coming to Hull in August. I s[hd] think Aug 10th w[d] be quite all right! M. sends regards. Here you see our hotel – we are in the tin shed on the left. Love Philip

1 Dixcart Hotel, Sark.

24 September 1961

Haydon Bridge, Northumberland

My dear old creature,

I am sitting in Monica's living-room on Sunday morning, having come over by bus from Hexham, w[ch] is only about 20 minutes' ride. It's very sunny and warm, and has been ever since I came up on Friday evening, a journey w[ch] took about 4 hours, through Newcastle.

I expect you'll be wondering what "1a Ratcliffe Road"[1] is like – well, it's a tiny house, attached to others on both sides, with a fairly busy road outside the front door, and the river Tyne outside the back. It has living-room, kitchen downstairs, & two bedrooms and a bathroom upstairs. On the whole it's in very good repair – the walls are so thick you couldn't hear the people next door if you wanted to. Monica is only half in, since the cooker & refrigerator have still to be attached, and the 100 gns carpet is coming on Tuesday, but she has borrowed a boiling ring & has an electric kettle. This Haydon Bridge place isn't a picturesque village, exactly, nor is her cottage a picturesque cottage, but in general it has a good deal of character. It's very well appointed – good bathroom & so on – and quite big enough for her. As usual I haven't helped her at all.[2] [. . .]

Yesterday – Saturday – we took a bus to Allendale, wch is near at hand and very pretty. We strolled about & had a small tea – 1/- each! – and Monica had a mild fit of remorse that she hadn't come to a really pretty village to buy her house, but after all it's more inaccessible there, and might be more expensive. As a matter of fact, 'buses to Carlisle & Newcastle pass the door in either direction where she is, & there's also a good train service.

I was glad to hear you had had an enjoyable trip to Dovedale & Matlock. [. . .]

There are plenty of gulls on the Tyne outside, & I can hear them calling as I write. They aren't our sort, though.[3] [. . .]

Love Philip

<*At top of first page, opposite address*> Thanks for Bunny news – The Mothers' Union there should be a flourishing organisation, I sh^{d} think![4]

1 The holiday home which Monica had just bought in Haydon Bridge.

2 On 25 September Eva replied: 'I was really anticipating your letter from Hexham with my "tongue hanging out" so to speak, and was most interested in all you described there. As you may know I have only had two ambitions in life, first to be a great author and the other, to have a little cottage in the country. Neither will ever now be realised.'

3 'Their sort' of gulls go 'oghoghogh'. See Philip's card of 27 May 1960.

4 On 13 June Eva had sent a cutting concerning the Bunny village clock, stuck at just after 10, and a visit by 'special coach' of thirty-one members and friends of the Bunny with Bradmore Mothers' Union to Bottesford to see the former vicar of the village. ('They toured the parish church before tea.') A cutting concerning a 'KEEN BUNNY CYCLIST' followed on 23 July, and one on a Bunny nonagenarian on 7 August. The cutting which prompted Philip's comment here was included with a letter of 19 September. It recorded the success in his examinations of the son of the secretary of the Mothers' Union.

28 September 1961

Hull

My dear old creature,

I got back here yesterday rather tired & not sorry to be home again: the conference, though agreeable enough, was exhausting like all functions. While I was away Farrell got a job at Bristol! So he will be going after Christmas. More worry.

I forget how much I said about Monica's house – it is really half a house, very solid & well-made, and once she has her purple carpet & chandeliers up – as I expect she has now – it will look very nice. It is solidly fitted & has this nice kitchen window onto the river. I didn't greatly care for the village of Haydon Bridge, & her position *is* rather noisy \though/ as you say this may at times seem an advantage.

When I got back there was a letter from Barbara Pym, answering one written by me on 5th March, the day before I was ill! I had imagined I had said something to offend her, but she seems quite affable. I want to do an article on her when her next book comes out, if I can.[1]

Friday A lovely fine day, though I do find it hard to get up in the mornings – I feel so tired! My physical wellbeing is still a trifle precarious. I'm so glad you read about Gdma Moses, isn't she marvellous?[2] All love

Philip

1 Larkin had first written to Barbara Pym on 16 January 1961.

2 The American folk artist 'Grandma Moses' – Anna Mary Robertson Moses (1860–1961) – died on 13 December 1961. She had begun painting at the age of seventy-eight, three years older than Eva was at this time.

28 October 1961

<*Letterhead*> 32 Pearson Park, Hull

My dear old creature,

I am sitting in front of my fire on Saturday night, & thought I would write you a page. It has been a dullish sort of day, & I've felt rather drowsy and below par: I was glad to get in from shopping and into my bath. After that I had two pikelets and some china tea.

Perhaps my drowsiness is due to going out last night with Betty. We went far out in her car to a place called The Trout, in the depths of the country, & had a very good dinner of duck & burgundy. Before setting out we had a drink at her parents' home, & her father tried to convert me to healthy feeding. I told you Betty wouldn't be immunised, didn't I? They scorn doctors & eat raw cabbage & things of that sort. Hull is full of polio germs going round in mortal dread of catching Betty. Anyway, the whole family looks very healthy. I have bought some cabbage & carrots to try myself. [. . .]

Well, I suppose I had better go and grate my carrot. The cabbage is simply enormous – as big as a football. I shall never get through it. However, I dare say it is very healthy. I keep expecting to come across a furry visitor ![1]

With all very best love
Philip

1 On 31 October Eva wrote: 'How did you fare with the raw carrot and cabbage? Raw carrots are very good for one. I remember Mr Bilston, the Borough Accountant at Warwick always had his vegetables raw, shredded. Walter and Rosemary also have raw cabbage. They like it very much.'

19 November 1961

<*Letterhead*> 32 Pearson Park, Hull

My dear old creature,

[. . .] Yesterday too I bought another cabbage. I find a good deal depends on one's cabbage of the moment. Last week's was tough & I am chucking away about half of it. This new one is much more tender. This diet renders shopping beautifully simple – cheese, carrots, cabbage, & perhaps tomatoes. \And some onion./ Nothing else. It's a great burden off my mind. As for whether I like it, well, I don't dislike it enough to stop doing it. As for whether it's healthy, well, I haven't been ill since I started it, but whether that means anything I don't know. Betty is always revoltingly healthy. [. . .]

Very best love, old creature,
Philip

26 November 1961

<*Letterhead*> 32 Pearson Park, Hull

My very dear old creature,

[. . .] Not a great deal has happened this week. I had a poem in the *New Statesman* on Friday wch I hope no one will notice, as it speaks somewhat critically of these parts.[1] It is all right up to the last verse, when it collapses somewhat to my ear. I have the feeling of having been out quite a lot, but all it boils down to really is attending one lecture. [. . .]

Best love,
Philip

1 'Here' appeared in the *New Statesman* on 24 November 1961.

1962

7 January 1962

<*Letterhead*> 32 Pearson Park, Hull

My very dear old creature,

This is my first letter to you of 1962, and of course it is your birthday letter. Indeed it may not reach you till your birthday. Let me be first of all then, [to] wish you a happy and comfortable day, and a year free from storms & worries and illness: may you keep your old friends and make new ones. [. . .]

Monica came on Monday & went back on Friday. She had left a pipe or two frozen, and was worried about them. She spent Christmas Day at home, & had a duck. About eleven the old miner next door called with a glass of neat whiskey & a piece of cake! As she hadn't had anything to eat she found this rather daunting, but she managed to swap the whiskey for port, at least. Your towels were a great success, & she is very touched that you should think of her. We didn't do much. She came into the Library a good deal and set examination questions. [. . .]

I'm glad to say the weather looks mild and agreeable & I might go out to Hessle to stir up the Hartleys, or I might just go out. It's 5 to 2 & of course I haven't had lunch yet! I expect you are just licking up your plate. Once again a very happy birthday & all best love.

Philip.

11 February 1962

<*Letterhead*> 32 Pearson Park, Hull

My very dear old creature,

A grey day, but not over-cold as far as I can see. I surprised Kelly putting my papers outside my door at 10.15! I think he is anxious to efface the bad impressions of last week, but they are a pair of fussers & meddlers, really. Still, better than Wilks who stole my *Observer* & still hasn't paid me the 3/6 he owes from last June, though he sometimes refers to it as if it concerned two quite different people.[1] I didn't shop very carefully yesterday, & forgot bananas (I eat these regularly now – they are easy things to manage) and have no caster sugar for my grapefruit. I might find some bananas today, but the sugar will have to wait.

This has been a better week once I got free of the Committee on Monday. What I find is that sometimes I am frightfully tired in the evenings, brain-tired chiefly but nerve-tired too, & unable to take up anything of my own. I don't as a rule try. Perhaps I ought to buy a television set! [. . .]

On Friday night I had to put in time listening to a poetry reading by William Empson – he is professor at Sheffield & a wellknown poet, in a slightly mad way. He used to teach in the east & affects a Chinese beard, wch looks very straggly. Afterwards he came with us to a pub & blathered on. Honestly, *all* writers are utterly awful when you meet them. This is one reason why I never undertake speaking engagements, but only one, as you can imagine.

Miss Moon has begun & will I think do well.[2] She is a tiny creature with a singsong voice, vaguely accented (she comes from Staffordshire), & seems cheerful & efficient & with a kind of inhuman pixie brightness. I'm sure she's a valuable addition to the staff. I am running into a bout of Wood-hatred: I can hardly keep myself from kicking him downstairs, through plate-glass doors, sawing his head off, etc.

Have you found out by now who has bought the house next door? I hope it is someone nice – not a gang of Pakistanis who will build a pile of empty kit-e-kat tins in the yard and grow marijuana in the back garden, nor yet some frightful crowd with gate-kicking children. I have wondered whether you had got any further forward with your holiday arrangements, fearful burden that they are. I should still like us – you & I – to have a week somewhere if possible. I thought Minehead was a great success. It w^d^, I suppose, be September, or perhaps late August.

I have bought a Valentine to send to Mary,[3] though I don't expect she is feeling much like Valentines! This month her baby is due.

I have an awful lot to do today – double load of laundry, & some washing – so I had better push on. Take *care* of yourself, dear old creature. You are always in my thoughts.

Love from Philip

1 The Kellys occupied the bottom flat in 32 Pearson Park at this time; the Wilkses occupied the middle floor.
2 Brenda Moon had been appointed chief cataloguer to replace John Farrell. Five years later, in 1967, she was promoted to be the second deputy librarian alongside Arthur Wood.
3 Mary Judd (formerly Wrench).

24 February 1962

<*Letterhead*> 32 Pearson Park, Hull

My very dear old creature,

[. . .] Most of the interest this week has been centred on Mary, who has gone into the maternity home but as far as I know hasn't had her baby yet. I told you she went to that odd film that we saw! It didn't seem to disconcert her. Stephen[1] says, "You can't hurry a Judd", but I'm sure Mary wishes it were all safely over.[2] [. . .]

My tongue varies from green to yellow: Betty's father says it is my system getting rid of its poison, and will go on for a year. He also said be thankful it's nothing worse! I don't know what he means by that. However, I continue with the raw salad daily, as far as possible, like Timmy Willie in Beatrix Potter's *Johnny Town Mouse* – I feel great sympathy with him. Do you know the story? It's about a field mouse that gets taken to town accidentally in a basket, and town life doesn't agree with him. Then he gets back to the country, & the town mouse comes & visits him. There is a wonderful passage when the town mice ask what he *does* in the country, & he explains how he sits shelling nuts & peas, and smelling the violets after the rain – it nearly makes me cry. You will think I am silly.[3]

I wonder if your wall has been repaired. [. . .]

Very dearest love Philip

1 Mary's husband.
2 On 27 February Eva wrote: 'I am rather surprised to know that Mary went to that horror film. Her waiting reminds \me/ of how I was kept waiting for your arrival. I had Mrs Poole in a month before you came. You were actually a fortnight late.'
3 On 27 February Eva wrote: 'Dearest creature, how I loved the story about the little field mouse. Whenever I~~n~~ think of ~~the~~ him smelling the violets after the rain, I feel I could cry, too. I'm sure this is not silly. (I have made a lot of mistakes here, but it is a bit difficult to write as Rosemary is practising on the piano. Rather deafening!)'

4 March 1962

<*Letterhead*> 32 Pearson Park, Hull

My dear old creature,

Self indulgence Sunday – I lay in bed till 12.15! I felt I needed it, having been out at a party wch was quite respectable & over by 11.30 but wch involved *a good deal of standing*, wch I found hard to take, poor old bones. Now it is a quarter to two, & snowing slightly – really, isn't the weather grim! We have a little snow each day, just to encourage us.

This weekend is the anniversary of my collapse: I have the same committee tomorrow, so I hope I survive. I think I shall. But think of me between two and three in the afternoon. Funnily enough, there is an item on the agenda that was on last time, & is the last thing I remember trying to speak about!

On Friday evening I went along to see Mary: she is in a pleasant little room, & looks very well. There were two women friends of hers there when I arrived, then when they went Betty looked in, & then Stephen, and I thought they'd probably prefer to be alone, so I went without really saying much. Helen Mary is reputedly a "rampageous" child, & has red hair, rather to Mary's surprise: she seems to have enjoyed the whole experience, though by all accounts it wasn't easy by any means. Hilary,[1] who was at the party last night & is expecting another baby in April, expressed the wish that Mary could deputise for her, as she found it less thrilling. But Mary was always rather tough, in her own way.

There's no more news of Miss Cuming:[2] she had a stroke a week last Wednesday, and has been unconscious ever since. It is saddening, but a painless condition as far as one knows. Life seems all birth and death at the moment. Ay, an' *Ah* doan't feel that gradely, Ah'm tellin' thee, so theer. [. . .]

Very best love, Philip

1 Hilary Penwill had been Larkin's secretary until 1957.
2 Larkin's predecessor as Librarian. She died on 9 March 1962.

25 March 1962

<*Letterhead*> 32 Pearson Park, Hull

My dear old creature,

[. . .] I haven't had any success with Easter yet, not that I've tried very hard. Bournemouth doesn't seem any good. Whenever I undertake the wearisome and disagreeable task of "booking holidays" – a task that quite abolishes the desire, if any, that prompted its undertaking – I get the impression that the entire population of Britain spends its time reserving holiday accommodation for every conceivable holiday period for five years in advance. Better prepare yourself for anything or nothing –

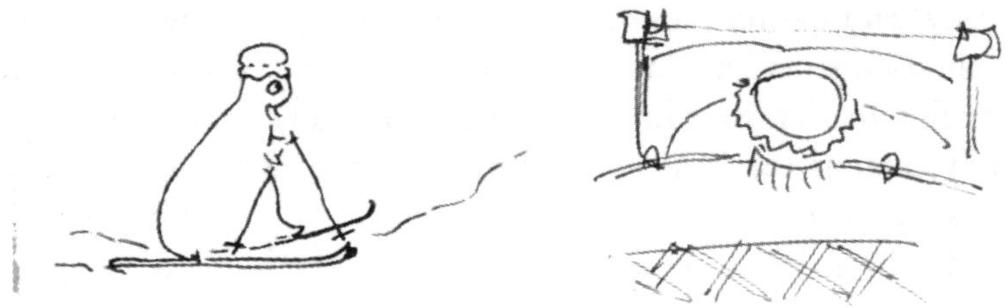

but probably *not* in the south of England.[1]

I ambled round the town yesterday & got as far as Marks & Spencer's,[2] where I bought a large size vest & pants in as warm-looking material as I could find – they came to 31/- in all, not unduly cheap. Then I went on to the Market Place, a horrible chip-infested place, and looked round the stalls, but what a mixture Hull is of the romantic and the drearily ugly – the redbrick Tudor school, where Andrew Marvell & William Wilberforce were educated, and the trawlers tied up in Prince's Dock, but the swarms of depressing cut-price kid-dragging people, caricatures of every vapid vulgarity, quite offset them. What a dump! What a crew![3] [. . .]

All very best love, Philip

1 Eva replied on 27 March: 'I wonder where else we could try? Hastings, Folkestone? I expect they would all be full up too. Don't forget to ask for a private bathroom. (I don't expect that would be available either.) [. . .] I managed to have an interview with the Bank Manager last Friday. [. . .] The first thing he said was "I don't know whether you have anyone dependent on you, Mrs Larkin, but I think, at your age you might spend some of your capital – say £2,000 and enjoy yourself. Go [on] a cruise round the world." He added, "you can't take it with you, you know". [. . .] The knowledge that I *can* indulge in a luxury now & then prompted me to make an appointment at the hairdresser's for a shampoo, set & trim. The Manager cut it and one of the girls did it in a new style, which I quite like – price 12/-!!!.'
2 This was 'the large cool store' in Whitefriargate, Hull, which inspired the poem of that title, completed on 18 June in the previous year, 1961.
3 Eva concurred in slightly different vein (27 March 1962): 'I quite agree with all you said about the people one meets on a Saturday in a large city. I am really tired of seeing so many "nobodies", dressed smartly albeit cheaply trailing round the streets, all busy spending.'

1 April 1962

<*Letterhead*> 32 Pearson Park, Hull

My very dear old creature,

[. . .] My photographs of Mary's baby came out moderately well, though she is a squalling little thing & looks quite agonised in most of them.[1] She has asked me to be god-father, wch is rather a tall order. I accepted though. Somebody will have to look after me when I'm old.

Betty is another godparent, I think. Miss Moon is gradually taking the Library in hand: she is also trying to *buy* a flat in Cottingham for between two & three thousand, but there is some hitch at present. I'm glad she is putting down roots – she is a tremendous acquisition. A very busy little creature. [. . .]

A fat volume – two fat volumes, in fact – of Lawrence's letters have been published & I am eating my way through them.[2] His life between say 1910 & 1914 seems very adventurous & idyllic, living in Italy & Germany with Frieda. Different from living in Hull with nobody!

Oh, I wish it were warmer!

Very best love, Philip

1 See Plate 10c.

2 *The Collected Letters of D. H. Lawrence*, ed. Harry T. Moore (Heinemann, 1962).

9 April 1962

Picture postcard[1]

Waiting for a connection here – it looks as if I have plenty of choice, doesn't it! Fine but cold.

Love
Philip

1 Largest Railway Crossing, Newcastle upon Tyne.

29 April 1962

<*Letterhead*> 32 Pearson Park, Hull

My very dear old creature,

[. . .] On Thursday a friend of the Hartleys' drove them & me to Bridlington – this place always reminds me of one of my boyhood friends, Peter Snape or Peter Sharpe or someone, who always used to go there – to hear a Louis Armstrong concert: this was a very great thrill for me, as Armstrong is the Shakespeare of jazz even now, & I've never seen him before. We got back about midnight. You'll see a picture of him in the *S. Times* today. And see all those poets in the Colour Supplement! Grim-looking crew. [. . .]

All love,
Philip

27 May 1962

<*Letterhead*> 32 Pearson Park, Hull

My very dear old creature,

[. . .] I expect you've been reading the *Sunday Times* feature on "Loneliness" – I just glanced at it. It is odd to think of young people being lonely, yet I remember how lonely I was at Warwick during vacations – at least, I think I was. Never knew anyone at Warwick, did we? I didn't, anyway. But as a family we were not very sociable. I remember that if there was "somebody in the drawing room" at Coventry I felt an intense emotion of fear mixed with shyness – a kind of embarrassment lest the door should open with its curious crackling sound (I can hear it now) and its awful occupants catch me crossing the hall. It wasn't so much that I was shy of people as that I hated the idea of them in "our" house. I expect you have been thinking of Coventry lately, now that the Cathedral has been consecrated. I wish I remembered the old Cathedral more clearly. I remember going with the school on several occasions – could they have been Founder's Day? – but all I remember was that it was very tall and very dark.[1]

Tomorrow I am going to the official opening of the new Library in Hull[2] – it is already open, actually, and I went in it yesterday. Perhaps I can pick up some tips for my opening in Wellington on September 12. Brrrr.

I had a letter from the Saturday Evening Post yesterday, offering a page, but I don't think I can take advantage of it – a pity, since it penetrates every living room in the United States. [. . .]

Love, Philip

1 Eva responded on 28 May: 'I expect you would be lonely at Warwick. I remember we did have Jim, Hughes and Kingsley to see us at times. / Daddy of course, made friends with Mr Bilson[,] Mr Champ and the Baker, I forget his name. I think I was too busy to make any friends there, for it was mostly war time and we had no cleaner.'

2 An extension to the Hull Central Library was opened by Alderman Lawrence on 28 May 1962, the Lord Mayor, Alderman George Frear, presiding.

17 June 1962

<*Letterhead*> 32 Pearson Park, Hull

My very dear old creature,

[. . .] *After a rather horrible lunch*. Am furious at the moment as I have discovered a spanner jamming the side-gate into the garden, which can only be the work of those sodding Kellys – I'll give him what for, obstructing a common right of way. I hope the University kicks them out in November, or whenever it is. Fuss, fuss, fuss all the time. Damned cheek.

What with that and my lunch – and an increase in hayfever – I feel less happy than I did, not I suppose that I did feel very happy.

I will keep in mind the business of writing to the Rector of St Michael's (was it?) Lichfield:[1] after all, I may want to go there myself one day![2] Of course, I think it w[d] be most appropriate if you *were* there, if you wish to be, and I don't think you need pay attention to such fancies such as disturbing those already there! They'll have enough on their minds already. Or else, as the Bible says, "The living know that they shall die, but the dead know not anything."[3] I expect Kitty would visit Lichfield twice as regularly if you were there! (Spiteful creature.)

Being disagreeable has made me feel more cheerful, even charitable, apart from making me want to ride over Kelly at the head of a troop of cavalry. I'm going to the Buildings Officer's tonight – I'll see I drop some poison in his ear.

Have you finished the Wodehouse? His autobiography – or, at least, a selection of his letters – called *Performing Flea* is quite readable, but of course there are plenty of novels left, not, of course, that you'll want to read them non-stop.

Thanks for finding the pennies – invest them wisely. All the money came out of my pocket when I was changing my trousers – I thought I'd found it all.[4]

Very best love, Philip

1 The site of the Larkin family graves. See David Gerard, 'Family Matters: The Fifth Annual PLS Birthday Walk, Lichfield, 11 August 2001', *About Larkin* 12 (2001), 30–3.

2 In a letter of 13/14 June Eva had written: 'I have thought a deal about the matter of Lichfield being my last resting place, and wonder if it is the right thing to do. I mentioned this at the time of our visit, if you remember. Also I rather shrink from writing to the Rector myself, and wonder if you could do it for me (if you think it would be right). Just a tentative letter asking if there would be room, for the churchyard seemed rather full.'

3 Ecclesiastes 9: 5.

4 In her letter of 13 June Eva had told him to check whether he had a hole in his pocket.

22 June 1962

Postcard

<*Postmark*> London S.W.1

Thank you for sending a letter as usual. I can't say the cricket yesterday was very enjoyable – play seemed dull, seats were uncomfortable, & I had bad hayfever all the p.m., most lowering. Today looks rather dull & grey. I hope to dash up to Austin Reed's for a fitting before going to Lord's.

I was glad to hear of the Bunny nonagenarian.[1]

There are a lot of very old bunnys at Lord's all wearing M.C.C. ties and taking a keen interest in what goes on. Monica sends kind regards.

Love P.

1 With her letter of 19 June Eva had enclosed a cutting concerning Mrs Edith Beecroft of Bunny village, who had received seventy-four birthday cards, 'countless gifts of flowers and many presents'.

26 August 1962

<*Letterhead*> The Collingwood Arms Hotel, Cornhill-on-Tweed, Northumberland

My dear old creature,

Rain is falling steadily. This is a pleasant solid hotel in quiet surroundings – on a road above a river opposite a church – and so far very comfortable, though I could do with about five more blankets till the cold weather comes.

I was glad to leave Pearson Park as the Kelly–Wilks fracas blew up again – Wilks had some foul friends to stay on Thursday: his friends always seem to arrive about 12.15 a.m. They kept me awake with talking till about 1.30, when they seemed to settle down, but about 2.20 a.m. there were three tremendous thumps below me, quite deliberate, & I was so furious I pounded on the floor in a frenzy. This produced a written apology (!) from Wilks, who said Kelly had been prodding on the ceiling with a broom to prevent *their* going to sleep. The spectacle of the three of us banging away is scarcely dignified! Anyway, I proceeded up to Newcastle on Saturday, where I met Monica & we journeyed on by stopping train into the lonely Border country. The trip was enlivened by my finding in a bookshop in Newcastle Anthony Sampson's *Anatomy of Britain*, [in] w[ch] in the section summarising the claims to distinction of Britain's universities Hull is described by "Only 48 public schoolboys. Many Africans. Poet-Librarian Philip Larkin." Plain to see there isn't much to be said about the place!

Last night we had "casserole of grouse" & a bottle of claret. It seems colder up here, and the chance of any summer weather very distant. I hope you fare better down on the south coast[1] – I expect you will. The grouse was all right though not much of it. [. . .]

Well, I must close & take another look at the weather, & perhaps write to Wilks, or he will think I am ignoring his apology. But what to say I don't know.

Much love, dear old creature, also to A. Nellie, Philip

1 Eva and Nellie were in a hotel in Bournemouth from 2 to 9 September.

16 September 1962

32 Pearson Park, Hull

My dear old creature,

For once I am sitting in my bedroom in the sun, in the chair I bought for doing so, though it spends most of its time holding clothes I am too lazy to put away. It looks a fine day, but so did yesterday, and that collapsed in torrential rain about 3 o'clock.

Well, my visit to Wellington was really quite successful.[1] You will recall I was staying with M[r] Buttrey who was chairman of the Library Committee in those days (and still is) – the first mystery was that I couldn't identify his wife – I am sure he must have remarried. The Mrs B. I remember was a much older person. Anyway, they gave me tea, & then we sat until it was time to go down to the Library. Actually the opening was fixed for 8, to allow members of the Council to finish a meeting. I was surprised by the splendour of the new extension – they have hollowed out the old building, and added a new one to it, entirely glass-fronted (and backed). There were a great many local government worthies there – Lady Jacqueta Williams (a great Shropshire figure), the Deputy Clerk of the County Council, the Chairman of the Urban District Council, & so on. The strain of keeping a smile on my face and not swearing for about 3 hours was considerable!

My "speech" seemed a bit long and dull to me, but I got through it without any great nerves. The atmosphere was so friendly that I could almost have sung a comic song. I don't think there'll be any tablet inscribed to me! They didn't even present me with anything, wch I thought they might have done. Still.

Since coming back I have been appalled by the amount of work there is here *of all kinds*, and should by rights go off my head with worry, but shall try not to.[2] [. . .]

Much love to you, dear old creature. Philip

1 Larkin had been invited to open the refurbished public library in Wellington.
2 Not to be outdone Eva replied (17 September): 'Like you, I am appalled by all the jobs, which ought to have been done much earlier in the year and hope I shall get some of them done before Christmas.'

7 October 1962

<*Letterhead*> 32 Pearson Park, Hull

My dear old creature,

Tomorrow is John Cowper Powys's 90th birthday! Just think of it! He certainly has learnt "the art of growing old", hasn't he – I believe he eats little and takes plenty of exercise, like me ogh ogh ogh.[1] It is marvellous, isn't it, considering how ill he used to be with ulcers. I believe what counts is the will to live, the basic psychic energy that you have & I haven't.

I have ordered all his books for the Library that we haven't got already. [. . .]

There is a poem by me in *The Spectator* this week, about advertisements[2] – not a very good one. [. . .]

Much love, dear old creature – how are your roses? Philip

1 See Philip's postcard of 27 May 1960.
2 'Essential Beauty'.

11 November 1962

Leicester

My very dear old creature,

How quickly these Remembrance Days come round! I wonder if you have been listening to the service on the wireless. I don't think there is any broadcast during the year that makes a stronger impression on me. Do your thoughts go back to 1918, and call up what you were doing then?[1] It must have been much more dramatic when there was no wireless and very few telephones, and news was published in special editions of papers and passed by word of mouth. You notice I never think of this day in terms of 1945! That date holds no romance for me: merely when a particularly dreary and depressing period in our history began.

Anyway, I don't feel unduly bright this morning – I find it awfully hard to get a good night's sleep out of my own bed, & it seems *cold* here: I must look after myself well in Hull! Add to this that I feel generally irritable. [. . .]

Betty keeps me supplied with apples and pears – rather sour some of the apples are too! Discomfort me with apples, I say.[2] I must have been on this raw-food diet for about a year now. Her father says it takes about two years to get a proper hold of your system, & that when it does I shan't have hayfever or anything! Certainly my health hasn't been too bad these 12 months – touch wood –

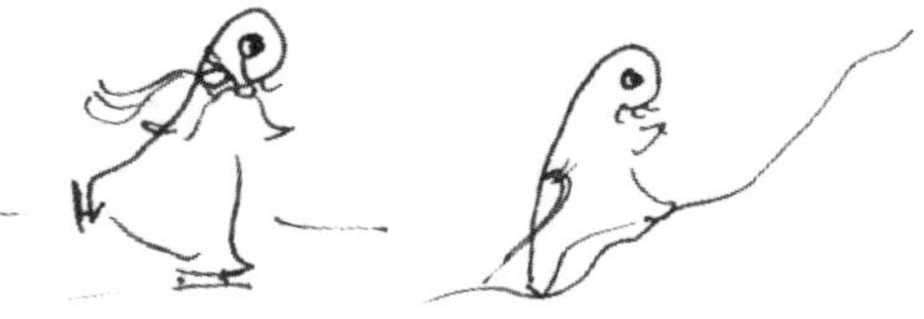

not my deputy Wood – touch him with a policeman's truncheon – However, I can't say it makes me any stronger – I had to move some books unexpectedly on Friday & it nearly corpsed me – my *back* felt *broken* –

I was glad to hear that vase in the front room was broken. It was extremely ugly. Also that you have got a cleaner again. It's cheering that one of your "old" women wanted to come back. You can't be so horrible after all! [. . .]

My dearest love, old creature – WRAP UP. Philip

1 On 13 November Eva replied: 'I agree with your remarks upon the two wars, although the first world war was more horrible in that a wholesale slaughter of our young men took place. I always remember Kitchener's cry, "More men, more men." I went to church however, and this reminds me to say that we have left the Parish Church and now go to Emmanuel. As you may know – Mrs Dexter does not like the alterations that the Rector intends making at All Saints.' Mrs Dexter was a fellow member of the Circle of Silent Ministry. See notes to the letters of 5 March 1964 and 11 July 1965.
2 'Stay me with flagons, comfort me with apples: for I am sick of love.' Song of Solomon 2: 5, King James Version.

9 December 1962

32 Pearson Park, Hull

My dear old creature,

[. . .] Yesterday a copy of the U.S. edition of *A Girl in Winter* turned up: it has just been published over there, at $4.50, jolly dear – about 32/-. There are a lot of complimentary remarks about me on the jacket – perhaps I will bring it home at Christmas. On Wednesday I am due to record two poems in London for a poetry record: I am not greatly looking forward to this. The poems are *Mr Bleaney* and *An Arundel Tomb*.[1]

Thou fool, this night thy soul shall be required of thee, the wireless has just said (*The Epilogue*). Ay, ah thowt it wor going to be required this mornin', an' all, let alone toneet.

Good night, dear old creature.
Philip

1 *The Jupiter Anthology of Twentieth Century English Poetry*, part III, released in November 1963. Bloomfield, *Bibliography*, F2.

1963

20 January 1963

<Letterhead> 32 Pearson Park, Hull

My very dear old creature,

[. . .] I did go to hear Duke Ellington though the journey was pretty fierce – 2½ hours each way, 6–8.30, and 11.30–2.00 a.m.![1] The bus was warm enough and not impossibly uncomfortable, but of course it was wearisome – and back to a cold bed! Awwghgh! The concert was in the main very good – to my surprise the Hartleys were there too. The City Hall at Sheffield is a huge place. [. . .]

Now do take care in walking, dear old creature – don't fling your feet about & lose balance – all best love

Philip

1 On 11 January Philip had written 'On Tuesday evening I am supposed to be going with a party of students by coach to Sheffield (2 hours both ways) to see Duke Ellington, or hear him & his band rather. [. . .] He probably won't come again – he's 64 this year. Quite a chicken by your standards, of course!'

27 January 1963

<Letterhead> 32 Pearson Park, Hull

My very dear old creature,

[. . .] I can't say I have very much in the way of news: the days go by with nothing especially colourful or alarming to mark them Perhaps this isn't a thing to be lamented! I thought I had lost my "credit card" at Austin Reed's, & had visions of some unknown being able to clothe himself at my expense, but luckily I found it again. Betty & I went to look at an "offset litho" machine that *might* be very useful in the office, and w^{d} *certainly* cost £475. Maeve is irritated by a Mrs Tanner on the staff who calls her "Mauve". This is inexplicable as "Maeve" is quite a well known name. Actually I have come to prefer Mauve. I think it's a rather distinguished name, like Coral I suppose, and after all there could be many Maeves but I'm sure there's only one Mauve. Maeve doesn't quite see this. [. . .]

Much love,
Philip

3 February 1963

32 Pearson Park, Hull

My very dear old creature,

[. . .] I can't think that much has happened this week. I just slog in & out, & eat raw cabbage. Some of the things I've done w^d need too much explaining to make clear, as they are tied up with business. Perhaps I should explain why Kelly hit Wilks! It seems that last Sunday Mrs K. asked the W.'s if they w^d mind being extra quiet as K. was ill, & the W.'s agreed. On the Tuesday evening Mrs K. rang again & called up the stairs to the effect that they seemed to have been noisier than ever since she spoke. W. replied in no very conciliatory style: K. then appeared, rushing up the stairs in his pyjamas in demented fashion and, in reaching the top, striking W. a light blow on the shoulder. W. rang up the police to find out how to charge people with assault! Luckily he didn't ring the fire brigade too. Next day he reported it to the Registrar, who passed it on to the V.C. There it rests for the present. Will keep you informed. [. . .]

Love
Philip

10 February 1963

32 Pearson Park, Hull

My very dear old creature,

[. . .] There isn't a lot of news from the Library – now there is some talk of the next stage of the Library being done by Sir Leslie Martin, the Festival Hall architect, at least "to sketch-plan stage". We have two additional typists starting tomorrow: our advertisement for two additional cataloguers, wch closes tomorrow, has so far produced two

Indians & a chap who was a trainee here last year & can't come till July! Of course there may be a rush of applications tomorrow, I don't

think. I shan't have the Indians.

Mr Wood still omits to win a football pool or fall down and break his neck – another 10 years to go! Oh God! I shall be 50, 51! Oh *god*!! The prospect is too ghastly for words. [. . .]

All best love Philip

10 March 1963

<*Letterhead*> 32 Pearson Park, Hull

My dear old creature,

It is rather a crushed creature that writes today, in that I have had a rather hard few days of it, here & in London & then yesterday in Leeds. This is a dim time of year, even though the cold has gone, and the sense of life being a bit too much for me is constantly at my elbow. Travelling about is not enjoyable, in that I find sleeping difficult & can't eat meals properly as it is hard to get water, and after a bit appetite goes. Today will be a thin day anyway, as I hadn't time to do much shopping yesterday. It must be nice to be like you, nothing to do but

shop, cook & eat!

Of course, I still have a few teeth, which is better than you, but I am sorry to hear from your Tuesday letter that your new ones are still giving trouble. I do hope they will come right in the end.

Bob Conquest came up on Wednesday and stayed the night here – I find I am rather unadaptable when it comes to having visitors! Their conversation palls rapidly & their presence is a strain. I travelled down to London and stayed at his flat on Thursday, wch was not much better – I hardly slept at all. I saw a very nice TV children's programme, though, with a sweet little animal puppet that watched a chap painting. Bob lives in a basement flat in a house belonging to his married sister – it was her husband who is the specialist I spoke of.

Then on Friday I lunched with a *Telegraph* music critic (I paid!) who got me the job of jazz reviewing, then went to an Arts Council Committee. I couldn't get on the Pullman,[1] so had to take the 6.12 which got in about a quarter to eleven. Saturday was a lunch & meeting in Leeds, from wch I returned about seven. So you see I had quite a full week.

Today I have caught up with *The Archers* & remade my bed. I don't know what to do with my white sheets: they are six or seven years old, quite sound as far as I can see, but disgustingly grey, almost greyish-yellow. Sending them to the laundry makes no difference.

I have finished the cabbage and need another – there seem to be none round here. I have bought two different kinds of cress instead.

Bob took me to a party on Thursday where I met a man who said he'd just finished reading *Jill*, and funnily enough in Friday's *Guardian* it was mentioned in a review of a book on post war English fiction – where, again, it is apparently mentioned. Dead but won't lie down, unlike its author who lies down without being dead – yet.

I wonder if anything is coming up in your garden. From the train I saw plenty of lambs, but few buds. Fancy you commissioning the new electrical fittings! I don't expect they'll be very extravagant – you won't use mine much. Best love dear old creat.[2] P

1 Originally Pullman trains were run by the British Pullman Car Company (PCC; founded 1874), and offered a luxury first-class service with stewards on board on mainline routes. On nationalisation in 1948 agreements with the privately owned PCC were continued by British Railways, and in 1954 the PCC was bought by the British Transport Commission (BTC). After 1962 'Pullman' coaches were included in some trains in some regions. The final Pullman coaches were built by BR in 1966 and the last Pullman service, operating between London and Manchester, was discontinued in 1985.

2 The text continues up the right margin, forcing a cramped conclusion.

17 March 1963

<Letterhead> 32 Pearson Park, Hull

My dear old creature,

[. . .] I have been *terribly* busy recently. There is something about March that puts a tremendous strain on one. Both at work and at home I have had more than I can handle. However, I am trying not to get into a state about it, and last night got my two current poems finished after a fashion – I shall have to work on them some more, but there is a great relief in seeing your way through a thing and knowing how it will end, or can end. Fabers appear willing to republish *Jill*! I don't know if I told you, but a new American (and not very good) book on "Post War British Fiction" begins "In 1946 Philip Larkin published *Jill* . . ." This may arouse interest in it. I am hoping to go up & see them soon, & shall suggest that they do my next book of poems simultaneously. I hope I have enough now. But I rather shrink from the publicity. "Mr Larkin has not fulfilled his early promise . . ."

This seems all about me. Last Sunday I pasted all the Bunny cuttings into a scrapbook. They look very quaint.[1] There are a few snowdrops in the front garden here – so pretty and heartening, The stairs still smell of cat. I spilled some disinfectant down them this morning. [. . .]

I have had a report from my bank about share transactions I can't make head or tail of. They seem to be buying and selling. One day when I have time I shall have to go & see them.

Wish I had nothing to do all day, like some people![2]

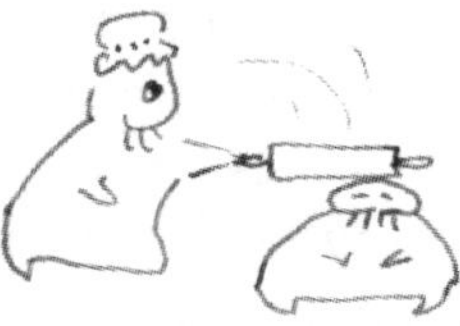

Try to go up & down the garden *for pleasure* when the sun is shining.

All love Philip

1 This may be a white lie. A good number of Bunny cuttings remain in their original envelopes and there is no Bunny scrapbook among Larkin's surviving effects.
2 On 26 March Eva wrote: 'Yes, it is a hard job to get any spare time, although I know you will hoot at the idea of *me* not having any.'

31 March 1963

<*Letterhead*> 32 Pearson Park, Hull

My very dear old creature,

[. . .] Mentioning food reminds me of your teeth. What a serious blow that the \new/ lot don't fit any better than the old new lot! I can understand your dislike of going back & reporting failure time after time, especially if he is a bit irascible, but what else can you do? It's strange how a set moulded from your actual gums still don't suit.

My literary news is that I am getting rid of my agent, & I have broken to George Hartley that I am giving Faber's my next collection. He was depressed about it, as I am about the only big name he has left, but I don't see the point of being published by a tiny spare-time back-room concern when I can be distributed by a proper publisher. Not that it makes any difference to the quality of the poems, wch is the main thing, of course. [. . .]

Very best love from Philip.

12 May 1963

<*Letterhead*> 32 Pearson Park, Hull

My dear old creature,

[. . .] There's not much to report this week. I have been typing out my poems slowly, in preparation for this next book. I'm afraid they are few & not very good. Brett[1] came in yesterday & said he was feeling rather worse – the shock treatment seemed to be wearing off, and his doctor was going to revert to "drugs". He seemingly feels depressed & unable to carry on. This doesn't really sound much like him, because he's a really very sane & humorous chap. Still, there you are. Betty says no more about her ailments. I do wonder about it! Anyone can have an operation, but two to four months! It *must* be serious. I asked if she was fit to go on working now, & she said she was. She is I think very tough & quite devoid of self-pity – a kind of character I find it hard to understand.

On Friday Maeve magnetised me to a dance at the University, where I felt my usual fish out of water self.[2] However, people were fairly tolerant. I do think I ought to know how to dance & drive a car! How badly educated I was! Quite unfitted for the modern world!

[. . .]

Has your sore spot from your teeth cleared up? I do hope so, & that you are "putting the bite on" all & sundry.[3] I wonder if you heard *Scrapbook for 1938* – ugh, what an awful time it was. Love!!

P.

1 Raymond L. Brett (1917–96): Professor of English at Hull (1952–82); best known for his edition (with A. R. Jones) of *Lyrical Ballads* by Wordsworth and Coleridge.
2 This occasion was the context for Larkin's unfinished poem 'The Dance', which he intended at first to include in the forthcoming *Whitsun Weddings*. Eva replied on 14 May: 'I'm glad Maeve got you to the dance. It would be a relaxation. You know I once said to Daddy "I think Philip should learn to dance", this was when we were at Warwick, but he thought it would put you off your studies.'
3 On 5 May Philip had written: 'P. G. Wodehouse calls borrowing money "putting the bite on" people. He also calls it "getting into their ribs." Both expressions make me laugh.'

16 June 1963

<*Letterhead*> 32 Pearson Park, Hull

My dear old creature,

[. . .] Faber's have now got my new book of poems & for the moment it is called "The Whitsun Weddings" [. . .] They say they like it, & will publish it "next spring", whatever that means. We must all try to live till then. Having typed all the poems out I find them gloomy &, in the main, mean-spirited.

My friend Bob Conquest is in America, & wrote to say he was off to Hollywood "to see Kim Novak" – this is a beautiful film star.

I didn't bother about this, but I had a postcard yesterday "Greetings from Hollywood" signed "Bob & Kim" – "Kim" had written her name in wavering green biro & added 5 kisses! This sent my stock up considerably in the Library.

Talking about celebrities, I had been fearing the coming to this University of Edith Sitwell, who was due to get an honorary doctorate – the VC asked me to dinner with (among others) her on Friday 28 June, & I went to great trouble to construct an excuse, arranging to go to Cambridge to see the architect. Now she isn't coming! and I have to go to Cambridge. It will be funny if I meet her there. [. . .]

I wonder what you are doing today, & if you have arranged to visit anyone. What a lovely tea you gave me & Monica, the cucumber sandwiches & cherry cake! Only at your house do faint traces of civilised living linger for me – sitting at table, etc. I haven't *got* a table, even. Nor has M.

Love!!! Philip

24 June 1963

Hull, of course!

My very dear old creature,

[. . .] In the course of turning out letters I have found a lot sent me in hospital in 1961 – people were very kind. I really have no idea what to do with them. To destroy letters is repugnant to me – it's like destroying a bit of life. Yet they mount up so. By the way, I don't think the card from Kim Novak was genuine – it was Bob pulling my leg. Well, I believed it for a while. Gullible creature! [. . .]

Very best love
Philip

15 August 1963

32 Pearson Park, Hull

My dear old creature,

I don't expect this will reach you till mid-afternoon on Saturday, when no doubt it will have "gone dark" & sea will be breaking over the promenade.[1]

It was very kind of you to send a letter when you were so busy. I'm sure the weather has got on your nerves – it has been so grey and sad here, I've been restless & depressed. Yet Monica said on the telephone last night it had been sunny all day there!

Do have a good time. I hope the hotel is comfortable and you find some congenial spirits –

let me know how you get on.

Love to both – I'll do a separate card for A. Nellie.

Philip

1 The letter is addressed to Mrs E. E. Larkin, Cliftonville Hotel, Cromer, where Eva was on holiday with Nellie.

1 September 1963

32 Pearson Park, Hull

My dear old creature,

[. . .] Betty didn't come back to work, she just called in to have tea.[1] However she looked at what I'd been doing & pointed out mistakes that had cost the University some £38. I don't think she will come back till mid-October! Apparently she tires easily, if she gets about much.

I smiled at the thought of you looking at the birds.

I sent *Jill* off yesterday, but the man who deals with me has gone on holiday, so I don't know what their reaction will be. I am on the point of signing a contract for it. I have written an introduction full of gossip about Kingsley & Bruce: I expect they'll be cross, but it's all quite complimentary gossip. [. . .]

Much love,
Philip

1 Betty was still on a prolonged medical break.

15 September 1963

32 Pearson Park, Hull

My very dear old creature,

[. . .] I have felt rather hunted recently – an awful literary layabout tried to force his company on me on Thursday night – I got shut of him – then I was in fear & trembling of two "fans" from Doncaster who announced their intention to be in Hull on Friday & Saturday. I didn't answer their letter – didn't answer the telephone on Saturday – didn't answer the doorbell – but eventually there came a tapping at the glass

& the dark shadow of bodies . . . They turned out to be two quite nice young men, & I gave them large gins & tonics while I ate some sausages & got dressed in order to go out to Betty's.[1] But it took 1½ hours of my time, during wch I had meant to write a letter . . . Awgh, awgh . . . [. . .] I went out to Betty's to play cards, which was all right. She was in fine form: the surgeon says she can come back to work on Tuesday week – and play badminton! – so she is full of high spirits. [. . .]

Love Philip

1 The visitors were Harry Chambers and David Selzer. See Harry Chambers, 'Visiting Mr Larkin', in Thwaite, *Larkin at Sixty*, 61–2.

6 October 1963

<*Letterhead*> 32 Pearson Park, Hull

My dear old creature,

Well, I am back after my tour, which I am afraid was too crowded to enable me to send my usual Saturday card. I went to London on Tuesday, where I handed in my final version of *The Whitsun Weddings* to Fabers and had a short talk with T. S. Eliot, who said, as he said before & as I expect he says to all young (!) authors, that he was glad to have me on their list. [. . .]

Very best love
Philip

17 November 1963

32 Pearson Park, Hull

My very dear old creature,

I feel in rather poor spirits this morning (for a change!), perhaps because of a late night last night, but I will try not to sound too doleful, as I expect by the time you read it I shall be in better fettle – I shall, as a matter of fact, be in the train going to London, as I have to spend tomorrow visiting the architects. A tiresome business, going there & back in one day.

My irritability (!) continues, and I really do find the people below noisy with their doors. The other night I counted the number of times they shut one or other (not necessarily banged) & it came to 38 in 2 hours – or nearly once every three minutes. It breaks my train of thought to say the least of it. I can't think how they move around so much! So much these days I feel things are wearing thin, and am aware of the bottomless depths that lie beneath them. No doubt I need more exercise, or something.

It is a damp chilly morning & I took a few photographs in the Park to finish off a roll. There was another person also doing so, a middle-aged lady with a cheap camera, & we had a brief talk about how the pond needed cleaning out (it is full of leaves). I thought of how we had walked round when you were here – I believe I took some pictures then, didn't I? I've quite forgotten what they were.

Oh dear, these slippers – well, I have a pair of Moreland's wine-coloured fleece lined ones at present, & they are very nice.[1] [. . .]

I expect you saw that Kingsley has published another novel – it is readable, like all he does, but not especially interesting or likable.[2] Monica says the Church Times reviewed it – I'd like to see what they say. He says a few things about religion which aren't designed to please: he makes his hero a Catholic, I don't know why.

An aunt of Betty's died this week, wch has depressed her. In fact I thought she looked ill this week. [. . .]

My best love: constantly thinking of you. P.

<*At top of first page opposite address*> Bought 4 pairs of pants yesterday!

1 Eva was considering giving him a pair of slippers for Christmas.
2 *One Fat Englishman* (London: Gollancz, 1963).

24 November 1963

32 Pearson Park, Hull

My very dear old creature,

I don't like Sundays as much as I used to, since I am in perpetual dread of a horn starting up from below.[1] Now it's just about 11.30 a.m., danger time as far as last Sunday went, & then we had *another* dose in the afternoon. Door banging has continued sporadically, & I am furious to relate that a *cat* has been imported. This event was celebrated by a fouling of the stairs unequalled since the age of Wilks. In fact, I feel things have deteriorated since his time!

Still, I won't howl until hurt. Thank you for your words of comfort – I'm sure you don't bang doors in the same way: it w^{d} be quite alien to your nature. I went to London on Monday, & talked with the architects, and then again on Thursday for a poetry manuscripts subcommittee. You may know that for some years I have been concerned with the drift of literary mss. to USA, & now a scheme has been set up to form a collection in cooperation with the B Museum – only in a small way, of course, but it has started. They now want some of mine! Oh dear! [. . .]

It's a dull windy day, not unfriendly looking, but I am not sure what to do with it. No horn so far! Touch wood! I hope your neighbours are quiet – funny how they keep hanging on, isn't it?

Very best love, dear old creature P.

1 A family called Burnett Hall had moved into the flat below Philip's, one or more of whose members played the horn.

9 December 1963 Postcard.

<*Postmark*> Hull

Arrived here 45 mins late after frightful journey – *all* trains unheated. Have written to the *D. Telegraph* about it!

Made some packet soup (leek) when I got in: the pie had vanished on the way!

There were no signs of fog or any other kind of hazard. Monica seemed well but her lunch compared very poorly with yours! Almost all cold, intentionally or unintentionally!

Love P.

1964

8 January 1964

32 Pearson Park, Hull

My very dear old creature,

This is to wish you all happiness on your birthday.[1] I wonder where you will be on that morning – at Kitty's, or at home? Wherever you are, I hope it will be a fine day, & that something especially nice will happen, like Mr Cann calling, or something.

Having said that, I must confess I haven't yet got any present to send you. I prowled all round Harrods on Tuesday, & all round Hammonds today,[2] but both places had sales on, & it was very hard to find anything that was not shopsoiled & reduced. I lingered a *very long time* this afternoon over a shopping basket on wheels:

I *nearly* had them send it you, but I didn't because I didn't want to *worry* you.[3] I am afraid lest you wd find it a nuisance – "driving" it, and where to keep it in the house, for instance, – but it seemed quite strong and light & easy to manage. And very capacious! So if you think you would find one useful, do let me know, and I'll have one sent. [. . .]

Maeve is off with a bad cold. She says people at work were treating her like a leper.

I haven't heard from Monica yet: she returned on Monday.

I am rather snowed under with work, and am missing Betty terribly. She is, as you know, staying with her married brother for a week. The architect called today & we had dinner together, discussing our plans. The present cost is £1,000,000! No doubt the government will step in and clip chanticleer's comb close. It all seems terribly unreal, lifts going 150ft per ¼ minute, and so on.

Well, once again I send my love, old creature: I hope you have a happy day with nothing to make you gibber. I shall be with you in spirit, and hope you will join me in a *glass*

to celebrate.

All love, Philip.

1 Eva's seventy-eighth birthday was on 10 January.
2 Hammonds was the largest department store in Hull at the time.
3 See Appendix for Eva's response on 12 January 1964.

12 January 1964

32 Pearson Park, Hull

My dear old creature,

[. . .] When I was in London, I bought 4 "beer goblets" at Harrods – reduced to 15/- each – and they came yesterday. They are huge, holding over a pint each. I don't suppose I shall use them for beer. They make even one of my large gin & tonics look pretty insignificant.

Well, I am beginning to get hungry again (2.45 p.m.). I do hope you are going along peacefully. If you don't want the shopping basket on wheels, what w[d] you like?

Very best love. P.

18 January 1964

32 Pearson Park, Hull

My very dear old creature,

I expect having folded this paper in this way will lead to trouble when it comes to putting it in the envelope! It's easier to handle it this way, though

Well, I am writing this on Saturday as Sunday may well be occupied, wch means I haven't gone into town for my shopping. For lunch I had a tinned s. & k. pie, & pretty horrible it was – I had one many years ago, & must have hated it then, as I never had one since. Strange flesh! (You remember Mark Antony – I think – said that as a soldier he was freed to feed on 'strange flesh'.)[1]

I'm glad to say my cough shows signs of departing. I must have caught it in London, & it has been really troublesome. I still cough early in the morning and have been taking Gee's.[2]

Lloyds Executor & Trustee Department has put my NALGO money into Dowty Group (machinery), Shell, and Scottish & Newcastle Breweries. They say "first class equity shares are the best medium for safeguarding capital against inflation." Don't ask me what equity shares are! This kind of thing, I suppose.

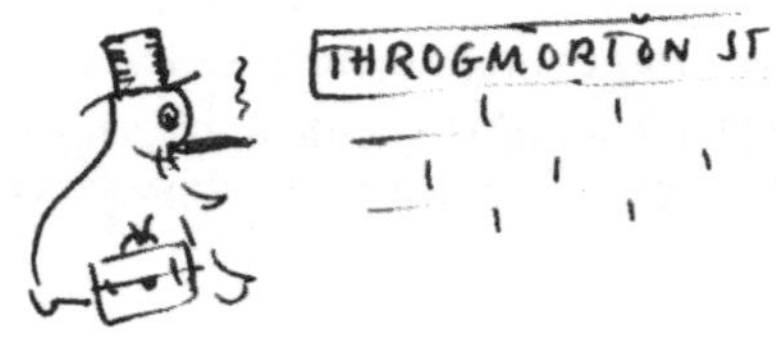

This has been quite a busy week, though I haven't been out except to dinner with a lecturer in American History & his wife. They have a little adopted coloured girl of 4½ who seemed extremely intelligent & pretty.[3] I had lamb & a nice sweet, but *suffered* through lack of water.

Bunny must have gone to sleep for the winter. "Immers'd in furs Doze the gross race" – Thomson, about the Eskimos,[4] but it sounds like rabbits, doesn't it? I was touched by your account of Beauty gazing at Kitty as if he understood what she said – I can't pretend I'm very fond of Beauty, but anything that loves & is loved is worth preserving. I hope his other abscess heals.[5]

The BH's continue noisy – they were playing the piano last night so noisily that I thought they had moved it into their bedroom under my sitting room – but when I went into *my* bedroom I felt as if I was *in* the piano, it was so clear! – and noisy! How the Phillipses stand it I don't know.[6]

Have you told me about the men lodgers next door? They are new to me. Today is very clear and frosty. The article you read by me provoked several letters of agreement and I shall try to get the record companies to do something.[7] I have been writing for the D.T. now for three whole years – never a month missed! I have to do 2 in Feb Ogh ogh!!

Would it be all right if I were to come home next Friday? I think I should spend Sat. in Leics. Sunday in L'boro, as I haven't seen M since before Xmas.

Sunday. I have just a little spare time, so I add a line or two.[8] It is a dull, slightly misty morning. I thought you might have heard from Alice's sister and Uncle, sorry Cousin, Walter, but the former may be busy & the latter too worried.

I am using the beer goblets for gin & tonics – I can put plenty of ice in without fear of overflowing, In fact I can see why they didn't sell – they are far too large to hold comfortably, even with my size of hand, but I like them because they are so outrageously large.[9]

The BH's have woken up down below – I thought I heard a strange note on a pipe. In addition to their horns & the piano, they have some kind of pipe, or clarinet. How I suffer!

Monica has been very busy & consequently tired. I don't know why she doesn't get organised more – it's easy to talk I know, but she could surely have written her lectures over Christmas, instead of leaving them till the night before. All these holidays lecturers have . . .

Well, I must do a little tidying and shoe-cleaning. I hope you are keeping yourself well & warm. Have you any flowers in your garden yet?

With best love
Philip

1 Shakespeare, *Antony and Cleopatra*, I. iv.
2 Cough linctus or pastilles.
3 P. A. M. (Philip) and Miriam Taylor. Philip Taylor later became Professor of American History in the Department of American Studies at Hull.
4 James Thomson, *Winter*, 943–4, *The Seasons* (1730).
5 In a letter of 14 January Eva had written: 'I am glad to say that Beauty is much better and is eating his food again. I don't know whether the abscesses will heal permanently. [. . .] "Poor Beauty", but how he does love Kitty. When she speaks to him he gazes at her in dumb devotion. I'm sure he knows what she says.'
6 Ground floor neighbours. See Moira Phillips, 'Larkin Recollected', *About Larkin* 33 (2012), 11.
7 The *Daily Telegraph* article was 'The Billy Banks Sides' (11 January 1964; *All What Jazz*, revised edition, 103–4). An LP of Billy Banks's recordings was made in 1970. See Richard Palmer and John White (eds), *Larkin: Jazz Writings, Essays and Reviews 1940–84* (Continuum, 2004), 168.
8 On a larger sheet of paper.
9 See Booth, *Philip Larkin: Life, Art and Love*, Plate 18.

2 February 1964

32 Pearson Park, Hull

My very dear old creature,

How profoundly thankful I am that the weather is mild & fine! When I think of the appalling time we had last year – the worst winter since 1740 – I think how nice it is now.

I had a big surprise this week on Friday, in that some advance copies of *The Whitsun Weddings* came. Now to save myself work – lazy creature – I have asked Fabers to send out copies in my name to people who live out of Hull (that small minority), & so you will be getting yours by post from them: however, it is not to be published until 28 Feb (why not 29th), so it may not arrive till nearer that date. I'm sorry for the delay. It is a thin book with an extremely ugly jacket: however, it's exciting to have it. The poems seem different in mood. Its motto might be: if you don't like it, turn over, the next one is quite different. But on the whole it's an unimpressive lot. I dread the reviews. There's no news of *Jill* so far – expect it won't be far behind. [. . .]

What are they all doing at Bunny? Much love Philip

1 March 1964

Hull

My very dear old creature,

My journey back was prompt, for once! We got in at 8.55 – there was no waiting at Derby at all.

You will be amused to know that a girl invaded my compartment with a copy of my book to autograph! Also, after Rotherham a young man I know slightly did the same! It all sounds very famous, but I expect the girl was a Hull student & knew me by sight. Still, she had the book.[1]

When I got in I ate the pork pie – very nice. Also had some Horlicks. There was an invitation waiting for me to the reception after Bob's wedding on 4 April, in the wilds of C. Durham or somewhere.[2] Can't think how I shall get there, if I go.

Thank you for all your kindness – that meat was really quite nice, wasn't it?

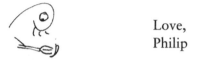

Love,
Philip

1 In her letter of 3 March Eva related that a Mrs Stubbs had suddenly asked at a meeting of the Circle of Silent Ministry: '"Have you brought the book of poems with you?" We were quite a small gathering, only five, so therefore more cosy and intimate. Miss Unwin, our Leader was very thrilled and interested, and would like me to take the poems for her to read.'

2 After two divorces Conquest married Caroleen MacFarlane, his third wife, in 1964. They divorced in 1978.

5 March 1964

32 Pearson Park, Hull

My dear old creature,

Thank you for your letter that arrived first post today as usual. I'm glad you found the weekend exciting – it was, really, wasn't it? Old poet-creature. The shops here have quite sold out – the university branch had 50! It was a very nice weekend & I did like my lunch. I'm sorry the meat doesn't look so nice. I have found a kind of frozen rissole called "porklet" or something – I do eat strange flesh![1]

You'll be surprised to hear that on Tuesday I bought a car! I don't suppose I shall use it much, but it will be very useful getting about in Hull & exploring the country. It is a Singer with an automatic gearbox w[ch] makes it very easy & (I hope) safe to drive. I must confess that I told K. & W.[2] last Sunday that I had ordered one as they knew I had learned to drive but it only came on Tuesday. I didn't want to have you worrying until I felt fairly confident about it: as long as I don't do anything rash I think it will be all right. So don't worry! Please!

The B-H's[3] have asked me to dinner on Sunday! and they have stopped playing their horns, at least for the moment, so that is good. I had a nice letter from Mary[4] that said Helen like[d] going down to the bottom of the orchard where there was a mass of snowdrops. Doesn't that sound nice?

Very best love P

<At top of first page opposite address> Yes. I hope Daddy knows of my writing, but he did know of some of it, didn't he?[5] I wonder if he w^d have liked my latest.

1 See note to letter of 18 January 1964.
2 Kitty and Walter.
3 Burnett Halls.
4 Mary Judd, formerly Wrench. Philip and Betty Mackereth were godparents to Helen, Mary's infant daughter.
5 Eva wrote (3 March 1964) that, after the meeting of the Circle of Silent Ministry, 'Miss Mee (spiritualist) walked along with me for a short distance coming home and during our conversation, which was mainly about your writing I remarked that I wished your Father could know and she replied "He does know. There is no death, you know, we live in another body."'

24 May 1964

32 Pearson Park, Hull

My very dear old creature,

[. . .] Reading about Whitsun makes me think I was lucky to get back alive! I think what the roads need is (a) a speed limit (b) plenty of patrolling police with power to fine on the spot. I drove out a little yesterday afternoon, as far as Brough, a place I have never been to.[1] It wasn't very interesting, but the sight of the river was nice. It is queer to feel I can "go anywhere" now!

I went to London & saw the TV man: he took me to Ealing where the famous Comedies were made, & showed me some films made of Ezra Pound, Robert Graves, & John Betjeman. They weren't very good. I also handed over "to the nation" one of my poetry notebooks – one of Auden's has just been bought for £600, so I thought as I gave it I was probably doing myself damage.[2] Mine covered 1944 to 1950, or Wellington & Leicester – curious unfocused years. It will go to the British Museum. Of course, the Americans have been doing this for years.

[. . .] I can hear a rook calling – ark, ark, ark. Go & clean the car, it seems to be saying.

Very much love, Philip

1 A small town on the Humber estuary twelve miles to the west of Hull; site of the Roman Petuaria.

2 On 26 May Eva wrote: 'By the way, what did you mean when you wrote that you thought by handing your poetry notebook over you might be doing yourself damage?' He replied on 31 May: 'I meant that in presenting my ms to the BM I was giving away something that might have fetched a lot of money. It doesn't show me as a v. good poet either. It's amazing how all through 1944–1950, or nearly, I wrote absolutely badly in quite the wrong way. There is absolutely no evidence that I should *ever* write anything worth reading – assuming I ever have, of course.'

6 June 1964[1]

32 Pearson Park, Hull

My very dear old creature,

I am just snatching a moment before they "come for" me at 10, if they do come for me – all arrangements are liable to sudden change. This whole affair is proving one of the most exhausting undertakings I have ever agreed to[2] – there is far too much to tell you: on Wednesday I was filmed in the Library, on Thursday in the fishdock (up at 6!) & a ruined chapel, & recorded in my flat, on Friday in a church over the river at Barton, on Saturday in my flat talking to Betjeman, who is here for a few days (he was much taken with Virginia!)[3] Today there are supposed to be further conversations with B. on the ferry, but the trouble is the weather. It has been dull & rainy all the time & is quite spoiling the whole project. When I think of all the fine weather in May I feel quite disappointed.

I'm not doing it at all well, but I suppose they will edit it till it looks better.

Betjeman was also much excited by the picture I have that Uncle Alf left me, & says it is a De Wint.[4] I doubt this!

I was interested to hear ab[t] the Sunnyville[5] – it sounds a shade homely but no doubt they will be friendly. I feel like coming home myself for a rest! but alas, there's no chance of this.

The BBC stood Betty a special hair-do so that she could appear as my "loaf-haired secretary". Betjeman has brought his Teddy-bear Archie, also a girl called Lady Elizabeth Cavendish.

I shall be relieved to get back to normal!

Love d.o.c. Philip

1 Larkin wrote '6 June (is it?) 1964'. The postmark is 7 June (Sunday).

2 Filming of the BBC *Monitor* feature 'Down Cemetery Road' took place between 3 and 10 June.
3 Larkin's wickerwork rabbit. See Plate 16A & B. Betjeman was deeply attached to his battered teddy-bear, Archie, mentioned later in this letter.
4 Uncle Alf had possessed a collection of fine china and glass. Peter De Wint (1784–1849) was a celebrated English landscape painter.
5 Eva had written to hotels and boarding houses in Southport, where she and Nellie were intending to take a holiday.

10 June 1964

32 PEARSON PARK
HULL

My very dear old creature,

I have a few minutes before "they" come at 10 a.m. for what is promised to be the last session of all – just one of me looking down into the park. Oh dear, what a week it has been. Yesterday Betjeman & I did our final conversation in my burial ground – what it will sound like I can't imagine: one just blurts out anything that comes into one's head. Funnily enough, the man in charge of the whole programme "Monitor" has resigned, or left, or something: it will be funny if the new man (not yet appointed) decides to scrap the whole thing! Towards the end it began to seem more like a programme about Hull introduced by Betjeman. I suggested they should call it "To Hull with John Betjeman."

Thank you *very* much for the letter that arrived on Monday. I'm afraid you are being sadly bothered by the weather. Dear old creature, remember that you have gone unharmed through so many years, it's unlikely that you'll be hurt now. Think more about crossing roads.

Last night I had dinner with the producer[1] (I paid) & we then went to a funny sort of music hall where you can sit at tables & have drinks & watch 3rd rate acts. They are interested in making a film of it, it strikes them as interesting. I must say it wasn't bad. Daddy might have liked it: it's rather in the German style.

Had better end now. Much love P

1 Patrick Garland.

14 June 1964

32 Pearson Park, Hull

My very dear old creature,

This is the kind of day *I* don't particularly care for – dull & still & warm. One is awfully hot at night – almost nothing is bearable. On the whole I feel rather low – physically as the result of a party last night, quite a nice one & I left well before the end, but fatiguing none the less; spiritually by reason of the feeling that what little of my life that isn't *irrevocably over* I am WASTING. I had one or two *bad* reviews recently, which I don't really mind but there they are. Some Australian paper thinks I embody everything bad in poetry at present! I don't think I do. Actually I don't embody anything at present, good or bad, since I don't write *anything*.

On Friday I fulfilled a longstanding promise and allowed Betty to drive me out into the country for dinner in my car. We went to the place at Holme where I went once before with the architects: I had duck again. It was very nice. Betty is an odd person: under, or alongside, her stern secretary manner is a completely frivolous, almost skittish person, a kind of schoolgirl that giggles at the back of the class. She was telling me how at 18 she was directed into industry (that w^{d} be about 1942) and trained as a factory inspector. She even learnt how to weld! This threw her into a pretty rough world and I sometimes suspect nothing since has ever made much impression on her. Of course, I may be wrong. She'll be 40 this month, and is much looking forward to her TV appearance.[1] [. . .]

My salary has gone up to £3950! Far more than I am worth. I expect everybody else is paid more, wch will be more than they are worth, too.

Thank you for the cuttings – I saw the *Yorks. Post* one. Bunny United have been in a bad way before.[2] I don't suppose they are very conscientious about gate-money! [. . .]

Best love – Philip

1 Eva responded on 16 June: 'I was very interested in all you wrote about Betty. When I first saw her I thought how serious, almost grim she was, but during the evening she relaxed and became quite gay and entertaining. She will enjoy seeing herself on T.V.' She continued: 'How is Maeve these days? and Monica, you have'nt [*sic*] mentioned her for some time.'

2 The cutting is lost.

26 August 1964 Picture postcard[1]

<*Postmark*> Carnforth Lancs.

We are here today, having eaten our lunch in Sawrey, where Beatrix Potter's house is. Nicer day, very warm (even *close*) – I hope you are enjoying yourselves & getting plenty of rest after lunch.

You w^{d} enjoy some of the views here, though mist & cloud tend to obscure the bigger hills. I'm feeling tired as usual on holidays!

Love P

1 The Square, Hawkshead. Addressed to Sunnyville Hotel, Alexandra Road, Southport, Lancs., where Eva was on holiday with Nellie.

6 September 1964

Haydon Bridge

My very dear old creature,

This is just a quick note to say that I've got so far safely and expect to return to Hull tonight. The weather broke as we left and *rained* all the way home, very disagreeable, & my car developed a leak!!! It's also cluttered up with numerous crumbs & a smell of apples, remnants of packed lunches.

We feel rather sad at the end of the holiday, wch has been successful and shown us a part of the country we didn't know before.[1] [. . .]

I'll send you a note to say I'm back, assuming I do complete the journey safely.

Very much love, in wch M joins,
Philip

1 Dentdale and Swaledale in Cumbria.

13 September 1964

32 Pearson Park, Hull

My very dear old creature,

Once again I am sitting in my bedroom in a patch of sunlight, embarking on my weekly task of "writing home". I suppose I have been doing this now for 24 years! on and off, you know: well, I am happy to be able to do so, and I only hope my effusions are of some interest to you on all the different Monday mornings when they have arrived. I feel a bit out of practice at present, and my handwriting isn't in consequence as steady as it might be.

From your saying that Kitty has invited you both to tea I conclude that "the Chelsea pensioner" is still with you.[1] Is this a little longer than she meant to stay? I hope if so that it means you are enjoying yourselves. I made a feeble effort to get Kitty's "handbag torch" for her birthday yesterday, but without any success: there seem to be pocket torches, some of them rechargeable, but they strike me as being rather large for a handbag. I don't want to weigh her down with something she doesn't want.

You'll be amused to hear that I left my tweed hat at Cally, but it was sent on. What a disreputable old thing it is! I always leave something behind. It has been a strange week of re-acclimatisation, not really very pleasant: I find I don't settle back to work at all happily. Betty seems cheerful & able to support my depression – she appears to be carrying on with a married lecturer in the Department of Sociology, wch no doubt raises her spirits & enables her to carry me. Every cloud has a silver lining! Not, I suppose, that she sees it as a cloud. People are trickling back, one by one – it really is awful, this prospect of another year's work![2] And yet I'd sooner have it than not. I suppose my next "loathly bird"[3] is a conference of librarians *here*[4] the week after next – 22nd–26th, I believe. I hope the weather is reasonably fine for them. I don't have to address them, apart from a few words of welcome when they come to see the Library, but I dread not having anything to show them. To make it worse, there are 11 Americans among them, and Americans have such wonderful libraries.

On Friday I spent a lot of time sorting out unneeded old clothes and made up a bundle wch Betty had offered to dispose of. Really, I don't know how I got some of the things. It was a little sad unpicking the name tapes – mine & Daddy's – wch you had sewn on years ago in your devoted way. What a good, dear old creature you are![5]

Thank you for all your care. A lot of the things are too awful to go to a jumble sale, and I am hoping to sneak up to the university dustbins this afternoon & cram them in. I hope they don't come home to roost in any way.

I don't know whether to come home next weekend (Friday 18th) or not – I should like to come some weekend soon, but it's not easy, with this conference in the wind. Perhaps I could let you know later in the week – I don't mind a bit of dust about!

There won't be anything in the *London Mag.* this month. T.W.W. is just being published in America – the U.S. ed. has a huge picture of me on the back, sitting by the sign "England".

Best love to the C.P.[6] & dearest love to you. xx P.

1 Nellie Day.

2 Eva replied on 15 September: 'Fancy you leaving your tweed hat at Cally. What a good thing it was returned to you. I found a vest of yours here, and washed it this week. It looks quite a new one. / Am sorry that you feel depressed at the thought of settling down for another year's work. Betty is very good, isn't she! How I wish I had been born with an optimistic temperament – like A. Nellie! She is busy knitting, a little coat for her \great/ grand daughter Denise. I hope she doesn't find it too dull here, for I seem to always have something to do.'

3 The phrase describes the shantak, a 'noisome and hippocephalic bird' in *The Dream Quest of Unknown Kadath* (1943) by H. P. Lovecraft.

4 Triply underlined.

5 In her letter of 15 September Eva wrote: 'I was also much moved at the thought of you unpicking those name tapes and I felt somewhat sad, and overwhelmed by your kind words. / Sewing on name tapes, boning the meat and cutting off the bacon rinds were things which I was brought up to do.'

6 'Chelsea Pensioner': Nellie.

22 October 1964

32 Pearson Park, Hull

My dear old creature,

Well, I am about recovered by now, Thursday evening – I still feel a bit aching in the back, but I no longer feel like drowning myself when I awake in the morning! Unfortunately, I still have a great deal to do.

I had much enjoyment from your letter this morning – you are funny about your face & hat! On the contrary, you have rather a nice rosy old face when it isn't screwed up in anticipation of a storm. And you being suspicious of your hat![1]

As if it was going to bite you, or get at your handbag.

I trailed in rather late in the mornings this week, which hasn't been too bad, but now has broken up and cooled considerably. I put the car away at about nine this evening in the rain, & floundered into a puddle in the dark, very deep, very wet [. . .]

On Saturday I go down to Swansea to stay two nights with Vernon Watkins – I am to try to get him to sell some manuscripts to the British Museum. I shall spend Monday getting back! So again, no letter – I may manage a card.

Love to all, especially you. Philip

1 In a letter of 20 October Eva had mentioned how her appearance in a photograph taken by Nellie's son Kenneth had displeased her: 'I don't like *my* face at all! I look so *plain* and I realize that my hat does not suit me at all. I have been suspicious about it all the summer. You must pass your opinion about them when you next visit me.'

29 October 1964 Picture postcard[1]

<*Postmark*> Hull 8.30 a.m.

Just setting off by train I'm glad to say, but have had y[r] letter. Hope Kitty's whine & jeers party goes well! It is dank & autumnal here. *The Jerusalem Post* (!) gave me a good review entitled "Toads At The Wedding", w[ch] amuses me highly – w[d] have called the book this had I thought! Now I must get train – back on Sunday.

Much love Philip

1 Kitten wearing a blue satin bow.

29 November 1964

32 Pearson Park, Hull

My very dear old creature,

Well, here I am back again, and as you will expect it has turned pretty chilly in my absence, meaning another blanket on the bed & some warmer underclothes. What a beautiful autumn it's been! How fond I am of mild days! I don't look forward to the cold weather at all – but then I never do.

I have duly seen my film, going down to Ealing for the purpose: I found it interesting, but I doubt if anyone who didn't know me or Hull would. It rather makes me the "poet of Hull" w[ch] is silly, as I don't really care about the place: in fact in retrospect most of my personal comments in the film sounded boring or silly. There's some nice camera work while the poems are being read, though, & a wonderfully dramatic appearance by Betty. It still has to be cut, alas – it was for 28½ minutes, now I think it'll have to be shortened to something like 20 – so some of what I saw you won't. They seem to think it *may* be put on on Dec 15[1] – is that Tuesday? – but don't believe anything until you see in the *R. Times*.

Afterwards I went with the producer & John Betjeman to the Ritz (!) for lunch. The room was pretty, but otherwise the experience was not remarkable.

I was glad to have your letter to take to London with me. Do you hold shares in Lloyds? I didn't know. I don't.

Every year I hate Christmas more & more – I just want to go into my burrow until it's over – and this year looks like being worse than most. [. . .]

Much love Philip

1 It was.

1 December 1964

32 Pearson Park, Hull

My very dear old creature,

Thank you very much for your "extra" letter wch I received yesterday – I thought I w^{d} delay answering it until I had heard from Hexham. I now learn they can take me, so I shall go.[1] I think we had better regard this year as a switch-round of the normal pattern – Christmas with you, Monica in January – and look forward to when *you* come here in January.[2] It will be nice to have you here for your birthday – perhaps we can have "a few people in" (don't groan!)

I think I shall very likely see you before then – at least I could spend the night of Friday Dec. 11th at home if you were kind enough to receive me.

I have a Conference in Nottingham Univ^{y}. on Saturday & Sunday (12 & 13) so shall be down this way. I have to rush home on the 13th as I have a publication committee on 14th here.

I think it would be a good idea if you & I came back here on January 1st (Friday) in order to be able to shop, & then I have this dinner on 2nd. I still haven't made up my mind about the Coveneys' Christening on 31 Dec. (in Nottingham). If I went to it I should have to come home on 30th Dec., I suppose. More of this later.

I did appreciate the kind things you said in your letter, and of course this is not the Christmas I would have planned myself; nor do I feel happy about your being on your own then. I will try to make it up to you in January!

Please do not *worry* about it, though: I think it falls to me to look after you while Kitty & Walter are away, & I don't want not to see Monica. That's all. [. . .]

Next Friday the Hartleys are coming round to settle up for *The Less Deceived* for the preceding year. I gather it is still selling at a copy a day! wch isn't bad after nine years. [. . .]

To keep warm just put on your big radiator full! I'll send you a cheque when you are hard up.

With very best love, dear old creature. Philip

<In pencil on different paper>

2 December 1964

This Bit First!

Like you, I doubt if I have expressed myself very well: reading what I wrote it seems a bit chilly! You know I'm not cross with you, & not really with K. & W., but I do feel bound to change my arrangements in consequence of the situation created by their holiday, & I don't see why A. Nellie sh^{d} be bothered. Whatever I do will hurt someone. It's all very difficult.

Monitor will be on on *Dec. 15th*.[3]

Love, d.o.c.
Philip

1 Philip had inquired about booking a hotel in Hexham for his visit to Monica in the New Year. Walter and Kitty, however, had decided to take a skiing holiday in Switzerland after Christmas, which would leave Eva on her own at that time. Philip felt under pressure to change his arrangements so as to be with her then. On 15 November he wrote to Eva: 'I think this holiday of Kitty's presents a problem – it puts me in a position of having to neglect either you or Monica.' His proposal was that he should holiday with Monica at Christmas and visit Eva afterwards while Kitty and Walter were away. On 18 November he wrote: 'I should dearly love *not* to come home for Christmas, just as a reprisal (& to get out of *that frightful tea*).'
2 In her 'extra' letter (29 November) Eva reproached Philip for not intending to visit her over Christmas: 'My real object in writing is to say how very sorry indeed we shall all be if you cannot see your way to come for Christmas. When Kitty mentioned it to Walter & Rosemary that you might not come, they were very sad. Kitty said last night that when Walter first mentioned the holiday, he thought vaguely that A. Nellie would perhaps come here, or I should go there. He did not dream of hurting your feelings in any way . . . Do you think I should ask her? /

The other alternative would be for me to stay here on my own while K. & W. were away, if you changed your mind and came.'
3 Doubly underlined.

3 December 1964

32 Pearson Park, Hull

My very dear old creature,

How kind of A. Nellie to offer, but this all complicates things even more, doesn't it?[1] It makes my arrangements seem rather silly. I don't know what to say. I acted quickly because of the hotel. I still feel W. should have given some thought for you & those who might be expected to keep you company.

I find it exceedingly hard to know what to do for the best! Certainly it w^{d} be easier to cancel Hexham, but I feel a little committed there now. And what do you feel? W^{ch} destination would seem more fun in January?

Friday Very late & tired – yesterday killed me. Many thanks for your letter – let us brood on it a little longer. Like you, I am scared of the weather!

How strange about the butterfly. What a wonderful experience. I must always remember it.[2] Don't you remember what one caterpillar said to the other as a b'fly flew overhead? "They'll never get me up in one of those things."

Love as ever
Philip

1 In a lettercard dated 1 December Eva wrote: 'This is a hurried note, really a S.O.S.!! I have had a surprise letter from A. Nellie this morning in which she asks if I am fixed up for the time when K. & W. go away. They offer to have me if I would like to go, although she says she cannot promise me a calm placid visit for over there it always seems hectic.'
2 In a follow-up letter to the S.O.S. lettercard, also dated 1 December, Eva wrote: 'I must tell you a strange thing which happened to me in church last Sunday morning. I was sitting in the pew (the only occupant) when I felt something hit the top of my hat and before I had time to investigate this unusual assault something bounced off my hat onto my lap. I was amazed to see that it was a beautiful butterfly! I gently picked it up and placed it on the ledge of the pew. It stayed there for some little time, I really think it was stupefied, and I was wondering whether to put it in my

handbag and take it home after the service and find it a sheltered nook somewhere in the garden, when it flew away across the church. What puzzled me was that there should *be* a butterfly about at this season. I thought they all turned into caterpillars at the end of the summer or something like that. (Have looked up butterflies in the encyclopaedia & find it is the caterpillar which turns into butterfly.)'

6 December 1964

32 Pearson Park, Hull

My very dear old creature,

[. . .] Regarding your butterfly, there was by coincidence a paragraph about butterflies in winter in the *Telegraph* on Saturday. Apparently they like cold – isn't that odd, when they are summer creatures? I'll send the cutting if I can find it.[1]

It seems they eat sugar or honey. I didn't know they lived through the winter.

I expect you are still worrying about Christmas, as I am. The only drawbacks about you coming here 1–11 January are that you would be alone for Christmas, & that bad weather might upset me in Hexham where *I* should be. If you came here I would fetch you on, say, 1 Jan., & take you back at some time suitable to myself. I don't want you to be unhappy at Christmas, dear old creature – w[d] you be? No doubt K. & W. w[d] do something to cheer you up. You sound as if you aren't too keen on going to Hyde.

Anyway, I shall be coming home on Friday, I hope, & we can talk about it then. Having made the Christmas suggestion to Monica it might disappoint her if I withdrew it now. We'll see. I haven't had any comments from her, but I'm sure she won't want to influence me either way. She never does!

I hope things are going well. I dreamed about you & Daddy the other night – *You* were dead & Daddy was alive. Tomorrow night is the University S.C.R. Christmas dinner – I tried to get a new dress suit for it, but there wasn't time – the trousers of the old one are too tight! Funny how one's clothes shrink over the years. It is quite a jolly occasion, but I shall have to keep sober this year as for the first time I shall have my car.

Fancy, you going to Church. I sometimes think I should like to – there was a fascinating programme on the wireless on Saturday about how people imagined God. I wish you had heard it. Now I must write a card to Monica. The Hartleys came on Friday (they departed in the small hours) & left me £135. Good old Less Deceived.

Love Philip

1 Larkin encloses a press cutting: 'NATURE NOTES: Butterflies prefer the cold.'

22 December 1964

32 Pearson Park, Hull

My very dear old creature,

I had your letter this morning, & was much relieved to hear that K. & W. had invited you along to their house for more than Christmas tea. That is very good of them, and I hope you will have a good time. I don't like to think of you sitting alone with your "Christmas globe"!

[. . .]

I got £125 for the Monitor film.[1] Betty had a letter yesterday saying she would get something too!

Well, dear old creature, I shall be thinking of you – I'll send word of my safety, somehow. The weather seems all right at present.

Much love Philip

1 In her letter of 20 December Eva recounts her friends' positive reactions to the *Monitor* programme, adding: 'By the way, would you be paid for doing it, I wonder.'

29 December 1964

Hull

My dear old creature,

Last letter this year! and only a short one, I'm afraid, but I was so pleased to get your letter when I returned (it *had* arrived – I just hadn't looked properly).

I think it sounds nice of K & W to have made such an effort on Boxing Day. Alas, people don't go to the cinema nowadays! Why didn't Effie drink? When I mentioned her to Monica she said 'The one they got drunk with?'! (You & Auntie Nelly!) I'm sure K & W will have earned their holiday in Switzerland.[1]

I expect your present is really a housecoat, if it says so, though I asked for a dressing-gown – I do hope you can wear it anyway. It is supposed to be very light and warm. [. . .]

Much love Philip

1 The final arrangement saw Philip spending Christmas with Monica, and Eva staying with him after the New Year in Hull. Eva declined Kitty's invitation to Christmas lunch and cooked a chicken for herself, going on to her daughter's for afternoon tea. On Boxing Day they drank champagne, and then Walter drove Kitty, Eva and their friend Effie McNicol, through the snow to the Victory Cinema to watch an Agatha Christie film ('Margaret Rutherford in it').

1965

24 January 1965

32 Pearson Park, Hull

My very dear old creature,

Life here resumes its normal pattern – rising at 10, now 2.25 and still no lunch. That is, if you can call it a pattern! I felt I had to concentrate on the car first, then the papers, and then you. Lunch will come next.

I thought I heard on the wireless a "flash" that Churchill had died – anyway, I put a black tie on: no doubt I shall hear at 6 p.m. I expect he has. I had respect for him, in a way, but not liking – most people w^{d} put it the other way round, I suppose. He seemed to me to be second rate in quality, but full of energy & respect for the right things. In a war you want second-rate energy, and he was clearly the best man.

The other news of the week was my old pal Du Cann getting made chairman of the Conservative Party! Truly surprising. And of course the Conservative victory at Leyton – jolly fine.

Well, I don't suppose you'll be very interested in Old Larkin's political reflections – on the personal front, I felt a *bit* dithery when I got back, but have recovered now. [. . .]

Virginia wonders where that nice old lady has gone who stayed in and had tea about 4 o'clock and kept the place warm![1] She doesn't seem to move about as she used, but is now sitting on a low table watching me. I wonder how Kitty's "mountain throat" is?[2] I reckon it's "kitchen throat", coming of working in an unheated kitchen in January.

Much love
Philip

1 On 21 January Eva wrote: 'Well, dear Creature, I must thank you *very* much for all your kindness during the past three weeks and also for the lovely warm dressing gown, the electric iron and the chocolates. I really did enjoy my stay at Pearson Park. Hope you have caught up with yourself.'
2 Kitty had picked up a sore throat in Switzerland.

13 February 1965

32 Pearson Park, Hull

My very dear old creature,

[. . .] Really, I'm much too late – I spent too long in the bath, & then I made a macaroni cheese, & a salad of raw cress, chicory, carrot, leek & cabbage. Awgh. Anyway, what with washing up it was 9 o'clock before I got out. I mean out of the kitchen. This afternoon I drove out into the country after shopping, just for half an hour. It's quite mild here, but all the trees are still quite bare – I'd hoped to see some lambs, or some birds building, but didn't. Still, I did see some snowdrops, and some tiny new ivy leaves on the ground. I felt the spring wasn't far off – a lovely time of year.

It's been a curious week, blighted by the awful cold in the middle of it – now gone. I'm glad to say – I had a very tough Senate meeting in the middle of it, too: a long argument which I won 22–9, but the 9 were rather narked. I don't know how they will take it.

Your letter was very nice and kind – please, old creature, don't get worried about Daddy's war diary. It upsets me to think of you puzzling over these old affairs. I think Pop used to let off steam in this way after a day's work – he was always "agin the government" and it must have cheered him up no end to rail against them. I shouldn't want to be living under the Nazis, would you? Better a bad English govt than any foreign one.[1] So don't worry. It gives me great joy to know you are liking the new iron! Nothing I can give you will equal all you have done for me. I only wish I had achieved a more satisfactory position in life. And of course I ought to find some solution for you. [. . .]

Sunday [. . .] I had a Valentine yesterday postmarked Wirral in Cheshire![2] [. . .]

Much love, dear old creature. Philip

1 Eva had been re-reading Sydney's twenty-volume war diary, 'The Fool's War'. 'It puts me in a peculiar state of mind, rather miserable and very astonished at all the hypocrisy of our Government' (9 February 1965).
2 From Nellie.

Above: Larkin's photograph of Graduation Day at Queen's University, Belfast, 1951.

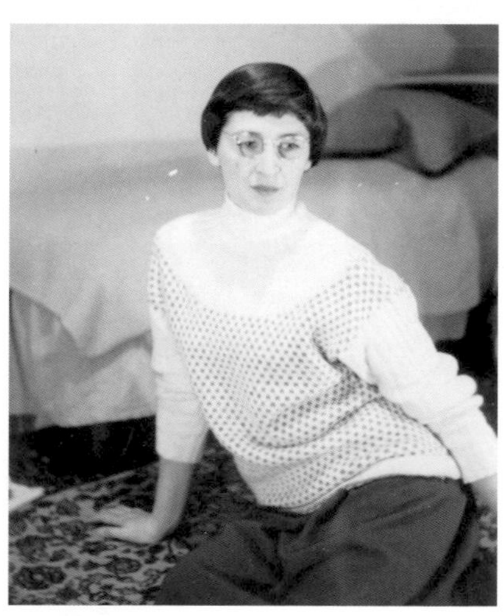

Right: Library Assistant Molly Sellar, who married QUB Lecturer in Spanish, Arthur Terry. 'I'm glad you occasionally do a bit at my pullover! Did I tell you Molly finished a very smart grey & white one [. . .] I hope to take a photograph or two of her in it before I go: it really looks very nice.' (6 February 1955)

Leo Japolsky, QUB Lecturer in French. 'I fancy I hear Leo playing his piano in the distance [. . .] he is a moody fool.' (30 May 1954). Japolsky later killed his father and was committed to a psychiatric hospital.

George Hartley. 'I heard from Hartley today that my book is in demand & that the first 300 have nearly gone. He is having another 400 bound.' (11 January 1956)

Betty Mackereth. 'My new secretary has begun, & seems all right in a way: no doubt she will learn. She'll probably stay all her life, though, now.' (26 May 1957)

Mary Judd (Wrench) with her newborn daughter Helen. 'My photographs of Mary's baby came out moderately well [. . .] She has asked me to be god-father, wch is rather a tall order. I accepted though. Somebody will have to look after me when I'm old.' (1 April 1962)

Philip and Eva with Walter, Kitty and Rosemary Hewett, late 1950s.
Probably taken by PAL with a delayed-action shutter release.

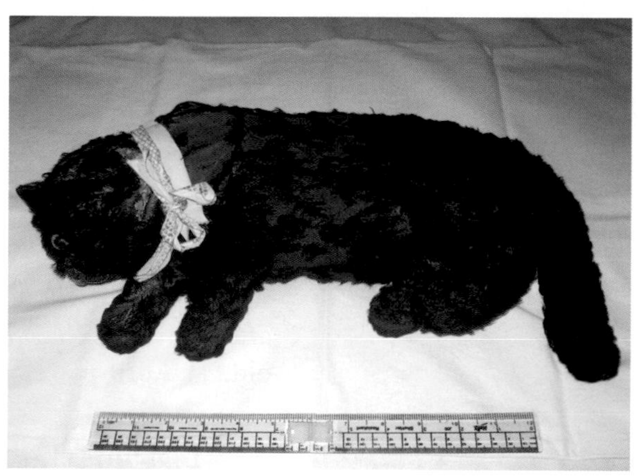

'Blak Pussy', Kitty's nightdress case (the spelling is the cat's own). 'You owe my mother 12/-! as Kitty's nightdress case used to say.' (26 June 1952). It was used to hold messages about money owed by Eva or Kitty.

Plate 14

Monica Jones's Haydon Bridge retreat seen (*left*) *c.* 1961, and (*below*) in 1977. 'This Haydon Bridge place isn't a picturesque village, exactly, nor is her cottage a picturesque cottage, but in general it has a good deal of character.' (24 September 1961)

Eva Larkin in the Conservatory in Pearson Park. 'I'm glad you approve of the photograph [. . .] I have one for you as well. Creature surrounded by flowers!' (27 June 1961)

Among seven portraits of Eva sent with a letter of 1 October 1967. 'Is there any one you like, or Kitty w^{d} like? Perhaps you think they're awful! I like 6 very much though: it shows you as the dear old creature you are.' Eva and Kitty liked nos. 6 (*left*) and 7 (*right*).

Plate 16

'Virginia wonders where that nice old lady has gone who [. . .] kept the place warm! She [. . .] is now sitting on a low table watching me.' (24 January 1965)

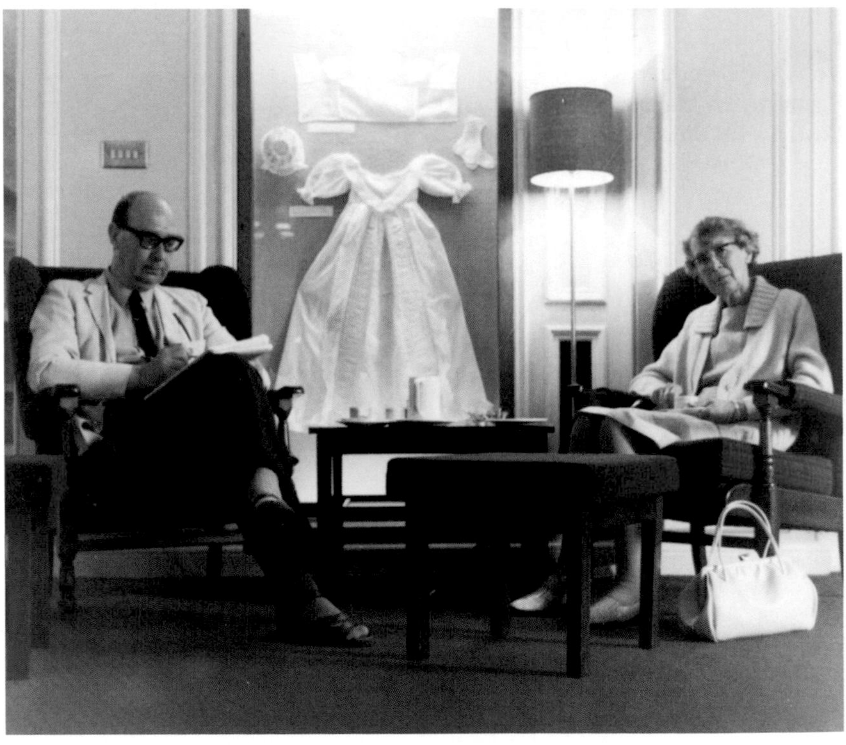

Philip and Eva in the Duke's Head Hotel, King's Lynn, July 1971 (with mob-cap behind). 'My froggy [. . .] greatly enjoyed his jaunt to King's Lynn with your froggy. [. . .] How they enjoyed sitting in the lounge when we had our tea on the afternoon when we arrived!' (31 July 1971)

28 February 1965

32 Pearson Park, Hull

My very dear old creature,

[. . .] I expect you got *Time*. In their next issue they included *The W. W.* in their list of best selling books – no, best *reading* (subtle difference) – and called me "the best living English poet". That'll make me popular with all the other living English poets. I wish I could do something to justify it. I'm sorry to hear you had such a traipse looking for it – I hope one of *my* assistants w^{d} have "looked on the pink list" for you![1] Lazy swine. On Friday *A Girl in Winter* was republished in paperback, just eighteen years (February 1947) after its first appearance.

This all seems very self centred. I hope your sciatica has gone. I hope to come home either this weekend or next – I'll see.

Be comfortable, dear old creature!

Much love
Philip

1 On 22 February Eva related that, after failing to buy *Time* in Smith's, she had gone to the library where an assistant had told her to 'look on the pink list, which would say which magazines they had'. But 'It wasn't on the list.'

1 March 1965

[32 Pearson Park]

Dearest old creature,

Snow here today! Not very deep though.

Yesterday I drove to Spurn Head, wch is a very odd promontory at the mouth of the Humber. It was quite nice, not lonely enough for my liking. [. . .]

Much love P

13 March 1965

32 Pearson Park, Hull

My very dear old creature,

[. . .] Today started with a terrible fright – a letter from a Chest Consultant saying he had sent a report on my mass x-ray to Dr Raines, who w^{d} "tell me about it"! You can imagine the fright this threw me into, as in the case of this x-ray "no news is good news", & probably the opposite is true also. I had a very unpleasant hour, & then saw Raines who quickly put me out of my misery by saying it was just my old oesophagus again, not lungs at all.[1] I'd been x-rayed after lunch & it was distended as usual I suppose. Needless to say I had been dead & buried several times by then, & my grave well grassed. Betty was very sympathetic, but she must have thought I was making a fearful fuss. How relieved I felt afterwards, how sweet the world seemed, how marvellous the prospect of seeing another spring! [. . .]

With much love from undead creature

1 Larkin died of cancer of the oesophagus twenty years later, in 1985.

21 March 1965

32 Pearson Park, Hull

My very dear old creature,

[. . .] London was all right but tiring: when I got back I found my feet were quite sore with tramping the pavements. I saw the architects, & saw the Editress of *Vogue*, & had drinks with the Features Editress who is a fat Belfast girl who won one of their competitions two years ago & is far less glamorous than, for instance, Kitty . . . Then on Friday I ordered another suit from Simpson's this time, playing safe on a kind I'd had before, & went and sat on a board for giving money to young poets to encourage them (what encouragement do middle aged ones get?): we handed out about £1000. May they get fat on it. When I got back I found a letter from a 21 year old girl in Istanbul begging me to go there & sending love! Such is my life.

I don't feel too bad this morning, but I have a kind of phobia about London – I feel great West Indian & Pakistani germs hopping on me in the tubes, wch are then artificially incubated in the stifling hot Pullman[1] on the way back, so that when I arrive I am ¾s ill already. It doesn't seem to have happened this time, but still. It may.

[. . .] You must stop putting the apostrophe in the wrong place in words like "isn't". It indicates that the "o" of "not" has been left out, & should go in its place. You are writing "is'nt".

How nice that your azalea is still flowering. There are a few green shoots in the garden here. I don't expect I shall get out today, but if I did I expect I should see plenty of signs of life. [. . .]

Much love Philip

1 See note to the letter of 10 March 1963.

5 April 1965

32 Pearson Park, Hull

My very dear old creature,

[. . .] Kitty makes me angry with her "wouldn't have made any difference" – can't the fool *see* that if she, by her actions, decides when someone else must go away, it's mere courtesy to let them know *even before she decides it*?[1] She hasn't the manners of a hog. In fact I feel very low all round. The Indians went today. Oh dear, this isn't a very nice letter – & it's after 11. Much love, dear old creature.

1 Most unusually Larkin has messily corrected and recorrected his text at this point:

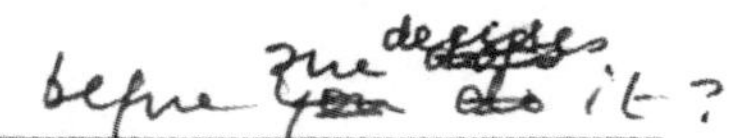

On 30 March Eva had written: 'About the holiday date, Kitty says that it would not have made any difference if she had told me earlier for they hadn't much choice on account of Rosemary's exam^{n}. They expect the results in August and don't want to be away then. I think it must be due about the end of August, I'm not very clear about this.'

25 April 1965

32 Pearson Park, Hull

My very dear old creature,

[. . .] The week has been a busy one – I went down to London & back on Friday, which is always a testing experience. My throat seems a bit odd, so I hope I haven't picked up any London germs. I can almost imagine them when I go down, waiting at King's Cross like porters. When in London I looked at a number of manuscripts that had come before the committee, and there was one belonging to Edmund Blunden wch was quite a small notebook with "For Eddy's poetry" written in the front, presumably by his mother, and dated 1921, I think it was. Blunden, who is still alive, wrote that it would have seemed strange then to think of anyone paying money for it – especially the £750 we offered – "but think of the price a tin of salmon was in those days!" I can't imagine what it was. Can you remember?[1] It's a strange business, pursuing manuscripts among the mothers & widows & girl friends & women generally of dead poets. Hope you'll never be approached. [. . .]

Glad to hear you are contemplating the telephone. I wonder if there is any special attachment for hard of hearing old creatures? There might be.

Much love as ever Philip

1 Eva replied (26 April 1965): 'I cannot for the life of me remember what a tin of salmon cost in 1921.'

28 April 1965

[Hull]

My very dear old creature,

Just a rapid note to say that I had a letter from the Poet Laureate (Masefield) this morning to say that the Queen had approved the recommendation that I should get her Gold Medal for Poetry this year! This will mean going to Buckingham P., I expect![1]

I fancy someone gets it every year, but I'm pleased.

Much love xx
Philip

1 Eva wrote on 3 May: 'I shouldn't be surprised if there were tickets to admit friends or relatives. You are adding to the honour of the Larkin family and keeping the name before the public as Daddy did before you. It is all very wonderful.'

3 June 1965[1]

[32 Pearson Park, Hull]

This is the last of these cards. This morning my medal came in the post! I was surprised. I suppose this means I shan't have to worry about going to the Palace, not for this anyway – am both relieved and disappointed. It's 9 carat gold & rather quaint: has my name on the edge! It is in a red case, & clearly isn't the wearing type of medal.

My record is of me reading the whole of *The W. W.* – the whole book. It costs 35/9d. Kitty has a leaflet about it. I can send you more if you like ogh ogh ogh.[2]

I was very glad to have your letter this evening. I can imagine you living on Guinness & being quite sorry when your teeth come back![3]

It's very steady weather here, fine but not warm. Have felt rather sluggish all day – think I want exercise or something. Shall be thinking of you at the weekend, & will ring up sometime – don't know when yet.

Much love xxx Philip

1 Double-sided plain card in envelope.
2 *Philip Larkin Reads and Comments on 'The Whitsun Weddings'* (Hessle: Listen Records, Marvell Press, 1965).
3 On 1 June Eva wrote that she was without teeth while her dentist prepared a new set of dentures, and was reduced to bread and milk and mashed banana. 'Don't know what to do about supper – perhaps a bottle of stout would provide the most nourishment.'

27 June 1965

<*Letterhead*> 32 Pearson Park, Hull

My very dear old creature,

No, I didn't thank the Queen for the medal. I remembered Dr Johnson's remark "It was not for me to bandy civilities with my sovereign", and simply acknowledged its receipt: I expect she is now thinking "That's the last time I do anything for that man."

It's a cloudy, warm but not unpleasant day. [. . .]

Reverting to the medal, well, it is of its period (about 1930) & the designer Dulac was very typical of the day. He used to illustrate Yeats's books. But I agree it's not much to our taste today.[1] [. . .]

Driving back from York last night I narrowly avoided a hedgehog that was travelling across the road (at least I hope I avoided it), & later on I saw a young hare behaving rather indecisively at the roadside. It's lovely seeing the wild creatures, but I wish they'd keep off the roads. They are so silly.

I still treasure the memory of coming home last Sunday into the cool and calm of your house, with a welcoming old creature & a delicious cold chicken – and flowers, & all so neat & peaceful.

Very much love Philip

1 On 22 June 1965 Eva had written: 'I have brought the medal back and put it away in what I hope is a safe place. [The Hewetts and friends] all thought it lovely, especially the Queen's Head on the one side and the letter from The Keeper of the Privy Purse. They weren't so impressed with the design on the other side. Kitty said she could have done better herself.'

11 July 1965

<*Letterhead*> 32 Pearson Park, Hull

My very dear old creature,

What a dismal weekend, so far anyway! It's hardly done anything but rain, or look like raining: the leaves of the chestnut trees hang down & look very resigned. Further, I've just weighed myself & I am certainly *no lighter* – I might even be *a bit heavier*. This is a great disappointment, as I had drunk less this week (no beer at lunch) and tried to use the car less.

But the needle on the scales still flickers uncompromisingly beyond 13 st 7 lbs – 13 st 8 lbs, 13 st 9 lbs, I don't know. *Very* disappointing. I shall just have to try eating less, not that I feel I eat a lot as it is. According to the fellow in the *S. Times* last week I ought to be 12 st 12 lbs *in clothes*. I eat very little bread, I never buy sugar, what can I give up?[1]

I wonder if the ebb & flow of life extends to weight! I could do with a spell of ebb.[2] Yesterday I noticed outside a church the Hull Samaritan telephone number – do you remember how you thought you w[d] ring up the L'boro' one? I do hope you haven't felt like it since you had your yellow telephone installed. Really, I don't think I'd know what to say, if I rang them up, not that I want to. I've felt fairly depressed recently for no very good reason. I think one is stamped with a particular kind of character, like a butter-pat having a cow or leaves stamped on it, and just has to struggle away with it. I can see that having other Circle members ring you up could be awfully interrupting, but surely it is comforting too. [. . .]

Very best love, Philip

1 On 13 July Eva replied: 'I must say that you don't eat a lot, in my way of thinking. Perhaps it is your big frame (bones) which weigh heavily. You don't eat nearly so much bread as *I* do.'

2 On 6 July Eva had written: 'At the C.S.M. [Circle of Silent Ministry] Miss Unwin spoke about the Ebb and Flow of Life. By this she meant that everyone has periods of elation and depression, and made the suggestion that the best way to deal with the last-named was to try to keep peaceful and "let go" and rest – if possible. I ventured to say how lonely I found it at times, and when they knew I was on the telephone each one put down my number, so now I am rather fearing that the 'phone will be always ringing and that I shall get less jobs done than ever. Still, as Walter remarked, when I told him last night, "You can't have it both ways". This is a queer letter, Creature, but it isn't often I moan in a letter. Don't take it too seriously.'

24 August 1965

<*Letterhead*> 32 Pearson Park, Hull

My very dear old creature,

Not a very nice night – a heavy downpour of rain, quite tropical: no thunder, but extremely wet! Actually it has been relatively cool here.

Thank you for your letter of Saturday & lettercard of yesterday. I fancy the easiest thing w^{d} be for me to drive to L'borough on Saturday morning – 28th – arriving about lunchtime. On Tuesday I should go to London for the day as I did before, returning about 9 p.m. Then I w^{d} drive back to Hull on Wednesday morning. Such are my plans at present. If I change my mind I'll ring up. I must stay on Friday to welcome the laundry back!

So they are moving on Thursday.[1] I suppose they meant well in not telling you, but it seems typical. Gibber gibber gibber. I wonder if you will be involved. Don't find yourself scrubbing floors while Rosemary lounges drinking milo.[2]

I don't make much progress with my weight-losing: I stay between 13 & 13½ stone, nearer the latter I'm afraid. Bisks are the thing, plain Bisks. Not Mini-bisks. I should quite like a chicken, but I should be happy with beef. Whichever you like, old creature. Whichever is easier.

I have paid for my spectacles and they seem better! Funny, isn't it? I do hope your stomach is better.[3] Drinkwater's elder daughter was married today.

Much love old creature

1 On 26 August 1965 the Hewetts, moved from 53 York Road to 'Oddstones', 283 Forest Road, Loughborough, a larger house more in keeping with Walter's salary. The new house was 1½ miles away.

2 A drink made with milk or water and a chocolate and malt powder, produced by Nestlé.

3 Eva had written on 23 August that Kitty had felt she must delay telling her the precise date of the move because of her 'tummy'.

12 September 1965

<*Letterhead*> Dixcart Hotel Sark, via Guernsey C.I.

My very dear old creature,

As you see from my pen, I'm not in the habit of writing letters![1] In fact I haven't written any so far. Well, we have certainly not done any better than anyone else for weather on this holiday – the first day was simply shocking, rain & wind, & then there followed some cold days & nights (the temperature went down to 41° one night) and perpetual showers. Add to this the hotel's 100% refusal to supply any kind of heat anywhere & you'll readily understand how this holiday has begun to seem like a fortnight under canvas with the Territorials. Bathing has been quite out of the question, and it hasn't really been warm enough to sit out – & sitting in is a chilly enough experience, as all the chairs are damp & the cold creeps into one's bones.

However, you can't expect to enjoy yourself on holiday like you do at home, so let me pass on to pleasanter aspects – after a day or two we got the hang of the place again, & are finding plenty to interest us among our fellow guests. One most obnoxious & loudmouthed young man who left, thank God, this morning tried to make everyone guess what he did, in the bar one night: after many unsuccessful suggestions Monica said "corset manufacturer" more out of rudeness than anything else, & he turned out to be a director of Spirella![2] Thank heavens he has gone, he & his sheepfaced wife. Now I must go too – to church. The day is what you would call "clouding over". So I must fetch my Regenmantel.[3]

Sunday p.m. Another cold afternoon: really, it is miserable here! I've snoozed on my bed a bit – only place to keep warm.

Thank you for your letter wch got here very quickly – day after, I think! I hope your telephone is working again. You'd not take too kindly to the idea of a Brush student, whatever they are. If you had any kind of student, a library one from the college w^d be fairly quiet, but I'm sure you're right in thinking your catering days are over, except for spongeing creatures who come & eat you out of house & home.[4] Talking about eating, the diet has pretty well gone by the board. It's hard to do otherwise. So I expect I shall have to start all over again when I get back to Hull. The food is quite nice on the whole, usually fruit juice & porridge for breakfast along with the principal dish; soup & salad & cold stuff for lunch, or else hot fish; *no tea* – actually it's a fearful long time between lunch & dinner, & we have once been to a café for a light tea; then dinner is four courses & eatable enough as a rule. We had a sort of stewed duck last night, & I think I caught the word "faisan" on the menu tonight.

But will it *ever* be warm? It's begun to rain again; half past three on Sunday. I bet *you* have a good fire & are snoozing on the sofa. I don't know where all the guests are: there are none in this "lounge", so perhaps they are all gone to bed in desperation.

I heard from Simpson's that to reface my jacket on *both* sides w^d cost £12.[5] Awgh! I think it w^d be best not to risk the jacket looking lopsided, though. I never looked to see if I was covered by insurance, but I don't suppose I was. [. . .]

Very dear love P.

1 The letter has been written with a ballpoint, and the first two or three lines are markedly scratchy.
2 Spirella manufactured made-to-measure corsets from 1904 until 1989, its 'corsetiers' calling at clients' homes for confidentiality.
3 'Raincoat' (German).
4 On 15 September Eva wrote to Philip on Sark: 'I have heard of someone who lived at the end of York Road, an elderly lady, now dead, who had several students and with the money received from them, employed a daily help to do all the cooking and work. She just wanted company at night – someone sleeping there. Not a bad idea I think.' A 'Brush student' was presumably a student funded by the Brush Company of Loughborough (see note to letter of 11 February 1951).
5 Larkin had scorched one side of his jacket while ironing it and the tailor (Simpsons, Piccadilly) could not find an exact match of material for the repair.

10 October 1965

<*Letterhead*> 32 Pearson Park, Hull

My very dear old creature,

I am slowly getting my room straight after the visitors on Thursday. What happened was that John Wain was given a dinner at The University, & then a few of the guests came back to my flat, where Maeve was already entertaining the Hartleys.[1] We were eight in all. God, don't people mop it up! All the cigarettes I put out vanished, all the bread & cheese I put out vanished, and the only reason all the drink didn't vanish was that I kept it in the kitchen & doled it out myself. One glass & one plate were broken, both belonging to Maeve, wch was a pity. John got very drunk, but was very nice about it. Oh dear, though, how exhausting I find such an occasion! The next day John had to give his lecture, wch I *chaired* – the ass forgot his notes, whether accidentally or on purpose I don't know: it was all very embarrassing. Oh, how glad I am it's all over!

Another burden is an artist called Sillince – to cut a long story short, I met him in the graveyard when Monitor was being filmed: he seemed to be a pal of Betjeman's. Now he is having an exhibition in the University, & I had to open *that*. Previously I had to go round and have a look at the stuff, wch resulted in my being given one & *buying* two (35gns).[2] Then after the opening I had to have lunch with him, his wife & two other people in Beverley. A rotten lunch, & rendered worse by the fact that his wife was clearly ill in some unidentifiable way – very fat & slow, & didn't speak easily, but ate neatly enough & read the menu for herself.

Anyway, after that peace reigned & I could begin Thursday's washing up. [. . .]

With very best love Philip

1 Philip had invited his friend the novelist and poet John Wain, to give a lecture in Hull. See note to the letter of 16 March 1952.
2 William Augustus Sillince (1906–74) contributed work to *Punch* between 1936 and 1974, including notable wartime political cartoons (sometimes assisting Leslie Illingworth). At this time he was teaching in the School of Art in Hull. The paintings Larkin bought, including an atmospheric watercolour of Spring Bank Cemetery, are currently in the Larkin Society Collection, Hull History Centre.

21 November 1965

<*Letterhead*> 32 Pearson Park, Hull

My very dear old creature,

[. . .] See the picture of Auden in the *S. Times* Colour Supplement. A chap from Auden's American publishers (also mine) said to me that Auden had told him to tell me to "keep writing". Nice of him. I saw him get an Honorary Degree at Reading but have never spoken to him. He sounds as if he has a comfortable enough life, doesn't he – but how early he gets up! I reckon I sh^d get up at 9, bath, breakfast, shave, dress – I shouldn't be ready for much before 11. Do you think I shall be living like him at 58?[1] No, nor do I.

My burnt jacket came back. The new panels aren't *quite* the same as the old cloth – how annoying! It means I can never wear the suit (& it's a *new* suit) on any occasion that really matters. It looks, if anything, worse in artificial light than daylight. My other new suit & sports jacket came too: they seem fairly all right. [. . .]

Much love,
Philip

1 Larkin had just turned forty-three.

1966

7 February 1966

Hull

My very dear old creature,

I am back at the flat just before going out to dinner with the architects: I've made up my laundry, wch is very thin this week. It's raining outside. I feel rather tired, but not too tired, though I should prefer to stay in by the fire.

Is the rain coming in the bathroom again?[1] Remember to get the scullery window unstuck if the men come again.

I'm sorry I was not more sympathetic during my stay. I'm not *really* unsympathetic, I just get mad with irritation.

I suppose you really want someone who would live in & do most of the work, & organise things, & *never* go away, but it's a remote prospect, isn't it. Failing that, live in fewer rooms.

I do feel rather tired now. Still. The roses would increase the value of the house, I suppose.[2]

There's no news here. I hope all the people at Oddstones[3] are well. Take care of yourself, & don't climb on those steps.

Much love,
Philip

1 On 8 February Eva wrote: 'I 'phoned Hammonds this morning and told Mr Freeman that the rain comes in even more than it did before.'

2 On turning eighty Eva had been considering selling 21 York Road. On 8 February she wrote: 'I mentioned to Kitty about the bungalow and she seems to be of the same opinion as I am, really. Thinks I should be happier staying here, where I know people. I think too that it is a comfort to hear your next door neighbours moving about – which one wouldn't have in a detached bungalow. She also said the upheaval would mean an awful lot of work. Perhaps I had better think about it a little more before making a decisive move.'

3 The Hewetts' new home, 283 Forest Road, Loughborough.

13 February 1966

32 Pearson Park, Hull

My very dear old creature,

[. . .] I have bought a Valentine to send to Betty, but I always have such trouble disguising my hand – even my printing seems recognisable. It says "You Make Me Feel So Young!" Rather an overstatement. [. . .]

Love from P.

13 March 1966

32 Pearson Park, Hull

My very dear old creature,

[. . .] Weren't those plums awful. I'm sorry I didn't buy the tinned ones. But you know, I thought they'd be extra good, home bottled and all that. I had a funny experience on Friday. I had got a copy of Kingsley's new novel, *The Anti-Death League*, also a tinned steak & kidney pudding, & when I got home I put the one on to boil & sat down to read the other. Fifty minutes later a strange smell crept to my nose! Yes – boiled & burnt & the whole flat full of smoke. Such is the power of the printed word.[1] I picked about in the remnants not very successfully. The smoke took a lot of cleaning.

Maeve is holding an Oxfam party next Saturday. She did this once before, filling the house with about 50 people at 2/- a time. I have promised to give a bottle of sherry as one of the prizes. There is a raffle & a bring & buy stall or stalls. She is on the local Oxfam Committee, & the object is to make money. I expect she will make a certain amount. You see how different she is from Monica – or from me, for that matter!

The ginger cake is very nice. Dear old creature, you make such nice things. I won't send the pictures this time as I want to consult my photographer about them – no, I will send them. I'll take more at Stratford. Send them back & say w[ch] you like best. Very best love.

Philip

1 A week later, on 20 March, Larkin wrote: 'Now the reviews of Kingsley's book are out I wonder if I really read it carefully enough. I found it pretty boring on the

whole. I wish I could write a novel! Sometimes I think I shall never write anything more. Of course, if I am spared I should like to write an autobiography.'

9 May 1966

Hull

My very dear old creature,

I drove back through rain last night, & today it is cool and dull. This is a note to say *how sorry* I am for upsetting you yesterday. Really I have no excuse. I just come home & belch & grumble.[1]

I had a letter from some student in Dundee enquiring about the poem "Reference Back" & saying that when she was 12 she refused to go & see her father in hospital because she wanted to go out with her friends, & he died that night! I felt I couldn't pose as being much better. I do hope you are no longer worried & can view things more calmly. I much enjoyed my visit until the shock![2]

Monica provided pheasant paté, cold trout & asparagus, & a queer sweet of egg & cream in half oranges!

This afternoon I shall go to Church for a memorial service for one of our councillors. I'm afraid I shall fall asleep. I hope the holiday brochures come in good time.

Much love
Philip

1 In a letter begun late on 9 May, Eva thanked Philip for telephoning to tell her he had arrived back safely. 'I [. . .] was sitting in the armchair thinking mournfully of the events of the day. I am ever so sorry that you had the shock from the scullery light and wonder which of us turned it on and why it was left on. I just cannot think. Anyway I am glad it did no serious damage to you.' She goes on to tell him that she has called Murcotts, the electricians, and will 'ask their man to look at all the lights and alter the two switches which are put in the wrong way'.
2 On 10 May Eva wrote: 'After reading your notelet I found the poem of yours "Reference Back" and read it. The Dundee Student must feel pretty awful. I know how *I* felt when I didn't go to see my father, Still, he didn't ask me to go. Of course you are not like the student. You have been a very kind and unselfish creature in visiting me always, as well as Monica, and Daddy. Remember how you came *every* weekend when I was in hospital, and in all the worst weather!'

5 June 1966

32 Pearson Park, Hull

My dear old creature,

A dark morning, no doubt cooler outside: the chestnut trees with their candles are shifting ceaselessly. I am rather late starting this letter, for no very good reason – I arose about 10.15, having slept till then. Then at breakfast I was much interested by reviews of this new Hardy book – I expect you read the one in the *Sunday Times*.[1] I shall have to get the book. I always thought his poem to Tryphena one of his most memorable (it is in *Wessex Poems*, one of the little red ones). I am in the middle of choosing poems by him for the O.B. There are so many! [. . .]

I dreamed about Kitty the other night, but have forgotten what. Fancy her saying we were utterly unlike each other! Only as one red is utterly unlike another red, I sh^{d} have thought. I'm glad she liked the poem.[2] Remember me to her. Monica thought she looked very smart.

Maeve looked at your photographs & opined that you look younger than her mother (a waddling old toad), though you're about 15 yrs older. Well, much love – w^{d} you please send the photos back – say if you want a copy of one?

Love as always P

1 Lois Deacon and Terry Coleman, *Providence and Mr. Hardy* (1966). The authors examine Hardy's early relationship with Tryphena Sparks, concluding that she bore him a son.

2 The poem is unidentified. Philip must be responding to a missing letter from Eva.

19 August 1966

Picture postcard[1]

<*Postmark*> Arrochar *Tuesday*

Many thanks for letter received this morning. I'm glad you got safely there: were the bags all right?[2] I am on a paddle steamer at the moment heading for Loch Lomond – weather not too bad but far from warm. Our hotel is beautifully done up & we are v. comfortable, but food c^{d} be more imaginative. I'm sorry I have not written a letter, but I hadn't any paper on Sunday; I will write. Glad you liked P. Strong.[3]

Much love to both Philip

1 Loch Lomond, Dunbartonshire.
2 Addressed to Strathmore Hotel, East Parade, Morecambe, Lancs., where Eva and Nellie were on holiday.
3 On 16 August Philip had written to Eva at Morecambe: 'I enclose a piece from Patience Strong – I thought it rather good advice for me & perhaps you too!' This cutting is lost, but see letter of 1 February 1953. Eva wrote on 21 August: 'How kind of you to send a letter to welcome us, and the beautifully expressed advice on the Patience Strong cutting which I shall read every morning.'

18 September 1966

32 Pearson Park, Hull

My very dear old creature,

[. . .] Many thanks for your two letters. The bookshop in Hull has bought endless copies of *The North Ship*,[1] silly trusting creatures: they won't sell. It looks odd to see my three books side by side in a shop – *The NS*, *The LD*, *The Whitsun W*. Funny they all begin with *The*. I wonder if there'll ever be a fourth. Not at the rate I'm going now. No one has reviewed *The NS* yet. [. . .]

With much love & constant thoughts

Philip

1 On 16 September Eva had commented on the 1966 reissue of *The North Ship*: 'I like the jacket very much and have read your introduction. I have never read Yeats and think I should like to. I like "Love we must part now" very much, also "If hands could free you[,] heart".'

16 October 1966

32 Pearson Park, Hull

My very dear old creature,

[. . .] It is certainly lovely at present – yesterday afternoon after shopping I drove out eastward, down that long road that leads through Ottringham & Patrington & Easington to far Spurn Head – country of flat land, red brick farms glowing in the sun, surprisingly beautiful churches, & of course the sea at the end of it. Everywhere looked beautiful. Of course it isn't so good as cycling, but at least I get there!

The haystacks are made up of rectangles of hay now – rectangular cubes – made by machines, I suppose – but the colour is the same.

The Vice Chancellor & I had a "cordial meeting" & flattered each other a good deal. I believe in buttering him up, as I think he is really very good to me & the Library. What the outcome will be I don't know. I am trying to get another deputy – what Wood will think I don't know.[1] [. . .]

The Abbeyfield houses sound very good ideas. You never actually stayed in one, did you? Really, though, as long as one can manage it, one's own place where one can shut the door on the world is the best. As for giving, well, do it in guineas – not less than one or more than five, I sh[d] say. Every little helps. The best way is a covenant over seven years, so that they can recover tax too, but this is probably too complicated for you.[2]

I have over £3,000 in my current a/c! I have lost faith in shares recently: still, I'll have to do something with it. It seems odd to have all this potential experience & not do anything with it. We could go a cruise at Christmas! I could buy a cottage. Anything. Really, I have little attachment to material things – silence, solitude, warmth, records, books: this is all I need.

I have been wondering whether to pay a quick visit home next Saturday – Sunday, as well as Nov 3rd etc. It seems a long time until November. [. . .]

Much love
Philip

1 Brenda Moon was appointed as Larkin's second deputy alongside Arthur Wood from 1 October 1967.

2 With her letter of 11 October Eva had enclosed a cutting from *The Echo* (Friday 7 October 1966): 'Mayor to Launch Appeal for Third Abbeyfield House', requesting donations towards the provision of a third Abbeyfield House in the town. Abbeyfield is a nationwide charity providing sheltered housing and care homes for the elderly.

29 October 1966

32 Pearson Park, Hull

My dear old creature,

[. . .] I had a letter from Rosemary this morning, referring to my projected visit. She says her hall of residence won't be ready by the time I go. She sounds very busy & in good spirits. The student who she thought was trying to get hold of me has been sent down for peddling drugs! Truly she lives in a more exciting atmosphere than I do.[1] I had to dine in a girls' hall here last Wednesday: I hadn't expected much in the way of food (stuffed marrow, in the event), but they all gobbled it up like dogs, far faster than me. Afterwards I had to have coffee with four of them in one of their rooms: they told me what was wrong with the library, then relented & said it was really the best they had ever used. [. . .]

Much love. See you Thursday. Philip

1 In a typed letter to Rosemary of 16 February 1966, headed with a creature drawing, Philip declined his niece's invitation to give a lecture at Warwick University, where she was studying English Literature. 'I don't even give talks here, so if word got back to my Vice Chancellor he would probably dock my pay or something. Still, one day I hope to come to Warwick, and perhaps we can then have the informal discussion in the bar without the lecture.' The visit was fixed for 7 November, and in four letters in October Larkin expressed his apprehension to Rosemary that he might be cornered and interviewed about his poetry by her student friends: 'I'm really coming to see you and the Library.' In the event he saw only the University Librarian, Peter Tucker, and Rosemary herself. (Email from Rosemary Parry, 7 December 2017.)

14 November 1966

32 Pearson Park, Hull

My very dear old creature,

Here's the second half of your letter. I feel somewhat the worse for wear: my visitor kept me up very late, & we drank a lot: today I feel like some old dented beer can. However, she's gone now.[1] It was a beautiful day today, sunny & mild.

I have just made up my laundry, two weeks' lot: my room seems untidy, but it will have to stay that way. Picture me hunched in my chair! Luckily Patsy wasn't very demanding in the way of meals. An omelette or poached eggs & mushrooms were enough for her.

She said Bruce is very far gone in drink & rather a pitiable person altogether.

I haven't done anything about my Christmas cards. Perhaps I have left it too late to order ones from the National Trust, as last year – as a matter of fact, I have quite a lot left from previous years. I wish I dare send them out! I wonder if people would remember.

I was able to show Patsy my gold medal, & felt quite proud of it!

No letter of thanks from Rosemary for the £5 I gave her: I suppose it's just possible it isn't required, but I should. Did you hear anything about it through Kitty? Really, R. seemed plain *bored* in a way that suggested I was boring her too! Heigh ho.

Telephone bill came today – £15 odd. Awgh. Awgh!! That's for 3 months. Most of it is talking to Monica at Haydon Bridge, in the summer. I'm glad you ate her cheese. I have a very nice piece of cheddar at present – & some celery. The refectory has started serving expensive dishes – one a day – I had steak today for 7/6, it was lovely! Goodnight dear old creature.

Much love P.

1 Patsy Murphy (formerly Strang). See note to letter of 12 October 1951. After her divorce from Colin Strang in 1955, Patsy had immediately married the Irish poet Richard Murphy (May 1955), by whom she had a daughter. They divorced in 1959. She died of alcohol poisoning in Dublin in 1977.

20 November 1966

32 Pearson Park, Hull

My very dear old creature,

[. . .] I have now got one of those pictures of Guy the gorilla yelling, & he looks fine, just like I feel sometimes.[1] On Friday I had the Hartleys round for the annual presentation of *The Less Deceived* accounts.

Maeve came to help, but with her things went better & it was 2 am before I got to bed. They sold 517 copies last year. Not as good as the previous year, but not bad – nearly 1½ copies every day! I gave them drinks, & cheeses, French bread, celery, tomatoes & pickled walnuts. They were especially enthusiastic about the last. "I never think you can just *buy* them," said Jean. There were also a couple of cakes – one of w^{ch}, a jam & cream sandwich, I have rather taken a fancy to, & shall finish.

Much love, very dear creature, Philip

1 Larkin kept a framed photograph of Guy the Gorilla (1946–78) on his desk in the University of Hull library. Guy was London Zoo's best-loved resident at the time.

1967

8 January 1967

32 Pearson Park, Hull

My very dear old creature,

[. . .] After my brief experience of house-keeping at Christmas I did feel that distances were very long & rooms very crowded, & stairs very steep! I do think it would be worth while *trying* a simpler way of living at York Road, based on sleeping in the front room & "living" in the kitchen, doing away with the open fire in the middle room, having a fire you can sit by in the kitchen, & having a storage heater in the front room. Agreed, it wouldn't cut out the necessity for going upstairs entirely, but it would reduce it, & I'm sure you w^{d} feel the benefit. Much labour-saving, *I* think, could be effected by having only things you really use regularly close at hand. I think the store cupboard should be on the ground floor, though, for instance.[1]

I know you quail at the upset & expense: it would be less upset than moving completely, though. I wish I could help. [. . .]

With very much love,
Philip

1 Eva turned eighty-one on 10 January 1967. On 4 January she had written: 'I'm glad that you managed to get a little enjoyment during your visit here at Christmas. I am so sorry that I was in bed most of the time, but I do thank you very, very much for all you did for me and the nice breakfasts you brought up for me. Whatever I should have done with no one here to care for me I *don't* know. / I agree with you about the house. There *are* too many things in it.'

19 January 1967

32 Pearson Park, Hull

Dear old creature,

[. . .] I had some photographs taken in connection with the MS exhibition[1] – I wish I hadn't got such a double chin.

Like a salmon![2]

Much love, old creature P.

1 Poetry in the Making: An Exhibition of Poetry Manuscripts in the British Museum, April–June 1967 (Cecil Day Lewis, W. H. Auden, Ted Hughes, Philip Larkin, Jenny Lewis, Dylan Thomas, Derek Walcott).
2 Eva replied on 21 January: 'O, what a caricature you have made of yourself, Creature! You don't look a bit like that.'

5 February 1967

32 Pearson Park, Hull

My dear old creature,

Another fine mild Sunday. I left the car out last night, not having the energy to put it away. There was something in the paper today about it being the most remarkable 'false spring' since 1817. I think it's lovely! *Carpe diem*, or enjoy the day, as Oldus Creaturus, the Roman philosopher, said. [. . .]

The snowdrops have come up by the garden gate, and there are plenty of green spikes to support them. Isn't spring wonderful!

I have just gone to fetch myself a drink, it being nearly one o'clock. I don't know if I shall get out today. I went to call on the Hartleys yesterday, but they were out – I had bought two 'gift boxes' of soap & talcum powder for their 'little' girls, now not so little – well, they are about 12 or 11, I suppose. I can never think of any presents for girls between giant pandas & bottles of *Extase*. The last time I called the Hartleys were out but the girls were in, & they made me very welcome with coffee & cake, wch I thought very nice of them.[1] They are at a convent school near *Swine* (funny name for a village).[2]

Well, my dear old creature, I do hope you are well & are not feeling the effects of your illness. How is your temperature? It occurred to me that your temperature might *always* go up & down, but that we might not notice it except when you were ill.

Remember me to Kitty. Much love Philip.

1 Alison Hartley, thirteen years old at this time, kept a page-a-day diary. The entry for 5 February reads: 'Larkin came – and with him he brought two presents for Laurien and I. They were Yardley talc and soap (16/3) because we were so nice to him. It pays to be nice. I got 2/- once for admiring his tie.' The diary also records that he gave Laurien and Alison 10/- each at Christmas 1967. Laurien recalls: 'He was always charming and talked to us children with interest.' Personal communication, Alison and Laurien Hartley.

2 It had been a thriving pig-market in the Middle Ages.

19 March 1967

32 Pearson Park, Hull

My very dear old creature,

[. . .] The new library building is rising above ground now, & we shall be moving into the new bit on the north end before term starts at the end of April. I have persuaded the university to call it after the Vice Chancellor, so he should back me up in future. The Brynmor Jones Library![1] Rather a quaint thing to have done, but I suppose it will last 50 years or so, by wch time everyone will have forgotten who BJ was, & I shall be in retirement (94).

Well, my dear old creature, it's getting on for 2 o'clock, & I have all still to do. I do hope you are all right and not spending too much time looking at the sky! I have a jazz article to write before I leave Hull, then heigh ho for a few days' peace under your blessed roof. Very much love, dear old creature –

Philip

1 On 5 March Larkin had written: 'I am now Librarian of the Brynmor Jones Library. He has done a great deal to build it up in all senses. Perhaps he will raise my salary! It was my idea to call the Library after him, but I made it so long ago that I had almost forgotten about it.'

6 April 1967

Hull

My dear old creature,

[. . .] I was shocked on Wednesday on returning from York to find a cutting saying Diana Gollancz had died. She became Princess Loewenstein-Wertheim. It was for her that I drew my first 'creatures' – she used to call everyone 'dear creature'. Isn't it sad! She was only 45. [. . .]

Much love Philip

14 May 1967

32 Pearson Park, Hull

My very dear old creature,

It seems to be raining outside on a dull morning – I'm rather behind this morning, although I got up at 9.30 to hear the Archers. However, I was rather behind on sleep too – Friday night 4 a.m., Saturday night 2 a.m. I shall have a nice quiet day today.

Last Monday I went over to York to have dinner with this Mrs Baily,[1] who is in The Retreat, & who I knew *very* slightly at Oxford. I was interested to see this place, & asked her to show me round before we went into the town. It looked comfortable enough, but the people sitting about looked rather forlorn! Mrs Baily said it was very expensive, but she was a NHS patient, got in by influence – her sister is the wife of a Governor, or *is* a governor. Mrs B. suffers from 'depression', whatever that is. I think she has tried to kill herself once or twice. Not very cheerful![2]

Did you see a tiny mention of me on p.55 of the *S. Times* today – in the panel headed *Modern, Not Modernist*? Rather equivocal, in that I'm praised by Betjeman & Betjeman by me, but still, I'm there, the youngest person on the whole double page. Kingsley isn't there, as far as I can see. I expect you saw that Masefield had died, the poet laureate. I wonder who'll succeed him. I *hope* Betjeman, I *expect* Day Lewis.[3] [. . .]

I have given my old record player to the Anglican chaplaincy. The Chaplain is a nice Irishman called Quinn. They came to collect it on Friday. Hope I don't get 'in with the Church', as you feared for yourself!

Still raining – I hope you are content in mind, dear old creature.

Philip.

1 Penelope Baily ('Pen'), formerly Penelope Scott Stokes: Larkin's early Oxford muse. She inspired Poem XXX in *The North Ship*, 'So through that unripe day you bore your head', and featured in caricature in *Michaelmas Term at St Brides* (1943).
2 For Penelope's account of this meeting, in a letter to her daughter, see Susannah Tarbush, 'From "Willow Gables" to "Aubade": Penelope Scott Stokes and Philip Larkin', *About Larkin* 26 (October 2008), 5–10.
3 Eva wrote on 15 May: 'It is chiefly an honour, for I read that the yearly salary if it is called that, is not very much.' Cecil Day Lewis's surname was normally spelt with a hyphen. However, as he wrote in his autobiography *The Buried Day* (1960, 17), 'As a writer I do not use the hyphen in my surname – a piece of inverted snobbery which has produced rather mixed results.' He was appointed Poet Laureate in 1968.

21 May 1967

32 Pearson Park, Hull

My very dear old creature,

Rather a windy day today, seemingly, though I haven't been out yet. It is warm enough to sit in my bedroom without a fire. I have found myself a large gin and so can join you & Omar Khayyam –

> Ah, my Beloved, fill the cup that clears
> Today of past regrets and future fears . . .

What a fine poem it is! have been looking at it, and my eyes are full of tears. I know you learned it in your youth, when Daddy gave you a copy. How terribly sad life is.[1]

Well, nobody has offered me the job of being poet laureate yet – I expect there is a subcommittee sitting on it somewhere. I personally hope Betjeman gets it: he is not only the right *kind* of poet, but a *good* poet, as *The Spectator* says this week. It would be a tremendous honour to be offered it, but I should be very worried about it. Anyway, I hardly think it's likely.[2]

I have discovered a new advantage in life: Marks & Spencers shirts. I bought 4 yesterday, 3 white & 1 cream. They are only 27/11 each, quite well cut, made of cotton & nylon, & the laundry ruin my shirts in 3 years so it's not worth buying good ones at 60/- or 70/-. If only I could solve the pyjama problem I sh^{d} be all set. [. . .]

On Saturday 20 May Betty completed 10 years in my service: I sent her roses, & she gave me (she wasn't in at work) a "steering wheel glove", difficult to describe, but you'll see it when I come. It is of leather & must have been quite dear. It was the most awful trouble to fit on – just the present for Walter, perhaps. I shall have to take her out to dinner sometime. But not yet, not yet. [. . .]

Much love P.

1 Edward Fitzgerald, *The Rubáiyát of Omar Khayyám* (1859).

2 Eva replied on 22 May: 'I'm glad you liked the Omar Khayyam poem, it is all so true. I wonder if the Queen would be allowed to make a choice regarding the next poet laureate. It would be strange if she mentioned you. I think many of your poems are really wonderful and Kitty thinks they are better than John Betjeman's. I agree though, it *would* be rather a worry to you, for you have so little time to write. You are a *very* busy creature, dashing off to London and attending so many meetings and social functions.'

24 June 1967

<*Letterhead*> Durrants Hotel Ltd, Manchester Square, London W.1

My very dear old creature,

A rather shaky creature is sitting at the writing desk in the 'lounge' this bright warm summer morning. We had a late night last night; it began quite pleasantly, dinner with Betjeman & 'Lady Elizabeth Cavendish' (I can't help putting her in inverted commas, but she's perfectly genuine),[1] but an actor & his wife came in later & we stayed much later than we intended. Anyway it was all very pleasant. I did *not* succeed in persuading Betjeman to come to Hull.[2] At least, I think he might have liked to, but Lady Elizabeth put her foot down. She seems to run him.

Of the three days' cricket, two stopped short at 3 p.m. – rain stopped play. This was disappointing. Still, what we did see was all right. It was warm enough, anyway, despite the absence of sun.

It was very nice to have your letter as usual here on Friday. I've never looked closely at St Peter's – I suppose the fête was in the vicarage garden? It isn't very leafy down there, is it, not like the Parish Church. As regards my poems, *Reference Back* (in *TWW*) recalls an incident at York Rd many years ago, but *Love Songs* hasn't any connection with you, except that I suppose I remembered some of your songs.[3] The actor asked if I was writing much, and I said I thought I'd said my say. Lady Elizabeth overheard this & snapped 'Don't be tiresome.'

I am undecided about next weekend, i.e. *this* weekend: in a way I should like to visit you as I haven't been for some time; also Monica is seeing a specialist on Friday about her hand, & she might like someone to talk to about it. I suppose I'll have to say I'll ring up, either Monday or Tuesday! I note all you say about the 'lonely' week.[4] I don't know what to think. I shouldn't want to make things harder for you.

Well, this creature is becoming more shaky, & a long day lies ahead of it – a long hot day, I fancy. I'll be in touch with you again soon, & in the meantime send very much love as always – dear old creature!

Philip

1 Lady-in-waiting to Princess Margaret, and Betjeman's lover and companion following the rift with his wife Penelope on her conversion to Catholicism.

2 Larkin had persuaded the Arts Council committee administering a bequest by the philanthropist Joseph Compton to set up a fellowship, installing a writer in Hull University for a year. Betjeman was his first choice for this Compton Fellowship.

3 In a letter of 19 June Eva mentioned that the niece of a friend of hers was a 'great admirer' of Philip's poems and had 'said something about a poem about *me*. Have you written another one besides "That's a pretty one I heard you call" and oh, I have just remembered "Love Songs in Age", no doubt that is the one she means.'

4 Eva had written on 19 June: 'Your letters were very welcome indeed as I have been alone most of the days as well as the nights [. . .] I really don't know what to say about your next visit to me, Creature. It certainly would be nice to have you in my "lonely" week, except that you might not find things so well kept or comfortable this assuming that Mrs. Slater [the cleaner] doesn't come again.'

24 September 1967

Haydon Bridge.

My very dear old creature,

Well, I drove up here on Friday afternoon, a dark and rainy one, taking the main road way by West Auckland and Corbridge instead of coming over the dales. I got in about 5, just as all the shops shut! However, I registered at my hotel, took a walk round the town, then drove over to H. Bridge at just six o'clock. M. had been ready since 5, so I could have come earlier. Usually she's having a bath when I arrive.

Yesterday – Saturday – was fairly fine – very fine, really, in an autumnal sort of way – and we went to Bellingham Show after lunch. This was a big agricultural show in a village about 20 miles to the north. It was large & well-attended. I don't know what they'd done in the morning, but various horse events were taking place in the afternoon, and also *wrestling* – this is a special local brand called Cumberland and Westmoreland Wrestling, in wch the combatants hug each other like bears & try to throw each other over. There was a big tent full of show dogs – every possible breed, almost: plenty of Zimbas![1] – and I found them rather noisy & tiresome. Then there was a wonderful 'horticultural' tent – flowers & vegetables – these were beautifully got up, the vegetables scrubbed clean & arranged exquisitely: they make a speciality of *leeks* round here, the short & fat pot leeks, & the long & thin blanch leeks. Beautiful carrots, too, and parsnips, & someone had even got a prize for parsley! We did wish you had been there & could see it all. There was another big tent of cakes, jams, home-made wines (I thought of Edie), bread, scones, *salads*, honey, & all sorts of knitting, sewing, & *walking sticks*, these with horn handles, another local speciality. At the end of the day there was more horse jumping, but it began to get cold – I was *terribly* cold as to the feet – so we drove home, rather tired but well satisfied with a novel experience. It's nice to think that people are still doing these homely things. As a matter of fact, I was quite hungry by about 4.30 & would dearly have liked to annex one or two exhibits – sausage rolls in particular – but they were thoughtfully protected by wire netting like so many post office counters.

I'm afraid I have gone on about this rather a lot. A good thing you managed to get rid of your cases – I know they were bothering you. Fancy Pop having all his teeth out before he was 30![2] I cling to mine desperately, though I think my dentist thinks I am robbing the country.

I bought some special toothpaste in Hexham, called Emoform, 4/- a tube, but I haven't used it yet. It's supposed to be good for bad teeth. My gum is all right now.

Monica says she fell over an uneven piece of pavement, but her knee is healing – it was the left knee, & really badly grazed. She sends her love. She is packing up now: after lunch we set off for Hull, & I expect I shall ring up when we have got in. There seems a lot of food to go. I'm not sure whether we are taking a cold duck! I hope we all arrive safely.

I'm glad M[rs] Slater has succeeded in adjusting the clock. I think it's a case of fools rushing in where angels fear to tread! Anyway, dearest love to you, dear old creature,

Philip

1 Zimba was a large boisterous dog belonging to the Richards family who lived next door to Eva.

2 On 19 September Eva had written: 'Daddy had all his teeth out (before we were married) his Mother used to mince all his food (meat etc). I was staying at Tamworth Street at that time. He took his holiday then, which was a sensible thing to do.'

1 October 1967

32 Pearson Park, Hull

My very dear old creature,

October! In the university world, the beginning of a new year. Today was a very bright morning, but it has grown rather cloudier now; it also seems very windy. I have hauled all the clothes off the bed, a way of making me make it – new sheets are due. [. . .]

I rang up last night about 8.45 but you weren't in: never mind. I hope it wasn't the weather annoying you again. Did you like the photographs? I showed them to my photographer & he said they had been printed wrong: at least, 4, 5 & 6 had been over-printed, too yellow. 7 shows what the proper colours ought to be. I thought I might get myself an enlargement of 6. Is there any one you like, or Kitty w[d] like? Perhaps you think they're awful! I like 6 very much though: it shows you as the dear old creature you are.[1]

I smiled at the American lady the Hewetts met.[2] Surely they have peas and beans in America? It's only you & Monica who give *me* fresh food. Monica said that when she got to Leicester beans were 1/6[d] a lb. whereas they are only 10^{d} here! She thinks things are very cheap in Hull, when you can get them. It's true, it is a cheap place – cheap & rather nasty.

I am just going to get myself a Guinness. Got it. Almost like home! I am wondering if I can drink Guinness for a bit instead of gin: gin is so expensive & no one pretends it is "good for you". Perhaps G. w^{d} be more fattening though: I'm still a pound or so over 14st. How wonderful you are, slim as a rake, keeping on working! Still, you could do with a bit more flesh. Rest *every day* after lunch.

The telephone rang mysteriously after 10 this morning: I was in the bath, & didn't go, A slightly crazy woman called Helen Spalding is pursuing me, luckily from Hampshire. I met her just before I had that blackout & she convinced herself that I was in love with her & that she was with me. After much trouble I got rid of her. Now she is starting again: letters & parcels arrive daily. I send them back unopened. I live in terror of her arriving unexpectedly. Oh dear.

Dear creature, I love you very much & look forward to seeing you again.

Philip.

1 Seven numbered photographs are enclosed. On 3 October Eva replied. 'I showed Kitty the photographs and we discussed them, and decided, like you, that no. 6 was the nicest and no. 7 good and just like me. If she may have one she would prefer one of no. 6. Do you want me to return them? If so I would like one of No. 6 also to keep. Kitty remarked that you had a very good camera.' Nos. 6 and 7 are reproduced on Plate 15.

2 On 25 September Eva related that Kitty and Walter, on a theatre trip to London, had 'got chatting' over dinner 'to an American lady from near New York. She was in raptures with "our country" and said how beautiful were the green fields and what a lot of flowers there were. Nothing like that in America! [. . .] She also liked the food and said "O, I must have some of your peas before I leave, I've had beans."'

5 October 1967

32 Pearson Park, Hull

My very dear old creature,

How *glad* I am your arm is better! What a difference it will make to you! I howled with laughter about you & the salmon – I read your letter walking along to the garages under the yellowing trees. I thought your letter was so interesting. I'm sure the salmon w^{d} have been all right.[1]

I rang up Mr Hooper at Leicester today, & left a message asking him to 'investigate the delay' about the fire. Hope it will do some good.

Friday There's a bit about me [in the DT] this morning, in a report on the Cheltenham Festival on page ? of *The Daily Telegraph* – the arts page.[2]

A fine day here today.

Much love, dear old creature.
Philip

1 On 3 October Eva had written: 'I have decided not to keep any tinned goods in stock, at least not for long. I had two tins of salmon, one a small one which had been in stock for almost twelve months, the other a larger tin, dated 1964. I opened the small tin on Sunday and really wondered whether it would be good. Then I looked up what to do in the Medical book if one were laid low with food poisoning and after that took it out and buried it in the garden! What shall I do with the larger tin, now. Kitty suggested I should throw it in the dustbin unopened! or ask Mrs. Slater if she could cope with it.'

2 A press cutting is inserted: 'Cheltenham Festival Introspective Poets Get Few Listeners' by Sean Day-Lewis, Arts Reporter.

28 October 1967

32 Pearson Park, Hull

My very dear old creature,

I am beginning this at 10.30 p.m., in a very hot room, having just put the car away. I went out to see the Hartleys this afternoon, and found them in not too good spirits – Jean depressed about her economics,[1] and George having been run into in the car, & nabbed by the police for a parking offence (parking without lights!). As usual they gave me tea, or rather coffee, plus a history of English literature that says I am 'less formidably intellectual' than Auden. Produced in Finland. George was having a struggle with the gas board, to make them come & take away old fittings!

I am glad NCB[2] & Brooks are showing some interest in your fire. Don't pay any bill! I can't believe the change in fuel will do any good, but of course I hope it will. Perhaps in the end a Parkray expert will come & see what's wrong. Like you, I think the chimney is at fault.[3]

Of course, I sympathise over the wretched Richards & their inconsiderate behaviour. As soon as I saw they were tacitly extending their ground to the entry gate I was cross, & I think I should have contested it. Let them keep behind their own gate. Let them mend that. Damned backstreet swindlers.[4] [. . .]

Tomorrow is the first Library Committee of the year, wch is always a bit of an ordeal. Brenda will be 'attending', the first time a deputy has ever attended – I expect it will upset Wood.

Do leave any little jobs for me to do on Saturday. Write them down. As long as they are things I *can* do – not requiring any brains or skill!

I go up to London and back on Wednesday, to attend an Arts Co. meeting. It's now quite settled that Cecil Day Lewis will start visiting Hull in January.

How neat and tidy your letter is! You are a wonderful old creature. I shall look forward to seeing you on Friday.

Much love. Philip

1 'A' Level examination. Jean was determined to take a university degree as a mature student.

2 National Coal Board.

3 On 13 November Larkin sent a typed letter to Messrs A. R. Brooks enclosing his second letter to The Director, National Coal Board, Heat Advisory Service, Leicester: 'Mrs. Larkin, however, informs me that the fire has been further inspected by one of your representatives, and also by the contractor who installed it. We are grateful for this response to my letter, but as in each case the matter appears to have been left rather in the air I think I should report to you that the fire is still not giving satisfaction. [. . .] / I look forward to hearing your report on the situation in due course. Yours faithfully.'

4 In her letter of 25 October Eva relates that she has had words with her neighbours about their dog Zimba. 'I opened my back gate and Nigel and Linda [father and daughter] were standing at their back door – plus Zimba. I told them they *must* keep their back gate shut and not let Zimba loose in the entry as the tradespeople were afraid to come to my back door. Nigel said "Zimba won't bite them." I said "I think he will, and they don't know that he won't." Then he said "Well, *tell* them that he won't"! I asked them to shut their gate else I should go down to the police station. I phoned Kitty and asked her what she thought about it. She advised me not to take any action for she thought it would be fatal not to be on good terms with my next door neighbour.'

26 November 1967

32 Pearson Park, Hull

My very dear old creature,

[. . .] Mrs Stubbs[1] was speaking about a so-called comedian called Alan Bennett. Four poems of mine were on four TV programmes of his: I saw one, but it wasn't very good. He imitated John Betjeman when introducing it, & it was then he said it was by a great friend of his, only I'm not a great friend even of J. B. A. B. I've never met.

It was pretty dismal in the town yesterday. Every weekend I think I'll have 'a good shop', & look round as well as buy lots of nourishing food, but in fact it's so crowded & depressing I just snatch up a packet of sausages & make for home, or rather for the Hartleys. George had gone to some film festival, so just Jean & the girls were there. The girls had been to Stratford on Avon to see *As You Like It*. Fancy going all that way! There was a special train for them, of course. Jean seemed to be getting on better with her economics. As I expect I've said, she hopes to get into the University next year.

In the post yesterday there was a pack of poems from some young man in London, saying he always came to Hull at Christmas & had rung my bell three times last Christmas, & could he see me this Christmas . . .

I never answer the doorbell, anyway, unless it is rung long and repeatedly. In any case I rarely hear it. Hazards of Christmas in Hull! I expect to arrive between 8 & 9 next Friday – shall stay till *Monday*.

MUCH LOVE Creature

1 Eva's friend from the Circle of Silent Ministry.

1968

10 January 1968

32 Pearson Park, Hull

My very dear old creature,

I feel extremely ashamed of my unsympathetic attitude on the telephone tonight – I wish I could take it all back. We started off happily, but then this fearful loss of temper on my part arose when I thought you were appealing to me to come & take you to Hyde should the occasion arise instead of even asking Kitty.[1] I quite see now that you weren't, and it was all most unhappy.

I certainly agree it w^{d} be a great strain for you to go, & I don't think you should in bad weather & certainly not unaccompanied. Of course I sh^{d} like to know – I w^{d} send a wreath at any rate even if I didn't go.

As regards the wretched fire, again I agree with you it is not right for you. Did Walter mean I should write saying to Brooks we didn't want it, & w^{d} B. knock anything off the bill if he had it back? This might be worth doing – I will if you like.[2] I can't think that any other solid fuel fire w^{d} be much less trouble, though. I still think you should be able to live in the kitchen as much as possible, though.

Oh dear! I have behaved wretchedly – I don't know what gets into me. I humbly apologise. I really thought we should have a nice chat & you would tell me about your birthday. All day I've been thinking of you on and off, & have told one or two people it was your birthday. Perhaps I'm not well – I have felt a bit odd, very tired & as if I want to be in bed, though no other symptoms. I only wish I could wish you an affectionate goodnight in person, instead of at long range like this.

Thursday[3] Your letter arrived by first post, quite in order, so I had it for breakfast. Thank A. Nellie for her messages: I'm sorry she hasn't been well. A ball pen is just a ballpoint pen – just like you use, only of course they can be more elaborate and expensive.

The car seems to have cheered up for the moment – they are mysterious beings, almost with a life of their own at times, it seems. There was a garage bill of £22 waiting for me when I got back – such little surprises are frequent in the life of the car owner.

It's about 20 to 2 – I haven't been to work this morning, felt too fed up. I can see the first half of this term is going to be hell, like the last. Got up at 11, had a not-quite-hot-enough bath, a large breakfast, etc & now am almost ready to set out. I don't expect there'll be any parking space at the university.

Much love, dear old creature, & I'm sorry for my awful temper.

Philip.

1 Nellie was ill, and Eva had irritated Philip by speculating on hypothetical arrangements for travelling to her funeral.

2 On 9 January Eva wrote: 'About the Parkray. It was so bright and fierce last night when I wanted to make it up for the night that I thought I'd better not to. My peace of mind was better than having a fire in when I came down in the morning.' On 13 January she agreed to Philip's suggestion that he write to the NCB: 'Mr Brooks has sent in his bill again this morning. I really do not want to keep the Parkray. It is too much work and worry for *me*. You may write and tell him so if you will please.' On 14 January Philip offered to take a day off 'to be with you & see further people representing kinds of fire or heating'.

3 Thursday 11 January.

21 January 1968

32 Pearson Park, Hull

My very dear old creature,

I am writing in my bedroom as usual. Week succeeds week, & nothing alters, not that I want anything to alter. When I met the new young man below moving in, & he said "I shall be here only till August", I replied "I've been here since 1956" – at w[ch] he stared.

After talking to you on the telephone last night I had supper & did the stew. I find it difficult to know how much water to put in. If you don't cover it the top gets dry. It is doing away now, and I hope will be ready for lunch. Last Sunday the potatoes were only just done.

I am sorry the fire is such a nuisance. Regarding electricity, all one can do is ask the local branch of the Electricity Board what they can offer. Personally, I think gas is more reliable – there aren't many gas cuts! And gas fires don't go wrong like electrical ones. However, you *must* please yourself. Would you like me to see if I could come home to see the E Board with you, or for you?

As regards cost, well, as I say I am willing to pay your bills on condition I can reclaim from the estate. I don't see why Kitty sh^{d} think this mean. You have plenty of money, but don't want to spend it, as you live on the interest. If *I* pay your bills I am lending you money, interest-free. When I get it back it will be worth much less than it is now. The arrangement w^{d} be through a solicitor, & I sh^{d} pay him too. I am offering you a chance to be warm now & pay later – much later!

Anyway, think it over. I wish I had time to see about my flat – the howling draught from the windows, the need for more shelves, cupboards, etc. Perhaps people fuss about houses too much. We are here so short a time, it hardly seems worth bothering.[1]

This is a grey but reasonably mild day. When I have had lunch I shall go to the Library, Do you know there's a new Al Read[2] programme on Sunday at 2 p.m.? I expect it is repeated later in the week: yes, Wednesday evening, It's mostly the old stuff. The dog sketch reminds me of Zimba ("Lie down!" "Woof!" "Lie down!!" "Woof!!" etc).

Did I tell you that we had a madman in the Library last week? He was a young man who spoke very wildly – he first appeared in the evening when only the evening staff were there, but then he came back next day and *I* had to see him! He was very well-dressed and had an E-type Jaguar! The medical officer sent him to the local mental home in the end.

I thought your letter was remarkable, so long and clearly written & small yet legible in script. Splendid old creature. I really haven't a lot of news. Day succeeds day as always. Tomorrow is a library committee, wch always means a lot of work & worry & nervous strain. Do take care of yourself, old creature & try to get to bed early.

Much love xx Philip.

1 Eva's letters at this time are crammed with anxieties about whether the house would be saleable without a fire in the kitchen, whether she could afford another storage heater, whether she should have a telephone extension in her bedroom, etc.
2 Al Read (1909–87). Very popular British radio comedian of the 1950s and 1960s.

28 January 1968

32 Pearson Park, Hull

My very dear old creature,

My handwriting looks a bit shaky, doesn't it? No reason why it should. Isn't the weather beautiful: a fine, mild, spring-like day. Perhaps there are some signs of spring, if one looks for them. It might be worth looking in the garden.

I really don't know what I can tell you about: I duly went to Leeds on Friday, and had lunch with this poet Geoffrey Hill[1] in a colourful pub called Whitelock's – *he* had a plate of cold roast beef that looked very good, but my chops weren't so good. They gave me 10/- short in my change, too. Aawgh! However, it wasn't too bad. He struck me as rather a dismal Jimmy. He teaches at Leeds University.

We then went to Leeds University & I left him to take the chair at a library group meeting – in the course of it I got out of being chairman, wch I have been for about 4 years, so that was good. My hearing aid wasn't much good. There was a man at my left elbow who roared like a sea lion, & a group of whisperers at the end of the table. However, I got through it somehow.

This week will have its busy side. The Poet Laureate is coming up again & I shall have to take the chair at his lecture, a thing I don't much like doing, but still. He's going to talk about Yeats. Then on Thursday evening there is a dinner for the Vice Chancellor to celebrate his knighthood – means dressing for it, too. On Friday morning at 11.30 a.m. there is a "topping-out" ceremony, to mark the completion of the shell of the new building, followed by a lunch. Then what is left of me goes to a coffee evening at Maeve's on Saturday, & drives home on Sunday. All very taxing. I found the Library Committee a great strain, though they were all perfectly pleasant, and I got most of what I wanted, but the nervous strain is fearful, I just fell asleep in my chair after it.

I hope you'll listen to Al Read today. I shall.

The Debonair fire sounds much too powerful for your little kitchen, wch would be about 1,000 cubic feet, wouldn't it?[2] We must be absolutely sure that you get something you like this time. I still feel an electric fire w^d^ be more likely to go wrong than a gas one, & of course there might be powercuts. But as I say you *must* get something you are really happy with.

I was glad to hear that Miss Langton had called on you. It would be nice if you had a few friends near at hand, who could be visited without long walks or taxi rides. With Miss Langton you could talk about your houses, as they're both much the same,

The bill for my hearing aid has come in again – £59. It's about as much use as the Parkray. Funny it should cost the same.

I wish I could find something new to read – I went through *Rebecca*[3] again & loved it, finding it very exciting. I never seem to have time to go to the Library in town, and there isn't much there when I do! Well, dear old creature, I shall be seeing you soon. I wonder if K & W are enjoying *The Spectator*. I can never get it here. Have early nights & easy days.

Much love Philip.

1 The poet Geoffrey Hill (1932–2016) taught in Leeds University from 1954 to 1980.
2 On 22 January Eva had written: 'Whilst looking for something else \just now/ I came upon a leaflet relating to the gas fire that Miss Unwin recommended, Debonair, but it is Debonair *Major* for the larger room, and will heat a large room of 2,500 cubic feet capacity. Weight 60 lbs (27 kg). I don't know what that means.'
3 The 1938 novel by Daphne du Maurier (1907–89).

18 February 1968[1]

32 Pearson Park, Hull

My very dear old creature,

[. . .] Rosemary's hyacinths are continuing to entertain me. The one that didn't flower seemed to break in half, and one half flowered & the other didn't. Now the bit that didn't flower is showing signs of life! I really ought to write & tell her.[2] One letter I did write was to a firm from wch 5 years ago I bought 6 pairs of socks. They are just now going into holes, & I wonder if I can get any more. They have done well, haven't they?

I haven't heard yet from Mr Brooks.[3] [. . .]

I must start to write to Monica now.

Much love from Philip

1 Larkin wrote '(Sunday anyway)' after the date; 18 February 1968 was indeed a Sunday.

2 Rosemary had given Larkin a bowl of hyacinths for Christmas, and he had written a ceremonious letter of thanks. On 19 March he wrote again: 'I thought you would like to know that your hyacinths did well. One, the blue, came out quickly. Then a second began to show signs of life, & was white. The third didn't stir at all, & I thought it was dead, but in the end it astonished me by splitting in two, and producing two separate yellow blooms. This pleased me no end. / The blooms smelt delightful & made my room much fresher than it usually is.'

3 After two formal letters from Larkin, copied to the National Coal Board, Heat Advisory Service, Brooks submitted a revised invoice, and Philip replied with a typed letter dated 1 March: 'My impression was that when we discussed this fire with your representative the cost given was below £40. The Supervisor of Buildings in this University tells me that the cost price to an ordinary customer for a Parkray 66 KF and smoke pipe is £36.10-. [. . .] I should be grateful to have your observations on his comment at your convenience.'

31 March 1968

London

My very dear old creature,

I'm just taking the chance to write you a page after breakfast at Bob's.[1] It's a beautiful fine morning and I should like to be out in it. However, my host shows no great desire to do so and I don't want to be a nuisance. [. . .]

I return to Hull this afternoon or evening rather, & shall perhaps ring up.

We saw Kingsley last night. He has a beard! He has just come back from America. You'll probably see that he has written another James Bond book – this will make him even richer than before.[2]

Well, I won't attempt a second page, but I wanted to send my love & tell you where I was.

Your affec. Creature

1 The envelope is postmarked Battersea, where Robert Conquest lived at this time.
2 *Colonel Sun*, published by Amis under the pseudonym 'Robert Markham' (Jonathan Cape, 1968).

7 April 1968

32 Pearson Park, Hull

My very dear old creature,

[. . .] The news from America is bad, isn't it.[1] Aren't you glad you don't live there? I shouldn't like a crowd of Negroes roaming around Pearson Park, or Loughborough.

This has been a disagreeable week in many ways, ending with my having to chair an all-day Conference on South-East Asian Studies library provision on Friday. It went off all right: there were representatives from the School of Oriental & African Studies, British Museum, National Lending Library, and one or two Dutch places. We had lunch, On the whole I find the prospect of working for the next 20 years & then dying rather depressing! It isn't really what I wanted to do.

Your letter was very interesting & beautifully written as usual, and I'm glad to hear the lumbago is subsiding. [. . .]

Love as ever P.

1 Riots had followed the assassination of Martin Luther King on 4 April 1968.

9 May 1968

32 Pearson Park, Hull

My very dear old creature,

This is just to say I am back safely on a very wet evening after my London trip, and was pleased to find your letter. London was rather tiring – wet underfoot, & very hot – but I am still in one piece.

While I was there I delivered in person to No. 10 Downing Street a refusal of the O.B.E.! I was offered it a few days ago, but felt I must turn it down. Still, I thought you'd be glad to know your creature has been offered it. There was no need for me to deliver my reply personally, of course, but I happened to be passing, having been to the House of Commons. I don't think you shd tell anyone – K & W, perhaps, but not the Hyde people. Not even Rosemary – I don't want it known in Universities.[1]

I was tormented by a shirt with a fearfully tight collar. It has left quite a weal. Awgh! I think these Marks & Spencers shirts shrink. It's supposed to be 16.[2]

Well, dear old creature, more on Sunday. Keep smiling.

Much love P.

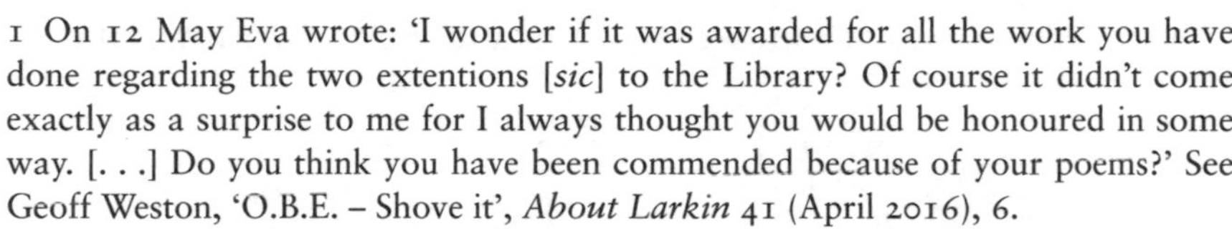

1 On 12 May Eva wrote: 'I wonder if it was awarded for all the work you have done regarding the two extentions [*sic*] to the Library? Of course it didn't come exactly as a surprise to me for I always thought you would be honoured in some way. [. . .] Do you think you have been commended because of your poems?' See Geoff Weston, 'O.B.E. – Shove it', *About Larkin* 41 (April 2016), 6.

2 Sixteen-inch collar size.

23 June 1968

Durrants Hotel, London

My very dear old creature,

Well! Not a very successful visit. No play after lunch on Thursday, & hardly any play at all yesterday: it *was* depressing, just hanging about the ground watching the rain fall. It isn't so much the waste of money one minds as the tedious waste of time – & it's so depressing, doing nothing. Worst of all, we had to wait about half an hour in the rain for a bus! Spirits were very low: mine were, anyway.

They are not too bright this morning, either: there is something about breakfast at this hotel that puts one's back up. It is intensely *mean*: one has positively to *extort* food out of them, & then it comes in *tiny* amounts – one pat of butter, a spoonful of honey in a saucer, the remains of somebody else's milk. Year after year it's the same. God knows what the Americans think of it.

Then there is the worry of these idle swine of railway-men. I hope I get back to Hull tomorrow night all right.[1] Awgh! I am starting to feel tired of being away. The continual brush with people exhausts me. I should prefer to be back in the silence of my flat.

I'm interested to hear you have been allocated a 'home help'. I do hope she turns out successfully – I believe Hilary Amis worked as a home help in her v. young days, & though I'm sure she meant well I can't imagine she was much use.

I don't imagine Rosemary will *not* get a degree, but it still seems rather vague. I expect it will be a fearful 'family' day, ending with humps all round! Why are they holding it in the Cathedral? It's not a religious ceremony. Grrrr. I'm not sure if you are expecting me to come on 3 August for a week: let me know some time. The pieces of cardboard can, I think, be thrown away.[2] I hope you managed to dispose of *some* of the rubbish in the store room!

You'll feel very luxurious setting off in a motor to Gt Yarmouth![3]

I wish I could come & see you. Perhaps nearer the time we could see. It's a freakish idea, though.

Today M. & I are going to lunch with the Day Lewises, out at Greenwich. I don't know whether to take my hearing aid or not! He tends to mumble, & of course there are children . . . M. is not greatly looking forward to it. I don't expect it'll be highly enjoyable, but D. L. is a genuinely friendly soul. Well, this is rather a bitty letter, but I mean well. Very much love, old creature. Have you had any strawberries yet?

Philip

1 On 24 June the National Union of Railwaymen rejected a pay and productivity offer from British Rail and began a 'work-to-rule' which lasted twelve days. The details of Philip's return journey are not recorded.

2 On 17 June Eva wrote: 'To-day I have been very busy and have sorted out all the things from the store room which were in the corner in the front bedroom upstairs. It *was* a job and I have wrapped most of the things up and labelled them before putting them back in the store room. Have thrown a few oddments away! / I found a box containing squares of cardboard really belonging to you. I think they are used to pack up records. Shall I throw them away or do you want them?'
3 Eva and Nellie stayed in the Windsor Hotel, Great Yarmouth, for a fortnight from 21 July.

30 June 1968

Hull

My very dear old creature,

I am sitting on the ground with my back against the car out of doors somewhere beyond Cottingham. It is such a lovely day that I felt I must get out to write my letters. The lane I am sitting beside is not very busy, but I expect everyone will be out as the day wears on. I'm looking over a field of green stuff – barley perhaps – that ripples almost like water. The sun is extremely hot.

Unfortunately I have left your letter behind! Awgh! I picked up two, but neither was yours. Very silly of me. I will look at it when I get back & see whether I have forgotten to answer anything. [. . .]

I have heard from the Leicester Elec. Bd. that they are willing to put in another immersion heater in your boiler at the bottom *for nothing*,[1] and connect the off peak connection to it. They will leave the present one in, dead, to save trouble. They are still doubtful if this will give full satisfaction, but they are prepared to do it. I take it you are agreeable? It will mean workmen coming, but not for long.

It really is a lovely day, hayfever or no hayfever. The country falls away before me very green & sparkling. Beside me the high nameless grasses are waving. I've had to take my jacket off, it's so hot.

On Thursday I'm taking my car in for a complete overhaul – they want it at 8 a.m.! Awgh!! They'll be lucky! Then Friday is my ordeal.[2]

Much love, old creature. P.

1 The correspondence reveals a long wrangle about Eva's newly installed immersion heater which heated only 4/5 of the tank.
2 A dental appointment.

1 August 1968

32 Pearson Park, Hull

My very dear old creature,

This is just to wish you a safe and enjoyable journey,[1] & to say there'll be a letter – small one – waiting among ALL THE BILLS at the other end.

Much love
Philip

1 Letter addressed to Windsor Hotel, Wellesley Road, Great Yarmouth, Norfolk. Eva was about to return home from the Yarmouth holiday with Nellie.

1 August 1968[1]

32 Pearson Park, Hull

My very dear old creature,

Found it? I have just looked out & seen a half moon – is this waxing, or waning? Everything looks very peaceful.

This is my seventh day without drink (alcohol)! On coming back from London I felt so fed up with it I decided to lay off for a week. On the whole I haven't missed it, but it's a bit awkward socially.

I was delighted to have your letter this morning. Fancy you watching TV, or trying to watch it. You don't mention other people specially in the hotel: has A. Nellie not 'cottoned on' to your fellow-guests as she usually does?

I actually bought some broad beans and had them with ordinary bacon tonight – shelled & cooked them! They were good – nicer than frozen ones.[2]

Please give my love to A Nellie. I think I can come on the *8th*, so you won't be alone.

Much love,
Philip

1 Addressed to 21 York Road, Loughborough, Leics.
2 Eva wrote on 4 August: 'I am very surprised to know that you are \giving/ alcoholic drinks the "go-by"! I hope you feel all the better for doing so. What a nice meal you cooked – broad beans and bacon. / We brought back a Pork Farms cooked chicken and had it today with peas and potatoes. It was very nice, but not quite done enough near the bone.'

4 August 1968

<*Letterhead*> 32 Pearson Park, Hull

My very dear old creature,

[. . .] Yes, the theatre is quite awful: I can't hear a word. You *might* have your ears looked at by an ear man, privately: I did & it cost 5 gns. He told me I was on the borderline of social adequacy, as far as hearing goes, of course! But I doubt if the hearing aid is much good, except for committees.

Queen (magazine) has offered me £20 or a case of champagne for a carol! I don't think I could manage it.

Has the water gone down in the cellar? I hope so, & that all is in order. I expect the garden has grown a bit. Does the hot water tank still make noises? [. . .]

Much love,
Philip

15 August 1968

32 Pearson Park, Hull

My very dear old creature,

[. . .] A man has just presented me with a copy of *The Letters of Wilfred Owen*, whch he helped edit.[1] Owen was an extremely good war poet. Most of his letters are to his mother! The book is 629 pp. long. He starts his letters 'Sweet my Mother', wch takes some living up to. I like mine better – my beginnings, I mean. My mother too, probably.

Chilly wet day here.

Much love, dear old creature,
Philip

1 Harold Owen and John Bell (eds), *Wilfred Owen: Collected Letters* (Oxford: Oxford University Press, 1967).

18 August 1968

32 Pearson Park, Hull

My very dear old creature,

[. . .] I went to the Hartleys' yesterday. Jean has got her two A levels, so presumably she will be coming to the University in October. They're bringing out another edition of my recording of *The Less Deceived*, with a new cover. This has another 1957 photograph of me, in the graveyard, looking very young and common.

It's been nice talking to you on the telephone, though I'm sorry the weather bothers you so much. Truly, it won't do you any harm. Roll up in a ball, and forget about it. You'll be quite safe. [. . .]

Love as always Philip

6 September 1968

Torridon

My very dear old creature,

It's Friday evening, & I've just changed for dinner, & am scribbling a page for you in the hope that it will arrive on Monday. To get it collected on Saturday I shall have to drive down into the village tonight specially!

It has been a glorious day here & we have spent it at Daibaig,[1] a tiny village near Torridon: just a few cottages, a jetty, sea, sheep, gulls, hens, looking out onto the loch & the sea beyond. Really, the beauty of these highland villages is beyond belief. I see the old creatures pottering about in aprons at their back doors, & I think that even you couldn't be nervous in such surroundings! There's one bus every day, to bring post, & connect them with Achnasheen, where there's a railway station. We ate our packed lunch, & took photographs, & peered in a few rock pools – extremely colourful and lively, & although there was nothing to do the day passed very well. Really, this was the nicest day here we have had. M. didn't care for the hens, especially the way they pecked about on the beach! She said perhaps their eggs w^dn't^ need salt. [. . .]

I must take your letter to the village box now: 2 miles! Awgh! It's a glorious evening, the sun (6.45) shining hot and unhindered.

My very best love, in wch M joins, Philip

1 Larkin has misspelled Diabaig.

22 September 1968

32 Pearson Park, Hull

My very dear old creature,

[. . .] This week I had to interview an Indian – a Ceylonese, actually – for a job as porter, and have offered it him, though I don't know if he'll turn up. He seemed a nice chap but I couldn't understand a word he said! He'd been in the Royal Navy as a steward and had good references. I hope he turns out a success. I'm also expecting to appoint a Ceylonese lady higher up the scale. Integration! I just can't get English people.

My dentist thinks he is making progress now, and expects to do the great fitting next Friday. I do hope it's a success, and doesn't drop out the first meal I have.

I had a pair of kippers for breakfast, & some oatcakes brought from Hexham. I can't get any good fruit these days – peaches woolly, pears woody.

I hope Rosemary is well again. I shall be interested to hear of her doings. I believe the new Library at Leicester has been shelved more or less indefinitely. Mine goes on apace.

Very much love, o.c. Philip.

29 September 1968

<*Letterhead*> 32 Pearson Park, Hull

My very dear old creature,

[. . .] I've had a second load of laundry back but haven't checked it – they cost about 30/- each. One pair of socks missing so far.

Yes, I appointed a Ceylon girl,[1] to match the Ceylon porter. I don't know how she'll be. She's quite well qualified. If she takes my job she will have to pay back a grant she came to England on – in instalments, I hope! She says life is awkward for a single woman in Ceylon – can't go anywhere. She starts on 14th October. [. . .]

Much love o.c. Philip

1 This was Lila Wijayatileka, Senior Library Assistant, Inter-Library Loans.

15 November 1968

Queensberry Court Hotel, London

My very dear old creature,

Here I am, perishing in cold London. The train down was awfully poorly heated, & instead of comfortably reading the work I'd brought with me I shuffled along to the bar to seek inner warmth. London is pretty nippy anyway. I wish I'd brought my overcoat.

Your letter was very kind – though it was mid-afternoon before I had a chance to open it. How exciting about the lavatory![1] I do think it will be nice & snug in there. 150w. is only like an electric light bulb – it doesn't take much power, if one bar of a fire is 1000w. (if! I'm not very good at home electricity).

I left my hat in the train!

Work continues to be extremely heavy. Really awful. I suppose I earn my £4,200 a year! I wish I could find a part-time job for £2,100. Or even a quarter time job for £1,050. Senate went on till 6.45 p.m. on Wednesday.

Do wrap up well, old creature, & don't stay too long in your newly-luxurious lavatory – I don't expect it's as warm as all that. Has the front room heater improved?

Very much love – Philip

1 In a letter of 11/12 November Eva wrote: 'The installation was quite a job, and took longer than I thought, but it is very nice to have the light in the toilet and the two foot tubular heater is set at 38° [F]. Any weather below that temperature will put the heater on. I don't know how it can do this!'

5 December 1968

32 Pearson Park, Hull

My very dear old creature,

A hard dreary week, leaving me feeling corpsed. As I said on the telephone, I didn't make much of an impression on the U.G.C.,[1] & it was a strain. Today hasn't been much better. Cold, too! Day Lewis was here today for the last time, & there was a lunch. He said that the students had begun by treating him as a sacred cow, but ended by treating him as a cow. I drove him to the station. Really, he's been very pleasant while he's been here. [. . .]

Much love, old creature,
Philip

1 University Grants Committee.

8 December 1968

32 Pearson Park, Hull

My very dear old creature,

I am sitting in my bedroom with the rug over my knees & my Shetland wool cap on, hoping I shall be warm enough. It looks a grey day out of doors – when did we last see the sun? However, I think it's milder. I awoke at 8.20, thought I was entitled to another hour, so got up at 9.20, then lay in the bath till 10.20. Brown boiled egg for breakfast. I finished my jazz articles last night so I feel a little freer, except that there's lots to be done in the Library.

Last week was a frightful week. I'm glad it's over. We are giving Day Lewis an Honorary Degree in July, & I took the opportunity to send the VC a letter saying that if he was thinking of me to do the citation, he'd better think of someone else. This is because I can't see myself standing up & saying that he's a good poet! Nasty creature. He's a very nice man, & I wouldn't mind standing up & saying that, but you don't get honorary degrees for being a nice man – not ostensibly, anyway.

I called on Hartley yesterday, to see how he was.[1] He's carpeted the back room, wall to wall, & painted it very professionally, so he doesn't seem to be grieving. There's still a faint unspeakable stench hanging about the house, but I can't guess its source. He never liked milk & has stopped taking it – bit of a disadvantage when giving people tea.

It was nice to have such an informative letter from you. Your parcels must be going *letter* post: there's no 1st or 2nd class *parcel* post. Really, I shan't mind if we have only bread & butter for Christmas, as long as there's enough of it.

Did you find the port? I'm sure it's there somewhere. [. . .]

I shouldn't care much for my mild honours if I couldn't tell them to you & Monica! There's no more news on this front so far. Fabers are making plans to publish my jazz articles next year in a book called *ALL WHAT JAZZ*. They've offered me an advance of £200, wch seems a lot. Incidentally, when M wrote she never mentioned the hon. degree! Awgh!

I hope I shall come home on 23 Dec. & be free to help you on 24 & so on. Pease don't get into a flat spin over it all. It's a fearful time of year, but we just have to grin & bear it. Or grin, anyway. Much love!

Philip

1 The Hartleys' marriage had broken down and Jean had left George, taking her daughters with her.

1969

5 January 1969

32 Pearson Park, Hull

My dear old creature,

The snow seems to be hanging about a long time – 'waiting for some more' they would say in the country, I expect – but the weather isn't cold. Just rather dull & dreary!

Well, New Year was quite remarkable. On New Year's Eve we drove to the small town of Allendale, arriving about half past eleven. There were lots of people out in the main square, where there was also a large unlit bonfire. Some of the people were in fancy dress, & there was a band dressed as crusaders! All the pubs in the square were lighted & seemed open, but we didn't go in. Then about 25 to midnight people began to thread their way through the crowd carrying shallow tubs on their heads, like wash tubs, full of wood & inflammable stuff: there must have been at least 20 of them. Suddenly a light flared, & two people were seen with torches, going round lighting peoples' tubs & also the bonfire. When all the tubs (still on peoples' heads) were alight, the carriers formed up into a line & marched off round the village – I think the band went with them. We could see them go down one street & along another: you can imagine how the flames looked against the darkness & the snow. Eventually they came back up to the market-place, marching round the bonfire & emptying their barrels onto it. By that time it was midnight & the band played *Auld Lang Syne*, & we joined hands & sang it. A complete stranger whose hand I held insisted on giving me a drink of whisky, & I wished him a happy new year. There was a lot of kissing going on, & many grotesque figures – rajahs, surgeons, witches – mingling with the crowd. All very jolly![1] After a while we went back to Haydon Bridge & had our own drink, & I drove back to Hexham, where the hotel's celebrations were far from over. However, I got to sleep eventually.

Next morning I had a flat tyre (?tire), w[ch] was a nuisance as New Year's Day is completely dead in those parts. However, I got it attended to eventually, & was ready to drive M. to her cousin's funeral at Rookhope. Rookhope is a wild and isolated place among snow-covered hills, & all in all it was very bleak. The funeral was held in a Methodist Chapel w[ch] was crowded, as the man had been a well known figure in the town. We went to the graveyard where it was even bleaker, and I noticed how all along the street the curtains were drawn. There was tea afterwards in the village hall, but M preferred not to go. [. . .]

Much love Philip.

1 In its present form the Allendale tar barrel ceremony dates from 1858, though it has ancient roots.

20 April 1969

32 Pearson Park, Hull

My very dear old creature,

I seem to have been talking with you quite a lot recently, so I haven't a great deal to say that's new. I had your letter on Thursday, and wasn't surprised to hear that you were finding it cold. It's pretty parky here even yet, although the birds are beginning to show themselves. The weather is more or less steady, & of course all our settled weather comes from the east, on a chilly wind.

My ailments seem to have mostly cleared up now: even the cough is on the way out. But my couple of days in bed did me a world of good. I really enjoyed being off. I must do it again some time. Yes, I got my laundry back from next door, & must now start collecting up another lot. Laundry never endeth.

I'm delighted to hear that the eggs have hatched. I hope the two birds grow up safely. You are probably right in saying that Zimba keeps the cats away. The collie dog that molests me has reappeared, & I have written to the Chief Constable again. Bloody nuisance. Why can't people keep their dogs under control?

Our term starts tomorrow. No doubt it will bring its quota of worry and upset. We showed the Vice-Chancellor round the Library on Thursday, & although he started off in rather a critical mood he was unwillingly admiring at the end. Of course, he's an awful ass, but the place is called after him. There's a small article about it in *The Observer* this morning, but you don't see it, do you.

I'm sorry you've been feeling worried about the prospect of holidays, and of things in general. I'm enclosing a copy of the letter I wrote to K & W, wch you can keep, about holidays: It hasn't produced any reply yet. It does seem rather complicated – too hard for Kitty to grasp, I expect – but all the same it's perfectly reasonable.[1]

I don't see why they shouldn't take you away sometimes, as I suggest, either. M & I are thinking of going to Ireland this summer, so I shall want to get things settled fairly soon. You'd perhaps better not say I've sent you a copy of the letter!

I can quite understand that in the long run, too, you're wondering how life can be made less of a burden. Personally, I should like to see you in a smaller set of living quarters, but with your own things, or some of them: someone looking in regularly & doing the shopping: preferably in Loughborough where you have friends, & your doctor knows you. To have someone to live with you at present w^d be another possibility, but it wouldn't get rid of the trouble of the house.

By the way, I am wondering if I could stay with you (between trips to London) on Thursday night, 1 May? I should arrive about six, I suppose, and be ready to overeat at supper. I shall have been to the RA banquet.

Much love again, old creature – don't forget the port & the wireless.

Philip

1 Larkin enclosed a copy of a two-page letter to Kitty and Walter (13 April). Auntie Nellie, he wrote, would not be available, which 'seems to me to have two consequences: one, that if Mother is to have a holiday at all you or I must arrange it; and two, that if she is not to be left alone in Loughborough your holidays & mine must be arranged in cooperation. In other words, it's Christmas all over again on a larger scale.' He proposed that he take Eva on holiday either at the beginning of August or the beginning of September, and ended: 'Apologies for style & writing – I'm "ill" & a bit feverish. Yr affec. Brother, Philip.' In her reply to Philip, on 21 April, Eva tried to side-step the quarrel between her son and daughter: 'It is most kind of you, Creature, to give up two weeks of your holiday to me. I wonder whether it would be any good my going down to the home help offices here. They sent me a very nice person for one day. I don't suppose they would be able to find anyone to stay with me for a week or so. The only other solution might be for me to enquire at Abbeyfield whether the "guest" room would be available for the time when Kitty is away. Somehow I think it might already be booked.'

18 May 1969

32 Pearson Park, Hull

My very dear old creature,

Changeable day, sun & rain alternating. Just at present it's sun, & the trees are all looking beautifully green. I rose rather late, not intentionally, but I had a rather disturbed night through this difficulty in breathing through my nose. However, I didn't have a bath, so have caught up a bit.

Yesterday there was a meeting of four Faber poets in a village near here – Richard Murphy is here, as you know, & Ted Hughes came over to see him, & so RM asked me and a young Scotsman called Douglas Dunn, who has just had a book accepted by Fabers, to lunch. So we went out and had a simple lunch at Murphy's cottage in Lockington.[1] I took a photograph of us all. I don't suppose you know Ted Hughes: he is as famous as I am, only younger: a great thug of a man, never does any work. I rather envy him. D. Dunn's book will be coming out in the autumn: I think some of it is good.[2]

The week hasn't been especially enjoyable: I felt very fed up by Thursday, but it's a bit better now. My suit came on Friday, & doesn't entirely please me, though of course I haven't worn it yet. Perhaps I ought to wear it to see how it fits. My pursuit of the Ideal Suit is rather laughable.

I haven't done anything about ~~my~~ our week in Norwich: Monica said she knew a man from there & would ask him what the Maid's Head was like, but I haven't heard from her.[3] I don't know whether to go on waiting, or trust to luck. It's not long till August!

I told you that I had been asked to 'reply for the guests' at the dinner for the honorary graduates at Queens – isn't this awful? It will spoil my whole visit. I think I must say I am no good as a speaker, but if they want me I will do it. Oh dear! From now on my life will be overshadowed by the speech for Day Lewis on 5 July & this wretched speech on 9 July. Oh dear! However shall I do it?

I think I shall make my way home on Friday evening next & stay till Tuesday morning – but I shall bring some work to do in order to salve my conscience. I hope this is convenient. It's not that I mind coming home, but the roads are so crowded at such times, & I feel ashamed of coming back late, when others are working.

Did you ask Kitty about Pitchforth at the RA dinner?[4] He used to teach her, didn't he? I believe he's quite deaf now – not the only one. I do think your doctor ought to have seen you, when you'd made an appointment.

M. love Philip

1 Richard Murphy had succeeded Cecil Day Lewis as the second Compton Lecturer in Poetry at Hull.

2 The Scottish poet Douglas Dunn (b. 1942) had graduated from the University of Hull, and then worked in the library under Larkin. His first volume of poems, *Terry Street*, was published in 1969.

3 They eventually stayed at the Duke's Head instead.

4 Roland Pitchforth (1895–1982) had been an official British war artist during World War II. Eva replied on 19 May: 'Kitty said that she had never heard of Mr. Pitchforth.'

19 June 1969

32 Pearson Park, Hull

My very dear old creature,

[. . .] I don't feel too good today: Hartley was here last night, & I didn't get him out till after one a.m. as usual. I never like his visits, but I have to put up with him. He is selling all his papers (including about 80 letters of mine), or trying to. I'm not too keen on this.

Our move has started, & is going fairly steadily, though one vital lift keeps breaking down. Most of the girls turn up in trousers wch makes them look very unusual, as normally they aren't worn for work. I'm about the only one who isn't helping. Idle creature!

Much love, take care,
Philip

22 June 1969

32 Pearson Park, Hull

My very dear old creature,

[. . .] The Library move continues to take up all our time. The staff is doing very well, working hard & in good spirits. They began on Wednesday & we have to get it done by 5 July. Did I tell you that Day Lewis has had a heart attack & won't be coming for his honorary doctorate? So I have ceased work on his citation. I'm sorry for him, as he was a very nice chap – *is* a very nice chap – & more so than some.[1] Wasn't it nice, John Betjeman getting a knighthood! Sir John! Well, well!

Your letter was very well written & full of interest. I wonder if you did get another meal from the chicken? I agree, food is a problem. I eat bacon & eggs, fish cakes, soup & cheese, tinned salmon. Actually I am down, almost, to 14 stone!! Isn't that wonderful? I wonder if I am wasting away. Recently I have been eating Ryvita instead of bread, & this may help. I agree the weather has been very up and down, but we certainly got out of the hot spell without any storms.

I am interested to hear of your new glasses[.]

One has to have a test every few years, I think. But certainly you are wonderful for your age! It's all this work that does it, though I wish you could do less. A little bungalow, or someone to look after you . . . I don't know.

I can't breathe through my nose. Things seem no better. Heaven knows when they will improve. Perhaps in the autumn. [. . .]

Well, it is 1.30 p.m. & I'm still not dressed. I have a quarter of boiled ham (cut off ye Bone) for lunch. For breakfast I had juice, yoghurt & boiled egg. In between I had gin. Awgh!!

Love dear old creature. Philip

1 The ceremony was postponed until 3 May 1970, when Larkin did give the speech.

24 July 1969

32 Pearson Park, Hull

My very dear old creature,

Oh dear, what a week. Today I should have been at Buckingham Palace garden party, but what with one thing and another I couldn't face it. I saw the surgeon at 9 this morning & he largely unstopped my nose, & told me to come again tomorrow: it's just about as good now as it was *before* I had the operation! He now says it'll be four weeks before it's fully right. Hum! I don't feel *any* benefit so far.[1]

How very kind of you to ring last night! It was so reassuring to hear you, even though the line was bad. Jean Hartley came round later, to seek support against her ex husband George – wch I don't really want to give. He is – according to her – trying to diddle her on various money matters.

I learned this morning that my D.Litt. robes would cost less than £50, so this is all right.[2] I can stand that! When I get them I will bring them home & put them on for you. My gown of glory.

I'm afraid we had a little thunder last night, but it didn't worry me. Hope you are free!

Much love, very dear old creature.
Philip

1 Larkin had undergone an operation to remove a polyp from his nose on 21 July, staying overnight in hospital.

2 Larkin had received an honorary D.Litt. at Queen's University Belfast on 9 July.

29 July 1969

32 Pearson Park, Hull

My very dear old creature,

[. . .] My nose is still not yet clear, & feels rather raw & unhealed. The surgeon says it will be some weeks before it's right, but it doesn't *really* inconvenience me. He rather staggered me by presenting me with my x-rays, on wch I don't look so fat as usual. The polyp is visible – quite large! Polyp Larkin. Did I tell you at the Nursing Home a rabbit came and ate grass on the lawn between 7.30 & 8 a.m.? [. . .]

A lovely day here!

I hope you're resting like this creature.

Much love
Philip

7 September 1969

Ballylickey House Hotel (Bantry, Ireland)

My very dear old creature,

I'm afraid this won't get on its way to you until Monday, as I believe in rural Ireland there's no Sunday collection, but I'm writing it all the same, & it can get on its way. Not that there's a great deal to report. We are comfortable enough here, & though the weather isn't fine it is at least dry. Our outings haven't been altogether successful: we went to Cork on Friday, and looked at the Cathedral of St Finn Barr, a large – nay, huge – 19th Century cathedral, all in marble & brass. As the distance to Cork was much further than I'd expected we had to leave quickly, & rather lost our way going back. Yesterday we lost our way too: we'd intended to drive round a coast road known as 'the ring of Kerry', but missed the way & had a good deal of driving about lonely mountain ways in consequence. Hum! However, it was pleasant enough, to be among the hills and see the sheep. I think Ireland is slightly less lonely than Scotland, though: there usually seems to be a cottage somewhere in the landscape. You would like the little donkeys that abound: they look very impassive & I expect they're pretty obstinate.

The car is behaving very well so far.[1] Most Irish cars seem to have a dent in them somewhere, wch isn't surprising the way some of them drive, but I have escaped up till now. This is rather a Frenchified hotel: many of the staff seem to be French, & certainly the chef has a heavy hand with garlic. The menus are all in French, and M's knowledge of the subject comes in useful. We usually have soup for dinner. Then a little course wch can be fish but wch can also be other things – I had brains once – then meat, beef, duck, lamb, & a cold pudding. There's choice of all these things, wch there wasn't at Newport. Some of the guests are French.

I am trying to get on with the Oxf. Bk. of 20thC Eng. Verse, reading different poets after dinner, but it's slow work & I don't do it well.[2] I'm almost tempted to start making my selection, so as to have something to build on. After all, I can pick only 200 or so poems, so there's no need to do more work than I require.

My bones ache rather. I think it may be the more humid atmosphere.

Dear old creature, I think of you so much. I wish I had given you a better holiday, in a quieter, cooler & less puzzling hotel.[3] I did enjoy sitting on the promenade at Southwold with you, in that beautiful sunshine, watching the waves & the people. I don't think you'd like Ireland, though. There are very few public lavatories. We couldn't find a single ladies lavatory in the whole of Cork & M was obliged to make her way into a cinema café in search of one. One of the two men's was out of order, too! And this is the second biggest city in Eire! Really, it was rather a shoddy place.

[. . .] There are a great many shops here selling tweed of different sorts: M bought a very stylish tweed hat, cream. I am not doing very well finding presents for Kitty – it will be a case of oddments, I'm afraid.

Much love, dear old c. \take plenty of taxis/ P.

1 Larkin's recently bought second car was a used 4-litre Vanden Plas Princess with a Rolls Royce engine. He told Barbara Pym that it was 'love at first sight' (8 October 1969, *Selected Letters*, 420).

2 Louis MacNeice had been the intended editor of the new *Oxford Book of Modern Verse*. But he died suddenly in 1963, and in 1966 Oxford University Press invited Larkin to take over the project.

3 In August Philip had taken Eva on holiday to the Duke's Head Hotel, Norwich.

14 September 1969

32 Pearson Park, Hull

My very dear old creature,

[. . .] Yes, we eventually got into contact with Richard Murphy, but only by going and calling on him! It seems that the local telephone operator is very slack & only puts calls through if he feels like it, and my calls had not been favoured. Very Irish. He took us out in his boat – it was a beautiful day – & caught a fish. I don't think I have ever seen a fish caught at close quarters before: it's not a very pleasant experience.

It seems odd to be back in dirty, crowded England after being in Ireland. On the whole I thought Ireland quite pleasant, but we didn't find as many solitary beauty spots as in Scotland, & spent more time in the car. I didn't take as many photographs as on some holidays. On about our last day we drove round the ring of Kerry, a famous coast road of great beauty, but could see virtually nothing for rain and mist. The car did very well, & I got it back almost unharmed – I believe a slight chip on the paint has appeared, but nothing worse – not like last year when a beastly caravan bent my rear bumper out at right angles! [. . .]

Much love, old creature – may ring tonight P.

5 October 1969

32 Pearson Park, Hull

My very dear old creature,

[. . .] I didn't catch the cold, I'm afraid, so have had to work all the week. Awgh! There are so many new members of staff that I feel like a stranger in my own building. Queer things happen: a lavatory was found *broken* off from the wall, with a resultant flood. It must have given whoever was sitting on it a terrible fright. Probably it was cracked to start with. Contrary to speculation we still have workmen in the place, finishing off various things at a snail's pace. The temperature in the place varies enormously: I really must get something done about this. My mainstay is Betty: boundless energy, always cheerful & tolerant, and if she doesn't do half my work she sort of chews it up to make it easier for me to swallow. I'd be lost without her. [. . .]

Much love, old creature,
Philip

26 October 1969

32 Pearson Park, Hull

My very dear old creature,

[. . .] It's a nice mild morning and I have eaten two large kippers – really, one would be enough, but I had two. I had some more kedgeree last night so I'm having a fishy weekend.

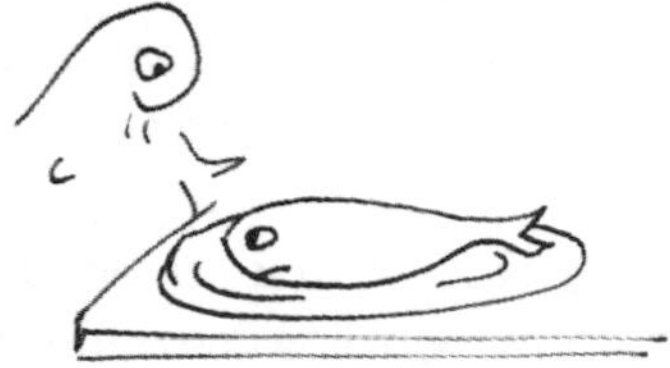

Thank you for your letter on A. Nellie's paper. I agree it's cheap, but unless you find it difficult to write on I think it's quite serviceable. [. . .]

My book (*All What Jazz*) is having a rough time. After agreeing to publish it in 'Autumn 1969', Faber's forgot about it until much too late to fulfil their promise: they are now saying January 1970. The printers have omitted to make the proof corrections, w[ch] I found out only by chance: more delay. However, since I shall be shot by maddened reviewers when it appears, I suppose there is no hurry. I had some funny photographs taken for the jacket, but I don't know if they'll use them. I look like a bald Turk.

About the mousse, the *packet* says that in a 2-star freezing compartment (like yours) the mousse will keep for a month, so tell Kitty to boil her head. Did you like it?[1]

The sun is coming out again. It really is a lovely autumn – this has been the best summer for years. I'm sure we shall remember it. I wrote a poem based on our visits to Southwold & have sent it to the *London Magazine*. If they print it I'll show it you. It mentions your \first/ meeting with Pop.[2] It isn't very good, I'm afraid.

I had a letter from America yesterday saying I had been made a Knight of Mark Twain, or something. Signed by a descendant. Crazy lot: only trying to get money.

Much love
Philip

1 On 20 October 1969 Eva wrote: 'I showed Kitty the mousse which we stored in the refrigerator, and she surprised me by saying that it would only keep for three days, so I suppose I should eat some of it to-morrow!'
2 'To the Sea'. Eva wrote on 3 November: 'I want to say how much I like your new poem. In a way the metre of it reminds me of The Whitsun Weddings.'

2 November 1969

32 Pearson Park, Hull

My very dear old creature,

[. . .] Not much to report. I went to a poetry reading by Richard Murphy on Friday, and afterwards asked him why he hadn't read a particular poem of his – he said he had! I must have been asleep, but anyway I can never hear spoken poetry, even with my hearing aid. My mind can't take it in. Before, we had a dinner that was ghastly – turf-like salmon, seemingly fried in engine oil. I left it. [. . .]

Well, I must get about my duties – the flat's in a fearful mess. I enclose the poem.[1] See you (all being well) on Friday about 9 p.m. Take care of yourself, old creature. Don't get cold.

Much love Philip

1 A two-page typescript of 'To the Sea' is enclosed.

15 November 1969

32 Pearson Park, Hull

My very dear old creature,

[. . .] As regards Christmas, well, I still feel that if I am to come home for it we should try to make it a happy peaceful time rather than one of overwork and tension and lack of rest. The principal cause of the latter are the fuss you make over presents, the Christmas dinner *and* having to go to tea at Kitty's. I suggest that if we go to Quorn (it's very generous of them to suggest it, of course), we shouldn't go to them on Christmas Day. I think *both* would be *too much*. Perhaps that's what they have in mind. After all, if I arrive on 24th and leave on morning of 29th (I don't know precisely when the Library is to be closed) that will give only five evenings. I have to keep something of my seven days for Monica at the New Year.

I haven't yet discussed all this with Monica – no chance, since she has no telephone.

What do you prefer? After all it's your sufferings that make me feel the Christmas dinner should be reduced in scale, & Christmas in general.[1]

Slight cough today, but feeling fairly all right – easily tired.

Much love Philip

1 Eva replied on 17 November in a slightly aggrieved tone: 'I quite agree that it *should* be a happy, peaceful time and, considering that I never make mincemeat, puddings or the Christmas cake \like I used to,/ it is a mystery why it should still be a worry. / I suppose it is not ready as early as it should be which leaves us no time to rest before going up to Kitty's. I cannot think how *she* manages to have such a wonderful tea ready, but perhaps Rosemary helps. She will be coming to see me to-morrow evening for an hour. Perhaps I had better tell her that we won't go to tea on Christmas Day as it is too much of a rush for us and leaves no time for a rest. In that case I should have to give them their presents before Christmas.' Then on an additional sheet ('Tuesday', 18 November) Eva ratcheted up the emotional blackmail, writing that she hadn't the courage to tell Kitty they would not be coming to tea, 'for I know how they like to have us – especially your company, which is one of the high lights of Christmas to them. / I won't say anything to Kitty this evening, perhaps you will reconsider your decision.'

30 November 1969

32 Pearson Park, Hull

My very dear old creature,

[. . .] When I went shopping I wore my duffle coat, my vermilion scarf, & my Shetland wool hat, & looked rather striking. Older people looked askance at me, but the young ones took me in their stride. People at the university look so queer these days that I expect I seemed quite normal.

Saw a man like this
yesterday →
I looked like this[1]
←

I can tell you are having difficulties over Christmas. [. . .]
Much love Philip

1 Scarf highlighted in red.

1970

4 January 1970

32 Pearson Park, Hull

My very dear old creature,

It's bright here, but cold and frosty: plenty of ice on the bedroom window! My bedroom faces south, so ought to be reasonably mild, but in fact the window fits so badly it's chilly in winter.

I wonder how you have been since I left? You sounded in better spirits on Tuesday, but I'm sure it would be wise to stay in as much as possible. Thank heaven for the storage heaters! I hope they never let you down.

You probably gathered I went up to Haydon Bridge on Wednesday: I sent you a letter from there, but it may not have reached you by Saturday. Of course we didn't go to the New Year's Eve celebrations at Allendale, just sat in & ate cold goose. The hotel was quieter than usual: I think some of the staff were off with flu. Monica had a bad cough & had lost her voice: I felt sorry for her, she must have had a wretched Christmas, & no one to get coal in or buy bread.

It certainly seems awful, term starting tomorrow – almost no holiday at all! Not even twelfth night reached! There were more cards waiting when I got back, but I doubt if I have as many as last year. I'm slowly choking people off.

I didn't much care for the drive up to Hexham – the road over the dales goes up to 2000 ft, and was covered with snow. I dreaded I shouldn't be able to hold the car with the brakes, & that in consequence it would slither off the road – still, I managed it, and it was nice to arrive at the hotel about 6.15 & have a pint of beer, well earned. [. . .]

I remember the sad mistake of your breakfast on Tuesday with much remorse. However, you did get breakfasts the other mornings, after a fashion! How is your foot? That was very strange. We must remember to get you a rubber end for your stick – or even a stouter stick.

Have you learnt how to manipulate the pedal bin? I'm afraid it's rather a silly present: it might be better if it stood on a mat of some sort.

I long to rearrange your house & get rid of half the things in it, so that it would be easier for you, but I expect you like it as it is.

I shan't know what to buy for your birthday! Have you been sleeping under the rug?

Much love. Philip

5 April 1970

32 Pearson Park, Hull

My very dear old creature,

I expect most of what I have to say will emerge from our telephone conversation tonight, if we have one. Since we last spoke I have become convinced I have another polyp in my nose, wch is annoying and presumably will mean another operation. I can breathe in but not out! Of course, the surgeon said that he had only half done the job, but as usual I hoped for a year or two's respite.

I haven't felt really well since returning, as if I had 'flu or something in a very mild form, but not bad enough to stay in. Can't taste anything.

Anyway, my cold has not been as bad as yours – what a streamer it was. I hope you are recovered, and that the weather is getting milder – I can't say it is here, really. It seemed warmer when I got back on Friday, but by now it just seems chilly & windy, although the sun is shining. I'm afraid I was not a very nice creature when at home. I wish I could explain the very real rage & irritation I feel: probably only a psychiatrist could do so. It may be something to do with never having got away from home. Or it may be my concern for you & blame for not doing more for you cloaking itself in anger. I do appreciate your courageous struggle to keep going in the old way, and am aware of your kindnesses – I did enjoy the duck, and all the other things – but I am worried about how long you can carry on without help.[1] Maeve's idea proved to be the Old Folks' Home in Pearson Park, wch she had heard praised. I don't know whether you'd like it! Perhaps I ought to go & talk to the manager. I always feel you're happier among your own things, if only they could be reduced by half, & if someone could do the shopping & keep an eye on you.[2]

I wonder how the hydrangea is faring. Keep an eye on it, too.

I am sitting in my bedroom in dressing gown & rug: it is nearly 2 p.m. I moved slowly today. Perhaps when I get out the air may clear my head. Perhaps!

I am due to go to London on Tuesday for a conference, returning on Friday, but do write here as usual. I enclose a few stamps. Have you managed to get any more drink yet? Maeve asked for the pic! Of course, I hadn't got one. Perhaps next time. If I don't feel better by Tuesday than I do now I may well not go to London anyway.

I do badly need some slippers here. I must make a serious effort.

Am drinking sherry now but can't taste it. Curses!

Much love,
Philip (Polyp)

1 On 6 April Eva wrote: 'Dear Creature, I don't blame you in the least for being angry and irritated when you were here, for you are on a higher plane (if that is the correct expression) than I am, and I must seem a childish and foolish old creature to you. I was sorry over the duck, and I don't think I shall ever have another, but you did warn me.'

2 In her letter of 6 April Eva also wrote: 'What you say is quite true about my being happier amongst my own things, but I feel terribly lonely, and the un-certain weather gets on my nerves. / If I went into a home I shouldn't want to say, play cards every evening or have to keep up a conversation with anyone about things I know nothing about!! / Some of them might be very clever!'

26 April 1970

32 Pearson Park, Hull

My very dear old creature,

[. . .] Next Thursday I shall be at Fabers (6–8 p.m.) to 'meet Robert Lowell', an American poet for whom I have no admiration at all.

I'm sorry the hydrangea isn't doing well: they are rather delicate, aren't they. Perhaps repotting would do it good. A pity we can't all be repotted![1]

Much Love, P.

1 On 20 April Eva reported: 'The blooms have faded and the green buds are not opening out. Mrs Slater said the dining room was too warm for it so I have put it on the hall stand but it still remains the same. *I* think the pot is too small for it.'

22 May 1970

Hull

My very dear old creature,

How nice to hear from you. Yes, you won't have had a letter from me for some time – me in person instead.

Don't worry about the Degree Day[1] – I'll take you & bring you back. We shall have to have lunch before we go. And I will take you to Abbeyfields on July 12.[2] I wonder if you've had a reply from M[rs] Hammond yet?

Life goes on here. I sleep very erratically at night: I think I have too much on the bed.

The architect rang up to say that our new Library has won a gold medal – it isn't official till July, but I'm very happy. I do wish you could see it one day!

Very much love,
Philip

1 Larkin received a Leicester University honorary D.Litt. in De Montfort Hall. He drove Eva to the ceremony.

2 Kitty and Philip had persuaded Eva to stay in one of the Abbeyfield houses in Loughborough for two weeks.

24 May 1970

32 Pearson Park, Hull

My very dear old creature,

It looks a fine day outside, & the glass is high,[1] so I dare say people will be going out in their hundreds and thousands. I'm glad I'm not travelling!

This has been a week of minor irritations – my laundry has taken to not replying to my letters, so I am taking it elsewhere. My garage does things wrong, & seems to have stolen the little purse of money I keep for parking meters. The replacing of the bedroom curtain rail will take some doing: it's rusty and clogged with paint. Very awkward thing to handle, too! on the top of a pair of steps.

However, they *are* minor irritations, so there's no need to dwell on them unduly. But it's been a dismal week altogether: I regret the banning of cricket as a giving-in to forces of disruption more baleful than any apartheid could ever be.[2] We shan't go to Lords this year. The prospect of another five years of Harold Wilson is enough to depress anyone. It's a gloomy spring.

The back garden looks very nice at present, full of white lilac. I ought to pick some & bring it in. Perhaps after lunch I may drive out into the country & see how it is looking. There's a special bit along the Humber to the west of Hull I like to visit, a group of villages such as Yokefleet, Laxton, and so on – very lonely & peaceful.[3] Then of course tomorrow is Bank Holiday: I shall try to work as usual. The Library will be open. I shall sit in my office – no Betty! – dictating into a tape-recorder, so that she can type it on Tuesday.[4]

Yes, it's very nice that our architects are to get an RIBA gold medal for the building. I look forward to its announcement (on July 1st) with a great deal of pleasure. This university hasn't been particularly appreciative of their work, & the award may vindicate them in the eyes of the Building Committee.

I hope you manage to write to Mrs Hammond:[5] I thought the letter you drafted was all right. I should add 'Perhaps you would also kindly let me know the terms I shall be paying, and also wch of the two rooms you showed me will be available.' It will be a bit like going to school. Had you thought of *post*? I suppose you could go up to York Road once or twice to see what *bills* had arrived – but otherwise it will be as if you were away on holiday. I hope it *will* be a holiday for you, old creature – I'm sure it will be!

Much love Philip

1 Larkin refers to the barometer indication of high atmospheric pressure.
2 The 1968–9 MCC tour of South Africa had been called off because of South African objections to the selection by the MCC of the mixed-race player Basil d'Oliveira. Subsequent years saw further sporting boycotts of apartheid South Africa, which did not regain international respectability until 1991.
3 Larkin dedicated a separate album to eighteen of these Humber village photographs (DLV/2/3). Richard Bradford reproduces four of them in *The Importance of Elsewhere*, 143.
4 Larkin had been set against acquiring a dictaphone for his office; but Betty insisted and he was won over.
5 At Abbeyfield House, Loughborough, where she was to stay in July.

31 May 1970

32 Pearson Park, Hull

My very dear old creature,

[. . .] One good thing. I found my purse of money – it was on the floor of the car, so it hadn't been stolen. Last Sunday afternoon, I pressed a switch that is supposed to squirt water over the windscreen to wash it (on the outside), & to my horror found a jet of water playing on my feet! There's always something going wrong. I took it to the garage, & when I was there a rabbit trotted by! They say there are several round there: it's in a residential district, near the nursing home I was in.

Well, we don't *have* to have Mr Wilson for another five years if enough of us vote for Mr Heath, but I don't know if enough will. I don't know who our member is. Some useless layabout, I expect. I see Mr Powell is still saying we must keep out the immigrants – a pity *he* isn't leading the Conservatives.[1] What with the election & football, we shall be properly bored in the next few weeks. I really am not much interested in the World Cup.

I'm sorry I didn't hear the poems read last Sunday that you mentioned, though on investigation I find that I had been asked permission for it. I'd like to have heard the audience reaction – did they laugh? At the funny bits, I mean.

I have still to write many more letters about this Scotch holiday: it's like organising a campaign of war, and I seem to have less & less time. Perhaps I am slowing down! We are going to Lochmaddy, on North Uist, in the Outer Hebrides – at least, if fates are kind.

It's very warm in this bedroom.

My dearest love, old creature, I think of you daily,

Philip

1 The election, held on 18 June 1970, resulted in a surprise victory for the Conservatives under Edward Heath. Labour, under Harold Wilson, lost power. Enoch Powell was a prominent Conservative MP with strong anti-immigration views.

13 July 1970 Picture postcard[1]

Hull

Not quite so warm up here – I hope you are enjoying your *leisure*[2] & finding plenty to do. I expect it'll seem lonely at first. Read that Monica Dickens book I saw on the shelf – can you find it again?

Much love P

1 The University, Kingston on Hull.
2 The card is addressed to Abbeyfield House, 17 Victoria St, Loughborough. Eva spent 12–24 July there. Philip set out for Scotland on 17 July.

2 August 1970

Invergarry Hotel, Invergarry

My very dear old creature,

[. . .] Well, our stay on Skye coincided with really rotten weather. So I don't remember it with much delight: the hotel was quite good, though, a large comfortable country house – somewhat on the cold side, though! Only about three rooms were at all warm, & that didn't include the bar. On Friday we left & had to wait 2½ hours for a car ferry at Kylerhea, wch was tiresome, and eventually got here about 5 p.m. We didn't like it at first – no real bar, public rooms too small, *too much* food – but we have become more reconciled. What we have been doing all the time is go out for the day with a packed lunch, & find some pleasant spot to eat it in. Not much exercise I suppose, but just occasionally we have walked a bit. M. keeps telling me that this is Ben this or Loch that, but it all looks much the same to me. When on Skye we went to Dunvegan Castle, the seat of the MacLeods, and were shown round, along with about 98 other people. Today we ate our lunch beside Loch Ness, but saw nothing untoward.

There is *no* postal collection today (Sunday), but there is one tomorrow, although it's Bank Holiday in Scotland, so I hope you'll get this some time in the week – it'll be stale news by then, I'm afraid. We move tomorrow to Aberfoyle for one night, then Hexham one night, then I suppose I go home on Wednesday, Aug 5 is it? When I get home I'll ring you up, to report safe arrival. It does seem a long time since I left you in the front room at Abbeyfield with the peach Monica had sent!

It sounds almost too good to be true that the gas has been successfully converted! Does it really work well? I am so glad. I know what a worry it was for you. I think I should eat meat if you can – protein is good for old creatures.

The flowers are beautiful up here, especially the wild ones. They don't seem to have been killed off by sprays as in England. M. collects them and presses them in her guide book.

With very much love, old creature – M. sends love,

Philip

4 October 1970

Set 3, Beechwood House, Iffley Turn, Oxford[1]

My very dear old creature,

It's a quiet dull Sunday morning, and I'm sitting in my sitting room at Iffley. I have no plans for today (rather a change) except to have lunch and dinner in college, so I shall have to get in either by car or bus. The other Sunday I was here I walked! Very hot it was, too.

The pictures I showed you were photographs taken by me & still in my possession. I'll bring them the next time I come (end of the month, or perhaps sooner). I've also taken some black & white ones wch I'll also bring. There is someone else living here now, a Danish professor. He seems very pleasant. Another professor is coming on Tuesday – a man from Belfast whom I know, called Connell. I'm afraid my morning baths will soon be a thing of the past. So far, I've managed to have my half-hour soak every day.

I don't know whether I have much news. Yesterday Charles Monteith and I motored out to a village called Steeple Aston and had lunch with Iris Murdoch and her husband. J.B. Priestley was going to be there but had a bad cold & didn't come (I thought of you). His wife was there.[2] It was a very nice outing. Next Sunday I have been conscripted to drive out the Dane to have lunch with Sir Max Mallowan & his wife Agatha Christie![3] Forgive all these famous names. For six months I shall be among them fairly constantly, I think. I feel very small and ignorant among them. John Wain turned up on Friday & we had a drink: he lives near here. [. . .]

Much love, dear old creature,
Philip

1 Larkin had taken sabbatical leave in Oxford to work on the *Oxford Book of Twentieth-Century English Verse*.

2 Iris Murdoch (1919–99), novelist; married to John Bayley (1925–2015), writer and literary scholar; J. B. Priestley (1894–1984), novelist; his third wife Jacquetta Hawkes (née Hopkins, 1910–96) was an archaelogist.

3 Max Mallowan (1904–78), archaelogist, second husband of the crime writer Agatha Christie (née Miller, 1890–1976).

21 October 1970

Beechwood House, Set 3, Iffley Turn, Oxford

My very dear old creature,

I'm sitting in my room at All Souls to write to you: tomorrow (my usual night) I am dining out, so shall probably not have much time. Last night I dined at New College, wch was very convivial! Also lunched at St John's, my old college, so I had quite a social day – left me feeling not very good.

I give frequent thought of your future, though I don't know whether this is the right letter to expatiate on it. It seems to me that you either give up having a home of any sort, and live with either Kitty or myself, or in someone else's house, or in Abbeyfield or somewhere comparable, or in a nursing home or hospital, OR you don't give up your home, keeping the present house or moving into a smaller house or flat, and either have someone to live with you or have someone to be a kind of part-time general daily housekeeper. Or, of course, you can just go on as you are!

Sell home	Keep home
1. Live with Kitty	1. Move somewhere smaller
2. Live with Philip	2. Have living-in companion
3. Live with ANOther	3. Have daily housekeeper
4. Live in Abbeyfield or some other institution	4. Go on as at present!

These are the eight alternatives as I see them – I've missed out *marriage*, or *having a lodger*, as impracticable. I think there's a good deal to be said for keeping the home in some form or other, unless you felt, for instance, that Abbeyfield suited you very well & that you'd like it as a permanency. On the other hand, I think you are reaching a time – have reached it – when for quite long periods you don't want to go shopping, & when it would be safer & more helpful to have someone looking in daily to see if you are all right & if you want anything. It may be that Kitty & the neighbours are kindly doing this already, but it seems to me that you don't *see* many people.

My opinion is that it w^{d} be prudent to put it about among your friends that you are looking for someone to be a kind of part-time general daily housekeeper, who w^{d} come in some days to clean and others just to see what you wanted from the shops. Do you think this is feasible? I've no idea what kind of wage they'd expect, but this is something that might be discussed. This, of course, assumes that poor Mrs Slater has to give up.[1]

I'll leave a little space to add anything that turns up.

Friday. Convivial night in Brasenose last night with Librarian of Bodley. Invitations seem to be pouring in. I shall be coming to see you next weekend – either Friday or Sat 30/31, probably Friday. Thanks for letter received today.

Much love,
Philip

1 Eva replied on 26 October: 'Like you, Creature, I am pondering about my future, although I'm sure I shan't live to be a hundred! Neither do I want to be. One thing I am sure about is that I ought not to live alone. / It wouldn't do either to live with you because of all those stairs, and also you would be out a good deal, and I should feel lonely. Neither do I think I could move myself, and sort out and throw away all the things that I no longer wanted. [. . .] I shouldn't mind living at Abbeyfield but unfortunately I think they do not want anyone that is not exactly fit and able to make their own bed and dust their room. It is a problem, and worries me now more than it used to. [. . .] I don't think I really want a stranger to live with me, and shouldn't want to do more cooking. I expect they wouldn't be satisfied with cold meat two or more times a week as I am!'

25 October 1970

Beechwood House, Set 3, Iffley Turn, Oxford

My very dear old creature,

It's a nice mild day here, with promise of sun, even. The trees are all very yellowy & fading, but still with plenty of leaves on. The squirrels that live in the grounds are always busy in the mornings, hunting for food I suppose, I expect when the weather gets cold they'll hibernate.

I'm sorry you felt rather low when I telephoned last night. No doubt the absence of Colemans makes you feel worse.[1] Despite your worries, you might take comfort from thinking that (a) you have a nice warm house no one can take from you (b) you've plenty of money (c) you can listen to the wireless and read books (d) there won't be any more storms for another eight months. Don't you think these are minor consolations? Perhaps we can think of some more at the weekend.

I'm afraid that All Souls is ceasing to be a haven of rest because I get so many invitations out, sometimes outside Oxford, & these take up a great deal of time and energy. I am going to London tomorrow to stay the night with the Day Lewises (Poet Laureate), and on Wednesday I am bidden to dinner in *Reading*, wch will be a tiresome drive. Last week I had a nice dinner in Brasenose College with the Librarian of the Bodleian. All these clever people make me feel rather small. [. . .]

– 4.15 p.m., and just back from lunch, with an Indian from Canada who has a wife from Hull! Very pleasant people. Of course they have a squalling little girl, but it was a delightful lunch. Preceded by drinks in College with none other than *W. H. Auden*, produced by Charles Monteith who is a fellow. He is I suppose the best-known English poet since Eliot died.

I must hurry and get this into the post. I do hope you feel better now than when we talked. I wonder *why* you fell? Had you been doing too much work, to make your legs wobbly? It perturbs me. As long as you didn't pass out, it may not be too serious. You didn't say what the doctor said.

Anyway, dear old creature, I shall see you on Friday evening – *don't* trouble about the bed, I'll do that, and I'll eat any odds & ends. Just to see you is all I want.

Much love – take care – Philip

1 Next door neighbours. Rosemary remembers that Eva 'found it comforting to hear Mrs Coleman clearing out her grate first thing in the morning and lighting the fire in the room on the other side of the party wall'.

5 November 1970

Beechwood House, Set 3, Iffley Turn, Oxford

My very dear old creature,

[. . .] Yesterday (Wednesday) I went to London in order to visit a picture dealer whom friends have been urging me to visit.[1] I looked at all his pictures & bought two, dating from Victorian days, but certainly at substantial prices. They both had sheep on, and I suspect the dealer thought I was a Yorkshire wool merchant.[2] [. . .]

Yours with much love,
Philip

1 Probably Abbott and Holder in Bloomsbury, where Judy Egerton bought watercolours.

2 On 8 November he wrote: 'This act of folly has been urged by Judy Egerton for a long time now, & I suppose it was interesting though expensive. I bought two 19th century oil paintings: not anyone special: hope I like them when they arrive.' One of these paintings seems to have been *Figure with Sheep*, by Peter Le Cave (Philip Larkin Society: Larkinalia Inventory 1, Hull History Centre).

15 November 1970

Beechwood House, Set 3, Iffley Turn, Oxford

My very dear old creature,

[. . .] The week has been quite interesting, though plagued with social engagements. Kingsley & his wife Elizabeth Jane Howard[1] came to Oxford on Wednesday, & we lunched with his son Martin who is at the University, & is rather an awe-inspiring spectacle with long fair hair & a velvet suit. In the evening Kingsley gave a reading of his poems in Balliol Hall, & we sat up rather late. On Thursday evening I had another rather late night at the house of one of the fellows. [. . .]

Very best love,
Philip

1 English novelist (1923–2014). Married to Kingsley Amis 1965–83.

17 December 1970

32 Pearson Park, Hull

My very dear old creature,

Well. I am in my own nook again, my draughty dingy book-filled flat. I don't suppose you'll get this on Saturday as post is beginning to silt up: however, I'll write it. I got back safely on Monday, as I said, and went to the Common room dinner, wch was fair, but a bit of a change from All Souls. The Vice Chancellor struck me as a terribly silly and vulgar fool.

Then yesterday we had the opening: speeches from Garnett Rees,[1] the new Chancellor Lord Cohen,[2] and yours truly: it was all over mercifully quickly, and there was a lunch of poached salmon. But alas there wasn't the magic of the day in June in 1960 when the Q Mother & you & Monica were there![3]

Then last night there was the Library Christmas Party, in the Library, fairly quiet & decent though some of the responsible girls still amaze me by their abandoned behaviour.

I wonder if you managed to get to the chiropodist. I do hope so. And did you remember to send your letter \to/ me to the Library? I don't seem to be getting any post. What a foul time of year it is. Chiefly I find it cold here, compared with All Souls. But it's nice to have my bed again.

I shall be seeing you next week – Wednesday, I expect.

Much love,
Philip

1 Professor of French at Hull from 1957 to 1978.

2 Henry Cohen, Baron Cohen of Birkenhead (1900–77), British physician.

3 Larkin inserted a cutting from the *Hull Daily Mail*: 'LIBRARY EXTENSION OPENED': photograph: 'Lord Cohen of Birkenhead (left) with Prof. Garnet Rees and Dr Philip Larkin at the opening of the western extension to Hull University's vast library complex.'

1971

10 January 1971

Beechwood House, Set 3, Iffley Turn, Oxford

My very *very* dear old creature,

I am wondering this morning whether I shouldn't have arranged to visit you today: the sun is shining so nicely, & I should only have to jump into my car. But perhaps it would 'worry' you, and I haven't done my jazz article, wch I must put in the post tomorrow. All the same, my thoughts are very much with you on this your 85th birthday, and I hope the day is as mild and peaceful with you as it is here. May you have a good day & useful and decorative presents, & a good sleep at the end to round it off. I wonder if you'll be able to open the salmon![1]

I suppose I have settled down a bit since arriving, though at first I felt rather sickish & unable to sleep. It's nice at All Souls in the vacation when there aren't many fellows in residence and *social life* is fairly quiet. Term starts next Sunday. Before then this house will fill up even fuller than before. In addition to the Irishman, the Italian, & the Dane who were here last term, then will be a Frenchman, a German & another Englishman. Since we all have breakfast together, and compete for bathrooms, life will be less peaceful! I must say I like to lie in a bath for half an hour before breakfast. It's when I get my reading done. [. . .]

Next week I hope to restart work on my anthology. I wish I knew how near finishing it I was! It still seems largely incomplete to me. When I have a kind of gross text, I shall take it up to Hull & get it copied (cheaper there) and then hand it in to the O.U.P. They'll then say it's much too long, & I shall have to cut it down. But that won't be hard. And by then it will be time for me to go back to Hull for another 15 years, like a beetle crawling back into the woodwork.

Once again, many happy returns, old creature – very dear & lovable one that you are!! & all love

Philip

1 On 13 January Eva wrote: 'What a nice sketch of me using the new tin opener. When I first used it I found it rather hard to turn, but suddenly the lid came off and I realized it was "opened"!' She mentions birthday cards from Maeve Brennan and Betty Mackereth.

14 January 1971

Beechwood House, Set 3, Iffley Turn, Oxford

My very dear old creature,

Your letter came second post today, & so I didn't get it till I came in after dinner about 9 p.m. How beautifully written it is for an old creature of 85! Your writing is smaller than mine. Truly you are a marvel.

I went to London today for a committee, coming back by the 5.15. Very misty! We had oxtail for dinner, and roes on toast to follow. I'm now back in Beechwood.

Well I suppose I ought to have come for your birthday, but I thought it would worry you, & also I had an article to write.[1] But it was such a beautiful day I thought it would have been nice to come. How nice to get cards from all the circle.[2] It makes me wonder whether you are not really happier in Loughborough, at least for the present, rather than, say, in Hull, or out at that village near Loughborough. I do worry about your future, of course, but I think your present set up is a *fairly* comfortable one. Much depends on Kitty of course.

If there is a postal strike you won't hear from me on Monday, but I'll write, of course. Aren't all the workers a nuisance! I bet they make special arrangements for their football coupons. To hell with them.

Good luck with the storeroom!

Much love Philip

1 On 13 January Eva wrote: 'Yes, my birthday was a very happy day. I did wonder whether you would surprise me with an un-expected visit, which wouldn't have worried me at all, and we should all have been pleased to see you.'
2 The Circle of Silent Ministry.

28 March 1971

32 Pearson Park, Hull

My very dear old creature,

[. . .] Did I say they had a little sherry party for me on Thursday evening? Brenda[1] did one of her iced cakes with 'Welcome Back to the Library' on it.[2] I tried to be nice to everyone, though it was quite an effort. That too was followed by deep depression. It made me want to hide away in a corner and never be seen again.[3]

When Doris Archer was talking about birds on *The Archers* it made me think of you and your little flock! I hope they are still faithful & that you are still finding something to give them. Is your garden coming out? There's nothing in sight here, except buds on the bushes.

Perhaps I'll ring again this evening.

Much love – Philip

1 Brenda Moon.
2 Larkin returned to Hull on Monday 22 March 1971.
3 On 30 March Eva wrote: 'I am so sorry to hear that you have felt so fearfully depressed since getting back to Hull and hope you have cheered up by this. I don't feel too sprightly either and don't like the thought of the lonely weekend – still, I suppose it is only the same as usual.'

25 April 1971

32 Pearson Park, Hull

My very dear old creature,

[. . .] This morning I weighed exactly 15 stone, wch is less than for a long time. I wonder if the non-gin routine is taking effect? Gin & tonic is very fattening. I had a little one at the Espinasses,[1] but nothing to speak of. It was quite a pleasant evening, but I couldn't hear what anybody said. I'm afraid my hearing is deteriorating. When I came back here after Easter I found a circular from the man who'd sold me my hearing aid saying he'd got some new lines and inviting me to come and see them. I think I shall, when I have time. No doubt they'll cost the earth.

It was nice to have your letter and to get the cutting. You are marvellous to write such long and lucid letters, & in such a good hand. Say what you like, you have lived a good life & are ten or fifteen years younger than your actual age! I wish you'd tell me how it's done – working all day & never enjoying yourself, I suppose.

[. . .] Today I have to go & see the celebrated George Hartley who is going to 'settle my accounts' up to Oct. 1970 for *The Less Deceived*. I believe he is finally going to leave Hull: Jean is making him sell their house, wch is half in her name, so he will no longer have a *pied à terre* here. I don't know how he will go on selling the book, if he moves! No one will know his address.

Slowly I have been easing my way back into work. It's rather delicate, coming back into an organisation that's been running itself for 6 months: one feels rather selfconscious about starting to tell them what to do. However, Brenda (who was Acting Librarian) is very welcoming. I feel sorry for her. She spent some time at Easter nursing a close friend who is seriously ill & who is in fact going to die. [. . .]

Fancy your not taking the sleeping tablets, when you make such a fuss about them! Well, it didn't do much harm. I shall have the remains of a shepherd's pie for lunch, & some broad beans (frozen).

Froggy is well, though he misses being 'put to bed' at night.[2] You spoilt him a bit! Much love

Philip

1 Professor Paul 'Espinasse (1900–75) was Professor of Zoology at Hull. His wife Margaret taught in the English Department.

2 'Froggy' was a soft toy filled with dried beans.

20 May 1971

32 Pearson Park, Hull

My very dear old creature,

Fancy Kitty making you a froggy! Do tell her that one of its chief characteristics is a certain floppiness, caused by being only 2/3rds full of beans or whatever it is. That is what enables it to sit up, & hang over your shoulder. It hasn't got a mouth, or any features except eyes. I think the material sh^{d} be fairly strong or stiff. [. . .]

A long day tomorrow, to London. Will write on Sunday as usual, dear old creature. Much love.

Philip.

20 June 1971

<*Letterhead with coat of arms*>
Durrants Hotel, George Street, London W1H 6BJ

My very dear old creature,

This has been the most disappointing visit ever! No play on Thursday until 3.30 p.m., no play on Friday *after* 11.50 a.m. (starting at 11.30), and no play on Saturday at all! Sheer waste of time & money, the money being £1.75 each every day, *paid in advance & irrecoverable.*[1] So you can imagine I feel pretty fed up. It was cold at Lords too, sitting in the bleak windswept stands: wonder I haven't caught my death.

However, hey ho for Hull again at 4.45, so all things come to an end.

I don't know that there's much news. Our rooms here are very tiny but have television sets: we saw part of *The Woodlanders* on Friday night, and lots of cowboy films and so on. I wonder if you'd enjoy it! But you'll have a good dose of it at Abbeyfield before too long, I expect.

What a hideous spell of weather! For the 3rd or 4th time, a dark drab morning, threatening rain. There are lots of Americans here. They eat toast and marmalade all through breakfast, along with egg & bacon & everything. One of them talked, too, like a machine left running by accident.

Hope you got my loyal cards.[2] TV showed us the Queen at Ascot, holding her own umbrella in pouring rain.

Keep warm & dry, old creature. Much love P

1 'irrecoverable' doubly underlined.
2 He had sent two colour postcards showing the Queen.

31 July 1971

32 Pearson Park, Hull

My very dear old creature,

[. . .] I hope your feet are not troubling you as much. My neck is about the same. Awgh!

Portrait of creature with bad neck.

My froggy is sitting in the window looking at the park: he greatly enjoyed his jaunt to King's Lynn with your froggy.[1] What well-travelled froggies they are! How they enjoyed sitting in the lounge when we had our tea on the afternoon when we arrived! Will you take yours to Abbeyfield? I think you should, unless you mean to go back and visit him often. [. . .]

I've started to work hard at the Library – don't know how long it will last! Brenda went off yesterday on the first stage of a tour of Finnish libraries. She is due to go to Leningrad in the course of it. I could have gone, but as you know I don't like abroad.

I suppose I'll be coming home at the end of the week. When would suit you best? I don't expect you'll want to get many big meals. But I'll ring up before long.

Be of good cheer, old creature.

Much love,
Philip

1 Philip had taken Eva on holiday to the Duke's Head Hotel, King's Lynn, between 15 and 22 July.

9 August 1971

32 Pearson Park, Hull

My dear old creature,

I hope you are getting on all right in Abbeyfield.[1] Your room looked rather nicer than last year! though I fancy you may have difficulty in turning your bedside lamp on and off. I'm sorry I rang rather late last night, after you had done your ears.

I've had a quiet sort of birthday: thank you for your very pretty card with the ploughman on, and kind words. There was a funny card from Auntie Nellie – a parrot with a bowler hat on. Other cards were from Kitty & Walter, Rosemary, Monica, Betty & Maeve. I wore a pair of my socks today – the ones you gave me. They were very nice.

I hope you are settling down in Abbeyfield, and have found one or two people to talk to, and aren't too bored! How many people are living in the house? I thought Mrs Clarke seemed very nice, as if she would look after you.

Do be careful about crossing the dangerous area round Murcotts! Ask someone to take you across. Send me a little letter when you have time. I bought six cakes for my staff to have for tea today.

Much love
Philip

1 This and the next letter are addressed to Abbeyfield House, 17 Victoria Street, Loughborough. Kitty and Philip had persuaded Eva to spend most of August there.

29 August 1971

Jura Hotel, Isle of Jura

My very dear old creature,

[. . .] The midges are bad here – not quite as bad as at another place we were at a few years ago, but I'm bitten all over the neck & head. Nothing seems to put them off! I suppose if I'd dipped my head in turpentine before setting out I might have been all right.

It was very good of you to send me a letter to await arrival. I expect what you said in it is rather stale news now – to you anyway – but it was very interesting.

I don't suppose you do much like the idea of living in a home, but I wish there was someone to look after you more thoroughly.[1] I don't think it would matter if you got up very early – you take a long time to get up & get breakfast – you might find yourself having breakfast at 8 instead of 10, & lunch at 12.45 instead of 2! Still, you please yourself, old creature.

Later We have been out: it's been a patchy day, sun & rain in turn. We listened to Al Read on the car radio! He did his 'We're not very popular, are we, pussy?' act, & I thought of you. Rather strange to be listening to Al Read in the wilds of Scotland. The car radio is our only contact with the outside world, as there are no papers.

Monday morning Grey & drizzling outside, & my neck is hurting badly. No, I don't like holidays!

Froggy is here, looking out of the window at the dismal scene. He asks how your Froggy enjoyed Abbeyfield. Did he have a comfortable bed? My Froggy sleeps in my wool hat, very cosy.

Much love – I feel a long way away –

Philip

Monica sends good wishes.

1 On 24 August, before her return from Abbeyfield House, Eva had written: 'I am finding time *is* hanging heavy on my hands and I don't think I should like to live in a "home" for some things.'

26 September 1971

32 Pearson Park, Hull

My very dear old creature,

[. . .] So Penvorn has finally gone![1] Colin Gunner wrote to me to say it had actually been knocked down. I expect it has. In a way, I should like to have given it one more look, as most of my memories are concerned with it rather than any other house, but no doubt it would have been rather a sad business. I find myself remembering the woodshed that was knocked down to make way for the air raid shelter. Fancy Mr Beardsley shouting! No doubt it was better than if he had muttered.[2] [. . .]

Much love Philip

1 Coventry Corporation had bought the remaining lease on Penvorn and demolished it for redevelopment. On 28 September, Eva wrote: 'I felt like you about Penvorn. I should have liked to see it once more before it was knocked down – perhaps it is as well that I didn't[.] I think I should have felt like weeping over it.'
2 On 21 September Eva wrote: 'My word! how Mr Beardsley [from Coventry Corporation] did *shout*. I think he had got the impression that *I* was as deaf as a post! I expect he has so much business with elderly people and many of them probably deaf that he gets into the habit of shouting.'

7 November 1971

32 Pearson Park, Hull

My very dear old creature,

[. . .] I don't know that I have very much news. Went to London on Thursday for the Gold Medal Committee, and was rather shocked by Day Lewis's appearance. He looks very ill indeed, and much older than his years. One can hardly believe he will survive much longer, yet he seems to be carrying on just the same, giving readings and so on. If he were to die, there would (presumably) have to be another Poet Laureate. Perhaps Betjeman would get it this time.[1] I've never really decided what I should do in the unlikely event of its being offered to me. My instinct w[d] be to refuse, on the grounds that poetry for me is a private, not a public, activity. But I suppose one could behave as one liked. Anyway, I very much doubt it I *should* be offered it.[2] Not really old and respectable enough!

How are you getting on with *The Rainbow*? It's a turgid piece of work. *Sons & Lovers* is much better. Still, I expect it has its points. There's a wedding, & some schoolteaching, that is vivid enough. It was written just about the time of the first world war – 1913 was it?[3] Lawrence was born in 1885, the year before you. [. . .]

Much love, Philip

1 Cecil Day Lewis died in May 1972; John Betjeman was appointed as the next Poet Laureate in October that year.
2 In 1984, following Betjeman's death, Larkin was offered the Laureateship, but declined. It went to Ted Hughes.
3 On 9 November Eva wrote: 'I'm afraid I have given up reading "The Rainbow" and am re-reading "Sons and Lovers", which I like very much. As I can only read it at tea and supper I'm sorry to say that I have finger-marked the covers. Do you think I could get you a new copy? Dirty creature that I am!'

14 November 1971

32 Pearson Park, Hull

My very dear old creature,

[. . .] The thought of Christmas depresses me. *Please don't go to trouble*. Every year I swear I'll never endure it again, & make you promise to be sensible, & now here you are talking about duck again, just as if I had never shouted and got drunk & broken the furniture out of sheer rage at it all. For two pins I'd stay here & have bread & cheese, & motor down on the afternoon of Christmas Day.[1] All I want is an ordinary lunch, and no *fuss*. Get a good piece of beef that will last a day or two, and potatoes for baking. *To hell with Christmas*. Let us have peace, & not all this blasted cooking and eating (and washing up!)

I'm glad you keep at the sherry. There's nothing like a little drink when you feel you need it. And I'm glad you enjoyed *Sons & Lovers*: it is his best book, I think, the most lifelike & not bedevilled with theories. It sounds as if it's all true, but I think there is a good deal of fiction interwoven with the fact. This reminds me that Colin Gunner has popped up again, & sent me a long typescript about his war experiences. It's very vivid! Sounds as if they spent most of their time (in Italy) stealing! Looting, I suppose it would be called.

Are there any roses in your garden? A fuchsia Monica gave me in the summer is still flowering – isn't that wonderful? It lives in the sitting room.

Much love Philip

1 On 15 November Eva replied: 'About Christmas Day[:] we can have a joint of beef (I'm not fond of duck) and I suppose you won't mind my having plum pudding and brandy or rum sauce. I hope there will be a few mince pies. These things are all ordered from my baker *and* a very nice Christmas cake – 90p!'

16 December 1971

32 Pearson Park, Hull

My very dear old creature,

Many thanks for your letter wch arrived today. A lovely day it is too – mild & sunny. I went shopping, Xmas shopping (groogh), spent all morning at it, not very successfully. I am not doing anything very special for this Christmas.

I went to the hospital on Monday & eventually saw a doctor about my neck. He really said & did nothing helpful – just said it was 'arthritis' & 'old age' & I'd have to put up with it. However he gave me a good going over (heart, bloodpressure, blood etc) and said I should 'lose 2 stone'! So I went along to the dietician who gave me a chart & told me to stick to 1000 calories a day. It really means cutting out drink but I can't bring myself to do this! I'm to go again on January 6th. So no Christmas indulgence!

I don't mind long or short socks. Preferably dark grey or buff or brown – not red or green or yellow or blue.

BBC say they are planning a programme for my 50th birthday!!

Much love, old creature Philip

1972

2 January 1972

as from 32 Pearson Park, Hull

My very dear old creature,

The first letter of the new year! I wonder if you will get it on Monday: they seem rather slothful about collections up here – they take the new year more seriously.

You remember that on new year's eve we go to Allendale (about 7 miles off) where they have a big bonfire, and the men of the village walk in a procession carrying tubs of blazing pitch on their heads. The town band plays in fancy dress, & at midnight old lang syne is sung. Everything went off much the same this year, but the bonfire seemed bigger than usual and when the wind blew it became quite uncomfortable and the flying sparks rather dangerous. I was afraid that the latter might burn holes in my expensive overcoat! I haven't really examined it yet. Anyway, it was all very jolly.

I shall be setting off today to drive back to Hull – miserable day it looks, too. I wrote to Kitty saying I didn't think I could get home for Al Read, and enclosed £2 for the Nottingham evening (little though I enjoyed it!)

Monica had some Christmas presents for me here, including a carving knife and fork! So I shall have to try buying meat myself. I wonder if you got rid of the remains of our Christmas beef. What a pity it wasn't nicer. You were very kind to me – I was a beast as usual.

With very much love, Philip

9 January 1972

32 Pearson Park, Hull

My very dear old creature,

Well, many happy returns of the day![1] I'm afraid this silly rabbit card isn't really very suitable, but in my brief journey to town to snatch something up it was the most attractive one I could see. Anyway, think of it as a frivolous spring bunny come to tell you warmer weather is on the way! Certainly yesterday & today have looked dreary enough. However as long as we have houses, and fires, and books, things could be worse.

I'm still as heavy! Really, I wonder if 14¾ st. is a kind of minimum below wch I can't fall. I shouldn't be surprised. I've given up virtually everything – drink, bread, butter, anything fried, chocolate, and anything that might be fattening. Yet nothing happens. And heaven knows I don't eat much in any case. [. . .]

I have cleared all my Christmas cards away – I didn't count them, but there must have been about 80 – and Froggy is sitting in the middle, highly satisfied with having got the mantelpiece to himself for once. He sends regards to your Froggy. He says *some* people are very lucky in being put to bed every night![2] [. . .]

Well, dear old creature, I hope you have a good day, and manage to give yourself a treat of some kind. Are you eating the frozen vegetables I left you? I shall be thinking of you, and wishing you many happy returns, as I do now.

Philip

1 On 10 January 1972, her eighty-sixth birthday, Eva wrote: 'Many thanks for your letter which arrived first post to-day and to which I had looked forward so much. Also the "rabbit" card with its' [*sic*] love and good wishes.'

2 In her letter of 10 January Eva also wrote: 'What a lot of things you have given up. It is surprising that you still weigh so much. I sometimes think that you have rather big bones which may account for it. [. . .] I have finished the biography of Beatrix Potter and enjoyed it very much. / I am now reading Hardy's The Trumpet Major which is very interesting and well written. [. . .] My froggy is sitting patiently waiting to go to bed. He could do with a bit more stuffing in him.'

16 January 1972

32 Pearson Park, Hull

My very dear old creature,

I have just been out to fetch more papers, and took the car to the car-wash, but there was such a queue I didn't wait. The atmosphere wasn't as mild as I expected, but not too bad really. Monica bought me a bowl of crocuses when she was last here, and one has just come out. It's a purple one.

I survived Maeve's evening well enough, though it didn't break up till 1 a.m. It was a curious mix of her parents & their friends & her own friends. There was sherry to start with, while they arrived, then we were herded into another room for soup – quite a good soup – then we had to fend for ourselves round a table with bread & cheese & other accessories like celery & radishes and what not. I spent a good deal of time pouring out wine. Then there was coffee, & port for some. At one point I disappeared into the scullery and washed up – or dried up – with my old secretary, Hilary Penwill, who was anxious to reclaim the soup bowls, wch were hers! On the whole it was a successful and respectable evening, but a shade crowded – there were twenty in all, and there wasn't really enough room, either to sit or move about.

I wondered if I should be heavier this morning but I'm not: still halfway between 14 st & 14½ st. Not bad considering I began only just before Christmas, I wonder how long I shall have to keep it up?

I don't know that there's much more news since I talked to you last night! One day next week I am having two new power points put into my sitting room. No doubt it will make a mess, but the result will be worth it.

I hope your neck is feeling better. Mine isn't. I do hope it's the sort of thing that goes away *in time* – do you remember how my foot hurt when I was about to leave Oxford? I limped about for weeks. But it went all right in the end.[1]

I found a passage in *Our Mutual Friend* that reminded me of you: 'She went through with whatever she had to do. She went through with me, she went through with the Minders [children she minded], she went through with herself. She wemt through with everything. O, Mrs Higden, Mrs Higden, you was a woman and a mother and a mangler in a million million!'

However, I hope you won't have to go through next week without Mrs Holmes, and I hope you won't go through *a day* without a rest on the sofa and perhaps a glass of port or sherry. Shall be thinking of you, and hope nothing happens to worry you.

All love Philip

1 On 17 January Eva responded: 'I'm so sorry to know that your neck is still painful. Of course it isn't old age. 49 isn't *old*. [. . .] Yes, Kitty had prepared a very nice tea for my birthday and Walter opened a bottle of champagne to celebrate it.'

19 January 1972

32 Pearson Park, Hull

My very dear old creature,

I was concerned to hear that you'd gone to bed! Your letter came this morning and I rang Kitty's number this evening, getting Walter. Did you really fall? What did the doctor say? I expect Kitty will tell me in due course.

I'm glad Mrs Holmes has started to come again. She will be worried about her mother.

What nice paper you have – mauve, is it? [. . .]

My dear creature, I shall be anxious till I hear you are better. Yesterday was a foul day here – today is better.

Much love, Philip.

21 January 1972

32 Pearson Park, Hull

My very dear old creature,

I was relieved to get your note this morning: I was very worried to hear you had fallen.[1] Dizziness is sometimes caused by bad circulation – blood not reaching the brain – and if it is this then lying in bed won't help. However, I'm no doctor.

It can't be very nice being ill alone. Do you have the wireless in with you? It can while away a lonely hour pleasantly enough.

It's a pity you don't like soup. It goes down easily and can be sustaining. I know when one is ill one doesn't feel like the most obvious things like chops & steaks: I find it hard to think of things to have in the evening now all my favourite foods are under ban. I grill bacon, & it is rather cheerless in consequence. But you must keep up your strength.

Isn't it cold? I put an extra blanket on the bed – I really needed it. Mrs Oates didn't come on Tuesday, it was so cold. However, the sun is shining today. I am nearly down to 14 st.!

Much, much love Philip

1 On 20 January Eva sent a notelet showing a bowl of flowers: 'I want to write you a short letter although I am still in bed and cannot get a really comfortable position in which to do it. Of course I *could* get up if I liked, the doctor said three days in bed and to-day is the third day. I may get up for tea. I seem to be existing on eggs mostly had a poached one for lunch. I seem to have gone off meat. Kitty comes every day and makes my Horlicks for supper does any job which wants doing. [. . .] Everyone is very kind. Mrs Richards offered to send me some soup but as you know I'm not fond of soup. / I can imagine how nice Monica's crocuses will look. Do you remember how I used to grow them on a plate in just water. I'm reading Thomas Hardy's Wessex Tales. / I read a bit too about Hazlitt. How he couldn't stand Lamb's poems. Have I spelt his name right. Well, dear Creature I haven't any more to say this week.'

24 January 1972

32 Pearson Park, Hull

My very dear old creature,

I got back all right last night, leaving Leicester about 8.30 & getting to Hull about 11.30. No difficulties, except that someone had stolen my Sunday papers that had been delivered here. Filthy swine.

I enjoyed coming to see you, and [was] relieved to find you not *too* bad, but I didn't like leaving you all alone, and don't think it is a good thing. I shall ring up Walter tonight for news: to see if any step was taken regarding a visiting nurse. If she were the right person it might be a very good thing. Anyway, do keep yourself warm and don't try to *do* anything strenuous. Remember 'flu is *very* debilitating and depressing. Just keep snug in your bedroom (not necessarily bed) until you feel better –

MUCH LOVE Philip

25 January 1972

32 Pearson Park, Hull

My very dear old creature,

I'm very sorry to hear that you fell over in the kitchen on Monday and hurt your leg.[1] I hoped you were getting on well & were on the road to recovery – perhaps you were being too bold. I'm sure it was a nasty shock and will have left a bruise. What a worry! I shan't rest till I hear you are feeling better. I think it's quite a good idea to *move* when you can, but don't go rampaging over the house in the cold. Just potter about the warm bedroom in your dressing gown, or sit with the rug over you.

I haven't much news. The car is in for a few days being repaired after its slight accident before Christmas, and I am having to walk to work and back – at least, I don't *have* to, but the buses seem few and far between. I suppose it's a mile & a bit, but a dull walk really. The poem I am trying to write for a government report, of all things, is sticking and isn't very good anyway.[2] Tonight I had an omelette & some curious tinned vegetable-mixture of tomatoes & peppers & little cucumbers. I hope you are still managing to eat!

With much love, from a worried Creature.

1 The fall, which broke Eva's leg, occurred on Monday 24 January.
2 'Going, Going', commissioned by a government working party on 'The Human Habitat'.

27 January 1972

32 Pearson Park, Hull

My very dear old creature,

I was sorry to learn that you had hurt yourself more seriously than was thought at first, and that they \have/ taken you off to Leicester[1] – though I'm sure that if this is the case then a hospital *is* the best place. Kitty says it seemed a nice hospital and that the nurses were kind. I think when one is actually there one feels a certain lightness of heart, as if one was no longer responsible for things – let them get on with it! Daddy used to say that everyone ought to go to hospital, once.

I shall be coming to see you on Saturday & Sunday, all being well, but I ring up Kitty at night to hear what news there is. In the meantime it's a horrible wet & windy day, & you are probably better where you are. My neck feels a bit better, not that that is any comfort to you! Our wretched students are 'sitting-in' – I hope they don't come near the Library.

Much, much love,
Philip

1 The letter is addressed to Fielding Johnson Ward, Leicester Royal Infirmary. For Eva's last lettercard from 21 York Road (26 January) see Appendix.

27 January 1972

32 Pearson Park, Hull

My *very* dear old creature,

This is my usual letter for Saturday – I wrote you a note this morning,[1] w[ch] I hope you'll get on Friday. I talked to Kitty on the telephone, & she said they had visited you: I hope to see you myself on the day you get this. What a trying time you are having! I do feel sorry for you: I know from experience that hospitals aren't very cheerful places, but there is some wry humour to be found in observing the people – types one w^d never see otherwise, I expect. I know I saw some extraordinary old men in Hull hospital who cheered me up in a way.

It's been a really horrible day, wet and windy, and at least you are out of it from that point of view. I had to entertain some visitors from Sheffield who came to see the Library, but I am so deaf, it's really awful. Even with my hearing aid I can't catch half what they say. I'm sure it's getting worse.

I have written to Eva[2] tonight to tell them that you've had a little accident, so I hope you'll get a letter. It's a change to tell *them* about illness! Didn't Auntie Nellie hurt herself in this way once? I hope they haven't gone off to Anglesey to their new home.

Poor creature, I feel so sorry for you, but you mustn't worry, just concentrate on getting well. Lie quiet and have the rest you must need. I'm sure they'll take good care of you. Do you remember our week at King's Lynn? What a sunny week it was! We both took our froggies, & they sat up for tea on the first afternoon in the lounge. I often think of it, and smile at the meals we had – do you remember how uneatable the chops were one night, but when the chef asked you if you'd enjoyed your dinner you said yes! Craven old creature!

I don't suppose you can sit up and read yet. Can you listen to the wireless through headphones? I expect it's all rubbishy stuff. Is there any television to be seen?

Well, I expect I shall see you soon after you read this, so I'll finish, but with all my love, dear creature,[3]

from Philip

1 Addressed to Fielding Johnson Ward, Leicester Royal Infirmary. See previous letter.

2 Nellie's daughter.

3 The envelope is addressed but not stamped. Perhaps Larkin failed to finish it in time to catch the post; he may have taken it with him and delivered it in person.

31 January 1972

32 Pearson Park, Hull

My *very* dear old creature,

I expect you are finding the days rather muddling. Monica & I came to see you in hospital on ~~Monday~~ \Sunday/ (getting muddled myself now!). I am writing this on Monday night after getting back to Hull, and you will be reading it on Wednesday (I hope), in a new place, the Berrystead Home. Kitty & I spent the best part of two hours there this morning looking at the rooms and talking to the Director, and thought you w^{d} be *more comfortable* there, & that it w^{d} be quieter & the nurses might be more considerate. As you have got to rest & get well, we thought you might as well do it in comfort. I hope it *is* comfortable. When you begin to perk up & the weather gets warmer, you'll see what a nice place it is. It's at Syston, outside Leicester on the Loughborough side.[1]

Oh, isn't it cold! For the first time for years I am wearing long pants. I drove back very slowly tonight, for fear of frosty roads. I left 21 York Road quite all right – Mrs Holmes (Sheila) will come in once a week to keep it in shape.

My neck is a little better – still hurts slightly, but not as much as it did.

There was a nice letter from Eva[2] when I got in – she says she has sent you a card. I hope it reaches you.

I hope you are in a softer bed now, and feel more in tune with your surroundings.

Much love old creature from your loving son Philip.

1 Eva was moved on 1 February 1972 into Berrystead Nursing Home, 1001 Melton Road, Syston, Leicestershire. It is here that her son's letters were sent for the remainder of her life: nearly six years.
2 Nellie's daughter.

1 February 1972 GPO Greetings Telegram

Hull

HOPE YOU ARE SAFELY INSTALLED AT BERRYSTEAD AND WILL BE WARM AND COMFORTABLE MUCH LOVE

PHILLIP [*sic*]

6 February 1972

21 York Road, Loughborough

My very dear old creature,

I've had my breakfast & washed up and put things straight, and thought I would write a note to you to get on Monday, even though I shall be seeing you this afternoon. On *The Archers* Tom Forest said that the trees were already starting to bud and spring is on the way! I can't say I see many signs of it myself. But of course it will come.

I have also rung up Mrs Stubbs and she sends her love. The Circle[1] will be meeting tomorrow (the day you read this) and they will all be thinking of you.

Monica gave me some roast lamb wch was very nice. You would have thought it rather underdone, but it will keep life in.

I do sympathise with you at present, dear old creature: days must be very long. But you are getting better slowly. One can't hurry nature. Just be patient.

Very much love,

1 The Circle of Silent Ministry.

7 February 1972

32 Pearson Park, Hull

My very dear old creature,

I returned home safely to Hull on Sunday night, though it was after midnight before I got in. A long drive! and I didn't go very fast.

I hope the weather is a bit brighter now than when I visited you – it is here, the sun shining and the weather quite mild. What a pity you can't see more of it! I'm afraid you will have to stay in bed until the x ray shows that the bone has healed satisfactorily: that will be at the beginning of March. Then you will have to learn to walk again, so make the most of your present rest.

I should try to cut your nails – I've asked Kitty to bring nail scissors.

I'm a little lighter still this morning – perhaps 13 st. 10 lbs! I shall vanish soon.

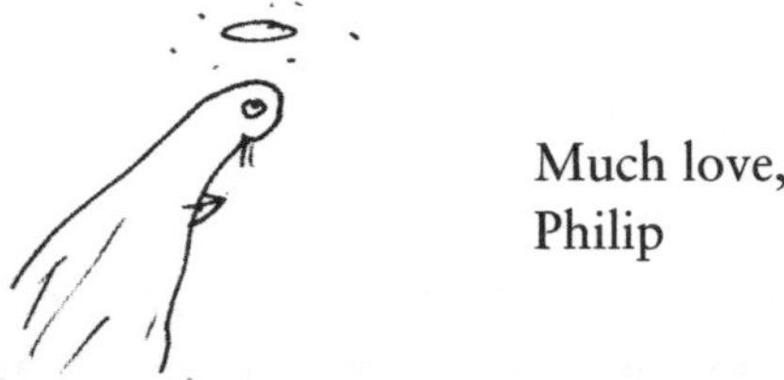

Much love,
Philip

10 February 1972

32 Pearson Park, Hull

My very dear old creature,

I hope you are not getting any power cuts. The miners are on strike, and this is threatening the power stations – it would be tedious to lie in the dark. We haven't had any yet, but I expect we shall. Lucky it isn't too cold at the moment.

Is the Home seeming any more like home? The thought of breakfast at 6 a.m. is very depressing: I wonder why they have to have it so early. Still, it is nice to have the longer days coming – I expect it will be light by 6 soon, even if it isn't now.

M[rs] Oates hasn't come this week: I hope she isn't going to let me down. She does drive herself very hard.

All being well, I'll see you on Saturday afternoon, and we can have a chat.

Much love,
Philip

16 February 1972

32 Pearson Park, Hull

My very dear old creature,

I hope you are still snug in your room, as it [is] certainly very bleak to be up and out. I have got out my very thickest wool underwear (including long pants) to counter it, and so look rather fatter than I have done recently.

So far I haven't suffered much from power cuts. The most inconvenient time is 8–midnight. It just ruins the evening: there's nothing to do but listen to a battery radio. Of course the gas fire keeps me warm.

Today is Ash Wednesday, the start of Lent, isn't it? I don't suppose you have had any pancakes. I didn't. Do you remember how you used to make them at Coventry?

My meals are drastically simple now – I have eggs one night, bacon the next. Of course, when I stop 'reducing' I can be more indulgent.

Much love.
Philip

23 February 1972

Picture postcard[1]

Hull

Would you like a picture for a change? This is rather a funny one. The grey skies and powercuts continue here as I expect they do with you. Have just found out that Arnold Bennett wrote to his mother every day! Betty has ordered a new car, having been told that her present one is about to collapse. She asks after you regularly.

Much love,
Philip

1 *The Lady of the Manor*, a stylised painting by Eden Box (1919–88) depicting a lady in a hat in a horsedrawn carriage with chestnut trees in flower around her, a country house in the distance and a children's picnic (with dog) in the foreground. 'Private Collection, London.'

24 April 1972

<*Letterhead*> 32 Pearson Park, Hull

Dear Kitty,[1]

I had a talk with my Lloyds man on the telephone this morning, & he said that while both groups of shares were all right he thought the second set (Industrial shares) had the edge insofar as if we bought from the first set we should be buying 'above par' & so if Mother lives until their redemption dates we shouldn't get back what we paid for them. This is Greek to me, but no doubt true. Any of the second set he thought all right, so should we go for those? He favoured Barclays, but I always like brewery shares. Presumably to invest in more than one increases 'charges', but perhaps this isn't significant: to do so spreads one's risks. It seems that any or all of the second set would do.

I found Mother rather less cheerful than on Saturday, but you will have seen her by now. She seemed cold – I do think she should wear more – and not very enthusiastic about the food. She confirmed the no-egg-for-breakfast story. She said she weighed 6 stone, wch doesn't seem much. I wish all aspects of the place were as pleasant as the building, etc! She walked along the passage with me when I left.

May I make clear my reasons for not wanting to pay the gas bill?[2] I think whereas there are charges wch definitely *are* my responsibility (e.g. telephone *calls* as distinct from t. *rent*), and charges wch definitely *aren't* (e.g. the garden), the middle area of charges (e.g. the cost of my being there at all) *could* be regarded as Mother's responsibility, since it is largely in her interest that I'm there, but not to be too scrupulous, might as well be split, me paying petrol & bringing her things like stamps and papers, & she paying house charges such as gas & electricity. You may say, & I quite agree, that it would be best for her not to spend money, but this seems a different argument to me, implying that we should divide the charges between us, as ultimately (as her heirs) we shall divide the money so saved. If I pay £100 to save Mother's £100, & this £100 is then divided between us by her will, I am £50 out of pocket.

This is a great fuss about a 30/- gas bill, but the principle may become important, if mother's expenditure exceeds her income, as it well may.

I am fatter after the weekend wch I ascribe to your excellent roast pork. Very nice lunch, & thank you. Don't have too many late nights, or early mornings.

Much love,
Philip

1 Apart from the formal letter to Kitty and Walter which Philip copied to Eva on 20 April 1969 this is the first letter from Philip to Kitty to survive since that congratulating her on the birth of Rosemary in 1947. This letter is preserved, along with nine further letters and two picture postcards sent between 1972 and 1982, in U DLN/3/8, a file mainly devoted to formal correspondence concerned with Eva's stay in Berrystead and the sale of 21 York Road in 1978. Intriguingly the file also contains the 1947 letter to Kitty.

2 These calculations relate to 21 York Road, where Philip stayed when he visited his mother in Berrystead.

10 May 1972

32 Pearson Park, Hull

My dear Kitty,

I thought you had better see this exchange before going on Friday.[1]

Stomatitis is simply 'diseases of the mouth', & a lot of these, according to Black's Medical Dictionary, are caused by, or symptomatic of, 'grave constitutional weakness'. Such weakness will only be aggravated by underfeeding. Hence my enquiry about special food, wch Bird studiously ignores. Tests won't feed her.

I am not answering this letter, at least for the moment, but I have written to Wynn-Williams[2] asking if I could see him this weekend. I do want to make sure that all is being done that can be done. This seems to me the plain duty of near relatives, let these sharks say what they will. No offence meant.

I'll ring on Friday at 9.30. as planned.

Much love,
Philip

1 Larkin enclosed a typed letter to Stanley Bird, the manager of the home, in which he asked that Eva be 'put on a diet designed to meet her problems'. 'Nourishing,

easily assimilable foods such as milk puddings, egg custards and so on suggest themselves, but you will know what is appropriate better than I.' Bird replied that the doctor had recommended tests, of which 'the results should be known in 7 to 10 days'.
2 Eva's doctor at this time.

11 May 1972

32 Pearson Park, Hull

My very dear old creature,

I often wonder when you get my letters – whether you are up and dressed and having your morning coffee, or whether you are still in bed & waiting to be 'got up'. It must be nice to lie watching the birds and the sun on the trees, now that they are so beautiful. I remember M[r] Bird telling me that he had the dressing tables made specially low so that people in bed could see out of the windows.

When I come to see you on Saturday I have to go out to dinner in the evening to some friend of Monica – *dinner jacket required*!! Isn't that a curse! I shall have to bring it all this way, & change somewhere. Perhaps I could wear it when I come to see you!

Don't be afraid!

I've been reading the letters of Llewelyn Powys again – one of Daddy's books, though my name seems to be in it. He had a *very* ill life, yet thought it was worth it as long as you could see the sun and feel the air.

Much dear love, Philip.

6 June 1972

32 Pearson Park, Hull[1]

My very dear old creature,

I am a rather fatter creature after Oxford – up to 13 st. again. I certainly didn't refuse anything, such as good thick soups, sausages for breakfast, even a pint of beer! That means I have had 3 pints THIS YEAR. Of course I drink other things.

Here is *Little Women*: I do hope you enjoy it. I have put your name in.

I feel very harassed these days, too many things to do and too many annoyances! Mrs Oates returns today – she was away last week – and will find plenty to occupy her.

I was so pleased to have letters from you this morning – I quite thought you had 'hung up your pen', or whatever the appropriate phrase would be. I wish you could join in with the others more – you need company. Dr Johnson said 'If you are idle, be not solitary: if you are solitary, be not idle.'

Must rush – much love – P

1 At the top of the first page opposite the address Eva has written 'P.S. I don't know whether this is the right sheet to write on next. / Have got all muddled up owing to the weather (sorry dear Creature.)' In a letter dated '2nd (a guess) June' she had written: 'O dear, forgive this awful letter – but this morning I was asked by Mr Bird to go downstairs and see how I thought I should like to be there permanent this. [*sic*] I won't try to write *another* copy. Anyway, apart from being with a lot of elderly ladies, and having Mrs Carter sitting next to me, there weren't many people there. I expect a lot of them were out, perhaps, shopping. I suppose I should get used to writing letters in a crowd of people, in time.'

23 June 1972

Durrants Hotel, London

My very dear old creature,

Well, we had a better day yesterday than I expected. The day started dull & dreary, & rain delayed the start of play till nearly 12: our seats are out in the open so there's no shelter! However, they started, & the game crept on, until eventually the sun came out & by teatime it was quite a good day. The cricket was interesting, though England did well to start with. We take our lunch. It's quite impossible to get anything to eat there, the crowds are so big. Queues for everything, including lavatories.

After play was over we went to have dinner at Stephen Spender's, where Auden was staying, so we had quite a poetic evening. Fortunately Auden likes to go to bed early so we broke up at a reasonable hour & were back here by 11 p.m. – bar just closed! There was a lot more about the laureateship in *The Times*, Auden has declared he doesn't want it & is an American anyway. I am still mentioned. Brr!

Today the sun's shining brightly and poor Monica has to go back to Leicester for an examiners' meeting, so she'll miss play today. We think of you very affectionately & wonder if you see the cricket on TV?

Much love
P.[1]

1 Eva has written on the back of the envelope: 'Stephen Spender '72 4th June'.

31 July 1972

32 Pearson Park, Hull

My very dear old creature,

Your letter arrived very early today, as early as the paper – thank you very much. You don't say if you have changed your room yet, so I expect you haven't. I'm glad you are sitting out in the sun. Make the most of it![1]

I got on with my proofs better yesterday,[2] but they are difficult things to finalise: one change can mean many other changes, especially in page numbers. I had the steak last night & some turnips – very good, really more than I wanted. My weight is up to 13¼ st! Perhaps one doesn't need food in summer.

In *The Times* this morning Sir John Betjeman says that if the Laureateship goes to the best *poet* it should go to me! I don't think I want it.

Closer examination of my armchair reveals it's in a bad way – perhaps I sh[d] buy a new one. But it's very difficult to buy a really comfortable armchair.

Much love Philip

1 On 29 July Eva wrote: 'the nurse has *brought* me out and the sun feels very hot. / I wonder what time Kitty will come? Nurse has just been and given most of us a tablet. Don't know what it is for. / The sun has gone in. Expect it will come out again. / I'm afraid you will find this a very dull letter. Of course there is not much to write about. / After lunch: – There was no time to finish this before. Kitty & Rosemary came about 11.30 a.m. bringing all sorts of things. [. . .] Fancy! it is only one o'clock! I expect there will only be a few visitors this afternoon. I wonder whether there will be anyone unexpected to see me. I forget when the Circle came last. [. . .] It is very quiet in the lounge most people are dozing.'
2 *The Oxford Book of Twentieth-Century English Verse.*

8 August 1972

32 Pearson Park, Hull

My very dear old creature,

Thank you for your kind letter wishing me many happy returns of tomorrow. I certainly feel the impudence of being 50 rather! I suppose it's all right when you get used to it, but I feel the grave is uncomfortably near!

It's nice of you to offer me a present – I told Kitty I needed a little plastic container to bring grapefruit juice in when I come home – they seem to have stopped making small tins – and she said she'd try to find one. Tomorrow I shall have to buy the staff a lot of cakes – Betty & I will go out in the morning. We shall have to buy about a dozen! So you can think of me.

Monica has given me some lovely music records – *very* enjoyable. I had a card from a complete stranger bearing a limerick:

> There was a young fellow of Hull
> Who found life distressingly dull:
> He would sit on the quay
> And gaze out to sea,
> Singing 'O for the wings of a gull!'

Very funny, isn't it? Anyway, dear old creature, I'll be thinking of you – as always!

Much love Philip[1]

1 On the back of the envelope Eva has written '8th August '42'.

9 August 1972

32 Pearson Park, Hull

My very dear old creature,

Many thanks for your birthday wishes. The card hasn't come yet, but I expect it will. I had a nice notelet from A. Nellie plus a funny card, so she isn't dead yet! Eva has had an operation, & A. Nellie is 'staying with friends'. Kitty & Rosemary sent very nice cards & I have had one or two unexpected cards & letters – one from Professor Brett, my first chairman here, welcoming me to the 'over-50s' club.

I shall certainly tape-record my programme, so we may be able to play it you.[1]

Betty has given me a silver cup – curious, but very pretty – & Kitty a book of stamps (you'll get most of them) & some soap. Monica gave me some records. Well, must go to lunch now, but thank you again and be sure of all my love –

1 'Larkin at 50: a birthday tribute', BBC Radio 3, 9 August 1972.

14 September 1972

32 Pearson Park, Hull

My very dear old creature,

Well, I did collect the watch this morning: they have thoroughly overhauled it and put in a new jewel. Cost £2.50! We shall see if it goes better. I don't like to abandon it without a struggle, as it was Daddy's watch & quite a good one.

I can almost remember him buying it: it was certainly before the war, & down Smithford Street in Coventry (if I remember aright).[1] He bought me one at the same time, wch was much appreciated as I could then tell how long each school lesson had still to go, & so feel less bored.

It doesn't seem a very bright day today, but I hope you are keeping warm. Have you been watching the Olympics on television?[2] You will be better informed on world events than I, wch wouldn't be difficult. You see the newspaper *and* television, I only see the newspaper.

Always thinking of you,
Much love,
Philip

1 Once the main shopping street in central Coventry, but engulfed by post-war redevelopment.

2 The 1972 Summer Olympics were held in Munich, West Germany, 26 August–11 September.

20 September 1972

<*Printed slip*> University of Hull, The Brynmor Jones Library.
With the compliments of the Librarian

Dear Kitty,

Exchange between myself and Bird enclosed.

His usual infelicities apart, it seems to me that either you or I sh^{d} be informed of any change in Mother's condition, & not be left to find it out when – and if – we visit her. What do you think?[1]

Did he tell you? P

1 Larkin enclosed a typed letter to Mr Bird noting that, after not visiting his mother for four weeks, he had discovered 'a minor but definite deterioration in her condition'. He asked whether Bird and Dr Wynn-Williams thought this would be a permanent change. Bird replied that the doctor had concluded 'that Mrs. Larkin has had a mild cerebral Thrombosis, and the prognosis is: there should be a gradual improvement, with the possibility of recurrent relapses. [. . .]' He added: 'Mrs. Larkin worried unnecessarily over your absence, but of course there was little we could do about that.'

11 October 1972

32 Pearson Park, Hull

My very dear old creature,

Well. I am *not* poet laureate! Sir John Betjeman has been appointed, so all is over. I have been asked to write an article for the *Sunday Times* about him – it all makes work! However, I am very pleased: long may he reign.

In fact I got up at 5.30 a.m. to do the article today: I woke & lay worrying, I thought I might as well be up.

I should like to think you are feeling better this morning: have you watered the plants? It's time you had another one really, isn't it. I'll see what I can find. Meantime, aren't the leaves on the trees beautiful? Or rather *off* the trees, for they're on the pavements mostly. You will see a lot of them from your window.

I think of you all the time, dear creature, and hope you are enjoying your rest.

Much love,
Philip

27 December 1972

32 Pearson Park, Hull

My very dear old creature,

Well, I am back in Hull again, where it is very fine and mild. I rose early at York Road this morning & was away by about 9.15, bearing certain provisions I hadn't managed to eat – and leaving others in the dustbin!

It was *so nice* seeing you for Christmas, & I hope you enjoyed your outing to Kitty's for lunch & tea. It was lovely to see your smiling face over the plates & to think you were having a good meal for once. [. . .]

My dear creature, I hope you don't feel too wobbly – take care. I know it's difficult. Keep your watch wound up. You are a lovely creature & we all love you. Kitty will come on Saturday. Hope the new slippers are being successful!

Very much love – Philip

31 December 1972

1a Ratcliffe Road, Haydon Bridge, Hexham, Northumberland

My very dear old creature,

Here I am up in Monica's village. It was a trying drive up, yesterday: quite thick fog from Hull to beyond Scotch Corner, and cold too. I stopped at Thirsk to eat sandwiches and have a drink, but it was hard going. Then, beyond Scotch Corner, the fog lifted and the weather became mild. It was like spring at Barnard Castle. I got here about a quarter to five.

It's Sunday morning, & I've rung up Kitty to see how she is and how you are. She says you are not too bad! I hope the upsets of Christmas have subsided.

Monica's Christmas goose has been thrown out at last, & remains only as a part of a big bean casserole we had last night. Tonight we shall go to Allendale to see the New Year bonfire & procession. I have brought my duffel coat & wool hat, as last year I was afraid of the sparks burning my good overcoat.

Well, 1972 is nearly gone – not a very nice year. Let's hope 1973 will be better. Dear old creature, I hope you are walking better & are able to sit with the others. You ought to talk to people occasionally – we get melancholy-mad otherwise.

Much, much love
Philip

1973

5 January 1973

32 Pearson Park, Hull

My very dear old creature,

The days get progressively mistier, & so do I! Monica's company is very nice, but it does lead to a lot of drinking, & I feel rather low of a morning. When I came in *this* morning I just sat in an armchair for an hour!

I shall be seeing you on Saturday – the day you get this – and Kitty says she is arranging a tea for you. That will be nice! I hope the day is mild, like this one.

I see Princess Anne has a suspected boy friend – I hope *he* likes horses![1]

Much love, old creature,
Philip

1 Princess Anne was to marry Lieutenant Mark Phillips of the 1st Queen's Dragoon Guards, at Westminster Abbey on Wednesday 14 November 1973.

31 January 1973

32 Pearson Park, Hull

My very dear old creature,

Another fine day, and another nice letter from you! I'm so glad you have found your stick. Certainly 10/- (50p.) would be enough for the benefactor who found it.

I'm so sorry your glasses keep slipping. Perhaps Kitty could take them and get them altered at an optician's. They bend the earpieces in a little, to grip tighter. The other stick is yours too. I carved the 'L' on it, for Larkin. Not 'L' for Learner!

There isn't a lot of news here. I am enquiring about some houses that are being built not far from Pearson Park, to see if they would suit me, but no information has arrived so far. I really can't stay in my flat for ever – it's only for as long as I work for the University!

However, the houses are a long way from being built – it is just a sea of mud at present.

I'm glad you like Monica's card, but they are *Siamese cats*, not foxes!! She is a bit better, as I think I said. Love as always,

Philip

1 March 1973

32 Pearson Park, Hull

My very dear old creature,

A rainy-looking day here, but still mild – so the heater I bought yesterday for my bedroom hasn't been used yet. Mrs Oates tells me that my lavatory brush is on its last legs and will have to be replaced! I dare say: everything is so old. Suddenly one finds things are 12 or 15 years old, that one thinks of as new!

I am heavier today, though I've been 'off my peck' generally this week. The rather dull rota of eggs, bacon, eggs in the evenings has come to pall, though I always eat my lunch hungrily enough!

Perhaps I should go more for meat. Yet it's rather difficult to buy – butchers seem to close earlier than other shops.

How I remember our trips to Bausons [?] and Palmers in the old days! The sawdust & the barrel of offal (not too nice!)!

Much love, old creature,
Philip

1 March 1973[1]

32 Pearson Park, Hull

My very dear old creature,

What a nice letter from you waiting for me when I got in this evening! I'm glad to hear you can be really warm in the lounge.[2] The weather is so changeable these days.

This is really only a note to say I hope to come & see you on Saturday – the day you get this – & we can have a good chat.

Take care of yourself!

Much love
Philip

1 Written on the same day as the last.

2 Philip kept up the residual dialogue. On 28 February Eva had written: 'It is a lovely sunny morning. It began with frost and fog and gradually these faded away but there are no flowers. I think it must be cold outside for there are no people walking about. Perhaps they are all resting for every where is very quiet. I have just peeped out of my door and saw the back view of a lady walking slowly down the corridor. I have made a journey next down into the lounge where it is very warm too warm, in fact so I came back. I feel rather "shivery" so have put on my thick cardigan. There is a lot of traffic along the road where Kitty waits for me sometimes. / I think they are making cups of tea in the corridor. Yes, here is a cup of tea.'

17 April 1973

as from Hull — Tuesday

My very dear old creature,

In fact I'm in London – up for the day, to have lunch with *another* publisher. I got the 6.45 a.m. train, wch meant setting the alarm for 5.30 a.m., and *that* meant I actually awoke at 3.45 a.m. – I'm so nervous of alarms. However, here I am, & came early to do a little shopping – a pair of opal earclips for Monica's birthday – rather a special present, to commemorate the Oxford book. And a dish mop for me! I had an awful experience last night: I put two mops and a dish cloth to boil – and forgot them!! About three hours later I was roused by a smell of burning –

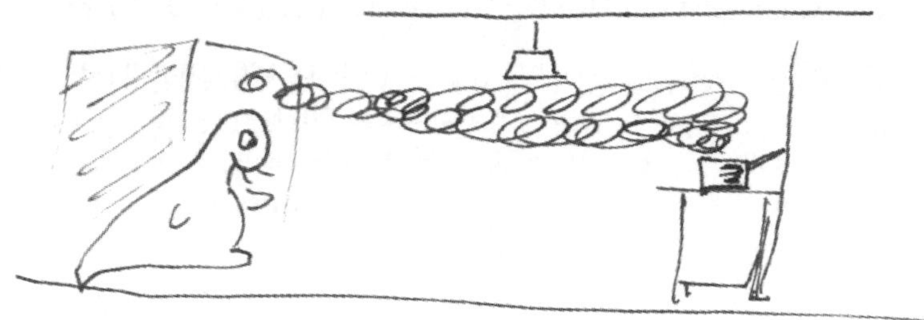

Everything ruined, of course!! Oh dear! So I had to replace them, before I can do any more washing up.

Shall be back this evening. I do hope you are feeling better. Wouldn't it be wonderful if you found your spectacles! Never mind. Kitty is getting another pair.

Very much love,
Philip

27 April 1973

32 Pearson Park, Hull — Friday

My very dear old creature,

The lunch yesterday was rather a strain[1] – you will see on p.18 of the *Telegraph* today that several tactless things were said. I was really hardly conscious of what was going on – what with being introduced to people, and photographed, & having to present people with prizes, &

then introduce speakers, and propose the health of the Queen, and sign copies of the book afterwards. Your poor creature felt very 'mithered'. Kingsley and Monica were there – I enclose a plan of the 'top table'.[2] Afterwards we went to the Oxford University Press and drank through the remainder of the sunny afternoon. I returned late at night a very worn creature.

M. looked lovely in a big black hat with artificial roses on it, a black suit & white frilled blouse with ruffled cuffs. She does do herself up well! She wore the opal earclips I bought for her birthday, although it isn't till May 7th.

Much love

Philip

1 Foyles literary luncheon, 'to mark the publication of *The Oxford Book of Twentieth Century English Verse*', held at The Dorchester, Park Lane, London W.1., 26 April 1973.

2 The list of attendees is enclosed with the plan of the 'top table'. Larkin was flanked to his immediate right by Miss Margaret Rawlings, Mr Kingsley Amis and Mr John Lehmann, OBE, FRSL, and on his immediate left by Sir Ralph Richardson and Lord Snow, CBE.

13 May 1973

32 Pearson Park, Hull

My very dear old creature,

What a gloomy day – wet, into the bargain, but not cold or windy. And the trees look so beautiful now, when the new leaves are just out. I wish I could hear the birds – I'm sure they are singing a lot these days, but too high for me to hear them. [. . .]

Much, much love, Philip

<*On first page opposite the address, in pencil*> Love from FROGGY!!

30 May 1973

32 Pearson Park, Hull

My very dear old creature,

Just a quick line, as this is committee day & I've not long to get this into the post. Isn't it exciting about Princess Anne?[1] I heard it on the car radio when I was driving home after work yesterday. It makes me very glad I'm not Poet Laureate. I shouldn't like to have to produce a poem. Will Betjeman, I wonder?[2]

The weather is still very hot and oppressive: I feel quite sick in the mornings.

Can't think of any explanation. I do hope you are well and look forward to seeing you on Saturday – the anniversary of Thomas Hardy's birthday

MUCH LOVE,
Philip

1 Princess Anne announced her engagement to Mark Phillips on 29 May 1973.
2 Betjeman's twelve-line poem, 'Princess Anne's Wedding Day. November 1973', was poorly received. Betjeman told *The Times* the poem was 'one of the most laborious things that I have ever written'. Labour MP Tony Pendry wrote to Prime Minister Edward Heath, asking him to 'reconsider his choice' of Laureate.

21 June 1973

Lords Cricket Ground, London

Dearest old creature,

Well, we are sitting watching the first session of this Test March between England and New Zealand. It's nearly one o'clock, and they play till 1.30 – then have lunch. The day is quite mild though sunless: the rain, that was pretty constant yesterday, seems to have retreated for the time being. I can see the TV cameras trained on the scene, but I don't expect you are watching. It isn't in fact *very* interesting. England are batting, & have made 48 for one wicket.

I always feel rather guilty coming away at this time of year, for my dear staff are slaving away at the Library, stocktaking. However, I've invited eleven of the more important ones out to dinner next Wednesday at the Beverley Arms, so perhaps that will console them. We are going to have melon & ginger, celery soup, roast duck, and fruit salad or cheese. I hope it's better than Monica & I had last night at a steak house! Awful uneatable steak. And not much else to eat either. Turkish delight with the coffee was the best.

London is *not very nice*: the stores are full of Indians & negroes (*serving*) who move like old tired snails & don't know anything about anything. Heaven knows what will become of this England! We shall have a picnic lunch in a bit – England have now made 62.

Monica joins in sending love

Philip

8 July 1973

32 Pearson Park, Hull

Dearest old creature,

Well, in the comparative quiet of Sunday morning I can sit back and feel that the fearful strains of yesterday are at last over.[1] Oh my! They really began on Friday, when I attended a Science degree congregation in the City Hall: it poured with rain, and traffic was at its peak. I put the car in a multi-storey carpark, but when the ceremony was over couldn't get it out as rush-hour traffic blocked the way. Since I had to meet Monica at the station I abandoned the car & rushed through the rain, fuming – then had to escort her & bags back to the carpark & resume my attempts to get out. Well, I expect this is all very dull, but I felt truly exhausted when I got back & got straight into a bath. Then I had to go to a dinner for the honorary graduands: dear old John Betjeman had arrived, & enquired if Monica was here – typical of his kindness. The other graduands included Lord Wilberforce,[2] whom I knew slightly at All Souls.

However, on Saturday it wasn't raining, at least, & we got to the City Hall in good order. Monica was looking stunning in a black suit with white blouse with frills & ruffles at throat & wrists, and a big black hat with luscious artificial roses on it. Very smart! I robed in the robing room (my scarlet Belfast gown), & we processed into the Hall about 10.30. John B. had on a turquoise blue silk tie & a light suit, but of course he had robes on too. After the VC had opened the Congregation

I was the first speaker – spoke for about 5 mins into a microphone with a huge audience of students & their parents, and staff – and press & photographers – I *hope* it went over all right: I didn't get the laughs I hoped for, but perhaps I went too quickly. Or perhaps the jokes weren't very funny! I could see Monica, perched up in the balcony, a tiny black & white figure with a huge hat. Anyway, it was over eventually, & I could relax.

Lunch was at the university: melon, then slices of beef, turkey & ham with salads of different kinds, then strawberries & cream and cheese & biscuits. Plenty of wine. Betjeman made a nice speech, paying me many fulsome compliments, & said nice things about Hull. We dispersed about 2.45, and did a little shopping in our fine clothes. Then home to collapse for a bit – though I did take some pictures of Monica in the garden before she abandoned her finery.

If there anything in the papers about it on Monday, I'll buy you a copy.

Of course I have thought of you a great deal in this 'rainy season', and hope you have not let it get you down – it really won't hurt you, old creature, and in any case you are *quite* safe among the dear old creatures in the lounge. Monica asks me specially to remember her to you. She is taking it easy today. I shall be coming to see you next Saturday & Sunday. Poor Kitty, going to Poland! Well, I hope she enjoys it.

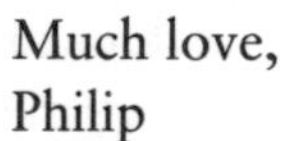

Much love,
Philip

1 Larkin had given the address at the award of a Hull honorary D.Litt. to John Betjeman.
2 Richard Wilberforce (1907–2003), British judge.

22 July 1973 — Greetings card[1]

Dearest old creature,

Since I can't visit you today, I'm sending one of Monica's notelets. I am going to London for a poetry reading from the Oxford Book, at the BBC.

I went to York Road today, & began mowing the lawn, but was alarmed to find that old Toad was in the roller part!! So I stopped, & borrowed a mower from M[rs] Richards. I'll have to buy a new mower.[1]

I did like seeing you yesterday & am sorry I was so sleepy. It was a hard day one way & another. Much, much love,

Philip

1 'St Valentine's Day' by Kate Greenaway: 'Best Wishes'

2 Two days later, on 24 July, Larkin wrote: 'I do hope old toad has settled down after his awful experience on Sunday. I feel upset about it still myself.' On 25 July he bought a new mower in Hull, which 'fits nicely into the boot of my car, so I'll bring it to Loughborough this weekend. Mowing the lawn will become a pleasure.'

26 August 1973

Haydon Bridge Sunday

Dearest old creature,

Well today is nicer than yesterday, w[ch] was sunless & not too warm. Monica & I went to Bellingham show, w[ch] was a big sort of country show at a small village some 16 miles away. We had been in 1967 and found it much the same. There was a great deal of dog-judging, and pony- & horse-judging, and of course jumping & that kind of thing. There were a number of stalls selling tweed & wool things, & I got inveigled into buying a sports coat – very loud, & countrified, with a hare pocket.

I think it will fit all right, but it will give you a fright when you see it.

Then after lunch we watched some Cumberland-style wrestling, w[ch] was interesting, & looked round the 'household' tent – all the prizewinning entries of vegetables, flowers, cakes, scones, jam, honey, lemon cheese and so on. It was fascinating. There were lots of other classes – crochet, knitting, rugs, draught-excluders! And in these parts they produce 'lambing sticks', or shepherds' crooks, with handles made of rams' horns: plenty of those.[1]

All in all a nice day – I wish you could have seen it. Of course it made one very hungry!

I see Princess Anne & her fiancé have been looking at their house, with a view to furnishing it. No expense spared, I hope.

I haven't got Eva's address:[2] so I can't send her a card. But I shall write to *you,* dear old creature, every day.

MUCH LOVE Philip

1 Larkin began drafting 'Show Saturday' two months later, in October.

2 Nellie's daughter.

31 August 1973

Cringletie Hotel (Peebles, The Borders)

Dearest old creature,

We are staring glumly through the hotel windows at rain – or drizzle, mild but persistent –

Typical Scotch holiday weather! However, I expect we shall go out & brave it: the car is always dry. Or nearly always: I remember it began to let in the rain in Ireland once, wch was very inconvenient.

Yesterday we visited Peebles, and did a little shopping. There were a lot of wasps, wch I preferred to avoid. After lunch we dozed, then drove round the neighbourhood, enjoying the lonely roads & the rolling countryside & the hills in the distance. I like small Scotch towns: they look so severe, & yet often they have lovely gardens, and the houses are gracefully designed in stone.

Today we are planning to go to Abbotsford, where Sir Walter Scott lived. I hope it clears up soon. I hope it isn't as gloomy at Syston as it is here, & that you are finding things to interest you as the days go by.

All my love,
Philip

10 October 1973

32 Pearson Park, Hull

Dearest old creature,

Gloomy day – raining – my 'illness' still hanging about. Luckily the pain has gone, but I still have no appetite. My weight goes down, though – every cloud has a silver lining. I have brought in two marmite sandwiches for lunch! Even they may disagree with me.

Today's post brought a copy of a book *about* me – written by one of the young men at Leicester.[1] I can't say it looks very exciting. Also a form saying my election to the MCC was a stage nearer. MCC is the Marylebone Cricket Club, but don't think I have to play cricket!

Don't forget to wind your watch, old creature: it does it good. I do hope you've found your glasses.[2]

MUCH LOVE
Philip

1 David Timms, *Philip Larkin* (Edinburgh: Oliver & Boyd, 1973).
2 Eva has inserted into the envelope a roughly torn half-page on which she has begun to draft a response: 'Oh I am so pleased to have / Oh I am so pleased to have a letter from you. Is \st/ it such to think that the ~~storms~~ storms have gone, although it ~~does nt~~ does'nt write much better than my old one! done. I doubt. Yes, it is nice to think that the storms have gone. I do hope they will not come back. They were

awful and I worried over what damage they had done. / Oh I am so pleased to have a letter from you and to ~~thn that~~ think that think that the storms I do hope that they will not come back.'

6 November 1973

32 Pearson Park, Hull

Dearest old creature,

I am about to go off to Edinburgh for one night – awful long way to go for so short a time – but I shall be back tomorrow night. The sun's shining brightly, so I shall have a nice train journey, seeing Durham and Newcastle.

I got up at 6 a.m. this morning to try to write a poem,[1] but didn't make much progress. It's nice seeing the light come, the almost-leafless trees outlined against the window. I expect you see them sometimes. It's better to get up than lie moping. I do hope you are feeling stronger, and are managing to put away your meals. I think of you all the time, & remember the happy times we had. You are a lovely old creature.

Much love,
Philip

1 Larkin sent Anthony Thwaite a copy of 'Show Saturday' on 10 December 1973.

14 December 1973

32 Pearson Park, Hull

Dearest old creature,

I'm writing this on Friday to say I hope to come and see you on Saturday, but I don't expect you'll actually receive it till next week, post being what it is. So I had better just say how much I look forward to seeing you. I feel rather low today as I had a heavy day yesterday with a dinner at night, but no doubt I shall buck up.

It's a time of year I really don't care for much!

I do hope you are managing to keep warm. Wrap yourself up in all you have.

There was a talk about me on the wireless on Tuesday called 'Larkin and Larkinism',[1] but I didn't hear it, so I don't know what Larkinism is! Something rather nasty, I expect.

Much love, my dear old creature,

1 By the American critic Donald Hall. The listing of the programme noted: '[Hall] develops a hard-hitting critique of some tendencies which he sees exemplified in Philip Larkin's recent anthology *The Oxford Book of 20th-Century English Verse*.' See http://genome.ch.bbc.co.uk/schedules/radio3/1973-12-11.

1974

10 January 1974

32 Pearson Park, Hull

Dearest old creature,

What a *miserable* day for your birthday! It's raining & blowing here, and so *cold* – poor creature, I'm sure you are feeling it. But it *is* creature's day,[1] & I have drunk your health in sherry *and* Guinness, and hope you have a comfortable and not too cold day.

I did buy you something for your birthday, but I don't know if Kitty will have given it you. Perhaps she is waiting for me to bring it on Sunday, when I come.

I was reading my diary for 1946/7 last night[2] – you remember that awful winter, when we were snowed up from January to March? You were at Warwick and I was in Leicester, at Joan Sutcliffe's. How awful it was – worse than now! Of course, we are older now and less able to stand it. I bought my duffle coat to wear *indoors*!

Wrap up well. I shall see you (all being well) on Saturday & Sunday.

Much love,
Philip.

1 Eva's eighty-eighth birthday.
2 Larkin's diaries were destroyed after his death on his instructions.

11 February 1974

32 Pearson Park, Hull

Dearest old creature,

I ploughed back to Hull last evening through wind & rain, arriving at 11, but very pleased to have seen you and sat watching the cows munching their straw & having drinks at the trough. It's very nice to have them to watch.

Today is *lovely* and mild, rather windy, but extremely springlike, wch is nice and comforting.

How fed up I am with all this election stuff! I really think I shall have to give up newspapers & the radio until it is all over.

Don't forget your nice *soap* – in the top half of the cupboard.

Much love:
Philip

29 April 1974

Picture postcard[1]

[32 Pearson Park, Hull]

Here is a gentle soul to wish you good morning! I feel a bit better this morning, but no doubt only because of work. It braces one up a bit. I hope you are well and comfortable, and finding things to amuse you. Kitty said you had a book about the Royal Family that was interesting. Perhaps I shall see it in due course.

Much love, Philip

1 'A Young Cocker [Spaniel]'.

30 April 1974

32 Pearson Park, Hull

Dearest old creature,

A much sunnier day today, and a bit warmer, wch is a comfort! A busy morning: we are being visited by the German Ambassador on 14 May, & I spent some time discussing the arrangements. Daddy would feel happier about it than I do! Still, they all speak very good English, so I suppose it will be all right. I asked the Professor of German if I should put our copy of the 1st ed. of *Mein Kampf* on exhibition, but he said he thought not!

I put on a suit today, thinking I had a special meeting but I find I haven't, & that the suit is very hot.

I hope you are having nice meals, and that *you* aren't too hot. There's quite a cold breeze out. See you soon. Much love,

Philip

4 June 1974

Picture postcard[1]

[32 Pearson Park, Hull]

Tuesday

I have just got back to Hull after my weekend. A beautiful day and a nice drive through Lincolnshire. As usual, on return I feel rather guilty about being away! However, I expect that will wear off. This is a picture of one of the students' residences here: isn't it ugly? I think of you & hope you are well.

Much love
Philip

1 The University of Hull: the Lawns.

23 June 1974

<*Letterhead with coat of arms*>
Durrants Hotel, George Street, London W1H 6BJ

Dearest old creature,

Well, as so often I am writing to you at the end of our Lord's visit, feeling a little flat now the mini-holiday is over and all I have to face is the journey home and then the grim realities of next week. It has been a nice visit: weather very warm and fine, and for the first time I have been a member of the MCC, able to stroll into the Pavilion wearing my bold red & yellow tie. On the debit side, hayfever wasn't at all good on Friday and I was

fairly miserable in consequence, but I kept going, & it was better on Saturday.

On Friday evening we had a simple dinner with Sir John Betjeman, in Chelsea where he now lives. He seemed a rather humble and crushed creature, and not in very good form, though quite ready to talk. He seems older than his years (about 68).[1] I think the Queen should give him a special pension.

Monica hasn't been well either, claiming that various meals upset her. At the match we first ate pork pie, lettuce & tomato, with some cherries & a banana, & a piece of cake about tea time. All the same, I don't suppose we've *lost* any weight. We both *feel* very fat.

I hope you are enjoying the quiet summer days, and aren't too hot. Let us hope there aren't too many mysterious noises from the passage, or overhead.

The *Sunday Times* today says my poems are selling well, w[ch] is a comfort. His sins were scarlet, but his books were read, as someone says somewhere.[2]

Monica joins me in wishing you a peaceful weekend, and in sending love,

Philip

1 Betjeman was showing the symptoms of Parkinson's disease by this time.
2 Hilaire Belloc (1870–1953): 'On his books'.

27 June 1974

<*Letterhead*> 32 Pearson Park, Hull

Dearest old creature,

This is *moving day* – the men have spent all morning loading my miserable belongings onto their van, & have gone off for lunch. I have had my sandwich in the Library and am snatching a moment to write to you.

I think my chief impression is how old and dirty all my things are! When the bookcases were moved, the dirt of ages lay behind. When a man put some sofa-cushions together, clouds of dust arose! I felt rather ashamed. I don't think Mrs Oates has been cleaning as well as she ought!

Heaven knows what damage I shall find when I come to examine my goods. The bed in particular had a hard passage. Oh dear! I will let you know.

Much love
Philip

30 June 1974

<*Letterhead amended in holograph*>
105 Newland Park ~~32 Pearson Park, Hull~~

Dearest old creature,

This is my first letter from my new quarters. I am still feeling rather strange and a bit upset – it's a time when one is easily affected, and finding little things wrong with the house, or missing things the removers have almost certainly taken, produces a kind of disproportionate depression. However, in the main things are all right, so I must try to take courage, and hope that as I get used to being here and work out routines for living it will all begin to seem more natural.

The house is in a very quiet residential district – virtually no traffic – and really isn't on the way to anywhere, so there are very few people about. It is nearer to the University than Pearson Park, but I don't pass any shops on the way, wch is going to make things harder. I had got into the habit of picking up things I needed on the way to or from work.

There is still a lot of things to put away – often things for wch there seem no places here – and with Mrs Oates being ill the house hasn't been properly cleaned; however, all will get done in time. Monica is coming on Tuesday, & on Wednesday we are setting out for St Andrews, where I am to get an Honorary Degree on Friday. St Andrews is in Scotland – the oldest Scottish university, older than Oxford.[1]

I shall be thinking of you always, and wishing I could be with you to tell you about it!

With much love!!
Philip

1 Larkin is wrong. St Andrews University was inaugurated by a papal bull in 1413. Oxford University had come into being in the twelfth century.

7 July 1974

<*Letterhead*>
The Old Course Hotel, St Andrews, Fife KY16 9SP Sunday

Dearest old creature,

Well, it all duly happened, but oh dear what a wet day Friday was.[1] I think it rained all day. Certainly Monica got her beloved hat wet, wch didn't cheer her up, because the queue for entering the hall moved slowly. The day was in fact a *science* day – don't know why I was there – *arts* having been done the day before; the other honorary graduates along with me included Sir Christopher Soames (Winston Churchill's son in law), Sir Andrew Huxley (some relation of Aldous & Julian),[2] & two other people. This time I wore a *cassock*, black with yellow buttons all down the front – very smart, but it was quite impossible to get at my handkerchief!!

The cassock was black. I had to kneel before the Chancellor, who dabbed me on the head with a sort of folded red duster (symbolising the cap of John Knox), then a beadle hooked my hood over my head (yellow silk lined with white) & I shook hands. Afterwards we had lunch miles away in some country hotel – still in the rain. By then I felt pretty exhausted.

In the evening we went to dinner with the Librarian, who has a nice house not far from the University.

On Saturday we walked round St Andrews – this was the first time we'd been able to do so – and then drove out through Dundee & lunched (rather late) at Glamis (Macbeth was Thane of Glamis, you remember). After that we went to Kirriemuir & saw J.M. Barrie's birthplace,[3] now run by the National Trust, & up Glen Clova, one of M's beauty spots.

Now it is Sunday, & we are setting off for home – at least, we shall stay overnight on the way, & get to Hull on Monday. My car seems to be *eating* petrol! Money, money. These jaunts are very expensive. I hope you are well, dear old creature, and settled comfortably. I shall see you at the weekend. Then I shall be on my way to Sussex![3] Wonder what it will be like there.

We both send love!
Philip

1 Larkin had been awarded an honorary D.Litt. at St Andrews University.
2 Christopher Soames (1920–87), British politician, husband of Mary Churchill; Andrew Huxley (1917–2012), British physiologist and Nobel laureate, half-brother of the writer Aldous Huxley and the biologist Julian Huxley.
3 J. M. (James Matthew) Barrie (1860–1937), Scottish playwright and novelist, creator of Peter Pan.
3 Larkin was awarded an honorary D.Litt. at the University of Sussex on 16 July 1974.

25 July 1974

<*Letterhead amended in holograph*>
105 Newland Park ~~32 Pearson Park, Hull~~ Thursday

Dearest old creature,

I have spent the morning at home, waiting for various workmen – mostly from the gas board. This house has a sort of central heating fired by gas, and they have been servicing it & finding a leak. It has a time switch so in the winter I can set it to come on before I return in the evening, and the house will be warmed up. That will be nice!

While I waited I had the Test Match on, but it is off now, wch must mean it is raining at Leeds. No doubt it will soon be raining in Hull!

Isn't it funny, me living all my life in Hull, a place I don't know or care about!

Dear old creature, I think so often about our days in Coventry, how the traffic used to go up and down St Patrick's Road, and I sh^{d} come in in the evening to find you 'picking fruit', with a cupful of water to put the maggots in – poor maggots! We should have put them outdoors. Do you remember how Daddy never liked *hot* pie, so his piece was always cut out & left to cool? Red currants, black currants, raspberries, blackberries – little I see of them now, except at Monica's or Kitty's!

MUCH LOVE
Philip

13 August 1974

<Letterhead amended in holograph>
105 Newland Park ~~32 Pearson Park, Hull~~

Dearest old creature,

I can't see the tortoise in the garden next door: I expect he has crawled out of sight. Perhaps the rain has put him off, although I should have thought he was pretty snug in his shell.

Of course he isn't as big as that.

Really, there is not much news. The University is very quiet. I am compiling my annual report, a task I find more & more tedious as the years go by. Yesterday I had a gas man in, and he found *two* gas leaks! I thought I could smell them. So that is a good job done. Today a man is coming to put up the remainder of the curtains, and a chest should be coming, for my bedroom. There is always plenty to think about – and pay for!

Much love, always thinking of you –

Philip

20 August 1974

<Letterhead amended in holograph>
105 Newland Park ~~32 Pearson Park, Hull~~ Tuesday

Dearest old creature,

Those wretched carpet-men left me with *both doors off* – I am *furious* at the inconvenience. God knows when I shall get them on again. It really is annoying.

In fact I feel rather fed up all round these days, though I suppose I should be a contented creature and count my blessings. It is certainly a nice sunny day, not too hot. I have bought a birthday card for Kitty, as I think it is her birthday tomorrow. Last night I made an attack on unmended socks – I have quite a lot – and mended about four pairs. I never seem to have the right coloured wool! In fact mending-wool is becoming scarce these days – I don't suppose anyone mends socks any more. Lord knows what they do instead.[1]

The tortoise has disappeared again. I envy him. Nobody takes his doors off.

Always thinking of you,
Much love,
Philip

1 Several of the socks recovered from 105 Newland Park by the Philip Larkin Society in 2004 following the death of Monica Jones have been darned with the wrong-coloured wool or in two colours. See Plate 5A.

30 August 1974

London

Dearest old creature,

I am feeling rather the worse for wear after staying a night at Bob Conquest's flat, where he had a lot of people in and much champagne was consumed. Kingsley and his second wife were among them, looking very well, and one of Kingsley's sons, who is now a writer himself. WE were not especially late to bed, or especially drunk, but the flat is in an awful mess (Bob's wife has left him) and I have a feeling that I talked too much. Such evenings are not good for me!

Anyway, it looks as if it's going to be another fine day. I hope you are not too boiled! [. . .]

MUCH love
Philip

4 September 1974

Cally Hotel, Gatehouse of Fleet — Wednesday

Dearest old creature,

This so far is a thoroughly wet holiday, and not at all enjoyable. The hotel is a large one – we were here 10 years ago – and harbours plenty of children. The food isn't too bad. Drink is fearfully expensive and so we have resorted to keeping a bottle or two upstairs, w[ch] is much cheaper, and much quieter.

There really isn't much news to report. We drove to Castle Douglas yesterday, and ambled about in the rain, then had a packed lunch by the wayside. A further drive took us to Moniaive near where Annie Laurie lived. In the evening we managed to catch a few lines of me reading my own poems on a portable radio I've brought.

I hope the zebra plant is well and that there are no problems at Berrystead. At least it can't be wetter than it is here!!

Much love
Philip

5 September 1974

Cally Hotel, Gatehouse of Fleet Thursday

Dearest old creature,

The waters are rising – it rained *all day* yesterday, hard and long. We went out and splashed about Newtown Stewart[1] – I bought myself a pair of yew cufflinks. Then we went on and lunched in the car by the roadside somewhere – found they had given us packed lunches from *yesterday*, barely eatable. Fortunately Monica carries extra supplies. It's always a fight to get the packed lunch even though we order it the night before.

I miss seeing you and hearing what has been happening chez Mr Bird. Is the zebra plant all right? Remember me to Kitty.

Monica sends love, as

I do –
Philip

1 Correctly Newton Stewart.

2 October 1974

Picture postcard[1]

Wednesday

Here is Prince Charles to keep Princess Anne company.[2] I am in the train going down to London where I shall see Betjeman and go to Westminster Abbey to see him unveil a tablet to Auden.[3] It's a grey day & I expect it is raining. The cows in the field all look resigned. The train is fearfully hot. So was my kitchen this morning – I had left the gas stove on all night!

Much love, Philip

1 Prince Charles in uniform, saluting.
2 He had sent Eva a card showing Princess Anne on 30 September.

3 On the following day, 3 October, Philip sent Eva a letter: 'It was a solemn ceremony. Poets' Corner seems to be getting rather crowded! No doubt there will be room for me.'

17 November 1974

105 Newland Park, Hull — Sunday

Dearest old creature,

Had two kippers for breakfast this morning – one nice, one not nice! I just fancied them. The lawn was white with frost this morning when I looked out, wch surprised me, as I hadn't felt cold in bed. But this is a much more air-tight house than my old flat at Pearson Park, when the curtains in my bedroom used to *billow out* with the draught.

Last Thursday was a very tiresome day, because a lot of students from other colleges came and 'sat in' in my Library, & I had to spend the afternoon wrangling with them and making arrangements to safeguard things as well as I could. It used up all my nervous energy, and I was flat out (metaphorically) on Friday. – – Hence my failure to write. Wretched little swine!

Yesterday I bought a mirror and hung it in the hall – too high, I'm afraid! I always hang things too high. Still, I can see *myself* in it, even if other people can't see *themselves*. It's a nice sunny day today, & I shall poke about in the garden after lunch. There are always leaves to get up! I hope you are well and comfortable, and finishing up your meals *with relish*. Pity you can't have a Guinness!!

Much love
Philip

1 December 1974

105 Newland Park, Hull

Dearest old creature,

Fancy it being December already! It's a very green one, and mild, so far: hope it won't fill the graveyard! Not with us anyway! I can do without the graveyard for a while yet.

I've just rung Kitty up & she seems fairly all right, though a bit depressed – Walter's been at home for a fortnight with a 'nervous cough', wch can't have cheered her, and of course she has had a cold herself.

I bought a new dustbin yesterday, as my old one showed signs of collapse, and painted my house number on it. I also bought a 'pruning saw', and did a bit in the garden – I am piling up an awful lot of rubbish at the end of the garden: I only hope it sort of decays and disappears. Surely it must. I suppose most people would have a bonfire, but it all looks too wet to me!

I am getting up early & listening to the cricket from Australia – of course I fall asleep again. Looking forward to seeing you next weekend, & Basil Brush (the fox on TV)!

Much love Philip

1975

8 January 1975

105 Newland Park, Hull

Dearest old creature,

I have just written cheques for some £1300 in TAX, an operation that makes me gibber like an ape, especially when I think of it being spent on criminals and layabouts and IRA members. What a world we live in!

I was delighted \to/ find myself about 2 lbs. lighter this morning – now Monica has gone I am not tempted to eat so much. Drinking remains a problem!

Perhaps I shall really have to observe Lent this year! Bread & water.

There really isn't much news here. I have been slaving away at an article for weeks, and it's nearly finished now.[1] My happiest time is reading in the bath every morning for half an hour or so but it doesn't last long enough.

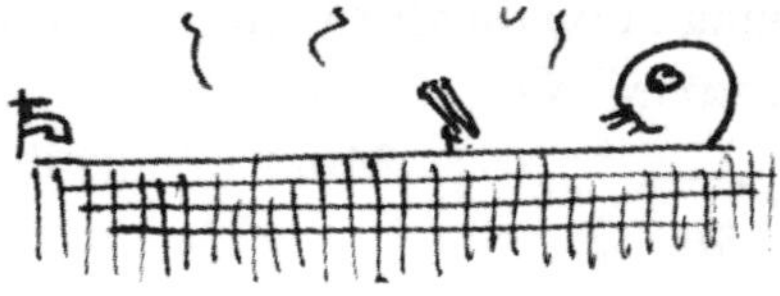

Much love
Philip

1 Perhaps 'The Real Wilfred: Owen's Life and Legends' (review of Jon Stallworthy's *Wilfred Owen*), *Encounter* XLIV, 3 (March 1975), 73–4, 76–81.

16 January 1975

Picture postcard[1]

[105 Newland Park, Hull]

There was a little frost last night, but the sun is shining & there are roses still out. Tonight I am actually going to a conjuring show – one of our professors[2] is a student of 'magic' & has invited me. Hope he doesn't make *me* disappear! Much love

Philip

1 The University of Hull: the Lawns. The same card as that sent on 4 June 1974.
2 Edwin A. Dawes, Professor of Biochemistry and long-time chair of the University Library Committee. On the foundation of the Philip Larkin Society in 1995, he became its first chairman.

27 January 1975

105 Newland Park, Hull

Monday

Dearest old creature,

Have you eaten your buns yet?

They w[d] make a nice change for you – and they were so well buttered! I found Monica had made a cottage pie when I got back, w[ch] was very welcome. Then I set out on the long dreary journey back to Hull, getting in about 11 p.m. M rang as soon as I arrived: I think she thought I'd come to grief. But I'd gone slowly.

Wasn't it fun, looking at all those peculiar birds and animals on TV? I liked the seals – they reminded me of someone!

Truly the world is full of wonders.

I have to go out to lunch today – a tiresome affair. But I remember sitting with you and watching the clear sky grow peacefully dark.

All love as always,
Philip

25 May 1975

105 Newland Park, Hull

Dearest old creature,

Well, we (Monica has come for the weekend) duly made our way to Ilkley yesterday.[1] We set off about 3.30 in the car, in our best clothes, & were able to arrive for the 'reception' at 6 p.m. It was cloudy & cold, & M was not happy in a long dress with nothing over it. We hung about in this central building, drinking about *three* (very few) glasses of red wine and getting very cold, until 7.15, then we were transported to another hall ('nearby') where presentations were to take place. More mismanagement – we had no tickets, so had to wait in a freezing porch until someone took pity on us & walked us in. The presentation of awards (*cheques*) to three people took very little time, then M & I legged it before the poetry-reading began, I saying that I had a dinner engagement in Hull. We ate sandwiches in the car & got back about 10 p.m. Ilkley Moor 'baht 'at!!! M said she certainly felt she had got her 'death of cold', but seems all right today. Awwgh!! Hope you are well & comfortable –

MUCH LOVE Philip

1 The Ilkley Literature Festivals had been launched by W. H. Auden in April 1973. In the first years they were biennial events, so this was the second festival.

3 August 1975

<Letterhead with coat of arms>
Durrants Hotel, George Street, London W1H 6BJ Sunday

Dearest old creature,

I am just recovering – at least I hope I am – from three days' watching cricket. Funny how tired it makes you! Of course, one is sitting for 6 hours on a hard wooden seat, and that must have its effect. But it has all been intensely interesting and exciting: I don't think I have ever watched a more exciting morning than on Friday, when England got 6 Australians out before lunch. We were all grinning like Cheshire cats, everyone friends with everyone else.

And the weather has been superb – hot & sunny. It's just the same today, though there's no cricket. I don't know what we shall do. Something restful I hope!

We've had some awful meals since arriving – very bad steaks on Wednesday, rather awful Chinese meal Thursday, too much whitebait & spaghetti (not together) Friday. Last night was better: some sort of sauced fish. But everything is so dear! A pint of beer in this hotel is 36p, whereas in Hull it's 23p – of course, it varies, but 36p! We have bought a bottle of whisky to drink secretly in our rooms.

I hope you are surviving the heat, & that your plants are still alive. Next Saturday is my birthday! I haven't thought what I shall do – it seems a long way off. Always thinking of you, dear old creature, & with much love in wch M. joins.

Philip

14 September 1975

Cringletie Hotel, Peebles Sunday

Dearest old creature,

Well, this is our week here nearly over. I'm sitting in the hotel lounge after breakfast (and after fetching the papers) & the sun is shining outside, though whether it will last I don't know. Thursday – or do I mean Friday? – was an awful day, rain all the time, in addition to wch I dropped my portable radio & broke it, wch put me in a rage. Very low spirits! Yesterday was better, though. We drove out & picnicked in a quiet spot, then went to look at Heriot Church wch we had visited two years ago. Monica found a hedgehog in the churchyard, busy rooting about, & we watched it for a while.[1] It was very young, but seemed to be able to forage for itself all right. If we went too near it 'froze' until we went away. It looked quite silky apart from the prickles. We also saw several rabbits – they're quite plentiful about here.

Really, the price of drinks in hotels is appalling. If M & I have a glass of sherry in the bar before dinner the cost is 56p. We can buy a *bottle* of sherry for £1.39 and drink in our bedrooms much cheaper! So we do. I feel very nervous going up the stairs with concealed bottles for fear I meet the manager.

Tomorrow we move to St Andrew's where I have a library conference: the first grim notes of reality will begin to make themselves known! It will be very dull for Monica as I shall be occupied all day, but we shall see. She has been doing some clandestine washing lately. Both of us send you *much* love – you are always in my thoughts.

Philip

1 Larkin took photographs of Monica approaching this hedgehog. Hull History Centre, U DLV 3 248.

8 October 1975

105 Newland Park, Hull — Wednesday

Dearest old creature,

The crisis of the beginning of term has begun to die down, leaving me rather mangled, but I expect I shall recover. Luckily the weather is mild and pleasant.

There really isn't a great deal of news. I lead a quiet life going to and from my house.

I usually telephone Monica in the evening to see what she has been doing (or vice versa). Sometimes I snatch up some shopping! I'm beginning to think I ought to buy a new raincoat to go to Buckingham Palace,[1] wch is 4th November. The old ones seem covered with marks of one sort or another. The Queen might think this a bit off!

Hope you are warm & comfortable, & enjoying your food.

Much love –
Philip

1 To receive his CBE.

16 October 1975

Hull

Dearest old creature,

Rather a frustrating morning: I drove into the town intending to do a little shopping, but found one now has to put shillings in the parking meters, so I came away – I hadn't any! Life gets more difficult daily.

I thought I might buy a new raincoat to go to the Palace in. Mine seems to have a great many inexplicable stains on it. I don't want to spoil the Queen's day! I shall have to try again when I have amassed some shillings.

There really isn't much news. Monica is trying to live on rice, fish & vegetables to cure her arthritis. She says it's a dull diet, & she comes in feeling very hungry. She isn't even supposed to eat eggs or cheese! And no drink of course!

Hope you are well and comfortable.
Much love,
Philip

28 October 1975

Picture postcard[1]

[105 Newland Park, Hull]

Tuesday I went today to try to buy my raincoat, but didn't like the ones they had. They are trying to get some from Leeds! It's a beautiful day here, & I am *almost* glad to be alive! Very rare for me! I hope you are seeing interesting things from your window. Has your watch turned up?

Much love Philip

1 'The Valley of the Stour' by John Constable.

4 November 1975

Picture postcard[1]

<*Postmark*> London

Tuesday

Here we are at the Palace, on a lovely day! I duly had my CBE looped round my neck by the Queen, & she asked if was 'still writing' – I said I was still trying! Lots of people here, all very good tempered & appreciative. Thought of you very much.

Much love, Philip

1 Buckingham Palace, London.

5 November 1975

Picture postcard[1]

[105 Newland Park, Hull]

Wednesday

I'm safely back after a gruelling day in London, & feel I need a good long rest. But the weather was serene and mild, & the new raincoat I bought wasn't really necessary. Monica devastated the West End with her hat! It is black straw heaped with artificial roses, & very pretty. My cold hangs heavily. Do hope you are better!

Much love P.

1 Horse and foal in a field.

8 December 1975

Picture postcard[1]

[105 Newland Park, Hull]

These pussies look a bit startled! Perhaps tea has come sooner than they expected. I did enjoy seeing you yesterday and watching the Laurel & Hardy film! Wasn't it funny? Much love

Philip

1 Two kittens in a wicker basket with pink roses.

14 December 1975

Hull Sunday

Dearest old creature,

It seems a little milder today, though it's drizzling in compensation. I have been washing some shirts before sending them to the laundry (!), and last night I mended eleven pairs of socks. It sounds as if I lead a very dull life, doesn't it? I suppose I do, by normal standards. If the rain would only stop I w^{d} wash the car, & perhaps cut off some roses that are still hanging about in the garden.

Poor Monica is not at all well, and is staying in bed with cough, cold, sickness and so on. I shall ring her up soon to see how she is. I rang Kitty up early this morning and she said you had been signing your Christmas cards! You're much further ahead than I am. I doubt if I shall send any this year – too lazy.

I remain fearfully heavy, and yet I don't eat much – just drink. Yesterday I had most of a (frozen) shepherd's pie & beans for lunch, and half a plate of soup for supper. Yet still I'm 15¼ stone!

If only you were fatter, & I thinner! Much love,

Philip

28 December 1975

Picture postcard[1]

<*Postmark*> Leicester

Here is a pussy to wish you all the best in the new year! Looks a bit indignant, doesn't she? Still I'm sure she sends all good wishes, as I do – with *much love*

Philip

1 Grey kitten.

30 December 1975 Picture postcard[1]

[105 Newland Park, Hull]

Here is a black pussy to wish you a happy new year! We are setting out for Haydon Bridge for a few days. Shall see you on your birthday – *much* love

Philip

1 Black cat.

1976

2 January 1976

Picture postcard[1]

<*Postmark*> Hexham

This is the nearest town, where we did our 'New Year' shopping. M. bought a new electric toaster, wch seems to take ages. We had snow last night, and I'm wondering if my car will start. We return to Hull tomorrow: hope you are well and comfortable.

Much love Philip

1 Market Place and Hexham Abbey.

4 January 1976

105 Newland Park, Hull

Dearest old creature,

Well, I am back at Hull, a wet Sunday, half-snowing, half-raining it is, very miserable. We seem to have escaped much damage from the storms, luckily. Weren't they awful!

I telephoned Kitty this morning and was glad to hear that she and Rosemary had been to see you yesterday, and you had been quite chirpy. I shall be coming to see you on Saturday, of course – weather permitting.

I had a nice New Year at Haydon Bridge with Monica, mostly sitting on either side of a 'real' fire, dozing or reading – and from time to time drinking.

We didn't eat much, & in fact I've actually lost weight! I expect I shall soon get it back.

I hope you are having a nice Sunday lunch. Monica is just pottering about the kitchen, getting ours. We both send love!!

Philip

12 January 1976

Picture postcard[1]

[105 Newland Park, Hull]

Monday

It was so nice to see you on your birthday, & to see you blow out the candles.

Look forward to seeing you again soon!

Much love
Philip

1 Kitten with blue and red balls of wool.

9 February 1976

Picture postcard[1]

[105 Newland Park, Hull]

This rabbit is wearing a mob cap like I used to draw for you! And the party cake is rather like yours. It's a lovely day here today – I hope it is with you.

Much love, Philip

1 'The Party Cake' by Willy Scherwele. Mother rabbit holding a cake, with infant rabbits, mice, squirrel and ladybird all holding spoons.

22 February 1976

<*Letterhead*> All Souls College, Oxford Sunday

Dearest old creature,

Just a little note from All Souls, where I stayed last night – had a good dinner & plenty to drink, so much so that I feel the worse for wear this morning. However, I had a walk round Oxford and viewed several old haunts.

A great many trees have gone from the Meadow – some because of disease, some blown down in the gales.

Am lunching with the Warden, then hey ho for the open road! Hope I am not too drowsy to drive.

Much, much
love –
Philip

1 March 1976 Picture postcard[1]

[105 Newland Park, Hull]

Isn't the weather beautiful? I did a lot in the garden yesterday, pruning roses (and getting scratched by thorns!) and even mowing the front lawn. How are you? I shall be coming to see you on Saturday – no doubt we shall both snooze, and watch football on TV!

Much, much love, Philip

1 'The Gypsies', rabbit family boiling a pot outside a gypsy caravan.

23 March 1976 Picture postcard[1]

[105 Newland Park, Hull]

Do you remember Basil Brush, the fox on television? I thought you might like to see him again. He's very cheerful, isn't he? I do hope you are well and comfortable! It's a grey day here, and even a little snow, but I try to keep cheerful.

Much love, Philip

1 'Basil Brush and the Train'.

6 April 1976

Picture postcard[1]

[105 Newland Park, Hull]

I seem to have run out of pretty cards for the moment, but this may interest you. Of course it doesn't exist yet! But one day I may drive over it to see you. I did enjoy visiting you on Sunday, and hope you are well.

Always thinking of you,
Love Philip

1 Artist's impression of the proposed Humber Bridge.

7 April 1976

Picture postcard[1]

[105 Newland Park, Hull]

Do you remember Scarborough? I think we went there before the war, and I'm sure I rode on a donkey like this one. Happy days! I am still slaving away at my quinquennial estimates, oh dear.

Much, much love,
Philip

1 Scarborough (head of a donkey and two sea views).

25 April 1976

105 Newland Park, Hull

Dearest old creature,

I see this is Daddy's birthday – he would be 92. I do wish I could have told him all about my Hamburg trip.[1] He would have been pleased, wouldn't he? Though I expect he would have found some reason for thinking it wasn't worth having!

It's a great relief to be back in Hull, and able to get down to ordinary jobs such as preparing the laundry and mowing the lawn – though the latter is more of a job than I care for. I expect Mr Bird is starting to fight the weeds in order to 'show off' the garden in the summer.[2]

I hope you continue well – now do watch out for your glasses! Both times I called recently you hadn't got them on. Surely you need them. Don't let them be mislaid. Otherwise you won't be able to see to cut the rinds off cucumbers, and everything else!

Dear creature, I'm always thinking of you – *Much* love –

Philip

1 On 19 April Larkin had flown with Monica to Hamburg to receive the Shakespeare Prize of the Alfred Toepfer Stiftung F.V.S. Foundation,which promoted European unification. They flew back on 21 April.

2 Berrystead held an 'open garden' day in the summer.

16 May 1976

105 Newland Park, Hull

Dearest old creature,

Now there isn't any collection of post on Sundays I sit down to write to you a bit later. I have had quite a busy day, mostly in the garden, wch is starting to grow quite fiercely, but I've also changed my bed and washed the car. Of course, there's heaps more to do! I really ought to get busy on my income tax, oh dear. Even though I employ an accountant it still means an awful lot of work for *me*, even though my affairs are relatively simple.

I talked to Kitty on the telephone this morning, and she said you had a book to keep your postcards in.[1] How nice! I look forward to seeing it when I come, wch will be next week-end – all being well.

I really haven't any news. I went to London last Thursday wch was tiring and expensive – in fact I haven't felt really well since. Must remember to buy some Eno's! Better than champagne!

I do hope you are feeling better than when I saw you last – I think you were a bit overcome by the heat then. Remember to eat up your meals and become a fat creature, like me. Looking forward to seeing you and with MUCH LOVE

Philip

1 This photograph album survives in the Hull History Centre, U DP(4) 9/47. It contains forty-seven postcards from January 1976 to March 1977, detached and in a state of disorder.

30 May 1976[1]

105 Newland Park, Hull

Dearest old creature,

End of a dull wet Sunday, wch follows a dull wet Saturday. I hope tomorrow won't be a dull wet Monday! I do seriously want to do a bit of weeding. The garden seems to be growing like a stage jungle.

But great news! I think I have a gardener! One of the University groundsmen! He says he will come round on Tuesday and 'talk things over' – but that will be a great help if he comes regularly.

I am slowly recovering from my visit to London and my recording of Desert Island Discs – I didn't think it went at all well, principally because I was very nervous. If only I could have had a few double gins beforehand! Doing it 'cold' was awful. It's to be put out on 17 and 19 July.

I talked to Kitty today on the telephone and she said you were in good form. See you soon!!

MUCH LOVE!! Philip

1 This is the last two-sided letter in the archive. From this point on Philip sent only postcards.

14 June 1976 Picture postcard[1]

[105 Newland Park, Hull]

What a lot of kittens! They look as if they were watching a football match.

Another hot weekend, and hayfever is starting. I hope you are well and comfortable, and not too hot. My roses are full of greenfly – I try to spray them.

Much love Philip

1 Eight kittens in a row.

15 June 1976 Picture postcard[1]

[105 Newland Park, Hull]

More kittens! ginger ones this time. I think I like the one on the left the best. I have been out this morning looking for a present for Betty (her birthday soon), but had no luck: everything is either so rubbishy or costs £100! Had such a nice letter from Mrs Newbold. She says she gave you some grapes.

Much love P.

1 Three ginger kittens.

13 July 1976 Picture postcard[1]

[105 Newland Park, Hull]

Oh dear, it is still very hot. I have stayed at home this afternoon to try to compose something to say about Betjeman for his 70th birthday, but am getting nowhere. I'm past it! Hope you are well and comfortable. I shall see you this weekend!

Much love Philip

1 Kitten in a basket.

3 August 1976 Picture postcard[1]

<*Postmark*> Dorchester

We went to Dorchester yesterday (Monday) but it is very noisy and full of people. Still, the weather was very good – hot and dry – and we drove about after lunch, eventually reaching Bere Regis, where the D'Urbervilles came from in *Tess*. You are always in my mind, and I hope you are well and comfortable. Have you killed many flies? There are not so many insects about down here as I'd feared. M & I send very much love.

Philip

1 Statue of Thomas Hardy by Eric Kennington, Dorchester.

6 August 1976 Picture postcard[1]

<*Postmark*> Salisbury

This is our last full day (Friday) here in Dorset. The visit to Anthony Powell[2] yesterday was all right, but he took us rather a long and pointless walk round his 'estate' and we got scratched and stung. The weather has held out well, but everywhere is very dry. I hope you are well and comfortable – you are always in our thoughts. We go to a place in Worcester tomorrow & shall be there for my birthday.

MUCH LOVE P.

1 Two white kittens.
2 Anthony Powell (1905–2000), English writer, best known for his novel sequence *A Dance to the Music of Time*.

28 August 1976 Picture postcard[1]

<*Postmark*> Hexham

Have come up to see Monica in Northumberland – today (Friday) – we had *rain*! Not much, but rain nonetheless. Tomorrow we hope to go to Bellingham show, that I wrote a poem about in *High Windows*.[2]

None too *warm* today – quite a change. Tomorrow is Betjeman's 70th birthday too.

Much much love Philip

1 The Roman Wall, Northumberland. Clag Lough.
2 'Show Saturday'.

4 October 1976

Picture postcard[1]

[105 Newland Park, Hull]

Have just given my first talk to students & feel rather corpsed. Two more this afternoon! Then it will all be over for another year. I never got into my garden at the weekend, it was too wet. I expect you had a lot of rain too! We shall be growing fins soon.

Much love P.

1 Labrador puppy.

21 October 1976

Picture postcard[1]

[105 Newland Park, Hull]

I expect I shall be seeing you almost as soon as this pussy, but I thought I would send him as he looks so appealing. Today started v. wet but has cheered up now. The leaves have started to come down now.

I talked to Bruce last night: he sounded v. old!

Much love to you Philip

1 Kitten. The same card as that sent on 8 October 1976.

30 November 1976 Picture postcard[1]

[105 Newland Park, Hull]

It's rather misty here today: I hope the fog isn't coming back, for I shall come to see you at the weekend. Looking forward to it! Hope you are warm and comfortable. I am still making porridge in the mornings – sometimes it is v. thin!

Love Philip

1 'The Party Cake' by Willy Scherwele. The same card as that sent on 9 February 1976.

6 December 1976 Picture postcard[1]

[105 Newland Park, Hull]

Here is Old Faithful again![2] hoping you are well and warm and comfortable. I did manage to drive back to Hull on Sunday night without mishap, but it's nasty weather for driving. The painter has come to paint my bathroom, so I shan't have a bath for two or three days! I shall look very grubby by the time he departs.

Much love Philip

1 Horse's head.
2 He had sent near-identical cards featuring a close-up of a horse's head on 2 July, 9 September, 9 November and 17 November 1976.

31 December 1976 Picture postcard[1]

[105 Newland Park, Hull]

I don't know when you'll get this card – we managed to get to Haydon Bridge after a dreadful drive, & it is all very cold & miserable here, Lucky you to be 'well wrapped up' and looked after! We are supposed to go to see the New Year's Eve bonfire tonight, but I don't feel very keen. Let's hope for a better New Year!

Much love P

1 'Blindman's Buff' by Margaret Ross (a rabbit Christmas Party).

1977

2 January 1977 — Picture postcard[1]

<*Postmark*> Newcastle-upon Tyne

Here is a pussy to wish you a happy new year! It is sunny today (Sunday) and I hope the weather will be clear and dry at least till I get back to Hull. On New Year's Eve we saw the fire-walkers at Allendale but it was v. cold & icy. I wonder if you saw the Coronation on TV?[2] It would be v. interesting.

All love from Monica & myself Philip

1 Head and shoulders of a cat.
2 On 1 January 1977 the BBC celebrated the twenty-fifth anniversary of the Queen's accession by rebroadcasting the film of the 2 June 1953 coronation ceremony.

4 January 1977 — Picture postcard[1]

<*Postmark*> Newcastle-upon Tyne — Tuesday

We are setting off back to Hull today – shall be glad to get there safely! It's not so cold, but the roads will be dirty. I hope you have survived all the festivities and are keeping an eye open for the first snowdrops. I don't expect they'll be long in coming! I shall see you at the weekend and we shall have another good chat. Much love,

Philip

1 'Hide-and-seek!' by Racey Helps. Rabbits hiding behind trees in a bluebell wood.

10 January 1977

Picture postcard[1]

[105 Newland Park, Hull]

Here are four Siamese pussies to wish you a happy birthday! I do hope you have a quiet peaceful day. It was lovely seeing you at the weekend and having a bit of your birthday cake. How gay the candles looked! Term starts today – back to the treadmill.

LOVE Philip

1 Four cats in a wooden newspaper rack.

11 January 1977

Picture postcard[1]

[105 Newland Park, Hull]

I expect you remember this old picture! There's snow on the ground this morning, but the sun shines, so things aren't so bad. Hope you are sitting up and taking notice.

Much love,
Philip

1 'Dignity and Impudence' (1839). Oil painting of two dogs by Sir Edwin Landseer.

21 January 1977

Picture postcard[1]

[105 Newland Park, Hull]

This is not a very interesting card, but it's all I have. Nice sunny day today! I do hope it is sunny in Syston. In my garden things are beginning to sprout through the earth, so spring must be on the way. Wish it was with me!

Love Philip

1 Altarpiece, Catholic Chaplaincy, University of Hull. Bronze bas-relief of the crucifixion.

9 February 1977 — Picture postcard[1]

[105 Newland Park, Hull]

Here's the cheerful Basil Brush to say hello! I hope he cheers you up. He looks smart in his velvet waistcoat, doesn't he? I brought a half-bottle of champagne into the Library today & drank it – very cheering. Wish I could give you some.

Much love, Philip

1 Portrait of Basil Brush.

4 April 1977

<*Letterhead*> 105 Newland Park, Hull

Dear Kitty,[1]

Back to base, & with many happy memories of Saturday – I know you said it was Rosemary's day,[2] and so it was in a sense, but you and Walter presided wonderfully, and made everyone feel completely welcome. Thank you for your hospitality – and the buttonholes – I'm sure everyone present will remember it as a splendid occasion. I hope David and Rosemary managed to get to wherever they were going.

I took the flowers to Berrystead & the big stone vase. The girls were very kind, & in the end Mother had five flower arrangements in her room, looking delightful. I hope they're still there when you go.

Not that she really took them in. She was physically all right, and ate her sandwiches & cake, & I think knew me & smiled & tried to talk, but as before something has gone and I'm afraid communication has broken down. She had upper teeth in but not lower: they were in the bathroom. Plenty of woollies waiting! Mrs G was in evidence, though I fended her off twice. Mother needs more tissues.

I'm sure you are feeling whacked after it all: time for you to recuperate. How smart Walter looked! And you yourself looked like something from the fashion pages. See you soon, & again thanks.

With love Philip

1 There are no letters to Kitty in the archive between September 1972 and this.
2 Rosemary married David Parry on 2 April 1977.

5 April 1977

Picture postcard[1]

[105 Newland Park, Hull]

I know this is your favourite pussy, so here he is again. He is well wrapped up, and I hope you are.

I mowed a lot of my lawns yesterday – feel very virtuous.

All best love, Philip

1 Kitten wrapped in plaid. The same card as sent on 16 September 1976 and also at an undetermined date in that year.

6 April 1977

Picture postcard[1]

[105 Newland Park, Hull]

These rabbits will be keeping warm at any rate. It's rather a grey day here – and I burnt the porridge, oh dear.

Much love as always, Philip

1 'The Sack Race' by Racey Helps. Sports day with rabbits, hedgehog, badger and squirrel.

4 May 1977

Picture postcard[1]

[105 Newland Park, Hull]

The horses look peaceful, don't they? I wonder what they are thinking about. It's Monica's birthday this Saturday, and I shall come and see her – and you!

Much love Philip

1 Mare and foal in field. The same card as sent on 5 November 1975.

Only three cards survive from May, no cards from June or July, two from August and four from September. Their frequently creased and stained state suggests that others were sent but discarded or destroyed.

9 August 1977 — Picture postcard[1]

[105 Newland Park, Hull]

Doesn't the Queen look nice here? I hope she gets back safely from Ireland.

This is my birthday – much love to you as always.

Philip

1 Her Majesty Queen Elizabeth II by Annigoni.

[September 1977] — Picture postcard[1]

<*Postmark*> Lochgoilhead[2]

It is still very wet and miserable here, though I dare say there are sunsets like this. Tomorrow we set out for Ballater, further east. Hope you are warm and comfortable.

Much love Philip

1 Sunset over Ben Bheula, Lochgoilhead.
2 The date on the postmark is illegible but Monica and Philip were in Lochgoilhead in early September 1977.

[September 1977] — Picture postcard[1]

<*Postmark*> obscure

Here's a colourful bird to greet you from Scotland! For once it isn't raining this morning, but it isn't sunny either. We both hope you are well and send love.

Philip

1 Head of a puffin.

16 September 1977

Picture postcard[1]

<*Postmark*> Newcastle-upon-Tyne

Here's the beaky old bird again, to say Monica & I are back in Haydon Bridge, safe & sound. We send all love. Shall be returning to Hull on Sunday. Always thinking of you.

Philip[2]

1 'The Golden Eagle of the Scottish Highlands.' Eagle at nest with a chick. Larkin had sent a slighly different card featuring a golden eagle at an undetermined date in 1976. He may also have sent an identical card to this, now lost.

2 This is the latest dateable card in the archive, though there are numerous undateable cards. It may be that Eva's state was such that Larkin saw no point in sending cards after September. It is also possible that he continued to send cards until Eva's death on 17 November 1977.

APPENDIX

Letters from Home

FROM Sydney Larkin 2 December 1943[1]

<*Letterhead*> ~~Penvorn, Manor Road, Coventry~~
73 Coten End – Warwick[2]

Dear Philip,

Mother asks me to write instead of her, as she has had a busy day. She will, however, write soon as she thinks much about you in your new "sphere".[3]

I was intending to write to remind you not to omit to write to Bedford, but no doubt you have already done so.

Your vivid description of Bruce's[4] quarters is interesting but, as the M. of V. reminds us, all that glisters is not gold[5] and, as A.T. says, kind hearts are more than coronets and the W.E.A. than Norman Blood.[6]

N.A.L.G.O. is a trade union.[7] It runs, inside itself, the "Nalgo Approved Society" which *is* the Friendly Society. Do not be persuaded to join any other. That is the *best*. I have been to London today and have just got back.

Love from both.
Your affectionate Father.

1 This is the earliest surviving letter to Philip from either of his parents. The letters from the Oxford period have been lost.

2 Sydney continued to use sheets with the old letterhead, but overprinted with cancellation lines and the new address above. The family had moved to Coten End two and a half years earlier, in June 1941.

3 Philip had taken up the post of librarian in Wellington the day before.

4 Bruce Montgomery.

5 *The Merchant of Venice*, Act II, scene 7.

6 Alfred, Lord Tennyson, 'Lady Clara Vere de Vere': 'Kind hearts are more than coronets, / And simple faith than Norman blood.' The reference to the W.E.A. (Workers' Educational Association) is Sydney's joke: the speaker in the poem advises Lady Clara to be less haughty and devote herself to educating her tenantry.

7 National Association of Local Government Officers. Philip had asked his father if he should join.

FROM Eva Larkin 5 December 1943

<*Embossed letterhead*>
Beauchamp Lodge, 73 Coten End, Warwick[1]

My dear Philip,

I have just written a long, long letter to Auntie Nellie, and am feeling a trifle exhausted in my brain and somewhat overpowered by the heat of the drawing room fire, but feel, nevertheless the urgency to write to you to thank you for your card and interesting letter.[2]

I hope by now you are getting more used to your new life and are comfortable in your little 'bed-sitter'. I sincerely hope you can keep warm, as it is so cold here, and I expect is the same at Wellington.

I was muchly interested in your visit to Bruce. He does indeed seem to be one of Fortune's favourites – for the present at least. Will he be able to get over to Wellington, I wonder? I expect his free time will not fit in with your's. [*sic*]

It was kind of you to think of me when the sirens wailed last Wednesday! As a matter of fact I was in the bus, coming from Leamington and only heard the "All clear"! I did quite a useful bit of shopping. I left your old, battered brolly to be given a new cover, and have it's [*sic*] ribs repaired, which will not be completed until the end of January!! I also got a pair of scissors at Burgis & Colbourne's for Eva,[3] which was a big surprise to us – *and* a bottle of orange squash at Shacker's.

When I went over to pay the milk bill on Friday, Mrs Hubbard (Mr Choat's sister) told me that the Art Master at the Warwick School was leaving. I *was* surprised.

Kitty came as usual this week end. She appreciated your letter, which also caused her much amusement.

I have been *ter*ribly busy since you left. Springcleaned, almost, our bedroom. There is a heap of things to be done before Christmas when we hope to see you again.

Daddy has gone to sleep over his book!

With our fondest love
Mother

1 In contrast to her husband Eva uses embossed notepaper.
2 See Philip's letter of 1 December 1943.
3 Eva, wife of Alfred, Sydney's brother in Lichfield.

FROM Eva & Sydney Larkin — 7 February 1944

<*Embossed letterhead*>
Beauchamp Lodge, 73 Coten End, Warwick

My dear Philip,

Your dear old letter came this afternoon much to my delight, and I read it after washing the 'handkies', and before starting on the tea towels! Incidentally I might add that I have also washed two pairs of Beau Brummelish yellow gloves of yours, which I found in a drawer, and one pair wants mending.

I am sorry to hear that you suffered from cold on Sunday morning – so did we, for our fire would not burn up quickly in time for breakfast and Ginger Pussy had many 'dead fingers' or rather paws.[1]

I am alarmed to hear of the bread famine. I am sure this can be ended at once. Do please ask for a loaf to be put on the table at meals, say at breakfast, lunch and supper. Bread is quite cheap and there ought to be no difficulty in getting it.[2]

I have wondered several times how your little tea party went off on Tuesday, and lo & behold you do not so much as mention it!

We were interested to hear that some of Bruce's music is to be published. I must read his book when it is out. Is he writing anything else?

I think you said that you were going to Birmingham to-morrow to buy some books. I hope you have a pleasant 'browse'.

By the way, when I went for our meat on Saturday, the butcher (not Mr Lees) asked how you were going on.

Last Tuesday evening we called upon M^{r} and Mrs Colbourne, to say how sorry we were to know that Bob was missing. It has been in the Coventry evening paper, and of course in the Warwickshire Advertiser,

It is very sad, and I *do* wish we could have some good news of him.

<*Sydney*> Have you heard anything of your Nalgo receipt? The point of difficulty is that you only started in L.G. Service on 1st Dec. therefore you may only pay 10 mos. sub., viz to 31st Oct 1944, and you should have 2/6 change. See your man and tell him this, as obviously he does not know.

<*Eva*> I think I have no more to add, except that I am now going to darn some socks. Much love from both, Mop.

<*Sydney has inserted at the top left of the first page*> P.S. I used a stick for many years – 26 years at least – and I always left off my right glove. *S.L.*[3]

1 'Ginger Pussy' is Eva herself.
2 Philip had complained that his landlady did not put bread on the table at meals.
3 Sydney is responding to Philip's comment in his letter of 6 February: 'I think carrying a walking stick (which I still do, vaguely as a Beau Brummelish or even defensive gesture) wears holes in the fingers quickly [? this last word illegible].'

FROM Sydney Larkin — 28 February 1944

[73 Coten End, Warwick]

Dear Philip,

It is suggested by "Mop" that I write a line.[1] There is little to say. I am getting to the end of Vol. 5. Of Gibbon. Seeing in the press that Carlyle's "Hero[es] & hero worship" ought to be suppressed as a Nazi publication, I read it and found, inter alia, the lecture on Mahomet most inspiring, particularly as I had just recently read the section of Gibbon dealing with Mahomet and the Arabs. I have also looked at the

Koran and conclude that it is a puritanical book and would appear to the Arabs much as Law's "Serious Call"[2] would appear to us.

Wavell's[3] contribution to the Sunday Times is a masterpiece. If he would stick to Generalship, I am sure it would be better for his reputation.

I am glad to hear your work (i.e. Library work) is progressing steadily. Stick to it and make a great success of it. I am at present about to engage in a battle with the Labour party and the Council on a question of "dishonesty" in expenses on the part of a Councillor. The trouble in this matter is that Councillors stick together on matters of this sort but I have "right" on my side. Local Government is made up (or should be) of this sort of thing. Love

S. L.

1 On half sheets with the edge roughly torn; enclosed in the same envelope as a letter from Eva.

2 William Law (1686–1761): *A Serious Call to a Devout and Holy Life* (1728) was a key influence on the eighteenth-century evangelical revival.

3 Field Marshal Archibald Wavell (1883–1950), British soldier. At the outset of World War II he was Commander-in-Chief, Middle East, then became Commander-in-Chief, India (1941–3). At the time of this letter he was Viceroy of India, holding this post until his retirement in 1947.

4 Sydney alludes to Wavell's enthusiasm for poetry. His annotated anthology *Other Men's Flowers* (1944) was very popular.

FROM Eva Larkin[1] — 17 April 1944

<*Embossed letterhead*>
Beauchamp Lodge, 73 Coten End, Warwick

My Dear Philip,

How nice it was to get a letter from you again – it has seemed such a long time since I heard from you.

First of all, I must say how sorry I am over your personal (or sweets) ration pages. I find that *I* have them, safely tucked away in my identity card case. I hope Miss Tomlinson was not annoyed over the matter.

By the way, oranges are here again. There are stacks in all the shops. This afternoon Kitty has got our ration, 8 lovely ones. I wonder if you have any in Wellington. If there are any, you can get them from any shop and the shopkeeper marks one of the squares on the back cover of the ration book. It is in panel 2, line 10.

I am surprised to hear of the state of the bath. Not very refreshing to see cigarette ash in it – but I wonder who put it there?

I have, this day, forwarded a communication from Gunner.[2] I do wish he would leave room for me to re-address his letters. I was absolutely baffled over this one. I feared to write your address on the back lest the post office should neglect to turn over, even though I inscribed P.T.O. to remind them. Finally, by obliterating 'England' I did the trick. How is he?

Mrs Colbourne called on us last night. She has had several letters and cards from Bob. He is quite all right, and said that they had formed a dance band in his camp.

I was *terribly* interested in your visit to Oxford. I am glad you saw Mr Costin. I agree that teaching is a good idea – specially if you could be at the university. This would give you time to write. I don't believe that your writing is "not any good", as *you* put it.

After you left I overhauled your winter coat. First I turned out the pockets. Holy smoke! what relics of forgotten hours! A little heap of tobacco shreds – a dry crumb of bread (rather large this)[3] a piece of chalk, a letter from Mr Buttrey, an envelope addressed to the Librarian, Shrewsbury, a library ticket (a new one) and this note-book – the only article I think I need return, oh, and lastly a dirty blue handkerchief, which I have washed.

There were also several sewing jobs to do at the coat, and I also took the vacuum cleaner over it – but of course that would not alter it's [*sic*] faded appearance.

Kitty and I hope to go to the Cinema, Leamington tomorrow afternoon to see Bette Davis in "Now, Voyager"![4]

Very much love, Mop.

1 Sent in the same envelope as the next two letters; written on full-sized letter paper.

2 Larkin's school friend Colin Gunner, who was on active service.

3 On 23 April Philip wrote: 'I thought "a dry crumb of bread (rather large this)" exquisitely funny.'

4 A 1942 film based on the novel by Olive Higgins Prouty, directed by Irving Rapper and starring Bette Davis, Paul Henreid, and Claude Rains.

FROM Sydney Larkin[1] 17 April 1944

[73 Coten End, Warwick]

Dear Philip,

I was glad to hear you had seen Costin. It is well to keep in touch with people like him and with your fellow English students. I don't believe the Clarendon Press man. *I* should not advise anyone to go in for my job, but publishers are always necessary as well as finance officers.

As regards the School of Librarianship, I suppose that *is* the thing to do, if you contemplate making a permanent thing of that profession. It is more expensive than passing the Library Ass-n Exams but probably no more useful for municipal purposes.

The other day at Hatchards[2] I picked up Conversations with George Moore by Geraint Goodwin postscript by G. Bernard Shaw.[3] You will be interested, if you have not already seen it. It is a slight book 240 pp of good sized print. Among other things he says "What has chilled Landor in the mind of the public is his unfailing wisdom. Nothing chills so much as his wisdom; the ordinary man will never like it."

Love. S. L.

1 This and the previous and following letters were sent in the same envelope. It is written on sheets roughly torn in half.

2 Bookshop on Piccadilly, London.

3 Published in 1929.

FROM Catherine Larkin[1] 17 April 1944

[73 Coten End, Warwick]

Dear Philip,

Just a short letter to keep up the old contact we used to have. I was much amused by your account of your trouble re baths. You did sound so disgusted.

I went to M[r] *Barnacle*[2] on Thursday. Do you remember the shivering and horror that name used to conjure up? He didn't find much to do[,] only one small filling on a tooth that is already ¾ filling but he DROPPED THE DRILL on my hand and made it bleed! I am afraid he is losing his grip.

When I visited Stratford again with Evelyn it (the Merchant) was not so good as the first night; the double curtain arrangement was not used!

I went to Loughborough for the day on Friday to take some work for an exhibition – I hope it *is* exhibited and not left lying about. I wish they wouldn't always have these exhibitions in the holidays.

I haven't quite finished "The Fly" but will send it as soon as I have.[3] A girl in a shop this morning was wearing a silver ring with an Egyptian insect on – very unusual.

No more room – excuse hurriedly written note but hope you will reply.

Love,
Kitty

<*Up left margin*> I saw Dilys Powell reviewed a new film which looks interesting: "The Halfway House".[4] She mentions "Thursday's Child".[5] That's about as far as I shall ever get to seeing it!

1 Sent in the same envelope as the last two letters; written, like the last, on a roughly torn half sheet. The only two surviving letters from Kitty to Philip (both from 1944) are inserted into envelopes containing letters from his parents. All other letters from Kitty to Philip are lost.
2 Wavy underlining.
3 *The Case of the Gilded Fly* (1944): detective novel by Edmund Crispin (Larkin's friend Bruce Montgomery).
4 A 1944 film directed by Basil Dearden starring Tom Walls, Françoise Rosay, and Mervyn and Dilys Johns.
5 A 1943 film directed by Rodney Ackland and starring Ronald Shiner, Stewart Granger and Wilfrid Lawson.

FROM Sydney Larkin — 8 September 1944

<*Embossed Letterhead*>
Beauchamp Lodge, 73 Coten End, Warwick

Dear Philip,

I have taken about half an hour to clean my fountain pen (fine nib) in order to write to you, a thing I have been intending to do for some days.

Thanks for this morning's letter. I had observed Cashmore's press notice. His style of referring to himself is going out of fashion, I think, but am not sure that Edward VII and possibly George V in his early years of kingship used to say "I and the queen" – which can be justified – but that has now been abandoned for "the queen and I", a much less impressive diction. I cannot understand J. C. Powys in his list. I should like to know the titles in stock.[1]

Thanks for Connolly's review of "The Razor's Edge".[2] It is nice to know that someone else shares one's opinion. I regarded it as a masterpiece. In view of Trilling's book on E. M. Forster (which I have ordered) I took "Howard's End" \(Penguin off your shelves)/ with me to Loughborough and read it with great pleasure. That, too, is a masterpiece. I propose to read "A Passage to India" some time.

I shall (D.V.) go to Oxford on Saturday 23rd Sept, staying at Balliol for Tea, Dinner, Bed, Breakfast, lunch & Tea, returning 24th Sept afternoon. Yesterday I ought to have paid a visit to London – the last chance I shall have at the public expense[3] – but we had booked for "Junior Miss" at Coventry.[4] It was very well done (competent, as all those travelling companies with one play are) and amusing. The weather was vile.

In your letter this morning, you mention that death is lonely and that to death we should all orientate.[5] That caused me to look up orientate, because, like the verb "implement" it is a word I have never used. It makes one wonder how one does without them! But the proper word is "orient" which in its literal meaning was used in 1727 "most religions . . . have their temples oriented". How, by 1850, it got to mean to bring into defined relations to known facts or principles is a mystery. But O. W. Holmes in 1867 tells us that "Mistress Kitty accepted Mrs Hopkins's hospitable offer, and presently began orienting herself, and getting ready to make herself agreeable." Orientate must have come from orientation, the best example is 1893 from Barrow's "World Parliament of Religions": "That is the best education which gives a man, so to speak, the best orientation which most clearly defines his relation with society and with his Creator."

At Leicester, I acquired The Collected Letters of Oliver Goldsmith, edited (very minutely) by K. C. Balderston. The price was the published price of 7/6, but, as books go nowadays, that is cheap.

I don't think there is any news here in Warwick. The abolition of fire watching will cause a good deal of trouble and many husbands will have to reorient themselves in their domestic life. When the home guard are disbanded the trouble will spread. In the meantime, I shall welcome any light that may be put on in the streets for the few occasions on which I am out after dark.

With love from both,
Your affectionate Father

<*On first page opposite the letterhead*> P.S. We heard from Ashton yesterday that you have a new 2nd cousin, Vivien Sutton.[6]

<*In Eva's handwriting*> Thanks for the dear "Mopcreature" and the poem.

1 See Philip's letter of 7 September 1944, and note on Cashmore's column in the *Birmingham Post*.
2 Novel by Somerset Maugham (1944). The reviewer was Cyril Connolly.
3 Sydney retired from his post as City Treasurer of Coventry in April 1944 at the age of sixty.
4 This play, adapted by Jerome Chodorov and Joseph Fields from the semi-autobiographical stories by Sally Benson, had a run on Broadway between 1941 and 1943.
5 See Philip's letter of 7 September 1944.
6 Ashton-under-Lyne, where Eva's sister-in-law Auntie Nellie and her family lived at this time. They moved later to Hyde.

FROM Catherine Hewett (née Larkin)[1] 23 October 1944

73 Coten End, Warwick

Dear Philip,

As I am detained at Warwick with a peculiar illness – intense pain and sickness all day yesterday – I am answering your letter \in order/ to put it in the weekly parental one.

Your letter was as amusing as ever. Glad you liked the photograph – the others we will show you when we meet. Yours was easily the best and we have had an enlargement of it by an expert photographer who is employed by the research department.

Your novel goes well I hope. How is Bruce? I read what I considered to be a good play on school life called "The Rats of Norway".[2] I thought of Bruce's play.

Work is progressing very well[.] We have enough students to make it interesting this year. Mr. D. is still telling wicked stories about Mr. P.[3]

I went to see "The Lodger"[4] and also "Laburnum Grove"[5] for the second time. How good it is, also with it was "Pack up your Troubles" with Laurel and Hardy.[6] It did bring back the old days. I haven't seen one of their films since the days I used to go with you.

About your cigarette case, here is the story[7] – intended to do it in gold as the lettering is on my books – managed to open the bookbinding drawer, (which is kept locked and does not come into my realm of work) found box of type – but all the letters were there but A! Also there is no gold leaf to be obtained anywhere. Decided to draw the letters and "blind" them in with a straight tool. P·A·L very simply like that. But it didn't look very nice so I tried to buy some gold paint but couldn't. Mr. P. raked up a dust covered tin of gold enamel – which I used when Walter[8] had reconstituted it. The result is that it looks rather crude and amateurish. Would you like me to send it to you?

How are you getting on with the brewery man?

With love from Kitty

<*Up left margin*> *Mr. Y* (not Mrs.) has told us we can stay as long as we like. There is a feud between those two.

1 On a roughly torn half sheet, in the same envelope as letters from Eva and Sydney.
2 By Keith Winter; first produced in London in 1933.
3 Kitty was teaching at the College School, Loughborough.
4 A 1944 horror film about Jack the Ripper, based on the novel by Marie Belloc Lowndes, directed by John Brahm and starring Merle Oberon, George Sanders and Laird Cregar.
5 The 1936 film version of J. B. Priestley's 1933 play, directed by Carol Reed and starring Edmund Gwenn, Cedric Hardwicke and Victoria Hopper.
6 A 1932 film directed by George Marshall and Raymond McCarey.
7 In his letter of 1 October 1944 Philip asked 'Do you think it is possible to put my initials on that cigarette case I passed on to you?'
8 Kitty's husband, Walter Hewett. They were married in August 1944.

FROM Sydney Larkin[1] — 4 November 1946

[73 Coten End, Warwick]

Dear Philip,

When I read letters in the press which interest me I almost always, either after reading a line or two or perhaps half way down, look to the end to see who has written it – it is nearly always G. B. Shaw, E. W. Birmingham (Barnes)[2] or W. R. Inge.[3] This time it was Bruce Montgomery. He goes wrong in attributing things to *Socialism* – he should have said *democracy*. The Conservative party do precisely the same thing as the socialists and any party wanting votes *must* do it.

I have read *Jill* with much interest. The story reads true, I think, and that is the test which generally satisfies me. It seems incredible on reflection, however, that so many catastrophes could happen to one person. Life, even in Gissing's novels, usually has some pleasant interludes.[4] The number of misprints, typist's errors and mistakes in spelling is rather large and they should make this first edition very valuable. "Huddersfield"[5] is an unfortunate one.

Ll. Powys's Life has not yet appeared.[6]

I meant to say a week or two ago that I enquired about your Nalgo approved Society. The position is that you remain a member of the Approved Society altho' not of Nalgo. The whole business of Approved Societies ends next year under new Act. You have, of course, sent your last completed cards to the Society?

Love,
S.L.

1 Enclosed in same envelope as a letter from Eva.

2 Ernest William Barnes, FRS (1874–1953), mathematician and liberal theologian, Bishop of Birmingham (1924–53).

3 Sir William R. Inge ('Dean Inge') (1860–1954): Professor of Divinity at Cambridge, Dean of St Paul's Cathedral and proponent of nudism. From 1921 until 1946 he was a columnist for the *Evening Standard*.

4 On 21 April 1947 Sydney wrote: 'I found no difficulty in "identifying myself" with Joan Ogden' (in Radclyffe Hall's *The Unlit Lamp*), adding 'Jill presented a slight difficulty in that respect.'

5 Sydney has spotted that on p. 59 of the first edition of *Jill* the copyeditor or typesetter has mistakenly 'corrected' Larkin's fictional 'Huddlesford' to the name of the real town, Huddersfield.

6 Malcolm Elwyn's *Life of Llewelyn Powys* was published in 1946.

FROM Sydney Larkin[1] 2 March 1947

73 Coten End, Warwick

Dear Philip,

Just a line to convey our hearty congratulations on Michael Sadleir's review.[2] I was quite overcome by it.

Hoping you had a nice week end with Jim, and with love

Your affectionate

Father

1 On a roughly torn half sheet.

2 Review of *A Girl in Winter* in the *Sunday Times*. See next letter.

FROM Eva Larkin 3 March 1947

<*Embossed letterhead*>

Beauchamp Lodge, 73 Coten End, Warwick

My dear Illustrious Creature!

I expect your first edition is sold out already.

Oh! what a day we had yesterday! We got up as usual, all un-suspecting that great tidings were coming to us, and when the Sunday Times arrived I opened it, remarking, "I wonder if Philip's novel will be reviewed?" Daddy peered over my shoulder and spotted it first and said "read it out to me." Well, I began to read it, but it was so marvellous that I had great difficulty in reading to the end – in fact both of us became very deeply moved. I consider it the most wonderful achievement, and am *very*, *very* proud.

Do you remember, when you were quite young, how you used to try to do big things in – I forget whether it was cricket or playing the drums, and I laughingly said "When you are famous, I shall be there waving my umbrella!" Well, my umbrella is waving wildly at the moment!

Your little sketch is lovely, but how fierce the great Creature looks! In a previous letter of yours you told us about the notice of 'Winter' in the T.L.S., and remarked upon the nice things that Faber's said on the jacket, in a later letter, so that I immediately added a halo to your last Creature, feeling sure that one would descend upon it in due course.[1]

This morning Daddy rang up the Editor of the Coventry Telegraph and told him about the review and he has quoted it in tonight's issue.

We were surprised to receive a letter from Mrs Bowen, Leigh, this morning. They had seen the announcement of "A Girl in Winter" in the Observer and wanted to know if it were you, or a namesake. She said they were going to order a copy.

We shall look out for the parcel from you. Thanks very much for signing Auntie Nellie's.

I am going to enclose the review cutting along with it so that she will read it in the right spirit!

On the whole we feel two very 'knocked into a cocked hat' creatures after the surprises of the week-end – yes, we had another surprise on Saturday. The postman brought us a box with a Copenhagen postmark upon it. It puzzled us very much until we discovered that it had been sent at the direction of Alan & Edith in Canada.[2] When we opened it we were astonished to find a nice piece of bacon, a tin of butter, a tin of honey, a tin of condensed milk and two packets of cream cheese. Isn't it very kind of them to remember us.

I thought of you a lot yesterday, and pictured how happy you would feel in London with your friends, your good fortune, and the lovely sunshine.

It is a pleasant pastime watching the birds being fed. We have seen them in St. James's Park upon the occasions when we have visited London.

Yes, the shortage of coal is a great calamity. Our dining room fire refuses to light, and so we have to stay altogether in the kitchen. I find great difficulty in drying to-day's washing. The cold weather will come to an end soon, I am sure.

I bid you good bye, and I likewise bows. [*sic*]

Much love Mop

1 See Philip's letter of 2 March 1947 for Eva's added halo.

2 Alan Larkin (b. 1906), son of Sydney's brother Alfred, had emigrated to Canada.

FROM Sydney Larkin[1] 14 July 1947

[73 Coten End, Warwick]

Dear Philip,

I said I would write but there is nothing to say of importance. You know of our Stratford Visit – it was a very fine show but there is something of the pearls and swine atmosphere in a visit of mine to a flower show – except, of course, that I can see that they are pearls, either real or sham. But in that junk shop between the town and station, where they have a few dusty books, I found "Holy Living" and "Holy Dying",[2] in nice condition, in Rivington's Devotional series (red borders, gilt edge, cloth, book mark ribbon, published in 1900 & 1898 respectively, by Longmans Green & Co). I offered the man 2/6 for the two, which he accepted. I wished then I had offered 1/-.

I have recently read "Still she wished for Company", Margaret Irwin[3] – a daft book, but someone must have recommended it to me when I bought it but failed to read it – "Friendship's Odyssey"[4] which I enjoyed, in spite of its bad print, "Three Act Tragedy" Agatha Christie[5] – silly as all crime stories are – "Sainte Colline"[6] – very good but not so good as Clochemerle – and now "Master Sanguine"[7] which, on second reading, is not so good as on first, but is much above the average of such books, if there *is* an average.

I went to lunch with the Mayor of Oxford (signalman on railway – "ex") and afterwards we went round various buildings with the Chief Constable and his daughter (as guides) Christ Ch., Magdalen, New College, Sheldonian, quite interesting. The Sheldonian we were told seats 2,000 exclusive of the floor. It seems incredible.

I will try to see Carroll about the Biro pen. He may have other suggestions but his opinion before was that the Biro or any other similar pen was not worth more than 5/-.[8]

I read with great amusement G.L.S.'s letter on the Crazy Gang but confess that I had not the wit to attach a name to the initials – but it is so obvious now.[9]

Love,
Father

1 On sheets of office paper roughly torn in half; in the same envelope as a letter from Eva on embossed notepaper.

2 By Jeremy Taylor. They were originally published as *The Rules and Exercises of Holy Living*, 1650, and *The Rules and Exercises of Holy Dying*, 1651.
3 Margaret Irwin (1889–1969), novelist and biographer; *Still She Wished for Company* was published in 1924.
4 *Friendship's Odyssey: The Autobiography of Françoise Delisle and the Story of Havelock Ellis from 1916 to 1939* was published in 1946.
5 Agatha Christie's *Three Act Tragedy* was published in Britain in 1935.
6 Gabriel Chevallier (1895–1969), best known as the author of *Clochemerle* (1934). *Sainte Colline* was published in English in 1937.
7 Ivor Brown (1891–1974). *Master Sanguine: Who Always Believed What He Was Told* was published in 1934.
8 On 21 July 1947 Eva wrote: 'Then about the Biro. Daddy has not seen the advt. about the *Roll Ball*, but he enclosed this about the Bell.' Enclosed with her letter was a newspaper cutting concerning 'A NEW PEN', priced at 29/4d (refills 4/11d). A letter from Sydney of 30 September is written with a ballpoint pen '(which, by the way, writes with unparalleled smoothness)'. However, on 6 October Sydney wrote: 'I took your "Rolball" back to John Carroll's and had my money back. He wasn't in himself but they said I could have one of the next lot of Biros – "new ones" they said, as though of an improved pattern.' Some draft passages in Larkin's unfinished novel, *A New World Symphony* are in ballpoint.
9 Not obvious to this editor.

THE REMAINING LETTERS AND CARDS ARE FROM EVA LARKIN

3 July 1951[1] [Extract]

53. York Road
Loughborough.
3rd. June 1951.

MY DEAR CREATURE

To-day has been such a lovely day and I have had such a big wash!!
Once again I admired and *loved* your dainty creature sketches. I *do* wish *I* could draw a creature as cleverly as you do. The faces of mine never look so alive as yours' and I cannot get the *aged* look.

1 Date as postmark. Eva has misdated the card 'June'. Between September 1950 and December 1951 Eva lived with her daughter at 53 York Road, Loughborough.

5 February 1952

21 York Road, Loughborough[1]

My dear Creature,

Have just come back from the sewing meeting, found my fire almost out, but being a well-ordered creature, I soon cheered it up with some sticks which I chopped a few days ago, and kept handy in case of an emergency like this.

Have also been busy in the cellar stacking the logs into a neat heap in the middle of the floor, ready for the workmen to clean it out and lime-wash it. During the process I came upon a toad, I *think* it is a small toad, but he has started to crawl about and I don't know what to do with him. I hesitate to put him in the garden for I don't want him to be frozen during the night. I hope he doesn't crawl up the cellar steps and I also hope I don't tread on him unthinking when I go down. It is queer to think that there is another live thing in the house besides myself. I wonder what he eats, but I suppose he *should* be asleep at this time of the year. I *might* make a pet of him.

I have this afternoon paid the gas bill and also the stop tap bill. Whilst at the builders I asked them if they would do the cellar and put a Yale lock on the storeroom door, and make all the windows so that they could be opened and shut. A man is coming to-morrow to see what wants doing and will give me an estimate as to what it will cost.

I seem to do nothing but pay bills just now, and I really want more coal – only about five large lumps left now. If they don't bring it I think I must make do with the Ideal boiler as I have plenty of coke.

I was so cheered by your postcard last Saturday morning, for I felt very depressed and miserable. It may partly have been due to my cold and the very cold weather, also being indoors all the time. Kitty had invited Mr & Mrs Deveril Mr Hewett and Connie and Ivor to tea for Saturday but Mr Hewett couldn't come, so she asked me if I would like to go 'to cheer me up'. I refused at first, but when I went down with some cutlery (lent for the occasion) she persuaded me to go. It was a very nice tea and did, I think do me some good, but I'm afraid they are all going to ask me to visit them now! Just what I don't want!

Anyway, I'm sure the postman must smile at the pictorial addresses on your postcards.[2] I have had a very nice letter from Mr Ralph in answer to mine.

Now I must answer your letter. I'm afraid you weren't the *only* late creature last Sunday morning. You see this intensely cold weather puts me off turning out very early and consequently I never really get going here until half-past ten or sometimes eleven. Then Walter comes to do any jobs. Last Sunday he put up the curtain fixture over the drawing room door. I actually sat down to dinner (roast lamb, savoy, potatoes, apple pie) at ten minutes to two!

It didn't take long to wash up and I soon caught up, and had tea at the usual time.

You would feel a trifle daunted when your visitors forgot the main course of your meal!

What a sacrilege though to turn chicken and ham in aspic into a 'fry'! I'm sure the sweet would be nice and I must try it myself one day.[3]

What a sweet little sketch 'at the grocers'. I'm afraid you are rather an extravagant creature though. Still I suppose you would spend more in rooms.

No. I have not seen the picture of the two sisters in the News of the World. I wonder what their recipe is for long life. Evidently *they* have made a success of living together and don't get on each other's nerves. What a lot must have happened during their 99 years!

About my sleeping here alone, I didn't really feel brave because it didn't frighten me one quarter as much as a thunderstorm, or the prospect of another war. I *would* sleep here always, but it would not do, the enforced loneliness all day and practically all night, and for ever, I'm sure wouldn't do. What to do about it, I really don't know. I *could* let the house, furnished, if the worst came to the worst (although I hope it won't) perhaps I could stay a few months with A. Nellie, which wouldn't cost as much as in a hotel or boarding house. They might not have room, though because Ian and Vivienne will soon need a room each.[4]

If funds will allow I think 'Old Creature' would like to have a little holiday with you somewhere. What county is Donegal in, Antrim? What a lovely drawing you've made – fancy an Irish Creature, too! One of our neighbours, on the opposite side of York Road died last week.

I am enclosing a cutting from the weekly paper. He was a very well known figure here.[5] I thought the 'appreciation' was very good, in fact I actually wept a little over it.

Contrary to my usual custom I haven't much left to write on this fresh sheet.[6]

Oh, one thing I wanted to ask you, were any walking sticks put in storage? I haven't come across any here.

Last Saturday, being hard up for something for lunch, and having some boiled rice left from a curry and also some cold potatoes, I remembered the cheese balls which you concocted when you were here, so I made some very nice ones, all golden brown, and fried an egg, and so had quite an enjoyable lunch.

Every week I keep meaning to tell you that my next-door neighbour actually wears (when doing her housework) a 'creature cap', whilst the other neighbour comes out arrayed in a cotton bonnet like I used to wear when I was in my twenties.

I heard from Mrs Dexter today that she thinks Miss Jepps[7] has gone into a sort of home in Surrey run to accommodate Clergymen who are visiting perhaps in London. I think she would try to help the staff in some way. I feel sorry for her, but it wouldn't do for me to have her here.[8] She could not help with the work or cooking and would only want to pay a small amount and I should have to buy her food, too. Her programme at Mrs Hunt's was. Breakfast in bed. Down about 11 o'clock drink a glass of milk, then if fine, a walk until lunch. Rest until 4 o'clock, and then I think she *did* get a small afternoon tea. They had an evening meal which I think Mrs Hunt's sister cooked. I expect Miss Jepps will come back though, in due course.

I suppose I ought to go down the cellar and see what 'toadie' is doing![9]

Do you ever see Miss McDonnell?

No more now. All love
Old Mop

1 In December 1951 Eva moved into 21 York Road, Loughborough, a few doors from her daughter's house on the same road. She lived there until admitted to Berrystead Nursing home two decades later in February 1972.

2 See Philip's postcards of 25 January and 1 February 1952.

3 In his letter of 3 February 1952 Philip wrote: 'The Strangs came round, having promised to bring supper, but when they arrived they had left it all behind. I therefore had to produce ham & chicken in aspic, a tomato or two, and some onions, which Patsy converted into a dubious fry. I had done my parti-coloured grapefruit as a sweet.'

4 The children of Nellie's daughter Eva and her husband George Sutton.

5 Eva enclosed a cutting: 'DEATH OF MR. J. A. MARTIN: Probably Oldest Working Journalist in Country', memorialising James Alexander ('Jimmy') Martin, who had worked for forty-eight years for the *Nottingham Guardian* and died, still in post, at the age of eighty-three.

6 The third sheet: sides five and six.

7 Two of Eva's religiously inclined friends.

8 Miss Jepps had originally responded to Eva's advertisement for a paid companion.

9 On 9 February Eva wrote that, since workmen were coming to lime-wash the cellar, she had rescued 'toadie', and put him in the garden: 'I found a nice sheltered niche for him, but after lunch when I went out to look for him, he had gone! Do you think a bird would eat him – he was only small.' In the same letter Eva recorded her reaction to the death of King George VI.

7 August 1961

21 York Road, Loughborough

My very dear Creature,

First of all, many very happy returns of the day. I hope you *do* get this and the card on the 9th. I look forward to buying you a present when I arrive in Hull. I was so pleased to get your letter on Saturday and hope the week end was not so lonely as you anticipated.

Saturday here was un-settled in the morning with heavy rain and thunder just as I had served my lunch. I left it and fled down to Kitty's. It did not last long so I came back and ate it, cold! I washed up quickly, and got washed and went out shopping for I had the usual Creature coming to tea on the Sunday.[1] It was a lovely afternoon so I sat in the park until nearly 5 o'clock when I went to Mrs Dexter's to tea. (What should I do without her!) Sunday was cloudy and unsettled. I went to the Communion Service with Mrs Dexter. We got caught in the rain coming back and just as I was getting lunch ready it thundered in the distance – so I went into Mrs Coleman's.[2] It didn't last long, but didn't look at all promising but I managed to eat lunch and soon after it started again, and was worse than before. I put on my mac, but the rain was so heavy so I sat on the stairs, hoping it wouldn't be too bad. It hailed and thundered, and lightened, but soon passed over, to my intense relief. I spent the afternoon in fear and trembling lest it should come on again. I managed to prepare tea, but, oh! What an upsetting time! Did you have any storms? I hope not, although I believe they were widespread on Sunday.

This evening is very gloomy, temperature at the back door 66°.

It is very good of you, Creature, to disrupt your day on Thursday to give me lunch and take me to the flat. I hope we shall arrive on time.

How kind of Mary[3] to invite us there, Tuesday.

Just received your letter. I expect you will not[4] be sorry to get back to the library after your lonely week-end. Mine would have been not too bad if the weather had not upset me.

What a nuisance over the fastening of the shed.

The morning is gloomy and rainy. I expect all our shops are shut, still, I don't want anything.

Have got plenty to do including ironing and assembling all ready for packing. Must see Mr Perry to-day, sometime. I am glad to have plenty of jobs to keep me going.

All love again.

Hope we don't keep you waiting on Thurs.

Old Creature

<*On first page, opposite address*> P.S. How is Virginia. I hope she has made herself at home.[5]

1 Philip.
2 Mrs Coleman was Eva's next door neighbour.
3 Mary Wrench (later Judd), assistant in the Hull University Library.
4 The letter concludes on a smaller sheet, as often.
5 Virginia was Philip's wickerwork rabbit. Eva has enclosed a cutting: 'BUNNY'S GRAND OLD LADY: On Wednesday of last week Mrs Parker of Rancliffe Cottages, Bunny (where she has lived for the past 56 years) was 90 years old. And on this memorable event she received 35 greeting cards and a telegram.'

12 January 1964

21 York Road, Loughborough

My very dear Creature,

How can I thank you enough for all the kind remembrances of my 78th birthday. The nice long letter, the beautiful flowers, with their card of good wishes and the very sweet birthday card. I think the wishes on this are so different from what one usually finds on such cards. "To wish you joy, to wish you fun, and when your 'Happy Birthday's' done, To wish you luck and joy and cheer for every day throughout the year".

Previously I have felt rather flat, and sad to think that it is all over for another year, but after reading this message I don't feel like that at all, rather full of hope, and a desire to get all the best out of the few 'borrowed years' which lie before me. (I hope.)

Now about the birthday itself. Cards from Kitty, (a lovely view of Lichfield Cathedral) Rosemary, and Mrs Slater, arrived first post. I have slept here since Christmas, with one or two exceptions,[1] so when I got up early on Friday, I silently wished myself a happy birthday, said 'Rabbits' for luck and went downstairs and made myself a cup of tea. O, I have forgotten A. Nellie's card, a lovely one which when opened discloses a cluster of pansies and heartsease, and has a sweet perfume. As the folks at 53 were coming to tea I went out early to buy cakes and cress and do the usual week end shopping. On the way I met Mrs Coleman[2] and asked her if she would mind answering the post for me if it should come again before I returned. When I got back she knocked on the wall, so I opened the front door, and she handed me a lovely lot of flowers. She said Miss M^c^Nicol had called with them. They are beautiful, daffodils, tulips and two bunches of freesias, the scent of those last named fills the room, and is very pleasant. As Mrs Coleman was speaking to me the postman called with your letter, and before I could get upstairs to put my coat and hat away, your lovely flowers arrived from Simpkin & James.

This page is crumpled, due to it being so difficult to tear off the pad.

Your flowers are two bunches of daffodils, a bunch of irises and a bunch of anemones. Really, the dining room looks as if Spring is here. How excited and happy I felt!

After this, I had to get down to preparations. Nearly all afternoon I spent making sandwiches, tongue and egg and cress, whipping cream and laying the table extra specially nice. I had a chocolate layer cake of Fuller's as my birthday cake and when I was buying it the girl at S. & James said "Have you ever had their *ginger* cake?" She told me it was gorgeous, the 'King' of ginger cakes. Do you like ginger, Creature? If you do I would get one the next time you come. (Just had a sleet shower). I accidentally heard a bit of the forecast at lunch time, 'snow in seventeen counties in the South but not so cold in the North!' Strange!

Kitty & Rosemary arrived about 5 p.m. bringing their gifts which we sat and opened before tea. Walter could not come (pressure of business!) but he sent me a linen cloth for the tea wagon. Kitty brought me a pretty cream jug and also two tea towels, very unusual. One, The Sunday Times Colour Guide to herbs, most interesting, the other, characters from Shakespeare. I think they are too nice to use, except on special occasions. Rosemary presented me with a gilt covered notebook and [—][3] pencil attached.

They seemed to enjoy the tea, and I sent Walter his share for supper when they left.

After tea we played Newmarket, and I found that some of the coppers which you left came in very handy. Rosemary won, and we had a lot of fun over the game, and the queer hands we got. During the evening they drank my health and we all drank to the absent ones, Philip & Walter. By the way Mr Cann didn't call, but when out shopping I met Mr Bacon from Cromer! They are over to help Mrs Bacon's sister May as Maggie (the other sister) is not at all well. I also met Mrs Welsh (next door).

How I laughed over your sketch of you, wondering whether to buy me a basket, or not.[4] It is so good of you to me. I think I would delay giving me the basket until I feel that it is an urgent need. I shouldn't feel very happy crossing busy roads with it. Thanking you very much for the beautiful flowers *and* the card and letter.

All dearest love. Old Creature.

<At the top of the first page alongside the addres> Am glad the people below showed you such kind hospitality upon your return.

Will answer your letter more fully on Tuesday. Did you get my letter card on Tuesday morning?

1 Eva still customarily slept at her daughter's house, a short distance from her own in York Road, Loughborough.
2 Next door neighbour.
3 Illegible.
4 See Philip's letter of 8 January 1964.

26 January 1972 — Lettercard[1]

21 York Road, Loughborough

My very dear Creature,

This will only be a very short letter just to say that I am sitting up in the bedroom and have just had my breakfast. I am much about the same. Dr Rainey came last ~~ny~~ night and prescribed some new tablets, to deaden the pain, which has been a\w/ff~~o~~ul every time I moved. O dear! I forget how to spell. The weather doesn't help, chilly and gloomy~~ng~~.

The Circle of Silent Ministry sent me a lovely lot of flowers yesterday. I still have yours' [*sic*] dear Creature.

I had a very long letter too, from Eva.[2] They are very worried about A. Nellie – she keeps sinking into unconsciousness. Eva too is not very well. George is the main stay.[3]

Dr Rainey said I had bruised the muscles of my leg. Dr de Villeniss[4] has given Kitty the address of a Nursing Home, I think she said at

Woodhouse Eaves. Of course I cannot do much for myself. Takes me ages to put on my stockings.

I hope Mrs Holmes continues to come. She was marvellous yesterday. Mrs Coleman, too has been to see me.[5]

Of course this last[6]

1 Bowl of flowers in colour.
2 Nellie's daughter.
3 George Sutton, husband of Nellie's daughter Eva.
4 A guess. Eva herself seems uncertain of the spelling.
5 Eva's next door neighbour in York Road.
6 The sentence is incomplete. Kitty has written at the end: 'I am sending this letter to you as I know you would like it, / Love Kitty.' Kitty addressed the envelope, postmarked 27 January.

11 June 1973 — Postcard[1]

[Berryfield Nursing Home, Syston, Leicester]

Don't put on such warm clothes now that Sumemsumer [*sic*] is coming is. You will be a ~~mornin~~ more comfortable ~~comcomfortable~~ comfortable creature. I find it too hot to write a long letter so please excuse me. Really it is awful! I had a visitor yester ~~a~~ day afternoon. She brought me some chocolates and several other ~~od~~ oddments. Oh dear, more mistakes. I don't think I shall ever write properly. It was nice of you to send me such a nice letter. Really I have now no decent notepaper, nor a decent pen. The visitor was ~~was~~ Mrs Stubbs. How busy you are, just now.

Hope it will not be too hot tonight. The sun has gone in now for a time. By the way it will be nice to see ~~Philip~~ you receive your prize? – Will Monica be there? Worr[y]ing time she has with the birds!

Excuse all mistakes. Much love to you both. Mother.

Hoping to see you both. Mother

<The above is written in blue ball-point. Enclosed in the same (white) envelope is a blue envelope on which the following is written in black ink in the place of the address>

I have neither pen, paper or decent ink. The last-named keeps slipping. Thank you for your nice letter about the duck.

Perhaps some day I shall be able to write again.

1 The postcard, addressed by Eva, is without a stamp. It is contained in a stamped envelope addressed in an unknown hand and postmarked 11 June 1973.

17 May 1974[1]

[Berryfield Nursing Home, Syston, Leicester] Sunday

Dearest Creature,

Oh it is such a horrible day not a tree moving. Really, I shall have a job to write to you. ~~you.~~

I mustn't give way, though, considering ~~considering~~ what a lot you have to do. I have just tried to wash my hands and find that neither of the taps will function. Strange!

It has suddenly gone very quiet – I wonder why.

I wonder if Kitty will pay me a ~~visitor~~ \visit/ I don't think so, it is too cold.

I wonder how you are getting on? Still, you will be able to take your time over getting straight. Perhaps Mrs Oates will come back soon.

I find it difficult to write a decent letter. I have just been into the toilet and was pleased to find one tap, the ~~in~~ \in/ use the cold water tap!

The birds are flying to and fro'

Whatever can I write about now. It all seems so desolate outside. There is not a person outside, plenty of doors banging inside. I should think it will soon be time for lunch!

There are two cars outside one, looks like the doctor's. Still, I don't think he will call here.

There ~~is~~ \are/ only two chairs now in my room.

I expect the lunch will soon be coming in.

Whatever shall \I/ be writing about now. Oh! Nurse has just set set my tray for dinner. I should like to go out but it is not suitable.

The flowers in the window are in bloom specially the the black and white ~~and the white~~.

Effie McNicol[l] has asked Kitty if she can come to see me? She says she can come, and would like to come.

There isn't a soul about, I do wish there was.

They winter jasmine is about all to be seen.

I do wonder how Philip is ~~gdting~~ getting on with the moving. I hope you can read this.

Much love and kisses with love to Monica

1 This is the last dated letter from Eva.

INDEX

INDEX OF RECIPIENTS

INDEX OF CORRESPONDENTS

GENERAL INDEX